DISRAELI, DERBY AND THE CONSERVATIVE PARTY

Journals and Memoirs of Edward Henry, Lord Stanley

1849-1869

DISRAELI, DERBY

AND THE

CONSERVATIVE PARTY

Journals and Memoirs of Edward Henry, Lord Stanley

1849-1869

Edited by

John Vincent

Professor of Modern History,
University of Bristol

BOOKS

10 East 53d St., New York 10022
(a division of Harper & Row Publishers, Inc.)

First published in the United States in 1978 by
HARPER & ROW PUBLISHERS, INC
BARNES & NOBLE IMPORT DIVISION
10 East 53d Street, New York 10022

Library of Congress Cataloging in Publication Data

Derby, Edward Henry Stanley, 15th Earl of, 1826–1893.
  Disraeli, Derby, and the Conservative Party.

  Includes bibliographical references and index.
  1. Derby, Edward Henry Stanley, 15th Earl of, 1826–93.
  2. Beaconsfield, Benjamin Disraeli, 1st Earl of, 1804–81.
  3. Statesmen – Great Britain – Biography.
  4. Great Britain – Politics and government – 1837–1901.
  5. Conservative Party (Gt. Brit.) I. Vincent, John Russell.
    II. Title.
DA565.D352A33   941.081′092′4 [B]   77-73294
ISBN 0-06-497214-3

Printed in Great Britain by
Redwood Burn Limited,
Trowbridge, Wiltshire

CONTENTS

TO NICOLETTE

PREFACE

This publication has its own history.

Neither the fourteenth nor the fifteenth Earl of Derby received an authorised biography. The elder Derby has been the subject of three biographies,[1] one of them a serious academic work, but none based on access to Derby's papers.

In the case of his son, the fifteenth Earl, whose diaries make up the present work, there is a tradition that his widow laid down terms which no biographer was willing to meet.[2] Only a selection of his speeches was published[3].

Between their deaths in 1869 and 1893 respectively, and quite recent times, the papers of both father and son lay undisturbed at Knowsley. Lord Blake's *Disraeli* (1966) was the first book to draw substantially on the elder Derby's papers. It did not, however, use the papers of his son. The Derby papers have since become generally available, and have been ably used by Stewart.[4] They have not however been used in this edition, and for a study of Derby one must await the forthcoming life by Lord Blake.

With the papers of the fifteenth Earl the story is different. Derby's private diaries and cabinet notes were cited by Disraeli's biographers.[5] They were therefore known to be in existence about 1920. Despite this clue, nothing was done or – more probably – could be done to explore the archives. An American diplomatic historian[6] was the first scholar to make good use of Derby's official papers, though not, apparently, of his diaries.

In 1968 a large part of the fifteenth Earl's papers, but not the whole, were moved to Liverpool Record Office. The division between what went to Liverpool, and what stayed at Knowsley, was an arbitrary one. Of the diaries, some (those for 1849–58) went to Liverpool, the rest stayed at Knowsley. Miscellaneous correspondence in quantities remained in both places. The larger amount went to Liverpool, where it has only recently (winter of 1976–7) been listed in a way that made it practicable to use.

From 1968 to 1974, therefore, the position was this: Liverpool Record Office housed Derby's correspondence as a minister, and his diaries for 1849–58, all in good order, together with much other unlisted material. Knowsley, it was vaguely known, continued to house the rump of the archive, to which little attention was paid. An edition of the diaries for 1849–58, which were all that were then known, was commenced in 1972.[7]

In 1974, during building operations at the Knowsley Social Club, whose cellars adjoin the Muniment Room, workmen came across trunks containing the diaries of Lord Derby from 1876 to his death. In autumn 1974 Professor

D. B. Quinn of the University of Liverpool informed me of the discovery of these later diaries. In summer 1976 I located a further series of diaries running from 1860 to 1875. The complete set had now been found.

NOTES

1 T. E. Kebbel, *The Life of the Earl of Derby* (London, 1892); George Saintsbury, *The Earl of Derby* (London, 1892); Wilbur Devereux Jones, *Lord Derby and Victorian Conservatism* (Oxford, 1956).

2 H. J. Hanham, ed., *Bibliography of British History 1851–1914* (Oxford, 1976), 93, based partly on Sir Herbert Maxwell, *Evening Memories* (1932), 270–1.

3 Thomas Henry Sanderson, Baron Sanderson, and Edward Stanley Roscoe, *Speeches and Addresses of Edward Henry, XVth Earl of Derby, K.G.* (2 vols, 1894).

4 Robert Stewart, *The Politics of Protection: Lord Derby and the Protectionist Party 1841–52* (Cambridge, 1971).

5 W. F. Monypenny and G. E. Buckle, *The Life of Benjamin Disraeli, Earl of Beaconsfield* (London, 6 vols, 1910–20), vi 264–6; hereafter cited as M. and B.

6 R. Millman, *British Foreign Policy and the Coming of the Franco-Prussian War* (Oxford, 1965).

7 Miss Colley, then a Bristol student, first drew my attention to this section of the diaries: cf. L. Colley and J. Vincent, 'Disraeli in 1851: "Young Stanley" as Boswell', *Historical Studies*, vol. 15, no. 59 (Oct. 1972), pp. 447–54.

ACKNOWLEDGMENTS

I am indebted to Lord Derby for permission to use and publish the material in this book.

My warm thanks are due to Lord Derby's staff at Knowsley, who bore my presence with good nature and patience, and in particular to Miss Agnes Rose, then Librarian, whose hospitality and kindness went far beyond the call of duty.

To Mrs Evetts, the archivist in charge of the Derby papers in Liverpool Record Office, one must pay tribute for her professional skill and helpfulness to visitors.

I would like to express gratitude to all other owners of papers, archivists, and fellow scholars whose assistance is indicated in footnotes, and in particular to Mrs John Montagu.

Finally, my thanks to Mrs Harrison, to Mrs Porter, and to my sister, who typed the manuscript.

INTRODUCTION

This diary is important, because diaries are important. By diaries one does not mean all diaries[1] – most are dull indeed – but those which fulfil the functions of chronicles. Intelligent political journals written from the centre of affairs are of decisive importance as historical evidence. They must be written from the inside. We have hitherto underrated the diary as evidence, because the diaries that happen to have come to light have chiefly been those of outsiders, of those who had their ear to the keyhole of history, but were not actually at the meeting. One thinks of men like Beaverbrook, Greville, Tom Jones, or Sir Edward Hamilton, men in the antechambers of power, but not themselves practitioners in the central areas of British public life. We admit the charm of these writers, their feeling for mood, their knack of representing great figures when outside public view; and in so doing we greatly underrate the stature of British political diaries of the last two centuries.

The modern school of history, as it emerged early last century, taught that we must read the private letters of statesmen in order to explain their public speeches, pronouncements, and political actions. The doctrine may now be carried one stage further back. It is that we need to read the diaries, or rather to hear the private conversations, in order to understand the private letters.[2] For 'private letters', in the politician's world, is a misnomer. A letter is a political action. It is not private, even if marked 'Private'. A political letter is an act of persuasion or deception taking place on a smaller stage. Its contents are conventional, not natural outpourings. It is not a message, but a form of art and craft[1]. We can no more be naive about private letters than about public speeches. We need to know, not so much the man behind, if that were possible, as the private speech behind the letters.

The gap to be bridged is that between what was written in letters, and what people actually said in cabinet, in the House, at dinner, at the club, or when staying in the country. Where a diary of the chronicle kind most differs from letters is in its power of reporting speech. Some even of the most industrious diarists do not report speech as they should, it is true. Gladstone and Gathorne Hardy, for instance, were not shining examples. Such cases of failure do not affect the general value of the better political diary. The case for diaries such as those of Lord Stanley is not that they are unduly honest, penetrating, or self-revelatory. That is too much to expect, though some degree of introspection normally goes with the habit. It is not even that diaries are written up daily (we owe much to the discipline imposed by Messrs Letts's page-a-day volumes which were in common use by the 1860's). Naturally evidence is better evidence if it is written up a day at a time as it happened. Even so, it is our desire to know what people said to each other, rather than what they wrote to each other, that makes us turn to diaries.

This quest for speech applies particularly to what was said at meetings. No record was kept of cabinets. The premier wrote a letter to the Queen, recording decisions reached; and even here some sugaring was not unknown. But cabinets spend most of their time failing to reach decisions; and it is here the interest lies. For this we have no official record. No secretary was present. No minutes were circulated. No record was kept even of papers circulated to the cabinet. Senior ministers might take working notes, though these have often not survived, and there seems to have been some doctrine that destruction should follow after an interim. The working of British central government has normally to be pieced together from fragmentary sources. The first question the student of any period of British government now has to ask himself is who, in the cabinet or very close to it, was keeping a diary.

With an opposition party, like the Conservatives between 1846 and 1886, the need for a diary source is still greater. Opposition generates much less paper than government. Shadow cabinets, of a very shadowy kind, existed; meetings, large and small, were held; and tactics and attitudes were certainly weighed and determined by discussion, without a word going on paper, again, save for the presence of some diarist. This dearth of information can lead to a wrong idea of the opposition as an inanimate body, out of power because out of office, and not part of the structure of government.

Moreover, letters are seasonal, and diaries are not. Letters, of the discursive kind at least, tend to bunch in the autumn and winter, when men were in the country, and met in London only for short periods. During the parliamentary season, the busier the pace, the fewer the letters. In British terms, what we most want to know is what senior politicians said to each other, or to themselves, between February and July. (After July, with parliament not sitting for five months, diaries become dull, while the corresponence becomes more interesting.) Diaries tend to treat of the whole year roughly in proportion to its intrinsic importance.

It will be seen that in modern history we are at the stage reached by mediaeval history in the middle of last century, when the chronicles, put into print by Stubbs and others, established the fundamental narrative for the period, leaving it to be tested against other, mainly administrative evidence. We have our modern Chroniclers; we have no modern Rolls Series, and no Stubbs, but the case for printing is the same, namely that the chroniclers (or diarists) while not giving any final answers, at least make it very much easier to see what are the questions.

In presenting Lord Stanley's[3] diary, therefore, questions have been left open, rather than solved. Something has been left for the next man, perhaps for the next generation to unravel. There are definitive modern editors. Miss Agatha Ramm is one. But, given the time that life allows, rather than the time the work requires, my task had to be one of discernment rather than elucidation; that is, selecting from a very large body of material that small proportion of historically significant material that someone, somewhere may wish to have on his desk.

Lord Stanley (as he was styled from the death of his grandfather in 1851, to the death of his father in 1869) was an ideal diarist in some, but not in all ways. He was painfully and obsessively concerned with truth. His lightest observations are marked by a straining after accuracy. If he is not entirely certain of something, he says so. He is concerned, and deeply concerned, not just with the political life of the ruling class, but with the effect of all its activities on the wider political public. He is, incidentally, the first statesman of high rank whom we can observe in some detail manipulating the press.

He was a lonely, shy man.[4] His diaries censor his ordinary friendships, so far as there were any to censor. He stands before us in the diaries as a man for whom public affairs, if not party politics, were his whole life. This is, historically, all to the good. The diarist had three main relationships. One was with his father, the premier, whom he respected and obeyed. One was with Disraeli, for whose friendship to him when young he was always grateful. The third element in his life was his friendship with Lady Salisbury and her family. In the 1860's Lady Salisbury was a central figure in the most powerful political circle in England. She and her circle wanted a coalition to continue the Palmerstonian consensus. Her candidate to run the coalition was Stanley. She was far from alone in her views. This diary is therefore an important source for studying the elder Derby, Disraeli, and the politics of coalition in the 1860's.

Stanley's diary as a source is an area where sources are much needed, because Conservatives, unlike Liberals, have tended to sink without trace. Liberal politicians, ever anxious to be in the public eye, have left most of the 'tombstone' biographies. The Conservatives put privacy before publicity in life as in death. It is not only the fourteenth and fifteenth Earls of Derby who conspicuously fail to become immortal in print. Of Disraeli's colleagues in cabinet, a hasty count suggested that about 23 were without a proper memoir. Even major figures like Cairns, a possible Conservative premier, and Cross have left only the most worthless printed records. The same is true of chief Whips. Only one Conservative chief Whip between 1846 and 1885, Jolliffe, has a volume devoted to his career. Against this background of shadowy figures, Disraeli has appeared without context or colleagues. It has been difficult to view the Conservative party through the eyes of anyone but Disraeli. Consequently, it is the non-Disraelian side of the story that historiographically now most needs examination. Stanley's diary, informative though it is about Disraeli, places him as one politician among many, thus giving a new perspective on Conservative politics.

The diary deals with a closed upper-class world which the rest of the political nation did not understand and was not meant to understand. The diary reports what did not get into the *Times*. Some may find this exclusive world offensive. It was certainly narrow, a matter of the same handful of people continually discussing the same questions of personal prospects. Other readers of the diary, more sensibly, may wish to use it to explain what went on. Unfortunately Victorian Society never generated a historian trained in its traditions. Unlike Lord Acton, most historians are not related to the Foreign Secretary. They are lower-middle-class professionals uncertain of themselves in the unfamiliar world of power, confidence, and leisure responsibly used. The professional man cannot interpret the nuances of this world; he needs to have it interpreted for him by someone like Lord Stanley. For instance, no historian can ever really know, from his own experience, what landed property involves. At the other end of the scale, he will have no experience of dealing, every day of his life, with begging letters, (every one of which in Stanley's case received minute and scrupulous attention).

Lord Stanley's journal starts in 1849 with his entry into parliament (he was then Mr Stanley, his Whig grandfather still reigning at Knowsley and his father sitting only as a baron in the Lords). The series of journals from 1849 to 1855 present a curious question. In 1855 Lord Stanley sat down and rewrote his journals to that date. When he wrote, he presumably edited and selected. He allowed himself to add retrospective comments, usually valuable ones. Why he should impose on himself the labour of writing out several hundred thousand words is not obvious. Perhaps he wished to blot out indiscreet comment or inconvenient memory (some fragments of the original which survive are more gossipy than the revised text). He may have felt that 1855 was a watershed in his life, as he ceased to be Disraeli's pupil, and became Lady Salisbury's friend. There is no real clue. What survives is a purely impersonal political diary, preserving only what Stanley wished to preserve. In the 1860's, on the other hand, the text is quite straightforward. It is what Stanley wrote at the time. It is lighter and more gossipy, at least until Stanley became Foreign Secretary in 1866–8. There are, for the years 1861–9, no additions, excisions, obliterations, or writing up in arrears – for Stanley was a punctual, exact, and careful man who did not suffer from second thoughts.

The diaries throw new light on old topics. In one case, that of the later history of Protectionism, the new version suggested by Robert Stewart is confirmed. The question is not why Free Trade passed in 1846, but why

Protection was not restored in 1849. The diary observes Protectionist buoyancy, Whig covert sympathy, and a general sense that Free Trade had collapsed in the face of events. Parliament talked Protection, and voted Free Trade. It did so because it believed there was a possibility of revolution. Predictions of a republic indicated this fear. British reactionaries, without any effort or merit on their part, were on the crest of the wave in 1849; but, for good reactionary reasons, they dared not show themselves master of the situation. The irony of the Anti-Corn League was that it made Cobden the true father of Derbyite Conservatism, and the irony of Chartism was that it made the world safe for free trade. If we consider not why free trade began, but why it survived, we must take Chartism very much into account, and must accordingly draw up a new reckoning of its effectiveness and of its supposed death in early 1848.

Palmerston is the next subject where the diary suggests a new approach. He figures much in the diaries, but in an unfamiliar guise. There is the Palmerston who in some furtive way used Disraeli as an agent, and kept him in mind for future employment. Lord Stanley (the elder) thought Disraeli feared exposure by Palmerston. Disraeli's moving speeches on the Jews in 1847 may have been intended to provide an issue of principle, sufficiently plausible and sufficiently liberal, to enable him to escape from the Protectionist corner into which he had painted himself. But to impute such motives is Disraelian. More important, there was the Palmerston who kept the possibility of becoming Derbyite leader under continual review; and the Palmerston who was looked to by average Tory opinion not only as an ideal, but also as a probable leader. Straightforward biographical treatments of Palmerston as a Liberal politician of reactionary leanings, but a party man for all that, miss not only the point but a whole gamut of points. They represent the eventual results of 1855 and 1859–65 as if they were causes. Palmerston was in the market. The question to be explained is why he did not become the Conservative leader. The short answer is that Derby, for his own good reasons, would not let him.

The more one knows of the elder Derby, the more one respects him for ruthlessness, clarity, and single-mindedness such as one does not find in Disraeli. If Disraeli was the jockey and Jolliffe the trainer of the Derbyite horse, Lord Derby was emphatically the owner, and behaved like one. He raced in politics as elsewhere for his own excitement. On the crucial issue of buying outside support, the diary confirms that Derby was generous and correct in the opportunities he gave to others to serve under him. What is equally apparent is the trouble he took to avoid serving, in name or in fact, under anyone else. He wanted to win on his own.

In the supposed fiasco of 1851, it is hard to fault his tactics once his aims are explained. As the diary makes clear, his aim in 1851 was to avoid premature office, and in 1855 he sought to force all rival candidates for the premiership into acknowledged failure. These were not the actions of a supine or unambitious man, or the miscalculations of a tyro, but finely judged wagers. In 1855 he played high and very nearly won. Derby sought much more than office on sufferance: he sought to reconstruct from a position of unchallenged strength. The picture given by the diary is that it was Derby, not Disraeli, who was decisive in fending off unwelcome mergers. It was also Derby who accordingly found it personally useful to maintain Disraeli's position in the Commons.

In 1853–4 the centre of political calculation was the abortive Reform Bill introduced by Russell in 1854. The diaries give the opposition view of the matter and delineate Tory resilience, interspersed with gloom and disarray, after the crash of December 1852. Enough is said to suggest that on the Reform issue, if not on anything else, the Derbyites held a winning hand, had they been given a chance to play it. War intervened; and here Conservative counsels, though certainly not Jingo, had little to say. The political crisis of 1855 caught Conservatives by surprise. They did not want a crisis over the war, and they did not get one. The question for them as a party was whether to respond to post-war liberalism. It was a question they were unable to answer in the sessions of 1856 and 1857. They were saved by the Indian Mutiny, and by the 1857 election. The Mutiny indicated an area of Indian reform where imperial diehards could unite with administrative reformers like Stanley who believed they were responding to the spirit of the age and the lessons of February 1855. The 1857 election reminded Conservatives that the electoral system of 1832 was, as Malmesbury said, 'cooked', and therefore ripe for amendment.

The diaries of the 1860's are harder to sum up, because they enter more into anecdote and individual character. Constant anxiety is shown by politicians about the Queen. While Bagehot was praising the Queen as an 'elegant facade', the London crowd was expressing very different opinions; the ruling few, knowing this, feared for the discredit it might bring upon themselves. There was also the intractable difficulty of doing necessary public business with the Queen. Students of today, taught that the Queen was not historically important, see matters very differently from the public men of the 1860's.

The same difference of view emerges with Gladstone. The student of today knows that he was a great Christian man informed by the highest motives. Fair-minded observers at the time, of whom Stanley was pre-eminently one, saw a different picture. They saw what to their colder blood was a pathological lack of self-control; and they gathered from the talk of the day much speculation as to whether he was of sound mind. It is notice-able in the diaries how little anyone seemed to know of the real Gladstone at this time. Because of its gross errors, and its complete lack of sympathy, the diary reminds one how rare Gladstonians were in the 1860's.

On Reform in 1865–7 it is still too soon for a general reconsideration of
the works of F. B. Smith and M. Cowling. One diary alone can do little.
The main function of the diary is to confirm and substantiate interpreta-
tions of the Reform crisis already put forward. There are some useful first-
hand accounts of Derby's and Disraeli's intentions. The discussions in
March and April 1866 over the impending break-up of the Derbyites are
dramatically presented. The diary also adds usefully to our evidence of what
ministers thought about the popular agitation. Stanley's comments mostly
pour cold water on the idea that ministers took demonstrators (or their
leaders) seriously. Stanley did not confuse the Hyde Park crisis with the
Reform crisis. The latter he took to be a parliamentary matter, incapable of
solution by a minority party once Derby had – to Stanley's mystification –
taken office without a Whig alliance. For Stanley the only remaining question
about Reform was how best to fail to pass a measure.

In matters of foreign policy, the diary is useful, not because it supersedes
the standard diplomatic material, but because it sets the despatches in the
context of a daily routine of office work. It also, by giving a synoptic, because greatly abridged, view of world problems, offers a guide to the links
between apparently unrelated diplomatic questions, as for example when
French policy on the Rhine governed France's attitude to the Cretan
question. Stanley, a detached observer with no real power to his elbow, put
British interest first to an almost unprecedented degree – a policy sometimes
denounced as indecisive, but in fact based on a deeply rooted conviction
that there was nothing to decide. Stanley was faced with intermittent
threats of risings or disturbances in Ireland, and Irish-American attacks on
Canada. More important, he had to consider the possibility that the United
States might suddenly veer towards war with Britain. American policy was,
to Stanley, supremely important and supremely incalculable. He and
Clarendon were not even able to guess whether the Secretary of State was
holding out for a bribe. With our relations with America so unpredictable,
Stanley did well not to tempt providence. Even his opposition to the
Abyssinian expedition, which Buckle cites with disapproval, made better
sense when viewed against the need to allow for Irish and American con-
tingencies. Stanley's assessments of men and events in foreign affairs are
instructive.

And here we must give our diarist his due. In most ways he was not a
remarkable man. He could not speak on his feet. He had no phrases. He was
overshadowed by the black genius of his father and by the arts of Disraeli.
He did not represent concentrated power in any form. But he represented
integrity. His diaries show a politician who is not an 'operator'. There are
rare lapses, often instigated by Disraeli, but his motives will usually surprise
the student of politics by their unaffected absence of deviousness. Stanley
gives us a combination of commitment to politics as a vocation, which he

had and which was the only interest of his life, with a singular aversion to politics as politicians normally practise it. For all that, he achieved his life's ambition, which was to avoid becoming prime minister. Few politicians can have so completely succeeded in their aims. (Indeed, he wished to give up the Foreign Office in order to devote himself to travelling abroad for the sake of his wife's health.) His diaries show him to be a disinterested, liberal English nobleman. He was disinterested and liberal, because, merits apart, it was entirely obvious to him that by these means the power of the ruling class might be best upheld, and the great estates and houses maintained in being. He wanted the territorial aristrocracy maintained, in turn, because it supplied a political system which enabled sensible decisions to be taken, which was all he really cared about.

Trollope imagined, in Plantagenet Palliser, a fictional equivalent of 'a perfect gentleman' who was 'scrupulous, and being scrupulous, weak' yet by his integrity justified 'to the nation the seeming anomaly of an hereditary peerage and of primogeniture'. In Edward Henry Stanley, fifteenth Earl of Derby, we have an historical equivalent to Trollope's creation, presented here with a view to extending the range of political understanding accessible to our middle classes of today. Stanley was, incidentally, like Palliser, favourable to decimal reckoning.

If any one person corresponded to Trollope's painfully sensitive and dutiful paragon, it was surely Stanley. Ironically, when Stanley served as chairman of the Royal Literary Fund, of which Trollope was a member, he was sorely tried by the novelist's middle-class bumptiousness and lack of political acumen.

FAMILY TREE

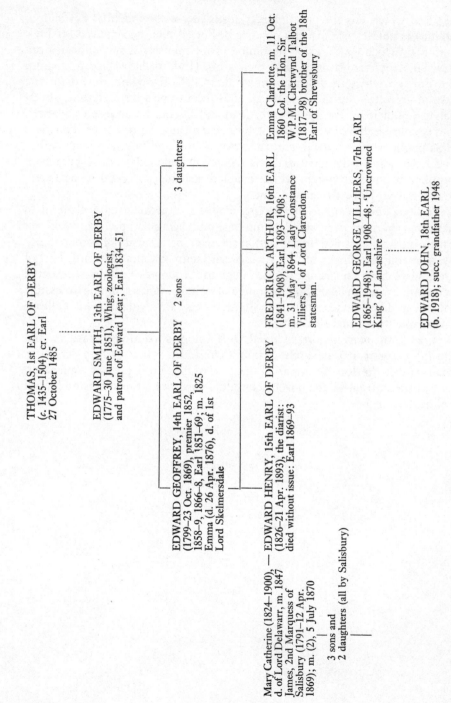

THOMAS, 1st EARL OF DERBY
(c. 1435–1504), cr. Earl
27 October 1485

EDWARD SMITH, 13th EARL OF DERBY
(1775–30 June 1851), Whig, zoologist,
and patron of Edward Lear; Earl 1834–51

EDWARD GEOFFREY, 14th EARL OF DERBY
(1799–23 Oct. 1869), premier 1852,
1858–9, 1866–8, Earl 1851–69; m. 1825
Emma (d. 26 Apr. 1876), d. of 1st
Lord Skelmersdale

2 sons

3 daughters

Emma Charlotte, m. 11 Oct.
1860 Col. the Hon. Sir
W.P.M. Chetwynd Talbot
(1817–98) brother of the 18th
Earl of Shrewsbury

Mary Catherine (1824–1900), — EDWARD HENRY, 15th EARL OF DERBY
d. of Lord Delawarr, m. 1847   (1826–21 Apr. 1893), the diarist:
James, 2nd Marquess of   died without issue: Earl 1869–93
Salisbury (1791–12 Apr.
1869); m. (2), 5 July 1870

3 sons and
2 daughters (all by Salisbury)

FREDERICK ARTHUR, 16th EARL
(1841–1908), Earl 1893–1908;
m. 31 May 1864, Lady Constance
Villiers, d. of Lord Clarendon,
statesman.

EDWARD GEORGE VILLIERS, 17th EARL
(1865–1948); Earl 1908–48; 'Uncrowned
King' of Lancashire

EDWARD JOHN, 18th EARL
(b. 1918); succ. grandfather 1948

1849

20 March 1849. I returned from America. Found my father,[1] by his account, ready to take office. He however feared that ministers would resign in order to force him into power prematurely. He wished for delay, as tending to heal past wounds, and reunite the party.

He repeated a conversation between himself and Mr Disraeli[2] on the subject of the leadership. He proposed the triumvirate as now existing (Herries,[3] Granby,[4] Disraeli). D. refused. My Father reminded him of his offer to act with Lord George Bentinck[5] under Granby. 'It is quite true' D. said 'that I acceded to such an arrangement when acting in union, and on terms of equality with, Lord George Bentinck: but I am Disraeli the adventurer and I will not acquiesce in a position which will enable the party to make use of me in debate, and then throw me aside.' My Father replied that the lead of the Commons was a question to be decided by the party in that house, and not by him: they had raised strong objections to Mr D. being sole leader, and he could not in such a matter attempt to coerce them.

Mr D. then declined all interference in party arrangements and said that he should be happy to give an independent support, but that he would speak only when it suited him as a private member. He wished to retire, and devote at least part of his time to literature.

'All this is very well' my Father answered 'but the position is one which you cannot hold. Peel[6] has tried it, and you see how his influence is gone. Your proposal, if it means anything, means that we are to lose you altogether.'

Mr D. thanked Lord Stanley for speaking so frankly, but said his mind was made up. My Father determined, as he told me, to try once more. He represented that Mr D. must be himself aware of the impossibility of acting alone. 'I would not apply to you any such terms as you have applied to yourself: but this I will say, that certain feelings exist, call them prejudices if you will, that will make many of our friends desire, in the man who is to lead them, a degree of station and influence which circumstances have not as yet enabled you to acquire: and if I were speaking to an ambitious man, and speaking for your interest alone, I tell you fairly, I could suggest no proposal which I think you would gain more by accepting. You escape the envy which attaches to a post of solitary and supreme command; you are associated with two men, neither of whom in point of abilities can stand in your way for a moment: but one of whom possesses a station and a private character which will ensure him support, while, so far from being ambitious of power, he has refused the lead when pressed upon him. The other is an

1

old man, not likely to remain long on the political stage, but having great business experience, and who will readily, give you the benefit of his knowledge. For a man desirous of distinction, I cannot see a better prospect than that which such an arrangement opens to you. I do not press for a decision, only think the matter over.'

Mr D. took his leave with many expressions of gratitude for the tone in which Lord Stanley had spoken, but repeated that his determination remained unchanged. On the first meeting, however, to which Herries and Granby were summoned, my Father thought it well to send him an invitation also. He came, sat down, discussed the Address, and without any formal acceptance, has ever since continued to act as one of the three.

23 March 1849. I took my seat, introduced by Jocelyn[7] and Granby. I sat on the second row, behind the lower part of the front opposition bench. This is the Protectionist quarter, while farther up, and nearer to the Speaker's chair, sit the Peelites. Sir Robert himself occupies the front bench: he, Disraeli, Herries, Granby, Stafford,[8] and Fergus O'Connor,[9] sometimes all take their seats close together. Behind, on the third bench, is Sir James Graham's[10] habitual post. He remains quite aloof, with no colleague or friend near him.

The Duke of Richmond[11] dined with us. A new government discussed. It is to be as follows:

Lord Stanley – First Lord
Lord Aberdeen[12] – Foreign Secretary
Lord Ashley[13] – Colonial Secretary
Henley[14] – Home Secretary
Herries – Chancellor of the Exchequer
Disraeli – Board of Trade
Granby – a seat in cabinet
Stuart[15] – Attorney-general
Walpole[15] – Solicitor-general
Parke,[17] or Pemberton Legh[18] – [Lord] Chancellor

The Duke of Richmond refuses the Home Office, saying he will never serve again. March[19] is named for an under-secretaryship if he will take one.

Lord Aberdeen's acceptance of the office proposed for him is doubtful. The rest, certain.

Herries consents to waive the leadership in Disraeli's favour, as a three-fold division is impossible in office. It was feared the party would not be well pleased with this change.

Returning to the House, I found that ministers had struck 14 out of 32 clauses from their Navigation Law Bill, leaving the coasting trade untouched. In return, and as we suppose by concert, Gladstone[20] withdrew his amendment: a sudden move, which he justified on two inconsistent grounds: first that he was unwilling to embarrass government, and second that he would not be supported. Disraeli attacked both for their vacillating conduct: Gladstone answered on his own behalf, Labouchere[21] on that of his colleagues. All three spoke well. We divided twice.

29 March 1849. The Duke of Richmond dined with us: expressed himself strongly against the possibility of forming a Protectionist ministry. My Father declares there are 110 seats, all of which his friends will contest on a dissolution. His only fear is lest the reaction against free trade should be so strong as to make it impossible for him to satisfy his supporters out-of-doors.

30 March 1849. Wilson Patten[22] proposed to me to take up the question of the repeal of the paper duties. I consulted my Father, and declined: partly as being too young a member, partly because it was doubted whether the country gentlemen would support such a motion. They contend that any remission of duties which may be financially practicable should be applied to relieve the agricultural interest of its burdens. The tax in question yields £400,000.

2 April 1849. Disraeli commented on Peel's Irish project which he condemned but in a tone of great moderation. A division was called for, but Government by a manoeuvre evaded it, thus losing us the votes of perhaps twenty men who had come up expressly from the country, meaning to return next day. Walked home with D[23]: we held our first political conversation.

3 April 1849. I met Peel for the first (and as it proved only) time at a private party. He was very silent, saying no more than politeness required, and grave even to melancholy.

10 April 1849. Visited [King's] Lynn for the first time. My chief supporter, R. Bagge,[24] met me at the station, and we walked round the town together. It is a fine old place, with two noble churches, public walks, and gardens. Local charities abound. The Corporation has £8,000 yearly to spend. Population 17,000: about 1,200 electors . . . One quarter of the town, the North End, is wholly inhabited by pilots and fishermen. The shipping interest has suffered severely from the competition of railroads. A large party was invited to meet me at dinner, and we had speeches afterwards.

11 April 1849. I addressed a meeting in the Town Hall – the same room where Lord George Bentinck delivered his violent protectionist declamations. The crowd considerable, but friendly. I was much cheered: spoke for half an hour. Another formal dinner with healths and much wine drunk.

14 April 1849. Returned to town, having paid 1,100 visits in the last three days. I was asked scarcely any questions, except about the Maynooth grant and payment of Roman Catholic priests, which it is supposed Sir R. Peel intends to propose. Lord George Bentinck's memory is held in great reverence: his faults of temper admitted, but forgiven: his liberality, energy, and devotion to the local interests of his constituents are in everyone's mouth.

Several electors said to me bluntly, not however meaning any rudeness, 'You may make us a good member, but you can never replace Lord George'.

The state of politics in Lynn is as follows. Bentinck had introduced Jocelyn to the borough,[25] becoming responsible for him: he therefore felt great indignation when Jocelyn joined the Peelites, and expressed his feelings, as was his wont, intemperately. He told Jocelyn that the latter ought to resign, which he (Jocelyn) naturally objected to do. Hence arose a quarrel, which is not yet set at rest. The Peelite section in Lynn is weak, but backed by an active though small Radical minority.

My Father talked of the Carlton dinner of 1847, at which Lord George had assailed him violently and without cause. He described the scene which ensued. 'I asked Richmond to come with me, and we called on him (Bentinck) next day. The Duke began, and I took it up, with an assurance that no offence had been intended. He said nothing. I repeated in so many words my assurance that the language used by me was not meant to refer to him. He answered that he did not believe me. I got up to go away, and said to him "Bentinck, you and I have been old friends: if you mean what you have just stated, and repeat it deliberately, I will not quarrel with you, but we can never speak again." He admitted that he had been wrong, apologised, and asked me to sit down and talk over the matter calmly. After this we never had a quarrel.'

He told me that Bateman,[26] who has lately professed Protectionist opinions, had consulted him on the Jew Bill, and that his advice was 'Don't go against your party unless your conviction is very strong indeed: if there is any doubt in your mind give them the benefit of it; hear what they have to say with an inclination to think them right.' 'By this disinterested kind of language' he added to me 'I am much more likely to secure a young man than if I showed eagerness to get his vote.'

He gave me an account of what had passed at the celebrated meeting at Brooks's, during the three or four days [in 1832] when it was expected that the Duke of Wellington would form a government, in the reform times.[27] His speech on that occasion had been repeatedly described as one series of invectives against the Duke. It was really nothing of the kind.

'When it was generally thought that the Duke was coming in, our party were furious. They called a meeting, and it was intended to pass some very strong resolutions, which would have had the effect of putting us wholly in the wrong. Althorp[28] came to me in the morning and said "for God's sake come down and keep these people from making fools of themselves." We went down together, and he spoke first. I made a strong party speech, assuring them that Reform was certain, that we had the game in our own hands, and that all we had to do was to see that we did not throw it away by any rash move. I said that the Duke, if he came in, could only choose between adopting our measures and opposing them, that as to the latter "the man must be a fool (and the Duke of Wellington is no fool) who thinks it possible, at this time of day, to carry on a government without Reform in parliament. If any parties hitherto opposed to us, be they who they may, are willing to take our places, and to carry through our measures, why then I say let the measures be carried, let us support them to the utmost, and let us leave contentedly to our successors their places and the infamy which must attend them." These were as near as I can recollect my words. I was afterwards charged with having called the Duke a fool, when Sheil[29] alluded to this speech. I wrote to Lord Ebrington[30] to ask him to confirm me in my recollection of what I had said. I have his letter now.'

19 April 1849. A meeting of Irish members of all opinions was held at Lord John Russell's,[31] to consider the vote-in-aid. This was much cavilled at, as resembling an Irish Parliament, and offensive to the English and Scotch members – especially to Irishmen representing English or Scotch boroughs, who were not summoned.

20 April 1849. Various rumours afloat: it is said that Sir R. Peel will join the government, with his followers, Lord John retiring on the ground of ill-health. It is supposed that Cobden[32] will also be included. We believe that Lord Aberdeen would join such an administration as readily as he would join us. He takes little interest in questions of domestic policy.

23 April 1849. The navigation law bill, third reading, came on at 6 p.m. Herries opened the debate: he spoke an hour, very slowly, sometimes hesitating, his voice feeble, but he made every argument tell upon the House. The absence of reciprocity, the reaction against free trade in the public mind, the risk of the experiment, were all urged with effect. Nothing followed until Sir J. Graham, arguing for the bill, declared himself in favour of 'progress', a declaration received with loud Radical cheering. Lord John declined to go into the question, spoke only half an hour, and rested his case in great part on the necessity of yielding in order to avoid agitation. Disraeli in reply said he had first made the agitation, then yielded to it: told him that the progress they spoke of, was 'progress to the devil': cited the falling off of incomes, and increase of rates, as evidence of distress: and renewed his pledges to protection on corn as well as ships. . . . We divided 214 to 275.

25 April 1849. I voted in favour of a bill for allowing mail trains on Scotch lines to carry passengers on Sunday. The Directors are bound to run these trains by their contracts for postal purposes: but by a strange piece of puritanical pedantry, they object to allow any passenger to make use of them . . .

30 April 1849. Much is said of the prospect of a Protectionist government: lists of its members are given, none of them accurate. My Father declared on Friday that he would oppose the navigation law repeal to the utmost, regardless of consequences. This is taken as implying that he is ready to accept office. Lord Brougham[33] votes with us on this question. Many think he would join us in forming a government. Lord Aberdeen on the other hand, though professing friendship, is much distrusted.

2 May 1849. Lord Aberdeen and many others dined with us. He strongly censured the Canadian policy of ministers.

Our lists bring the numbers on Monday next (navigation law debate) within 8: allowing government 16 of the bishops, whose votes, though uncertain, are in such matters usually given with the minister. Much vague talk about Prince Albert canvassing peers for the bill. He is said to have written to the Duke of Wellington, who gave an evasive reply: but these stories rest on little foundation. Lord Brougham has given us strong pledges, but many say he will yet change his mind.

3 May 1849. The Duke of Richmond dined with us: our cabinet was discussed: my Father thought Lord Ashley ought to go to the India Board instead of the colonies, he being thought impracticable: Disraeli to hold the Colonial Office: Stafford or T. Baring,[34] Board of Trade.

We had in the House a bill for allowing marriage with a deceased wife's sister. I had thought and read much on the subject, but did not vote, my own opinion being favourable to the relaxation of the law, while that of my Father, Gladstone, and the Conservatives generally, is the other way.

5 May 1849. Dr Whewell,[35] Master of Trinity College, Cambridge, wrote to me avowing himself a Protectionist, and pointing out the course which he thought we ought to take. He was a Whig in early life, appointed to the mastership by Peel in 1841. He is notoriously ambitious of a bishopric, and earned Court favour by exerting himself to return Albert as Chancellor of the University. His accession, therefore, shows that he thinks the tide turning. I showed his letters to my Father: and urged the Dr to express his opinions publicly in a pamphlet. This he was too cautious to do.

We hear of nothing except the canvass which the Court is supposed to be carrying on. The arguments used are that the rejection of the bill would lead to a dissolution, that parliament could not meet again till late, and that the Queen would be seriously inconvenienced by being prevented from going to Scotland. Others are threatened with a renewal of the Corn Law battle: and as a consequence, with an agitation of free traders for an extension of the suffrage.

From later calculations, we have now no doubt that the division must go against us. This is however kept secret, lest the knowledge of the fact should swell the majority.

My Father had lately a conversation with Lord Aberdeen, in which he told him that on his vote (if the bill were thrown out) depended the formation of a Protectionist ministry: since, if he went against us, it would be impossible to include him in the arrangements, and without him as Foreign Secretary we could not succeed. He bade him consider well the responsibility which he was incurring.

On going down to the House, we heard that the majority would be at least 16 against us. Lord Aberdeen also had pronounced for Government.

Lord Lansdowne[36] opened the debate. Brougham followed, spoke for 2¼ hours, connectedly, very amusing in parts, but on the whole prolix. He did not however digress much. He argued the case, he said, as a free trader. He moved no amendment, but spoke on the original question. Lord Colchester[37] moved that the bill be read this day six months. Ellenborough[38] closed the debate in a speech of remarkable power. Altogether the advantage of argument and eloquence was on our side.

In the Commons, the second reading of the Jew Bill came on. . . . Disraeli remained silent, though called upon repeatedly by name. He voted with Government. . .

6 May 1849. Less interest was shown in the second night's debate (Lords) because the result was already known. But both last night and this the House was crowded, indeed yesterday the attendance in the Commons was was very thin, and today we were counted out, in consequence of the number of M.P.'s who were listening to the peers. . . . Lord Grey[39] rose late, argued the question well and powerfully, but in too dry a style: his unadorned reasoning, however effective, was ill-suited to an audience which having passed seven hours in listening, was at once exhausted and excited. The speech was, oratorically, a failure: though none but an able politician could have made it. My Father followed. He rose at past 2 a.m., was obliged to throw overboard all his statistics, and deal only with the general bearings of the question. He kept the attention of the House alive throughout, ridiculed Lord Grey, and appealed to the Duke of Wellington in a singularly beautiful peroration. The old man appeared moved, turned restlessly in his seat, and covered his face with his hands. It was past 4 a.m. when Lord Stanley sat down. Lord Lansdowne replied feebly: the division took place at 5 a.m. On our side, one vote was lost by the holder giving his vote from the Woolsack, which is not within the House. One peer (a ministerialist) came down too drunk to be presentable, but was paired nevertheless. Two insane peers were brought in and made to vote, the keeper of one being in attendance in the lobby.

7 May 1849. Dining with the Jerseys,[40] I met Lord Hawarden,[41] who was profuse, and even abject, in his apologies. He said that he owed everything to Peel, and could not oppose him. Lord Wilton[42] told me that the Duke had pronounced my Father's speech 'not only the finest which he had ever made, but the finest ever delivered in parliament.' The Duke makes no secret of the reluctance with which he supports Government.

A singular, and I hope rare, case of parliamentary corruption[43] occurred in relation to this question, when it was before the Commons. A shipowner much interested in the maintenance of the laws as they stood, received from a parliamentary agent, whose name was mentioned to me, an offer of ten votes for £1,000. The members implicated were supporters of the government, and offered to stay away for £100 apiece: the money not to be paid till after the division. The offer was rejected, chiefly, I believe, because ten votes could have done nothing to turn the scale. I did not hear this directly from the shipowner (whose name I know) but from an official member of our party to whom the proposition was referred.

15 May 1849. I began a series of articles in the *Morning Post* on the Canadian question . . .

19 May 1849. I called on Disraeli to discuss with him the Canadian question. He undertakes to bring it forward. It has occupied a good deal of public attention, in consequence of the riots which broke out at Montreal, when when Lord Elgin[44] was pelted, and the Parliament House burnt. D. then entered on another subject: the want of a party organ. We agreed to see what could be done provisionally with the *Morning Post*: to try and revive that paper in the first place, and if it succeeded, then to purchase it. I promised two weekly articles, or three if required. John Manners[45] and Powis[46] were also to be taken into the scheme. We thought Adderley,[47] Baillie,[48] Ker Seymer,[49] and several others, might be applied to for occasional assistance. We are sadly crippled by the want of a journal . . . Nothing could exceed D.'s civilities and confidence to me on this occasion. He suggested a weekly meeting, or council, of his principal friends, which he asked me to join. (This fell through. I heard no more of it. The *Morning Post* scheme ended in my writing a few articles, but no one else did so, and I gave it up.)

He took an opportunity in the course of this conversation strenuously to disclaim any special forbearance towards Palmerston. There had been some misunderstanding on the subject of a proposed attack on the Sicilian intervention. D. accuses my Father of having changed his mind, and refusing to allow it to be brought forward. (This may well be, without any inconsistency, inasmuch as Lord Aberdeen's final alienation from us makes it useless to displace Palmerston.) My Father in his turn thinks that D. is afraid to hazard an attack, it being in Lord Palmerston's power to retaliate with a charge of having volunteered to take office under him. The report, industriously circulated at the beginning of the session, is to the effect that while it was doubtful whether the lead would be conferred upon him or no, D. was in treaty for the office of Minister at Vienna – that Lord P. objected on the ground of his being a Protectionist, whereon D. replied 'Search my speeches through, and you will not find one word of Protection in them.' This last saying, whether genuine or fictitious, is near the truth. His great displays on the Corn question have all been attacks on opponents, not assertions of a principle. (I repeat this absurd story simply because it was very current at the time.) He is now anxious to drop the subject of a protective duty altogether: but this the party will not allow.

20 May 1849. Some conversation with my Father on the question of Protection. He does not think it hopeless to restore a moderate fixed duty: and proposes to combine this with a sliding scale, to commence when the price of corn is very low: the two extremes of said scale being (say) 35s. per quarter and 60s. Between these the duty to remain fixed: to decrease at 60s.; and increase when the price fell below 35s.

25 May 1849. Disraeli is negotiating for the [*Morning*] *Post*: says they ask £15,000: which is just £10,000 less than last year, when it was offered to Bentinck. Except the Duke of Richmond, I doubt whether any peer will subscribe largely: and on all accounts a public subscription is inadvisable. It may be possible, however, to find some capitalist who will take it on as a speculation, paying £10,000 or £12,000: and that we may make up the difference.

House adjourned for the Whitsuntide recess. I went to Cambridge, and lodged with Dr Whewell, meeting there Bancroft[50] and Lord Monteagle.[51]

1 June 1849. Another conversation with Disraeli on the press. I found him desirous of buying the *Morning Chronicle* which appears to be on sale. It is not, as commonly supposed, the property of the Peelite party, but was purchased as a speculation, and constituted the organ of that party. The sale is not remunerative, and the proprietors wish either to part with it, or to place it under new management. The price given by them is said to have been only £5,000: but they have spent large sums on its improvement. The literary reputation of this journal is higher than that of the *Post*, and its purchase besides securing a friend, would silence an enemy.

D. also tells of moving for a Committee to inquire into the state of the nation, as was done by Tierney[52] many years ago. Such a motion if carried is equivalent to a vote of no confidence.

5 June 1849. Hume[53] brought on his motion for ballot, household suffrage, triennial parliaments, and electoral districts. He spoke two hours, having passed the morning on a committee, where he took a very active part. He is 72 years of age, and is only just recovered from a severe illness. A fortnight ago his life was despaired of. Bright[54] delivered an angry tirade against the aristocracy, and told Government that they had always been more aristocratic than the Tory party. Lord John replied in a Conservative strain, called the Manchester party 'narrow-minded', and opposed the motion. He was cheered loudly from our side, but by us only. He threw out something like a hint as to future extension of suffrage.[55]

7 June 1849. Sir A. Macnab,[56] who had come over from Canada yesterday as agent for the Loyalist party, (of which he is leader), went with me to breakfast with Lord Brougham and state his case. He and Lord B. talked both together during the whole time, but Lord B. contrived to get a fair knowledge of the case. We then went (Sir A. and I) to Herries, and to Lord Lyndhurst,[57] who rather threw cold water on our expectations. Sir A. wished to call on Gladstone, which I dissuaded him from doing. Mr G. has taken up the question, but it is suspected that he only does so to prevent it from falling into our hands. In the evening, I drew out a statement of the facts, for parliamentary circulation. A meeting was fixed for the next day at Lord Brougham's. We tried also to collect opinions from former Canadian governors – Sir F. Head, Sir G. Arthur,[58] and others.

In conversation, we referred to the swamping of the Canadian Upper House, or Council. This was compared to what took place here in 1831–2. Lord B. said, the question of making new peers in case of resistance had been discussed between himself and Lord Grey: finding that not less than 80 creations would be required, they had determined not to carry out their threat.[59] The chief argument that swayed them was the following. They thought after a period of such excitement a strong reaction must follow: a Conservative ministry would succeed to power: and the Lords being so thoroughly liberalised, a fresh batch of Tory peers must be made in order to restore the balance. Thus the mischief would perpetuate itself.

10 June 1849. An interview of three hours with Disraeli: we went through the Canadian case: he then explained to me his plan of attack in moving for a Committee (v. above). . . . He said he should drop protection, but dwell on the necessity of reciprocity.

11 June 1849. Jew Bill read a third time, [passed] by 272 to 206, after a dull debate. Disraeli voted, but kept out of the House until towards the close of the debate.

I called on Macnab, who talked of the future prospects of Canada. Two schemes have been proposed for the purpose of destroying the political influence of the French interest: the first, to join Gaspé and the eastern townships with Nova Scotia, Montreal and the Ottawa settlements with Upper Canada, thus leaving the French settlers isolated, and allowing them to form a separate province: the second proposition is of a nature directly contrary: to join all the British N. American provinces in one league, with a single Governor and legislature. Neither of these plans appear feasible: the latter is the more so.

14 June 1849. The Canadian debate came on . . . We pressed hard for a division – the Peelites, as we had expected, tried to avoid one. Herries had brought the matter to an issue by making a motion, but Government came to the rescue by moving an adjournment, which they carried.

15 June 1849. Debate resumed: Macnab sat under the gallery all night, and put into my hands some important papers which I supplied to Disraeli shortly before he rose. D. spoke well, in his peculiar style . . . Peel supported ministers, who carried their vote by 291 to 150. We had many defaulters, Henley among them, but gained some converts, from the other side. We reckoned our loss of votes on which we had counted, at 25. Many were influenced by distrust and dislike of Gladstone . . .

17 June 1849. Called on Disraeli with facts and figures for his speech. He expressed himself strongly on the necessity of making an effort next year, and making it on new principles. He seemed to intimate that we, the Conservative party, were engaged in a losing cause: but said if we became more democratic, what would England be but an inferior copy of America?

20 June 1849. . . . Rumours of Lord John's resignation have revived, in consequence of his having fallen down in a fit yesterday at Norfolk House.

22 June 1849. Wood[60] opened his budget, in a very full House. He has risen in general opinion since his speech at the beginning of this session, and Peel's compliments upon it. His gesture is awkward, his voice brazen and disagreeable, but the articulation distinct. He was held to have succeeded tonight. I heard some candid expressions of regret at the financial state of affairs being so prosperous under free trade. No debate ensued, only a rambling speech from Hume, on whom years begin to tell.

23 June 1849. A great Protectionist dinner at the Mansion House.

26 June 1849. The Drury Lane meeting came off. I did not attend: and doubt the policy of such demonstrations, though they are deemed useful. Malmesbury[61] is said to have spoken well. But Conservative leaders are out of place conducting an agitation.

30 June 1849. This week has been chiefly taken up with debates on Irish poor law: very tedious, yet involving some important principles. There is among Irish members on all sides a strong tendency to communistic legislation, such as throwing the burden of pauperised unions or electoral districts on those which are better managed – in other words, taxing the good landlord for the support of the bad. This is the theory of the rate-in-aid, which Government has introduced and carried through, and it is not strange that private members also should act upon it. . . . Disraeli rose at 5.30, spoke 2¼ hours, unequally, in a style free from sarcasm, and somewhat didactic. He dwelt most effectively on foreign affairs, which seem to be his favourite subject. Some closing sentences about the 'hierarchy of classes' were incomprehensible to the country gentlemen, and indeed not easily comprehended by anyone . . .

3 July 1849. . . . Dined with Gladstone. Mr G talked much of an attack which he meditates on the Hudson Bay Company's charter.[62] He did not say, nor seem to know, what form of government he would propose to substitute among the wild Indian tribes of that country.

6 July 1849. . . . [Peel's] language towards us was conciliatory: he seemed to treat Disraeli with a studied and pompous courtesy which provoked some amusement. He ended with an eloquent warning against a return to the protective system . . . Granby tried to reply, but failed totally, breaking down in the statistical part of his argument. Lord John followed: and at near 2 a.m. Disraeli replied. His speech was amusing, though inconclusive:

but he woke up the sleepers, put the House in good humour, and did away the bad effects of Granby's failure . . .

17 July 1849. Henley brought on a motion for financial reform, proposing a reduction of official salaries, on the ground that free trade had reduced prices, and thus increased the value of money. This motion was not well received on our side. Herries and Granby voted against it, and Disraeli for. *25 July 1849*. Dined with Disraeli, meeting only George Smythe.[63]

On 28 July, Stanley left town for Knowsley, remaining there, apart from an excursion to his father's property at Buxton 'which I had not before seen', until he set off on a tour of Ireland about 17 August. Travelling alone, he took a predictable route from Cork to Bantry and Killarney, noting incomparable scenery and squalor, and meeting John Bright on the public car to Killarney. Bright 'avowed his preference for a republican form of government very frankly, but not offensively'. On 26 August, Stanley returned to his father's estate at Ballykisteen, Tipperary, and his thoughts on his visit were published in three letters to *John Bull*. On 4 September, Stanley visited the Isle of Man, staying with the Bishop and then with the Governor. Stanley then crossed to the Lake District where he stayed with Lord Brougham. In mid-September, Stanley sailed for the West Indies, visiting Madeira, Barbados, Trinidad, Guiana, Jamaica, the Spanish Main, and Cuba, returning, via the U.S., in March 1850. His original journals of this voyage were later condensed by him into a memorandum separate from his main journals.

1850

On returning to England in the beginning of March 1850, I found a change in the state of political parties, especially in that of ours. Towards the close of last session, and still more during the winter, Disraeli had become unpopular, partly as the hostility to Sir R. Peel, the expression of which by him constituted his chief claim to confidence, began to diminish: partly also because he appeared desirous of giving up the contest for a re-enactment of the corn laws, on which the Protectionist M.P.'s and the farmers out-of-doors were still bent. The more violent of these, under the leadership of G. F. Young,[1] seemed inclined to imitate the proceedings of the League, which they had always denounced as unconstitutional. Meetings were held, angry speeches delivered, and in some cases riots ensued, which did us no good in the opinion of thinking persons: while Disraeli, who stood aloof from these manifestations, was maturing a plan of agricultural relief which he wished to have accepted as the substitute for a protective duty.

However little the Protectionists might approve this change, the want of a parliamentary leader left them no alternative but to submit. And the tactical skill of their chief was shown in the success of the resolutions brought forward by him early in the session. I was not in England at the time, therefore judge of their effect by hearsay only. They fell like a shell in the Peelite camp, and for a time completely divided that party. All who wished to stand well with both sides, and looked forward to a future reconciliation, voted with us: our members were largely reinforced, the wavering were strengthened, the discontented confessed themselves satisfied. Disraeli became once more popular, and the speedy fall of ministers was predicted with confidence. It was perhaps equally advantageous to our leader, that immediately afterwards he was seized with a serious illness: whereby all lingering feelings of discontent were merged in regret for his state, fear of losing his services, and a sense of helplessness without him. In his absence little was done: nor did any event occur worth noting except a debate on Hutt's[2] motion for the withdrawal of the African squadron. This motion caused great alarm to ministers: every engine was put in motion by them to retain the support of their followers, which was not easily secured: the results of keeping up this armed force had been small, the cost was heavy, and circumstances had occurred threatening quarrels with other states. We might have obtained a victory by coalescing with the Radicals, which many were anxious to do: my Father himself, though disliking the motion on its abstract merits, hesitated as to the propriety of this course. One reason which inclined us in the opposite direction, was the calculation that, were Government turned out,

13

they would take the opportunity of reconstructing their cabinet with the help of Sir James Graham and his friends. We should have had fair parliamentary ground for supporting Hutt, even though intending to retain the squadron: since we should have argued that it was useless as a means for the prevention of slave trading, without the additional safeguard of a differential duty on Cuban and Brazilian sugar, which we meant to propose. However, it was ultimately decided to do nothing: and on the night of the debate, I carried down a note to Beresford[3] with secret instructions not to bring up his whole force, and not to urge doubtful members to vote against their wish. Hutt, Cardwell,[4] Gladstone, and Russell spoke powerfully: there was much perplexity and cross-voting: Graham and Mahon[5] went away before the division. With the former I had much conversation. He admitted that, but for fear of turning out the ministry, he should support the motion. I voted against it, with Russell, and against the majority of the Conservatives.

22 March 1850. We had a debate on the constitution of the legislature in Australia . . . I observed with pleasure the appeals made on all sides equally to the precedent of America, as indicating a diminution of prejudice among Conservatives.

26 March 1850. We adjourned for Easter. Much comment on Lord Westminster's[6] acceptance of the post of Lord Steward: Court office being in general designed for, and held by, men whose fortune is inferior to their rank, while Lord W. is supposed to possess something like £150,000 income. This piece of avarice was severely, and most justly, censured in a *Times* article.

A vehement pamphlet by the Bishop of Exeter against the Primate, on the Gorham controversy, drew general attention by its style and unepiscopal tone. (Of this pamphlet, 100,000 copies were sold).

No attack was made for a week after the Houses met again: the first occasion of dispute being a proposition of Government to appoint a committee of enquiry into the salaries of public officers. This, Opposition determined to resist: and a meeting was held accordingly in St James's Square, at which the subject was debated, and the various arguments gone into. My Father objected, on constitutional grounds, to a ministry delegating its functions to a committee, and thus relieving itself of responsibility. We proposed – direct and immediate reduction, to a definite amount, instead of vague enquiry where no fresh information was needed, which could only serve to waste time, and might lead to no result. The discussion was not animated: in the division we were beaten by 91: 250 to 159. All the Radicals except Hume voted with Ministers, notwithstanding their professions of economy: a course for which at the time they were much censured, but in truth they had cause to doubt the sincerity of the Conservative party, the great mass of whom disliked the vote which they gave, and probably would have found means to avoid acting up to it.

(I had occasion on this, and other similar votes, to remark the want of unity and cohesion in the Protectionist party. The more sensible had already ceased to believe in the possibility of restoring the corn laws, or at most desired a fixed 5s. duty: yet they had no other definite aim, no great hope of power, but seemed content to offer an unmeaning and unavailing opposition to every act of Government. This policy of frequent attack was encouraged by the leaders, as tending to keep up discipline, and prevent desertion. The non-abandonment of Protection as a cry was however not optional with many: the farmers whose minds had been thoroughly pervaded with that idea, refused to let it drop: even in the heart of the purely rural districts, where reverence for rank is greatest, farmers' meetings were frequently held, at which landlords supposed hostile or lukewarm to the cause were very roughly handled. In some cases, by an express resolution, all land-owners and magistrates were excluded (this occurred near Belvoir, in Leicestershire, to my recollection, and also in other localities): the cry of 'lower rents' succeeded to that of 'higher duties' and as the country gentle-men would not concede the first, they felt themselves all the more bound to speak and vote for the latter. The Duke of Richmond, whose influence with the agricultural class was and is very considerable, expressed to me extreme alarm at the course which affairs were taking among them. Prophecies of the early advent of a Republic abounded,[7] my Father being among the prophets, but I think not seriously or deliberately meaning what he said.)

17 April 1850. After some unimportant debates on stamp and paper duties, Fox[8] of Oldham brought forward his motion for a general system of educa-tion – an injudicious one, for besides the total exclusion of religion from all schools established under his proposed bill, by which proviso he incurred the enmity of all the clergy of every sect, he had so framed it as to vest a power absolutely despotic in the Privy Council, and to extinguish all schools actually existing. Such a measure could not pass: nor was it designed so to do. It gave the Radicals occasion to display their oratory, and that was all. In the debate Stafford spoke with an artificial theatrical cleverness which belongs to him, and which one may admire, but not like. Lord Arundel,[9] a simple-minded bigot entirely in the hands of his priests, imprudently likened the effect of this bill to that of the Reformation, which gave Roe-buck[10] an opening, and would have added several votes to Fox's list, had we that day divided. Though favourable to what is called a 'secular system' of school teaching, I had no hesitation in voting against Fox: on the plain ground that his plan would not work, and could only have led to a vast waste of public money. The mover is a man of considerable talent, a So-cinian preacher, lecturer, and political writer, professing extreme democratic opinions, apparently without personal views. His size is about that of Louis Blanc: his large head and singular face encircled by long grey hair which streams down to his shoulders. There is some likeness between him and the prints of Franklin, perhaps aided by art. In the House he has preserved, but not increased, the peculiar reputation for talent which he brought into it. His personal friends seem to be few: and he speaks but rarely. (He has now, 1855, subsided into a silent member: but writes for the *Weekly Dispatch*, and perhaps for other journals) . . .

(My journals here contain a long account of negotiations for the purchase or setting up of a Conservative newspaper, in which Disraeli took a leading part. We proposed first to buy the [*Morning*] *Chronicle*, then to supply the [*Morning*] *Post* regularly with articles, lastly to establish a weekly organ of our own. All these projects came to nothing: but I contributed a good many articles both last year and this, to the *Herald*, although disliking the general principles and tone of that journal. We consulted those members of the party who were thought most likely to take an interest in the scheme, but to no purpose. Some were jealous of D.: others disliked the press without knowing why: few liked the notion of paying down money without getting something tangible, like a new vote in parliament, to show for it. They had no faith in an ultimate result on public opinion.

26 April 1850. We joined Macgregor[11] in a vote for repealing the duties on marine insurance. The object of those who thought of anything beyond the amusement of putting Government in a minority, was to drive them to reimpose a corn law for the sake of revenue, by holding over them the threat of a deficit. A false and foolish calculation, but Opposition seldom require more than an excuse to oppose. Disraeli pleaded to me the necessity of keeping the farmers amused, and of not seeming to abandon our post. I did not like either the vote or the excuse, but accepted both. (At this stage of my parliamentary life, I like most beginners, thought an independent vote a mere feat of audacity, only to be resorted to in extreme cases: nor do I greatly blame myself, for it requires some legislative practice to weigh both sides of a question: and it is but reasonable to give one's friends the benefit of a doubt.)

. . . [Lord John Manners] possesses a fortunate audacity not to be expected in so modest and mild a man: and if called upon (though never for his own pleasure) will grapple with any speaker on any topic, whether known to him or not.

We voted in this week £300,000 for the relief of distressed Irish unions: by a needless delicacy, this gift was termed a loan, though certain not to be repaid.

30 April 1850. Henley moved for a reduction of all official salaries by 10%: a motion which caused much dissatisfaction on our side. He rested his argument on a double basis, first that officials in general were overpaid: secondly, that free trade had rendered cheaper the necessaries of life, and indirectly, all articles of purchase, whether necessaries or not. The latter ground was ingeniously taken to please our Protectionist friends, and to a great extent succeeded. The debate went off indifferently: Henley argumentative but tedious, plodded steadily through his case, omitting nothing, and reasoning strongly, though in an uncouth manner ... Peel in his pompous, plausible way eulogised the clerks of all the offices – in short everyone employed by government. D. who had announced to me his intention of giving Henley a 'silent and sullen support' roused himself to reply, and delivered an odd, rambling speech, in the course of which he averred that all reforms in finance had originated with the Tory party – a startling assertion, but which our benches cheered to the echo. I noticed that he referred again and again by name to the 'Tory party' as if wishing to substitute that term for 'Protectionist' – but it was indifferently received. He also took occasion, and this I believe was the main object of his speaking, to allude to Protection. 'The time was past when that question could be settled in the House: it must now be referred to the people: and it was only by experience that the people could be instructed.' A clever but ineffectual endeavour to shelve a disagreeable topic. Lord John [Russell] exposed his tactics very neatly: his reply told on the division. Numbers, 173 to 265. Many Conservatives stayed away. Some voted with ministers, as did also Cobden and Bright, to the disgust of some of our own people who had absented themselves solely from dislike to go into the same lobby with these two men. Graham was absent. It was generally believed at this time that in the event of any reconstruction of the ministry being necessary, he [Graham] would join it, perhaps take the lead in our House, Lord John [Russell] going to the Lords.

7 May 1850. Sir E. Buxton,[12] a Whig philanthropist, had fixed for this day a motion on the state of the West Indies: Beresford, anticipating a possible victory, made great efforts to bring up Conservative members from the country. When the time came Buxton was ill and the debate had to be postponed. Many over-shrewd politicians suspected a trick, but this suspicion the character of the man refuted. The contretemps caused no small annoyance, for many of the country gentlemen never attend, unless expressly summoned for some particular division.

10 May 1850. The Irish Reform Bill passed its third reading, after a debate not equal to the interest which the measure had created out-of-doors. Its effect is supposed to be that of placing the parliamentary representation of Ireland almost entirely in the hands of the priests. So Sheil predicted, and most Irish M.P.'s on both sides say the same.

The Duke of Argyll[13] brought on the case of one Mr Ryland, a colonial officer, alleged to have been improperly removed from his situation. The Duke is 27, the youngest peer who takes part in public affairs: he has some talent, more confidence, a diminutive figure, an affected style of dress, with long red hair loose over his shoulders, and a deep sonorous voice, capable of great rhetorical power. There is nothing to prevent this young man rising to a very high position except his too visible arrogance and conceit. He spoke very well, with logical force not inferior to his fluency. His style reminded me of Gladstone. When he sat down, Brougham, who during his speech had been noisy in applause, clapped him on the back, with a 'well crowed, little Highland cock!' which the Duke did not appear to like.

11 May 1850. A meeting of delegates was held at Lord Eglintoun's[14] house, for the purpose of presenting an address to my Father, expressive of confidence in him, and of their desire that increased efforts should be made for the restoration of Protection. He had previously received private letters, signed and unsigned, complaining of his lukewarmness, and urging the necessity of more vigorous action. Some went so far as to suggest the possibility of other leaders being substituted. These instigations, I think, he might have disregarded: he certainly attached to them more importance than they deserved: and determined accordingly to address the delegates in such a tone as should leave no excuse for discontent. He began by a defence of himself and his friends. It was not in parliament, he said, that the battle must be fought. A constitutional agitation must be carried on. 'You ask me for advice. I say go on, and God prosper you. Do not tire, do not hesitate, do not falter in your course. Maintain the language of strict loyalty to the Crown, and obedience to the laws. Do not listen to rash and intemperate advisers, who would urge you to have recourse to unwise and disloyal threats. But with a spirit of unbroken and unshaken loyalty to the Crown, and with a spirit of unswerving obedience to the laws, combine in a determined resolution by all constitutional means to enforce your rights, and to urge upon those who now misrepresent you the duty of really representing your sentiments and supporting you in parliament.' He then explained the objection to Protectionist motions in parliament: namely, that each successive division involved a renewed pledge in favour of free trade on the part of such members as might be wavering, but not yet converted. It was wiser to point out the working of the system, and let conviction do its work gradually. Meantime the feeling of the country ought to be roused. 'If you ask my advice, I say, persevere in the course which you have adopted. Agitate the country from one end to the other. Contrive to call meetings in every direction. Do not fear – do not flinch from discussion . . . . . . if there be but one district in which a suspicion is entertained that I am flinching from, or hesitating in, my advocacy of those principles on which I stood in conjunction with my late lamented friend Lord G. Bentinck – I authorise you – one and all of you – to assure those whom you represent that in me they will find no hesitation, no flinching, and no change of opinion: that attached as I have ever been to the principle of Protection, that attachment remains unchanged, and I only look for the moment when it may be possible for us to use the memorable words of the Duke of Wellington on the field of Waterloo, and to say "Up Guards, and at them!" '

Singularly enough, the press took little notice of this very strong appeal. It delighted the ultras, and both annoyed and alarmed Disraeli. (The explanation of its being made is simple. My Father, not only at this time, but even so late as the winter of 1851, believed a partial return (at least) to a protective system possible. Nothing more irritated him than to have it thought that his continued support of such a system arose from unwillingness to resign his post as party leader, or from any personal motive. On the other hand, Disraeli was well known to be desirous of abandoning the cause altogether. My Father wished, therefore, perhaps not without some little mischievous amusement at the idea of disconcerting an intrigue of his subordinate, to give, in the name of the party, a pledge from which there could be no receding. He may also have been glad to shift the scene of combat from parliament to the country, so that the agitators could only blame themselves in the event of failure).

23 May 1850. . . . George Smythe spoke, for the first time during two years. He is, or rather was, a young man of great promise, but an incurable habit of indolence has marred his prospects. (In the four years 1851–5 Smythe has done nothing. He promised assistance when we set up the *Press* but though a well-wisher to Disraeli, never gave it.)

I wrote and published a pamphlet on the West Indian question[15] at this time, in the form of a letter to Gladstone. It had some success, and was largely quoted in the debate of the 31st.

Lord Aberdeen again renewed his overture to my Father, stimulated by the hope of organising an attack on Palmerston. He professed great friendship etc. but carefully avoided giving any pledge.

6 June 1850. . . . A great Protectionist meeting held this day in Liverpool, passed off peaceably and well. 4,000 persons attended: Wilton was in the chair: the speeches were better than is usual at such gatherings. The mass of those present were tradesmen, artisans, and others from the towns, not connected with land – a circumstance much noticed. Macneile,[16] the actor-preacher, was there, and delivered a vehement anti-slavery harangue in the old style. Butt,[17] an Irish barrister of local reputation, also distinguished himself. I declined to go down, excusing myself on the score of my grandfather's well-known opinions.[18]

9 June 1850. Much conversation with Disraeli: speculations on the fate of the motion relative to Greece:[19] D. predicted a victory in the Lords, a whitewashing motion in the Commons, but whether this would be carried or not, he could not judge. It was thought the Peelite party would be divided: that Gladstone and Graham would turn against Palmerston, but Peel support him: the latter no longer desiring office, and dreading a Protectionist ministry: the two former aiming at a reconstruction, and the lead of the Whig party. Lord Aberdeen was greatly suspected, D. said (and I had heard the same from others) of making us catspaws in this business:

intending to overthrow Lord Palmerston and then supplant him with the Whigs. I told this to my Father, who scouted the idea, saying that he did not particularly admire Lord Aberdeen but thought him wholly incapable of such treachery as this. Both D. and I agreed as to the extreme importance of drawing off men's minds if possible from the free trade question, but also as to the difficulty of effecting this object. He, like myself, has long given up the idea (if indeed he ever entertained it) of a return to protective duties on corn.

The next week, being that of Ascot, little was done in either House. My Father's absence from London while the Australian bill passed through the Lords, caused some amusement, the more so as it passed only by two votes: but he was paired off. Of course he was at the races.

17 June 1850 (Monday). After two postponements, the Greek debate at length came off. Long before 5 p.m. the House of Lords was thronged . . . (Up to this date, February 1855, I have never seen so great an interest shown in any question, nor so dense a crowd about the House). . . . it was 5.15 when my Father rose, and he spoke until past 8. Not for an instant did the attention of his 800 or 1,000 listeners flag: the most profound silence, broken only by cheering and laughter, prevailed during the entire time. The exceeding clearness of the style, pointed, without so much of ornament as would have seemed to direct attention from the substance to the words: the skill with which each thought, or argument, or fact, led to on that which followed, as if the speaker had been carelessly pursuing the course of his own ideas, while no one could have removed or transposed without disturbing the whole chain of reasoning: the rapid transitions from ridicule to grave reasoning, or indignant denunciation, often startling in their abruptness, but never unnatural – astonished even me, long accustomed to hear from him similar displays. George Smythe, writing in the *Chronicle*, said of this speech that it was 'accurate as an official précis, terse and close as one of Sir James Graham's official despatches, luminous and graceful as a page of Macaulay, and as entertaining as the last new novel.' Fifteen Blue Books had been digested to furnish the evidence: and in the immense labour which this preparation involved, my Father, as his custom is, would suffer no one to help him. Don Pacifico's claim was laughed out of court: even those who voted with Government could not mention the name of this unlucky adventurer without a smile. But the feeling excited was not that of ridicule, when the orator, changing in an instant his look, voice, and tone, reminded his hearers that it was in support of demands ilke these – demands which could hardly be named with a grave face that the peace of Europe had been disturbed, and a fleet employed greater than that which fought at the Nile. The peroration, contrary to usual practice, was quite extemporaneous (Lord D. himself told me this): he had prepared a few closing sentences, but did not use them, the inspiration of the moment supplying a more effective conclusion. . . . No ordinary debater could hope to produce an impression after the great effort of the mover. The division gave a majority of 37: 169 to 132: we had reckoned on 10 at the outside. Lord Roden,[20] whom we had supported (somewhat to our discredit) in his quarrel with the Irish Government, stayed away with two proxies in his pocket. In the Commons, we had a debate on the Irish lord-lieutenancy which was ill attended, half the members being at the Lords' bar.

18 June 1850. I met Disraeli returning from the House, and walked with him in the Park for near an hour. He told me that the first intention of ministers had been to resign: but that they had changed their purpose, after a three hours' cabinet. He repeated his suspicion that Lord Aberdeen, the author of this motion, had planned it with a view of displacing Palmerston, and joining the Whigs with Graham, Cardwell, etc. He evidently thought the attack a mistake in point of tactics, though praising the ability shown in its execution. We then talked of our want of organs in the press, a subject which he seemed to have much at heart. He thought it quite on the cards that we might be called upon to take office, but that we had no chance of holding it long, even if we could form a cabinet.

19 June 1850. I passed the morning in correcting my Father's speech for publication, from the newspaper reports: a laborious task, as much of it had to be rewritten altogether. In the evening I presided at a public charitable dinner, a duty not much to my taste, but which I did not think it right to decline . . .

20 June 1850. [Lord John Russell] . . . declared an unaltered intention of persisting in that course of foreign policy which the other house had censured. He affirmed that Lord Palmerston, while in power, would be neither the minister of France, of Austria, nor of Russia, but of England – a declaration which drew vehement cheering, and was understood to convey a sarcasm on Lord Aberdeen . . .

24 June 1850. . . . Graham's position at this time was peculiar, and commanding. With few friends, and no party, for he seemed to have withdrawn himself from the little circle of Sir R. Peel's personal followers: with a cold, even contemptuous demeanour that repelled familiarity, and with no well-defined political creed: always present in his place, attending every debate, even the least important, he found his support courted, and his enmity deprecated, on all sides. It was commonly thought that in the event of the Whig party being reconstructed, he would supersede Russell as its leader. I find papers of this date which show that by many Conservatives, who disliked quite as much as they feared him, he was regarded as personally abler than Peel: and certainly his opinion weighed quite as much with the House.

25 June 1850. . . . Palmerston then delivered his own vindication in a speech of 4¾ hours, of extraordinary talent and power. It also showed a remarkable memory, for his notes were few, and he scarcely used them for reference, except when reading documents. He concluded with an expression equally eloquent, popular, and indiscreet: likening the English people to Roman citizens . . . it cannot be expected that other states shall acquiesce in the doctrine herein laid down.

A Conservative victory is confidently predicted, and my Father's cabinet drawn out on paper, as follows:

Lord Stanley – First Lord of the Treasury
Lord Aberdeen – Foreign Secretary
Gladstone – Colonial Secretary
Redesdale[21] – Home Secretary
Herries – Chancellor of Exchequer
Disraeli – Board of Control

Malmesbury, Granby, Ellenborough: seats in cabinet, offices uncertain.

27 June 1850 (Thursday). My Father, Palmerston, and Russell met at a Court Ball: they spoke in a very friendly way, exchanging compliments and jokes. . . . Gladstone spoke in this night's debate, . . . with uncommon force and earnestness, in defence of a policy of non-intervention. His tone unusually bitter and sarcastic, he charged Palmerston with forcing quarrels on all governments, despotic, constitutional, or republican, for the mere love and excitement of quarrelling. Walking home with Sir J. Graham, I was amused by his excited and triumphant mode of commenting on the past debate. It was the first and only time I ever knew him throw off his habitual reserve. He recapitulated to me some of his earlier victories in parliament . . .

The Times steadily supports our attack on Lord Palmerston, giving a leader every day to the subject. Among other matters, it states with an air of authority that nothing except the state of foreign affairs had prevented Graham from joining the ministry last year, on the death of Lord Auckland.[22]

28 June 1850 (Friday). Cobden rose, . . . denounced Palmerston, and persevered in this strain for more than an hour, amidst hooting and yelling from his own friends, answered by Conservative cheers. His language was plain, earnest, and sensible. In the division he carried only some eight or ten members of the Radical party with him. Peel, who came next, commenced by disclaiming all connection with us, and all desire of returning to office . . . Lord John Russell and Disraeli closed the four nights' debate: neither were up to their usual mark, but the length of the discussion, and lateness of the hour, made against them . . . Had we come in on this question, I believe a 5s. fixed duty would have been proposed by way of compromise: and to this I am almost sure, from the language held by him at the time, that Lord Aberdeen would not have objected. The numbers, 310 to 264; 46 majority . . . On the whole, this great struggle has raised the reputation of the House for talent, a reputation of late years somewhat diminished.

Scarcely any of the rank and file spoke: all was left to the leaders: and they had prepared themselves with unusual care. The best speech, *longo intervallo*, was Palmerston's: in style and arrangement it appeared absolutely faultless: no other man in the Commons could have made it.

3 July 1850. The death of Sir R. Peel has startled and shocked all London. . . . He had attended the Exhibition Commission at 11 on Saturday morning, where my Father sat next him, and says he never saw him in higher spirits: an elation which Lord Stanley ascribed to his satisfaction at having spoken and voted according to his conscience, without thereby producing the result which he had apprehended – that of upsetting the ministry. My Father described him as amusing himself at the expense of some of his fellow Commissioners, and commenting humorously on the proceedings by means of little slips of paper passed to his friends. In the afternoon he rode in the Park: and according to the newspapers was thrown by his horse kicking. Several persons however who were standing near, declare that he had previously lost all control over the animal, and that while riding quietly on, the reins dropped out of his hand, whence they infer that he was suddenly seized with a fit. This seems the more probable, because when taken up he recognised no one. From the first his recovery was thought doubtful: latterly it was despaired of. Lord Hardinge,[23] Sir J. Graham, the Bishop of Gibraltar,[24] and his immediate relations, saw him on the day of his death. The usual religious ceremonies were performed, but I was told that he remained nearly unconscious during their performance, as indeed he had done throughout. He died on Tuesday at 11 p.m. An excessive constitutional sensibility to pain was exhibited by him under the surgeons' hands: and even while he lay unburied there were not wanting those who made this a matter of reproach. I myself heard a Duke say 'Well, he lived a coward, and he has died one.' During all his illness Whitehall was besieged with inquiries: the police had to close the court, or roadway, before his house against carriages: a temporary gate was built outside: and at this, bulletins were issued every two or three hours. Palmerston was among the first to call: and sent off a special messenger to summon Robert Peel the younger from Switzerland.

I was not in the House when an adjournment was moved: but on my way down met H. Lennox,[25] who related what had passed. He said that Gladstone was unable to speak for tears: that two members (whom he named) sobbed aloud: and that the scene resembled that which might follow a family bereavement, rather than the formal and ceremonious mourning of a public assembly. The sitting lasted only some twenty minutes.

I went up to Disraeli's – on business – and found him at breakfast, between one and two. He made no parade of regret, but seemed bewildered by the suddenness of the event, and the prospect which it offered of new combinations. He speculated on the possibility of recovering Graham and

Gladstone, whom he assumed to be completely alienated from Ministers by the late debate. He also thought the time favourable for definitively abandoning a protective duty. I told him I quite agreed so far as my personal opinions were concerned, but that the mere suggestion of such a course would raise a mutiny in the camp. I therefore recommended him to leave it alone. (And this advice was sound. Judging by the temper still, 1855, evinced towards Gladstone and his friends by the Opposition, I am satisfied that no reconciliation was possible in 1850, and that had we adopted D.'s suggestion, we should only have been left in the ridiculous plight of having neither a principle nor a party. Besides, my Father's speech to the delegates only rendered an immediate change impossible.) D. was full of a plan for removing Peel's restrictions on local banks, which he thought would be accepted as a substitute for corn laws. This also I disputed, inasmuch as not one farmer out of 10,000 knows anything about currency. At intervals in our conversation, he would break off suddenly and pace up and down the room, exclaiming 'What an event!' I remarked that the two chief obstacles in the way of his success had been Peel and Bentinck: while either remained, the Conservatives could not reunite: as matters stood, there was no insuperable barrier to surmount. He assented. We called together on Lord Lyndhurst: found him cheerful and conversable, in no way affected by the death of an old colleague. He enquired curiously about the details of the accident, and speculated on the future.

Dining at Lord Brougham's, I met [Lord] Douro:[26] he, though styled a Peelite, did not hesitate to say that he thought Peel had inflicted a grievous injury on the landed party, and had made the matter worse by treating their remonstrances with contempt. Lord Brougham, who repeats his good sayings more than enough, lectured on the folly committed by Peel in omitting to take counsel with his friends during the winter of 1845–6. 'If he had only written, or talked the matter over with a dozen of the leading country gentlemen, he might have kept them still in hand. I don't say they would have voted for the repeal – there would have been a debate, a division, some sharp things said, but there would have been no personal offence given, and the quarrel would have been made up in six months.' Lord B. has used almost the same language to me at Brougham last autumn, and he used it again, for the subject is with him a favourite one, this same winter, 1850, at Cannes. It therefore expresses his deliberate belief.

Douro, notwithstanding his censure of Peel, pressed strongly for our acceptance of free trade as a *fait accompli*, reminding me of the precedent set by Peel himself, and his (Douro's) father the Duke, in 1834, when they accepted the Reform Bill, which they had so fiercely contested two years before. I reminded him that this act, however necessary and inevitable, had laid open Peel and his colleagues to one of the bitterest invectives, by Brougham himself, that human tongue ever pronounced.

4 July 1850. [Parliamentary tributes to Peel]. . . . Disraeli thought it more decorous to be absent . . . The Protectionists in general show more regret for, and appreciation of, their former chief than from their late language could have been expected. The newspapers teem with reviews of his character and career, several above mediocrity. (Disraeli has drawn so admirable a portrait, from his peculiar point of view, as probably to supersede all others. But a character like that of Peel can never be mapped out and made plain to all the world. How can the world understand a man, who during a great part of his life, never understood himself?)

I shall make only two remarks concerning him, and they are impartial, for in the corn law quarrel I at no time mixed, nor greatly sympathised with those who did. First, I think his death in 1850 fortunate for his fame: called again to power, he could not have regained the lost confidence of the Conservatives: the attacks of Bentinck and Disraeli had cut too deep for that: nor could he with satisfaction to himself have acted with the extreme Liberal party. The high strain of Liberalism which some of those who admired his conduct in 1846 were pleased to attribute to him, was, so far as I can judge from observation and from the testimony of his living friends, entirely the creation of their fancy. I do not believe he would willingly have enlarged the franchise: nor dealt with the Church: nor yet dared to grapple with the question of a non-sectarian education. The whole bent of his mind was Conservative: he did not give up the corn law until satisfied (and the event has proved him right) that the change would do no real injury to the landed interest: and if in his later days he ever held language of a contrary tendency – as in the compliment to Cobden – I conceive such phrases to have been momentary ebullitions of wounded pride than expressions of his real feeling. His celebrated wish, left in writing, that his children should not take a peerage, may have originated in some such pique: but it was more probably owing to a conviction that in the House of Commons alone, in the present day, can a great political position be achieved. There was also in it something of the habitual plausibility (I can find no other word) which had become part of his nature. He liked to show forth to the world the disinterestedness of his public services.

Secondly, I have remarked since his death, and especially since the extinction of the corn law quarrel in 1852, that the language of his political friends is far less eulogistic than formerly. By a natural effect of reaction, while Protectionists could find no milder term to apply to the transaction of 1846 than 'cowardice', 'treachery', and 'desertion', the Peelite party, and the Liberals generally, represented his conduct on that occasion as a sublime sacrifice, and a model to future statesmen. This doctrine they were accustomed to maintain with a vehemence, not to say irritability, caused perhaps by some lurking doubt of its soundness. Extreme opinions have now drawn nearer to one another. The question, 'What ought an honest man in

Peel's position, to have done in 1829 and 1846?' is less often discussed: and his own solution, of it is now rather excused, or at most vindicated as necessary, than held up to admiration. I may here state the view which my Father has always taken upon the subject. He says that in resigning when he could no longer honestly support a corn law, Peel was right: but that he ought not to have taken office again unless in the absolute, proved impossibility of any other Government being formed: and if he found it necessary to do so, he should have appealed to the country by a dissolution, and not have placed his followers in the painful position of having to break pledges solemnly given to their constituents.

Three years later, dining with Fitzroy Kelly,[27] he told me (Disraeli was of the party, which included no one else) that as early as July 1845, Peel had warned him, being then on his way to his constituents, not to pledge himself too strongly on the corn laws. Kelly's impression was that he had already decided on the change which he afterwards effected. He [Kelly] went on to say 'Peel's contempt for his party was very apparent to those who were in office with him. He seemed to take it as a matter of course, that go where he might, they would follow. He thought no more of them than I do of the labourers who work for me. He never contemplated for a moment the possibility of their leaving him on the corn question: he expected a few hard words, and a little murmuring, and then that all would go on as before. This belief he retained even in the spring of 1846, and his disappointment was proportionate. Certainly he never was the same man after his resignation: anxiety and annoyance destroyed his health.'

Kelly, though not an intimate friend, continued on terms of familiar acquaintance with Sir Robert to the last: and was therefore probably well informed as to the facts he related.

Between Peel and my Father there was at no time great cordiality: their characters differed too widely: and my Father had reason to believe, from expressions dropped by the Queen on his taking office, and from the report of persons about the Court, that Peel had lost no opportunity of prejudicing the Royal mind against him. She certainly said to the Duchess of Gloucester[28] 'How different Lord Derby is from what he had been always represented to me!' I do not think their mutual coldness arose from any actual dispute, but rather from a totally different manner of viewing all subjects, and from the formal, somewhat egotistical temperament of Sir Robert, which shrank from anything like familiarity.

5 July 1850. A vote taken on the malt tax. Cayley[29] moved its repeal, Disraeli went into the lobby with him: I left the House, choosing neither to vote against my party nor my opinion.

The same day, I had a conversation with Sheil, the Irish orator and Whig placeman: he spoke with great and sincere alarm of the new question of tenant right, saying that it would lead to a new predial agitation more dangerous than any merely political had been. He seemed to take pleasure in sneering at the hollowness of those Irish movements in which he had been so prominent a leader.

(I here pass over several stories of imputed parliamentary corruption,[30] in the direct form of a bribe, which I find in my original notes. They affected the Irish, and one English M.P. It is certain that a general belief prevailed in the existence of such corruption: Beresford, a hot-tempered, intemperate, but truthful Irishman, has stated to me in detail, and with the names of the parties, offers made to him of votes for money: and I am afraid the fact cannot be doubted. The occasion of these offers was the division on foreign policy.)

9 July 1850. The Duke of Cambridge[31] died, a foolish, kind-hearted old man of amiable but rather eccentric habits. His manner of speaking resembled that ascribed to George III: and he practised in society a habit of perpetual interrogation which caused his neighbourhood to be shunned by timid or reserved persons. Though his general abilities were below par, his memory of persons and families was very extraordinary. It was a common remark that he knew more about everyone's relations than the person addressed did about his own. He gave away large sums, not very judiciously, and it was one of his chief pleasures to preside at a charitable festival. . . . His political opinions so far as he can be said to have had any, were High Tory, but as a member of the royal family, he thought it right to abstain from active opposition to the government of the day . . .

17 July 1850. Returning to town after a few days passed at Knowsley, I found some alarm, and a good deal of excitement, about the financial prospects of next year's Exhibition, Not being an incorporated company, the Commissioners were severally and jointly liable for any debt incurred in the cost of construction. This cost amounted to £210,000, of which only £50,000 had been raised, and the receipts expected at the doors, on which the projectors relied for their profits, could not be calculated beforehand with any certainty. After consultation, and a special meeting being held, they resorted to a guarantee fund, which within 24 hours was signed to the amount of £180,000. The Rothschilds alone put down their names for £50,000, Peto[32] for the same sum, the Prince for £20,000, and other Commissioners in proportion. The most cautious, and the most reluctant to subscribe, was the millionaire, Lord Overstone.[33] (At this time Government thought ill of the Exhibition project, and seemed anxious to clear themselves as far as might be from the responsibility of originating it. Their usual language in private was to describe it as a magnificent scheme, but one which could never pay. I myself heard such predictions from two cabinet ministers. The credit of persevering in the scheme, and carrying it through, belongs mainly to the Prince).

19 July 1850. . . . I dined with Lord Brougham . . . [who] seemed in high spirits at the success of an attack which he had made in the House on the new Chancellor, Truro,[34] whose appointment, by the way, is much censured, Campbell[35] and Rolfe[36] being regarded as abler lawyers on that side. I do not know that these criticisms are well-founded, but it is possible that Lady Truro's peculiar position, and connection, may have had something to do with the choice.

20 July 1850. My Father talked much of the prospects and plans of Government. He thought they must do something to conciliate the Radicals, who were daily more and more alienated from them; he considered it likely that they would keep things quiet for the short remainder of this session, and next year introduce a bill for extending the English franchise,[37] as they had done with that of Ireland: that they would press it to a division, get beaten, and dissolve with a popular cry. It is certain that by the great bulk of his followers Lord John is reluctantly and coldly supported. (The foresight shown in this prediction was made manifest next spring, when the very course here marked out was followed, though interrupted before the final step had been taken, by the Palmerston quarrel).

He then spoke of a conversation which had passed between him and the Prince Consort; the subject, the proposed allowance to Prince George, now Duke of Cambridge.[38] The Prince told him that Lord John had offered £10,000 only: that the Queen protested strongly, saying this would not be enough, on which the premier reluctantly gave way, the Court apparently undertaking to secure the support of the opposition leaders. Of course my Father made no difficulty . . .

My Father then spoke of Bunsen,[39] whose influence he regarded as very considerable, and dangerous: that he, Bunsen, was always trying to set the Court against the aristocracy.

21 July 1850 (Sunday). I called on Disraeli: he said the session was over – nothing remained to wait for – he had intended to close it with a review in the style of Lyndhurst, but this he had done once before, and did not like to repeat himself. Besides, it would be difficult in such a speech to avoid throwing out some hint of our own future intentions, 'and who can say what they are?' I had nothing to suggest except patience, and the probability of a quarrel between Whigs and Radicals. He (Disraeli) totally discredited the rumours about a new Reform Bill: called it mere idle gossip – why should Ministers build a wall to run their own heads against? He thought the Radicals would be glad to have us in (Bright had said as much) since they would then be relieved from their present irksome position, as involuntary and unthanked supporters of a ministry which they disliked. He believed Graham well-inclined to join us: but distrusted Gladstone, whose professions of friendship he thought officious and over-acted.

We again discussed the question of an organ: the *Spectator* was named as likely to be on sale: D. named £4,000 as the least sum with which it would be possible to begin.

25 July 1850. I dined tête-a-tête with Disraeli, who had asked me 'to talk over a matter of great importance'. It seemed that a Buckinghamshire neighbour had undertaken, on certain terms, to find the requisite capital wherewith to carry out our scheme. In course of talk I made some remark on the greater scope for journalistic talent which the Liberal side afforded in politics. 'Yes' he replied 'we are both on the wrong side, but there is nothing for it except to make the best of our position.' I told him that he wanted, like Canning, to combine Liberal ideas with Tory connections: but Canning had failed. There is certainly a very prevalent impression that Disraeli has no well-defined opinions of his own: but is content to adopt, and defend, any which may be popular with the Conservative party at the time.

30 July 1850. [*On the attempt by Baron Rothschild,*[40] *the elected but unsworn M.P. for the City of London, to take his seat by swearing on the Old Testament only.*] ... The acrimony of feeling elicited by the controversy certainly bears no proportion to its practical importance: every Whig or Radical seemed to think every Conservative a bigot, and the Conservatives treated the arguments of their opponents as if they had been insults to Christianity.

I voted with my party, reluctantly and in much doubt: what chiefly weighed with me was, first the often-expressed and well-known opinion of Arnold upon this subject – Arnold, who of all men had the least tincture of bigotry in his nature: and next, the fear which I felt of giving an impulse to the demand for an ecclesiastical parliament (Convocation) independent of the temporal one. (I leave these arguments as they stand, *valeant quantum –* 1855). But I voted in considerable perplexity, and should have been glad to absent myself: but that seemed like evading a public duty.

At the close of the Rothschild debates I went abroad, and meeting some friends at Baden, remained there a fortnight. Thence I made a brief tour of Switzerland: and from Geneva returned to Paris, where I passed several weeks, going little into general society, but reading much, and watching the course of political affairs. So far as I could judge, there was no revolutionary fervour in any class of society ... The prevalent feeling appeared to be one of uneasiness, a timid desire for order under any regime, a complete scepticism as regarded all political creeds, and a general distrust of, and contempt for, public men of every party ... The Prince-President, though supposed to aim at empire, was neither generally understood nor feared. At the English Embassy, and among the diplomatic body, it was the custom to ridicule his pretensions and depreciate his abilities. He certainly had not then the general popularity which he has since obtained ... The leaders of all parties seemed to acquiesce patiently in his possession of power, each regarding him as a mere temporary stopgap, who could be got rid of whenever their plans were matured, and who in the meantime kept their opponents out of the field. I was presented to him by Lord Normanby,[41] and received with that marked courtesy which he extended to all Englishmen, especially to those engaged in political life. He had the true royal faculty of remembering persons and places: on my being admitted to his presence, he at once reminded me how on the 10th April 1848, in London, where he served as a special constable, we had perambulated the Haymarket together. (It had chanced that we both belonged to the same section, and this was my first introduction to the future Emperor). The state and ceremony maintained in his palace was very great: nothing could be less republican . . .

I had projected a voyage to, and tour in, Algeria, and collected a considerable number of French works, government reports, pamphlets, and travels, relative to that country. These are now in the library of the Geographical Society. But on mentioning my intention to my family, they took up so exaggerated a notion of the dangers and difficulties of such a journey (though travelling in French Africa is as safe as travelling in France) that I thought it right, not without regret, to abandon the project. I went instead to Madrid . . .

. . . On my return I passed a week at Lord Brougham's villa at Cannes, being alone with him for several days. He was much engaged in optical experiments, but found time nevertheless to discharge the duties of hospitality in the kindest manner. All at Cannes knew him, rich and poor: with all, especially the poor, he was a favourite, and the conversations which he used to hold, in almost unintelligible French, with fishermen and peasants, were not a little amusing. It was said at Paris, not long after, when he read a paper before the Institute, that in addition to his other gifts, he must have the gift of unknown tongues.

I returned to England about Christmas [1850], after an absence of between four and five months.

1851

Before the meeting of Parliament, I passed a week at Hughenden, with Disraeli.[1] The house is small but comfortable, the situation pleasant. The neighbouring country singularly picturesque: undulating hills, hanging beech-woods, a wide stretch of open down and common close by: a pure air, and a complete solitude, within two hours of London.[2] It is a very fine retreat for an overworked politician, or man of letters desiring undisturbed seclusion. Here I first became intimate with D: our conversations in London, though frequent and unreserved, having been almost exclusively on business.

In this place D. takes great delight, and passes there the greater part of the autumn and winter months of every year. For what are usually called rural pursuits, as shooting, farming, gardening, laying out plantations or roads etc. he has no taste: nor does he exert himself much as a magistrate, though occasionally attending quarter sessions. But he has a good library: and in fine weather passes the whole day in walking about the neighbourhood, either alone or with a companion. Here he rests from the work of one session, and plans that of the next: for whether in town or country, politics constitute his chief, almost his sole, pleasure.[3] One other topic is a favourite: the philosophical discussion of religious questions: I mean by this the origin of the various beliefs which have governed mankind, their changes at different epochs, and those still to come. This was common ground to us both: of the new German school of criticism I had perhaps read more than my friend, but his acquaintance with the earlier phases of the great controversy much exceeded mine. Often and often were these matters discussed between us: so far as historical criticism is concerned we had both reached the same result, but there our agreement ended. He seemed to think that the sentiment, or instinct, of religion, would by degrees, though slowly, vanish as knowledge became more widely spread: an anticipation which I believe, as I most sincerely hope, is unfounded. If it be just, the conditions of life must indeed change widely, before life will be worth having. Yet Disraeli is no materialist: he has always avowed his expectation of some form of future existence, though whether accompanied with any consciousness of personal identity with the self of this present life, he thought it impossible to foresee. He told me that Bulwer Lytton and he had frequently conversed on these subjects. He used to praise Gibbon's history as being on the whole the most important literary undertaking ever achieved by a single man. Of Voltaire he spoke more slightingly: admitting his extraordinary talent, but describing his books as not profound, and as partaking more of the nature of journalism, or review-writing than of authorship. Byron he was

31

much in the habit of mentioning as one who would have done great things had he lived longer, but who died almost before he had discovered where his true powers lay.[4] Of persons whom he had met in society, D'Orsay was the one whose character seemed to have impressed him most deeply.[5] He defended his apparent frivolity by saying that the position in which he (D'Orsay) had early placed himself, alienating him from his own country, had put a public career out of his power. Otherwise, he thought him likely to have been one of the first men of the age. Louis Napoleon he had known familiarly: but did not rate his genius as high as the world now (1855) does. He described him as a man of one idea: the ideal of a conspirator: almost a monomaniac on the subject of his right to the Empire. He allowed him also the merits of silence, enterprise, and judgment: but considered his intellectual qualities as not much above the average.

On one occasion, during this very visit, he talked to me with great apparent earnestness on the subject of restoring the Jews to their own land. I recollect it well: we were walking in Lord Carrington's park, by Wycombe: the day was cold: but though usually very sensitive to influences of weather, he seemed to forget the thermometer in the earnestness with which, halting to enforce his views the better, and standing by the side of a plantation, he explained the details of his plan. The country, he said, had ample natural capabilities: all it wanted was labour, and protection for the labourer: the ownership of the soil might be bought from Turkey: money would be forthcoming: the Rothschilds and leading Hebrew capitalists would all help: the Turkish empire was falling into ruin: the Turkish Govt would do anything for money: all that was necessary was to establish colonies, with rights over the soil, and security from ill treatment. The question of nationality might wait until these had taken hold. He added that these ideas were extensively entertained among the nation. A man who should carry them out would be the next Messiah, the true Saviour of his people. He saw only a single obstacle: arising from the existence of two races among the Hebrews, of whom one, those who settled along the shores of the Mediterranean, look down on the other, refusing even to associate with them. 'Sephardim' I think he called the superior race. He went on to say that the power of the Hebrews was under-valued. Massena, Mozart, Soult[6] and other considerable names, he claimed as of that descent: as also a large part of the Portuguese aristocracy. The only two religions which had influenced Western Asia and Europe – 'the Galilean and the Mohamedan movements' were founded by men of Arab blood. It was the race that produced these great results.

... I have often recalled to mind, and been perplexed by, this very singular conversation: he never recurred to it again: his manner seemed that of a man thoroughly in earnest: and though I have many times since seen him under the influence of irritation or pleasurable excitement, this is the only instance in which he ever appeared to me to show signs of any higher emotion. There is certainly nothing in his character to render it unlikely that the whole scene was a mystification: and in the succeeding four years I have heard of no practical step taken, or attempted to be taken, by him in the matter: but which purpose could the mystification, if it were one, serve? scarcely even that of amusement, for no witness was present. There is no doubt that D.'s mind is frequently occupied with subjects relative to the Hebrews: he said to me once, incidentally, but with earnestness, that if he retired from politics in time enough, he should resume literature, and write the *Life of Christ* from a national point of view,[7] intending it for a posthumous work.

D. has not been successful in forming and retaining personal friends. By none of his colleagues in office and opposition is he personally beloved: and his principal confidant, a young man of rank,[8] whom I will not here name, wrote to consult me only a few days ago, on the expediency of quitting [his] flag for that of some other leader. I myself feel that there is much truth in the bitter portraits painted of him by Phillips[9] in the *Times* . . . it cannot be pretended that he is attached to any political principles as such, or that his objects are disinterested and patriotic: yet singleness of purpose – contempt of obloquy – energy which no labour can exhaust – indifference to the ordinary pleasures and pursuits of men, which he neglects in search of power and fame – a temper usually calm, and patient under annoyances of the most trying kind – all this, joined with such intellectual powers as not one human being among a million can lay claim to, forms a combination rare in political or private life, and surely deserves some degree of respect.

In two things D's character is more amiable than most persons suppose: the one his willingness, disinterestedly, and often with considerable trouble to himself, to encourage and help on rising men of talents (of which several instances occur to me): the other, which would be well understood by those who knew his domestic position, but which I only mention by allusion, the gratitude which during many years he has never ceased to evince towards a person to whom he owes much of his success, but whose claims upon him in return are neither slight, nor easy to satisfy.

He possesses in a remarkable degree the art of listening, or seeming to listen: and always sends away visitors well pleased with themselves. He assumes vanity to be the ruling passion with all, and treats them accordingly. This theory succeeds with many, especially the young, and those on whom the prestige of his talents and position has an effect: in practice he carries it too far: and not seldom disgusts, where he means to please: by overdone and manifestly artificial compliments.

These notes, hastily set down, are not meant for a complete character: they are merely such as occur to me after a somewhat intimate knowledge of their subject during four and a half years.)

We talked, during this visit, of many political subjects: a report came that the Ministry had quarrelled: D. took the occasion to speculate on a probable junction between Russell and my Father. Why should it not be? he argued: both are Whigs, of great aristocratic Whig families, both have been reformers, and both are now inclined to be Conservatives. Both have taken up the Protestant cause: the only difficulty arose from our quarrel with Palmerston: which he regretted, as it threw us on Aberdeen for a foreign Minister. He thought P. [almerston] of the two the better inclined towards us: (a prescient judgment, as the result has proved).[10]

We also again, and still without effect, canvassed the plan of establishing an organ: a point which D. had much at heart. He seemed to think it discreditable, intellectually, to a party, that it should not be thus provided.[11]

But the principal topic discussed was his forthcoming scheme of agricultural relief.[12] He developed it in considerable detail, assuming as a basis of argument, the state of the country to be one of 'general prosperity, coincident with agricultural distress'. This is an advance on the ideas of the thorough Protectionists, who regard every interest in the country as on the verge of ruin: and the fact of agricultural distress is patent, whatever the cause. He proposed to move for a Committee of the whole House, to consider upon the means of relieving the distressed interest, partly explaining his plan, but at this stage pledging no one to vote for it. He thus reckoned on reducing the majority to 20. (It was 14 in February and 13 in April). If ministers should grant the committee, or be beaten upon it without resigning, four distinct measures to be brought forward, each of which might be affirmed or negatived separately, and which in union formed a large and comprehensive scheme.

These were (1) union rating substituted for parochial, and law of settlement done away (2) removal of various small local charges onto the consolidated fund, (3) change in currency laws, restoring certain facilities to local banks, (4) a 5s. duty on corn.

On the No-Popery agitation at this time raging furiously, D's ideas were moderate and wise. He disliked the movement, would do nothing to increase it, but if it must be dealt with, would try to direct it as much as possible away from the English Catholics, against the Pope and his foreign adherents.[13] He had no measure, but would wait and see that of Govt.

He read me passages from a life,[14] or account of the public career of G. Bentinck. He said it had occupied many months of his time, especially a character of Peel, which 'had almost turned his hair grey'. He had composed it over and over again, not on paper, but in his memory: and was at last satisfied with the result. He read it out: but I think it was not then complete, or has been since altered.[15]

24 January 1851. Beresford came up at 11 p.m., asked to see my Father, and admitted told his errand. He considered himself charged with a negotiation from Sir James Graham to know if we would give the latter the post of Chancellor of the Exchequer. The communication however only came through Lord Londonderry,[16] who, from incapacity and love of meddling, is no competent agent in such matters. My Father however took it so far seriously as to begin to discuss the risk we ran, in the event of a junction, of being swamped by our allies. 'It will never do' he said to me 'to man a prize-vessel with her own crew, unless we have men enough of our own aboard to keep them under.'

28 January 1851. I met D. in high spirits, confident that the ministry could not stand. We talked over the distribution of offices: he offered me to serve under him in the Home Dept, which I accepted. He mentioned a widespread rumour which he disbelieved, that Lord John was about to propose a 5s. duty.

1 February 1851 (Saturday). An evening meeting at my Father's, consisting of Lords Redesdale and Malmesbury, Disraeli, Beresford, Herries. Granby had been asked, but preferred his hunting. Redesdale, whose election as Chairman of Committees in the Lords is certain, was in great glee. D. put out all his powers of entertainment, but his good things were rather in the manner and style than in any pointed saying which one could carry away. He described a conversation with Peto, the destined seconder of the Address, whom he had drawn on to rehearse his intended speech, indicative of the tenor of the Royal Speech, the victim only awaking to a sense of his indiscretion when he had told all he knew. This however was but little, and the narrator had his labour for nothing. In conversation D. repeated what he had said to me respecting the papal question: 'We must attack the ultramontane party and the Pope, not the Catholics of England.' This was well received, as was also his descriptive formula applied to the state of the country, 'general prosperity concurrent with agricultural distress'. Lord Redesdale was, I think, the only dissentient (but except Herries, all denied the prosperity in subsequent debates). In the course of the evening it was remarked that Grattan and Canning were of one mind on the subject of securities, and that the latter, when endeavouring to remove the disabilities, had framed an elaborate scheme for preventing the assumption of territorial titles. The story goes that Lord Minto,[17] accredited to the Pope, was discoursing largely to His Holiness on Italian affairs, when the latter, perhaps desirous to hint to him, the propriety of attending to his own business rather than theirs, laid his hand on a paper near him, the rescript in question, with the words 'Questo tocca l'Inghilterra'. The minister had either too much discretion, or too little curiosity, to press for a further explanation.

Little was arranged at this party, but all separated well content. Lord Aberdeen, whose visits in St James's Square become more frequent as our prospect of power brightens, has called there three or four times during the last week, foretelling a crisis as a Mother Carey's chicken foretells a storm.

4 February 1851. A meeting held, which 120 of our friends attended, including Sir R. Inglis,[18] who appeared for the first time. [Inglis has retired from politics, and a word on his career may be allowed. He made no pretence to talents, spoke verbosely and pompously, though never quite without meaning: yet though all persons knew beforehand what he was about to say, inasmuch as to be able, on certain topics, to predict not the substance only but even the actual words which would be emoloyed, his age, his long attendance in the House, and a certain consistency of character displayed by him throughout, created an impression in his favour. He spoke chiefly on religious topics, and seldom on any topic without introducing religion, often in a manner offensively dogmatic. His language was usually wild, his sentiments always intolerant, his piety may have been, and I dare say was, sincere, but it did not show itself in ascetic practices. Sir Robert drank like a country gentleman of the old school, and except when expecting to be called upon for a speech, passed the latter part of the evening in a half-drunken sleep. I am bound to say I never saw him intoxicated, but neither did I ever see him, with the above-named exception, thoroughly sober at night. It was the custom of his early days for all gentlemen to drink, and very probably (like Lord Eldon, of whom he must have been an admirer, for they had three things in common – love of wine, scholarship, and High Toryism) he saw nothing in the practice inconsistent with his profession of sanctity. Privately, I knew him only as an acquaintance, and in the slightest degree. I believe that he was a good scholar, after the manner of Oxford, and a kind friend: hospitality is a virtue which no enemy can deny him. He sat, or dozed, always in the same seat, the first below the gangway on the ministerial side. His dress never varied, nor his general appearance – the white hair, the purple face, swollen with good feeding, the metal-buttoned coat of the fashion of 1828, and the flower in his buttonhole, form altogether a parliamentary portrait which habitués of the House will long remember. I do not think his religious opinions told much either for or against him in parliament. He was listened to on account of his long standing: of the important constituency which he represented: of the shortness of his speeches (the only good point they had): and, it is fair to add, his independence in a party point of view. I am willing to believe that he never asked favours of any ministry, as assuredly he gave his vote implicitly to none. Right or wrong, wise or foolish, his judgment was his own: and his independence, rare in the House of Commons, gave a certain weight to what he said. . . . Probably in the entire House there are not 40 members . . . who can be styled really independent. Of that small minority Inglis was one: a good deal used to be said, and sometimes to his disadvantage, about an appointment which he had held in connection with the East India Company, and which was supposed to be little better than a sinecure: something of the kind there was, but in Inglis's early days no man was thought the worse of for accepting a sinecure: indeed the abolition of such places now is due, not to the scruples of the few, but to the jealousy of the many . . .]

My Father spoke at length: dwelt on the unusual importance of the measures to be brought forward, in a religious and constitutional, as well as a merely political point of view: then urged the necessity of unanimous action: next proceeded to allude to the Queen's Speech, which he described as 'milk and water, with a decidedly larger proportion of the latter element': and read it paragraph by paragraph, interspersing brief comments as he went on. He remarked that last year the land was spoken of as 'complaining' now it was an 'important interest' and acknowledged to be in distress. Still, though there was a surplus in the Treasury, no measures of relief were proposed.

The 'Papal aggression' – as for shortness he would call it – he thought 'insolent, not insidious'. 'Ministers say they mean to resist it. If they are honest, let us support them in their honesty: if not, pin them down to the pledges they have given. They had taken on themselves the responsibility of action: and it was the duty of parliament to see that their action was real and effective. If they meant to do nothing, if their language has been held merely to turn off unpopularity from themselves, what punishment did they not deserve? As for the Pope, it was impossible to ignore altogether the existence of his power – the only effect of so doing was to make it absolute and un-controlled – it might be better to sanction it to a certain extent by law – to legalise, with a view of limiting it. He would not consent to any modification of the Act of 1829: he thought the penal laws ought to be revised, and all merely offensive and inefficient Acts struck off at once: while those that were retained should be no longer dead letters. Some people had asked, what difference did the Pope's rescript produce in the position of the R.C. Church?' He answered, it gave the hierarchy a synodical action, the nature of which he explained, and had the effect of making the Pope's will absolute, whereas formerly each Bishop had been guided only by his own conscience. He instanced the case of the Irish colleges (on this some controversy has since been raised). He ended with an earnest hope that into the debates of either House, no controversy would be admitted.

Inglis put two questions: first, whether Lord S [tanley] had any idea of a concordat, which was denied: next, whether it was meant to draw a dis-tinction between the English and Irish Churches? Answer: 'certainly not'. The meeting then broke up, having sat an hour.

A dinner of Conservative peers, held the evening before, went off well. Lord Winchilsea[19] alone was dissatisfied, and in a state of profane piety 'swore by the living God' that if no one else would move an amendment, he would. But he has not done so.

6 February 1851. . . . In the evening my Father repeated to me a conversa-tion which he had just held with Lord Aberdeen on the possible reunion.

My Father asked if he had expected the results which have followed from the repeal of the Corn Laws? 'No.' 'Then why should you be ashamed of saying that you anticipated a quite different result – that your anticipations have proved wrong – and that you will therefore consent so to modify your measure that it shall produce that effect which you originally desired?' Lord Aberdeen agreed, but answered that he was ashamed (using that word) to alter his vote: 'if Graham and his friends would join me, we should divide the responsibility, and I should not care': but on this point, he added, Graham was 'stiff'. My Father went on 'I have all along predicted what is now happening, and the prediction has come true. You confess that you have miscalculated. Which of us then makes the greater sacrifice – I in joining you, or you in joining me?' Lord Aberdeen owned that in honour and consistency they, the Protectionist party, could form, or coalesce with, no government that should not propose measures of relief for the land. Then they began to talk of possible coalitions – my Father with the moderate Whigs, in the event of the Radicals seceding. He knew one at least who would not be scrupulous about free trade. 'Who is that?' asked Lord Aberdeen. 'The Secretary for Foreign Affairs' my Father answered, laughing. Lord Aberdeen's surprise was extreme – he rose from his chair. 'It is impossible – quite out of the question.' The hint was broad: 'if you will not join me, others will', and in this sense it seems to have produced some effect.

7 February 1851. Lord John introduced his proposed measure of repression, directed against the Roman Catholic 'aggression' . . . His speech occupied two hours, and was well received by the opposition, coldly by the Whigs. His nervous embarrassment while delivering the first few sentences attracted general attention, and some minutes elapsed before his elocution became animated or fluent. . . . The chief fault in his otherwise clever speech consisted in the disproportion between the indignation which it expressed, and the measure to which it served as an introduction. The premier seems to have thought that his words would be taken instead of deeds: exactly the reverse has happened: and he has raised, as before in his letter, expectations which he cannot fulfil . . . Roebuck, who followed, destroyed at one blow the force of a great part of what had been said . . . (Since 1852 Roebuck has been struck down by paralysis, from which in this year 1855 he is beginning in part to rally: but his career as an active politician is closed).

Disraeli closed the evening's performance with a speech that gave universal satisfaction. The contrast between ministerial measures and language was finely and forcibly dwelt upon, each hit rising above the last in power. He exposed Lord John's inconsistency out of Hansard, but in temperate language: and with a rare ingenuity of debate continued to express no opinion whatever as to the remedies necessary for the occasion, while criticising and commenting on those of Government. In this act of censure without self-committal he peculiarly excels.

8 February 1851. Heard much talk from the Irish camp: so great is the indignation of this section, that they profess readiness to join us in turning out Lord John. It makes no difference to them that we vote for the bill to which they object. From us, no other course was expected: nor did the measure originate with us, though it will have our support, nor is it so much the Bill itself, as the introductory speech, which has provoked their enmity.

9 February 1851. My Father related another conversation with Lord Aberdeen, who again repeated that nothing except the fear of being thought inconsistent kept him from consenting to a junction, on the basis of a moderate fixed duty. He laid the blame, as before, on Graham, who, he said, was immoveable on this point. Some indirect communication has nevertheless been opened with him. It is a singular feature in Graham's character, that while often ready to acquiesce, and even to lead the way in large measures of large change, he at all times, and before any audience, indulges in the most gloomy predictions. Thus he habitually informs his acquaintance that he shall outlive the monarchy, a prognostication in which my Father also, though less often, joins.[20]

10 February 1851. ... From Graham, a final answer has been received, refusing positively to do anything for the agriculturalists. Consequently for the present Lord Aberdeen keeps aloof. My Father thinks that in the event of a Conservative ministry being formed, he might be gained over by Court influence: but for such an attempt royal favour is necessary and we are not supposed to be in the way of obtaining it.

11 February 1851. Disraeli moved for a committee on agricultural distress in a three hours' speech which by the confession of all parties has seldom been exceeded in point of ingenuity and tact. Its merits were different from those which his speeches on such occasions usually display: there was nothing showy, and not much that taken separately was striking ... the words of the speech, and the bearing of the speaker, were equally those of a leader, not unmindful of official responsibility. His line of argument seemed to be to admit the existence of general prosperity, concurrent with agricultural distress: the concession seemed to be unexpected, for Wood had framed his reply to meet a widely different assumption, and the inapplicability of his figures to meet the requirements of the debate was amusing. For this night at least, victory remained with us.

12 February 1851. Adjourned debate on Ecclesiastical Title Bill, dull, except for a bitter and vehement invective against Lord John, by Keogh of Athlone:[21] once a Conservative and member of the Carlton, now hesitating between Peelism and Radicalism: generally supposed to have applied to the present Govt for solicitor-general and to have been refused in favour of Cockburn. *Inde irae.*

A story, that when Lord Clarendon[22] first heard of the Durham letter, and had it read to him, he expressed admiration at the cleverness of the forgery, nor, until proof arrived, would he admit it to be genuine.

13 February 1851. The division was anxiously looked to. It was thought on our side that many Irishmen, indignant at Lord John's raising the No-Popery cry, would put in practice their often repeated threat of voting against Government. When it came to the test, however, only 18 out of 105 did so. There was much talk, just or unjust, I know not, of corruption being employed. The manner of proceeding was said to be the giving of small places, which the recipients put up to sale among their friends. (The subject was investigated before a committee last year, but with no result. There prevails in Ireland itself a general belief in the prevalence of such practices, which is not refuted by the ordinary character of Irish M.P.'s . . . From 1849 up to this date, 1855, I remember no important [division] which has not been followed by imputations of venality against some member . . .[23]

The numbers were 281 to 267: great excitement – in the lobbies considerable disorder, and many practical jokes were played: supporters of Government dragged into our lobbies, and *vice versa*.

14 February 1851. More talk respecting the Irish M.P.'s, who are now unpopular with both sides . . . It is noted of many, that from the late change in the franchise, or for some other reason, they have no hope of a seat at the next election: whence their sole object is, to trade as largely and profitably as they can on a capital which is so soon to be drawn out of their hands; the more so, as in many cases their seats had been obtained at the expense of bribery which they could ill afford . . .

16 February 1851. I called on D. with facts and figures relative to the income tax, and we walked together in the Park. He was full of a new scheme for organising a ministry on a broad basis – in other words, by means of a coalition. Nothing could be more magnificent than his programme. He aimed at securing at least one leading Whig from the cabinet: at effecting a junction with the Peelites, Graham excepted: and counted also on an Irish alliance of a very comprehensive character. With these materials he thought we might form a powerful administration. I did not doubt it, though I did doubt whether we should form a united one: but I felt some curiosity as to the nature of the machinery by which such great results were to be brought about. These as stated to me, appeared quite inadequate. Of the Irish he made no account: it would be enough for them to continue the Lord-Lieutenancy, to distribute some small patronage among them, and give office to one or two of their number: Keogh should be solicitor-general, under Napier[24] as attorney-general. He treated the present agitation lightly – thought it would end as quickly as it began suddenly – the Catholics could be no worse off in our hands than in those of the Whigs. He wanted, he said, to break off the connection between Toryism and Orangeism, it was merely accidental, of late growth: the first Orangemen were Whigs. The real struggle of the present day was between country and town: Ireland was wholly agricultural, therefore ought to side with us against Manchester. (Last autumn – 1854 – Disraeli employed himself sedulously in blowing up the extinct No-Popery agitation, from which attempt he desisted, less in deference to the opinion of all his friends, than from perceiving its utter hopelessness). He predicted Lord John's early defeat and resignation: thought he would then retire from public life: that Graham, who had as yet kept aloof on the Catholic question, would take command of the Liberals, whereon many of the leading Whigs would secede, and come over to us. Again and again he recurred to the idea of a coalition between my Father and Palmerston: said Aberdeen had played us false: that we ought not to trust him: we had been more than once his catspaws. 'Palmerston was a man who bore no malice, who liked office, whose tendencies were Conservative, and who would find no difficulty in throwing over former colleagues, especially as he and Russell were not on the most cordial terms. He felt confident that he, D., could arrange with him in 24 hours, if permitted.

The Chancellorship of the Exchequer *in futuro* was this day offered to T. Baring, who had in 1841 refused the vice-presidency of the Board of Trade. He expressed surprise and pleasure at the offer, withheld a definitive answer, but expressed a hope that we should not be compelled at this moment to take office, as the state of prosperity actually existing, while it falsified our predictions, seemed unlikely to last. He spoke with confidence, and even with some alarm, of the reaction that must ensue: but at any rate it would not do to give opponents an opportunity of ascribing it to the re-enactment of a Corn Law.

17 February 1851 (Monday). Sir C. Wood brought forward his budget . . . The financial scheme involved in it produced no strong impression, being received at first with great indifference.

20 February 1851 (Thursday). Lord John, in a debate on Locke King's motion to extend the franchise, volunteered a reconsideration of the question – i.e. a new Reform Bill – next year. Notwithstanding this concession, the Radicals refused to yield, wisely thinking that they should best impress the minister's promise on his memory by showing the strength of their party. They accordingly divided, beating Government by 100 to 52. The Conservatives stayed away purposely: indignant at the evident intention of the cabinet to throw on them the burden and unpopularity of resistance. Lord John's colleagues either were, or affect to have been, taken by surprise, at this declaration on his part. To many of them it is doubtless unpalatable, and many more think they ought to have been consulted. The premier evidently feels his weakness, and seeks to remedy it by an alliance with the democratic leaders. His early resignation is much talked of: he himself on being applied to for the reversion of a place which would be vacant in a few months, recommended the applicant to address Lord Stanley; which the latter in his simplicity did.

21 February 1851 (Friday). . . . Lord Fitzwilliam[25] took an opportunity, within the last two days, of intimating to my Father a partial adhesion saying that he at least, though he could not vote for a low fixed duty, should not object to see one carried.

A meeting in St James's Square to discuss the income tax, and consider how it should be opposed. The business began and ended with a speech from my Father, who exposed the inefficiency of the pretended measures of relief: criticised the budget generally, explained the grounds on which he and his then colleagues had supported the income tax of 1842: and expressed a conviction that if that now proposed was suffered to pass, it would be saddled on the country as a perpetual burden. He pointed out the method of gradually repealing it as a surplus arose, and deprecated union with the Radicals for a merely factious purpose. They had had a long run, he said, after their fox, and were on the point of killing him in the open: but they must kill him with their own pack, and not let any straggling curs come in and finish their work for them. He hinted that the less said of free trade in the impending debate, the better: and suggested the advantage of closing it, if possible, in one night.

At 6 p.m. the same day, in a very full House, Herries rose to open the debate when, unexpectedly to all present, Lord John interposed, and begged that the debate might be postponed till Monday. No explanation was added . . . Within ten minutes the House adjourned, and 500 members poured out into the streets . . . The secret had been well-kept. The Whigs shared fully in our astonishment: even Sir James Graham . . . seemed to be taken unawares. Not a rumour had reached non-official members. To add to the bewilderment, it so chanced, by a merely accidental coincidence, that my Father had been invited to dine at the Palace, from which fact premature conclusions were drawn.

Four different theories are afloat on the subject of the mysterious delay. Some expect a dissolution: others a mere abandonment of the unpopular income tax: others the removal of Sir C. Wood, the admission of Cardwell to fill his place, and a fusion with the Peelites: while a fourth and more numerous party predict a simple resignation.

22 February 1851 (Saturday). The *Times* announced that ministers had resigned. At 2 p.m. my Father received a summons to Buckingham Palace. His interview with the Queen lasted 70 minutes. He repeated to me afterwards what had passed, and also permitted me to read a paper drawn up by himself containing the substance of their conference, and which was afterwards submitted to the Queen. I believe therefore the following summary to be accurate.

He found the Queen and Prince together. They both received him with apparent cordiality. The Queen's manner showed little embarrassment, and she entered on business at once, saying that she had sent to ask his advice under the following circumstances. The government had, last night, tendered their resignations, which had been accepted. Lord Lansdowne being unwell, and in the country, she had seen him only at an early hour that same day, and had therefore been unable to communicate sooner with Lord Derby. My Father requested her permission to ask two questions leaving it wholly to Her Majesty to decide on the propriety of giving or withholding a reply. First – whether the resignation was that of Lord J. Russell alone, accompanied by his colleagues *pro forma*, or whether it was the act of the entire united cabinet? She replied without hesitation that it was the latter. Next, whether any other person had been sent for previous to himself? The Queen apparently misunderstanding the drift of this question, answered earnestly and quickly 'No, I assure you it is not so' adding that as he was the head of the most powerful party opposed to the late government, she had thought it her duty to summon him without delay. My Father then, on her invitation, proceeded to explain his views on the actual state of parties. It was true, he said, that the present or late cabinet had met with a defeat, but that defeat had not come from a side of the House over which he, Lord Stanley, exercised some influence: that it certainly furnished clear evidence of the weakness of ministers, but no evidence of his (Stanley's) strength: that a third party existed in the state including men of great ability and experience whose views, on at least one important subject, agreed with those of Lord J. Russell and his colleagues: and that considering the strong objection which always existed against a complete change of policy, especially if accompanied by a dissolution of parliament, he humbly submitted that it would be desirable in the first instance to see whether the present holders of office could not strengthen their hands, by a junction with other men of influence and weight, whose opinions coincided with theirs. If the latter refused to accede to such a proposal, it remained to be seen next, whether they would coalesce with him (Lord Stanley): or if they did neither one nor the other, but held aloof from both parties, being themselves unable to form a government, it would then become obvious that they either would not, or in their own judgment could not, do H.M. any service: in which last event he was prepared to stand by H.M. at all risks, and use his utmost efforts to prevent her being left without a government. In that event he felt sure that H.M. would look with indulgence on a list of names less known to the public, and less distinguished, than he should have ventured to present to her in any other case. He then continued 'The expression is not a flattering one to myself, but I venture to believe that I shall be able to serve Y.M. more effectively if I appear as Y.M.'s chief minister in consequence of a necessity, and not of Y.M.'s selection.' The Queen said little, but listened with profound attention. My Father went on to speak of his principal followers, Herries and Disraeli: one, he said, had extraordinary talent, but no practice in official duties: the other, with considerable knowledge of routine, was not possessed of distinguished ability. Here the Prince interposed, and began to ask many questions as to the course contemplated in respect to free trade. My Father said he should not alter the tariff of Sir R. Peel in any important particular except those of sugar and corn: even in reference to those items he would endeavour to make his demands as moderate as might be, consistently with justice to that interest whose claims he had been accustomed to advocate, and with his own honour: he must respectfully add, that were he to be induced, on any pretence, to waive those claims altogether, not only would he do his friends a great injury, and suffer in personal character, but he would be utterly and forever depriving himself of the power of serving H.M. by the loss of influence and of public confidence which must follow such a retraction of avowed opinions.

The Prince seemed inclined to press this subject and enter into argument, but my Father saw that the Queen wished to change it and hinted that the details of whatever measure he might have to introduce, would be better discussed bye-and-bye. It was probably at this state of the conference that the principles of the Manchester school being alluded to, my Father thought it necessary to protest most strongly against them. 'Not only' he said 'would they destroy all the existing institutions of the country, but if suffered to gain strength, endanger the stability of the throne itself.' He felt, he told me, that this was delicate ground: and while uttering the last words, his voice trembled so that he scarcely finished the sentence.

The result of the interview was this: my Father neither accepted nor declined office, but advised that a junction should first be tried between the Peelites and the existing government. He thought the former of these parties must then be placed in a dilemma: if they refused, it must be purely on personal grounds, which would damage them with the country: if on the other hand they, or a part of them accepted, the rest, being too few to stand alone, must return to him: and it was probable that some of the Whig party, disliking their new allies, would secede. At any rate, if it should so turn out, that both this negotiation, and one to be subsequently set on foot between Lord Aberdeen and himself in case of the failure of the first, should fall to the ground, the formation of a Protectionist ministry would then be felt as inevitable, and on that account more willingly acceded to by the country.

My Father expressed satisfaction at his conduct of this affair: he considered the resignation as a plot arranged by the late ministry, with the connivance of the Prince, to throw upon him the ridicule and discredit of having attempted to form a government and failed. He said 'It is a bungling fisherman who strikes at the first nibble: I shall wait till my fish has gorged the bait, and then I am sure to land him'.

23 February 1851 (*Sunday*). I saw Disraeli: he expressed alarm at the turn affairs were taking, feared the effect on Conservatives out-of-doors would be bad, if it were thought we had declined power: and showed me a note he had written to my Father, which was very characteristic. It contained a proposal for a 5s. duty to be laid on 'for the sake of revenue' coupled with a professed abandonment of Protection, and declaration of adhesion to the new commercial system. I thought such an arrangement would only create suspicion on both sides; but D. pressed it strongly. He predicted our early success – a dissolution – and the almost total elimination of the Peelites from the next H. of Commons. Walpole on the other hand asserts that a return to protective duties is out of the question, and that till that controversy is decided, we cannot take office.

The evening was passed at St James's Square in arranging the distribution of offices, on the two suppositions that Aberdeen and Gladstone do, and do not, join us.

24 February 1851 (Monday). Explanations in both Houses: these explained nothing except what had already gone the round of the papers. John Russell used the phrase 'that Lord Stanley had "declined" to form a Government' which though true in the letter, conveyed a false impression. Disraeli thereupon contradicted his statement in general terms: Lord John repeated it, with the qualification 'that he spoke to the best of his belief': this discrepancy, perplexing the public, led to a belief that the Queen had insisted on my Father's not dissolving, and that he had declined to comply with the condition.

In the Lords, Lord Lansdowne made a speech generally understood to mean that he should not again take office. (Brougham said of him lately 'Anyone who goes into our House is sure to hear Lansdowne taking leave of the Peers for the last time'. I have heard from Lord Lyndhurst also more than one final farewell publicly delivered). Sir John Hobhouse[26] is also announced as a Peer: never of late years an active politician, he had in the present parliament contracted so strange an aversion to speaking, even on the affairs of his own department, that the threat of a hostile motion would induce him to concede almost anything that was desired.

Much discussion respecting the propriety of D.'s contradiction of Lord John. It was contrary to etiquette, confessedly: for the theory is, that Royal conversations are never repeated to third parties without express permission. It was also unfortunate, for the Queen especially dislikes having her words quoted or repeated in public. There may also be a doubt whether the misstatement was worth setting right: but Lord John's object could not be mistaken: he wanted to show that we had finally, and through weakness refused to take advantage of the offers made us.

Rumours circulate, first vague, then assuming a definite form, that the attempted coalition between Graham and Lord John had broken down. The former held language of the most desponding kind, saying to Naas seriously, that he had hitherto hoped to die under a monarchy: but now feared to outlive the throne. This startled our friend: who asking explanation, was told by Graham that the negotiations would probably end in a Protectionist Government being formed: of which the result must be civil war.[27]

25 February 1851 (Tuesday). At 11 this morning, my Father received a note summoning him again to attend at the Palace. He did so, and immediately afterwards called on Disraeli, whom I saw in the afternoon. The subject chiefly discussed was the constitution of the new Cabinet, which is to consist of 13 members, 7 in the Lords and 6 in the Commons. In the event of our failing to obtain help from without, the filling-up of the latter would create our chief difficulty. D. expressed his willingness to serve under Gladstone if the latter could be brought over. He (Disraeli) said he was well aware of the prejudices which existed against him both at Court and among the party. I denied this, so far as the party was concerned: of the Court I knew nothing. I told D. also, as I really thought, that Gladstone as a leader would be equally obnoxious to Protestants and Protectionists: that the farmers never could be brought to understand that his, (Disraeli's) supersession had been his own act: they regarded him as their representative and would take it ill that those who had borne the burden and heat of the day should be set aside to make way for allies who only at that moment ceased to be enemies.

D. offered me the Under-Secretaryship of the Home Office in very flattering terms: saying that his duties as leader of the House would throw all the administrative work on my shoulders: that this must be the case: it was almost without precedent that a Home Secretary should lead the Commons: nothing but the urgency of the occasion would induce him to take such a responsibility: he should rely on me as a friend, and one not unwilling to work. I promised, if need were, to stand by him: and there the matter dropped.

In the evening I went to St James's Square, where I found my Father more despondent and depressed than I ever remember to have seen him. All had gone wrong: Lord Aberdeen had refused to take office, but recommended Canning,[28] whom he called his 'alter ego' and said he loved as his own son. He would not however attempt to influence Lord Canning's choice, and disclaimed having held any communication with the latter. This conversation led to an immediate application to Lord Canning, who affected to hesitate, but in fact intimated his intention to decline, should the proposal be formally made.[29] As a last resource, my father has thought of applying to the Duke of Wellington, whose name would have been to us as a tower of strength, though he himself, by age and infirmity, is disabled from taking an active part. It was believed, from some communications that had passed, that he would hold the Foreign Office *ad interim*. The Queen however objected to this. Thomas Baring also had expressed his reluctance to take part in the formation of a government. To add to these difficulties, the Queen professed herself seriously offended by the language which Disraeli had held on Monday. She thought an unwarrantable use had been made of her name: it was only on Father's repeated assertion that without D. a cabinet could not be formed, that she would consent to his inclusion. Her last words were 'Remember that you make yourself responsible for him'. My Father answered that he would take the responsibility. He told me that on his admission to the Palace, he could see plainly that she had been in tears. His impression was that since their communication began, she had become much more cordial and unreserved in her manner towards him. With the Prince the reverse was the case: he remained present during every conversation that passed, suggesting difficulties faster than they could be disposed of, and endeavouring to alarm the Queen as to the results of a Protectionist Ministry. Among other things, he began to talk, in my Father's presence, of the unpopularity of the Minister affecting the Sovereign personally, quoting the instances of Polignac and Guizot. My father bore this insinuation with temper; and the Queen, feeling it to be offensive, used some words intended to do away its effect: I know not exactly what they were. It was suggested by her that he might himself take the Foreign Office:[30] to which he replied by naming the obstacles: one, the constitutional practice, which renders it impossible for the Prime Minister to occupy any other post than that of head of the Treasury: the other, his own constitution, which a year of such double labour would break down. He did not communicate a project which at the time I know he entertained, of recalling Sir Stratford Canning[31] from Constantinople to fill that post. The Queen evidently feared that Disraeli would be the person selected.

During the day, which was one of unceasing occupation, my Father's spirits sustained him, but at night they failed utterly. After dinner, a note from the Queen being brought him, he answered it rapidly and in few words: then leaning his elbows on the table, and resting his head in his hands, he sat in that posture without speaking or moving during at least a quarter of an hour. Yet in all this agitation, he has not once missed giving my brother (a boy of ten) his usual lesson in the morning: and when he went into the drawing room he called for his chessboard and played two games in succession, in which he became as entirely absorbed as if no such thing as Courts and Cabinets existed.

Without his having stated a positive opinion in words, it is now clear to me that he will not persevere, unless strengthened by the accession of Gladstone.

26 February 1851 (Wednesday). Gladstone arrived this morning in town, and without the delay of an hour called in St James's Square, having made a rapid journey from Rome.[32] He asked a few hours for deliberation, and went to consult with Lord Canning. The Duke of Northumberland[33] also came by appointment, and received an offer of the Admiralty. His claim consists of having been long engaged in the naval service, really understanding and liking his profession, and possessing, besides his social influence and wealth, a pleasing, popular manner. (The Duke's career was unlucky: I say unlucky, for fault on his part there was none, except the fault of overtrustfulness. He became nominally responsible for proceedings with which he had nothing to do, and which in themselves harmless or at the worst very venial, were magnified by the spirit of party into political crimes. All that skill both in tactics and argument could effect was done to turn the current of public feeling, but to no purpose, against a hostile majority, which the Duke not understanding, considered his cause to have been abandoned, and is even now – 1855 – scarcely reconciled to his former colleagues).

I accompanied my Father to the levée, on his way to which he was two or three times cheered by the crowd, although it was neither large nor noisy. On our return there was a similar, though fainter, demonstration. He stayed only a few minutes, having at all times, and now more than ever, a strong dislike to being made the object of public curiosity. The diplomatic corps were particularly friendly in their salutations.

27 February 1851 (Thursday). Gladstone's refusal was made known as early as 4 or 5 p.m. yesterday, and it was by his influence and that of Lord Aberdeen united that Lord Canning was induced to give a similar reply, as did likewise Henry Corry,[34] whom we had counted on securing by an offer of the Colonial Secretaryship – a post above his claims, and indeed above his abilities. He had filled a subordinate post in the Admiralty under Sir R. Peel. For a time it was intended to apply to Lord Ashley,[35] but this idea was abandoned, partly on account of the probability of his declining, partly because of his impracticable ideas in matters affecting religion. Lord Ellenborough was also tried, but would have nothing to do with an import duty on corn. Even Sir R. Inglis declined what he might well call a 'very unexpected' offer of Cabinet. The leaders of the party met in St James's Square, and about 4 p.m. my Father determined to abandon the attempt, a decision which he lost no time in communicating to the Queen. I saw him about half an hour later, when past anxiety and present relief were equally depicted in his looks. I am convinced that he himself had long despaired, but thought it right to persevere while any, the slightest chance of success remained. (Subsequently, he has often told me and others, that at no time during this crisis did he look forward to a different result from that which actually occurred: there were however, moments when he seemed to take a more sanguine view.)

(The free trade journals, including the entire press except *Post* and *Herald* were vehement against us at this time: nor were their invectives without effect. I find here in my original journal a lamentation on the low state of

Conservative journalism, mingled with speculations as to its cause: these need not be preserved. The fact still remains, the causes are not hard to find.)

Had Gladstone not joined, the Cabinet stood as follows:

First Lord – Lord Stanley
Chancellor – Sir E. Sugden[36]
Colonies – Lord Malmesbury
Admiralty – Duke of Northumberland
Post Office ⎰Lord Hardwicke[37]
President of Council⎨ uncertain: Lords Exeter[38] and Salisbury[39] named
⎱ for these posts.

In the Commons:
Foreign Sec. – Sir Stratford Canning
Home Office – Disraeli
Exchequer – Herries
Woods and Forests – Granby
Board of Trade – offered to Henley, who took fright and declined: this and Board of Control not filled up.

No doubt this administration would have been one of the weakest ever formed: we regarded it, however, as provisional only, and had we gone on, we should have done so in hope of bringing over some of the Peelites who, we thought, might have accepted as existent a government which they would not help to make.

One obstacle to success was the absurd vanity and self-confidence of some of the least capable of the party. 'It is bad enough' said my Father 'to have to deal with mere sticks instead of men: but when these sticks all fancy themselves great Ministers, what can one do?' Two exceptions deserve mention. Sir E. Sugden had nothing to lose, and everything to gain, by the construction of a ministry in which he should be included, even for a day as Chancellor. The peerage and pension are equally permanent, whether the actual tenure of office be short or long. Notwithstanding these personal considerations, he was the first, and the most earnest, in dissuading my Father from the trial.

Walpole has shown equal disinterestedness in a different manner. He knew the difficulties under which our party laboured, and though entitled to claim, and having indeed a promise of the Solicitor-Generalship if he had chosen to demand it – though poor, having a family, certain to rise in his profession, devoid of political ambition, and disliking responsibility, he at once offered to take any political appointment which he might be thought capable of filling. The post of Home Secretary was accordingly allotted to him.

28 February 1851 (Friday). I called on Disraeli at his desire, and found him in very low spirits. He had counted on success, and felt the disappointment keenly. He did not expressly affirm that we ought to have persevered: but said the defeat was decisive – it was a confession of incompetence: for himself he should retire from public life, and return to literature, leaving those who had brought him and themselves into this trouble to find their own way out. In this strain he continued for some time. I pointed out that we were now free from the Protectionist incubus, that no one could ask us to reimpose a corn law, the formation of a government on that basis being proved impossible: that, therefore, the Conservative party might now be reconstructed on a wider and sounder basis. He concurred, but thought it would be a work of time to 'reunite the fragments' after such a crash. He added that there was a fatality about his own career – he had turned out two successive administrations, but it was fated that he should never himself succeed.

My Father did full justice to D.'s management on this occasion. 'But for him' he said 'I should have given up the game too soon. He was hopeful to the last, and did all that man could do'. Both described the closing scene alike: a panic seems to have fallen in a moment on all their colleagues: it was as though their senses had suddenly forsaken them. Yet these men seek to dictate our policy, and would if it depended on them, reject all assistance from without.

Explanations in both houses this afternoon, but no new fact elicited, except a declaration from my Father which though important has attracted little notice. He announced that if the next parliament should pronounce in favour of free trade, he should feel himself bound to yield, in acquiescence to what must then be regarded as the deliberate decision of the nation. (This declaration has been purposely overlooked by opponents, and not sufficiently adverted to by our friends. It furnishes a complete answer to those who accused us of having changed our policy for the sake of holding office.)

The position of the Peelites at this moment perplexes all parties. Separated from us by the corn law question, from the Whigs by the dispute on Papal aggression, they seem to have no option except that of uniting with the Radical section – a course, however, which they show no disposition to pursue. Their only obvious principle of action is close coherence. Like the Duke of Bedford's followers, Rigby etc., as described by Macaulay, they are 'only to be had in the lot'. (This state of things applies now (1855) notwithstanding the many changes intervening, but at the time here spoken of. I believe that Gladstone and Newcastle,[40] if they had any definite policy, aimed at forming a Cabinet exclusively out of their own party, with the aid of a strong recruit or two from other camps. This was certainly their idea in the autumn of '52: perhaps is so at the present moment.

Meantime the Queen's summons to the Duke of Wellington is regarded as a mere manoeuvre to gain time.

1 March 1851 (Saturday). A clever article in the *Daily News*, which exactly describes the true state of affairs, as regards our attempted ministry.

I may here insert one or two miscellaneous remarks belonging to this time. It was supposed that my Father, immediately on taking office, would dissolve: this was never his intention, though he would have done so at the close of the session. He argued that a dissolution was impossible until the supplies had been obtained, and afterwards it mattered little what might be said or done by an expiring parliament. But he would have run any risk rather than dissolve while all the country was still under the influence of violent religious excitement.

The Queen told my Father that she had insisted on Palmerston's exclusion from the new arrangements. The feeling of the Court against him is most violent (the cause to us unknown) and as he is of all the Whigs at present the most popular, and next to Russell the most important, this prohibition creates no small embarrassment.

So earnestly did the Whigs court the Peelite alliance, that at the first interview between their respective chiefs, Sir James Graham had *carte blanche* offered him to do what he liked, and turn out whom he pleased. This we heard directly from the Queen.

Brunnow[41] had several interviews with my Father during the crisis. He expressed in his own name and that of the diplomatic body, a strong desire that Lord Stanley should unite the offices of Premier and Foreign Secretary. They feared Disraeli's nomination to the latter post, and Brunnow was privately assured that this was not intended: perhaps he would have been little better pleased to hear that Lord Stratford, the bitter enemy of Russia, was the individual selected. He (Brunnow) added, what is not easy to believe, that Lord Aberdeen would have joined us after a time, as soon as the Papal question should have been disposed of.

I have nowhere mentioned the intended appointment of the Duke of Cambridge[42] as Lord-Lieutenant of Ireland. The proposition pleased the Queen, who mentioned it, when all was over, to the Duke himself. This my Father had thought of doing, but forbore, not wishing to pledge himself to the same selection under possibly altered circumstances.

In speaking of some over-eager partisans, who expressed annoyance that the intention of forming a government had been so quickly abandoned, my Father remarked that they had more reason to find fault with his moderation, than he, with their patience. 'I have little to gain by office, and everything to lose: they have nothing to lose, and much to gain'. So Pitt wrote concerning his followers in 1802–3, when Canning was intriguing to put him in Addington's[43] place.

My Father gaven an explanation of Lord John's Protestant zeal of last winter which to me at least was new. 'Johnny had heard that I meant to publish a strong Protestant manifesto (which I never thought of doing): he remembered how he had tripped up Peel by his Edinburgh Letter in favour of entire corn law repeal: and he thought I was going to trip him up in the same way. As it turns out, he has only upset his own government. It is quite a case of retributive justice.' He added that in asking for a committee of inquiry on the subject, he had two objects in view: one, the chief, to allow time for the popular heat to cool down, the other, to bring to light the oppression which he believed to be practised by the R.C. priesthood on the laity of their own persuasion. To the appointment of such a committee, I have the authority of Moore[44] and Keogh, the two most active partisans of the R.C. hierarchy, for saying that they would not have objected. I suspect however, that if Lord John had not, by publishing his letter, put himself at the head of the Protestant movement. Disraeli would have assumed the vacant post of agitator. (I believe this, first, on account of the general character of the man: next because of some remarks which he made to me about this time: lastly, because in the autumn of 1854, he actually made some moves towards conciliating the Orange ultra-Protestants of Ireland.)

3 March 1851 (Monday). Parliament met again: it was announced that no change had taken place: but that the late ministry had resumed their offices. It is not now easy to understand why they ever vacated them. Their reception by the House of Commons was cold: the few speeches that were made, all either openly or covertly hostile, and scarcely a cheer to be heard. A stranger would have thought that nothing of interest was passing. After a few words, the House adjourned to Friday.

The Duke of Wellington summed up the state of parties in few words, in a conversation held with the Queen, which he has repeated everywhere. He says that there are two sections of the Conservative party: on one side officers without men, on the other men without officers. He had thought the best thing they could do was to unite and form an army, but since personal differences prevented this, nothing remained except to recall their predecessors. This is the whole truth in short compass.

5 March 1851. Certain Protectionist delegates, headed by the indefatigable G. F. Young, waited on my Father, professedly to express their confidence in him, but in reality with the object of eliciting another declaration like that of May last, and on the strength of it beginning a new agitation. They were however disappointed. No reporter had been admitted a circumstance which materially tended to shorten the speeches delivered: and a gentle hint was given to their leader, that Lord Stanley's engagements rendered a long interview inconvenient. So all passed off easily, and nothing occurred that could provoke hostile comment. The delegates then visited Disraeli, who, though taken by surprise, addressed them at length, but in a cautious moderate tone.

In the afternoon my Father saw the Prince, who took him apart (it was a meeting of the Exhibition Commissioners) and began a conversation ranging over many subjects of foreign and domestic policy. The ostensible purpose was to discover which course the Protectionists meant to pursue respecting the Ecclesiastical Titles Bill, but they diverged into many other topics. Two points my Father especially noted: first, that the Prince's mind appeared to have been formed by Sir R. Peel, whose sayings and acts he continually quoted: next that there had manifestly been instilled into the Prince's mind a feeling of strong prejudice against him (Lord Stanley) approaching to personal dislike. He described it as amusing to witness the Prince's un-disguised astonishment and pleasure at finding his opinions so much more moderate than he had been taught to believe. Nothing pleased him (Albert) more than the distinct understanding now entered into, that after the next election the question of Protection should not be mooted. He talked much of the necessity of a Conservative policy, expressed alarm at the policy of Manchester, but said 'What is to be done? Here are your rising men, sons of the aristocracy, educated in the best schools and universities, and among them there is not one that can compete with the self-taught middle class manufacturers'. (Unluckily this is true, or was in my day at college, 1844–8. At that time the noblemen and fellow-commoners were the jest of the University for their idle, indolent, and often disreputable lives. Something of this was due to the then system of teaching, which has of late been greatly improved.)

We hear from various quarters, as this conversation shows, that the feeling of the Court towards my Father is greatly altered, since they have come to know him better. It is evident that pains had been taken to prejudice those in authority against him.

The Prince broached one subject of vast interest and importance. He thought the state of the English Church unsatisfactory, and that it was necessary to try and settle those questions of discipline which of late years have led to so much controversy. He proposed to summon together three or four times in each year, all bona fide members of the National Church, in what may be called a lay convocation, for the arranging of such matters as are now referred exclusively to the Bishops. These latter to have a veto on the proceedings of the meeting. I did not understand whether he meant such a meeting to be held in each diocese, or for England generally: I presume the former. The plan never went beyond a mere outline. My Father on the whole approved it, but the difficulty of properly apportioning power between the clergy and laity is obvious.

7 March 1851. The House met again. Sir G. Grey[45] introduced the new Ecclesiastical Titles Bill. He spoke without force or animation: seemed hardly to believe, certainly not to feel, what he was saying. Nor was the House in a more excited mood: all parties listened in languid silence, as to a farce played by very indifferent performers, and the conversation which ensued, a debate it cannot be called, was both short and full. Ministers now propose to strike out all except the declaratory enactment, to the effect that

Popish titles are not good in law, and the penalty of £100 on their assumption in any public act. And this is the sole result of a Bill, to bring in which England had been convulsed by an agitation, at the head of which, cheering them on, stood the Prime Minister!

9 March 1851. Disraeli earnestly pressed a combined attack, with the aid of the Irish party, on the anti-papal bill, as nugatory and objectionable. This proposition was rejected: it was doubtful whether all the Conservatives would support such a move: by the country it would not be understood: and its failure might expose us to the charge of faction.

11 March 1851. Ministers were again defeated, by 120 to 119, on a motion of Lord Duncan's[46] for the reform of the Woods and Forests. They and their supporters ascribed their defeat to a coalition between the Radicals and Protectionists: unjustly, for none such existed: only 54 of our men voted with Lord Duncan, and the result was attributable to the indifference of the ministerial supporters themselves, who can now hardly be induced to come down even on the most pressing emergency. (I did not know it at the time, but I have now little doubt that Duncan acted in concert with Disraeli. He, Duncan, was right in his propositions, and it is a pity they have not been more largely acted upon).

12 March 1851. Sir C. Wood called on my Father, and entreated him to prevent, if possible, his followers from voting for a motion to be made by Williams[47] of Lambeth, for transferring the Customs and Excise Departments from the control of the Crown to that of parliament (I state the case as he put it.) He pleaded, he said, not for the existing government, for he believed their time had expired, and they had better quit office at once, but for the cause of government generally: the influence of the executive was declining daily: party combinations had ceased to exist: 'no man would now walk across the House at the bidding of another'; with more in the same strain. He was answered, that the defeat of yesterday had not been due to any preconcerted plan, but that there existed a general opinion that ministers were endeavouring to throw on Opposition the odium of defending unpopular measures, a belief which led many to withhold their support. Wood repeated again and again, that they (ministers) could not influence their own friends, that the country was tired of their government: that they had had their turn, and now it was ours: we might come in whenever we pleased: he supposed we should do so on Baillie's motion. The only person of whom he spoke with bitterness was Graham, whose conduct he described as a mixture of rashness and cowardice.

A day or two ago, Lord Lansdowne had spoken in nearly the same sense to my Father saying, among other things: 'My political life is ended: I only hope not to be succeeded in office by such men as Bright and Cobden'.

About this time it was arranged that in the event of our coming in, Disraeli should take the Exchequer instead of the Home Office: the change was made partly to get him out of the way of the Court, partly to relieve him from the excessive labour of the H.O. Malmesbury was suggested for the Colonies, with me as his under-secretary.

It is calculated that we shall gain on an election 60 seats, most of which will be lost by Peelites and Whigs: the latter section are dying out rapidly: except Ebrington[48] there is not in existence a young Whig.

14 March 1851. For the first time since the late resignations, a meeting was called in St James's Square. Inglis, Sir J. Pakington,[49] and others who have hitherto held aloof, attended. My Father's task here was delicate. He had to explain the cause of his declining office, that cause being the incapacity of the friends whom he addressed, for the higher departments of administration. He undertook it with entire frankness: and drew such a picture of a hostile House of Commons, threatened impeachments, a combined opposition headed by all the ex-official members, and the helpless situation of even the ablest minister until he has grown familiar with the routine of his business, that though silent and ill-pleased, they acquiesced, and applauded to the very echo when he appealed to them to say 'whether he still possessed their confidence, or not?' Then, diverging to the position of the actual government, he urged the necessity of sparing them a little longer, until the supplies should be passed, and parliament could be safely dissolved. He recommended the postponement of Baillie's Ceylon motion, and deprecated any attempt to force ministers into a minority. 'We have them like chickens in a coop: we may keep them as long as we please, and put an end to them when we please: their existence is always in our hands.'

This speech lasted an hour, but much of it was a repetition of what is here set down, and of arguments used in the Lords. Barring some necessary differences of language, the explanations given in private by Lord Stanley to his family and friends were identical with those addressed to parliament and the country. There has been literally no *'dessous des cartes'*; no material for secret history. A few questions were put by Adderley, Inglis, and others, but not a word of dissent was uttered.

In the House, the second reading of the new Papal Bill was discussed, the most interesting feature of the debate being a maiden speech from Sir R. Peel. It was well-composed, well-delivered, the voice good, the remarks not wanting in acuteness, but exceedingly rambling, and the manner of the speaker theatrical even to the verge of ridicule. Sir Robert was at one moment on the point of breaking down, but saved himself by dint of courage. He was in no way discomposed, but pulled his notes out, referred to them, refreshed his memory, then went on as before. The speech left behind an impression of considerable cleverness, combined with a plentiful lack of judgment. It is impossible to conceive a contrast more marked than that between the late and present Sir R. Peel. (This gentleman's subsequent career has admirably corresponded with the beginning here described.

Half-insane, wholly inconsistent, insomuch that no set of men can at any time wholly count on his vote,[50] he yet commands some respect for talent and independence of character: it remains to be seen whether the latter quality will be extinguished by office.)

15 March 1851. I attended a committee of the Carlton Club, composed of Malmesbury, Salisbury, Mackenzie,[51] Forester,[52] and others, and organised for the purpose of attending to election affairs. (The functions of this body were various, but ill-performed, the more so as some of them might not have borne publicity, though ostensibly our objects were consistent with the most entire purity. I cannot now recall the circumstance that led me into this business, from which I soon retired, and in which I believe my services were of no value. At the few meetings which I attended, I remember being not a little surprised to find applications from boroughs wanting members, in quite as great number as the letters of candidates wanting boroughs: the idea of choosing men personally and locally known seemed scarcely to occur to anyone. We found that we had been grossly practised upon in our choice of agents. Some fifteen persons acting for the National (Protectionist) Association were removed as being notoriously strong Liberals, who had taken our pay to betray us. The chief managing man was one Brown,[53] a shrewd parliamentary practitioner.)

Malmesbury called on me to supply him with a list of works on political economy, which I did, marking out for him a course of reading. He is full of zeal, able and willing to work, but has never studied this class of subjects.

16 March 1851. We decided reluctantly, and after much deliberation, to withdraw Baillie's motion for the time, Government having offered us a day: a challenge which we thus declined. The reasons were trifling, turning upon the absence of some few votes counted upon. (This was a mistake, put us in the wrong, spoilt our division, and caused the acquittal of a great political offender.) The Duke of Wellington was consulted by Lord Stanley. He replied in the terms that from his peculiar ideas of government, and jealously of parliamentary power, might be expected. He said 'the conduct of the army had been approved by the Sovereign' (i.e. by the Ministry) and ought not therefore to be called in question. There might be a doubt whether martial law had been administered with sufficient conformity to established rules, but in the nature of things it must be arbitrary: it had been so under him, the Duke: on the whole he disapproved the debate. I saw the letters to which reference is here made: they were almost illegible: but my Father said that in conversation the old man's mind was still clear. They had a long conversation: when the Duke took occasion to deplore the weakness of the Executive, and the recent advances of Liberalism.

Our determination to postpone, in other words to abandon, the Ceylon motion, has given great cause of triumph to ministers, and proportionally discouraged our own partisans.

17 March 1851. I went down, on business, to see the veteran politician and reviewer John Wilson Croker.[54] His house at West Molesey, crowded with books, pictures, busts, and MSS., suited well the character of its owner. He pressed me earnestly to become a contributor to the *Quarterly*, saying that the political department of that review would, but for him, be entirely neglected. I neither accepted nor declined, but left it open. The truth is, quarterlies are well nigh superseded by the growing influence of the daily and weekly press, which draws off the ablest writers. In discussing this subject, I chanced to mention the *Herald*, and express a wish that volunteers could be found to write for it. Croker immediately went back to his reminiscences. 'I remember that in 1818, or '20, I forget which, but it was before the Queen's trial, our organ, the *Courier*, had fallen off greatly both in merit and circulation. Peel, Palmerston, and I took it up and worked it daily: and in eight months we had raised the sale from 6,000 copies to 20,000'.

With reference to the politics of the day, Croker's views are gloomy in the extreme: he thought it was not now merely party, but property, that was at stake: the next parliament would be thoroughly democratic: we ought by all means to remain in opposition, because the Whigs were only to be kept quiet by office: he might be reconciled to a *de facto* republican government as such, but did not see how it could be brought about in an old country without violence, etc., etc. I listened to the old man without agreement or sympathy, but with a strong feeling of respect for his laborious life, acute intellect, and singleness of purpose. He pointed with some pride to a dozen thick volumes of his own contributions to the *Quarterly*, in which he still continues to write. He spoke of his death as near, but this is a habit of his: I remember him doing the same when I met him at Wimpole in 1848. (He is alive still, an active invalid, always complaining and criticising, and convinced of the impending ruin of England.) His conversation was peculiar: the slow pompous delivery, meant to be impressive, seemed to me rather tedious: but the matter, though diffusely stated, always worth hearing. On the whole I went away pleased to have seen a man of note, but not desirous to repeat the visit.

19 March 1851. Walpole came up to me at the Carlton, began to discuss his own prospects, and those of the party, both in a tone of despondency: he thinks he is placed too high, is too old to take office for the first time, might have succeeded better if brought up to the profession of politics, etc. Walpole is not an unambitious man, but fear with him is stronger than hope, and principle than either.

20 March 1851. ... Newdegate[55] and Drummond[56] delivered two of the most offensive speeches ever heard in a British parliament – Drummond the worst: he described nunneries as either prisons or brothels, a phrase which raised a storm of some minutes' duration. At one moment I thought actual violence would have followed: many Irishmen rose from their seats, calling aloud and gesticulating: Lord Arundel rose to order: the Speaker behaved well, and though unable to pronounce Drummond's language disorderly, contrived to convey both in his words and manner, a severe rebuke of the Protestant orator. He failed nevertheless to appease the tumult, and was at last obliged to call on the House to support him: an appeal rarely made, and never without effect. On Drummond's sitting down a fresh explosion ensued. Eight or ten Irishmen rose together: Grattan[57] the first, in a paroxysm of passion: the speaker called on Graham, then left the Chair, thus interposing a quarter of an hour, and allowing time for all sides to cool. Furious outcries and great excitement continued even after he had retired: Drummond sat near the Irish benches: whereon fearing lest he should be openly insulted, three or four friends crossed the House and took their seats also near him.

Graham's rising restored order: he commented severely, but simply on what had passed: then plunged at once into the heart of the subject, and for two hours kept the House in breathless, and not displeased, attention. I say 'not displeased', because though his sentiments were opposed to those prevalent out of doors, and to the votes of an immense majority of M.P.'s, yet most of those votes were given in compliance with the wishes of constituents, and nothing could contrast more strongly with the tone of bigotry assumed in debate, than the private conversation heard in the lobbies night after night. Hence, when a champion of the unpopular cause could be found to rise, he was listened to with respect and secret envy, by those whose want of moral courage alone restrained them from taking the same course. Graham's argument tonight was admirable, his manner dignified, calm, and even solemn: his advocacy of the Catholic Church perhaps too extreme: but his closing appeal to Liberal statesmen could not be exceeded for beauty and rhetorical skill ...

21 March 1851. A conference in St James's Square on the postponement of Baillie's motion: this was decided on finally, chiefly on account of my Father's apprehension lest it should be too successful, and lead to a second disruption of the ministry ...

My Father showed me a letter from Lord John, entreating aid to carry the Papal Bill, 'lest it should slip through our fingers, and then Cardinal Wiseman may toss up his hat for joy!' In a party view, it is clearly our policy to defer the passing of the Bill as long as possible, thus keeping open the breach between Graham and Russell, whose coalition has been the object of Disraeli's unceasing fears. It is also our interest to keep the debate going as long as possible, for every speech uttered by the Peelites places them in a worse position with their constituents.

I had an interview today with Samuel Phillips, a well-known journalist, whose object was to get the *Herald* put into his hands. He is a man of talent and energy, though weak in health: is ill looked on by the journalistic profession for his secession from Liberal principles, and the Conservatives who regard all journalists as hacks, join in the cry without a reason. (Phillips is since dead. He published two volumes of *Essays* from *The Times*, very cleverly done: and did not reprint an article on Disraeli, the bitterest and the most masterly of all his writings. He died of overwork) . . .

. . . The violence of the popular organs against R. Catholics is at this moment very great, and certainly not creditable, when one knows that of those who write in this style there is probably not one who does not feel that he is playing a part. The agitation has now lasted three months, and continues without sign of abatement.

Lord Aberdeen called on my Father for the first time since the resignations, and entered into a long confidential conversation vindicating his conduct. He had previously given the strongest assurances of his resolution never under any circumstances to coalesce with the Whigs, and as it was notorious that a coalition had been attempted, he felt bound to explain the part he had taken. His explanation was amusing. The Queen, he said, had sent for him (as indeed my father had recommended) to sound him on the subject of a junction with Lord John. The purpose of the meeting, however, was not stated in her note of summons: and he accordingly wrote to the Palace in the full belief that he was invited to form an administration on his own account. On this supposition he discussed with her for some time the state of affairs: and was disagreeably surprised when she told him that Graham and Lord John were in the next room waiting to see him.

He repeated a characteristic answer of Sir James Graham, when urged himself to take the highest office. Graham's words were 'I am the most unfit man in parliament for a prime minister: there are two things which I can do: make a speech and manage an office: but I have no followers, and I know myself to be more unpopular than any living statesman'. No description could be truer, and it evinces remarkable self-knowledge.

A postprandial indiscretion of Lord Broughton's, at an India House dinner, in which he spoke of the Government (himself included) as virtually defunct, has caused some gossip. The old minister's habits were formed in less temperate times: and cabinet secrets are said often to leak out in his cups.

24 March 1851. The endless length and general dreariness of the Papal debate relieved by a speech from George Smythe – quaint, brilliant, desultory, yet carefully prepared. All admired, no one was convinced. It was the failure of a clever man. He spoke about twenty minutes: his best point, a defence of the Catholic hierarchy as combining the freedom of a voluntary system with external magnificence and religious discipline.

25 March 1851. Some debate continued . . . the House narrowly escaped a count-out which would have been fatal to the Bill, and in the present temper of England, to the parliament also. The speech of the night's, Gladstone's: it occupied two hours, and surpassed in eloquence and animation, though not in argumentative power, even the great display by Graham. The peroration was one unbroken torrent of energetic declamation marred only in its effect by being too long: Gladstone did not know when to stop: for half-an-hour his audience expected him to come to a close at the end of every sentence, and the attention so long strained, began at length to relax . . . We divided 414 to 95.

The violence of feeling provoked on both sides is very great. I have heard an English Catholic, of generally moderate opinions, say that the conduct of the British government towards those of his own faith excused, if it did not justify, insurrection: and I have also heard Wakley,[58] a staunch and violent radical, say that in his belief the Emancipation Act of 1829 was a mistake, and ought never to have been passed .These are only samples, and I could add to them many more, of the extent to which popular passion has been roused. Ollivier, the publisher, showed me a collection, supposed complete, of pamphlets published on this controversy in the last four months. It amounted to fourteen thick octavo volumes.[59]

2 April 1851. A dinner given to my Father at the Merchant Tailors Hall, where Peel was entertained in 1838. The report of this festival being in the public prints, I shall not notice it here. Of peers and commoners 300 attended: my Father spoke an hour: never on any occasion have I known him so embarrassed both beforehand and at the moment of rising: with him such agitation usually precedes a more than common success. The opinions announced in his speech had been previously stated in parliament: the passage most rhetorically successful was one which contained an eulogium on Lord G. Bentinck: it was a model of declamatory art, admirable both for matter, words, and rhythmical structure. Disraeli alone expressed disappointment at the general result, having expected either a more explicit declaration of policy, or a larger attendance. He now predicts a new Reform Bill, the swamping of the agricultural constituencies, and the permanent defeat of the Conservative party.

3 April 1851. The only fault found with the manifesto of yesterday is the overcaution displayed in it – a new charge! I passed the morning in assisting my Father to revise his speech for publication: he refused scrupulously to do more than correct errors in reporting, contending that anything beyond this is a fraud on the public, and that a professed republication should contain only what was actually spoken.

8 April 1851. Malmesbury came to see me with a proposal that we should remove from the Colonial to the Foreign Dept. I did not much like it, having carefully prepared myself for the former post, while of the latter I know nothing. But I assented, not thinking a change of government likely for some time.

. . . Here follows in my journal a long account of a negotiation in which I took a leading part, having for object the improvement of the Conservative press. It came to nothing: the party in general seemed to regard the news-paper interest as their natural enemy, and any attempt to turn it into a friend as mere waste of time: my Father sympathised in this view. Disraeli thought nothing could be done with existing journals, and that our only hope lay in founding a new one. I find journalists a difficult class to deal with. They have the irritable vanity of authors, and add to it a sensitive-ness on the score of social position which so far as I know is peculiar to them. Having in reality a vast secret influence, rating this above its true worth, and seeing that it gives them no recognised status in society, they stand up for the dignity of their occupation with a degree of jealousy that I never saw among any other profession. Moreover as from the anonymous nature of their writing, the separate work of each can never be distinguished, they consider their individual reputation as involved in that of the paper to which they contribute: and refuse accordingly to act except with colleagues whose abilities they recognise. The actual state of Conservative journalism is as low as it well can be.)

. . . Barron[60] moved for, and nearly obtained, a committee to enquire into the state of Ireland. He failed by only 9 votes, 129 to 138. There is truth in the remark of a daily paper, 'that the ministry resembles one of those Cornish rocking-stones, which the finger of a child can shake, but which twenty strong men cannot overturn.'

11 April 1851. Disraeli brought forward a motion on agricultural distress, which was discussed until 2 a.m. His speech, though good, was coldly received: the party in general expected a bad division, in which they were agreeably disappointed, for ministers had only a majority of thirteen. The debate was not remarkable. Robert Peel rose at midnight, was received in dead silence, and having apparently not prepared himself in any way, broke down utterly. A more painful failure I have never witnessed. It is the more unlucky as Peel, whose talent and originality are undoubted, has of late incurred considerable personal obloquy, partly from an affectation of eccentricity, which goes beyond the ordinary license of society, partly in consequence of a quarrel in which he got involved, not creditably, in con-nection with some gambling transaction.

The state of the House towards midnight was disgraceful: eight or ten members were visibly too drunk to know what they were doing, and others not sober. Of the Irishmen, two, Magan[61] and John O'Connell,[62] quarrelled, a challenge passed between them, and Roebuck, in the character of peace-maker, had to threaten both with the Speaker's interference. The threat answered its purpose. The scene passed in the lobby.

15 April 1851. A conversation with Disraeli, given at length in my journals: he expressed general despondency at the state of things, thought he ought to have taken office when it was offered, lamented my Father's indifference on the subject, and censured our tactics on the Papal Bill. He wanted the debate on this last protracted as long as possible, with a view to detach more thoroughly the Irish and Peelite M.P.'s from Government, and foster division in their ranks. He also spoke of the existing institutions of England as dying out, and the progress of democracy as certain: but I have heard language from him, equally confidential, and exactly contrary: therefore attach less importance to these predictions.

24 April 1851. The House adjourning for Easter, I went down to pass two days among my constituents.

A meeting was arranged to come off at Edinburgh, Eglinton in the chair; it was meant as a great Protectionist demonstration. My Father, who is not usually favourable to such gatherings, had promised that I should attend there: I thought it unwise to refuse, but at the last moment took to my bed on the plea of illness. The cause of Protection being lost, I wished to leave it without giving offence. The meeting succeeded well: Alison the historian the chief speaker: 700 persons were let in by ticket, and many more came. Within a few days, the Boston election[63] was decided in favour of a candidate who had little to recommend him except Protectionist opinions, against a strong free-trading opposition: which is naturally viewed as a sign of reaction. A few such victories will force on the new Reform Bill.

30 April 1851. I returned to town from Goodwood, where I have passed a few days. The Duke of Richmond appears nowhere to such advantage as in his own house. Surrounded by a tenantry among whom he is deservedly popular, engaged in the personal superintendence of his large property, or in local business, which he understands well, extending an abundant hospitality, not to a few fashionable friends, but to all in the rank of gentleman with whom he has anything to do – enjoying life, and helping others to enjoy it – he is far more in his element than when addressing the Lords, or ranting at a provincial meeting. His attachment to my Father is of twenty years' standing: they have constantly acted in concert: and I do not believe that on the Duke's side there has at any time existed even a momentary jealousy of the superior distinction attained by his old colleague and friend. In the Duke's manner there is something so peculiar that it can neither be imitated nor described. It is frank, open, brusque, and by a very timid or very fastidious person might perhaps be felt as disagreeably unceremonious. But the sincerity and unreserve of the man show through it, and his real goodness of heart, and freedom from affectation, are almost as easily perceived. I cannot imagine the Duke of Richmond saying anything he did not mean, nor except on very rare emergencies, suppressing anything that he felt strongly. In public estimation, he has suffered from the latter cause: few politicians have so many hasty or violent speeches to answer for: and it is commonly supposed that these represent his general manner of thinking, whereas they are in reality mere ebullitions of the moment, undignified, doubtless, and unwise, but for the most part forgotten as soon as uttered. In action this heat of temper vanishes: as a magistrate, a landlord, in committees of the Lords, or anywhere else where the duties to be discharged partake of a judicial character, it is impossible to show a more entire freedom from prejudice. His habits are active: he rises early, is out in all weathers, gets through a great deal of business, and nevertheless has time to attend to the convenience of his guests, who are generally numerous. He loves to talk of the Peninsular War, in which he acted as the Duke of Wellington's aide-de-camp, and for some time (I think) as his military secretary. I have often urged him to put on paper some record of those days: but he has always declined, disliking the act of writing, and perhaps distrusting his memory.

A Protectionist meeting held this morning in Drury Lane Theatre, where 2,500 persons were present, nearly all above the grade of labourer. The speaking was inferior to the numerical demonstration: Butt, the Irish barrister, being the chief performer: his style creates by its very vehemence a suspicion of insincerity, and would not suit the H. of C. without great modification. It is certain that the cause of Protection has of late gained ground among the farmers, and also that it has lost among politicians, few of whom support it with any earnestness.

1 May 1851. The Queen opened the Exhibition in Hyde Park: a grand show absurdly magnified in importance by the press. (It was the common language about this time of the Liberal free-trading party, that the epoch of unrestricted commerce being inaugurated, that of war had ended, and a general disarmament of nations must ensue. Few perhaps went this full length but many even of the most sober-minded of men fell in more or less with the prevailing delusion. At last the popular enthusiasm produced a reaction of weariness, and the scheme and its authors were talked of in a tone of depreciation as unjust as the preceding excess of panegyric. I suppose this effect was limited to a comparatively small class. Each year, since I remember society in England, has had its prevailing mania: some one subject eagerly seized upon by the people, and dwelt on to the exclusion of every other. In 1848-9 this favourite topic was foreign politics: in 1850, reduction of expenditure, and free trade: in 1851, the Exhibition: in 1852, hunting down the Derby administration: in '53, spirit-rapping and the Russian quarrel: in '54 and '55, the war.)

I know of nothing relative to this ceremony of opening that is not already related in the newspapers, except the ludicrous blunder of treating as a mandarin, and inviting to walk in procession with some 15 or 20 of the most distinguished men of England, a Chinese speculator who had come, or been brought over for the purpose of exhibition and who, as I afterwards learnt, had left China during the campaign there as the servant of an officer in the Madras army.

2 May 1853. Hume moved to reduce the income tax from three years to one: he carried his motion by 244 to 230. Ministers have accepted their defeat very quietly, knowing that a second resignation would place us in power. My Father observes that a marked change is perceptible in the conduct of the Court and of foreign ministers towards him, Bunsen alone of the latter standing aloof. Brunnow said at a recent visit 'I know who your Foreign Secretary is to be, and though he is no friend to our country, yet he will find us ready to act frankly and cordially with him'. Stratford Canning was here indicated. ·

Sir E. Lytton Bulwer,[64] a professed liberal, has joined us, and published a pamphlet[65] in our favour. More O'Ferrall,[66] late governor of Malta, now an Irish M.P. whose talents are well spoken of, has done the same . . .

5 May 1851. A meeting was held to discuss the provisions of the Papal Aggression Bill which stood for this evening: but in the interim between the summons and the assembling, it had been postponed for a week, and this change, and the diminished interest now attaching to the subject, made the meeting a dull one. My Father declared himself ready to take office if required. This was cheered. No violent anti-papal speeches were made: on the religious subject men seemed to have become more rational.

We got an urgent message, professedly emanating from the Court, begging us not to make any attack on ministers, as they proposed dissolving parliament at the close of the session. (It would have been well for all parties if they had done this. We should have shaken off the Protectionist incubus, have entered office free from the burden of a pledge which could not be redeemed, and possibly in union with the Peelite section: above all we should have avoided the plausible, though unjust imputation of altering our principles on succeeding to power.)

Our parliamentary strength is increased by Whiteside,[67] one of the leaders of the Irish bar, who has obtained a seat for Enniskillen. (Whiteside's debut in parliament was but partially successful. He spoke well, but too vehemently: he worked himself into rage on small matters, a fault of which the House is very intolerant, nor could he ever forget the feelings of a provincial partisan while dealing with questions of imperial moment. For three years he scarcely made a speech that did not contain some attack on the Pope or the R.C. priesthood. Hence, with all his energy and eloquence, he gained little ground: until the present session, when he denounced Gladstone and the Government in terms indeed too bitter, but with great dexterity and parliamentary power. This one speech has effaced the memory of many previous failures. I write impartially, for in the opinions therein expressed I neither did nor do sympathise.)

6 May 1851. Naas[68] carried a motion in support of the claims of Irish distillers, by the Speaker's casting vote . . .

8 May 1851. Cayley raised his annual debate on the malt tax. My Father, in a printed letter, had declined to strike five millions off the revenue without equivalent. Disraeli voted for the motion, guarding himself in an ingenious harangue. I stayed away purposely, as did many of the country gentlemen.

Lord Lyndhurst has had offered him the Presidency of the Council, in the event of a Conservative government being formed: he hesitates on the ground of expense (his pension being diminished by the amount of any official salary which he may receive) but raises no other difficulty. His age precludes him from holding a laborious office . . .

11 May 1851. I returned from passing two days at Syon . . . Disraeli and my Father got into deep conference, walking together: and in their abstraction missing the path, wandered into a swamp by the riverside, a bad omen, as all agreed: they came home in a state neither clean nor comfortable. I had some conversation with Lockhart.[69] He seemed a disappointed and soured man: neither smiled nor laughed at all: his remarks were epigrams, mostly in disparagement of some one. He seemed to think the old Conservative cause lost, so far as journalism was concerned: said all the best writers had deserted the *Quarterly*: his only volunteer was John Manners, of whom he spoke in terms of unmeasured contempt . . .

15 May 1851. Again the Irish party wasted the entire night. They consumed two hours in reading petitions at length, with the double object of causing a delay, and of thinning the House, in hopes of effecting a count-out, which would have stopped the Bill. They were prepared, if at any time the numbers had fallen short of forty, themselves not included, to have left the House en masse, and thus carried their point. But these tactics were seen through, and the annoyance caused by such merely vexatious delay lost them the sympathy which they would otherwise have received from impartial persons among all parties. Indeed, except dogged perseverance, and the never-failing fluency of their nation, they showed no one quality of parliamentary tacticians during this struggle. Whiteside made his first speech: a rich brogue, a redundant oratory, and an unnecessary energy recalled the idea of his country, but he had something to say, and said it well, though rising at midnight in an impatient House.

16 May 1851. . . . . Grattan, son of the great orator, delivered a wild harangue accompanied with the most extravagant gesture: he is a man of some talent, but on some subjects little less than insane.

I had some conversation with my Father at this time on a plan of his for appointing a committee to enquire into the relations of the R.C. Church with the state. At first, as a means of gaining time, of allowing the popular ferment to cool, and as a substitute for the Titles Bill, such a proceeding would have been of great use: now, it is plainly superfluous. He saw this, and abandoned the project, displeasing thereby the fanatical Protestant party, who are ready to go all lengths. He said to us respecting these persons, when expecting to succeed to office, 'I hope you' (his family) 'are prepared to hear me denounced as a traitor within a month's time'. He again repeated to me, as he had done before, his fixed purpose not to stir the question of Protection again, if a new parliament should prove unfavourable to it: but added he should feel great reluctance in such circumstances, in attempting to form a government.

18 May 1851. Lord Aberdeen called: held most friendly language: repeated that the Peelites were only holding aloof until the one obstacle to reunion was smoothed over: that disposed of, no further difficulty would exist. He even hinted at Stratford Canning's unfitness for the Foreign Office, and at the possibility of *his* accepting it again. (In my journals, this conversation is given at length: but being only at secondhand, I could not guarantee accuracy. The substance, as here related, was communicated by my Father) . . .

27 May 1851. After a week barren of incident, Baillie drew a full House to hear his long-deferred charges against Lord Torrington. . . . Roebuck stood up for Government, as he never does except when they are unpopular and in the wrong: his argument, briefly stated, came to this, that all savage populations require strong measures to keep them down: that the rising in Ceylon had been suppressed, and that it was not our duty to enquire further.

22 May 1851. Baillie's motion was lost by 282 to 200, a result mainly owing to bad tactics in bringing it on.

. . . During the last few days I have received from the editor of the *Morning Herald* a collection of fifty or sixty articles by Lord Brougham, written for that paper during the years 1844–6. Their authenticity is proved not only by Knox's[70] assertion, but also by the style, which cannot be mistaken: their merit varies, some indicate labour, but the majority are hasty and careless in the extreme. There is much repetition: the best are personal attacks on Palmerston, Campbell, and O'Connell. In quite one-half of them there is panegyrical mention of the writer himself.

30 May 1851. I met Thiers[71] for the first time, at a dinner given by Edward Ellice. A party had been made expressly to meet the French statesman, and nothing could exceed the deference with which he was treated. His person, manner, and voice, are all unprepossessing. In height he does not exceed Sheil, whom he also resembles in appearance: a short squat figure, pot-bellied, with a strange restlessness of movement, and eccentricity of gesture, such as would draw attention in a crowd. He ran rather than walked about the room, bowing profoundly to all present as each in turn caught his eye. During the dinner and evening his tongue scarcely rested. Ellice told me that it was his habit to rise between five and six in the morning, and that since his arrival in London, he had passed nearly the entire day in walking about to see sights. The face is not intellectual, until you come to observe the breadth and squareness of the forehead: the voice is worse than that of any public speaker whom I have known. When in animated conversation, it rises to a shrill scream: but the general tone is low and husky, like that of one suffering under a bad sore throat. His difficulty in first obtaining a hearing must have been extreme, but this once overcome, his style is wonderfully pointed and vivacious. He did not talk, but spoke: interrupted only now and then by a question: used much gesticulation, flinging round his arms like the sails of a windmill: and conversed on political matters, among a circle of strangers, with a degree of unreserve which an English politician would scarcely think allowable except in the society of intimate friends. His sketch of the days of June '48 was an historical essay delivered offhand. Sidney Herbert,[72] sitting near me during its delivery, could not forbear whispering 'We ought to have had a reporter to take this down'. It was chiefly a narrative, interspersed with remarks, but contained little that could be carried away and quoted separately. I remember that he scouted an idea thrown out by somebody, that the French army would not act against the people. 'The officers' he said 'are mostly republicans, but they are in favour of order, and dislike mobs – the soldiers are soldiers'. Towards eleven, when he had discoursed above an hour without pause, he made a sudden stop, looked at his watch, rose, bowed round the room, and darted through the door abruptly, giving no time to take leave. Between him and Guizot[73] the contrast is complete: the *pondus in verbis, severitas in vultu* of the latter is altogether wanting. Peel and Lord John were not more unlike. I once met Guizot at a breakfast, where he sat silent and the cause of silence, freezing the company by his reserve, imperturbable as a statue and not more sociable, but commanding a kind of involuntary respect by the natural dignity of his demeanour. The ideas of dignity and of Thiers are incompatible.

2 June 1851. After three weeks of expectation and delay, Walpole succeeded in bringing on his amendments to the ministerial bill: to these the more ardent Protestants had looked anxiously, as calculated to supply the deficiencies of the original measure. They consisted chiefly of provisions against the introduction of fresh papal rescripts, and in safeguards, or what were meant to be such, against the evasion of the law. On the whole they contained little that was calculated to excite either the hopes of one party, or the fears of the other; but such as they were, a large body of Conservative members had come down to support them, and the disappointment was proportionally great when after a short, unanimated debate, they were withdrawn. The reasons of this withdrawal were, first, the general coldness of the House, which in this respect represents the now prevalent temper of the country; and next, some legal difficulties, overlooked until that moment. The Carlton was in a ferment: Beresford and a few of his set raving and staring, talking of treachery etc., but Walpole's character stands so high that he could not be attacked with any show of plausibility, except for his self-acknowledged tendency to vacillation. It was a mistake to bring down 200 men to support propositions which after all were to be withdrawn.

Sheil's death was this day announced: an early and melancholy end for one who though not a great was certainly a remarkable person. He had faults which made his rise to a really high station impossible: words were more to him than things: the rhetorician prevailed in his nature over the statesman: his acceptance of a diplomatic post was a mere job: nor was he capable of the labour and responsibility of administration. Devoted to the rhetorical art, he has left behind some of the most finished models of the Irish school of oratory which we possess: O'Connell wanted polish, Curran[74] taste: except Grattan, Sheil has no superior among the speakers of his country. But the perfection of the orator was the weakness of the debater: he could not reply readily, except where the attack was foreseen, and the retort previously prepared, not yet argue closely: and he feared to trust himself on ground which he had not fully explored. Hence his inferiority to O'Connell, who cared not one farthing for the judgment of critics, and if he had anything to say, would rather make a bad speech than none. Nor had Sheil studied politics as a science: his great displays are limited to a narrow range of subjects, and even on those he argued like a partisan: the accident of nationality and religion made him a Liberal: the prejudices against his race and (nominal) creed were met by him with well-acted indignation and pointed sarcasm, never with calm argument and reasoning: the party which he supported went away from the delivery of one of his harangues exulting in their triumph, but opponents were irritated rather than converted or made to doubt. Though violent in language even to the verge of sedition, his sincerity was always questioned: in later years his energy died out, and his political objects became avowedly personal: accepting a place from the Whigs, he lost caste, and affected to laugh at his own venality. I knew little of him in private life: he seemed to me an unhappy man: there was a bitterness, approaching to cynicism, in his conversation which was not entirely put on for effect. Domestic distress, failing health, and disappointed political expectations, concurred to make his last years gloomy. He did not sympathise heartily with the agitators of a new generation, the champions of tenant right and communistic doctrines. (Since this was written, his magazine articles have been reprinted: they are slight, sketchy, exaggerated, but their cleverness indisputable.)

3 June 1851. Grantley Berkeley[75] was to have brought forward the case of the West Indies: but so great was the annoyance of the Conservatives at Walpole's withdrawal of his amendments, that they refused to come down and vote on any question. Knowing this, and fearing a bad division, Beresford continued a 'no-house' at four o'clock.

6 June 1851. The great cause of Pope v. Premier again occupied all this evening ... We again beat ministers on Naas's motion respecting Irish distilleries, and with this small success, the second division of the session (i.e. Easter to Whitsuntide) ended.

Almost immediately after the Whitsuntide holidays, I was summoned to Knowsley by the illness of Lord Derby,[76] and remained there three weeks, after which I set off on a tour to India, of which the details are elsewhere recorded.

1852

June 1852. In June of last year I left London for Knowsley, where my grandfather lay ill. He died in that month, and in July I sailed for India, where I passed the autumn, winter, and early spring. The news of my Father having formed a ministry reached me in Scinde on 2 April: on May 21 I landed in England, and after a brief visit to St James's Square, went to the Foreign Office and House of Commons. I had learnt in India that the post of undersecretary for the F.O. was reserved for me, Lord Malmesbury, a personal friend, being my chief.

The first thing I learnt was that practically, though not quite avowedly, Protection had been abandoned. The farmers, and country gentlemen generally, appeared satisfied that nothing more could be done for them: at least no complaint was heard from them, nor did any unreasonable expectation seem to be excited: a few M.P.'s expressed suspicion, but they were very few, and on the whole the most obstinate resistance to the order of things was within the cabinet, Lord Hardwicke and John Manners being particularly refractory, and sometimes abetted by Henley.

I heard a good account of the manner in which the new ministers had conducted departmental business: the experiment of their appointment was a bold one, for except Lord Derby himself, and the veteran Herries, not one of the cabinet had ever held high office before.

(The Duke of Northumberland, at the head of the Admiralty, was at this time much censured by whippers-in for distributing all his patronage according to professional merit, without regard to party claims: I know that letters of remonstrance were written to him, and that his secretary, Stafford, was loud in complaint. Unluckily, these remonstrances had too much effect, as was found later.)

Malmesbury, my immediate superior, threw himself heart and soul into the business of his office: from early morning to midnight he was busied over its affairs, though hitherto a man of leisure and pleasure. His attention had been turned to this department, and his ambition excited, by editing the letters[1] of his grandfather, the first Earl. He has been more attacked by the press than any of his colleagues, partly from a certain awkwardness of phrase in speech and writing, which does not do justice to his real ability: partly because almost any successor would contrast unfavourable with Lord Palmerston, to whose experience and talent are added the advantages of great social popularity, and of a strong interest with the profession of journalism.

(It is impossible to describe the exaggerated vehemence of tone with which Lord M. was inveighed against by the popular journals. He was daily

70

spoken of as being in league with Napoleon and Count Buol to establish a despotic system throughout the Continent: there being no foundation for such charges that I could ever discover, except his personal friendship with the French President. But the constant reiteration of these attacks in every form ended by half persuading even sensible men of their truth.)

The legal strength of the cabinet is considerable. Lord St Leonards stands high in reputation as a lawyer, though subject to infirmities of temper: Thesiger,[2] Kelly, Whiteside, Napier, are all at least equal to the average.

Irish affairs are thought unsafe in the hands of Lord Eglinton, who shows a strong leaning towards the Orange faction, which is too much identified with Conservatism in Ireland. (I let this passage stand as written at the time: in the event, Lord E. disappointed both his enemies and his too zealous friends, proving a fair, liberal, and popular administrator.) He has however a marked advantage in his hospitality, munificence, and personally pleasant demeanour to men of all ranks and parties. He has gone to Ireland with the avowed intention of spending not only his whole official, but his private income also. The two amount to £50,000 a year. Lord Clarendon, his predecessor, is damaged in public opinion by a transaction in which he appeared as having spent nearly £4,000 of public money in bribing a worthless journal, called the *World*: money, it is fair to add, which he replaced on an intimation from his colleagues that he ought to do so.

Walpole, our Home Secretary, was at one time extravagantly praised, by way of disparaging Disraeli. He is now respected as a useful and amiable official, but with no idea of his becoming a party leader which indeed he does not himself desire to be. His career as Home Secretary was commenced by an extraordinary and most unlucky blunder: a proposition to give the electoral franchise to every militiaman. This plan, of his own exclusive devising, he announced one day from the Treasury Bench without having consulted any colleagues or friend upon it. The surprise of the House was great: greater still the dismay of his brother ministers: and not less the amusement of both friends and enemies, when the plan was withdrawn as abruptly as it had been proposed. (Of this proposition, Macaulay said in a speech delivered at Edinburgh, that the Home Secretary's qualifications for an elector were 'youth, poverty, ignorance, a roving disposition, and five feet two'.)

Pakington, as Colonial Secretary, has accomplished a success. Till his appointment, he was known only as an intelligent and active country gentleman, an occasional speaker in the House, and a quarter-sessions authority. He offered his services to my Father, expecting an under-secretaryship only, and quite prepared to accept one: but the failure of negotiations with Lord Aberdeen and Sir S. Canning having compelled Malmesbury's withdrawal to the F.O., the colonies were left without a chief, and Pakington has been pitchforked into the vacant place. A love of detail, a certain clearness of statement, joined to a strong desire to give satisfaction, have given him a position which he himself could scarcely hope for. It is said that when the Duke of Wellington heard of his appointment, he asked simply 'Who is he? I never heard of him'.

Attempts were made at the first formation of the ministry, to induce Lord Palmerston to join it. He played a cautious game: hinted that nothing except corn-laws stood in the way: would give no pledge: promised forbearance, even support if possible – in short, would say neither yes or no.

None of Peel's followers have joined us except Lord Hardinge, who is more soldier than politician. It is supposed that this party, which remains compact and united, will wait till after the elections, organise a vigorous attack, compel a reconstruction of the cabinet, and thus either enter it by force, or supersede it.

One of Lord Derby's chief difficulties at first was with the Court. He found the Queen reserved, the Prince manifestly unfriendly. A considerable change has taken place, and he is now better received at every visit. Their real acquaintance with one another began last year, when the Queen told the Duchess of Gloucester, 'They never would let me know Lord Stanley before'.

Disraeli appears to have acquired a certain degree of influence over Prince Albert's mind. Disraeli describes him as one of the best educated men he knows, indeed over-educated, something of a pedant and theorist, but a man of talent nevertheless.

I had, naturally, an opportunity of hearing how the leaders in Lords and Commons spoke of each other. Disraeli said of my Father 'He astonishes me – his mind always clear – his patience extraordinary – he rises in difficulty, and his resources never fail'. My Father's estimate of his lieutenant was different: he admired his temper, tact, and ability, but seemed jealous lest he should aim at the first place, and sneered at his tendency to extremes of alternate excitement and depression.

The most strenuous opponent of the ministry, notwithstanding former professions of friendship, is Lord Aberdeen. Graham is equally hostile, Gladstone neutral.

Disraeli, to quiet the fears of those who expect a return to Protection, has put out an election address, containing explicit declarations to the contrary.

There seems still on the part of the Court a nervous dread of being implicated in any unpopularity which the government may incur: of which proof occurred in some difficulty which was made about the prime minister accompanying the royal party to the Ascot races. By singular mismanagement, the secret of their objection was allowed to reach us: and having been thus awkwardly made known, was not less awkwardly disclaimed.

The chief want to the government is the want of a daily or weekly organ, the *Herald* being imbecile, and no other existing. I drew out for the cabinet a scheme, which was proposed through Malmesbury: each member to subscribe 2% of his official salary towards a fund for supporting the press. This passed with little opposition (but though we found money, we never found writers, and part of the sum thus raised was returned).

. . . A more serious blunder is the recent issuing of a proclamation against Roman Catholic processions, by which an obsolete law of 1829 has been revived. The ostensible object is to secure peace at the approaching elections: the Protestant interest applauds, the Catholics complain and threaten. Napier and Walpole are mainly responsible for this step, which Disraeli told me he had supported only to please the Irish Protestants. (The effect was to give a handle to agitation, and create far more disturbance than would otherwise have existed.)

I dined (June) with the East India Company. . . . Lord Hardinge spoke of the Sikh war. I asked why he had made a peace which he knew could only be a truce? He replied, because to gain four or five years' rest for India was an object: in that time some of the leading chiefs might be gained over: and if the Sikh empire could be saved, so much the better, because that people, spreading between India and the Mahometan East, would prevent any movement of fanaticism extending to India from the westward. He repeated several times, that the dangers of India were all internal: what he seemed to fear most was disaffection in the native army, under religious or national excitement. The frontiers were invulnerable.

Lord Hardinge was lately exposed to an awkward misunderstanding. Lord Londonderry in February last consulted him as to whether he (Lord Londonderry) should apply for the post of Master-general of the Ordnance. Lord Hardinge said 'By all means, and you shall have my support'. Coming home, Lord Hardinge found on his table a letter offering *him* the place, which he accepted. Lord Londonderry thought he had been betrayed and made ridiculous, whereon a quarrel ensued . . .

. . . The most important in its possible results of recent F.O. transactions, is the signature of a protocol (May 24) by the representatives of the five great powers, respecting Prussian rights over Neufchatel. That small state, attached to Prussia previous to the French Revolution, was by the Treaty of Vienna placed in the anomalous position of being constituted a member of the Swiss federation, the King of Prussia appointing its Governor, and exercising other sovereign rights . . . The double allegiance thus created has caused perplexity: since 1848 frequent disturbances have arisen, and from the divisions of parties in Neufchatel itself, they may arise again: the simplest and completest remedy would be to alter the terms of the Treaty, as in their nature self-contradictory, but this cannot be done. Diplomacy dislikes change: and many persons fear (mistakenly as I think) that the precedent of altering the Treaty of Vienna, once set by England, would be followed by Napoleon on his own account. Prussia, moreover, by no means consents to yield her sovereignty, nominal though it be. Bunsen went so far as to propose the separation of Neufchatel from Switzerland, and a return to the state of things before 1792. But this proposal can only have been met by him as a test of our feeling on the subject, since it is out of the question that Switzerland should freely cede her rights, and equally so that force should be used to make her do so.

A positive settlement being out of the question, the next best course was to prevent recourse being had to arms to assert the Prussian claim, either now or in future time. With this view the rights of Prussia as now existing were guaranteed, Napoleon being a consenting party, but this seeming concession was neutralised by the imposition of a pledge on all the contracting powers, binding each of them to forbear from measures of force pending negotiations. Now as these negotiations never can end, neither party being willing to waive its rights, the pledge in question amounts to a guarantee of perpetual peace so far as this subject is concerned. Such at least is Lord Malmesbury's view: it certainly is not Bunsen's. Bunsen during the discussions assured us that Prussia only wanted her rights admitted in order formally to waive them without loss of honour. The Protocol signed, he has found it convenient to forget these assurances, and asks when his master's troops will be allowed to occupy the canton. My Father, however, protested vehemently, and threatened, if the matter were pressed, to make public his (Bunsen's) private declarations, a hint which had its effect . . .

21 June 1852. I published an election address, intentionally of a more liberal character than those of my colleagues generally. It was however not disapproved in St James's Square. It contained an express abandonment of the protective principle in finance.

26 June 1852. Granby, in a conversation at Lord Salisbury's, took me to task, though very courteously, for this address. I asked, being curious to know his views, 'Had you remained leader of Opposition, and held a place in the present cabinet, would you have tried to put a duty on corn?' 'Certainly.' 'And do you think you should have succeeded?' 'Probably not' (with some hesitation). 'Well, for this bare chance of success, would you have risked an agitation, and rendered a reform bill inevitable?' Answer: 'I should have thought it my duty to assert my principles.' This devotion to a financial tenet is hard to understand.

Conversation with Disraeli. He says the post of Chancellor of the Exchequer goes well with the lead of the House. There is much work to do, but not routine, not drudgery, like that of a Secretary of State: and he can take his own time to do it, if debates press. He thought we ought to have 330 supporters returned: full one half the House. We could not get on with less: if we had those numbers Palmerston would be sure to join us. Peel in 1834, he said, had 300 followers, yet failed.

12 July 1852. A long canvass, tedious from the heat of the weather, and the necessity of seeing every elector . . . The victory proved easy at last,[3] but up to the day of polling we remained in suspense. The Liberals gave out that they expected 100 majority. Jocelyn my colleague, wavered, and had indeed formed a partial connection with Pashley, his friends to stand neutral, so far as I was concerned, and he to receive the Liberal second vote. By management and temper, and especially by showing confidence in our prospects of success, we won back the authors of this combination, to the extreme disgust of Pashley's friends, who complained, not entirely without reason, of having been tricked. We canvassed daily from 10 a.m. to 7 or 8 p.m. The mass of the electors, 1,100 in number, were quite indifferent to politics, the determining cause of their votes was generally local, or more properly speaking, personal: dislike to, or respect for, some leading person in the town. Had there been no canvass on either side, I doubt whether out of the 1,100 votes, 200 would have been recorded.

(It was an unfortunate coincidence that while I abandoned the principle of protection, as Disraeli had done before, in express terms, Christopher,[4] in the neighbouring county of Lincolnshire, held precisely opposite language. This diversity of sentiment led to many comments.)

The elections went off tolerably, but not more than tolerably well, for Ministers. Liverpool and Dublin gained, Westminster, though lost, well contested: my Father, always sanguine, claims 330 supporters, Disraeli is less hopeful, thinks that without some accession of strength we cannot face parliament. He proposes two methods of making room for Palmerston: the one to replace the present Speaker, who would willingly retire, by Walpole, the other, to transfer Pakington to the upper house. (I never heard that Pakington's consent was asked to this proposition: it seemed to be assumed that he would submit to such honourable shelving). He, Disraeli, argues that when Palmerston has joined, Gladstone and Herbert will follow. With such a party, nothing can shake us except a sweeping extension of the franchise, which Russell and Graham would not hesitate to attempt, but for which he doubts whether England is prepared. My Father approved of the attempt at a coalition being made: and at this juncture peculiar facilities offered for its execution, the Canadian and Indian governments being both vacant . . .

15 July 1852. Little of importance doing in foreign affairs . . . The only serious matter under discussion is one between Russia, Prussia, Austria, and England respecting the course to be taken in the event of Louis Napoleon declaring himself Emperor.

18 July 1852. At dinner with Lord Malmesbury met Lord Stratford, whom I had not before seen: an elderly man, keen-eyed, white-haired, his manner grave, the expression of his face severe, so as to give countenance to the prevalent belief in his harsh and overbearing disposition. His return to England is by the press ascribed to an intention on the part of Lord Derby to put him in Malmesbury's place. This report dates from 1851 when the F.O. was actually offered him. Though gratified with a peerage, he is not content, having expected the offer to be renewed in 1852. (It is singular to reflect on the possible turn which events might have taken, had an opposite decision placed Lord Stratford in the F.O. His removal from Constantinople could not have failed to make the Turkish councils more pacific: his noted hostility to Russia doubtless exasperated the quarrel which grew into a war: while, had he remained in England on our quitting office, which he must have done, his withdrawal from diplomacy would in an equal degree have conciliated the Russians, by whom he was and is detested. I have always regarded him as, whether intentionally or otherwise, one of the prime movers of the Russian war of 1854.) . . .

. . . Lord Malmesbury told me that there were three members of the cabinet who had agreed to resign, if there appeared a prospect of filling their places with more valuable recruits from without. These were Hardwicke, Lonsdale,[5] and himself. I agreed as to the other two, but told him, what I really think, that he cannot retire in the face of such attacks as have been made upon him, without seeming to acknowledge incapacity. He proposed that Palmerston, whom he assumed as willing to join, should take Pakington's place, and that Pakington should take that vacated by Lord Lonsdale, or one equivalent. He also wishes Beresford and Christopher to withdraw, their posts to be put at Palmerston's disposal, to be had, probably, by Lords Cowper[6] and Jocelyn.

19 July 1852. I had a curious letter from Disraeli, in which he repeats the expression of his alarm concerning the elections, and ascribes the loss of several seats to our taking up with the 'Protestant cry'. I don't differ from this view: but who allowed that cry to be raised?

21 July 1852. Saw Disraeli, who spoke despondingly of the elections, laying all the blame of what he called our failure on the proclamation respecting R. Catholic processions, which has created great exasperation and alienated many moderate men, even on our own side. But this proclamation was carefully framed, with his approval, with a view to its effect upon the Protestant voters! He talked of Palmerston, whom he had been sounding through Lady Bulwer:[7] of Beresford, whom it was expedient to remove, his hotheaded blundering having done mischief, and for whom a colonial governorship might perhaps be found. Beresford is not without average ability, but his temper the worst I ever knew. I have heard him curse men to their faces on very slight provocation, and his conversation is one perpetual reviling of the opposite party. He appears to be always angry. His constitution is very gouty, and his blood Irish. Being hooted lately on the hustings at Braintree, he told the people 'they were the vilest rabble he had ever seen, and he despised them from his heart'. Language like this from a minister is sure to provoke comments, and the matter is made worse by unlucky imputation of bribery at Derby, resting on doubtful authority, but plausible enough to give credit.

Walpole sent for me to the Home Office on pretence of business, when he made an opportunity to talk about Palmerston, and pointedly expressed his willingness to give up the H.O.

28 July 1852. The negotiation with Lord Palmerston has ended for the present in failure. It was managed through Lady Palmerston and Lady Bulwer. Lady P. speaking for him, said, she knew it to be his opinion that in England change of principle was more easily forgiven than change of party: he had been looked upon as fortunate and as having shown sound judgment, in joining Lord Grey's government before the Reform Bill: but he himself had always spoken of that transaction, not indeed with regret, for he had thought, and still thought it, his duty, but as the most painful sacrifice that he had ever been called upon to make. She then went on to explain that he had few followers, that he did not like to walk across the House alone: consequently could not accept our proposition, but wished us all success, and would assist us to the best of his power. Meantime the negotiation was to be treated as though it had never taken place – no further word to be spoken concerning it.

Beresford's business is worse than we at first supposed. He wrote from the Carlton to one Frail at Shrewsbury, a man of noted bad character, desiring him to send down a 'good and safe' man to Derby to serve as agent there during the election. The good and safe man went accordingly, and shortly after his arrival was taken into custody, while engaged in committing acts of bribery, with a bag of gold by him, and Beresford's note in his pocket. The only circumstance in Beresford's favour is the publicity of the whole affair: had there been a guilty intention, as may be argued, there would have been more secrecy: but Beresford's reckless imprudence of character lessens the weight of that argument for those who know him.

. . . Malmesbury told me that he had been suggesting to Lord Derby the appointment of Beresford to a colonial governorship. This is a good idea taken up too late. It would be worse now to try to evade enquiry than upon enquiry to be censured. So my Father has thought, and Beresford remains.

Disraeli requested my presence at an interview with Joseph Hume, on the subject of Sir James Brooke's[8] conduct. There are against Brooke six distinct charges, all put forth with much animosity, arising apparently out of private quarrels . . . Disraeli treats this question, as he does most others, solely with a view to the strength of the government, and inclines to throw over Brooke in hope of securing Hume and through him the Radicals. He affects to listen with profound deference to the old man's senile garrulity, and cajoles him with compliments grossly and even absurdly exaggerated. (I afterwards went over the subject with Pakington, and we came to the conclusion that Brooke, though not faultless, deserved support. But D.'s wish to please Hume prevented any decisive approval being given.)

Lord Derby having distinctly stated, after the failure of the Palmerston negotiation, that we must meet parliament without reconstruction, no farther attempt has been made on the doubtful Conservatives – Jocelyn, Canning, and the like. Some talk arose of sending the Duke of Newcastle to India (his acceptance was reckoned upon) but nothing came of it. This place was applied for by many whose claims were perceptible only to themselves, among them by the Duke of Buckingham,[9] whose character suffered almost as much as his fortune in the crash which his extravagance had caused. Almost as unreasonable a demand was that of Baillie Cochrane,[10] the butt of the H. of C., for an appointment as Minister at some foreign Court. Jamaica has been offered to Lord Harris[11] by Pakington, a good selection, which disgusted some of the cabinet, who wanted to job the place for parliamentary support. Harris's sole claim consists of an efficient discharge of his duty at Trinidad. Canada and the Ionian Islands remain to be filled up. The question is being discussed 'What can be done with Lords Elgin and Dalhousie[12] when they come home?'

. . . Tennent,[13] who lately wrote a pamphlet in our favour, entitled *The Ministry and the Session*, called upon me to discuss the possibility of obtaining journalistic assistance. I did not tell him of the cabinet fund, but assured him generally that money would be forthcoming if good writers could be found. He asked me to meet Mr Delane senior,[14] father of the *Times* editor, which I did at his house. Mr Delane's notion was that a series of letters should be written for the *Times*, shadowing out the ministerial policy, by which he considered that the support of that journal might be gained. This course was so obviously impolitic, as putting us in the power of enemies, that it seemed to me difficult to believe that the advice to follow it was honestly given. Disraeli of course rejected it on the instant. Mr Delane said the conductors of the *Times* were prepared for a violently retrograde policy on our part: whence their hostility.

2 August 1852. I went down to St Leonards . . . Lord Malmesbury came down in the evening, and discussed affairs with my Father. Both complained of the interference of Prince Albert in matters of foreign policy. Lord Howden when last in England was desired to correspond privately with the Prince, and keep him informed of whatever passed. He bowed, expressed his sense of the honour intended, but never wrote. Others have been less scrupulous. Lord Normanby's course at Paris has been guided by instructions from Windsor, unknown to Palmerston, who was nominally responsible. The Prince is constantly in the habit of expressing to Lord Derby and his colleagues what he states to be the Queen's wishes on this and that point. Of late these communications have become friendly and confidential: they were at first cold and even dictatorial.

Much passed respecting Bulwer's[15] secret mission to Rome. Malmesbury hopes so to arrange matters, that we may have a permanent legation there, while the Pope has a layman acting as his representative in England. He thinks the effect of this friendly understanding on the R. Catholics of the U.K. would be considerable. My Father looks to Ireland: wishes to lay before the Court of Rome the conduct of the Irish priesthood: and to obtain a condemnation of their proceedings from the highest spiritual authority. With this view, he has collected through the Irish Office a large number of proved cases of priestly intimidation and violence. These he has forwarded to Bulwer, with a letter meant to be shown to the Pope pointing out the injury done to the R.C. cause by its own supporters.

7 August 1852. The measures preparing for parliament are large and numerous, more so than I had expected: they include exemption of dissenters from church rates (a plan suggested by the Bishop of London): an enquiry, by Commission, into the capitular revenues of the Church: another into the relations of the R.C. Church with the state: some amendment of the law of settlement and removal: a plan for the revival of Convocation with admixture of the lay element: and a budget concerning which Disraeli is sanguine. He tells me he thinks he can satisfy every interest except the West Indian, to which he knows not what to concede, unless it be a re-opening of the African labour market: by some scheme, the nature of which I understand but imperfectly, of dealing with the terminable annuities, he anticipates a margin of £4½ millions out of which to make reductions: his expectations of success are unbounded.

Tennent has not relaxed in his efforts to gain over the *Times*, which however refused to be converted, and is now more hostile than at any preceding period. Bulwer talks and writes vaguely of doing something by which the class of literary men and journalists may be propitiated. At present the assistance we get from Conservative newspapers is rather worse than none.

13 August 1852. I find here in my original journals a long and minute account of the origin of the dispute relating to fisheries on the British N. American shore. Enough to set down that the treaty of 1818, excluding American fishermen from the sea within three miles of the British shores, admits of a double construction. We claim that the line of exclusion shall be drawn across from the headlands bounding any bay ... while it is argued on the other hand that it ought to follow the course of the shore in all its windings, at a uniform distance of three miles. Each claim is plausible, that of the U.S. perhaps the more so of the two ... Meantime the trespass on these protected fisheries by American ships has increased yearly. We used to make the mistake of sending, for protective purposes, only vessels of large draught, too few in number to guard the whole line of coast, and too heavy to follow trespassers into shallow water. That error has been remedied: and the appearance in June last of Sir G. Seymour[16] with a more effective squadron than had before been employed (though not a larger one) having for the time put a stop to the aggression complained of, has raised a storm of indignation in Washington. Mason and Cass made violent war speeches: even Webster at Marshfield (our Minister, Crampton,[17] being his guest at the time) committed himself to a strongly worded promise of protection to his countrymen. Some days before, he had published Pakington's despatches in a semi-official form, with comments of his own, and very material omissions. Fillmore, the President, an upright and plain man, is understood to disapprove these tactics. Lawrence,[18] with his accustomed frankness, explains them by saying that Webster, disappointed of the nomination for the Presidency, wishes to be sent to England as Minister: that the cabinet, fearing his opposition, will be glad so to get rid of him: and that he is now engaged in blowing up the fire that he may be employed to put it out.

Lawrence read to Pakington, Malmesbury, and me, the despatch which he was about to send to Washington . . . My Father's object in mooting the question, was not so much to protect our colonists against competition, as to make America feel that there were some rights which, if we were willing to cede, she might find it for her interests to buy. The chief of these is the opening of what is called the coasting trade to California, now closed to British ships. We have to grant in return free navigation of the St Lawrence, and equal fishery rights. We have also in hand a plan of convention between England, France, and America, for the purpose of checking designs on Cuba. It is doubtful, however, whether the Senate will ratify such a treaty, or if they do, whether the South will act upon it . . .

17 August 1852. Malmesbury and Addington[19] being both absent, the whole routine duty of the office devolved on me: though nothing important was to be done, the variety of subjects became to an unpractised person almost perplexing. We have 33 clerks: despatches written and received last year were 30,000, being at the rate of 100 every working day in the year: while those for 1849, the last which are bound up, fill 450 folio volumes, nearly one and a half daily, excluding Sundays.

Of my predecessors, G. Smythe seems to have done nothing: Lord Canning worked hard and steadily, Lord Aberdeen leaving most matters of detail in his hands: my namesake Stanley of Alderley,[20] took his fair share of duty and no more. Palmerston's activity and restlessness are extraordinary: there is no subject, however dry or trivial, on which long minutes in his handwriting may not be found. This is the more remarkable, because he has always borne, and rather carefully assumed, the manner of an idler: his late hours are notorious: and in this respect he has set an undesirable example to the office. I have come down between 11 and 12 in the day, and found difficulty in getting access – the day's work had not begun!

Disraeli sent for me, and sketched out in conversation his plan of a budget: it is brilliant, taking, includes various sweeping changes, and is framed so as to satisfy the different interests concerned. It is however liable to the

charge of sacrificing the future to the present. The main features are reduction of malt tax by one half: reduction of tea duty, gradually, to the
same extent, but this to be spread over several years: removal of light dues
on shipping, and of other small charges: rural police and highway charges to
be thrown on the consolidated fund: newspapers relieved from advertisement duty. To meet these concessions, he proposes to effect reductions in
the services to the extent of £500,000: to increase the house tax and extend
its area: to retain the income tax with large modifications, extending it to all
incomes above £100, and drawing a distinction between temporary and
permanent income: and to spread over a longer term of years the payment
of certain annuities, which would naturally terminate in 1860. To this last
proposal I ventured to object, as improvident. It is not exactly borrowing,
but it is next to borrowing. It is refusing to complete an arrangement
entered into many years ago, for the paying off of a portion of the Debt at a
certain time. The rest of the budget I cordially and fully approved.
(This plan varied a good deal, as will be seen, from that subsequently
adopted.)

Disraeli proposes at the same time to do away with removals, and with
the law of settlement on which they are based. The Irish emigrants into
England are the chief difficulty here.

21 August 1852. Another trouble impending. Napoleon and his advisers
are naturally jealous of the almost republican system of Belgian administration: and they are, or profess to be, extremely sensitive to libels, which,
published principally by French refugees, continue to be sent out in
thousands from Brussels. Some of these are fair critiques on the French
government: others mere tirades of abuse against Napoleon and his family,
and undoubtedly such as might be prosecuted in a court of law. But the
President apparently did not expect the outbreak of feeling against him
in England on the occasion of the coup d'état: he is still sore from its
effects: and being unable to deal with us, he has openly declared that unless
the Belgian freedom of the press be restrained, he will march in troops and
occupy the country. For some such announcement we were prepared: and
arrangements were made with Austria, Prussia, and Russia to guard against
it: but it is now believed that if the occupation proposed be only temporary,
and if its object be to establish an arbitrary, in lieu of a constitutional
régime, these powers will not interfere, but leave England to fight the battle
single-handed. It is of course possible that this threat – which has not been
made in public, though plainly worded – is meant merely to intimidate: but
the reverse is equally possible: and the excessive susceptibility to libels
which marked the character of the elder Napoleon renders it likely that his
feeling may be shared by the nephew. Every peaceful means has been tried
to weaken the Liberal, and to strengthen the absolutist party in Belgium.
Clerical influence has been exerted to the utmost: money has been largely

spent at elections: menaces of invasion have been used in quarters where they might have effect, and the renewal of a commercial treaty, established August 1846, to the great advantage of both nations, is refused.

In this crisis the Queen's visit to Belgium has been of use, as indeed it was meant to be. It has more than hinted at the closeness of the connection which exists between the two countries, and revived proportionally the drooping hopes of the Constitutionalists. Malmesbury has spoken to Bunsen and Brunnow, and plainly says that the distinction between permanent and temporary occupation is one which we cannot consent to recognise. In a word, no effort, nor expression of feeling, has been wanting on our part.

... The invasion panic has subsided: while it lasted, few persons would listen to arguments founded on the improbability of one great nation committing against another an act of piracy which would put her out of the pale of civilisation. The mode of reasoning which had most weight with alarmists was to say that Napoleon, not being a general, could not command in person, and that he would fear to place any one in a position of such high power and popularity as that of a conquering general ...

24 August 1852. ... Various stories were told me by Mure [British consul at New Orleans] of the venality of subordinate officials in America. These are partly confirmed by Sir H. Bulwer, who once said in my hearing that there was no confidential despatch on American affairs which he could not get a sight of for fifty dollars. I have heard the same from Lord Derby, and a recent instance is alleged by Pakington ...

26 August 1852. Discussions as to the admission of Lord Stratford into the cabinet (if he would consent, which seems to be assumed). Malmesbury strongly opposes. A Garter is vacant: Disraeli supports Lord Londonderry's claim ... I suggested to my Father an offer to Lord Shaftesbury, but he did not think this expedient.

Much consideration on the subject of the Burmese war ... Three plans seem open to adoption:

1. To annex Pegu, tell the Burmese government that we mean to keep it in satisfaction of our claim, and remain there on the defensive, asking no further reparation, and being ready to make peace if desired.
2. To move on to Ava, in order to make peace at the capital, but with no intention of remaining there.
3. To move on to Ava, occupy it, annex the country, and depose the sovereign.

The last proposition is generally thought unwarranted both in regard of policy and justice.

... The second is objectionable on this ground – that a temporary occupation of country afterwards abandoned, leads to cruel retaliation on those natives who may have joined or come to terms with the invaders: while the ultimate retreat conveys an impression, however unfounded, of failure.

The first plan appears on the whole preferable ... Disraeli however objects on grounds of finance, saying truly that late annexations have not been profitable.

28 August 1852. Bunsen called on Neufchatel affairs: introducing an English officer, one Capt. Ibbotson, resident in the canton. This gentleman complained that the royalist party was proscribed, that its members were living under a system of terror, unable to exercise political rights, and even liable to insult whenever they went abroad. Bunsen thereon urged our declaring Neufchatel separate from the Confederation, and acknowledging the rights of the King of Prussia over it. He argued that such a step was necessary for the peace of Switzerland. Failing that (for of course I told him it was impossible) he wished we should obtain a pledge from the Federal Government not to occupy the canton with its troops. This was equally out of the question, the F. Govt having a right to do so in case of disturbance. Lord Malmesbury, to whom I reported, approved the language I had held.

... The fear of the Federal Govt is lest Napoleon should intervene. Bunsen holds the language that 'Prussia has nothing to gain by possessing Neufchatel, it would be a source of weakness, not of strength, but the King's honour is pledged to his faithful subjects' – and the like. He feels that the Protocol lately signed – a mistake on our part – has given him an advantage. He sent through me a Memorial to Lord Malmesbury and to my Father.

19 November 1852.[21] French designs on Elba are talked about: for no other reason than that Europe believes Napoleon to be desirous of striking a blow somewhere, and each state thinks itself the one specially threatened ...

I may here note the course which has been pursued in regard to the approaching declaration of the French empire. Lord Malmesbury and the cabinet decided on calling a Congress in London, of representatives of the Four Powers, to concert measures jointly ...

The Queen sensibly attaches no importance to this question: the diplomatic body, to an extent that is ludicrous. After the President's explanations, the Congress becomes a mere formality.

Lord Cowley called also, bringing good news: he felt confident no mischief was on foot: at none of the dockyards have preparations been going on: the number of men employed was very small: little activity in any department of marine, except in the building of steamships, and these were being constructed by every government which possessed a navy. He thought the President would find no trouble in reducing the army if he wished it: conscripts were always glad to be discharged before their term was out.

Lord Cowley thought that the Empire had been forced on by Persigny and others of the Emperor's friends: who had organised a system of *claqueurs* to meet him on his late tour, and produce a show of enthusiasm greater than the reality. The reception was warmer than had been expected by Napoleon himself: who found it expected of him that he should change his title, and accordingly did so. Otherwise he would have preferred to wait until the people required fresh excitement.

Lord Cowley's opinion of political parties in France is very low: he thought all the French statesmen dishonest, except perhaps Guizot, and he used the word dishonest in no figurative sense, but in its plainest and broadest meaning. Of the Legitimists, many were coming round to the President.

Lord Cowley believed the President's government to be a necessity: that no other at this moment could hold power, at least with so little active exertion of force . . .

21 November 1852. Disraeli sent for me, I called, found him greatly excited and annoyed by the charge of plagiarism, at an anxious moment . . . 'I can bear a great reverse' he said 'but these petty personal vexations throw one off one's balance.'

22 November 1852. Fresh despatches from Vienna and Berlin. Buol declines, for Austria, to recognise Napoleon III: is doubtful whether to recognise the Empire: asks for delay, that a plan of joint action may be arranged: approves the idea of a London Congress, but thinks it should precede, not follow, recognition of the Empire. Buol says the President is putting forth extravagant pretensions, in order to have something to resign, as a proof of friendly inclinations. Austria is wavering between her fear and her dislike of France.

Manteuffel approves the memorandum: thinks the sooner the Conference is held the better . . .

24 November 1852. Villiers[22] moved his resolution on free trade . . . Disraeli followed, rising at half past six in a very full House which contrary to custom, scarcely one member left during the dinner hour: his harangue was very elaborate, very original, and not a little audacious. He reviewed the events of the last six years, placing them in a new light, startling friends and foes alike by the boldness of his assertions, justifying his own course by reference to that of Gladstone and Russell, and ending with a dignified admonition to the new members, whom he entreated not to mix themselves up with 'obsolete parties and exhausted factions'. He did not allow attention to fail for a moment, and was cheered with more enthusiasm than ever before in my recollection. Bright followed, declaiming vehemently in a voice which I could hear so as to follow his meaning through entire sentences, through the closed door of the lobby . . . Palmerston rose between 11 and 12, assumed a judicial tone, affected to hold the balance, talked of 'fair play', 'English gentlemen', 'not establishing a political inquisition' etc. etc. all which was received with grateful cheers from our benches. He suggested a resolution of his own by way of compromise. He saved the Govt by this: we looked upon ourselves as beaten men. Palmerston is willing to help us as far as he can without danger to himself: he wishes to show his power, and our weakness: if we pass through the winter safe, he may probably join us, but he does not care to run risks: and personally, he is right. After the rejection of an overture made by us in the summer, it is his turn to speak.

25 November 1852. . . . Jocelyn came to me after midnight yesterday, having roused up my servant with some difficulty, saying that he had a communication of some importance to make. This proved to be the report of a conversation by Gladstone, Graham, and others, who agreed that Palmerston's amendment would be accepted by the Liberals generally, and hoped that we should accept it also, so as to make the affirmation of the free trade principle unanimous, or nearly so. Jocelyn observed that possibly the House might object to Disraeli withdrawing his amendment. This was scouted, Gladstone saying that no one would venture, through mere faction, to impede the giving of a pledge which all wished given. Graham had remarked that we should be madmen to refuse the amendment: and that in that case he and his friends must vote for Villiers. Jocelyn then went on to hint at the possibility of future alliance, of Newcastle accepting India, Herbert, Gladstone, and Canning joining the cabinet: all however dependent on Palmerston's taking the first step. This was so vague, and seemed so like sounding, that I did not encourage it: more so as the question of leadership might cause negotiations to be broken off at the last moment. The *Times*, though not friendly in general to ministers, praises Disraeli on all occasions, a subject on which the country gentlemen are sore. They feel an attack on him to be an attack on themselves, and resent it: but when he is complimented, it is for possessing qualities which they do not share, and holding opinions which are not theirs: thus the compliment offends them as much as the censure. It is natural that journalists should sympathise with one himself an author and a journalist, who has risen by the undivided force of talent: and equally natural that they find some mischievous amusement in contrasting the leader with his supporters. Nor has the wish to annoy Lord Derby by unfavourable comparison been wanting.

. . . The meaning of these transactions is simple: the Liberals, affecting fear lest Protection should be restored, sought to force upon us a resolution intentionally offensive to those who had been Protectionists: the more moderate party, Palmerston at their head, thought it just that we should be made to give in our adhesion to free trade, but wished to make this disagreeable process as little humiliating as possible: Ministers disliked both alternatives, but accepted the latter, knowing that if they rejected the offered compromise, they must be defeated and driven out, without time even to propose any measures.

26 November 1852. . . . We divided against Villiers 336 to 256: on Palmerston's amendment 468 to 53.

28 November 1852. A long conversation with Pakington in which he spoke of Disraeli in very hostile terms, as 'not a gentleman' and expressed hopes that Palmerston would take the lead. Pakington then went on to lament the tone of Tuesday's speech, treating it as an ingenious mystification, very clever, but a mere trick, and almost too audacious a misrepresentation of facts to mislead anyone. Such is certainly the popular impression, and notwithstanding its cleverness, it has done more harm than good. The fact is, that it represents fairly enough the position which Disraeli himself has assumed: but while abstaining from irrational pledges on his own account, he has allowed, and even encouraged his followers to go all lengths. It has sometimes occurred to me that he was not unwilling to mark the distinction between his position and theirs, like a skilful counsel, who while defending some client whose conduct cannot be justified, takes pains not to lose the sympathies of the jury by carrying his vindication further than is necessary for the purpose of getting the verdict.

3 December 1852. The Speaker has said publicly that on no occasion in his memory had a budget excited so much curiosity, or its nature been so little guessed at. Westminster Hall was lined with strangers; all the lobbies and galleries full to overflowing. Disraeli rose at 4.35, evidently ill. He spoke at first without animation, but warmed as he went on: his statement was very clear, very full, perhaps a little too minute: he dwelt on the state of the shipping and W. Indian interests: his proof of the flourishing condition of the latter was well received, the more so as being unexpected: the reductions on malt and tea were loudly cheered from both sides: his proposal to put the whole revenue under parliamentary control, pleased the Liberals: it was received on our side with indifference. The extended house-tax provoked no murmur, which was all that could be expected. Disraeli spoke for $5\frac{1}{4}$ hours: he might have got through what he had to say in 4 hours, but for the exhaustion from illness which at times almost overcame him. This took off from the effect of what was otherwise a remarkable address. He had a fair hearing: the House, never enthusiastic, was throughout attentive and patient.

5 December 1852. Among the northern powers, the recognition of the Empire continues to be discussed. Nesselrode and the Czar differ upon it. The minister is reported to have said to his master 'Your Majesty is prepared then, to trample under foot the memory of your brother Alexander?' It is believed that the course taken by these courts will be: to recognise the Empire as such: to refuse the title of Napoleon III: but to do this only indirectly, by addressing all communications to the 'Emperor of the French'. Prussia wisely professes indifference to the whole question, though likely to follow the Russian lead. England accepts the Emperor's explanation, to which he consents to give a formal shape. No Congress will now be held: there being nothing to discuss.

. . . No rational cause can be assigned for the panic which still prevails on the subject of French invasion, but it exists, and constant applications are made for an increased naval and military force. (It is remarkable that the budget, and indirectly the ministry, was destroyed by this panic. At the last moment, the Duke of Northumberland, a zealous administrator in his own department, an old sailor, and an ignorant politician, insisted on raising his proposed estimate for the next year by £800,000. Disraeli in vain dissuaded him: the country party, as represented in the cabinet, shared his fears, and supported his demand: Lord Derby, though not believing in the likelihood of war, had always held the opinion that our military and naval defences were too much neglected in peace: thus the vote passed, rendering impossible certain boons by which Disraeli had proposed to sweeten the unpalatable house-tax. But in assigning this as the proximate cause of the fall of the ministry, I do not forget that from the first, a majority of the H. of C. was against us: whence Disraeli's desperate though unavailing, exertions to secure the Tenant League (Irish party) . . .)

7 December 1852. Serjeant Shee,[23] M.P. for Kilkenny, introduced a tenant-right bill in opposition to Napier's, speaking three hours. Shee is an English lawyer, moderately successful in his profession, converted to the Roman Catholic faith, and now sharing with Moore of Mayo and Keogh of Athlone the leadership of what is known as 'the Brigade'. He has some qualifications for an agitator: the chief, a deep sonorous voice, of extraordinary volume, insomuch that the House cannot choose but hear him. (Serjeant Shee has pursued a more moderate course than was expected from his outsetting: though not listened to with much pleasure, he is respected as sincere: perhaps his Irish friends would have been better pleased if he had indulged in more of their characteristic exaggerations.) He asked to have his bill referred to a select committee, expecting the request to be refused. It was however granted at once by Walpole, in pursuance of the policy forced upon ministers, of securing the Irish vote if possible. (This policy lost us the Irish landlords, who were with difficulty reconciled – indeed are only partially so now – though most of them voted for the budget.) Napier's bill being sent before the same committee, it was thought that the latter could not fail to pass, and Shee's to be thrown out, thus guarding our concession from becoming dangerous.

. . . (The parliamentary agitation for tenant right, now extinct, was for the most part insincere. The agitators were generally landowners, and had pledged themselves to support some measure like Shee's, as the readiest means of securing their return. They purposely decried every attempt at a practicable settlement of the question, by which they would have been both personally and politically losers. Extreme and impracticable propositions suited their game, since they had thus the credit of demanding what they knew English members would take the odium of rejecting. One of them came privately to Mackenzie,[24] who told me the name, entreating that Government would not seem to countenance the principle of Shee's bill. That same M.P. voted for it in most of the divisions of 1853.)

8 December 1852. The Lord Mayor's dinner to ministers ... My Father used a remarkable and touching expression. He said he was proud to be the countryman of those masses who on the 18th[25] had shown such an example of good conduct and self-restraint, and that when he saw them he had asked himself with a feeling of self-humiliation 'What have I done to hold so high a place among such a people?'

11 December 1852. Palmerston is, or pretends to be, ill with gout: his retirement causes more surmises than his presence could, and is generally imputed to policy. He is willing to save us if he can do it without injury to himself: to join us, probably, if we pass safely through the session: but will run no risks. Jocelyn told me that the Liberals of Brooks's have sent him a message, to the effect that they admitted he had been ill-treated, that they did not blame him for resenting it, but they thought he might now be satisfied, and that if he continued to support the Govt they should regard him as having abandoned his principles. The old Whigs vacillate: being unprepared with a cabinet of their own, and yet afraid lest we should gain strength, they try to persuade us to recall and amend the budget: a course which might delay but certainly could not avert our fall. It is their policy to discredit the ministry without destroying it: to keep it alive, but so feeble that, when convenient to themselves, they may extinguish it without trouble. This policy is intelligible: not so that of Newcastle and Gladstone, who treat the Whigs with studied contempt, hint at a Govt of their own, and affect to believe that, Disraeli once removed, the Conservatives will transfer their support to them! The Duke of Newcastle especially holds this language.

Malmesbury and the more clear-sighted of Lord Derby's cabinet, have given up hoping for success: Lord Malmesbury even declines initiating fresh plans of foreign policy, regarding himself as holding office only *ad interim*.

I have long determined, in the all but certain event of our leaving Downing Street, to connect myself less with party, and act more as an independent member, than I have done hitherto. Among other impelling causes to this determination is the doubt whether my Father may not carry into effect his often talked of purpose of retiring from politics.

12 December 1852. Nothing doing in Europe that affects England. The French are much gratified at our conduct about the Empire ... In the New World, fresh apprehensions for Cuba, which America is bent on having, and Spain knows not how to retain.

... Turkey is threatened again, this time both by France and Russia: Rose writes from Therapia (Nov. 23) that Lavallette has been holding most intemperate language, threatening 'une vive demonstration' and even an expedition to Jaffa, which must end in the occupation of Jerusalem. The object of Russia is increased influence over Moldavia and Wallachia, perhaps the annexation of those provinces. The nominal ground of quarrel is one which recalls the crusades: a difference between the Greek and Latin Churches as to the respective rights of each over the Holy Places at Jerusalem. But it is well understood that this question is chosen as a battlefield whereon to try the strength of the French and Russian interests. The Porte has been coaxed and coerced by each alternately, until he has ended in so far giving way to both that their respective privileges as conceded by firman are quite incompatible. Matters look serious: Napoleon attaches an importance to the question which it is difficult to understand: Rose suggests that England should interpose with an offer to mediate.

13 December 1852. . . . *The Times* of today defends the budget, ending however with a suggestion that if parliament thinks differently, it ought to be altered. The *Post* (Palmerston's organ) tells us that to go out on a defeat such as any ministry must expect, will be considered as a mere excuse for escaping responsibility, with more in the same strain. As yet there has been no strong expression of feeling against the house tax in any of the great towns.

15 December 1852. . . . I dined at home. My Father wrote a long letter to Disraeli, counselling him not to modify the budget, unless it were possible, by leaving both malt tax and house tax on their old footing, to retain a surplus sufficient to allow of some other remission of burdens from the land. He told me Disraeli and Mackenzie had been with him, and had represented the carrying through of their scheme as it stood, as hopeless. I urged the uselessness of modifications: if there was a majority against us, concession would only delay, not avert, our fall. Better to avoid needless humiliation. My Father seemed perplexed: nothing was decided: his wish was to resign on defeat, but he knew the reluctance with which this decision would be accepted in his cabinet.

16 December 1852. 'The evening's debate opened with a long and dull, though important, dispute, as to the meaning of the vote which we were about to give . . . The debate languished until Disraeli rose, at about 10.30 p.m., and delivered, I think, the most remarkable speech I remember to have heard in the Commons. He took little notice of other critics, but applied himself seriously to answer Graham and Wood. The latter he attacked again and again, demolishing him at each onset, and closing with a personal invective which maddened the House with excitement. Never did one parliamentary speaker receive a severer infliction at the hands of another. Gladstone replied at past one in the morning: he rose choked with passion, for which he could find no vent in words, and his first utterances were the signal for fresh explosions from each side of the House alternately. He cooled as he proceeded, spoke with great effect for a time, but in the end wearied the House, which grew impatient for a division. We divided about 3 a.m. and were beaten by 19: we had expected a majority against us of 10 or 12. In the debate we might certainly claim a victory'.

The above was written by me next morning to a friend in the country. Disraeli's attack on Wood exceeded the usual limits of parliamentary vehemence: but the provocation was considerable . . . Gladstone's look when he rose to reply will never be forgotten by me: his usually calm features were livid and distorted with passion, his voice shook, and those who watched him feared an outbreak incompatible with parliamentary rules. So stormy a scene I have never witnessed. I went to the Carlton after the division: those who had voted with Gladstone prudently kept away: they could not have escaped insult.

17 December 1852. Lord Derby went down to Osborne, a cabinet being previously held *pro forma* to settle the question of resignation. Several quarrels in the Carlton: the ultras want to break it up, and substitute a club purely Conservative, in the commonly understood sense of the word.

It seems that the idea of a purely Peelite government, if ever entertained, is now given up, for the chiefs of that section are in daily communication with the Whigs.

The present H. of C. is supposed to be thus divided:

Derbyites	300 nearly
Peelites	35 to 40
Whigs	probably about 170
Irish Radicals (Brigade)	60
English Radicals	80
	——
	650

The first and second class admit of something like accurate computation. The Whigs and Radicals blend so closely that distinction is impossible, but I take Mackenzie's estimate.

. . . My Father repeated what had passed at the Palace. The Queen received him cordially: she seemed grave and anxious: the Prince entered into confidential discussions on many subjects, appearing desirous to take upon them the last opinion that he could receive from his ex-minister. He spoke often of Disraeli, extolled his talent, his energy, but expressed a fear that he was not in his heart favourable to the existing order of things. My Father defended his colleague: said he had been unnaturally kept down for several years, and then suddenly raised to the highest position. 'He has better reason than anyone to be attached to our constitutional system since he has experience how easily under it a man may rise'. The Prince was glad to hear it, but still thought Disraeli had democratic tendencies 'and if that is the case, he may become one of the most dangerous men in Europe'.

My Father, with his accustomed frankness, related the substance of this conversation to Disraeli, who naturally replied with assurances of devotion and fidelity. These my Father appears to distrust (as the event has shown, without cause). He talked much of his indifference to office, his willingess to retire if it were not for public considerations, and the danger which he foresaw to the monarchy. He said 'When I was a boy I remember thinking that to be Premier of England, with power so restricted as it necessarily must be, was no worthy object of ambition: and I think much the same now'. He then recurred to Disraeli: said there was a strong feeling against him at Court: the Prince feared his example would raise up a host of inferior imitations, instancing Osborne.[26] This conversation means one of two things: either, which I think most probable, that the Prince, wishing ill to both leaders, seeks to disunite them by prejudicing my Father's mind on a point on which it is very susceptible or else that he has contracted (though himself a man of talent) something of the mingled dread and contempt with which persons in high places are apt to look on satirists. Gladstone is reported to have said of Disraeli 'No words can express my hatred of that man, or my admiration of his genius'. These words are probably not genuine: the sentiment they embody, however, is so.

My Father claims credit, justly, for having resisted the pressure put upon every Minister to create peers. He has created only three: the [Lord] Chancellor, Lord Raglan,[27] and Lord Stratford de Redcliffe, all men who had earned their honours fairly.

I went to Jocelyn's in the evening. Palmerston had just been dining there. J. owned that P.'s gout was political: P. had been offered Ireland, but had refused. He told Jocelyn positively that he would never act under Lord John or Aberdeen: if Lord Lansdowne formed a ministry, and Lord John went up to the Lords, he might then consent to lead the Commons. It seems this arrangement was proposed three years ago, Russell's health having failed, but abandoned, Russell not liking to leave the Commons without introducing a supplementary Reform Bill. This is curious, as showing that the concession made to Locke King in 1851 was not, as supposed, the result of an impulse, but the execution of a purpose long entertained. Palmerston told Jocelyn, with a hint to repeat it to me, that he hoped we should not take any step as regarded the new ministry, that could be represented as factious: but wait, and keep our party together. Jocelyn felt sure that he meant to join us.

20 December 1852. My Father held a meeting in Downing Street, at which 160 of his followers, peers and M.P.'s, attended. Many had gone into the country. The speeches were fairly reported in the *Herald*. The cordiality shown by those present was very great: Lord Delawarr proposed a kind of vote of confidence in Lord Derby: and was so affected as to hesitate in his speech. The cheers, according to the hostile testimony of the *Daily News* 'could be heard three streets off'.

. . . In the Lords, Lord Derby explained the reasons for his retirement, denounced the coalition in language stronger than he perhaps intended, but promised his support if the ministry founded upon it should act in a Conservative spirit. He had already, he said to me, decided on his course, which was 'to kill them with kindness' – to alienate the Liberals from them if possible.

Lord Aberdeen has taken Delane into his confidence to an extent hitherto unusual, and has thus conciliated the support of the *Times*. But the pure Liberal journals – *Daily News* and *Globe* – begin to show suspicion already.

A dinner was given to Beresford last night at the Carlton, Sir J. Buller[28] in the chair: about 24 present. This is by way of counter-demonstration to the report of a committee which last week, though acquitting him of direct participation in bribery, severely censured his conduct on the ground of indiscretion. When the dinner had ended, some of the guests went into the news room, where Gladstone was: they being heated with wine and the late excitements, spoke to him roughly, so that he left the place, fearing insult or actual ill usage. This unlucky incident is much noticed, and not to our advantage.

Jocelyn came, with the news that Palmerston had refused a place in the new cabinet, as Lord St Leonards has also done.

23 December 1852. I attended at the office for the last time, and took leave of the clerks. All were friendly, some even cordial, in their expressions of regret. Hammond, a Liberal, a protégé of Palmerston's, (now under-secretary) said at parting 'We have never had so hardworking an under-secretary before, and I don't expect that we shall have one again'. This compliment gave me pleasure, because it seemed sincere, and I hope it was not altogether without foundation. Except when making these notes, I have since May last given every available hour of my waking time to office duty, sometimes writing and reading despatches from 9 a.m. till midnight with only a brief interval for meals. My position has been one of more than common enjoyment: without responsibility I had the confidence of those who were responsible: my advice was often asked, sometimes taken: I had little anxiety, and no ennui: nor, so far as intention goes, has mine been wasted time.

. . . Napoleon has asked in marriage the Princess Adelaide of Hohenlohe:[29] the Queen, whose consent is asked, hesitates, but dislikes the match. She likes the Orleans family: objects to the Emperor personally: and fears to compromise England. She said to my Father 'You know *our* family (the Coburgs) have always been accused of being too ready to pick up any crown that had tumbled in the dirt'. It was understood before we left office that the marriage would not come off.

Lord Malmesbury who visited us at Knowsley in January 1853, placed in my hands two letters, one from Bulwer, the other from Petre,[30] relative to a secret mission sent by us to Rome in the autumn. The history of this mission is as follows. One M. Mahé, a R.C. priest resident in England, offered his services to Malmesbury to bring about three objects (1) the withdrawal of Wiseman[31] from England, (2) a formal abnegation of any claim by the Pope to territorial jurisdiction here, (3) permission to have a Minister accredited to, and resident at, the Court of Rome.

Mahé appeared so well acquainted with the state of the R.C. church here, as well as with that of parties at Rome, and displayed in conversation so much acuteness, that Lord M. struck with his ability, gave him the employment he solicited. The result of his expedition is stated by Petre, under date Rome, December 24, as follows.

'Mahé has seen Cardinal Antonelli, was very well received, found the Cardinal full of erroneous notions respecting England, but willing to be informed and to enter into discussion. Mahé is well informed as to the feelings of the moderate R.C. party in England, and will have been able to give useful intelligence. But he does not venture to enter on the question of Wiseman's recall without first returning to England and obtaining, which he expects to do, a written declaration of the opinions of the majority of English R.C. bishops on the course pursued by the Cardinal. It would be necessary that they should condemn this course, and point out the mischief which may befall the Catholic interest from dissensions among themselves, and especially from quarrels between the Cardinal and the episcopal body. The Cardinal is supported only by the ultramontane party and the new converts, a large majority lay and clerical being against him . . . To all propositions of diplomatic relations between the Courts, Antonelli had one reply: that so long as the English refused to receive an ecclesiastic, nothing could be done. M. Mahé in vain tried to persuade him that no ministry however disposed, could succeed in cancelling the prohibition alluded to, embodied as it is in an act of parliament. With regard to the Ecclesiastical Titles Bill, the Cardinal appeared willing to make some sort of declaration that no aggression, no interference with the prerogative of the English Crown, had been contemplated'.

From another letter, December 29 [1852]:

'M. Mahé has had an audience of His Holiness, whom he found much prejudiced against the English Catholic clergy: he spoke angrily of them, called them Gallicans, but excepted the younger members. M. Mahé asked whether H.H. included the episcopacy? "By no means" the Pope replied. "Then" said M. Mahé "Your Holiness will listen to a representation from the majority of the bishops?" To this the Pope consented, and promised to see him again on his return from England.

. . . Bulwer's just comment on this is that M. Mahé has done nothing, and that the Court of Rome, though they could not refuse to receive an English mission, were the Eglinton clause repealed, had much rather be without one, disliking the personal presence of a Protestant of rank and influence at their capital.

Bulwer himself, who has been on an unofficial visit to Rome, wished and applied to be sent there in the dignity of a special mission: this Lord

Malmesbury declined, not seeing any likelihood of important results being obtained, while suspicion was certain to be excited here.

24 December 1852. Palmerston joined the coalition. Up to the last moment his friends represented him as determined to refuse all offers. My Father says 'Wait – don't attack ministers – that will only bind them together – if left alone they must fall to pieces by their own disunion'. He expressed fears that Disraeli will lay himself out for radical support.

Went to Turvile, Lord Lyndhurst's place ... I stayed there until the 27th. Lord L. cannot read much, but likes to be read to, and to hear all the news of the day. He talks little: prefers listening, but his memory is extra-ordinary: he seems to recollect everything he hears. He told me of his visit to Washington, the President, at Mount Vernon, but added few details: described Washington as a grave silent man, of whom his guests and visitors stood much in awe: and that his presence checked conversation. Lord L. expressed regret that he had never kept a journal of political events. He said among other things 'Newcastle and Herbert were brought into the cabinet by Peel at the same time. Peel did it in order to have two young pliant men trained in his school, to keep his older and more independent colleagues in check. He must then have foreseen the Corn Bill. That measure would not have passed, Peel would not have ventured upon it, but for Graham'. 'Graham' he went on 'said to me one day "What malignity there is in Disraeli's character!" I told him he was quite wrong: that D. was only playing a part: I have known him many years, and there is no malice in his disposition. There never was a man so absorbed in one idea: I don't think he will like retirement and a Sabine farm, eh?'

28 December 1852. Some talk on politics with Lord Derby: he said 'I knew as long ago as 1845, that I was playing a losing game: I said so then: I thought I was left high and dry for ever: the tide has risen once, high enough to float me again, which was more than I expected: it will never do so again: the game is lost, but I think it ought to be played, and I will play it out to the last'. By this he means resistance to democracy. He does not object to extension of franchise as such: but thinks it important to maintain the balance between town and country, land and trade, the permanent and the precarious sources of income. He thought a double franchise, borough and county, might be extended over the whole of England.

Talk about Louis Napoleon: said that Mrs Howard[32] was his Josephine, that though no longer in love with her, he has shown reluctance to marry on her account: also that at the time of one of his unsuccessful attempts on France, she sold nearly all her property, amounting to £7,000 to help in paying his expenses.

We hear that John Russell said to Walewski that the manner in which Lord Derby had conducted the business of the country during ten months '*était une gloire pour lui*'.

1853

5 January 1853. I went to Heron Court [Lord Malmesbury's . . . It] stands in a very wild country, thinly peopled, and barren: the site low, and often flooded. It is a good house, not too large, and comfortable. The scenery round it picturesque but sombre. The Hampshire farming wretched; the population poor and undersized. They object strongly to emigrate, no matter how ill off . . . Malmesbury said that in many parts of the country near, farmers durst not put their ricks together, for fear of incendiary fires, but scattered them apart. When Phillips' Fire Annihilator was tried on an adjoining estate,[1] the peasantry gathered round, and cheered when it failed to put out the fire.

9 January 1853. Malmesbury made some remarks which surprised me from him, about the annoyance of keeping up an establishment, and the superior comfort of a perfectly private and unostentatious life. 'When I am alone here with Lady M.' he said, 'it is a positive annoyance to me to see four or five servants waiting on us two during dinner-time'. This is exactly what I feel at Knowsley, and on that account I record it. I cannot but think, that if anyone dared to begin, a great deal of the show and parade might be got rid of. Indeed a great deal that was once thought indispensable has been got rid of already. The persons who object to give up any part of that parade on which they fancy their importance depends, are the millionaire fundholders and merchants – not the landowners.

10 January 1853. I saw Disraeli. He said many Whigs were offended at the new arrangements, by which they were shut out: did not think their disappointment would show itself at once, as no man liked to seem to be acting from personal motives: but they would take the first opportunity to embarrass the govt on any fair pretence: the Irish brigade too were hostile: the Radicals distrustful, and would wish to see their programme before they did anything. The Reform Bill would be the test: England did not want one: if strong, it would drive out the Conservative part of the cabinet: if a mere readjustment, the Radicals would cry treachery. In either case we should have a fine opportunity, if we knew how to use it. Disraeli had no settled plan of operations. I advised waiting, 'kill them with kindness', as the true policy.

14 January 1853. I saw Disraeli again. He had conversed with Stockmar,[2] who came to him from Albert, expressing a wish that communications should be frequent. He had negotiated, through Emerson Tennent, with the Irish Brigade, who promised the support of from 30 to 33 men. He said the Manchester radicals were discontented, and were forming themselves into a separate party, with a whip of their own. There was some talk of putting Milner Gibson forward as their leader. The Whigs were also angry, Carlisle,[3] Seymour, and G. Grey especially. Could we form a coalition with these?

16 January 1853. I named this last idea to Lord Derby. He rejected it, and that decidedly: I thereon said no more. Disraeli had offered to surrender the lead to Sir G. Grey.

9 February 1853. Saw Disraeli, and walked with him down to the House. He had no plan of action: said his only object was to avoid the appearance of utter defeat, and to keep his friends together: matters were not ripe for change: immediate return to power could not be expected: it was better, if possible, to avoid a decisive engagement.

On the reform question he thought ministers would neither act nor refuse to act: but demand twelve months for reflection and decision. The country was not ready for reform, and would accept the delay with pleasure: but a quarrel between Government and the Radicals appeared inevitable.

Disraeli had been in frequent intercourse with Milner Gibson and others of that school, but secretly, fearing the effect on Lord Derby and the party if these confidences were known.

He complained loudly of the apathy of the party: they could not be got to attend to business while the hunting season lasted: a sharp frost would make a difference of twenty men. They had good natural ability, he said, taking them as a body: but wanted culture: they never read: their leisure was passed in field sports: the wretched school and university system was in fault: they learnt nothing useful, and did not understand the ideas of their own time. Disraeli had just come out of Yorkshire, which might explain this just invective.

Mackenzie has not given satisfaction as whipper-in: it was debated whether Stafford or Jolliffe[4] should succeed: I strongly urged the latter: the wonder is that independent gentlemen will accept such a post. While we sat in the Carlton, Disraeli picked up a piece of news which altered the whole tone of his spirits. It was to the effect that France had taken serious offence at the language held, first by Graham at Carlisle, and then by Wood at Halifax, respecting the character of Napoleon. Graham's speech had been in part explained away, but that of Wood was even more offensive. The report ran that Walewski had orders to demand either the retirement of Wood from the cabinet, or his own passports. 'The opportunity' said D. 'is too good to be lost. We must press for an explanation, and failing to get one, give notice of a resolution complaining of language being used by a Minister calculated to disturb friendly relations with France'. He urged me to consult my Father without delay. Not liking the business, I did not do this, but arranged that Disraeli should see him next morning. In any case, there would have been little opportunity of discussing politics with him, for he had just returned from John Scott's stables, full of good stories and racing details.

10 February 1853. The intended interview did not take place, but I communicated D.'s views to my father. He thought the way of proceeding by resolution inadvisable: we knew of the words imputed only through a newspaper report. It was without precedent to found so grave a procedure on such grounds. The first step was to ask whether the language in question had really been used. The next, to call attention to it simply, not attempting to divide. My Father thought that for the honour of England it was better to take up the affair in parliament, rather than wait till Walewski should have made his demand. In the former case Wood's apology would be made to the House and not to France.

Malmesbury called on me. I found him fully persuaded in his mind that our quitting office had caused a marked change in the feeling of foreign governments towards this country. He wanted to make as much as possible of the Wood business, but not to take the lead in it himself, being already thought too strong in his Bonapartist predilections. He and Lord Derby both expressed alarm lest the policy of 1848 should be renewed on the part of England, the probable result being to leave us without one ally in Europe. I was surprised that they both contemplated the possibility, though not probability, of an invasion: thinking that Napoleon might thus retrieve his fading popularity.

My father expressed fears lest the Continental powers jointly should arrange a partition of Turkey, France taking Egypt. I do not know on what facts this idea is based.

. . . In the Lords an attack half-serious, half-comic, was made by my Father, who pressed for a statement of measures. No answer followed, nor indeed was one expected, but the scene amused its author, who rehearsed to me what had passed, in a very animated manner.

11 February 1853. Apropos of a rumour that ministers intended largely to increase the army, my Father maintained that this was a favourite idea with the Prince, who had often pressed it on him, but he had always refused. He thought Lord Aberdeen meant to give way, but that his cabinet had objected.

We spoke of Canadian politics – the clergy reserves, a subject on which Lord D.'s convictions as to what must be done, and his wishes as to what ought to be done, are directly at variance.

12 February 1853. . . . Information from a person employed at Court, that lists of the present Ministry were in the Prince's hands some time before our fall: in fact that it was formed by him. The person in question also spoke much of correspondence carried on between Albert and foreign courts, without the knowledge of the Secretary for Foreign Affairs: this I cannot disbelieve, knowing it true in some instances.

13 February 1853. Disraeli wrote asking me to call upon him: I did so: found he wanted me to communicate with the French Ambassador, for the purpose of stimulating him to complain, and assuring him privately that he would be backed in his demands by a powerful party here. He said he could not go in person, being so well known. He spoke exultingly of his case, of the materials he had at command, in the speeches of Palmerston, Grey and Russell: said his one real apprehension was that the quarrel might be settled peaceably: that Walewski might accept an apology, but he hoped there was no danger of that.

I liked this mission very ill, but thought it useless to state my grounds of objection: therefore only advised delay, and renewed conference with either Malmesbury or Lord D. Next day (Monday) I wrote to D. having seen my Father in the meantime: the general purport of whose advice was to be cautious and not make too much of a small matter.

On a repeated application from Grosvenor Gate I consented to call at the French Embassy, limiting myself, however, to a simple enquiry as to the state of feeling there existing. I found Walewski much more moderate than his amateur champions: he entered on the subject frankly, though as usual with him, in a confused way: remarked that the same insulting language had been held by two leading ministers, and loudly justified by their press, at a moment when the relations of France and England were not only friendly, but cordial to an exceptional degree: regretted this the more, as the French Govt were grateful to ours for the prompt recognition of the Empire, an act which had favourably affected the Emperor's position in Europe: believed that an apology was contemplated: its purport, though not very intelligible, would be satisfactory. Lord John had disclaimed all intention of justifying his colleagues' words. Had it been otherwise, he, Walewski, should not have returned to England. He did not understand how the persons implicated could remain in power: it was *inoui* but that was their affair.

I repeated this, with further details, to Disraeli, and dissuaded him strongly from the meditated attack ... D. answered little but his countenance expressed annoyance. It was evident that he had a speech in readiness, and had made up his mind to deliver it. We went down to the House together: Russell read the apology, as Walewski had foretold: it was clumsy, but honest, indicating a desire to avoid giving offence ...

15 February 1853. . . . Stories current of Lord Palmerston being disinclined to remain a member of the cabinet. These are vague, probably groundless, but being put about by his friends, indicate a wish to escape sharing, at least, in the enmities of his colleagues ... .

16 February 1853. Disraeli announced to me his purpose of making a speech on foreign affairs generally, choosing Friday evening for the time. He excused himself, in a half apologetic tone, pleading the necessity of keeping his party in good humour.

17 February 1853. . . . Walking up with Wilson Patten, he told me that out of 120 election petitions only 35 would be proceeded with: all the rest were compromised: the law as it stands, respecting bribery, was so strict, and the observance of it is so lax, that, he said, not one tenth of the entire House was legally elected ...

I saw a letter written by Napoleon to Malmesbury, apparently with the view of stopping discussion on the alleged insult to France. Of course it availed nothing, though shown to Disraeli.

The prospect of a personal debate had drawn a full House: Disraeli rose at 5, opened in a manner too solemn and prolix for the occasion, expatiated on the past relations of the two countries, sketched French politics at the present day, magnified the value of the alliance, criticised Wood, Graham, and Aberdeen, sparing Palmerston throughout, and closed with a most pointed and amusing review of the state of parties at home. This was evidently what he had risen to deliver, the rest being only accessory. It was characteristic that every joke had a purpose as well as a point: he represented the Whigs as made subservient to the followers of Lord Aberdeen, and the Radicals as the tools of both. It was certainly a most skilful and ingenious rubbing up of old sores: the brilliant satire, the offensive personality, yet all couched in the language of good humour. Some of his sarcasms have proved prophecies, as where he spoke of 'a ministry of progress under which everyone stands still': and of the peace of Europe being made an open question. Somewhere in this harangue D. alluded to himself as 'a gentleman of the press, who has no other escutcheon'. Laughter followed, which the Conservatives, by a generous impulse, drowned in their cheers ...

The general effect of this attack was to please the party, especially its more violent members, in the Commons: to exalt D.'s reputation for power of satire, at the price of what reputation he may possess for prudence: and to draw upon him, and on us generally, the indignant denunciations of the hostile press. I suspect it was the attacks made upon this occasion that revived in his mind the long suspended project of setting up an organ for himself, a project of which I had heard since 1849, but thought it hopeless.

Sir J. E. Tennent (of the Board of Trade) communicated to me a scheme of which the purport was to obtain, by some concessions, the support of the Irish brigade. I made this known to D., refusing further interference. What came of it I know not, but D. both then and later expressed a full conviction that the Irish party wanted only encouragement to join us, and meant to have done so until deterred by a speech of my Father's in the Lords, which they regarded as hostile to tenant right. In this business, the chief of Tennent's friends was Gavan Duffy of New Ross.

22–23 February 1853. Debate on Maynooth ... I have long abandoned the idea, at one time popular, and put forward by Lord Lincoln at a public meeting, that the R.C. priesthood ought to be endowed: that step is impossible: the feeling of the English people forbids it: Maynooth must one day be deprived of the grant: but that very determination on the part of

England not to sanction or recognise the religion held by the Irish must react on the general principle of establishments, for it leads directly to a voluntary system in Ireland, and that once found to work well, will not end there. The Conservative leaders took care to keep out of this division and debate.

24 February 1853. Lord J. Russell moved for leave to bring in what is mostly known as the 'Jew Bill'. Inglis, Napier, and others opposed him: among them Sir R. Peel, in a clever but eccentric declamation, to which the House listened with a forbearance due rather to the speaker's name than to his merits. This extraordinary harangue decided his reputation in parliament, placed him among the guerrillas, and out of the regular line of battle.

I voted in the majority, numbers 234 to 205 [for the bill], my conviction on the subject being strong, but found I had not estimated the strength of party ties till called on to break them. Nothing that had passed up to that time in the House gave me so much pain. (And the recollection of that pain, long afterwards, has induced, and always will induce me, to protest against the attempt made by all parties, to cry down independent voters, and to substitute an artificial for the natural conscience in political matters.)

I walked home with Walpole. No man living is more placable in disposition: but though as a matter of theory, he would doubtless have admitted the duty of everyone to follow his judgment, he could not avoid betraying some irritation at my vote.

27 February 1853. Conversation with Disraeli on Indian reform. I found him satisfied that many changes were necessary, but inclined, naturally, to look at the question with reference to party interests. I pressed the issuing of a commission of inquiry in the country itself, and limitation of the Charter to three, or at most five years. He appeared to have made up his mind that ministers would bring forward no plan on a large scale.

I saw Sir E. Lytton: we discussed closely the state of parties. He thought the Whigs nearer to us, in point of opinion, than Gladstone and his friends, who had no territorial connection to restrain them: we talked of the latest ill-feeling between Russell and Palmerston, and probability of the latter taking occasion to break up the cabinet.

28 February 1853. Fifteen millions voted in seven and a half hours – army and ordnance estimates. After this, we disputed more than an hour over the salaries of certain officers in the Court of Chancery.

1 March 1853. . . . Much talk in the smoking room with Bright on India: the contrast between his vehemence, and Disraeli's calculating coolness, was more amusing, from their views being substantially the same.

. . . Disraeli this day showed me a letter from Lucas, of the *Tablet* newspaper, an ultramontane organ, containing overtures towards reconciliation. The letter was well-written, temperate, and skilful. After some flattery of D. it proceeds to say that 'Irish Catholics have been in the habit of considering the Conservative party as their natural and implacable enemies. There is a traditional hostility, kept alive by local disputes. Many Conservative magistrates seem to think that with a Tory Lord Chancellor in the Castle, they are sure of impunity for any moderate amount of unfairness'. It rests with us to remove this belief!

... My comment on this letter was to the effect that, while suggesting reconciliation ... it held out no terms on which union, or even neutrality, could be brought about ... in fine, I thought the project visionary. Lucas however was sincere: he even wrote a penitent letter to Walpole, apologising for some violent attacks made upon him in the course of last summer.

3 March 1853. Hume moving a resolution to do away certain protective duties, and Gladstone opposing, Disraeli suddenly gave Hume his support, and tried to steal a division. Some of his followers voted against him and we were beaten by 158 to 101. (I retain this entry because it indicates the commencement of a practice afterwards largely indulged in by the opposition leader, and which to some extent damaged his position among members of his own party; I mean the practice of effecting a sudden coalition with some discontented section of the Liberals, and by their aid, and taking advantage of surprise, securing an unexpected victory.)

4 March 1853. In Indian Committee, Wood announced his intention of bringing in after Easter a bill for the government of India. He would not answer, being questioned, whether this would be a permanent or a temporary measure. From his language we inferred the first. Herries almost committed himself to approve this course, which has for object the maintenance of British Asia on its present footing, and for effect utterly to stultify the proceedings of the committee. Cobden, Gibson, Disraeli, and I all protested strongly. We two left the room for some time, conferred, and on our return successively explained that we were not prepared to renew the Charter for more than five years at the utmost. In this step Baillie was our most zealous and sincere Conservative supporter: the rest for the most part standing aloof, indifferent, or hostile.

7 March 1853. ... My Father suggested a scheme by which a certain number of writerships should be given to the Governor-General for distribution among natives, on the condition that the youths selected shall receive their education at Haileybury, thus gaining some knowledge of England and the English.

I find in my notes of this date much mention of an Irish quarrel, noticeable only as indicating Disraeli's new tactics. There was a strong case against Ministers for acting partially in forbearing to try certain rioters on the Catholic or priestly side: our Protestant friends were of course eager to take advantage of it: Disraeli steadily refused, I think on the whole wisely, though he provoked thus a good deal of obloquy among the more violent.

14 March 1853. I have omitted from these notes the mention of a new project which for three weeks had been frequently discussed between Disraeli and myself: that of founding a newspaper to be the organ of moderate Conservative opinions. The want of such an organ had been felt since 1849. D. at first proposed to call it the *Week*, thought a capital of from £2,000 to £3,000 contributed would be enough, for the rest it ought to be self-supporting: literary critiques, and satirical illustrations, pictorial, were also a part of his scheme. Against the last I protested vehemently, knowing that a Tory *Punch* would soon degenerate into ribaldry. He wanted only one paid writer: Lytton, Stafford, Smythe, etc. would all help: I promised to do my share. He afterwards added the names of Stirling, G. Bentinck, and one Cayley. (But I doubt whether many of these took any active part. Smythe did nothing: Lytton contributed one series of letters: Stirling nothing: Stafford five or six papers: I wrote about a third of the original matter of the first and second volumes: Disraeli likewise worked hard, for a time, with his own pen.)

An editor was quickly found: one Lucas:[5] the idea of comic illustrations, chiefly suggested by the accident of having secured a half-promise of assistance from Doyle, was abandoned: volunteers offered help, as volunteers always do: and some leading members of the party took up the project warmly. The Duke of Northumberland, especially, undertook to put down £2,000, if four other persons would do the same. He estimated our total necessities at £10,000, proving in this more nearly right than D. himself.

D.'s ardour, great from the first, rose higher and higher as the plan assumed a definite form. He talked of a circulation of from 10,000 to 15,000: of driving all other weekly journals out of the field: even of shaking the power of the *Times*. I have never seen him so much excited[6] on any subject, except once in a conversation at Hughenden, in 1851.

It was on this subject that I now (14th) consulted my Father. He expressed himself decidedly hostile: thought we should be compromised: offence would be given: it was impossible not to hold D. and even himself responsible for whatever appeared in a paper confessedly their organ: such a connection could neither be acknowledge nor disavowed: Peel, while in office, had always repudiated the claim of any journal to represent his ministry: he thought this a sound principle, and had said as much to Malmesbury, by whom it was repeated to the Duke of Northumberland. The result of this statement was, that the Duke withdrew his offer.

I answered that for a party to be without organs was impossible: it had two already, the *Herald* and *Standard*: its only choice lay between being represented and misrepresented. We could not silence these supporters, though they did us more harm than good. We were judged by them among the general public. In fact, they did very accurately convey the feelings of a part of the party: unluckily it was the lowest and least enlightened part:

what we wanted was that the other and more reputable sector should be equally able to make its voice heard. My Father objected that this would divide us into sections. I thought the attempt to enforce uniformity was already carried too far: that it tended to drive away men of talent: that a party could not be disciplined like a regiment. Lord Derby then expressed distrust of all the individuals engaged in the new design, not entirely excepting Disraeli. He promised however to say nothing in disparagement of it: there being in return a clear understanding that his name was to be in no way used.

At this time, and for some weeks afterwards, Lord Derby was living at St Leonards, in almost entire seclusion, seeing few of his former colleagues, and attending debates in the Lords only on a few great occasions. He objected to call a meeting, and generally, thought it best to leave ministers alone.

This unfavourable opinion expressed by Lord Derby had the effect of putting an end to our expectation of large subscriptions such as that promised by the Duke of Northumberland. Disraeli was not dispirited: said they must go on now, it was too late to retreat. He showed me a letter in which Malmesbury warned him 'as an old personal friend, apart from politics' not to embark in an undertaking certain not to repay him in any sense.

Hints begin to reach us of differences on the Indian question. Lord Lonsdale especially takes the side of the Directors.
17 March 1853. . . . Bright told me not long ago, that when he and Cobden were sounded as to the support they would give Lord Aberdeen, they named two conditions as essential – ballot, and abolition of the newspaper stamp.

Some talk already of disunion in the ministry. Indeed from the first there has been no cordial alliance between its subordinates and followers. The same distrust exists on our side: the ultra party disliking Disraeli, and placing most confidence in Pakington. To set matters right, a meeting is announced for after Easter. The very docility of the country gentlemen on questions which do not touch their prejudices renders them more exacting, since they cannot go on without guidance: every sheep wanting a shepherd.
20 March 1853. Kelly had asked Disraeli and myself to dine with him . . . it turned out that he had a modicum of parliamentary reform to propose: the admission to vote of all persons exercising professions, or who had graduated at any University. He had also a plan for the repression of bribery (I omit its details, as they are for the most part embodied in his Bill of 1854). D. asked quietly whether he thought our friends would consent to secret voting? It is their special abhorrence, though probably they would suffer little or nothing from its adoption.

Kelly talked of Peel: said that on his, K., taking office early in the summer of 1845, Peel had warned him not to pledge himself on the subject of corn law. He took little notice of this warning at the time, but remembered it afterwards. He felt sure that Peel had at that time decided in his own mind on the change. He went on to say that Peel's contempt for his party was very apparent to all who were in office with him. He took it for granted that wherever he went they would follow. On the corn law question he expected a few hard words, a little murmuring, and then that all would go on as before. This belief he retained even during the spring of 1846, and his disappointment was proportionate when compelled to resign.

24 March 1853. . . . . Much conversation and correspondence at this time about Walpole's acceptance of the Chairmanship of Ways and Means: which it is thought ministers will offer, if understood that he would take it. Walpole, with his usual vacillation, put off a positive reply, but with his usual uprightness of purpose, ended by a refusal, fearing misconstruction, although his position is that of a very poor man.[7]

My Father, in several conversations, held this week, repeatedly expressed his expectation of never again holding office. He thought if the present Ministry refused to bid for Liberal support, and gave Conservative measures, they might, with their strength and prestige, destroy his party within two years. He thought Disraeli ought to see more of them, and try to gain their confidence. He seemed to have occasional misgivings that D. was aiming at the first place – doubts which I believe, and said, were needless. The truth is, D. could not stand alone, any more than Lord Derby would retain his position without a lieutenant in the Commons.

My Father repeated more than once a conviction which he said had been forced upon him early in public life – that real political power was not to be had in England: at best you could only a little advance or retard the progress of an inevitable movement. Even in America, a President could do much by his own will: an English Minister had more responsibility, more labour, and less authority, than the ruler of any people on earth. I assented, and said the only posts of power which appeared to remain were the Governor-Generalship of India and the editorship of the *Times*.

4 April 1853. . . . . I dined with Disraeli at the Carlton: found him full of a project of alliance with Lord Grey and the discontented Whigs, Lords Carlisle, Clanricarde,[8] and Fitzwilliam: his agent was old Lord Ponsonby.[9] I would not discourage him: but should be curious to see the cabinet in which Lord Grey and my Father should sit together. As formerly in regard of his newspaper, so now with this plan:[10] his mind was so full of it that he could think and speak of nothing else.

5 April 1853. Saw Malmesbury, who regrets my Father's absence: thinks it will lead to suspicions that he is indifferent to politics, contemplates resigning the leadership, etc. At the same time he dislikes Disraeli's vehemence, and counsels delay – saying of Disraeli rather bitterly that to get office he would do anything, and act with anyone. His views of home politics were of the most despondent order. We then fell on French affairs.

M. read out of his journal the conversations he had held with he Emperor and other persons. His reception was cordial: Napoleon on seeing him broke through the circle, went up to him, shook him by both hands, and added in the hearing of all 'I thank you, and I beg you to thank Lord Derby, for all that his government has done for me'. The Empress was friendly: M. spoke highly of her beauty and manners. The etiquette of the palace is very stiff: the obsequiousness of the courtiers disgusting ... The Emperor's general views on politics seem to be these:

'There are two states' he said 'both semi-barbarous, but both young, powerful, and growing in strength – Russia and the United States. Russia had great influence over Austria, and some over Prussia. There was danger of his uncle's prophecy being fulfilled to the letter, and of Europe becoming literally Cossack. The only safety for Western Europe lay in the close alliance of England and France. The Northern Powers were all in reality against England. They had pressed him to join them in a remonstrance on the refugee question, saying that if England persisted in protecting revolutionary exiles, they would follow up words by war. They had told him this plainly. He had replied, that having resided as a refugee in England himself, he knew that what they asked was impossible: no English Minister could do what they desired. He was so well aware of this, that he would not embarrass the British Cabinet by even a remonstrance: though he thought a culpable laxity was shown as regards attempts at assassination. . . . He complained in strong terms of the speeches of Graham and Wood, and also of the Queen's Orleanist predilections. She ought to remember that it was not he who displaced Louis Philippe . . .'

He then explained the cause of his own success. Each party had accepted him as a compromise each preferring him to the candidate of their opponents. Thus his friends had had time to gather strength.

Returning to foreign policy, he expatiated on the dangers of Russia. It was absurd to suppose that, because his government was strong, France was not governed by public opinion. If he lost public confidence he could not last an hour. It was by the people he was elected: a fact which the good citizens of London forgot, while they enjoyed the attacks of the *Times* over their breakfasts. France, England, Portugal, Sardinia were all in their several ways constitutional countries. The fashion of the dresses might not be alike: but they all came from one tailor. The really despotic powers recognised no rule of government except divine right; this principle they sought to propagate by the sword. . . . There were two points, he continued, of pressing importance at that moment: one, the integrity of the Turkish Empire: the other, the new international code put forth by America. (He meant the Monroe Doctrine . . .) Both these equations would require to be settled. He spoke with complacency of the material condition of France . . . All he desired was peace internal and external . . .

14 April 1853. . . . Conversation with Walpole, who names Gladstone, Bright, Disraeli, as the three men of the future. I agree with him.

We combined this day with Milner Gibson against the advertisement duty, and carried a resolution for its discontinuance by 41. This vote gave annoyance to many Conservatives: they disliked it as coming from the Radical side of the House: as being given in favour of the press: and because the opposite line had been taken last year when we were in office. It was however in the first draft of D.'s budget, and he was reluctantly induced to keep the tax on by finding the year's expenses exceed by £600,000 the sum at which he had estimated them. This fact could not be known: whence a cry of faction came to be raised.

16 April 1853. A meeting in St James's Square, very crowded and enthusiastic: my Father spoke 1½ hours, chiefly dwelling on personal politics: alluding to the 'Liberal–Conservative' phrase, he said 'the black was not to be so very black, nor the white so very white, but it was odd that the one colour carefully excluded in their union was that of Grey'. He laid down no general principle of political conduct.

18 April 1853. Gladstone's budget, which occupied five hours, an extraordinary effort of rhetorical skill: no fault could be found except too great length, and a hackneyed quotation from Virgil spoiling a fine peroration: it was said that for three nights before this display he was unable to sleep from excitement, but the success was worth the suffering. Every party except that of the landed interest took away something in the shape of a boon: Manchester had the succession tax: Ireland a remission of debt: the working classes cheaper tea and soap: the press, the advertisement duty taken off.

The general feeling on our side was opposed to any attempt at a contest, although the succession duty is much disliked.

25 April 1853. Another meeting in St James's Square, at which I was not present, but heard that my Father had thrown out some hints about retiring unless the party kept together. He and D. believe they can still count upon 260 out of the 305 who voted with them in the winter.

26 April 1853. . . . Disraeli about this time expressed great confidence that Palmerston would resign, and break up the ministry: no doubt some negotiations have passed, but of what kind or how far sincere, I cannot tell.

5–6 May 1853. A scene between Gavan Duffy and Ministers, whom he charged with corruption . . . His explanation was skilful: it seemed strange to see the English country gentlemen cheering and vehemently encouraging an Irish Roman Catholic of the ultra-radical party, and whose language in the press has been ostentatiously seditious: but the circumstance shows how strong is their feeling against Lord Aberdeen and his colleagues.

Only 61 voted against the extension of income tax to Ireland.

I dined with Disraeli: found him less interested in politics than literature: the success of the cheap reissues of his works seemed to have turned his thoughts into that channel. He talked of retiring from affairs, of writing an epic poem, and a life of Christ from the national point of view[11] – mere talk, but characteristic. He surprised me by speaking of his unlucky epic as the best thing he had done – that most to his own taste.

7 May 1853 (Saturday). First number of the *Press* appeared, Disraeli, Lytton, Smythe, Maddyn, Butt, and I all being contributors . . .

9 May 1853. The debate was feeble. Irish members tried to extort from Hayter[12] a confession that he had promised that the income tax should not be extended to Ireland, if they would vote to turn out the Derby Govt. He prevaricated a good deal, but escaped. It is certain that some intimation to this effect was given.

18 May 1853. I sent to press a pamphlet on the Church Rate question, carefully drawn up, so as to convey my own opinions against the tax, while not actually professing to abolish it, but only to exempt Dissenters. I believe that this plan, if adopted, will infallibly, though indirectly, lead to abolition. I inserted, tentatively, some passages adverse to the general principle of Establishments of an ecclesiastical kind: but confined this to theory, though it may be that a practical application to the Irish Church is not far distant. The scheme supported by me is that of Walpole and the Bishop of London, though adopted by them with some reluctance.

21 May 1853. Third number of the *Press*: too much of essay-writing, too little news, but on the whole successful. Only 600 subscribers, though 3,500 copies are distributed.

I tried to open an attack in the *Herald* on the Indian Directors. The editor refused, being friends to them.

31 May 1853. Moore brought on the subject of Irish Church: Lord John strongly opposed all enquiry, or attempt at change: I did not vote. The permanent maintenance of the Irish Establishment cannot be defended: but it is reasonable and expedient to wait until the cessation of emigration shall have settled the relative numerical strength of the two creeds and races.

3 June 1853. Sir C. Wood brought in his India Bill, speaking five hours. When he began there were 300 members in the House: when he sat down, about 100! He defended the double government: and his reforms were few, the chief and best being the opening of the civil service.

Bright followed in an admirable harangue, full of fire and force, strong sense in plain words, with some touches of humour: and occasional outbreaks of natural eloquence. His style has lost its old coarseness: he improves daily: and may one day lead the House. It is creditable to Cobden, that when himself most successful, he always predicted a higher success than his own for his then unpopular colleague. This speech was loudly cheered by Conservatives: in 1849 they would have hooted. Bright has risen almost as rapidly as Disraeli, but by different means . . .

Russell's Irish Church speech has caused offers of resignation from Monsell, Keogh, and Sadleir: it is said (in the manner in which low and personal motives are always imputed to politicians) that this was the object, and that the vacant places may now be filled with Whigs: I do not believe that any such design existed. It is clear that the Whigs are now the Conservative element in the cabinet. Gladstone is the least popular of the ministry on our benches: his financial scheme is reported a failure. Disraeli exults over him.

Dined (yesterday) with Lord Hardinge: meeting Lord Ellenborough: two relatives who are not friends. Lord Hardinge calls Lord Ellenborough a madman: Lord Ellenborough thinks Lord Hardinge a courtier and time-server. Lord Hardinge took a gloomy view of foreign affairs: expected war: talked of India: and disparaged the Sepoy troops, saying that in the first Sikh war they had been taken with a panic, and that if the enemy had known their real state, nothing could have averted defeat. He said that on the morning after Ferozeshah, when Taj Singh came up with fresh troops, it would have been impossible to resist an attack, the more so as ammunition had fallen short. If a retreat had then been begun, all northern India would have been in arms: none can say where the movement might have ended.

6 June 1853. . . . *The Press* (fifth number issued on Saturday) has 1,200 subscribers. Disraeli remains enthusiastic about it, and there is scarcely any secret made of his and Lytton's contributions.

30 June 1853. The second reading of the India Bill passed by 322 to 140: the causes of this defeat being (1) general disorganisation of the Conservative party, arising partly out of ill-success, partly out of distrust of Disraeli, partly out of real differences of opinion: (2) the vast influence of the East India Company, felt in every profession and rank of life: (3) my own mistake in dealing with the subject in a spirit too strictly judicial . . . (4) perhaps too (though I write this with doubt) we erred in not having a scheme of Indian government drawn out ready . . . But the real reason of the failure was, that both Disraeli and I were at this time extremely unpopular, being thought to differ (as we did) from the Conservative masses on most political subjects. This feeling showed itself in many ways. The *Herald*, *Standard*, and *John Bull*, frequently wrote at or against us: Alex. Lennox,[13] a son of the Duke of Richmond, whom though our tastes widely differ, I have known from childhood, one day remonstrated with me, saying that I ought to exert myself to become personally acceptable to the party, who regard me with a feeling approaching to personal dislike: and Malmesbury took me to task more seriously on the same subject. He, Malmesbury, argued that Disraeli could not be and ought not to be leader, that place was reserved for me, I might fill it when I pleased, if it were not understood that my sympathies were on the Liberal side. M. argued that political talent being scarcer among the proprietary opposition, I should there have the field to myself, while the other party was already well supplied with leaders. I replied merely that while my Father remained in politics I would stand by him[14]: if he retired, I should hold myself free to form any connection that might then seem suitable. I would not enter into the subject with M. partly because it was needless, the case discussed not having arisen: partly because I saw that he regarded a certain type of Radicalism as belonging to a particular brand of youth, and no argument would have shaken him in this belief, which indeed is general, and based on common experience. But from any wish to lead the Conservative party the fate of Peel is enough to set me free.

Here ends my journal of the session. A few recollections are added as they occur.

Towards the close of July, a rumour prevailed that Lord Aberdeen would resign in consequence of the Turkish difficulties, and the cabinet break up. It was surmised by many that in such an event, Palmerston and Russell would join my Father. *The Morning Post* at this time began to write up the claims of Lord Palmerston for the premiership.

The *Press* has continued to flourish: reaching by the end of July a sale of 2,000. As many as 4,000 copies have at one time been printed. The transaction, however, has proved unprofitable. The party subscribed about £2,500: the same amount was supplied by Disraeli himself, but even thus a heavy deficit remains, to meet which the sale of the paper to some capitalist was contemplated. I declined to give money, but wrote in every number, not on personal subjects.

The question now in all men's minds was that of peace or war: all the press, without exception, save only the *Times*, advocated war: in society opinion was more divided and I think a desire for the continuance of peace might still be said to preponderate. I regret to add that among the most violent advocates of hostilities were the owners of Whig boroughs, endangered by a Reform Bill, and hoping to avert the risk of this by turning off public attention. Newspapers joined recklessly in the cry, as promising excitement, news, and an increased sale: besides which calculations, there seems to be something in the profession of journalism that inclines men who follow it to adopt rash and extreme counsels.

In contrast with this excitement, was the perfect apathy on that of Reform. The *Edinburgh Review* took a Conservative line on the question: when mooted at all, it was so in a speculative spirit, and with little vehemence. Scarcely any attempt at agitation was made: and such attempts as were made, failed.

The Preston strike, the chief domestic event of this autumn, came under my notice only in an indirect manner ... It cost £500,000: 80,000 hands were out at one time: and the movement originating in one town spread over the whole of Lancashire. Two remarkable features characterised this transaction: one the general good conduct of those who turned out: the other, the extreme vagueness of their objects, of which an increase of wages was only one. The sole permanent result of this agitation has been to accelerate the passing of bills to establish limited liability, so that operatives may have, if desirous, the means of setting up mills on their account. A privilege, however, which they are not likely to use to any great extent. It was observed that neither poverty nor want of intelligence could be pleaded by those who took the most active part in the strike: but a clear majority of the whole were under 25 years of age.

The month of September was passed by me in Ireland, a part of it on my Father's Tipperary estates, where I had daily occasion to mark the steady progress made, and the absence of those disturbing elements which neutralised all attempts at improvement before 1847–8. Even religious bitterness had much diminished, though the Protestant clergymen exercised no influence. Except the ecclesiastical grievance, I could see no political difficulty remaining for Ireland to settle. Tenant right was and is acted upon amongst us: but as a parliamentary cry, its advocates had made no way, and the movement was looked upon as fictitious rather than real.

In October I visited Lynn, a duty towards constituents which by the representative who pays it is very generally felt as irksome: I cannot regard it in that light. I found confidence and respect evinced on all sides: no question was put to me on any political topic: local quarrels had nearly disappeared: and great efforts were being made to carry out plans of improvement mainly projected by myself. Among these were a Free Library, to which I have subscribed £1,000: baths and washhouses: an Athenaeum, or union of literary and conversational societies: a new corn exchange, etc. It is singular how much the standpoint of the person proposing any change affects its reception: I have taken and carried through, with little trouble, the principal plans which the local Liberals had long advocated in vain, and [with] quite as much bitterness as vigour.

Shortly before the end of the session I analysed the divion lists to ascertain the average attendance of M.P.'s. Taking the first 200 divisions, the result came out like this:

In the first 50 there were taken votes					13,006
„ „ second 50 „	„	„	„		11,573
„ „ third 50 „	„	„	„		9,717
„ „ fourth 50 „	„	„	„		8,410
Total of the 200 divisions					42,706.

Tellers in each case included.

This gives an average attendance of 217½ members, or nearly one-third of the House. I did not however take in the last fortnight, when few attended, which would have reduced the average. The falling off towards the end is perceptible. The number of absolutely silent members is about one-half.

The division list is no complete or accurate measure of diligence, since many M.P.'s, living far from home, and not frequenting clubs, pass their spare hours in the library or smoking-room, not scrupling to vote on questions which they have not heard. Generally, the representatives of commercial boroughs attend most steadily: these constitute the middle class Liberals: next to them came the office-holders: then the Irishmen: the country gentlemen, as a class, are rarely present after dinner.

Politics remained in abeyance during the autumn: reform feebly discussed: most eyes fixed on Turkey, where war had begun in earnest.

Lord Palmerston's letter to the Presbytery of Edinburgh is now so well known as to need no special mention. Instead of the day of humiliation which they had proposed on account of the cholera, he bade them clean their houses and drain their streets, not asking Providence to do for them what they could do for themselves. It is likely that under Perceval, a newspaper writer or pamphleteer would have undergone prosecution for this language, as tending to infidelity. Yet this act of moral courage lost the Home Secretary no popularity, even with the Tory party, who were almost unanimous in praise of his ability. Their praise, it is true, being intended as disparagement of the Premier, Lord Aberdeen.

A foolish proposition was put forth by Lord Mayor Challis[15] about this time, for a statue of Prince Albert to be erected in London. I wrote against it both privately, and in the *Press*, thinking the affair a mere piece of adulation, unworthy of England, and a bad precedent. The newspapers on all sides did their duty in exposing this folly, which died a natural death.

My Father placed in my hands, during our stay at Knowsley, a mem. of conversation between himself and Prince Albert, of which, as it is preserved in his papers, I will give no extract. The substance of it to the effect that Palmerston had given grievous offence by insisting on his right to manage foreign affairs after his own fashion. The instances alleged were numerous, relating to Austria, the French *coup d'état*, and the German Powers. Palmerston had once told Albert 'that he was a German, and did not understand British interests'.

20 November 1853. The Duke of Beaufort's[16] death was made known yesterday amidst many newspaper lamentations. He was the ideal of a great peer, such as peers were in the beginning of this century, princely in his personal bearing, profuse in hospitality: generous from habit and impulse: careless of money, and thus always embarrassed: a soldier in early life, devoted to his profession: fond of women: a sportsman: no reader: courteous to men of all parties: Conservative by tradition and sentiment, not a professed politician: an attached follower and friend of Lord Derby. He kept open house at Badminton, especially to country neighbours. He was a man well fitted, had he ever desired office, to be Lord Lieutenant of Ireland. Towards the end of his life he suffered continual torments from gout, which he bore with a kind of epicurean fortitude, enjoying to the utmost whatever pleasures his state allowed.

22 November 1853. I went to Bury for the inauguration of an Athenaeum of which Lord Derby laid the first stone in 1850. Though the town has 40,000 inhabitants, with an immense trade, I found remaining an almost feudal respect for our family, which has not been duly cultivated. The Rectory is worth £3,000 yearly: held of course by a cousin (Rev. E. Hornby).[17] I lodged there, and was well pleased to observe the good terms on which all sects appeared to be. Indeed the chief Dissenters (as in some other manufacturing towns) are Unitarians, whose creed excludes fanaticism.

It was in Bury that the Peel family made their fortune: others, less distinguished, have succeeded equally, in point of money: one Wrigley,[18] a papermaker, began life as a worker with his own hands, and now owns £10,000 to £15,000 yearly: another family, the Grants, have erected a monument on the hill where the eldest of them, walking from the north, a penniless boy, halted to rest before entering the town in search of employment. They are now large employers, owning several mills. (I saw much of these men: their force and shrewdness of character greatly impressed me: in these requisites for success no class that I know in English life equals them. The contact of this visit fixed me in a purpose which general considerations had prompted: that of shaping my political course so as not to lose their support, if it can once be gained – and I think it can.)

They talked often of the strike, which had partly reached them: their tone respecting it was that of the most invincible determination to win, without either anger against, or compassion for, their opponents. They seemed to have, except in church matters, many Conservative tendencies, but are kept aloof by the mingled timidity and pride of the country gentlemen.

28 November 1853. Rumours of ministerial change, quarrels, etc., the two supposed subjects Turkey and reform. They were sufficiently loud and general to produce letters from Disraeli written in an excited mood.

Much conversation about this date with the Duke of Richmond, whose views are interesting as being those of probably a majority of English farmers. He surprised me by dissenting from the common agricultural hostility to what is called 'centralisation': he thought gaols, hospitals, lunatic asylums, and the like, ought to be thrown on the consolidated fund.

He related a good deal of what may be called the secret history of the Peninsular War, chiefly anecdotes concerning individuals which I do not set down as I could not do it with accuracy. The moral of all was this, that the Duke, though he never overlooked, never made public the fault of an officer if it could by any means be kept secret. He feared, not public opinion at home, but the effect on the troops, if the prestige belonging to military rank were destroyed. He spoke also of the Duke's extreme coolness, amounting to apathy, in critical positions; how he could lie down and sleep for an hour or so in the very presence of the enemy, after making every disposition for engagement. He thought there was in this something more than self-command: a kind of constitutional insensibility, peculiar and innate.

6 December 1853. Malmesbury arrived from Fontainebleau, where he had been staying with the Emperor as a guest: he described the French Court as earnestly bent on peace, Napoleon having plans of social improvement and financial reform on hand, both vast and for the time costly. 'He is as much' M. said 'of a philanthropist as Lord Shaftesbury, only with more sense'. The failure of vine crop and harvest had caused discontent, which increased the anxiety of the French Govt to avoid war. All the French generals were averse to the employment of a French force in Turkey . . . Napoleon did not hesitate to express to M. his disgust at the weak policy of Lord Aberdeen, who, he said, had thwarted him at every turn, and even seemed desirous of showing publicly that the governments were not on good terms.

. . . Malmesbury assured me that he has, or had, in his hands, papers which prove that in 1850–1 the French Govt had made up its mind to the necessity of a war with England – the cause being a discovery of certain letters addressed by our Court to leaders of the Orleanist party, which were construed into expressions of goodwill to their cause, and of enmity to the existing government of France. Malmesbury adds that Russell is fully aware of these facts.

Malmesbury related an interview with Napoleon, as follows: 'I visited him at Ham, in 1845, when he had been several years in prison. He then said that he had lost hope, that his health had begun to fail, and if I would intercede for him with the British Govt to use its good offices on his behalf, he thought they might be effective to obtain his release. He had received an invitation from the republic of Ecuador, where a revolution had just taken place, to come over and be its president: this offer he was willing to accept, and to give a written promise that he would never cross the Atlantic again. He also assured me that many of his guards were gained, that he might have escaped before, but that he suspected the French Govt of trying to induce him to make the attempt, in order that they might have an excuse for shooting him in the recapture. In proof of what he had asserted as to the friendly disposition of the sentries, he made a signal to one who stood in the court below: the man, after glancing round to see that he was unobserved, replied by laying his hand on his heart.

I went back to England, saw Peel, and pressed him to comply with the Prince's request, which he seemed not indisposed to do, but put me off without any definite reply. I called again the next day, and found that in the interval he had seen Aberdeen, who had thrown cold water on the plan. Napoleon knows of the refusal and its cause'.

Napoleon, when starting as candidate for the Presidency, applied to Malmesbury and Eglinton for funds. He wanted £5,000: they jointly offered him about £3,000, but, this he declined, having got the money from some other quarter.

Willis, the American, relates that between 1830 and 1840, Napoleon proposed to Lafayette to marry the latter's granddaughter 'with a view' he said 'to unite the imperialist and Republican parties'. Lafayette, it is added, referred him to the lady, refusing to influence her choice: and by her the offer was rejected. The story is plausible, but I have no authority for it except that named . . .

14 December 1853. News of the battle of Sinope . . . [*On Reform*] . . . it is hardly credible that while entire apathy prevails on this question among the masses, the Conservative class has worked itself into a paroxysm of alarm, and talks everywhere of revolution, as impending. The members of this class do not see that this revolution, such as it is, has been caused by their own unfitness to exercise the function of government: or, which is the same thing, by the indolence which all but excludes them from it.

17 December 1853. News of Palmerston's resignation: he goes out alone, the ostensible cause the new Reform Bill . . . I went up to town on the 19th, and saw Disraeli, who was full of confidence and exultation, speculating on the juncture of Palmerston and the old Whigs generally with us, and on our having in consequence a numerical majority in the House.

We talked about electoral and other changes. He did not fear ballot, though rather disliking it. He objected to reform, thinking you could not find any point to stop at short of the absolute sovereignty of the people: what he most dreaded as fatal to territorial influence was the equalisation of the representative area – the principle of electoral districts.

22 December 1853. Jocelyn called upon me with a minute account of the circumstances which had led to Palmerston's resigning. It seems that on first going into the Aberdeen government, he had told Lord A. that they should probably differ about Reform. Lord A. said 'no matter, there would be time to consider that subject'. The Bill was referred to a committee of the cabinet, P. being one: he opposed it, and wrote to Lord A. threatening to go out if it were not modified. The premier after consulting with Russell and Graham declined modification, but afterwards conceded it on Lord Lansdowne's request, not however saying anything in deprecation of P.'s avowed purpose. P. accordingly thought it was wished to get rid of him, and persisted in leaving them. Gladstone, Newcastle, and the rest, appear not even to have been consulted. P. on his retirement was immediately visited and congratulated by Lord Fitzwilliam and others of the discontented Whigs, who dislike the Peelites as much as they love their pocket boroughs.

25 December 1853. After some days of suspense, Palmerston's return was announced. The transaction, exhibiting as much vacillation as had been shown by him on his juncture with the Aberdeen cabinet, has damaged his position seriously. Lord Aberdeen's friends exult, saying 'He has done for himself now', language which does not exhibit much cordiality. The events I have noted, assuming Jocelyn's version of them to be correct, throw little light on the real causes of the split. It is possible that P. himself may have desired to escape from an office which he does not like, and from the society of uncongenial colleagues: but the more probable version is, that Lord Aberdeen and Albert jointly have contrived the affair, the latter being the prime mover, the former only his tool. This last is certainly the idea commonly received out of doors: and has led to loud and growing complaints of the secret influence exerted by the Prince Consort.

27 December 1853. We had letters, and subsequently a personal visit, from Jocelyn, whose minute account of the negotiations between P. and his colleagues I do not think worth inserting. P. though reconciled remained strongly of opinion that his expulsion, had been planned by Graham, the Prince, Russell, and Aberdeen: the first of these is said to have been most violent against him in Cabinet, Gladstone on the other hand adopting a conciliatory line. Jocelyn thought that P. had calculated on detaching Gladstone together with himself, and failing in that, had consented to give up the attempt . . .

31 December 1853. More reports of P.'s return. He appears to have come back without conditions of any kind. In the words of one of his colleagues 'he had come to the door of the cabinet, whining like a dog to be let in'.

. . . I know not if it be worth noting that during this autumn, I engaged actively in promoting the educational movement throughout Lancashire. In addition to the Lynn library, set on foot early in the year, though not yet opened, I established public libraries at Prescot, Ormskirk, and St Helens, and endeavoured to do the same at Bury, where it fell through, owing to local party feeling. I also attempted with some others the setting up of a literary and scientific institution in London: which failed, owing to fraud practised on the promoters, causing a considerable loss.

1854

3 January 1854. A letter of mine, written on the 29th to the *Herald*, with signature 'M.P.' and relating to the conduct of Prince Albert, appeared today. Part of the facts stated rest on the authority of Malmesbury, part on that of Lord Howden, the diplomatist to whom I have referred: part have long been known to me. One story, which I mention as a rumour only, reached me through Malmesbury, but this I expressly decline vouching for.

War is more and more loudly called for: and now seems inevitable . . .

23 January 1854. Settled in London, after a visit to Hatfield. The M.P. letter still discussed everywhere: great excitement produced by it: nearly all the provincial papers copied it: between 300,000 and 400,000 copies have appeared: on the part of Government it caused much anger, and a prosecution was talked of, but it is said the Attorney-general gave his opinion against such a procedure. (This was stated by Knox, editor of the *Herald*, but I now incline to doubt the fact.) In the provinces the prevalent rumours were absurdly exaggerated: inasmuch that in our neighbourhood the farmers asked whether it was true that Albert had been sent to the Tower? It will hardly be credited that this folly was ascribed by ministerial organs to the Derbyite leaders. I did not follow up the attack farther than by a single letter under a different signature, and that rather in defence of M.P. than with any intention of rousing farther passion.

About this time appeared a long and heavy attack on Disraeli, in form of a biography, an octavo of 600 pages, the author not known. I mention it only as having furnished the opportunity for a review by Phillips in the *Times*, which is perhaps the bitterest piece of invective that has been produced within my recollection. It described Disraeli as the impersonation of intellect alone, without feeling or sense of right: one to whom politics are a game of skill only. There is some truth in this sketch, but also some exaggeration.

Sir F. Kelly, Walpole, Disraeli, and I busied ourselves in a bill for the prevention of bribery, its chief features being the appointment of an election officer, through whom all expenses shall be paid, and the taking of votes by voting papers, instead of orally. (This last provision the House struck out: the first passed.)

25 January 1854. Malmesbury, Walpole, Disraeli, and I, consulted with my Father on the Turkish question. We sat three hours, analysing minutely the documents which have appeared, and the history of the subject. Malmesbury read to us the mem. of 1844 (since printed and published) the effect of which is to exclude France from all participation in the settlement of European affairs, confining this to Russia and England jointly. Nothing was

116

really settled, except that we agreed not to attack ministers for having resisted the warlike feeling as long as they could: but rather to blame them for general diplomatic blundering, and to point out the very slight difference between the terms offered by Russia and those which they could accept.

At the end of the session, each parliamentary party was split in two. The Irish brigade sat half on one side of the House, half on the other. Whigs and Peelites, though outwardly at peace, had trouble in suppressing the quarrels of their hangers-on. Disraeli had lost his hold of the more extreme partisans, and the English Radicals, 100 strong, were divided into a war and peace party, the last represented by Bright and Cobden, the first by the *Daily News*.

It is certain that at this time Palmerston was looked to as the most popular candidate for government. My Father's followers were distrusted, nor was protection forgotten: Russell was regarded, justly or not, as worn out in body and mind: Newcastle had not sufficient standing, though in favour at Court and generally respected: Lord Clarendon wanted debating aptitude: Graham's talents were, and are, neutralised by his reputation for inconsistency: Lord Grey's health and temper put him out of the question: Gladstone, though at the height of his financial fame, lost, as he still does, by his junction with an unpopular ecclesiastical party, and by his vacillating habit of mind. Bright and Cobden have never aspired to be more than sectional leaders.

One remarkable prediction was uttered by [Disraeli], for the genuineness of which I can vouch. It took place either at the end of May, or the beginning of June [i.e. 1853]. He said 'There will be no reform bill next year, and there will be a war'. This he repeated to me more than once, adding that he wished he could see his way as clearly through the affairs of Europe as he did through this.

He prophesied also, what has not yet come to pass, the relapse of the old Whigs into Conservatism, and the progress of the Peelite section until they united with Manchester. He argued clearly and well against the folly of treating the Manchester interest as democratic, it being essentially middle class in its nature: the workingmen had no representatives, except Cooper the Chartist and Reynolds.

He often repeated to me a favourite theory, the truth of which I am not inclined to deny. 'The H. of Lords is the weakness of the aristocracy. It is a security to the people against their power. It possesses privileges on condition of never using them. Thus it is invidious without being formidable. Put the great territorialists into the Commons, and what influence they would have. Lord Derby, for instance – Newcastle – Argyll.' In support of these views he would quote a saying of Odillon Barrot,[1] to the effect that without laws compelling the subdivision of landed property, parliamentary reform was *une mauvaise plaisanterie*. We discussed emigration, its present and ultimate influence. I contended, and he agreed, that for the time it tended to content, as taking off the most aspiring of the working class: but that the later effect would be to spread a sense of power, and desire for equality among that class which would not be easily resisted.

It seemed to be thought that the war would soon become unpopular and that as a matter of policy, it would not be wise to connect oneself too strongly to its support. Of all the party, both now and later, Lytton held the most warlike language, and Walpole the most pacific. I inclined to the latter side, and expressed myself decidedly in private, but did not choose to take a strong part publicly.

31 January 1854. A meeting was held at my Father's house, according to custom. About 150 came. He addressed them in a high Conservative strain, speaking nearly 1½ hours, at times with great effect, and being received with enthusiasm, though the heat of the room, and want of seats, exhausted some of the older members present. He began by commenting on the construction of the ministry 'founded on a fusion, or rather a confusion, of all principles' – of which the result was visible in the present [Queen's] Speech and in the state of affairs. He commented on the high price of provisions, which he said would have been cheaper under a protection system, and which contrasted with ministerial boasts of prosperity. Education had not been mentioned in the speech: he thought a rate for the purpose was unobjectionable and even necessary, he was willing to deal liberally with all sects, but no teaching could be worth anything that was not based on religion. Hotham's mission to La Plata ought to have been mentioned. He touched on the Palmerston resignation on the franchise, and University reform. He disclaimed any intention (which had been imputed to him) of bringing in a Reform Bill. As to the Russian affair, so far from being inclined to join in denouncing the Czar, he thought the latter had been ill used, and had more reason to complain of Lord Aberdeen than Lord Aberdeen of him. Lastly, he spoke of the party: its position, prospects, and the necessity of union. If he saw it gradually diminishing in numbers, he should retire, with much regret on account of the public, but with none on his own. He eulogised Disraeli, who might have made mistakes, dropped expressions which would have been better unuttered, but whose ability and devotion to their interests could not be doubted.

I went down to Westminster about 2 p.m. with a new member, R. Cecil.[2] We got shut up in the crowd, and saw the Queen's reception. It was not so good as in the newspapers; cheers over-powered the hissing, but of this latter, where I stood, close by Whitehall chapel, there was a plentiful sprinkling . . .

2 February 1854. About this time I called on Lord Shaftesbury, hoping to be able to cooperate with him in some of his many philanthropic enterprises though not in those of a sectarian character. We discussed several of them, but in general Lord Shaftesbury's zeal appeared stronger than his judgment. As I rose to go, Lord Shaftesbury took leave of me in these words 'I thank God that he has put it into your heart to come here'. (Not much came of this interview.)

6 February 1854. Knox came by appointment: told me that the M.P. letter had been copied by himself and the MS. destroyed: the secret was perhaps suspected by one person in his confidence, but not known to any. There had been great curiosity as to the authorship: my name was mentioned, but less positively than those of Malmesbury, Mandeville,[3] Beresford, and Glengall.[4] He explained the sensation created by saying that the assertions there contained had given definite shape to rumours which were floating in all men's mouths, but which wanted verification and detail. He had not heard of an intended prosecution, but had expected to be summoned to the bar of the House.

. . . I discussed with Knox the subject of a cheap weekly journal to circulate among working men, but found his ideas of what such a journal ought to be widely different from mine. Also he thought the stamp duty would be an obstacle.

Meeting Disraeli in the House, he conferred with me on the Reform Bill: wanted someone to oppose it on the ground of unsuitableness in point of time, while a war was impending: thought this language ought to be held by a Whig, as in the mouth of anyone else it would seem like an excuse: named several who might be made available – H. Vane, Vernon Smith, Jocelyn, Lord Seymour: the latter was preferred: it was agreed to sound him through Lord Malmesbury. Disraeli thought that whatever Lord Seymour might do, would be seconded by Lords Clanricarde, Carlisle, and Fitzwilliam.

9 February 1854. Beresford's persecution ended today in a manner creditable to him and disgraceful to his accusers. They had threatened him with a prosecution in Queen's Bench for bribery: put him to an expense of several hundred pounds for defence, and caused him to pass months of anxiety with the stigma of an expected trial upon him, aggravating his sufferings from bodily ill health. At the last moment, the prosecution was withdrawn, but without a word expressive of apology or regret, though it was admitted that no compromise had taken place. Beresford is poor, and a subscription will be set on foot for him. Thesiger and Kelly, who were engaged, have returned their fees. There is no doubt of Beresford's imprudence, but of anything beyond imprudence I firmly believe him innocent. The case has been commented on and prejudged without scruple by the Liberal journals.

. . . Councils were held as to the best mode of opposing Reform in parliament: the Tory leaders agreed to wait until the second reading, hoping thus to force the old Whigs to declare themselves, and by the seeming absence of attack from without to give time for mutiny to break out within the camp.

Palmerston is intriguing busily against the bill: secure to win in either event, disliking his actual post in the cabinet, yet resolved not to sacrifice it till he sees his way to something better. He has friends on all sides, spies in every camp, even age tells in his favour, since statesmen are willing to accept terms from him which they would otherwise decline, thinking the arrangement must of necessity prove purely temporary.

10 February 1854. In the Lords, the Whig party, represented by Grey, Beaumont,[5] and Clanricarde, attacked ministers for bringing in a needless reform bill in time of war. My Father protested against the bill, but declined opposing the first reading: in other words, he wished his opponents to fight it out among themselves.

13 February 1854. Lord John introduced his reform bill . . . its chief features are: £10 franchise in countries, £6 in boroughs, disfranchisement of 62 small boroughs, the seats to be distributed between towns and counties: with various minor additions to the franchise, and a plan for the representation of minorities.

When first enunciated, the plan seemed to startle the House, from its magnitude: Lord John's speech was clear, but dry and feeble, on the whole unequal to the occasion. He seemed to suffer while delivering it, and went away immediately afterwards. Out of doors was no visible excitement: the galleries not full: nor any crowd about the lobbies, or in Westminster Hall. Within was more curiosity than enthusiasm: I did not hear one hearty cheer: the speeches which followed were mere desultory comments: a month was allowed before the second reading.

20 February 1854. . . . On the Conservative side the war is not popular, at least not to the extent that the newspapers, and our acquiescence, would lead a looker-on to suppose. Out of doors it is vehemently applauded, partly out of sympathy with Kossuth and the Hungarians, partly out of the mere mob-love of fighting in any cause, partly also from the intense monotony of that life of unbroken labour which millions lead in England.

I abstained from taking part in this debate: disliking the quarrel, thinking that we should have done better to keep out of it, feeling certain that public opinion must veer round before long, but unable to see a present remedy, now that matters have been allowed to proceed so far. Of the country gentlemen some joined in the war cry out of mere thoughtlessness, some out of fear of Russia, some in order to annoy the Government, some to stave off Reform: a few because they liked the prospect of popularity which was to cost them nothing in the way of a sacrifice of class interests: but there remains a large number who dislike prospective disturbance in Europe, who object to fight where England has nothing to gain: and who in their hearts agree with Cobden . . .

22 February 1854. Overtures of a personal kind from Gladstone. I reply alleging duty to Lord Derby to whom I owe my seat in parliament, etc., but hint that I know of no other obstacle.

. . . Attended, on Saturday last, a meeting in the City for the construction of improved lodging-houses on mercantile principles: Baring in the chair.

. . . Printed and circulated a letter addressed to Pakington on what is called the private business of the House, and also a proposal for the more extended circulation of parliamentary papers.

Began a pamphlet, the second on church rates, and another on national police: both of which were suppressed.

23 February 1854. In the House, Disraeli called me aside for a conference: we went into the private room behind the Speaker's chair: he seemed excited and elated, in one of his sanguine moods. He spoke of civilities received from the Queen and Prince, which he construed into proofs of political reconciliation. He mentioned a Whig meeting lately held against the Reform Bill: and said that he was in communication, directly or indirectly, with most of the leading Whigs, Lord Grey, Sir G. Grey, Seymour, etc. A junction with them was quite possible: all depended on Palmerston, who was playing fast and loose, throwing out hints that might mean much or nothing. D. had got tired of this, and had proposed that if P. was in earnest, he should at the next cabinet express his determination not to go on with the bill in time of war. It seemed that P. himself had hinted that he might stand neutral, and keep away from the division on second reading, but without quitting office: this notion D. justly ridiculed as both offensive to his colleagues, and unbecoming a public man in high office. Palmerston once gained, he felt sure of the rest: as to the lead, he was willing to give it up, P. being an old man, not capable of sustained exertion: the real power would always remain with himself, Disraeli. He exulted in the notion of revenge on Gladstone and the Peelites, who would be driven to Manchester, and must act under Bright. He even began to arrange offices: wanted Walpole made Speaker, and Pakington a peer. He treated the latter with much contempt, which of late has been his habit, and tried to excite me against him, saying that Pakington had urged my Father to offer Palmerston the premiership, and serve as leader of the Lords under him. He wanted to send Lord Grey to India, where his impracticable temper might be out of the way.

25 February 1854. A meeting at Disraeli's, where we discussed an intended motion of Sir E. Dering,[6] in which Reform is deprecated. Now that the withdrawal of the ministerial bill seems likely, Disraeli dreads the escape of its authors, and wishes to force them into going on with it: this Walpole, Pakington, and I all deprecated.

26 February 1854. From various quarters came reports of an angry debate in cabinet yesterday: Palmerston had declared that nothing should induce him to agitate the question of the franchise at such a moment . . .

28 February 1854. ... Dining at home, I found my Father confident of victory, planning future measures and framing his cabinet. Disraeli had been talking to him of the possibility of securing Gladstone – his bitterest enemy. 'Politicians neither love nor hate'. The Liberal journals busy in writing down what they style the Vane–Dering conspiracy. Silence, absolute and significant, of the *Times*. Palmerston did not appear in the House, nor vote with his colleagues.

Serving on a committee which sat to investigate the forms of parliamentary business, I obtained from an officer of the House (Mr May) the following returns which are amusing, and not likely to be printed. The two longest sessions of recent times have been those of 1847–8 and 1852–3: in these the undernamed members spoke as follows:

	1847–8
Russell	229 times
Hume	203
Sir G. Grey	192
Sir C. Wood	179
Lord G. Bentinck	122
Palmerston	100

	1852–3
Gladstone	432 times
Hume	307
Russell	290
Disraeli	185
Bright	148
Palmerston	137
Pakington	133
Wood	123
Henley	114

All questions and answers recorded in *Hansard* are here counted as speeches.

In 1852–3 there were noted 1,106 speeches, including all those of any length or importance. These, analysed, gave:

Under half an hour	877
Half to one hour	148
Above an hour	81

Of the 81, 3 exceeded 4 hours each: 2 exceeded 3 hours, falling short of 4: 14 exceeding 2 hours: 62 occupied more than one and less than two hours. The 81 speeches were delivered by 47 members.

In the present parliament, out of 646 members, 342 are not reported as having spoken at all: i.e. more than one half the House still consists of silent members.

3 March 1854. Lord John, with reluctance hardly disguised, announced the farther postponement of the Reform Bill . . . nobody appears to entertain an idea that the bill will ever be heard of again.

11 March 1854. . . . It is singular that Graham, who is even unpopular with the multitude on account of his supposed cold and calculating temperament, who is regarded as eminently an intriguer, as skilful and unscrupulous in using other men for his tools, himself remaining safe and irresponsible-should be one of the most imprudent speakers now in parliament. I never heard him make a speech of any length or weight in the House, in which he did not say something that he had not meant to say, and that had better have been left alone. And it is more singular, that these rhetorical escapades occur usually, not in his argument, which may be improvised, but in declamatory passages, which he elaborates with the utmost care.

15 March 1854. Debate on truck systems, which I defended, at least excused, on the ground of legislative interference being impolitic. Country gentlemen are apt to vote on these questions merely with the view of spiting the manufacturers, whom they dislike.

17 March 1854. St Patrick's Day: Irish M.P.'s mostly drunk, whence a disorderly quarrel ensued . . .

22 March 1854. Disraeli attacked the financial policy of ministers in one of his best speeches . . . Gladstone's reply, delivered at 1 a.m., failed of its purpose, partly by reason of the late hour. This is Disraeli's first victory over his rival in finance . . . .

I received from Capt. Hay of the Metropolitan Police an account, first verbal, then written, of Louis Napoleon's Boulogne expedition. His story went to show that the attempt was by no means that mere piece of folly which we in England are accustomed to consider it: not rashness, but treachery, caused its failure. Napoleon, in short, walked into a trap. The paper is preserved among these records.[7]

24 March 1854. More projects by Disraeli against Govt: intrigues with the Whig party continued: his last scheme is to press, on war being declared, for an explanation of the objects of the war, and failing to get an answer, to move for an Address to the Crown, praying that those objects may be stated. He relies, as before, on Palmerston's secret support . . .

27 March 1854. Baines's bill postponed for a month, the adjournment being opposed by ministers. This is the first important defeat they have sustained during the present session. It is made more serious by this fact – that the blow has been struck more by friends than by enemies. Bright and the Radicals disclaim against them everywhere partly on account of the war, partly because they feel themselves of less importance under a coalition ministry than they would be either as supporting a Liberal government against a Conservative opposition, or the contrary. To neutralise parties is to neutralise agitation. I asked Bright one day what his object was in trying to bring down Lord Aberdeen? Did he think his party was strong enough to take office? He said frankly 'No – a change of hands would probably put the Tories in power'. Then parties would be reconstructed, the Whigs and Radicals would once more come together, and theirs must be the next turn. He added, that he should like an avowedly Tory government better than this one.

28 March 1854. Breakfast at Mahon's: talk of the Duke of Wellington, his leading idea in politics that he was pledged to do whatever the Crown desired, irrespective of other considerations. Mahon said that he had refused to join in some censure on Lord Durham's Canadian administration, of which nevertheless he greatly disapproved, on the ground that he was 'the sword of England', a part of the Executive as it were, in virtue of his personal character. Conversation fell on Louis Philippe: his prudent, bourgeois, but unkingly qualities. In England he affected utter poverty: had no wine at table: even grudged medical assistance to some of his household who were sick. This was like Napoleon at St Helena selling his plate, a demonstration, not a necessity. The ex-king might at any time have raised £50,000 to £100,000 on the security of his French property . . . Milnes, who was present, spoke of his extreme loquacity: he could not help talking to all who came near him of his most private affairs . . .

War declared by proclamation, but without pomp or form: a simple message to parliament. The levity with which it is talked of might surprise anyone whose experience did not show him how ignorance in the lowest class, business in the middle class, and frivolity in the highest, preclude all serious attention to public matters. It seems impossible to doubt that the whole Continent is against the Allies – Turkey herself alarmed by our interference: and the Russian force far more effective than our journalists admit it to be.

10 April 1854. Talk with Ellice[8] of Coventry, the Whig Achitophel, about ministers and the new Reform Bill. He predicts a break-up, says the Peelite element is too strong, the Whigs are already in rebellion against our allies, Russell and Aberdeen both disgusted from different causes, and would be glad to see the thing at an end. Ellice argues that no small measure of reform ever can pass – it must be large, or it will not rouse interest enough to overcome obstacles. Hostile interests can only be overborne by strong external pressure. 'In the old time we had a complete organisation. I could raise the steam or let it off as Govt chose. We had 16 leaders in the provinces, who managed the constituencies, and sent instructions to Liberal M.P.'s. One of our men used to vote steadily, but did mischief by foolish speeches. We gave a hint to the agitators, and they sent him orders to vote silently in future'.

11 April 1854. The abandonment of the Bill announced. Russell deeply mortified, and burst into a hysterical fit of crying: a painful scene. It however called forth the good feeling of the House, and averted what might have been an angry debate.

(From this date, transactions of a public nature are recorded in my letters to Lynn, printed and collected into a volume.)

20 April 1854. Being in Lancashire, attended and spoke at a meeting for the establishment of a public library in Warrington. It however proved a failure, partly on account of a church rate quarrel going on at the same time.

(Most of this and the next month was passed by me on a railway committee: I also wrote in support of the stamp duty repeal, and attended the House regularly, but took no leading part. The war occupied all minds: no other topic attracted any interest. I lectured at a Greenwich institute, and wrote much in the *Press*, as indeed I have done since its first establishment.)

23 May 1854. I spoke and voted for total abolition of church rates, having last year proposed a plan for their modification, which was rejected by the House.

Engaged about this time in an attempt to establish a free, rate-supported, or voluntary, library for the parish of St James's. It fell through. I could not induce the clergy to promise even neutrality. They seemed to dislike it on two grounds – the one, interference with their more especial charities, by the drawing off of funds for this purpose: the other, fear lest 'radicalism and infidelity' should be thereby encouraged. From their point of view, they are probably right.

27 May 1854. At Sir F. Kelly's, I met Sir H. Seymour,[9] the lately returned diplomatist. He talked freely. I asked, apologising for the question if indiscreet, 'Do you believe that if the Czar had been made to understand from the first that this invasion of the Principalities would be a *casus belli*, he would have provoked a war?' 'Certainly not' Sir H. answered: Brunnow and others misled him, saying that England would not fight. 'Then might not this quarrel have been averted by our taking a more decided line at first?' 'If you ask me, I think it might, and I recommended this course. But I was also misled by knowing that Nesselrode was strongly for peace, and that his opinion had more than once before prevailed over that of the Emperor'.

29 May 1854. Some talk with Disraeli about this time: he said in his judgment Walewski had done more than anyone to stir up the war, being a Pole. His (D.'s) private information has been singularly good since the war began: he told me that whatever news he got of foreign transactions, he wrote for the *Press* in the style of one translating from a foreign language, so that it might appear to come direct from abroad.

13 June 1854. I know not if I have anywhere noted that a plan of franchise extension was drawn out about this time by Disraeli and Lord Derby, intended to remedy one evil of the present system, the disfranchisement of persons who would be qualified to vote for a borough if residing within one, but who are excluded therefrom by living in the counties, the higher franchise of which does not admit them. My Father's intention was to enlarge the area of the boroughs so as to include among them all the counties, and thus establish a double representation over the entire area of England. He did not, however, desire to propose their scheme unless Ministers should reopen this question . . . .

22 June 1854. Heywood obtained the admission of dissenters to B.A. degrees at Oxford, by 252 to 161, a good work wherein I took part by speaking and voting. (Not much else of moment occurred during the session, in which I took part until its close. The Whigs and Peelites continued their quarrels: Layard threatened Ministers continually with a motion which he as continually postponed: the public mind grew impatient for decisive military action, whence ensued the Crimean campaign: and Gladstone, with his friend the Duke of Newcastle,[10] suffered greatly in public estimation by the disgrace of a friend of theirs, Lawley, whom they had attempted to send out to South Australia, while under suspicion of violating official confidence for stock jobbing purposes.)

I left London in August, and returned to it for the winter session.

1855

Memorandum on the Change of Ministry, January–February 1855

22–30 January 1855. My Father came up to town alone, and for nearly a week I dined with him daily tête-à-tête.[1] Some rumours had spread abroad of the intention of the Aberdeen ministry to break up, they being universally unpopular on account of their mismanagement of the war, following on the many defeats they had sustained in the session of 1854. It was also known that the leading members of the party were not on good terms. Consequently Lord John Russell's resignation, though its suddenness caused a momentary surprise, did not greatly astonish anyone. It was kept secret to the last moment: I heard it at the Carlton at about 3 p.m. on Thursday, and an hour later it was officially made known in the two Houses.

Lord John's explanation was given on Friday January 26: his statement occupied about an hour: it was not generally regarded as fully vindicating the course he had taken: too much personal animosity seemed to be shown against the Duke of Newcastle. Many found fault with the reading of letters originally private, which however of late years has become an ordinary occurrence. By others, Gladstone among the number, it was urged with more force, that Lord John himself had consented to waive his objection to the D. of N. and that at the very moment of his resignation the cabinet were unaware that he intended to revive it. To this Lord John had no reply, except that all the circumstances of the case were not known to the public: doubtless this was so, but the public could only form its judgment from the explanations actually offered, and if these did not contain the whole truth – if material facts were of necessity suppressed – it would have been better to pass over the subject in silence. In reality, it was obvious to all that Lord John's sudden determination to resign arose not from one, but many causes: a sense of uneasiness at his personal position: reluctance to make himself responsible for the errors of colleagues who were not friends: slights supposed to be put upon him by those colleagues, who presumed on court favour and the support, until lately, of the *Times*: possibly also a growing conviction that the Liberal party, if set free from Peelite supremacy, might be reunited under his guidance.

I think it likely that the design of breaking up the cabinet by retiring from it was one which Lord John had for some time past entertained: and that the abruptness of the final step arose from his perceiving the crisis to be nearer than he had expected. It was a dexterous leap out of a sinking boat: and perhaps many persons felt that the Peelite party had not itself been so

127

scrupulous in its relations with other sections as to be entitled to complain. Nevertheless, the feud between Whig and Peelite has by this move been so much embittered as to make an early reunion impossible. Lord John's reputation has suffered: no one seems to have gained politically, except Lord Palmerston, whom for reasons elsewhere stated, I regard (January 30) as proximate premier.[2]

My Father at first seemed inclined to try the experiment of forming a government even if unsupported by any other party than his own, and to this course, assuming no combination to be possible, Disraeli vehemently urged him. Malmesbury, Walpole, and I thought the experiment hopeless, and dissuaded. Disraeli even said to Malmesbury 'He must do it. I will make him – if he does not I will break up his party'.

He (Lord D.) secured a promise from Lord Ellenborough on Friday 26 January. They discussed together what should be done as regards the war: and Lord E. advised the instant recall of Lord Raglan, the making him, Lord Raglan, commander-in-chief in lieu of Lord Hardinge, who was to have, I think, the Ordnance, if he would take it, to break his fall: Sir Colin Campbell to command the expeditionary army. My Father approved of the recall of Lord Raglan, but thought Lord Hardinge's removal impossible, although desirable.

My Father's idea was, in the event of being called upon, to prosecute the war much more by commercial means than has hitherto been done: imposing a prohibitory duty on all goods the produce of Russia, so as totally to destroy that trade. I am not aware what course he designed to pursue with respect to the forces now before Sebastopol.

Returning to the debate of Friday, it was noticed on all hands that the House took slight interest in the subject, absorbing as that subject was and is. The reason, that nothing, or little, could be said upon it, which was not already familiar through the newspapers: and also that the conclusion was anticipated throughout. During the first night's discussion (Friday) very few Conservatives, about 130 as I was told, were present: the rest being still in the country: of those present some disliked the motion because it was brought forward by a Radical, others because they thought a direct vote of censure should have been proposed: a third section thought a parliamentary enquiry dangerous, if not impossible. Altogether the result seemed to Disraeli so doubtful, that he became unusually excited and impatient, answering sharply all who spoke to him, and to his friends deploring the loss of an opportunity which might not return. His apprehensions were shared by a few, but I think the public, and most members of the House, considered the defeat of ministers certain from the first. The speeches were dull – Roebuck broke down through bodily infirmity, and Sir G. Grey, the chief ministerial advocate, spoke feebly though with his accustomed fluency. The adjournment demanded by our side was not opposed.

Rumours were rife during the interval from Saturday to Monday night. It was sedulously put about by the Treasury officials that in the event of a ministerial success, the Duke of Newcastle would at once be removed, and Lord Palmerston substituted. The obvious intention of this manoeuvre was to disarm criticism, by representing the most obnoxious member of the cabinet as already fallen, and his colleagues as willing to disavow his acts. But like the Duke's war measures, it came too late.

By Monday the House showed a different aspect from that which it bore three days previously. The Irish members had come up: so had the country gentlemen: the benches on both sides were crowded: and Stafford, who on the strength of a personal inspection of the camp and hospitals, both in the Crimea and at Sebastopol, had prepared an elaborate speech, delivered it with considerable effect to a breathless audience. He had to enter much into details, some of a disagreeable and even disgusting nature: and this part of his work was executed with a straightforward simplicity which on such a subject was the truest delicacy. His rhetoric was very bad, and flowery: Irish of the worst sort: but he argued the case with remarkable candour for a partisan speaker, inculpating the local officials quite as much as the War Office: a discriminating censure of which some of the more violent oppositionists complained loudly. He was followed, I cannot say answered, by B. Osborne, who vindicated the Admiralty, but although holding office, handled the War Department quite as roughly as any opposition speaker, amidst the laughter of all parties. It was a feat of audacity unique in its way, and merited the credit which it got. From 7 to 10, as usual, the debate languished: at the latter hour, Gladstone rose and delivered a very powerful, ingenious harangue, which considering its rhetorical merit was but coldly received. He caused surprise by estimating the English force actually under arms before Sebastopol at 30,000 men: it is generally believed not to exceed one-half that number fit for service. Disraeli followed: his chief aim appeared to be to inculpate the entire cabinet, and prevent them from making a scapegoat of Newcastle which was their obvious design ... At no time was the House greatly excited. The interest of the division had destroyed that of the debate: no one knew within 150 what the vote would be, though nearly all expected the defeat of Government. When the numbers were announced – 305 to 148 – there was no cheering, but a slight, incredulous laugh: the extent of the victory had astonished one party and stunned the other. I chanced to be one of the first who came out, and watched with amusement, the surprise of those sitting immediately round Ministers, as the human stream continued for several minutes to pour forth from the opposition lobby ...

30 January 1855 (Tuesday). Nothing occurred, except that as a matter of form, Lord Aberdeen went down to Windsor to tender his resignation. It was rumoured at the clubs that Lord Lansdowne would be sent for to give advice: some added that he would be requested to hold the premiership for a time, but this was generally discredited. The House, after an hour's sitting for routine business, adjourned to Thursday. I walked up with Disraeli and Walpole: the former I found in one of his most sanguine moods: he thought that Palmerston would be deterred by age, infirmity, and the consciousness of an overrated reputation, from undertaking the Government: and that after a little hesitation he might be induced to lead the Commons under Lord Derby, bringing with him Gladstone and Herbert. My Father also seemed inclined to favour this view.

Edward Wilbraham dined with us: in the evening my Father read aloud: while thus engaged a royal messenger came with a note summoning him to Buckingham Palace next morning: he took it, handed it round, then resuming his book, finished the chapter. This was about 9.45 p.m. By his desire I immediately went off to tell Disraeli, stopping on my way there at the Carlton, where there prevailed a general expectation that Lord Palmerston would be sent for. This opinion I did not contradict.

I found Disraeli sitting alone with his wife: and handed him the note which I had written in expectation of finding him engaged, or in company. He said little, but his countenance betrayed great excitement: Mrs D broke out in exclamations of joy and surprise. I sat with him a few minutes only: and was glad to perceive that he agreed as to the impossibility of forming a cabinet if Palmerston held aloof.

Next day, Wednesday 31 January, none of the newspapers announced the summons, nor was it known at the clubs so late as from 12 to 1 o'clock.

My Father returned from the Palace a little after 2 p.m.: he said he had paid two visits there: first to ask leave to treat with Palmerston: then, after having seen P., to report his success. He had offered him the Presidency of the Council, with lead of the Commons: on the understanding that Gladstone and S. Herbert would also join. Palmerston accepted readily on his own account, but said he must consult the two friends named, and would report their answer in the course of the day.

No objection was made to Lord Ellenborough for the War Office: and his willingness to accept it is ascertained.

The Queen expressed a wish that Lord Clarendon should be induced to remain at the Foreign Office, to which my Father assented without difficulty, only expressing a doubt whether Lord C. would accede to the arrangement.

The Queen thought, as did also my Father, that in the event of his (Lord D.'s) failure, John Russell should be the next to try: Lord Derby added that though, without help from some other quarter, he considered the chance desperate, still in such an extremity the country should not be left without a government: and if all others declined the task, he would, though most reluctantly, and though feeling that his own reputation might be sacrificed in the attempt, consent to take office again with the men of 1852.

While this negotiation was pending, and before Lord Derby had returned, I saw H. Lennox, who told me, from Disraeli, that the project of fusion had fallen through: that Gladstone insisted on retaining the Exchequer, which Disraeli could not with honour or consistency surrender, as they had been so directly and personally opposed on questions of finance: that both parties meant to [and] would stand firm, and he could see no possibility of a compromise. All this Lennox communicated in a tone of hopeless despondency, as befitted the disappointed aspirant for £1,000 a year.

At 2.30 I went to Grosvenor Gate to summon Disraeli to meet my Father: D. was, or professed to be, more sanguine: thought the Peelites sincere, and that under Palmerston's management they would give way. In the afternoon, notwithstanding the worst of weather, – high wind, frost, and snow falling – I found the clubs crowded. I heard there a strong report that our arrangements were complete, the visit and offer to Palmerston being well known, except as regarded the exact nature of the latter and it was also said that Newcastle meditated a bitter attack on John Russell. The press, up to this time, has been rather perplexed than violent in favour of, or against, any particular leader. The *Times* supports Palmerston for premier, with Grey for War Minister: the *Chronicle* simply laments over the downfall of Lord Aberdeen: the *Herald* declares for Lord Derby, as against all coalitions: the *Daily News* defends Russell, as the only real Liberal leader: the *Post* and *Advertiser* both pronounce for Palmerston alone, with unfettered discretion as to colleagues.

The afternoon was passed by us in ignorance and suspense: not until 9 p.m. did a messenger arrive from Palmerston, bearing a courteously-worded refusal, accompanied with the usual assurances of support etc. E. Wilbraham dined with us again, and was witness to the reception of the letter. My Father thereupon wrote to the Queen advising that someone else should be called in, and for the present declining the duty of forming an administration. This letter he despatched overnight, and early next morning (Febuary 1) went down to Windsor calling on Disraeli en route. The Queen seems to have expressed her regret at his decision with more warmth than mere civility required: in which she was probably sincere, for her aversion to the inevitable Palmerston seems increased rather than diminished by time. She took time to consult, and Lord Derby thought it probable that Lord Lansdowne would be summoned to give advice.

In the House of Commons, nothing was done this day. I there saw Disraeli, who seemed to doubt whether we had done right in throwing up the cards so soon: he argued that a party which had twice failed to use its advantages, was thus self-proclaimed as incompetent: and thought many desertions would ensue. He appeared in low spirits, believing that Palmerston had got the game in his own hands: said that in a time of war and disaster no effective opposition could be formed, etc. I reminded him that Palmerston had never yet been more than a departmental minister: that his health and strength were failing: that his reputation, always overrated, would break down under the weight of the premiership: and predicted that should he now take office, his government would not last out the session of 1856. The Whigs were drawing together under Russell: they, if not hostile, were by no means friendly to P.: they mustered 100 votes, we 250: the Radicals under Bright hated P. if possible worse than the Court did: the country doubtless was with him: but the country would expect impossibilities, and cry out if the army system were not reformed in three months. 'All this may be true' D. replied 'but for whom shall we be fighting? Not for ourselves: we shall be as incompetent next year as we are now: If P. goes out, Russell is the natural successor, and he will, when this quarrel is forgotten, again unite the coalition'.

. . . While events were doubtful, Jolliffe called upon me with a letter from Taylor,[3] containing a strong remonstrance against the admission of Gladstone to our cabinet. He said the 'Protestant party' would leave us to a man, especially the Irish part of it: Napier and Whiteside, by joining such an alliance, would lose their seats: that we should not know whose support to count upon, etc., in short that the union would be to us a source not of strength, but of weakness. From other conversations, and reports that reached me from various sources, I have no doubt but that this representation was in the main just.

In the Lords, the Duke of Newcastle defended his conduct against Russell, and produced a favourable impression . . . My Father reviewed the state of affairs in a clever, good-humoured speech, which by some was thought more jocular than the occasion required. It appeared to be relished by none more heartily than by the members of the late cabinet. His speaking on this occasion indicated the failure of his attempt to form a government: since it is not usual for one actually charged with that duty to appear in public, or to offer explanations,

The Queen had not as yet sent for any minister: Lord Lansdowne was summoned to give his advice.

2 February 1855 (Friday). No change took place in the state of affairs: Lord Palmerston's name was in all mouths. Towards evening we heard a rumour that Lord John had been summoned to the Palace: as also that Clarendon had been requested to take the Government, and had declined. Of these tales the truth was not known: and equal uncertainty prevailed during the following day (Saturday 3rd): interrupted only by a startling announcement in the *Globe*, that Lord Derby had again been called in. This announcement, which for a moment produced a marked sensation at the clubs, was quite unfounded. I called on Lord Brougham, to ascertain his views on the crisis: he received me with unusual cordiality, shook me by both hands, and in a very excited manner, and with much gesticulation, proceeded to declaim against Palmerston, for his refusal to join Lord Derby. I think I have never heard any man, in his sober senses, and not under immediate personal provocation, curse and swear so vehemently.

4 February 1855 S(unday). It was announced this afternoon that Lord John had given up the attempt: rumour adding, that only three of his offers of office had been accepted: viz. by Vernon Smith, Labouchere, and Granville Berkeley. Palmerston's success was hereon considered certain, as it was unlikely that he would allow the opportunity to pass, and still more so that the Peelites would, by declining any offers made them, suffer Lord Derby to try his fortune again. But beyond the fact of his being engaged in cabinet-making, nothing was certainly known.

5 February 1855 (Monday). Vague rumours during the day of a 'screw loose'– some quarrel as to division of the spoil – one common report was, that the Queen insisted on Lord Aberdeen being a member of the new Government, as some check upon Palmerston.

Disraeli asked to see me, and entered into a detailed statement of the situation, as regarded our party. He said many were annoyed, on two grounds – first, they thought our giving up the trial was a slur upon them, as incompetent to form and support a cabinet – second, they disliked Gladstone, and were indignant that overtures should have been made to him. Something ought to be said by Lord Derby to remove this impression. Their feeling was, that any party leader professedly pretending to the premiership ought to be ready to take office with the help of his own followers alone: or if he could not do this, resign his claims to be First Minister. I could not allow the justice of this reasoning, which seemed to me inconclusive: but the feeling of which he spoke certainly does exist . . . .

6 February 1855 (Tuesday). Much talk, and among persons who should be well-informed, of an intention to give a seat in cabinet to Lord Aberdeen. This, of course, the Court's doing, if true. It was also said that Gladstone had refused on two grounds: first, because his ready money policy was not approved: second, because he could obtain no sufficient guarantee that peace should be made on fair terms. These details were conjectural: the existence of a difficulty in some quarter is certain. Towards evening we heard that all was made up: Disraeli complained to me bitterly that we had lost our opportunity – he saw no prospect for the future: this failure was final. I reminded him that this was not the first time, by half a dozen at least, that he had held such language. He took this well, but was little comforted . . .

7 February 1855 (Wednesday). . . . It is known that an attempt was made to force Lord Aberdeen into the cabinet; but with what support it met, or by whom it was opposed, we are not aware.

8 February 1855 (Thursday). Explanations in the Lords: my Father stated the circumstances of his being sent for, and exculpated himself to his party

for not having taken office. The *Times*, which is Palmerstonian only in deference to the feeling of the moment, compliments this speech, and regrets the
failure of our attempt . . .

It was noted that the debate on Roebuck's motion took place upon the
anniversary of that of Walcheren. About the time of its coming off I heard
from good authority that the French Emperor had said despairingly to one
of his ministers 'What can one do with an ally who has neither an army nor a
government?'

I learnt also from Malmesbury and my Father the nature of Napoleon's
plans for the next campaign: as likewise his intended terms of peace: but
these are not proper to be set down here.

P.S. The plan here announced never took effect. It was, in substance, to
send 48,000 French and 12,000 English troops to land somewhere on the
Baltic coast: this force to be under a French general. The fleets to cooperate,
and to be both under the English Admiral: thus giving unity of command,
and making each nation supreme in its own element.

The plan was drawn out, in the Emperor's own hand. I supppose the reason
of its not being executed was the enormous drain of men for Crimean service.

Memorandum on Public Affairs, November 1855

The session of 1855 closed more tamely than it had begun. Some trials of
strength came off, especially one on the guarantee of the Turkish loan, in
which ministers had a narrow escape in the H. of C. though backed in this
instance by opinion out-of-doors. The position of eminent public men under-
went no material change, except that Lord John Russell's mismanagement
at Vienna, following on the rather equivocal transactions of the winter, put
him out of the question as a leader. Lord Palmerston, on the whole, held
his ground. He has lost the factitious popularity which surrounded him
during the days of the Aberdeen administration, but the equally violent and
unjust outcry raised against his ministry has also died away: and his possession of power is acquiesced in by the nation, the more readily as a return
to the cabinet of 1852 would be deprecated by all, while the Radicals are
numerically weak, and Mr Gladstone's friends unpopular in consequence of
their opposition to the war. He stands therefore in the singular, but strong
position of the only possible minister: though his personal following is
small, and he can scarcely rely on a working parliamentary majority.

The debate on Laing's motion, early in August, and especially Gladstone's
part in that debate, injured the peace party in general opinion. They spoke
with great force, had the best of the argument, but went farther than the
country was prepared to follow: and the failure of this attack strengthened
the government.

Shortly before the prorogation I went out of town, dismissed from my mind all thought of political combinations, and engaged, during the intervals of abundant leisure, in a variety of local duties. I passed some weeks in Ireland, and one in Wales:[4] was present at Knowsley during the reception of the Duke of Cambridge on his visit to Liverpool: and had entered into correspondence with Fitzroy Kelly on the subject of law reform, designing to make that my chief occupation during the winter.

Disraeli, meantime, had not been idle. In July he sounded me as to the feasibility of a triple combination, which should include the Peelites, the Manchester men, and ourselves. I named the difficulty which occurred to me – viz. that neither Lord Derby, nor the mass of our supporters, would listen to such a proposition. The only possible basis of union was peace: and both Lord Derby and Malmesbury inclined decidedly to the party of war. Most, though not all, the country gentlemen, took the same view: and the farmers, connecting the idea of war with prosperity and high prices, supported them to a man. But I added that personally my feelings were strong in favour of such a junction, assuming its possibility, of which I doubted. In the meantime the less said on the subject the better.

Disraeli did not keep his own counsel. The rumour of such a coalition as he had sketched to me, though at first discredited, spread far and wide. Even now though officially contradicted, it prevails, and has been largely discussed by the newspapers. D.'s principal argument, a very characteristic one, for taking the side of peace, is that Palmerston represents the war, and is recognised as war minister. If the opposition support the war, they must support him: which is to occupy a subordinate and uncongenial post. Their only chance of independent and successful action lies in adopting an exactly opposite course. In a word, as D. had written up the war in the *Press* during the summer of 1853 in order to turn out Aberdeen, so he now prepared to write it down, in order to turn out Palmerston. But the motives of an individual cannot affect the merits of a policy: and having spoken in H.C. for peace on the Four Points, as early as May of this year, and having from the first endeavoured (along with Walpole) to moderate in lieu of stimulating the military spirit, I could only rejoice in, and approve, the change of tone indicated in these reasonings. The duty of reopening negotiations was, and is, vigorously urged in the *Press*: and with effect on the public mind: for hitherto no journal of any influence has held this language. Much alarm and astonishment, however, has been caused in the minds of Conservative M.P.'s, who had gone to their homes and constituents unprepared for so sudden a turn. Indeed, no longer ago than Whitsuntide, Disraeli had rested a motion of no confidence mainly on the alleged danger of ministers concluding a disgraceful peace during the recess of six days!

So matters stood: the Conservative party disunited on this vital question, the ablest politicians inclining towards peace, but the numerical majority of M.P.'s, the cabinet, the *Times*, and the general public, still bent on con-tinued war.

On the 31st October [1855] I chanced to be passing through town on my way to attend a meeting in Norfolk, when I was told that a messenger from Lord Palmerston had called the previous evening, and had again enquired for me that day. He came a third time, and brought a note re-questing an immediate interview. I, of course, lost no time in obeying the summons: and about 2 p.m. was received by the premier at his house in Piccadilly. He came to the point with little circumlocution: said he had an offer to make me: that out of respect for his late colleague, Sir W. Moles-worth,[5] he had abstained from taking any step towards filling up the vacancy caused by his death until after the funeral: that I had been pointed out in many quarters as a fit successor, and that if I were so inclined, the post of Colonial Secretary was at my disposal. He was aware that it was not usual to make such a proposal to one who was not a habitual supporter of Govt: but he had reasons for so doing. He thought, apart from the question of personal fitness, that my adhesion would give strength to his cabinet, as an indication of the desire of parliament to support a ministry whose function was to carry on a great war: domestic questions were much in abeyance: I had assumed a position independent of party, and he thought no blame or discredit could attach to a junction between us. There were points on which I had censured the conduct of ministers: I had said, that peace ought to have been made on the terms proposed at Vienna: but that question was set at rest by the issue of the negotiations: I had scouted the doctrine of nationali-ties, and he himself had never laid it down in any general form: he was in favour of Austria giving up Lombardy, should any revision of the map of Europe become necessary: but he recognised the necessity of Austria con-tinuing to be a great central power in Europe, and should object very strongly to the separation of Hungary from her: he had wished, as everyone must, to see Hungary better governed, but not to see her an independent state: as to the Polish question, it was impossible to say what turn events might take. Here he paused, and I asked whether he would give me an assurance that the war, as conducted by him, had no other object than the protection and safety of the Turkish empire? He replied at length, but vaguely: talked of the possibility of the Russians being driven north of the Caucasus, out of Poland, and even out of Finland. I cannot set down his language, which seemed purposely ambiguous: the impression it left on my mind was that he looked forward to a long, and ultimately a revolutionary war. But I cannot affirm that any words actually implying this meaning were used by him. I then reverted to the immediate subject, said that though on abstract principles of domestic policy there might be little difference of opinion between us, yet that in the eyes of the world suspicion at least, if not dis-credit, attached to any politician who quitted his colleagues to join another party, especially if that party were at the time in power: some evident justification of such a course was necessary: there were three difficulties which I felt strongly: one relative to the war, on which I should at that time say nothing: one arising out of the obloquy which attached to political conversions in general: the third, reluctance to place myself in an attitude of almost hostility, at any rate of complete and permanent separation, from Lord Derby, to whom I owed my introduction to political life, and, indirectly the honour of this offer. I could only regard the overture as made to him equally with me: I must consult him upon it: I would do so that night: but I felt it right to state then and there, that I thought it more probable that I should not be able to accept the proposed post. Lord P. answered with great courtesy, that of course he did not wish for an off-hand answer: nor could he expect that I should decide on such a matter without consulting my Father: that he should be happy to allow me whatever time I chose to take for consideration: he could very well carry on the routine of the office *ad interim*: he only hoped there would be no unnecessary delay. This I promised, and thanked him warmly for a proposal so little expected and in itself so flattering. The conversation lasted scarcely half-an-hour: I went home, telegraphed to Knowsley and also to Norfolk, where I was expected to take part at a public meeting next day: and went down to Knowsley by the 5 p.m. express. I found some guests in the house, among them Malmesbury: on their retiring my Father came into my room, and the subject was discussed between us. He was no more prepared than I had been for the offer, and received it with expressions of surprise.[6] He had arranged to go out shooting early next morning, but came again to my room before setting out, when I told him that a night's reflection had decided me, and that I should refuse. He approved entirely, thinking that it would have been difficult to accept without injury to political character: he should have done the same in my place, but was unwilling to bias my judgment. He had however said enough overnight to make his opinion evident: and it was in substance mine.

I remained at home, and wrote to Lord P. the letter which is here subjoined. I wrote confidentially to inform Disraeli, but did not tell Malmesbury: I found, however, at night that my Father had done so.

Knowsley, November 1st, 1855

Dear Lord Palmerston,

The very flattering offer made by you in our conversation of yesterday took me so entirely by surprise that I could only promise a definite reply after some interval of consideration. I have weighed it well, and have consulted, as I felt bound to do, with my Father: and the result is a clear conviction on my part, that in joining your cabinet I should both fail to bring you the strength which you have a right to expect, and should also compromise my own political future to an extent which nothing except the pressure of a great national necessity could justify.

In the first place, I could bring you but little strength. If anything in the nature of a junction between your friends on the one hand, and the leading members of the Conservative party on the other, were involved in my acceptance of office under you, such a step would no doubt materially strengthen your position both at home and abroad. But no such junction is proposed or contemplated . . . The amount of assistance, therefore, which I could render to your Govt would, therefore, be limited to such personal sacrifice as I could contribute in council and debate; and your chief object, namely, the conciliation of parliamentary support, and the disarming of parliamentary opposition, would not (I am certain) be attained. Nay, more, the very fact which under other circumstances might have facilitated union between us – I mean, the sympathy which on more than one question of domestic policy I have avowed with the views of the so-called 'Liberal', rather than with those of the Conservative school of politicians, makes it still more certain that in stepping across the H. of C. to join you, I should have to go alone.

Next, as to myself. It is true that of late years, the lines of demarcation which separate political parties have been finely drawn, and have even at times appeared to be altogether effaced. It is true that, on subjects relating to internal policy there may, for aught I know, be but little difference between your conclusions and those at which with far less experience, I have arrived. One question however there is, on which I fear we differ widely: I mean that of foreign policy. And though during a state of war questions of intervention or non-intervention may not often arise in a direct and positive form, yet the differences of temperament and principle which lead one public man to assert in peace the doctrine of diplomatic interference pushed to its utmost limits, and another, on the other hand, to seek to reduce that interference to the minimum amount compatible with harm and safety, are differences not accidental, but permanent, and which must of necessity affect the spirit in which war is carried on, or concluded. I should ill requite your courtesy, if I did more than indicate a divergence between our views on this class of subjects: a divergence which I fear time will not diminish, while the subjects themselves were never more prominent or more important than now.

But this is not all. I do not rate as highly as some incline to do, the obligations imposed by party ties. On the contrary, I hold that where any large question affecting the nation is involved, on which a deliberate opinion has been formed, no sacrifice of personal alliances or friendships ought to interfere with the expression of such opinion, nor with the taking of whatever steps may be necessary to carry it out in practice. If, for instance, one who has habitually voted with the Conservative party were to differ from that party in thinking a large and immediate measure of parliamentary reform necessary, I should hold him bound to vote for that measure, and, if his aid were required, even to take office with those who were prepared to pass it, though in so doing he placed himself in a position of hostility to all his former associates. The public interest would in such case override the claim of private connection. But is that plea available to me? Domestic controversies, as you yourself stated, are in abeyance. The sections into which political men are divided, the banners under which they have ranged themselves, represent individuals rather than ideas. I regret this state of things: it is an unfortunate and unnatural one: but assuming its existence, can I, attracted on the one hand by no peculiar identity of sentiment, repelled on the other by no difference of opinion which makes itself peculiarly felt at this moment – transfer my services from the section which is headed by my own nearest relative, to that over which you preside, without incurring at least the suspicion and discredit which attaches to political change, when accompanied by obvious personal advantage to the individual, and not obviously prompted by considerations of public policy?

. . . I have stated at length, and with personal frankness, the motives which influence me in declining, respectfully and with thanks, your proposal. Let me add in conclusion that to the close of my public career I shall look upon it with pleasure, and not without gratitude. It gives me a political status to which I had not attained, and hardly yet aspired. And whether our future paths in political life lie together or apart, I shall equally feel it an honour to have been selected for such a post, at such a time, by one whom all parties agree in recognising as among the foremost of English statesmen.

Believe me,
My dear Lord
Faithfully yours,
Stanley.

My letter to Disraeli was brief, containing a mere intimation of what had passed. In next day's *Times* (November 2) appeared a paragraph anticipating my adhesion to the government, and also a letter which I had addressed to the gentleman in Norfolk, Sir W. Jones, whom I had been on my way to visit when detained. The return of post (November 3) brought a brief note of acknowledgment from Palmerston, containing expressions of courtesy and regret.

In my letter of the 1st I had stated the truth, but not the whole truth, nor was it possible I should. Palmerston's hold over the Whig party is uncertain, depending much on the line which Russell, the real chief of that party, may think fit to take: and the two men are mutually hostile. By the independent Liberal, or Radical, section, he, P., is supported for his warlike propensities, but suspected, justly, of Toryism at home: thus neither Whigs nor Radicals would be secured by a junction with P., while the Conservatives would be not only alienated but embittered. Again, the friends of Gladstone, and the Manchester party, agree in nothing more cordially than a dislike to the present premier: Disraeli, Gladstone, Bright, are the three strongest men now in the H.C. and all in energetic opposition. Thus the proposed junction would have been on my part a secession from the stronger to join the weaker side – a sacrifice of permanent results for temporary distinction. Further Palmerston's age (now past 70) enters as an element into all calculations on the duration of his Govt: and between the various members of his administration he personally forms the sole connecting link. Add to this, that my views in favour of peace have been broadly stated, both in public and private: and though it is true that circumstances have changed since the spring, yet Palmerston is so identified with the ultra war movement that in joining him I could hardly avoid the reproach of interested inconsistency. To the bulk of the Conservative party I owe nothing, nor do I admit their claim upon me: but Disraeli would have had a right to complain of desertion: and (to write unreservedly) I feel assured that a political separation from Lord Derby, however friendly at first, would soon be widened by the influence of his partisans (when our mutual communications being interrupted their misrepresentations could neither be known nor answered) into a personal breach. Nor is a great House divided against itself a seemly spectacle.

From these transactions generally three results to me are clear again. At whatever time, or under whatever circumstances, my connection with the Conservative party is finally dissolved, I stand free from the imputation of leaving it from motives of self-interest. Also (and this is not less important) having declined union with any other political body, I may without suspicion, and with a good grace, stand aloof from all party moves and combinations: in short, act as an independent private member. I have long done this in effect, but not avowedly or consistently.

It does not seem that Lord Derby contemplates, or even desires, a return to office: nor has he any definite policy. He is content to watch events, keeping under his command as large a body of Conservative Peers and M.P.'s as will remain satisfied with inaction. But Disraeli is not among these: and as he and Lord D. are necessary to one another, no separation will ensue: so that the leader in H.C. will have his own way, Lord D. probably dissenting, but not offering opposition. But although thus powerfully reinforced in the Commons, the peace party will fear to put forth its entire strength, dreading a dissolution: and, if the two offices now vacant (Post Office and Colonies) are given to men of decided Liberal opinions, that section, Manchester excepted, will follow Palmerston with little demur. So, in my judgment, stand parties at the present time.

After a few days spent at Knowsley, I returned to town, and there began at once to carry out a plan of reading on subjects connected with reform of the law, with a view to assist [Fitzroy] Kelly in the enterprise to which I had long been urging him. We easily came to an understanding on the main questions at issue: but these need not be touched on here.

It was announced (November 18) that the Colonial seals, after being refused by S. Herbert, had been accepted by Labouchere. This appointment pleased surprised and disappointed no one. It appeared inevitable, and really was so . . . Labouchere is an amiable, honest, and not incompetent Whig of the old school: speaks seldom when not in office, and suffers from bad health. He has taken no decided part either in support or disapproval of the war.

27 November 1855. Within the last few days events have taken a new and startling turn. It is affirmed on authority which I believe to be good, that of an unknown but hitherto accurate correspondent of Disraeli's, that the Austrian Govt. has proposed to Napoleon terms which the latter is willing to accept, which Russia will not refuse, and which therefore wait only the determination of our ministry to become final. These terms were communicated on Monday, 19th: except in the *Press*, no notice is anywhere taken of them by the newspapers: on the contrary we hear of the accession of Spain, Sweden, etc. to the alliance as probable, and of the consequent prosecution of the war with increased vigour and extended objects. These reports are supposed to be put about by the agents of ministers, in order to mask the real state of the case . . .

Disraeli, whom I met at Hatfield, consults me on a plan of administrative reform which he is bringing forward, on which he expatiates in his customary strain, saying that it will be a greater measure than the Economical Reform proposed by Burke. As yet I have not seen the plan.

30 November 1855. Returning to London, Malmesbury called on me, fresh from Paris. He had not heard Disraeli's tale, but knew the fact that negotiations were going on. He reports that the French Court, Government, and people, are all weary of the war: thinking that it can bring no practical or tangible good to France: there is no disguise about Napoleon's sentiments on the subject: Morny, Walewski, etc. talk of the necessity of a peace . . . Malmesbury believed that our government was holding back, thinking another campaign necessary: and he naively advised me to keep silent on the war, as he himself should do, until it was seen whether Palmerston would consent to peace or not, since it would be equally easy to attack him for having made, or for having forborne to make, it. I thought comment on the morality of this proposal needless and inconvenient, therefore said nothing . . .

1856–1857

In 1855 Stanley ceased to be a regular diarist, perhaps because he had Lady Salisbury to confide in instead.[1] For the following year, 1856, nothing substantial seems to exist, which is not to say that something may not yet be found. For 1857 Stanley left a volume of desultory notes,[2] sometimes with dates attached, but not closely linked as before to the events of the day. 'As the events of every session are recorded, I preserve no notes of them, except as means of reference'.[3] (It was not until January 1861 that Stanley again kept regular journals,[4] maintaining the practice almost without a break until his death.) His notes for 1857 nevertheless have a value, albeit not mainly a political one. They reveal Stanley as he might have been, rather than as the forces of party eventually made him. They show a Stanley who put social amelioration before parliamentary life,[5] who believed that in social science lay the key to a better life for the artisan, and who was examining the subject of military hospitals 'at the request of Miss Nightingale'. Stanley's notes are those of a student rather than of a politician; perhaps moreover of the disinterested student, for the purpose of his thirst for knowledge is never made explicit. Economics and social reform occupied his mind much more than before (or later). They were perhaps his reaction to the Crimean War, but he did not say so. Social reform, however, was in the air. When in October 1857, Stanley was chairman of the sanitary section of the Birmingham conference on social reform, and when he spoke there on reformatories, the audience on each occasion reached 3,500.

In quieter moments we find Stanley relaxing with the census reports, musing over the excise returns, eagerly seizing on the latest report of the Factory Inspectors, looking into the question of law reform, and giving some thought to pauper emigration, the nearest thing to a panacea[6] that his cautious mind allowed. Some of his jottings might have served for an economic history textbook. Recondite problems of taxation and the national debt were examined at length, revealing the extent to which Stanley at this stage was training himself to be more than just a future foreign secretary or a colonial and Indian specialist. When Stanley described Buckle as 'a work wh. more than any other I have seen, embodies the results of recent discovery, and the tendency of modern thought', he illustrated not only how estranged he had become from his party and mentors, but how the Palmerstonian reaction of the Sixties was preceded by a post-Crimean period governed by quite different ideas.

Stanley's notes are generally unsuitable for quotation in full. They tend to analyse the case for and against a proposal with a painful fairness which says much about the writer (whose own views rarely obtrude). More interesting than this highly cerebral process of private study was a zealous programme of visiting institutions not usually seen by the higher orders; Colney Hatch asylum, the building of the *Great Eastern* at Millwall, Lancashire County Asylum, model lodging houses in Spitalfields ('there used to be baths in the establishment, but being little used they were discontinued'), the transatlantic cable being made at Birkenhead, and a tour of a Cornish mine. With Lord Salisbury, whose widow he was to marry, he went round the Bank of England, noting that 'about 1,000 persons are employed within the walls; nearly 100 sleep within them'.

Behind both practice and theory lay a knowledge that social, economic, and legal reforms would constitute the politics of the future. The Palmerstonian war fever was seen as an interim in which wise men were to prepare for new times; and the meaningless opportunism of the Derbyite party appeared in this perspective as worse than irrelevant. A Tory undertow in favour of parliamentary reform and the ballot was a significant element in this preparation for a progressive future. The slogan 'Conservative progress' which incapsulated Derby's second ministry of 1858–9 so well, was already stirring in indefinite form in 1857.

In foreign affairs Stanley's position, though not elaborated, was that of a classical liberal internationalist. Talking (1 February) to Lord Grey on foreign policy, he noted, significantly, 'among the best points of Lord Grey's character is an inflexible adherence to the peace policy'. Stanley's own adherence to the peace policy had not passed unnoticed during the Crimean War, least of all by Lord Derby. In spring 1857 the issue had shifted to the British attack on Canton, which Stanley thought 'worse than that of the Russians at Sinope' for its disregard of life. Later in the year Stanley, like Disraeli, was strongly against the demand for revenge upon atrocities committed during the Indian Mutiny. Apart from rereading the *Idées Napoléoniennes*, Stanley's interest in foreign affairs mainly took the form of disapproval of Palmerston's manipulation of public opinion.

Stanley's relations with Pakington, which had hardly existed before 1855, were important in bringing his departure from Derbyite orthodoxy into the open. Once Stanley had thought Pakington 'ought to begin his educational theories upon *himself*',[7] but a visit to Westwood, Pakington's house, from 11 to 15 January 1855 led to several years of amicable communication. Pakington wanted a patron: Stanley gained a sincere admirer of some standing. By 1857, indeed, Pakington found 'I concur with you more often and more closely, than with any other man'[8] and had earlier acclaimed his collaborator: 'You have a great future before you, and the Country, which now begins to see the importance of attending to social progress, will look to you (and not to the D. of Newcastle, as he seems to suppose) as the "coming man".'[9]

Stanley helped the cause in drafting and in debate, but especially in journalism. He offered 'to work the subject in four or five leaders'[10] in the *Morning Herald*, though regretting 'I can't work the whole press single-handed'.[11] A comment on the organ of the licensed trade shows a Stanley who, unlike his father, was not above a little manipulation of press opinion: 'The *Advertiser* is managed by a half madman, but its sale is next that of the *Times*. The editor has gone out of his way to be civil both to you and me – to you as a Protestant, to me as a partial Liberal. I think he might be influenced, if necessary, so far as to open his columns to communications'.[12]

The 1855 Education Bill was by no means modest in the hopes that it engendered. Pakington's ideas went beyond those of 1870; he argued 'the American Experience in favour of *free* education is *very* strong'.[13] Nor was free and compulsory education enough; Stanley wanted 'a recognised Minister of Education',[14] and there were shared views on the purpose of education. Pakington wrote: '. . . I quite concur in what you say about industrial training, as forming part of any good education system for the labouring classes . . . Every village school ought to give industrial instruction . . .'[15]

There was no chance of accommodating this mixture of vanity, energy, and idealism within the context of the Derbyite party as it actually was,[16] or within the situation created by the ministerial crisis of February 1855, a crisis so unexpected by second-rank Derbyites that Pakington was writing shortly before the storm: '. . . The programme is so meagre that unless we have something spicy from the Crimea I think M.P.'s in general will prefer the country to the H. of C.'[17]

Pakington's 1855 Bill floundered on, with Pakington dependent on the government and receiving no official help from his own side, until he gave up hope in June. Stanley, Miles, the Bristol member, and Adderley assisted Pakington in debate; but 'from Disraeli who asked me to proceed and wished me to move my Bill as a party measure, and from Bulwer who is on the back of my Bill', Pakington received no aid.[18] Palmerston had given the measure just sufficient countenance to create a cave of disgruntled educational reformers on the Derbyite side, a grouping and an issue which remained alive until the second session of 1857, and was only finally laid to rest by the impact of the Indian Mutiny.[19]

Both Stanley and Pakington concluded that the lesson of February 1855 was that the Derbyites could never come in on their own. Stanley's and Pakington's attempted secessions in 1856–7 must be seen in the light of this doctrine; they were seceding not to go into the wilderness, but to occupy the independent central position from which Derby would have to recruit if he ever took office. How Pakington's attempt to bolt early in 1857 was smoothed over, as it was, is not clear, but his ideas remained much the same at the end of the year: '. . . I also think it essential to our being either useful or hopeful as a party, that we should stand on a broad basis. I do not see how I can continue to occupy my seat, unless this is an accepted principle'.[20]

There was a difference in motive between Stanley and Pakington. Stanley was not only prepared to concede, but actively wanted both social reform and 'parliamentary innovations',[21] whereas Pakington wanted social reform as a bulwark against democratic tendencies. Both men envisaged a post-war future in which Russell 'would fling up his cap for democratic reform – and will again be our leading antagonist'.[22] It was this assumed Russell recovery, this conjectural creation of a popular Liberal party, against which thoughtful Conservatives of the left sought to guard. Pakington wrote: 'I think it is very desirable for us to give every proof, as public men, that if not in favour of parliamentary innovations, we are not the least forward party in the country in supporting social reforms and improvements'.[23]

Why was Stanley becoming, so generally and in so many different fields, a typical liberal intellectual of his time? Many reasons may be cited. His writing for the *Press* had much to do with it. In 1853 it suited Disraeli that his apprentice should take up the questions of the day and pronounce on them in a liberal spirit. The tactical need soon vanished; but in the process Stanley acquired an embarrassing number of liberal principles. In 1854 Stanley began to distance himself, in politics if not in friendly regard, from Disraeli. In 1855 he found at Hatfield sources of solace and confidence which nerved him to greater independence. The incident of Palmerston offering him office in autumn 1855, gave him for the first time the sense of being an independent political personality; that sense of existing in his own right governed his conduct in 1856–7, and very nearly determined his absence from the 1858–9 government. Palmerston's investment was not ill repaid.

One other consideration should not be overlooked. Stanley's constituency at King's Lynn was itself, in a sleepy East Anglian way, becoming liberal; or more liberal by far than the run of Conservative ministerial seats. Now this need not have mattered, for Stanley was regularly fending off entreaties to stand for more prestigious constituencies, and could in theory have defied his electorate to do its worst. However, Stanley very much wanted to be member for Lynn, and for nowhere else. It had the normal advantages of a decaying borough – little public speaking, little correspondence, small expense, few contests – but over and above these it had one special advantage: it was as far as possible from the influence of 'my Father'. If Stanley had sat for a Lancashire seat, he would, while his father lived, have been the nominee of a patron to greater or lesser extent. And this he was determined against.

The electoral politics of Lynn were therefore not as unimportant as they might seem. Party feeling in the decaying borough was weak, and most elections were uncontested. In 1848, 1854, 1857, 1858 (twice), 1859, and 1866 a Lynn election went unopposed. Only in 1852, 1865, and 1868 did

Stanley have to face a contest. This did not mean that there were no currents of opinion, or that Stanley was free not to conform to the increasingly liberal tone of Lynn politics. In 1848 Stanley had arrived in the borough very much as the political heir of Lord G. Bentinck. In 1852 he and the other sitting member, Viscount Jocelyn, Palmerston's son-in-law and a nominal Peelite, had fended off a radical challenge from a London barrister, Robert Pashley, who continued to wait watchfully.

In 1854 Jocelyn died suddenly of fever contracted while on military duty in the Tower of London, leaving it to the 'moderates', in Stanley's view, to fill the vacancy. If a second Derbyite had stood, it would have risked uniting the Peelite–Liberal majority in the town, and Stanley was much against this. Stanley was also at pains to point out to party headquarters that Lynn was by no means a close borough. The Duke of Portland had influence (built up by Lord W. Bentinck, the Indian governor-general) but no paramount control; Lord George Bentinck's influence had been personal, not proprietary; there were two or thrée families without whose consent no member was likely to be returned, but otherwise everything turned on personal standing. Pashley was quick to reappear in town as a potential radical candidate for the vacancy. The Conservatives simply lacked a candidate of their own hue, though Stanley thought his own chief supporter, Richard Bagge, twin of the county member, might succeed if willing, which apparently he was not. The Tory chief whip, Jolliffe, though fully informed, had little to suggest. The Jocelyn section, despite its Peelite past, solved the problem by putting forward J. H. Gurney, a rich and respected Norwich banker with strong local ties, who was a moderate Liberal of Anglican (but ex-Quaker) background. This satisfied the radicals, who told the unfortunate Pashley he might go home again. The Derbyites, and Stanley in particular, were happy to let Gurney walk over, and to allow him to be returned unopposed until he retired in 1865. Gurney's £20,000 a year, and the conversion of the former Peelite section into moderate Liberals, had shifted the centre of political gravity in the town far away from the rural and marine protectionism of Bentinck's day.

At the 1857 general election Stanley and Gurney were returned unopposed 'as it seemed, by almost unanimous assent'. Gurney canvassed from house to house, but Stanley paid no visits except to a half-dozen of the leading men, having decided instead to elevate his constituents by delivering a political lecture in Lynn once a year, a practice he maintained, with some gaps, until he took office in 1866–8. On the hustings, Stanley condemned the China war, and interventionism generally; said that some extension of the suffrage had become inevitable, but gave no definite pledge: and omitted to mention the question of ballot.

The main entries of the year may now be summarised. In 1857 Stanley was busy with law reform, presiding at a meeting of the Law Amendment

Society, attending the Juridical Society, going to a conference on bank-ruptcy law, and attending a meeting on patent law reform, a cause he after-wards pressed. He attended the Statute Law Commission, where the guiding spirit was the Conservative lawyer Fitzroy Kelly, who had given up part of his immense practice to further his consuming interest in law reform. He discussed the government promotion of science with the British Association; he received from a Post Office official plans for telegraph nationalisation ('the general outline of this plan has often before passed through my mind'); he dodged requests to become a parliamentary spokes-man for the ex-king of Oudh, the indigo planters of Bengal, and the sup-porters of legalising marriage to a deceased wife's sister. In short, without having made any distinct move, he had established his position as a public representative of liberal causes.

This was unhelpful. Stanley, like other junior Derbyites (Adderley, Pakington, Northcote, Fitzroy Kelly) could play to a liberal gallery with some hope of being noticed, now that the Peelite monopoly in the spheres of efficiency and practical reform had been broken by the Crimean disasters. Boys' reformatories,[24] the symbol par excellence of Christian Conservatism as a progressive force, and law reform were appropriate vehicles for showing that individual Derbyites had heart and zeal. The immediate effect in 1856–7, however, was not to extend the appeal of the party outside parlia-ment, so much as to risk fragmenting its forces in the Commons. Pakington and Stanley both applied to secede early in 1857, essentially because they were too liberal for their party. Their secession was inconvenient to the leaders; and 'Conservative progress' made its appearance, partly as a lesson drawn from the 1857 elections, but partly to stop a weak Commons front bench from becoming weaker. A greater question weaving its way through 1856–7 was what to do about Gladstone. Had Derby come in when Palmer-ston fell in 1857, Gladstone was, by all conventional signs, at least as avail-able for Derby's Exchequer as he was to be for Palmerston's in 1859. Palmerston's decision to dissolve put a stop to moves towards a strong Derby–Gladstone ministry implied in Gladstone's dealings with Derby and to a greater degree in Gladstone's vehement criticism of government finance in the first month of the 1857 session. Here Disraeli's behaviour in leaving Gladstone to make the running implied collusion.[25] Gladstone and Derby knew, by late January 1857, that the question was not so much how to secure Gladstone, as how to force him on hostile back-bench opinion. In February, therefore, Gladstone devoted his efforts to financial points cur-rently exciting deep prejudice among the squires. The sudden election, itself partly the product of Derbyite–Peelite reunion, left politicians adrift for the rest of the session, though Reform again became a topic after three years interval when Palmerston conceded, in the debate on the Address, that the cabinet would have to consider Reform in the 1858 session. This hint, and nothing else, gave Disraeli a theme to work on – the necessity, as in 1853–4, of using Reform as a party issue to dish the Whigs.[26]

19 January 1857. At Pakington's[27] earnest request, I had promised to put my name on his Education Bill: at Knowsley he had a conference with Lord Derby, who seemed to fear inconvenience from the differences between him and Henley on this subject: the conference ending in his deciding to do one of two things, either give up the Bill or give up his seat on the front Opposition Bench: he was undetermined when he left us, but wrote to me two days later, saying that he was bound in honour to persevere, though as an independent member only. I have since answered his letter, repeating my promise of support, under these altered circumstances. . . . Nothing was arranged about income tax: all condemned (most justly) the Naples, China, and Persia affairs.

1 February 1857. From hints casually in conversation, I am led to believe that the strength of the Opposition will be directed against a continuance of the income tax; thus using the present popular cry to procure a virtual return to the principles of Protection: high duties, and restricted trade.[28]

2 February 1857. Dined with Disraeli, as leader of Opposition, officially. Some 50 of the Conservatives were present: the Speech was read, various comments made. Disraeli appeared in the highest exultation, alluded mysteriously to certain disclosures which he should make tomorrow, and said in my hearing 'By this day fortnight we shall be in office'. He has passed part of his winter in Paris, in frequent communication with the Emperor, his object being to gather material for an attack on the foreign policy of ministers. . . . This dinner at Disraeli's was preceded by a curious correspondence.[29] I at first declined to attend it, giving no reason. Disraeli thereon wrote in a tone of friendly reproach, appealing to our former intimacy, and treating my refusal as indicative of a desire to break it off. My real reason was simply a wish to be free as regards political action, especially on the subject of income tax, on which I foresee probable difference between the Conservatives and myself. I answered by a statement in detail of the points of difference that had arisen between us since 1852: church rates, religious tests, education, newspaper stamps, military purchase, etc., expressing my belief that the number of these would increase rather than diminish. I said, that being so situated, I could neither take my seat on the front bench again (I had left it last year) nor give pledges as to political conduct. On that account I had declined to join his guests. But if he chose, accepting this state of things as inevitable, to invite me, I would, by accepting, give him proof that no personal alienation existed on my part. He replied in terms which made it clear to my mind that he anticipated an early return to office, and trusted to the prospect of power, to overcome all scruples of principle.

3 February 1857. Pakington called: said a heavy pressure had been put upon him to postpone his notice of an Education Bill. Disraeli especially had pleaded for delay: he would have yielded if he had thought that only a temporary postponement was desired: but felt sure that the real object was to stave off the measure altogether: in this I agreed with him, and confirmed his resolution. I told him not to look for support to the Conservative party at large: he might perhaps get a few supporters out of it, but that would be all. He next discussed the question of where he ought to sit: his habitual seat being on the front bench, and Lord Derby and Disraeli not having formally rejected his plan, it seemed best that he should remain for the moment where he was, so that the rupture, if it took place, should not come from his side. If they rejected his measure, he being pledged to go on with it, the time for secession would then have arrived.[30]

We talked over the extraordinary excitement in which Disraeli seemed to be, and agreed in thinking his anticipated triumph premature. We went over the income tax question also, but briefly and with less agreement.

11 February 1857. Read ... Simon's collected reports on the sanitary state of the City ... I propose to write to Dr Simon and find out what, if any, assistance can be given in parliament to his plans. The Board of Health will work no worse for his pressing.

13 February 1857. Lewis brought forward his budget ... His style is ungraceful, his delivery embarrassed, he speaks without animation, often repeats the same words, and often ends a sentence without saying what he meant to say when he began it. His demeanour tonight was that of a clerk reading accounts, and intermingling with them here and there an explanatory remark. A more marked contrast to Gladstone can hardly be imagined. As a speaker, Lewis has two merits: he says what he has to say in few words, and those words never leave a doubt as to his meaning. Lewis is a sensible and laborious student, better versed in the affairs of the last century than of the present: devoid of any special knowledge of finance, and in consequence prone to argue points which financiers usually take for granted.

... Conservatives still talk of the succession tax as a measure of confiscation, by which large landed properties are certain in the long run to be destroyed: indeed the recollection of this measure, next to differences of ecclesiastical policy, constitutes the most serious obstacle to Gladstone's rejoining the country gentlemen.[31] My vote against this tax is of all I have given in parliament, that which I most regret.

24 February 1857. It would appear[32] that in every case the fathers of those who competed held the status of gentlemen, in the conventional sense of the word. ... No reform of our time has passed so easily into a fact – scarcely any can be more important in its results – than the introduction of the competitive test for office in lieu of patronage.

6 March 1857. Gladstone moved reductions in the tea and sugar duties, speaking long, forcibly, and with that peculiar vehemence, like that of a man under personal provocation, which has marked his displays during this session. Many Conservatives would not vote, or voted with Ministers, and Govt beat us by 60. Gladstone made the mistake of not indicating with clearness enough the quarter from whence the deficit, caused by his re-reductions, was to be supplied. This lost him votes. Truth is, there must be a new direct tax when the Income Tax ceases, or else an extended and greatly augmented House Tax: this fact most statesmen are aware of, but none of them like to contemplate it. The last alternative, is that which Gladstone used to prefer.

14 March 1857. Number of public[33] Acts passed:

1853	137	1855	134
1854	125	1856	120

26 March 1857. Feb. 3, debates began in both Houses: Gladstone in strong opposition, as also Lord Grey: a singular dispute between Palmerston and Disraeli respecting the existence of a secret treaty with Austria, guaranteeing her Italian dominions: Disraeli at first was ridiculed on all sides, but persevered, and got out so much of the truth as to show he had grounds for his statement: this second battle came off on the 12th: on the 18th Pakington moved to bring in his Education Bill, which excited little interest: on the 19th Locke King brought forward the £10 [county] franchise, Spooner Maynooth: both beaten: 20th and 23rd [February] we debated the budget, Disraeli moderate, Gladstone vehement, in hostility: Govt had 80 majority, carrying off many Tories: we had with us Cobden, Gibson, and most of the economists: 24th, Lord Derby raised the Chinese question in the Lords: Cobden did the same two days later in the Commons: this great struggle lasted four nights, nearly every member of influence speaking: Gladstone more decisive in his censure, and by far more eloquent, than any other: we divided 263 to 247, majority over Govt 16: next day a dissolution was announced . . .

On the dissolution being known, I had two offers of seats, one from North, the other from South Lancs., but preferred remaining at Lynn, where no new pledges will be required. I told Lord Derby that I must support a Reform Bill if brought forward, and on that score offered to resign my seat: this he would not hear of.

9 April 1857. Analysis of votes of 1856.[34]

Of 653 applicable M.P.'s	*Of total 198 divisions*
1 (Duncan[35] of Dundee)	voted 198 times
1 (Hayter[36])	190
14	absent 10–50 times
79	absent 50–100 times
243	100–150 absences
226	150–180 absences
82	from 150 to 197 absences
7	absent from all 198 divisions!

We have thus 315 members, or nearly half the entire House, absent from at least 150 out of 198 divisions, i.e. from three-quarters of the whole number. We have 558, or more than five-sixths, absent from above 100 divisions, or from more than one half of the entire number. It is however to be noted that the session of 1856 was absolutely devoid of important business.

7 May 1857. Kelly called, with a plan[37] for Parly Reform ... This in addition to whatever extension of the franchise in a downward direction Ministers may propose.

18 May 1857. I had, a few days back, a conversation with Disraeli on political subjects: an event now rare, though frequent enough in 1851–4. He utterly despaired of present success for the Conservative party: saw not a prospect of it, even in the future, so far as that future could be looked into; but continued to entertain vague hopes that the next year's Reform Bill would cause some change. He now seems to take in the idea, by him long rejected, that Lord Derby really does not desire office, his health having of late become unequal to its fatigues. He repeated one remark which is striking, probably true, and which as I heard it from him years ago, is no temporary paradox, but a fixed idea in his mind. He says that the H. of Lords, as a legislative assembly, is an ingeniously devised contrivance for lessening the power of the aristocracy.

23 May 1857. Disraeli has been delivering to his constituents at Newport Pagnell a speech on electoral reform–probably that which he was so anxious to deliver in parlt on the first night of the session, but suppressed at Lord Derby's request. He deprecates hostility to reform as such, but contends that a fair reform bill must greatly increase the parliamentary power of the land.[38]

4 June 1857. Nothing, or next to nothing, has been done this session: and but little will be. . . . We have voted estimates on a large scale, with hardly an attempt at reduction; Gladstone, either from ill-health, pique, or prudence, stays away, and there is no check on ministers. Out of doors, entire apathy;[39] within the House, party spirit is dead. I see no violence, no extravagance of opposition; we are all moderate in sentiment; moderate also, I fear, in talent. But I hear that patronage is bestowed both in army and navy with more regard to personal, and less to political claims than has been usual in this country.

Walked up with Wilson Patten, whom our debate led to talk of Ballot,[40] and the progress which it is making. He expects to see it adopted, but fears the result will be bad: arguing that a Govt is always unpopular except when newly appointed, and that its members, on any change of office, or on a dissolution, will be liable to be turned out of office.

. . . Lytton said to me in casual talk that he thought the time was come when Ballot would be taken up by some leader in earnest; and when it was so, it would be carried.

5 June 1857. Walked up with Stafford, who related an odd story. He said that John Russell had told him that the cause of his (Russell's) speech on the estimates, in which he complained of their extravagance, was an application from Cornewall Lewis,[41] who agreed in all that he had said, but durst not say it, nor act upon it, himself. Lewis had complained that Palmerston would refuse no one, had granted every request for money indiscriminately: while as a natural consequence, his colleagues were never weary of asking for it. What a state of administration, when a Finance Minister entreats a doubtful friend to attack his estimates, in order that he may have a pretext for reducing them!

Stafford went on to talk of the overbearing tone assumed by Hayter and the Govt subordinates towards their Radical allies: how the latter were told if they did not vote steadily, Govt influence wd be applied to turn them out at the next election: with more to this effect. Partisan bias may colour Stafford's opinions, and render his inferences doubtful: but I have found him always accurate on questions of fact.

Vernon Smith[42] complained to me, in conversation the other day, of Palmerston's extreme unpunctuality: he keeps people waiting for hours, then tells them to come again another day.

22 June 1857. ... I lodged[43] with Platt[44] M.P. for Oldham. He and his brother employ, as machine makers, 3,000 hands: their production was last year to the value of £400,000, of which £150,000 went in labour, and about £50,000 was clear profit. These facts I have from themselves. Their three principal managers receive £1,500 yearly, the salary of an under-secretary of state! These men are almost always promoted from the ranks.

31 July 1857. The Divorce Bill was this and yesterday night argued in the Commons ... Gladstone was learned and impassioned, but his harangue lost great part of its effect when Sir G. Grey[45] published the fact of a similar Bill having been brought in by Lord Aberdeen's cabinet, of which Gladstone was a member, thus showing that his religious scruples dated from less than three years back.

7 July 1857. Debate, raised by Roebuck, on the abolition of the Irish viceroyalty. He proposed no substitute, and of course the motion was lost. I voted for it. This question was last debated in 1850. The abolition was then supported by a large majority of the Commons, but the D. of Wellington pronounced agst it on military grounds, and Govt durst not go on. The arguments seem all on one side.

Stanley's status as a political intellectual was recognised by his presence at an unusual, if not profound, discussion:

6 July 1857.[46] I met at breakfast with Macaulay, De Tocqueville, the French pol. philosopher. Talk on the state of America. He thinks disunion not probable. The impulse of the moment, which at present tends towards disunion, is less strong in America than it would be in a like case in France:

and the interest of both North and South is against a rupture. He thought the South stronger than is usually supposed – the slaveowners had all at stake – local nationality, personal interest, even personal safety: while their opponents are fighting for a principle wh. does not directly concern them. But parties had never before been so violent: slavery used to be excused, palliated, represented as an inevitable evil, inherited from former times and for which the present age was not to blame: this was a few years ago the language of the slaveholders: now they identified themselves with the practice, boasted of it, sought to extend its area.

He said a French squadron had lately touched at San Francisco: the officers had examined Californian life: they saw it 'with a mixture of admiration and alarm', saying that a race of such energy and organising power must conquer the world. But California represented an exceptional state of society – not so much a particular class, as a particular stage, and that the most energetic, in the life of a large number of young Americans. He noted the power wh. America seems to have of absorbing other races. The Irish disappear at once, losing any national peculiarity. This he explained by the community of language, and to some extent of ideas. The French do not hold out long. The Germans live in masses, and retain their nationality longer than any other people.

The U.S. are now for the first time learning what it is to have among them (in the emigrants) a class unfitted by ignorance and previous habits for the exercise of pol. power.

We spoke of the physical change produced on race by the New World: the loss of flesh, the increased height, the greater nervous excitability, the bad health so common, especially among women, and the change of voice. De T. said, no corresponding change could be traced among the French settlers. I observed I had heard of it in Australia among British colonists.

I have noted here what passed between us, not carefully distinguishing what was said by each.

Notes on the New Ministry, February 1858

20 February 1858 (Saturday). An unexpected change has taken place in politics. The Bill against conspiracy, lately introduced by Ministers, was unpopular, great pains being taken to represent it as an Alien Act: though this statement was far from the fact: but anger was created by Walewski's despatch, in which he expressly complains of the right of asylum as sanctioned by our law: by Persigny's speech at the Mansion House: and still more by the unmeasured language which the latter has been in the habit of holding in private companies. In short, the arrogant tone of the French Govt had excited resentment, and it was thought that Ministers had replied too tamely. In particular, the leaving unanswered of Walewski's manifesto was regretted and blamed. On the second reading of the Bill, Milner Gibson moved an amendment, which was in effect a vote of censure on this ground: this amendment was debated during an entire evening, and the division gave 19 majority against Ministers. The majority was composed of Whigs, Tories, and Radicals: Russell, Gladstone, Cardwell, Graham, Disraeli, Bright, all voting together. In the minority none voted except Palmerstonian Whigs, and a few Tories like Bentinck, whose most lively apprehension is that of a union with Gladstone. The result surprised both victors and vanquished. Probably it would have been different, had either side expected it: but as always happens in chance combinations, no party knew what strength any other could bring. I gave a hesitating and rather reluctant vote to the opposition: but I should have stayed away rather than precipitate a crisis, had I anticipated the carrying of the amendment.

It was not generally supposed this morning that Ministers would resign: but retiring from the Speaker's dinner, I learnt that they had done so, and that the Queen had sent for Lord Derby, with a view to discuss the state of affairs. His words to me were 'I don't know whether I am Minister or not'. He had given the Queen a day to consider whether she would make him an offer of the premiership: intimating that in the event of her doing so he would attempt to form a Govt. Being asked by one of his family if he had a majority in the Commons, he replied that to choose her own Minister was a prerogative of the Crown, which he would not consent to surrender. He appeared rather depressed and anxious than sanguine of success. He had seen Disraeli since his visit to the Palace; and thought D. was disappointed at his not having at once grasped at the offer made him. He appeared to doubt whether the offer of resignation was not a ruse: and remarked that in that case the course taken by him would soon unmask it. He dwelt two or three times on the Queen's right to choose her Minister, and his duty of acceptance.

22 February 1858. Offers were made in the course of yesterday to Lord Grey, to Gladstone, and to the Duke of Newcastle, by Lord Derby. All declined. Gladstone answered for S. Herbert as well as for himself. Lord Grey has been for some years past drawing nearer to Conservative views, and as early as 1853 Disraeli entertained the idea of seeking his assistance:[1] it does not seem, however, that any ground existed for this hope.

The most friendly reply came from the Duke of Newcastle: he hesitated at first, but consulted his friends, who had refused already: whereupon he did the same.

Lord St Leonards refused the Great Seal on account of age, Thesiger taking his place.

The cabinet may now be considered as formed. It is substantially that of 1852, with the addition of Ellenborough and B. Lytton.

Disraeli called on me about 3 p.m. and vehemently urged my joining the Ministry. He pleaded that I was bound in honour so to do: that Liberalism in the sense of the only really progressive party, that of Gibson, Bright etc., was impracticable for twenty years to come: that whatever was possible to be done in the meantime might be done as well by himself as by the Whigs: that the chances of success were great: it was not a case of 1852 over again: the Ministry must have a year's respite: they had to restore peace in India, and good understanding with France: no measures would be expected for the present: in twelve months time there was no saying what might happen. He appealed to our past personal connection: spoke of the antipathies of Russell for Palmerston: of his own prospects: of the necessity of someone who sympathised with him to give him strenth in the cabinet: there were no difficulties in prospect: the Reform agitation was a delusion: church rates would be an equal embarrassment to any cabinet: etc. etc.

He left me unconvinced but disturbed and doubtful in mind. I did not however retract a refusal, rather hinted than expressed, which I had previously given in conversation with my Father.

The two papers which follow explain my views of this crisis, as it regards Lord D. and myself. I must add that for my Father to have refused office would, in general opinion, have been impossible, and unfair to the party with which he has acted.

21 February 1858. Reasons why a Ministry formed by Lord Derby at the present time is not likely to stand:

1. Because the present H. of C contains a large majority of members professedly Liberal, elected under a pledge to support Lord Palmerston, and most of whom, though not all, would follow him into opposition.

2. Because even in the Lords parties are so balanced, as to make it doubtful whether a Conservative Minister could avoid defeat.

3. Because neither the creation of new peers, nor the dissolution of a parliament which has lasted during only a year, are practicable expedients.

4. Because the character of Disraeli, who must lead the Commons, does not command general confidence, either in parliament or among the public. If in difficulty, he would probably resort to desperate expedients rather than resign: whence might arise differences between him and the premier: a danger only averted in 1852 by the short duration of the ministry.

5. Because Lord Derby's views on political matters are greatly and unfortunately misapprehended by the public.

6. Because, for obvious reasons, it would be necessary to form a junction with Mr Gladstone and his friends: whose extreme unpopularity could only be a new source of weakness, and would alienate some of Lord D.'s habitual supporters.

7. Because it is, and since 1853 has been (I write from personal knowledge, not heresay) the earnest wish of the more advanced Liberals to see a

Derby Ministry formed. They reckon on the effect of such a step being, to unite every section of the Liberal party in opposition.

8. Because a new Reform Bill is expected by the public: who, however indifferent at present, will be easily stirred up to agitate for it by the Liberal leaders, instigated as these will be by the hope of regaining office.

9. Because of the Indian Mutiny being in the main put down, and no serious alarm existing among the people as to the safety of that part of the Empire, the plea of urgent public necessity cannot be put forward, as in 1855, as a reason for attempting to govern without a majority.

10. Because there seems reason at least to suspect that the object of the Court is only to give time for the reconstruction of a Liberal administration, on a broad basis, as in 1853: which end would be most effectually served by the union of the Liberal party in common opposition.

On these grounds, I regard the attempt now being made as hopeless, unless a coalition be formed including men of various parties, such as Lord Clarendon, and other of the Whigs, who would, however, find it difficult to act under Lord Derby.

Disadvantages of joining Lord Derby's government:

1. Connection with Disraeli. Able as he is, this man will never command public confidence.

2. Connection with the worst section of the political world, though only temporary, and though there be no real union in the case.

3. Difficulty of avoiding being mixed up in unpopular transactions, such as opposition to necessary reforms, and the like.

4. Impossibility during many years of taking office with the dominant party, without suspicion of interested inconsistency.

5. The rule *noscitur a sociis* is applied and rightly to politics. It is naturally thought, though a man's language be unlike that of his colleagues, that he sympathises with them, else why should he have joined their party?

6. Risk of seeming to play a double game: losing credit for honesty and simplicity of purpose.

Advantages of joining Lord Derby's government:

1. The plea of personal attachment to its head lessens, if it does not wholly remove, the reproach of inconsistency, both as regards the past, and the future, if I afterwards join the Liberals.

2. Whatever Liberal measure (if any) this cabinet adopts will by the public be ascribed mainly to me, while to measures of an opposite tendency I shall be regarded as having been opposed.

3. Administrative failure will be excused by the weakness of the general body: success will be imputed to myself personally.

4. The influence and position given by high office will increase my power of advancing Liberal opinions hereafter.

5. Whatever principles the present Ministry repudiate, can never be taken up again as a part of 'Conservatism' – whatever that word may mean. Extreme opinions in that direction are neutralised by our resistance, more than they could be by avowed opposition from the other side of the House. In this way I may indirectly serve the Liberal cause.

6. India may fall vacant – though on this I don't count.

7. There is always the power, though with some difficulty and annoyance, of resigning in case rash proposals are brought forward: a popular course, if taken at the right time.

In addition to the reasons given above for joining Lord Derby's cabinet, there is the difficulty of finding any other course free from objection. The alternatives were:

1. To take a subordinate office. This I actually proposed to do. It would have lessened my responsibility and proved that no desire of power influenced me: but it would have lowered my position, diminished my influence, rendered it impossible for me, by any display of personal qualities or of Liberal opinions, to redeem my character from the general unpopularity of the connection: and after all, I should have been almost equally implicated in any unpopular vote that might be given.

2. To remain in parliament, but out of office. Here the responsibility would have been less, and to this plan my feelings strongly led me: but here again the personal position in which I stood would have hampered me, and in some respects even more than it does now. On no great question, involving the overthrow of the ministry, could I have voted against them without exposing myself to misconstruction. It would have been difficult, considering how strong the influence of family ties is among the English people, who judge the conduct of politicians, to take office with the party which turned out Lord Derby, and thus to appear to rise on his fall. But if I declined office with the Liberals, after declining it with the Conservatives, what would have remained for me – never an efficient parliamentary speaker, nor likely to be – except sheer inactivity, or activity which could lead to no important result?

3. To retire from parliament altogether for a time. Objections: the difficulty of getting back – losing the thread of events – losing the habits of public business – wasting the best years of life – probable mental deterioration in consequence.

I imagine that few public men have been placed in crises of greater perplexity. No possible choice was free from actual inconvenience and possible risk: it will mainly depend on management and caution whether these few months to come injure or advance my parliamentary prospects.

Means of escape from office:

1. An appointment abroad. But there is no colonial post which I could take except Canada or India: and there are obstacles in the way of both.

2. Resignation professedly on political grounds. Disagreeable, and has a tendency to injure future prospects, as suggestive of a quarrelsome, impracticable temper: but under the special circumstances of this case, that imputation is less likely to be ventured on than usually would be the case. A possible solution of the difficulty.

3. Resignation without public cause assigned, or on the ground of health. The first is not easy, though B. Lytton would be ready to take my place: the second expedient can always be resorted to, but there is something unsatisfactory in it, and it suggests doubts of future efficiency, which are unfavourable to political success.

25 February 1858 (Thursday). The formation of the new administration occupied the last few days. On Sunday evening I had, not in express terms, but unequivocally, declined to take part in it: for the reasons stated in the preceding note, and also because the principles professed by Lord Derby and most of his followers were inconsistent with those which I have often asserted in debate. Nothing more was said to me on the subject: the *Times* suggested that the Gov.-Gen.ship of India was reserved for me, in case Lord Canning came home: and this supposition was favoured by some hints thrown out by the premier.

On Thursday morning the state of affairs altered. Sir E. Lytton, either fearing the loss of his election in Hertfordshire, or as some affirm, desiring his adhesion to be rewarded by a peerage, declined the Colonial Office: it was then transferred to J. Manners. Meanwhile Malmesbury and Pakington came to me, imploring that I would reconsider my decision, and both affirming that after Lytton's secession the ministry could not go on. I took some time to reflect: and then went to Lord D. I told him that I felt all the difficulties that had weighed upon me before: that I had no great hope of the success of the experiment: that it was still my earnest wish to remain a private member: but that if he told me he considered my support essential, considering the relations between us, I thought myself not justified in withholding it. He expressed regret that I should feel any difficulty on the subject: and recommended me to offer myself as the subordinate of Lord Ellenborough in the Commons, in which position, he said, I should have less responsibility for the acts of the cabinet than if a member of it. This offer I accepted: and was actually on my way to Lord E.'s house, when Lord Malmesbury and Pakington (I believe) having heard from my Father what was proposed, and in turn informing Disraeli, procured the alteration of the arrangement: displaced Manners from the Colonies, and persuaded Lord D. to appoint me. All was settled by 4.30 p.m., the discussions I mention having begun about 2 p.m.

The recommendation given to me to serve under Lord E. was undoubtedly with a view to my succeeding to the Gov.-Gen.ship. Indeed Lord Derby said so.

How this experiment will end seems doubtful: it is just possible the ministry may survive one session, quite impossible, without some special favour of fortune, that it should survive a second.

Personally, I can only lose by what has occurred: it seemed to me, however, that I had no alternative, and I believe my motives will be understood.

The changes of heads through which of late years the Colonial Office has passed are remarkable.

	Colonial Secretaries
Lord Stanley	1841
Mr Gladstone	1845
Lord Grey	1846
Sir J. Pakington	1852
D. of Newcastle	1853
Sir G. Grey	1854
S. Herbert	1855
Lord J. Russell	1855
[Lord Palmerston	1855]
Sir W. Molesworth	1855
Mr Labouchere	1855
Lord Stanley	1858

The Duke of Newcastle took the War Dept. when they were separated in 1854. Sir G. Grey succeeded *ad interim*. Herbert took the office under Lord Palmerston, but resigned on the quarrel about the Sebastopol Committee. Lord J. Russell then held it, but went to Vienna, Palmerston doing the work. Molesworth succeeded on Lord John's resignation, but died in November [1855] when it was offered to me.

Thus, including Palmerston, the C.O. had, in about 15 months (1854–5) 7 different masters. It might be expected that all unity of management would thus be lost. But the excess of the evil works its own cure: for the real conduct of ordinary business falls into the hands of the permanent officials (Merivale[2] and Elliot[3]) who being able and sensible men, manage it well, though without responsibility.

The Boulogne Expedition of 1840

I had often heard from friends of Louis Nap. that they considered this seemingly wild enterprise as a really rational, though audacious, design, which but for accidents had a fair chance of success: I knew also that treachery had been suspected. Therefore, when in the F.O., I took an opportunity of making private enquiries as to the fact. The diplomatists could tell me nothing: but from Capt. Hay,[1] one of the Police Commissioners, I got the following statements, which seemed worth preserving as a piece of secret history. The police keep no records: and Hay (he is since dead) was not a man likely to write Memoirs for his private amusement. I believe therefore that the facts are not recorded except in this paper. Hay had been a Peninsular officer, was an honest, truth-speaking man whatever the professional expedients to which he may have found it necessary to have recourse. I believe his narrative to be accurate: and have copied it exactly as it was received.

The Boulogne Expedition

'In the autumn of 1840 there was a considerable feeling existing among revolutionary parties connected with France, at that time living in London, which I believe had been encouraged by the Chartist disturbances in this country. It was believed the time had arrived to displace Louis Philippe and proclaim a Republic. Proceedings from a movement by communication between parties in this country and in France, had gone so far as to cause a degree of uneasiness in the French Government. The Minister of the Interior had been informed that a plot was on foot in London: and application was made to the Foreign Secretary to ascertain through the police if there was any foundation for the report. Sir Charles Rowan then one of the Commissioners of Police, declined to act officially in the matter: as the Sec. for the Home Dept. did not see just grounds for the police to interfere: at the same time telling me he would be glad if I would put myself in communication with the Foreign Office and the French Embassy, and give them any assistance in my power (in those days there was no regular Detective Police): I set to work by getting introduced to an old German who at that time knew all the foreigners of distinction at that time in London. This person had formerly been employed as a private courier to George IV when Prince Regent: a Capt. C-. Through his means I was made acquainted with the leading men of the French republican party: I soon ascertained there were two plots by different parties to upset the Government. The first I had to look after was headed by Cavaignac, who was chairman of the committee of thirteen who held their meetings once or twice a week at two different public houses in Air Street, and were in communication with the revolutionary party in France. A book was written by the heads of the party in Paris, containing orders and regulations for the republicans, and was printed here for distribution in France, but only in very small numbers. These copies were intended (for those?) in France who had presses, (which were afterwards destroyed) by whom copies were made, and sent to every other member of the society: these copies were destroyed after they had been perused and undertood. A man named Fleenden, a pilot, a desperate character, and a smuggler, was the person employed to carry intelligence from the party in this country to France, not deeming it prudent to trust to the post. From enquiry I found the French Govt. had nothing to fear from them, they being all extremely poor; and I gave such information as enabled the French Govt. to deal with them in their own way.

To obtain information as to the proceedings of Louis Napoleon was a much more difficult task: but after some trouble I found there was a French doctor and two women in the secret: the doctor was a man in needy circumstances: and measures were taken accordingly. A medical man in whom I could confide was instructed to make his acquaintance and on some consultation case to take his opportunity to extract the information required, the names of the ladies, etc., one of which was a very fashionable Englishwoman, the other, a beautiful French girl: letters from France, from a Doctor Montmalière in Paris, who had undertaken to assist Louis Napoleon, were sent under cover to them: I by an excuse to obtain tickets for a concert made myself acquainted with Mad^{lle.} Bettecourt: and after a few visits found out enough to satisfy myself of the information being correct.

Mrs Edwards, the English lady, I found was quite in the confidence of Louis Napoleon: and was employed to communicate with his party through the above-named Doctor in Paris: and on the information I gave steps were taken by the French Govt to intercept and open letters addressed as stated: when enough was discovered to satisfy them, proceedings were taken by the French police, and a trap (was) laid, frequent letters were sent under cover to Mad^{lle.} Bettecourt's mother, to Mad^{lle.} B., describing the enthusiastic feeling of the people of France and their anxiety to receive Louis Napoleon. Money was also liberally supplied. On the day which had been fixed for his departure from this country to Boulogne, where he had in reality a considerable party ready, but was precipitated by a false representation that everything would be ready a month before the day intended by his real friends, and urging him immediately to take advantage of the feelings in his favour. . . . He was therefore induced to start for Boulogne.

Mrs Edwards got her recall from Paris, where she had been staying, watching proceedings, for two months previous, and was on a given day to return to Paris and to take in her charge a portfolio containing a proclamation to the French people from Louis Napoleon as their emperor. She was directed to meet him at the entrance of Place Louis XV and see him make his triumphal entry. On the evening of her arrival at Dover there was waiting at the hotel a young Frenchman on his way to Calais. On board the packet the gentleman was very attentive: offered his services, the passage was rough, and on their arrival at Calais he offered her a seat in his carriage and safe escort but to remain at Calais to dine and stay that night: to which she consented. Suffice to say, the lady in the morning found her friend gone, her room door locked: the box containing all Louis Napoleon's papers absent: and on enquiry she was told he had taken his departure en route for Paris that morning at 3 o'clock'.

Here the mem. ends: the result was, that Napoleon's accomplices were arrested; a regiment much in his favour and on which he relied was changed, and replaced by one of undoubted fidelity: in short, he walked into a trap.

1860

Spring 1860.[1] . . . Called on Lord Cowley, who talked frankly of politics: said he did not think the Emperor had been wilfully false in his language respecting Nice and Savoy: he was sincere when in the Milan proclamation he disclaimed all wish for the aggrandisement of France: but since that time circs had brought him into conflict both with the protectionists and the priests, two of the most powerful interests in France, and he had felt the necessity of doing something to conciliate opinion, the more so as the Villafranca peace was very unpopular. There was no doubt, he said, but that the Austrian quarrel was planned ever since the end of the Russian war. Napoleon had during that war expressed a strong desire to reconstruct Poland. Baffled in his Polish project, he had then turned his eyes to Italy. The defence of Turkey, he used to contend all along, was not an object in itself worth the cost of so great a struggle. It was certain however that he was not ready at the moment when the war broke out: he would have delayed it another year if he could.

He added that Napoleon had made an offer to the English govt to agree on a proportion of force which should give England a preponderance at sea, and himself the same on land: this (as I understand) was after the Crimean war. The arrangement fell through from distrust on the part of our ministers. Napoleon then warned Lord Cowley that he must increase his fleet, and expressed a hope that his doing so would not be misunderstood.

29 July 1860.[2] Ernest Jones,[3] the ex-chartist leader, applied to me for pecuniary help, which I gave him. He had given up politics, and taken to the bar, where (1863) he is now getting on moderately well. He was heir to an estate of £2,000 a year, which he lost by joining the chartists: and his motive for leaving them was the jealousy with which he was pursued by rival agitators, the most virulent of them being one Reynolds,[4] who is believed to have given Govt. information of the plans to which he was privy in Feb. and March 1848.

1861

Flyleaf. Total received by me since July '51,[1] about £21,600. Total given, in charity or for public objects not political, up to 31 Dec. 1859, £5,800: since that date, to Jan. 1 1861, £947 3s 6d (say £940). Total given from July '51 until now, £6,740.[2]

1 January 1861. Knowsley. My Father recovering, but has not yet left the house. . . . Wrote, among other letters, to wish Lady J. Russell joy of her step-daughter's marriage.[3] There had been for the last two years a foolish story going about to the effect that I was to marry this young lady: insomuch that in 1859 Talbot wrote to congratulate me on the choice: I do not know whether Lord and Lady John desired it, but the rumour made me, of late, unwilling to accept invitations to Pembroke Lodge.

3 January 1861. . . . Wilson Patten[4] spoke to me about a certain Church Association which is forming, its centre in London, and having branches in all the main towns . . . He thinks it more likely to do harm than good, that it will alienate moderate men, provoke the nonconformists to active hostility, and revive a class of controversies the most injurious to social peace. He wished to speak on the subject to my Father.

. . . Mr Melly[5] talked much about volunteering: he has been a strong Liberal in politics, but is in process of conversion: he assured me that the effect of the movement on political opinion could not be overrated, and that it would lead to the return of a thoroughly Conservative H. of Commons. But as though to save appearances, he added (wh. is certainly true) that it would train a large number of persons to habits of self-government, and thus to a real Liberalism.

12 January 1861. Colville[6] has no country house, but lives during the autumn and winter in his yacht, and among his friends: his estate is said to be between £3,000 and £4,000 a year, but I know this only from report. He has been unfortunate in domestic life: his wife, a daughter of Lord Carrington, a very pleasing person, went mad after childbirth, and though recovered, is not secure from relapse, remaining eccentric in her habits. He is sensible, intelligent, has considerable knowledge and much tact. He acts as manager for Lord Derby's party in the Lords, and does it judiciously.

27 January 1861. Hatfield by 9 a.m. train: found Lord Salisbury recovered, and able to walk as usual. No guests.

Lord Delawarr's[7] affairs discussed: they are worse than before: out of £18,000 to £19,000 which is the rental, £10,000 are absorbed in payment of interest on his debt; some part of which seems to have been incurred on personal security, and at cost of 14%. . . . They are running through their property in mere carelessness: though the trustees have entire control of estate matters, they have not power over the household, and bills of large amount are presented them from time to time, which they must either pay or create a public scandal.

29 January 1861. London by 9 a.m. train . . . Went to see Disraeli, and found him. He is lately from Windsor:[8] says the Court is utterly disgusted with the state of foreign affairs, and apparently not well pleased with the conduct of its own ministers: this last was rather a conjecture than a certainty, for neither the P. nor Q. would speak on the subject. The Q. complained that there was a deficiency of armaments, that the country was undefended: although the expenditure for purposes of war is greater than at any time since 1815. D. made some allusion to the strength of the Conservative party: 'What is the use of that,' said the P., 'the country is governed by newspapers, and you have not a newspaper.' He then went on to say that the whole English press, except the *Times*, was influenced by foreign governments: (which is true of some journals: the *Chronicle* being in French hands, the *Daily News* acting as the agent of Sardinia): the Q. broke in, saying the *Times* was as corrupt as the rest. D. repeated to me what he had said before in letters: that it was the business of Conservatives to support the ministry: he evidently looks to the death or retirement of Lord P. as an event not likely to be long delayed, and expects a general disruption of his followers to succeed. He said it was certain there could be no reform bill: and probably the immense deficit now existing would check Gladstone in any attempt at financial change. As to Italian, and foreign affairs generally, he did not see his way: thought the Emperor himself undecided, thought there were no present designs on the Rhine: did not see what would come out of the Italian complication, and knew no one who could give any information. He appeared to expect a quiet session, so far as in the uncertainty of politics anything can be foreseen.

30 January 1861. . . . I have been reading during the last few days De Tocqueville's correspondence, just published. I had known the writer slightly, having met him at Macaulay's house. His manner was very agreeable, simple, natural, and lively. His two great works on democracy in America and on the *ancien régime* in France have both been long familiar to me; the first I have read twice, and made an abstract of part of it, which is probably among my papers.

3 February 1861. . . . The Duke of Newcastle's son, Lincoln, is to marry[9] a natural daughter of Mr H. Hope: his father-in-law pays or compounds for the payment of his debts, with £35,000 down, and allows them £10,000 or £12,000 a year. They will in the end have four times as much. The marriage is said to be made by Lord L.'s mother – Lady Lincoln that was. The Duke of N. has quarrelled with his son, as last year with his daughter: the match is not brilliant as to rank, certainly, but it saves the dukedom from ruin, otherwise inevitable.

4 February 1861. . . . Dined with Disraeli: present, Pakington, J. Manners, Peel, Northcote, Jolliffe: we read the Queen's speech, wh. is moderate and conservative in tone: no mention of reform. It was discussed, but there seemed nothing in it to object to. D. talked much about church rates, on which he said he had been consulting with the Bp. of Exeter: I thought his ideas very wild: and no two of the party agreed as to what should be done.

8 February 1861. . . . Talk with D., he says the quarrel between Whigs and ultras is irreconcilable, that overtures are made to him daily, asking him to turn out the Ministry, which he declines: renewal of our old conversations on the possibility of a fusion – Grey, Lewis, perhaps Clarendon, to join Lord D.

9 February 1861. . . . Dined at home: talk with Lord D. who has been reading the report of the Civil Service committee of last year: to my surprise and pleasure I find that he is willing to go farther than I had ventured to recommend in this report: he strongly supports, and claims to have originated, Mr Mann's plan, by which every person is invited to qualify himself for an appointment by entering into an open competition, success in which does not necessarily imply success in obtaining employment, but the Minister is bound to choose only out of the list of those who have passed. . . . But that my Father should recommend a plan by which patronage, as such, is utterly swept away, is almost in itself a guarantee of the ultimate success of the principle.

10 February 1861. . . . The report is that Herbert's health is seriously affected: that he has an incurable, though slow, disease of the kidneys. If he breaks down, his loss will be felt . . .

11 February 1961. . . . Jolliffe tells me that the present calculation of Conservative strength gives 304 members, which it is expected that coming elections will increase to 307 or 308. But it is only on great party occasions that this full strength is available, and perhaps not always then, if an attack were made on the Ministry which the country gentlemen thought premature.

14 February 1861. . . . Dined with D., Pakington, and Jolliffe: Sir C. Wood told us what ministers mean to do with the four vacant seats . . . The seats are assigned to the W. Riding, S. Lancashire, Birkenhead, and Chelsea-with-Kensington: one to each: on the whole, this seems as fair a disposition as could have been made: it is only inadequate so far, as that each of these constituencies ought to have had two members instead of one, except Birkenhead. By our statistics of 1859, there are 62 boroughs having two members each, which have electors fewer than 1,000. A partial disfranchisement, not extinguishing any borough, but taking away one of its two members, would give from these, 62 seats disposable. And this was about the extent of disfranchisement at first contemplated by Lord D.'s government: afterwards it was reduced to 15 seats, partly in consequence of opposition within the cabinet, and partly because of the general apathy out of doors.

16 February 1861. . . . Walk from H. of C. with Disraeli: he exulted in the gain of Aberdeenshire, said Cork would follow, and that happen what might, Palmerston durst not dissolve for fear of losing all his Irish seats – result of the old quarrel with the Pope. We talked of Locke King's motion of Tuesday next, and how to meet it.

17 February 1861. . . . Last night, Brand, the Whig whipper-in, began, uninvited, to talk to me about the agreement of opinion between Whigs and moderate Conservatives (in wh. he is quite right): it was a pity that their divisions should throw power into the hands of the extreme party: could there not be a fusion? I do not suppose he was authorised to hold this language, but coming from him, it is significant.

18 February 1861. . . . Dined H. of C. with Disraeli: who was full of the expected victory at Cork: he says the union of the R. Catholics with the Conservative party has been his object for twenty years.

6 March 1861. . . . Lord Lyndhurst's only unmarried daughter[10] has been, and still is, ill: a rumour spread through London, now generally believed, that her illness is a confinement: Gen. Armitage the father. This explains Lady L.'s looks of anxiety and misery, which I had ascribed to her husband's health.

Adolphus Vane,[11] who has been several times mad and has recovered again, is now sent to an asylum. He broke out violently, made a riot in the streets, and was with difficulty taken in charge by the police.

15 March 1861. . . . Dined H. of C. with Disraeli: who gave me a long account of a conversation he had had with Bright. He described Bright as utterly disgusted with the state of politics, as expressing himself only anxious to retire, and as convinced that he had been duped in the arrangements of 1859, by which he, and he alone, of all the prominent liberals, was excluded from office. D. who enjoys such disclosures, fostered his discontent by an affected sympathy. Bright complained that even Milner Gibson had turned Whig and left him. Of Cobden, who has in effect retired from public life, he said nothing.

20 March 1861. . . . Talk with D.: he lamented the apathy of the country gentlemen, said it was impossible to induce them to attend, even where their own interests were concerned, there was nothing new in this, it had been so ever since he knew the House: in Buckinghamshire there were many men of large income who took no part even in county affairs, hunted all the winter, and seldom stirred beyond their estates. I agreed in what he said, but thought in my own mind that considering what bad judges they show themselves of their own interests, as in the Corn Law case, their absence from the House is not much to be regretted. Nevertheless, it is unsatisfactory to see the opposition benches completely bare, except the front bench, from 7 to 10 every night, unless an important party division is likely to come on. The real work of the House is done by less than 200 out of 654 members: and of these the majority are either liberals of the middle class, or officials past and present. The only unofficial member on our side who attends regularly is Spooner,[12] now 80 years of age: and he is a banker, not a squire.

23 March 1861. , , , The Duke of Bedford[13] is supposed to be dying: his estates are little less than £200,000 a year, clear of debt: he has in his lifetime paid off £1,100,000 of encumbrances: an almost incredible sum. He has done this without incurring the reproach of avarice, though always accounted saving and prudent. It is understood that these vast possessions will be left in the hands of trustees, to accumulate still farther: Ld. Tavistock[14] being incapable from the state of his health of attending to business. He will live in London, and receive an allowance, it is said, of £20,000 a year.

Lord Tavistock's life is a mystery: he was once in the H. of C. but left it early: never goes into society: his occupations and pursuits are absolutely unknown: he is not married, but has a mistress, and several children by her. Hastings Russell[15] is the next heir: unless, as some suppose, Lord T. is secretly married to the lady with whom he lives, or used to live.

26 March 1861. . . . Hayward[16] spoke of the Duke of Newcastle's affairs, his quarrels, his habit of complaining of ill-luck, he had never entirely forgiven being passed over when the last vacancy for the Gov.-Gen.ship occurred, though always saying that he should not have accepted the place, that his health is not good enough for India: the Duke ascribed his not having the offer to Vernon Smith (Lord Lyveden) who had either misunderstood, or affected to misunderstand, something he had said about not wishing for it.

9 April 1861. . . . The editor of the *Standard*[17] called, wishing to know, he said, something of the policy of the party: I could tell him but little, for in truth there is no policy at this moment, except that of keeping quiet and supporting ministers. He seems an intelligent and moderate man.

11 April 1861. . . . Edwin James[18] has resigned his seat for Marylebone, in consequence, it is said, of being totally ruined: he had lived fast in his earlier days, and raised money of the usurers at enormous interest. The *Times* has a leader referring to his case, but without mention of his name.

15 April 1861. Called at 11 on Sir C. Wood[19] to discuss the question of legislative and executive councils for India: sat with him till 12.30 . . . Gladstone opened his budget . . . I endeavoured to collect opinions as to the chance of this budget passing: Walpole and Estcourt were disposed to consent to it, though doubtful: Disraeli angry and annoyed. We dined together, and there was much talk of war: J. Manners, as usual, saying that it must come, and we be involved in it. D. seems more than ever convinced that Naples will be separated from the Sardinian Kingdom, and put under a Murat dynasty.

18 April 1861. . . . E. James's resignation has made a vacancy for Marylebone: three candidates came forward: one Lewis,[20] an Irishman, hitherto unknown, who, Dunne tells me, offered himself not long ago (I suppose in 1859) as a Conservative candidate, but was refused, since which he has become an ultra-liberal . . . Lewis won, with no trouble. – It is now said that James has been compelled to retire by Lord Yarborough, who threatens to expose him: he has induced Lord Worsley (Lord Yarborough's son) to assist him in raising £30,000 by bills, which the Worsley family must pay: in this transaction there is nothing illegal or fraudulent, but as James must have known when he raised the money that he never could pay it, and as Lord Worsley is, or then was, a young man and weak, it is a disagreeable affair.

Talk with Herbert,[21] whom I met at the Travellers, about the Lord-Lieutenant of Ireland: he says Lord Carlisle is more unfit for the office than any man he ever had to do with. He cannot say no: he grants things which he ought to refuse, promises which he cannot perform, all out of good nature, and then, 'when I used to go to him to complain, instead of defending his conduct he would apologise, beg pardon humbly, and promise that it should never happen again: so I went away disarmed, and next day things were as bad as before.' One of the jobs in question was so outrageous that he wrote to Palmerston through Hayter[22] to complain of it. Palmerston answered, that it certainly did look like a job, but a Lord-Lieutenant ought to be able to do a job now and then.

Herbert wants the office done away with, and a thorough centralisation of all business in London: he thinks this might have been effected in 1850, but it is now less easy, there is an organised agitation on the subject, and the country would be up in arms. The failure of the measure in 1850 (which I voted for, and which was supported by more than 300 members) was owing to the Duke of Wellington: he took a view of the matter, which no one well understands, saying the military command ought not to be left to any person in a position inferior to that of a Lord-Lieutenant. His authority, not his reasoning, convinced the H. of Lords, and the bill dropped.

19 April 1861. . . . Long talk last night with Disraeli about the budget: I urged him, whatever he did, not to press for a further reduction of the income tax after the penny already conceded: to this he assented: we then discussed the question of tea and sugar as against paper: he would come to no conclusion, thought it better to protract the debate as long as possible, and watch the temper of the House. We agreed, however, that if a division were expedient, it could not be taken on a better question: since to reduce tea or sugar duties is a concession, not to the richer, but to the poorer class.

He threw out a hint that if the ministry of 1858 were formed again without a coalition, Malmesbury ought to go to Paris,[23] and I should be placed at the Foreign Office, as being the post of difficulty, as India was in 1858. This is flattering, but the bare idea of such a responsibility weighs on my mind: nor do I believe that my health would endure it. It is however possible that Lord Clarendon would join us, and then that office would naturally fall to him.

20 April 1861. . . . My Father told me of an agreement between himself and Ld Palmerston, negotiated through Malmesbury at the beginning of the year.[24] The terms were, that Conservative support was to be given to the ministry, on condition that they did not support France or Italy in any attempt forcibly to dispossess Austria of Venice: that they did not make church rates a government question: and that they would check Gladstone's projects of increased direct taxation. This last article was vaguely worded, and he and D. now seem to think that in spirit at least it has been violated.[25]

13 May 1861. . . . In the House a debate concerning Mr Stewart,[26] M.P. for Cambridge, who is subject to fits of lunacy, and expecting one of these had lately placed himself in Dr Forbes Winslow's[27] asylum as a certified patient: retaining however entire freedom to go in and out, and visiting London from time to time: while in this state the budget debate came on, and Mr S. went up and voted: being, as appears by the evidence of several members, in full possession of his faculties at the time: but nevertheless being registered as a lunatic patient . . . Roebuck brought on the question of his vote . . . It is curious to see how entirely the House regards itself as a club: great indignation was expressed at the private affairs of Mr S. being brought into question, much was said as to the pain to his family: but of the main question, his fitness to vote at the time, only a few words. The truth is, we require a law to prevent persons of insane mind, being members, from voting: they may do so at present, and the case has often occurred: oftener, as is natural, in the Lords than among the Commons.

14 May 1861. . . . News this evening of the Duke of Bedford's death,[28] which had been long expected. Though seldom seen, he filled a considerable place in society, not only from his rank, wealth, and connection with Lord John, but from his large acquaintance, and the sound judgment which he is said always to have shown on matters affecting the Whig party. He was a great letter-writer, and his correspondents kept him acquainted with whatever passed either at home or abroad. His chief merit lay in the admirable management of his vast estates: on these he found a debt of £1,100,000, the whole of which he continued to pay off, while building model cottages, and making necessary improvements on a large scale.

23 May 1861. Hatfield by 10 a.m. train for the day: returned by 4.30 train: on way back read a pamphlet by Maurice on the *Essays and Reviews*, which I tried hard to understand, but could not.

... Navy estimates discussed all the evening, little progress made. The House was very empty, not more than 60 members when I came, not more than 100 at any time: the benches below the gangway, as usual, the most crowded. Not one country gentleman on our side was present, except Henley: Pakington and I had the front opposition bench for upwards of an hour to ourselves.

Met D. going away: he stopped me, I turned back to walk with him: he was full of some great project of attack for Monday, in which he expected to beat the government: he had been in communication with Lord Normanby, with the Irish Catholics, with the disappointed Whigs; and anticipated great results. The Irish M.P.'s are dissatisfied with the cabinet, because Gladstone, who has always been hostile to the Galway contract scheme,[29] has taken advantage of some failure of duty on the part of the Galway company to cancel the contract. He had a legal right to do so, but appears to have strained this right to the utmost: and they have some cause of complaint, for their failure to fulfil the contract arises mainly from the uncertainty in which they were kept during more than a year as to the probability of Parliament sanctioning their subsidy. Till that question was decided, it was impossible that capitalists should come forward, or the building of ships proceed in earnest.

29 May 1861. ... Dined Sir J. Hogg's[30] ... Mrs Gladstone, whom I sat next, could think and speak of nothing but her husband and the division of tomorrow: she seemed astonished at any of his measures being opposed, and almost intimated that she looked on such opposition as personal to him.

30 May 1861. ... The division[31] was taken at 1 ... Numbers, 296 to 281 ... Many [Conservatives] stayed away; partly because they thought the Irish members had entered into a conspiracy against Lord Palmerston on account of the Galway contract, and did not choose to be mixed up with that: partly also, I believe, because they do not really want the government disturbed, though they like to see it kept in check.

31 May 1861. ... Ld. D. much put out at the result of last night's division: he professes not to wish to return to office, but he would undoubtedly have liked to defeat ministers, and especially Gladstone, of whom he speaks in very angry terms.

Conversation last night with Kelly[32] about a case in which he has been concerned respecting the law of succession duty. He has had before him the returns made to the Inland Revenue office, and is startled, he says, to see the extent to which the largest landed fortunes are encumbered. He gave three instances: the Duke of Sutherland has nominally £200,000 a year, but his encumbrances amount to £130,000 leaving him £70,000: the Duke of Devonshire has charges upon him to the amount of £120,000, out of a rental of about the same amount: the Duke of Norfolk has £80,000 nominally, and £40,000 after deducting encumbrances. Many of these, however, are charges for life only, not permanent. Lord Bute with £100,000, and Lord Brownlow with £80,000, are entirely free from debt. The truth is, fashionable society discourages and ridicules any man who looks after his affairs, while it has a very strong sympathy with those who have ruined themselves, no matter how much by their own fault. A certain contempt of economy and prudence has always been characteristic of an aristocracy.

3 June 1861. . . . Kelly and others asked me what truth there was in rumours that had reached them to the effect that Disraeli meant to throw up the leadership. I took on myself to deny their truth: and soon after, meeting D. led him to talk of Thursday last. He seemed vexed by the number (about 20) of Conservatives who had stayed away from the division: taking it as a mark of want of confidence: he had also had an interview with Ld D. whom he seemed to find impracticable on some plan which he had suggested: I did not ask details: but it was clear that there was no intention of resigning, only a little natural ill-humour, perhaps incautiously expressed. Taylor[33] likewise talks of treachery: though a division lost by only 15, on a question of confidence, is no discredit to an opposition.

. . . Hammond,[34] whom I met, described Lord John Russell at the Foreign Office. 'He is very indolent, lets things go their own way: but when a difficulty arises, he seems to wake up, he becomes another man, and his courage and resource carry him over all difficulties.' These were not Hammond's words but they express his meaning pretty accurately.

5 June 1861. . . . Lord Clarendon talked much about the late Duke of Bedford: says the property is tied up in the strictest manner, the present Duke having only a life interest: so that the stories of its being put in trust are rather exaggerated than untrue. The late Duke's anxiety to improve his property, he says, grew to a monomania: so much so that in his last illness he would not allow himself little delicacies which the doctors ordered. His wealth was a torment to him.

17 June 1861. . . . Debate on appropriation of the four [vacant] seats resumed: the House got into confusion, a dozen plans being laid before it at once: Ministers would propose nothing: Disraeli interposed, but solely with the view of making mischief, and increasing the embarrassment: he wants to throw out the bill altogether, for no reason except that its rejection would humiliate his opponents. Indeed, he acknowledged as much, and a rather sharp dispute arose between us: but it passed over, leaving us good friends. The proposition of giving a third member to Middlesex was thrown out, though supported by the cabinet: Palmerston then announced that they would consent to the scheme of giving four members to the West Riding: this I was glad of, having supported it when proposed by Collins, though only about 80 members followed him into the lobby. Birkenhead does not seem to be opposed . . .

A meeting of my Father's friends was held this day at Lord Salisbury's: I did not attend, but heard it went off well. I doubt whether these meetings do good, except in emergencies: those who come require no stimulus, and those who want advice mostly stay away. There is discontent among a considerable section of the Conservatives, especially the Irish: they want office, and have no idea of a party leader not using every exertion to get into power, whether he can stay there or not. Ld D. is well known to prefer the indirect and irresponsible power which he holds in the Lords, to office: and this preference naturally disgusts the more ardent of his supporters. Others dislike Disraeli as not sufficiently prejudiced for them: others again object to the Irish alliance. Of this alliance D. says, 'Ireland is agricultural, aristocratic, and religious: therefore Ireland ought to be Tory', but he does not allow enough for the antipathies of religion and race.

18 June 1861. . . . Page Wood,[35] at dinner, told me that on principle, he had never taken the life of any animal for pleasure: he condemns utterly all shooting, hunting, and I suppose fishing also.

25 June 1861. . . . D. told me last night, in conversation about Bethell, that my Father had made Chelmsford[36] Chancellor without consulting him (D.) and against his wish. He would have preferred to go on with St Leonards,[37] who would probably have served if pressed. D.'s leading idea in such matters is the wealth of the persons promoted to the peerage. Chelmsford has made nothing, for both his habits and those of his wife are expensive: he has moreover six children.

4 July 1861. Mr Entwistle[38] called to urge me to stand for Lancashire: he pressed me to consider the matter, which I said I would, and answer next day.

5 July 1861. Much talk last night with D. as to representation of Lancashire: he is anxious to bring forward Sir R. Gerard,[39] who has every good quality, but is unlikely to succeed, being a Catholic. Entwistle called again. I gave him my final answer, in the negative: he pressed me hard, and I felt some regret in refusing what is undoubtedly an honour, and probably one within my reach. My reasons for refusing are: that I have often pledged myself to the people of Lynn to remain their member: that to abandon Lynn would be to sacrifice the results of several years exertion and considerable expenditure, the object of which has been to create an influence there which should be permanent in the Stanley family (if my brother were of age he might succeed me, and the case would be different): that my present seat is quiet and safe, whereas Lancashire would involve frequent contests: that my political independence, which is at present complete, would be considerably lessened: that the great cost of contesting Lancashire would put me entirely in Lord Derby's hands, since without his assistance I could not venture to stand, and he could therefore withdraw me from Parliament whenever he pleased:[40] and lastly, that to accept what I have so lately refused in positive terms, my refusal having been made public, would look like vacillation on my part, and might even be considered as involving a breach of faith towards other candidates.

13 July 1861. . . . I do not think it expedient, on various accounts, to spend another winter at Knowsley: and the three months from Nov. 1st could be passed by me abroad without breaking any engagement except that of attending the January quarter sessions. The matter will bear further considering. If I could get any employment of public utility, no matter what, I should not care to stir: but action in some form I must have.

Eglinton told a singular story of an Earl of Buchan,[41] his immediate predecessor in the Scotch peerage, who succeeded to his brother: he had been left absolutely penniless, and used to ride races (nominally as a gentleman rider) for money: latterly he got into the habit of selling himself to lose races which he was engaged to win, and being detected in a too obvious attempt of this kind, was hooted off the course at Manchester.

14 July 1861. . . . Lord Granville lately told Lord D. that if Herbert had retained his health, he must have been Palmerston's successor, and even hinted that an arrangement to that effect had been made! Every one regrets the loss of H. to public life: he was a ready speaker, amiable and accomplished in society, well-intentioned in politics, and kindhearted: though bitter in his invective, and not (I think) always sincere in his professions: at least there was a wish to please which made him often say what he did not mean. His retirement weakens the H. of Lords, which can ill afford it. There is much comment on the utter inactivity of that body during the present session . . . All the business is carried on by a few members: of young peers who take an active part, there are none, except Carnarvon and Wodehouse: by far the larger proportion of those who speak often are peers newly created, such as Chelmsford, Lyveden, Taunton, Llanover, Stanley of Alderley, Brougham, Cranworth, etc., and the rest with few exceptions, peers whose political training has been in the H. of C. . . . Observation and thought confirm me in the belief, recorded already in this journal, that to those peers who have wealth and social influence, the right of sitting in the Lords is a diminution of political power. They could always get returned to the Commons, if willing to sit there; and in that House they would exercise the reality, not as at present, hold only the show of power.

1 August 1861. . . . Walk with Sir E. Lytton[42] in Hatfield park: I find he takes much the same view as I do of the state of politics: not expecting or wishing a Derbyite administration to be formed.

3 August 1861. Talk of the Duke of Buckingham's[43] affairs – Hayward gives instances which are almost incredible of their mismanagement. E.g. the Duke liked to have a sum of ready money by him, not less than £10,000. To keep up this fund he was compelled to borrow, and it cost him in 8 or 9 years, not less than £90,000, for which there was absolutely nothing to show. In another case, an estate was bought for an annuity of £4,000 a year during the Duke's life, the estate yielding £700 only. It was wanted for election purposes.

. . . News, in afternoon, of Herbert's death: which will surprise no one, though it has come more suddenly than was expected. Cardwell, it appears, was removed from the Irish Secretaryship without being consulted, in order that it might be offered to C. Fortescue, who refused it:[44] Cardwell was then told that he might remain, but with a natural feeling declined. He is very ill pleased, as are all parties in the late changes, except Lewis, who says that one government office is like another, the system is the same in all.

4 August 1861. . . . Stanhope has discovered, in his researches for the life of Pitt, that Mrs Fox, the wife of the great orator, had previously been the mistress of Lord Derby, and to the day of her death received an annuity out of the Knowsley estates: a singular proof of want of delicacy on her husband's part. I think he said that she had also a similar annuity from the Duke of Bedford. He told me also that it was established that Fox had had a son borne to him by Lady Sarah Bunbury: this child's existence was kept secret, and its end not known. The proofs of this were conclusive.

6 August 1861. . . . Lord Granville said to Hayward, that he had known both French and English society for many years, and never remembered anything like the social corruption which prevails in both countries at the present time. I report his words as they were quoted, though not well understanding them.

25 August 1861. . . . Much talk with Mr Ellice:[45] he says, in his view the most formidable symptom in the state of modern society is the growing indifference to public affairs, and even to society, shown by young men of rank. For one that takes an active part in politics, there are ten that take none: nor are great houses opened as they used to be: Holland House, Devonshire House, Holkham, Woburn – how are they now represented? It is mere idleness and egotism and indolence, by which they are sure to suffer, and the radicals to gain. I did not altogether dissent . . . As to the alleged seclusion from society of those who naturally ought to lead it, I cannot deny the fact, nor explain it.

He spoke of the proposed creation of peers at the time of the Reform Bill: said that Lord Brougham's doubt[46] whether the threat would have have been acted up to was absurd: he had the list made out: the names contained in it were 97: out of those only 11 would have been permanent additions to the peerage: the rest being sons of peers, or heirs of peers, or childless men of fortune. He said he had always objected to the profusion with which titles were granted by Lords Russell and Melbourne: he had stopped many such grants: at the time when a reform of the H. of Lords was largely discussed, he had given his plan, which he still thought the only one applicable: he would enforce a pecuniary qualification of £5,000 or

£3,000 a year, clear of all charges, without which no peer should be admitted to sit in the House of Lords by descent.

3 September 1861. Ellice: 'The danger of the present day is a war of classes: I am never afraid of a war of parties, there are some of all classes on each side: but I fear to see our parties broken up, democracy on the one side, wealth and aristocracy on the other.'

. . . Talks of the old royal family: George IV: his madness on certain points: he had a mania for buying up foreign orders, wearing them, and relating stories of how and where they had been conferred upon him. Told the Duke of Wellington that when living at Brighton, he had charged at the head of his regiment down the Devil's Dyke (an impossible feat). 'Very steep, Sir,' was the Duke's answer. William IV used to say of himself that neither he nor any of his family told truth, that it was in the family, they could not help it: but (Ellice added) 'when he came to the throne we never found him out in a lie. He seemed to feel that in his altered position he must be careful.'[47]

After Sir R. Peel's failure to form a govt, and quarrel with the Court, in 1839, the Queen wrote to Lord Melbourne to come and see her, adding that she was sure he would not desert her in her difficulties. Ellice was present when the letter was received: said Lord M. cried like a child. Lord M. on his deathbed declared he was innocent of the relations imputed to him with Mrs Norton.

6 October 1861. . . . Examined the list of the peerage to ascertain how many of the hereditary peers take part in public affairs, or are in any way before the public. The result gave only 81, out of about 380. I do not include Irish or Scotch peers, nor bishops sitting as such. Here is the list. Argyll, Ashburton, Auckland, Belper, Breadalbane, Brougham, Buccleuch, Buckingham, Canning, Cardigan, Carlisle, Camperdown, Carnarvon, Chichester, Clanricarde, Clarendon, Colchester, Combermere, Chelmsford, Cowley, Cranworth, Clyde, Dalhousie, De Grey, Derby, De Ros, Devon, Dufferin, Ebury, Eglinton, Ellenborough, Elgin, Egerton, Eversley, Fortescue, Glenelg, Gough, Grey, Granville, Hardinge, Hardwicke, Harris, Harrowby, Hatherton, Heytesbury, Howard De Walden, Howden, Kingsdown, Lansdowne, Lucan, Lyndhurst, Lyons, Lyttelton, Malmesbury, Marlborough, Melville, Monteagle, Newcastle, Normanby, Northumberland, Overstone, Redesdale, Richmond, Russell, Rosslyn, St Germans, St Leonards, Salisbury, Sefton, Shaftesbury, Somerset, Stanhope, Stanley of Alderley, Stratford, Torrington, Tweeddale, Wensleydale, Westbury, Wodehouse, Wrottesley. In all, 81, of whom new creations count for 27. A second list of those whom I hesitated whether to include or exclude gave the following names: Abinger, Albemarle, Bessborough, Cathcart, Colville, Lonsdale, Montrose, Plunket, Ravensworth, Rokeby, Strangford, Teynham: 12 more, or 93 altogether. It is impossible in such cases to draw a line with accuracy and certainty: but in any case the number does not exceed one quarter of the total number. I was astonished in making this and the former statistical calculations with regard to the peerage, to find how many names in it were utterly unknown to me, and I believe also to most people.

14 October 1861. ... Sir E. Lytton[48] came to dinner ... Sir E. in good health, full of life and animation, but says to Lady S.[49] pointedly that he will never hold office again. In this decision there is as much of disappointment as of weariness: his ambition has always been to obtain a peerage, which was refused him in 1859, partly on account of his comparative want of fortune, partly because of his wife's character and conduct. He has forgiven, but not quite forgotten, the failure of his hopes. Jolliffe[50] had, perhaps has, the same wish, and is in a lesser degree alienated in consequence. There is in Lytton's mind a singular mixture of feelings towards Disraeli: he admires him, sneers at him, envies his position, yet cannot quite forget their long-standing intimacy, and the somewhat similar careers they have run. On the whole, his feelings of dislike prevail, and they are expressed with sufficient plainness.

18 October 1861. ... Met Disraeli, who asked after my Father. I gave an unfavourable account as to strength,[51] thinking it well he should be prepared for a possible refusal of office, or retirement from public life. He had heard nothing, thought events would not alter, either in Italy or here: said Napoleon was watching for the separation of Naples, which he expected, and desired: as to Germany D. thought there was no idea in the Emperor's mind of regaining the frontier of the Rhine, but that what he wanted was the frontier of 1814 instead of that of 1815, which would do away the consequences of Waterloo. Europe could not, the Emperor argued, object to a settlement which she had personally imposed on France.

10 November 1861. ... In the evening my Father left for town by night-train: he has a meeting of the Wellington Coll. governors to attend. It seems that a son of Gen. Ridley has been removed from the college for indecent practices, which have spread widely through the school: he thinks the boy has been hardly used, complains of the headmaster to the governors, and thus necessitates this meeting. It is said that these practices are increasing rapidly in the great schools: and that from Eton especially many boys have been removed in consequence.

17 November 1861. ... The only public event of the last few weeks is the conduct of Sir R. Peel[52] as Irish Sec. He seems to have determined on indulging the Irish by a display of their own national character, and presenting as marked a contrast as possible to his predecessor, Cardwell. Dr Cullen having attacked him in the ordinary style of the Catholic priests, that is, very violently, he has retorted in the same strain, and got rather the better in the dispute. The Protestants are loud in their rejoicings: the Catholics equally loud in censure. Ireland is thoroughly stirred up. Many people suspect that Peel's apparent indiscretion masks a well-planned design on the part of his chief, to break with the Catholic party ostentatiously and openly, in such manner as to secure a considerable amount of Protestant support. By this device nothing is lost, for the Italian policy of ministers has alienated the Catholic support they might otherwise have reckoned on: and something may be gained, for Disraeli, by coquetting with the Pope's party, has roused a good deal of suspicion among their opponents. I do not think Peel capable of a political calculation: but he may have been permitted by Palmerston to indulge his temper, without being told why.

It is a proof how naturally men love fighting, that Peel has undoubtedly increased his popularity, though not his reputation for good sense, by getting into this dispute.

There is in Ireland no Conservative and no Liberal party: only Catholics and Protestants, with a small sprinkling of nationalists, men who talk of '98, and dream of a revived Irish parliament. But among both Catholics and Protestants there has undoubtedly grown up, in the last 20 years, a strong feeling of resistance to the factious agitators on both sides. Unfortunately, this feeling does not reach below the upper middle classes: and in forming a jury, the religion of the jurymen is still a consideration of primary importance.

26 November 1861. . . . My speech of Friday last[53] [at King's Lynn] has been discussed in *The Times, D. News, Star, Telegraph, Standard,* and probably other papers. The general effect which it seems to have produced is favourable: it is admitted to be, what I most wanted to make it, a fair statement of the position of affairs: the Liberal journals endeavour to represent it as a protest against Conservative policy, which it is not, but at the utmost only an indirect and implied caution against an exaggeration of that policy. Several persons, Lord Ebury[54] among them, have written me letters of congratulation. I shall be sorry, but not surprised, if offence has been given to strong partisans: but the circs under which I took office in 1858, the language held by many Conservatives, especially of late, the silence which I have generally observed during the last two years, and some charges of inconsistency which I had to meet, made an outspoken statement of my views expedient. I carefully avoided giving new pledges, so that there is nothing for criticism to lay hold of hereafter. It is really the first political move I have made since quitting office in 1859. – I could not avoid noticing that Ld D.'s reception tonight was cold: he would barely speak to me: but these alternations of mood in him do not indicate serious annoyance: they pass off as quickly as they come. (Note. Perhaps it was not worth while to mention this, but as it is set down, I must add that next morning I saw no trace of annoyance).

27 November 1861. . . . Talk about Eton. E. Wilbraham[55] says that boys now write home to their parents (his son has done so, and it is a common custom) for champagne to entertain their friends with at supper. He thinks the masters encourage this sort of thing, as tending to distinguish the school from others, and to limit admissions to sons of rich men. Bad policy! But they, like many men in the middle class, think a display of wealth aristocratic, whereas it is anything rather than that. Aristocracy in its days of power cares little for show and table luxury, which it leaves to rich merchants and the like, desiring for itself influence and recognised superiority.

30 November 1861. . . . An article in today's Press on the Lynn speech, praising the statement of foreign affairs, but hostile as to the rest. The writer gives me credit for intellect, logic, industry, and so forth: but accuses me of being under a necessity of disagreement with other people, of having no sympathies or feelings, of looking exclusively to the material side of public questions, and of being conservative by conviction only, not by temperament. I have heard these things said before, so there may be some truth in them. It is a mistake, however, to think that I am not willing to follow a leader: on the contrary, I should be only too apt to leave in other hands than my own the responsibility of deciding on the questions of the day, if I could find a politician among those with whom the course of events has associated me, in whom to place implicit reliance. My Father's nature and mine differ too widely for me to follow him in this way, however I might wish it: the only other possible chief is Disraeli: with whom I have been long allied: I owe him many hints, old habit has drawn us together, and I admire his perseverance not less than his talent· but how can I reconcile his open ridicule, in private, of all religions, with his preaching up of a new church – and – state agitation? or how can I help seeing that glory and power, rather than the public good, have been his objects? He has at least the merit, in this last respect, of being no hypocrite. – As to Walpole, Pakington, Malmesbury, they are at best colleagues, not chiefs: Lytton has genius, but neither judgment nor health – and– there is no one else.

1 December 1861. . . . At dinner, much talk on American affairs (I took no part, but listened). Lord Derby, C. Stanley, and Talbot all angry, strong for war. Lord D. says 'If they don't give back the men taken their apologies are worthless: and as to withdrawing our minister, that is no punishment.' The others 'Better let them punish one another, without our interfering.' All agree in wishing a long war between north and south, that both may be effectually humbled. There is in this kind of language some national feeling, but there is also a good deal of class jealousy. America is the country of equality, and has thus succeeded, in the minds of our upper classes, to the place which France filled in the days of the great revolution, when France was regarded as the enemy of aristocracy, monarchy, and church establishments.

16 December 1861. News (at 8 a.m.) of the Prince Consort's death, after a few days serious illness, which however was not thought dangerous till yesterday. It is impossible to calculate the consequences of this event: no change could have occurred in politics which was less expected. The effect on the royal family will be unfavourable: the P. of Wales, though good-tempered, and apparently likely to be popular, is, by general report, not gifted with much ability, and a natural reaction from the somewhat excessive strictness of the restraint under which he has been hitherto kept, has led him into some outbreaks, not seriously discreditable, but undignified, and which may be precursors of worse excesses. Between him and the Queen there is not much confidence or liking: it is quite a chance into whose hands he may fall. The Queen herself has long shown indications of a nervous and excitable disposition, requiring care, lest hereditary eccentricities should develop themselves. By the testimony of those who have the best opportunity of knowing the truth, this care has been bestowed, incessantly, and judiciously, by her late husband: her letters were written by him, he was present when she received ministers, nothing small or great was done but by his advice: I have myself, when dining at the Palace shortly after taking the Indian department, heard him, at dinner, suggest to her in German to enquire about this, that, or the other: and the question never failed to follow. No one can replace the Prince as her adviser in daily life: she will probably be guided by someone, but who the person may be, or what the degree of his influence, is necessarily uncertain. The worst consequence possible is one, unluckily, not unlikely: that without being absolutely incapacitated for affairs, she may fall into a state of mind in which it will be difficult to do business with her, and impossible to anticipate what she will approve or disapprove. In such a condition of the Sovereign, the position of an English minister is peculiarly trying: he cannot allege the cause of his embarrassment, nor yet get over it if the royal determination to oppose what he considers necessary cannot be shaken. His only remedy is resignation: and resignation is not to be justified, especially in a case of such delicacy as that supposed, unless the cause of quarrel be grave. It is true that the H. of C. has always shown justice and forbearance in perplexities of so delicate a character.

I have more than once observed, when in office, the contrast between the Queen's letters on business, and the hasty notes which she would occasionally send relating to matters of slight importance. The former were always well-written, sometimes models of good sense and clear style: the latter for the most part slovenly, many words underscored, and the whole full of scratches and corrections. I have no doubt now, from what others have told me, of the cause of this difference.

The Prince had undoubtedly a fixed determination to increase the personal power of the Crown: had he lived to add to his great industry and talent the weight which age and long experience would have given in dealing with statesmen of his own standing, he might have made himself almost as powerful as the Prime Minister of the day. Under the conviction that such was his design, I have watched his career with some jealousy: but who, in his place, and with equal powers, would not have done the like?

25 December 1861. . . . Much gossip is circulating about the P. of Wales, his doings at the Curragh camp: how he got out of his hut at night by the window to visit a woman who was kept by one of his acquaintance, and got stopped by the sentinel on duty. Also how he picked up another woman when at Windsor (or one who followed him there) and introduced her at night into the Castle. The Prince found out something though not all, of what was going on, and the agitation is said . . . to have increased his illness.

30 December 1861. . . . Called on Mrs Moss at Roby: she tells me they are thinking of selling Roby Hall, and moving elsewhere, being crowded by the influx of new inhabitants from Liverpool . . . She talked of the Prince of Wales, whom she met in Switzerland, and heard a good deal concerning him, having been laid up by illness in the house in which he lodged at Interlaken. He was thought by the people of the house to be young and childish for his age: it was observed that his suite talked to each other, seldom addressing him when serious subjects were discussed, but treating him as a boy: he played a boyish trick upon them one day, being nowhere visible at dinner-time, and when all were tired of looking for him, appearing suddenly from under the table. This is just like the story of his firing a gun loaded with powder among the boatmen at Muckross, to frighten them, when the wadding cut open a man's face, and frightened the author of the trick as he deserved.

31 December 1861. . . . My Father told me of the family arrangement which he was contemplating: viz. to put the estates in trust, naming as his trustees F. Hopwood and C. Stanley, without whose consent no sale or exchange is to take place. As I understand him, they are to have no other power of interference with the management. The reason of the arrangement I understand to be, that there are legal difficulties in the way of entailing an estate on two brothers successively, in default of male issue of the elder brother: so at least Lord D. seems to think: and that this, his projected plan, is the only alternative to leaving in his successor's hands an uncontrolled power of disposal, which he is naturally averse to do. . . . In the course of conversation I told Lord D. that I did not care for the power of selling land, provided that of exchanging were left. He however thought it would be for the advantage of the estate that a power of sale were given. The legal necessity for this plan of Lord D.'s is not clear to me, and indeed I suspect some confusion in Lord D.'s mind as to what the lawyer has told him: the plan is however unobjectionable and Lord D. has, morally and legally, a right to settle the estate as he thinks best.

1862

21 January 1862. . . . Much talk about the Wellington College, from which the Salisburys are removing their son. Its popularity was great about a year ago, but has been shaken by the disclosure of indecent practices prevailing there in September last. Between thirty and forty boys have been removed privately though not without a great deal of scandal and gossip. I do not hear that blame is imputed to the headmaster, Mr Benson: on the contrary, he is generally praised: the fault is in bringing together a large number of boys who from the poverty of their parents have been for the most part badly educated, who know little, are not easily made amenable to discipline, and have not the manners or ideas of gentlemen. The school was originally a charitable institution, and the idea of grafting on to the charitable foundation a school for the sons of the wealthier classes, is an afterthought. Besides Lord Salisbury, Hardwicke, Pakington, and the Duke of Argyll have sons there: Hardwicke has withdrawn his, and Pakington will probably do the same.

23 January 1862. Long walk with Disraeli: and political speculation. He considers Albert's death as the commencement of a new reign: it is the destruction of that long-mediated plan of establishing court-influence on ruins of political party which the late Prince had for years been working out with perseverance equal to that of George the Third, and talent infinitely greater. He expects, he says, that Palmerston will be succeeded by another minister of the same party, probably Lord Russell, but that his ministry will not be strong nor durable. He remarked often on the singular fatality which had attended the followers of Peel – the whole party scattered and destroyed in a few years: Graham, Aberdeen, Dalhousie, Herbert, dead: the last two prematurely: Newcastle supposed to be going blind: Cardwell having joined the Whigs: Gladstone trusted chiefly by the Radicals, and at war with the Church, with which all his real sympathies are. Some discussion as to possible arrangements in the event of our being required unexpectedly to take office: but nothing conclusive was settled. He expressed strong dislike to having the F.O. represented in the Commons by an under-secretary: repeating several times that if Malmesbury was to hold that post again, he himself (D.) would represent the department in the Commons. He also said, what I was glad to hear, that he had had enough of being a minister on sufferance, and did not wish for such a position again: and I believe, this is sincerely meant: for since 1859 there has been a marked change in his tactics: less apparent eagerness for office.

3 February 1862. . . . Met W. Cowper, and much talk with him on the way up. . . . The late Prince, he told me, was in the habit of keeping a regular record of public events, in the form of a journal, amplified with copies of letters, extracts from newspapers etc., to which he used often to refer in conversation with his ministers, making no secret of its existence. – I led him to talk of the Prince of Wales whom he described in terms substantially agreeing with what I had heard before: saying that he is no reader, quite devoid of application, popular in manners, quick in receiving ideas when instilled into him by others, not likely to take much interest in affairs: and as yet unusually young for his age. 'In short,' Cowper added, 'he will make a very good constitutional king.'

22 February 1862. . . . Speaker's dinner: sat next Walpole, who talked of Sir J. Graham . . . Walpole said that among Sir James's papers were found notes on every subject discussed, or about to be discussed, in parliament: these often very copious, as though he had been preparing himself to speak on each question as it arose: the practice of making them he continued even through the session of 1860, in which he took scarcely any part: they were tied up in bundles and marked 'Not used.' He added that Graham had given him this piece of advice, 'Speak as seldom as you please, but always prepare yourself as if going to speak.'

23 February 1862. . . . Disraeli said to me yesterday, the Prince's name being mentioned, 'A few years more, and we should have had, in practice, an absolute monarchy: now all that is changed and we shall go back to the old thing – the Venetian constitution – a Doge.' Again, there being talk of a bill which is being brought in to save the Queen the trouble of signing officers' commissions: 'It is all wrong: talk of saving trouble! what you want is to make the public believe that the Sovereign really has something to do.'

2 March 1862. . . . Talk about the Cowley family: it appears they are in absolute poverty: he is a bad manager, spends all his salary and more, has debts, and nothing to fall back upon except his diplomatic pension, with five children to bring up, three of them sons. Nor is there much chance of things mending, for his eldest son, Dangan, has taken to the army as a profession, and shows no sign of talent. He wants to retire from diplomatic life, of which he is heartily weary, but is held back by fear of the entire obscurity into which he and his family will fall.

3 March 1862. . . . Dined with Peel and Disraeli at Bellamy's. D. full of his prospects of forming a cabinet, and busy about the distribution of office. He appears to have abandoned the idea of transferring me to the Foreign Office, of which I am glad.

21 March 1862. . . . Much talk in society of a quarrel between Royston, Lord Hardwicke's son, and Hartington. It seems to have arisen while playing billiards after dinner: Royston being drunk, perhaps the other also: R. used some expression which Hartington disliked, on which H. threatened to kick him if it were repeated: it was repeated, and the threat was executed. A scuffle followed, and blows were exchanged. Royston, who has long been unpopular, from his overbearing manner and general folly, is considered as most to blame. Altogether it is a disagreeable business: and the more so, as several affairs of the same kind have happened of late. Men of the old school shake their heads, and say, 'This will not do. We must have duelling again, it was the only check on violent acts and words.'

8 April 1862. . . . Patten talked sensibly of the folly of the squires, whose first thought is, now that opinion is turning a little in their favour, how to make the game-law more stringent. There is an association forming for this purpose, and returns are being moved for, of the number of convictions under the existing law, with a view to show its inefficiency. This is as Patten truly says, playing into the hands of the enemy.

17 April 1862. Knowsley by 2.40 train with Lord and Lady D.: the train stopped at Huyton: we arrived about 9 p.m.: my father happily less tired with the journey than we had feared. He had a bed-carriage, and lay down all the way. His spirits, which in London had been latterly depressed, revived as soon as he got into country air, the sunshine and fine weather helping. On the way he told me of his intention to print (not publish) some of his translations into English verse from Homer, Horace, and Catullus: on which it seems he has consulted Stanhope. He told me also that he meant to sell all his horses (of which he has but few left) and retire from the turf, keeping only a stock from which to breed.

21 April 1862. . . . Lord D. remembers the time, in his childhood, when the hour of dinner at Knowsley was about quarter past five: it would be followed by a long sitting, perhaps two hours: then the gentlemen would come out, and between ten and eleven there would be a supper, when those who came sober from dinner had an opportunity of making up for lost opportunities. Such was the routine but I suppose only when a party was in the house. He told me (I had heard it before, but forgotten the story) that in his childhood he often recollects to have heard a sort of political catechism, beginning thus. 'What does A stand for?' 'An axe.' 'What is an axe for?' 'To chop off kings' heads.'

'I remember as if it were yesterday,' he said, 'hearing of Perceval's death: I was a boy at school, and my comment upon it was, that it was too good news to be true. Such was the feeling of the Whig opposition of that day.'

'The Prince of Wales came here in 1806, just after Fox's death, he affected great grief, and was in very bad humour. The Liverpool people were prepared to give him a cordial reception: but he would drive into the town in a close carriage, showing himself as little as possible. They were disgusted. Next day he found out the mistake he had made, and wanted to go again, but it was too late, nobody would have cared to see him.'

He talked of the politics of those days: said the man whose reputation increased as he was better known, was Pitt: Fox went much too far in opposition, was violent and factious, but he had the excuse of contending for a principle: he thought that England was fighting on the wrong side, and ought not to succeed. Grenville had less principle than either of them: with him the leading idea was the importance of his family connection, and to this he was always ready to sacrifice the public interest. Grenville undoubtedly had more to do with the French war than Pitt, who went into it against his will.

27 April 1862. . . . Lord D. spoke of his claim to the Hamilton titles and estates, a subject which at one time occupied much of my grandfather's attention. He said he had gone into it, and satisfied himself that he could have made his claim good to at least the Marquisate of Hamilton and Earldom of Arran: but no landed or other estate would have accrued with the titles, and he did not think it worth while to press his claim to a title less distinguished except in point of precedence, than that which he actually holds, at great cost, and to the annoyance of the Duke of Hamilton, his kinsman.

30 April 1862. . . . A meeting of Lancashire members was . . . held in the tea room . . . I moved Patten into the chair, and the whole question[1] was fully gone into. . . . Cobden advised our going on a deputation to the Poor Law Board to have the labour test done away: contending that it was inapplicable in a case where the pauperism of the applicant arose from a case obviously beyond his own control, and cruel to the operative, whose hands were unused to the rough work of breaking stones. This was agreed to . . .

20 May 1862. . . . Talk with Whiteside about the state of the Irish business, which is unsatisfactory: six or seven important bills are brought in, talked about from time to time, no progress made, and the time passed on them is merely wasted. Peel is now admitted, by those who know and like him best, to be too flighty and incoherent for administrative usefulness. He cannot keep to a subject, nor do one thing at a time. Lord Carlisle, though liked, is not respected: there is no directing head. I hear the same opinion from all sides.

24 May 1862. Meeting at Lord D.'s of twenty members of the H.C. to consider how far reduction of expenditure might be possible. The general feeling, elicited by nearly three hours discussion, appeared to be in favour of reduced estimates, but against any vote that might seem to censure ministers for the largeness of theirs. We having passed the estimates without criticism, are responsible for them: and it would not be decent to use the votes of the economico-radical party as a means of defeating Lord Palmerston in a party division. Peel and Pakington were for keeping the expenditure at its present amount: Disraeli opened the case: I spoke strongly for reduction: Lord D. appeared not to disapprove, but he expressed no opinion. Sir M. Ridley talked sensibly, as indeed did most, except Banks Stanhope: and he was only asked in order to mollify him by the compliment of being consulted.

2 June 1862. . . . A meeting was held at the Duke of Marlborough's house, to consider the course to be taken in tomorrow's debate. Stansfeld had made a motion which in plain terms affirmed the necessity of a reduction of expenditure: Lord Palmerston had given notice of an amendment directly approving a large expenditure as necessary· and it was agreed that in order to avoid voting with Stansfeld, a resolution in the same sense as his should be voted as an amendment to Palmerston's. This was drawn up, I believe, by Lord D., was entrusted to Walpole, who agreed to move it.

3 June 1862. . . . Debate on the question of economy, raised by Stansfeld's motion. The House began by an irregular conversation, which the Speaker had not firmness to check, and which ended in a sort of agreement to withdraw all amendments except Palmerston's and Walpole's, so that the debate and division might proceed without impediment. But Palmerston at the outset took an opportunity of declaring that he should consider the motion as one of confidence: and Walpole, either acting in concert with him, or seized with a sudden panic, intimated that under those circs he must ask time to consider whether he should bring on his amendment: which was in effect equivalent to giving it up. This unexpected change took the House by surprise: on reflection that the debate was, for all practical purposes, at an end. Disraeli spoke, though under the mortification, not only of defeat, but of desertion, with more tact, skill, and power, than I have known him show since 1852. He referred to the state of other countries as proving that there was little danger of European war: argued the question of the relative military and naval strength of France and England: contended for the absolute necessity of reduction; and to prevent misunderstanding distinctly explained where and how he wished it to take effect. He referred to the abandonment of Walpole's resolution, in good humour, saying in reference to the Derby tomorrow, that 'the favourite had bolted': and, on the whole, put as good a face on matters as the case allowed. Cobden spoke later in the evening, but the interest of the question was gone.

Stansfeld's resolution was negatived by an immense majority: I should have voted for him, had I voted at all: but as no result was to follow, and the vote might be misinterpreted, I thought it better to go away. Walpole's conduct is blamed by all parties. If he had meant to withdraw his resolution at the first threat of a minister to resign if it were carried, he ought not to have accepted the office of moving it: since the possibility of such a threat being held out was from the first to be contemplated. If he changed his mind in the short interval of twenty-four hours, and broke the engagement into which he had entered, his infirmity of purpose unfits him for public affairs. But there is something besides infirmity of purpose in the course which he has taken. Since 1859 he has been courted by the opposition, who conceived hopes of gaining him over when he left Lord D.'s government, or if not of gaining him over, yet of establishing such a hold upon him as to be able to use his influence with the Conservatives in their favour, and against Disraeli's. This game has been played by the Whigs with considerable success. They have flattered him until he finds it difficult to do without their applause. But they have done more than flatter: it is well known that the object of Walpole's ambition is the Speakership, and they have given him hopes of obtaining it: Denison is unfit for his place, said to be tired of it, and likely to resign: Walpole's election would not greatly offend the Whigs, who have no very available candidate of their own, and would (until now) have gone far to conciliate the country gentlemen. Personally, Walpole is unambitious: but he is poor, has a family, the pension is an object, and Mrs Walpole, a daughter of Spencer Perceval's, who with her father's narrowness of mind has much of his ambition, never ceases to urge him on. (This he has told me himself.) She is farther stimulated by an extreme jealousy of Disraeli, as a Jew, and as having counselled the admission of Jews to parliament: a subject on which her feelings are fanatically strong. Walpole shares her dislike, but in him, according to his nature, it is greatly mitigated. I believe that Walpole accepted the task of moving his resolution without consulting his wife, for which indeed there was no time, that she saw the impolicy of the move for his and her objects, persuaded him to give it up conditionally on Lord Palmerston making the question one of confidence, and having obtained this promise from him found means of communicating with the cabinet. My reasons for this belief are: I know that Mrs Walpole has entertained confident expectations of getting the Speakership from the Whigs: I know that he never acts without consulting her: as he, indeed, has more than once owned to me: I know that to several members of the cabinet Walpole's private intention not to press the motion was made known before an idea of it reached Walpole's own colleagues, and I know that it was on this intelligence that Lord Palmerston acted in taking the bold and as it proved successful course which he did take. It remains to be seen how far the event will affect Walpole's own position on the benches where he sits. Undoubtedly there is a large section of the country party who, not from feelings of interest, but from traditions and prejudices which have come down to them from the days of Pitt, dislike economy and peace establishments: forgetting that while in Pitt's time the armaments of England were employed against the French Revolution and in support of their general views, the exact opposite would be the case now, were any intervention to take place.

16 June 1862. ... My Father had an interview with the Queen on Saturday which he related to me. He thinks her really better, both in health and spirits, but she will not admit it, and does not like to hear it said: she was much annoyed at a paragraph to that effect which appeared in *The Times*, and has ordered it to be contradicted. She asked many questions about people of her acquaintance, what they were doing, how they were: showed a good deal of curiosity, but in the midst of her questioning broke off abruptly, and began to talk of the Prince. She told over again, for the fourth or fifth time, the story of his illness and death. She said he had always predicted that he should not recover from a serious illness, and added, very oddly, as it seemed to my Father, 'Some people rally much better from illness than others: it is all pluck.' (Lord D. says she must have heard one of her children use this phrase, and has repeated it without exactly understanding what it conveys.) She has the papers marked for her by Phipps, and reads only what he points out. She sat during the whole interview, but kept Ld D. standing, which is now always her custom. Phipps told him that her finances were getting into confusion, in consequence of her determination to carry into execution all the Prince's plans, employ everyone whom he was in the habit of employing, and act generally, as though he were still living. The increased cost is heavy, now that his allowance has ceased. She allows nothing to be touched in the room where he died: all remains as it was during his last illness.

24 June 1862. . . . Dined at The Club, meeting Lords Lansdowne, Stanhope, H. Vane, Reeve, Milman, Sir E. Head, Sir H. Holland. Lord Lansdowne talked of parliamentary speakers whom he had known in early days: among them Lord Grenville: who, he said, had once told him that he knew he was accused of a supercilious manner in speaking, holding his head aloft, and speaking into the air, but that it arose from his nervous dread of seeing the expression of the faces of those opposed to him: a sneer or a mark of disapproval put him out, so that he found it necessary to avoid looking at them.

. . . Meeting Lewis in the House, a day or two ago, he engaged me in a long conversation on army-purchase. He said personally he agreed, or was disposed to agree, in the view I took of it . . . The Duke of Cambridge would prefer to keep things as they were: but he was so divided between opposite apprehensions that no reliance could be placed on him. He was afraid of the officers on one side: afraid of the newspapers on the other: and disliked having the question mooted. Lewis thought his excessive timidity arose from the fear of newspaper criticisms on his domestic arrangements, which are not such as this moral age approves having made public, though they are known to all the world.

25 June 1862. . . . House, where a singular scene. Digby Seymour, who had been censured by the benchers of his Inn for unprofessional practices, and narrowly escaped being disbarred, took the occasion of a bill being debated which regulated the jurisdiction of the Inns of Court, to go into a personal defence, in the course of which he accused the benchers of unfairness. Bovill, as one of those who had sat in judgment on the case, followed, and gave an explanation which abundantly justified the benchers . . . There was only one opinion among members as to Seymour's impudence, and the undue leniency of the tribunal before which he had appeared. He received a recordership in the winter of 1854–5, as the reward of having supported the

Foreign Enlistment Bill introduced by the Aberdeen ministry, and which was hotly opposed. How he afterwards got a silk gown is unexplained: it caused much discontent at the bar. There was also a transaction at the time of the last election in 1859, of which I do not well know the particulars, but the substance was that he tried to sell his vote on the question of confidence to both parties in turn, but asked terms which neither would give. It is unlucky for the bar that this case should follow immediately after that of Edwin James.

Dined Sir G. Lewis: met among others the Clarendons ... Lady Clarendon told me, in talking over Irish affairs, that her husband had gone to Dublin, in 1846 or '47, for three months only, and in order to make arrangements for the abolition of the Lord-Lieutenancy: then came the famine, then the Ballingarry affair, and the office became one of real importance: so little had they expected to stay, that even their house in London had not been parted with. She lamented Lord Carlisle's unfitness for the office, and his utter want of dignity, which indeed is everywhere acknowledged ... She mentioned that Lord Clarendon thought highly of the talents of Mitchell – that he might have been a dangerous leader in a real insurrection: of the others he had no opinion.

7 July 1862. ... Dined with Disraeli, Bellamy's: he told me among other things that Lord Londonderry[2] is shut up, the hereditary madness of his family having shown itself. D.'s keen interest in politics seem to have gone off of late, though he attends the House regularly.

20 July 1862. ... A meeting was held yesterday at Bridgewater House, my Father in the chair, to organise a subscription for relief of Lancs. distress: he gave £1,000, Ld. Ellesmere and Egerton, the same, Patten £300, Lords Ducie and Skelmersdale £100 each: altogether £10,000 was subscribed in the room.

Yesterday Mr Glaisher, the meteorologist, went up in a balloon to the height of five miles (26,000 feet) which I believe to be a greater elevation above the surface of the earth than has yet been reached by man. ... The ascent seems to have occupied ninety minutes,

23 July 1862. ... Debate in H.C. on a bill which has for its object to give to the police power to search and apprehend persons suspected of poaching. The bill, which was hotely contested on its second reading last week, and carried by a majority composed of members from both sides, is objectionable in some of its features, but especially unsuited for discussion at the present moment. Lancashire is starving, and when 2,000,000 of Englishmen are in doubt where to find bread for the winter, it is not good policy that the H. of Commons should be occupying itself, in the last few days of the session, with a bill which will be regarded out-of-doors as intended to protect landowners in their amusements at the expense of the public. Some words to this effect I uttered ... It is probable my speech, short as it was, will have given great offence, but I am sure I was right, not only in the interest of the nation, but also in that of the Conservative party.

. . . (Note. It did give great offence, especially to Ld D., who used very strong language on the subject: his anger, however, did not last long. I declined all discussion, as is my habit in such cases.)

27 July 1862. . . . [Talk] with Sir G. Lewis, chiefly on points of history, not much of present affairs: the only thing he said bearing on live politics was that in his eyes the real difficulty of the day was the Irish Church. While it remained there appeared no chance of the Catholics being satisfied, yet to reduce would do no good, and to abolish it wholly would be impossible, the country not being ripe for the voluntary system, and the middle classes looking on the Irish Church in particular as the defence of Protestantism. In all this I expressed assent. He consulted me as to whether it would be worth while to suppress the vacant archbishopric, the reduced salary of which is £10,000. I said no, that to make any change of that kind would create as great a stir among the Protestants as though the property of the establishment were to be taken away: it was not worth while to raise a disturbance where no result was to follow, except the saving of £5,000–£6,000 a year, for the see must still remain, even if cut down, and £3,000–£4,000 would be wanted to endow it. We had a truce existing since 1837 on this question: keep it while you can, and if it must be broken, break it for some larger object than one which if attained, will leave both parties in the same relative position as before.

2 September 1862. . . . Into Preston by 10 to see the laying of the first stone of the Town Hall by the mayor. It was a masonic ceremony, and the masons had to walk round the town – up every street and down every lane – which occupied several hours. (There is nothing that the people of the Lancashire towns like so well as a procession, no matter how composed, and weather makes no difference to them.) . . . The crowd recognised Ld D., and cheered him vehemently: some carried their welcome so far as to shake hands, slap him on the back, lay hold of his arm, and ask if he remembered them, all which familiarities he took in excellent part. It was an honest welcome, though a rough one.

3 September 1862. This day was devoted to the agricultural show [at Preston] . . . [The] dinner was at 4 p.m., Ld D in the chair, 1,200 tickets given out. The place of meeting was a large tent, which let in the water so freely that during heavy showers we had to sit under heavy umbrellas. Most of the leading gentry of the county were present: Gerard, Hesketh, Skelmersdale, the High Sheriff, etc. My father spoke for about an hour, in his best style: he dwelt very much on the necessity of manuring, utilising sewage, and so forth: he went into details like a practical farmer. He was very cordially received, as was I also, in rising to propose the health of the High Sheriff.

4 September 1862. Into Preston early to see the procession of trades. . . . The procession occupied about two hours, the trades represented were bakers, butchers, tailors, coachmakers, blacksmiths, whitesmiths, engineers, printers, spinners, etc. All had with them a car, or large truck, on which the occupation of their trade was carried on while the procession moved. Thus the printers had a press at work, and distributed copies as they were struck off, among the crowd: the blacksmiths had a horse which they shod as they went along: the bakers an oven, and hot loaves being drawn out of it, the tailors a sewing machine, and so forth. Nearly all halted opposite the window where the mayor, Ld D., and the other notabilities were posted, and gave a hearty cheer. After the trades followed a second procession, of R. Catholics exclusively, for the most part boys and girls out of the schools.

. . . It was curious to observe, yesterday and today, how little the weather affected popular enjoyment. Men and women stood in the rain for hours, wet through, but laughing, shouting, and quite indifferent to the discomfort of draggled clothes. It was also observed by all of us that the distress of the last few months could not be traced on the faces of the multitude. Men and women both appeared hale, hearty, and good-humoured: not a sign of suffering or discontent. Yet of suffering, unless a mass of trustworthy evidence is to be set aside, there has been a great deal.

16 September 1862. . . . I don't think I noted at the time a conversation with Cobden shortly before leaving London. He laughed, though in a kindly way, at Bright's ardour for the cause of the north: saying of him that he was a good partisan: he himself deplored the waste of blood and money, inclined to think the contest useless, acknowledged that England alone could do no good by interfering, but thought it possible that a mediation by all the leading European powers jointly might succeed, in the event of the summer's campaign leading to no decisive result.[3]

20 September 1862. . . . In evening, news of death of Lord Ellesmere,[4] aged only 39. He had always been an invalid, but his illness was not announced, and his death came to all of us as a surprise. From youth he had been sickly and partially deaf: he took no active part in public affairs and mixed but little in society. His estates were well managed, and his affairs, I believe, properly regulated. He was always spoken of with respect in Lancs. though not personally well-known. He leaves a son aged fifteen, said to be, like his father, in poor health. The property is very large: I have no certain knowledge, but it is generally estimated at £80,000 a year.

A letter from Lord Hardwicke,[5] in which he says that Royston's marriage hangs fire: the young man's debts being so heavy as 'nearly to break him down.' They have been brought about mainly by gambling. There is no good in the man, whether he marries or not: his folly is a heavy disappointment to Lord Hardwicke who by economy and good management has brought round a property nominally large, but heavily encumbered.

Lord Granville is reported very ill. I hear no more of his marriage.[6]

Ld D. says that if his racing engagements turn out badly, Lord Canterbury[7] must leave England. He has been living recklessly all his days, and dissipated the little property that was attached to the title, until now he is driven to subsist as best he can from hand to mouth. He was, and perhaps is, a constant guest at St James's Square, where he makes himself popular by retailing or inventing gossip. I have heard surprise expressed that with his notoriously debauched character, and absence of any other recommendation, he should be admitted to Lord and Lady Derby's intimacy. His being on the turf explains it to some extent.

21 September 1862. . . . Whether it be the climate of Lancashire, which after a certain time always affects my spirits, or the east wind which has blown for a week (and with us the east winds come loaded with foul vapours from the towns inland) or mere accidental indisposition, I have suffered for the last three days from a very disagreeable depression of mind: the more disagreeable as it is absolutely without cause. I have, I think, concealed it from my family: and have combated it to the best of my power by occupation. But the ailment is bodily and real: change of air, or perhaps of weather, will remove it.

8 November 1862. . . . Heard that a new weekly paper is talked of, Disraeli much interested in its success, Lytton also concerned in it, Sir H. Wolff[8] the chief promoter. Wolff is a son of the missionary, the converted Jew Dr Wolff, whose eccentric and conceited autobiography set all London laughing. The son has quite as much vanity, some talent, and a turn for intrigue: he is reputed dangerous to deal with by those who know him best. I doubt the experiment being tried, after the failure of the *Press*, and still more doubt its success if it be tried.

18 November 1862. . . . Talk yesterday with the American minister . . . He said in answer to a question which I put, that the border states were the real difficulty, he did not see how either party could do without them. He admitted that the cotton states might be abandoned as gone beyond hope of recovery.

21 November 1862. . . . Dined W. Cowper's, meeting Gladstone . . . Much discussion about America . . . Gladstone made no secret of his views[9] as to a separation. He thought Virginia must be divided between the two federations, and probably Tennessee likewise.

7 December 1862. . . . Declined an invitation to attend a meeting of the friends of Greece, on the ground that as everybody was agreed to leave the Greeks to settle their affairs in their own way, I saw no occasion for special declarations of sympathy with them. – Much laughing at Frederick and me, because a newspaper (the *Post* I think) quotes the resolution come to by some Greek club somewhere, that if they cannot have an English prince, they will vote for 'a son of Lord Derby'.[10] – Gladstone has been seriously talked of by some English Greeks as a candidate for the vacant throne.

16 December 1862. . . . There is a strong rumour that our government propose the cession of the Ionian islands to Greece. . . . I remember Gladstone contending strongly for this view at Hawarden: he would have ceded Corfu as well as the rest.

19 December 1862. . . . Sir G. Lewis came. I found an opportunity of asking him about the Ionian islands: he admitted at once that the report was in substance true, and discussed the whole question freely, as though it were one in which he had no personal concern. Nothing has been done which is irrevocable: but proposals have been made to the other great powers to call a congress with a view to the cession of the islands, including Corfu, and Sir G. admits that to withdraw from the offer thus made will now be difficult. He went on to tell me that it had been decided upon in great haste, that it was the doings of Lords Russell and Palmerston: Palmerston he should have thought the last man in England who would take such a step: Gladstone had supported the cession warmly, on the ground of economy: he himself did not know what parliament would say to the executive having acted on its own responsibility: the public mind was not prepared: there would be a great deal of talk, general surprise: he let it plainly be seen that he doubted whether his colleagues had not been hasty. It was argued that the islands cost for military defence £300,000 a year, but he had never been able to make out that they really did so. He believed one motive in the minds of Lords P. and R. was the wish to place England in a position in which she could honestly and consistently advise Austria to give up Venice. He thought it possible that the Ionians might themselves feel some reluctance to be handed over to an unestablished govt like that of Greece, and in that case the unreality of the cry for annexation would be effectually exposed. It was also on the cards that Austria might object to the transfer of the islands to a power not strong enough to hold them during war, since if they fall into enemy hands (say, into those of Italy) they might cause great inconvenience to Austrian trade.

. . . There has been some talk of my name being suggested as a candidate for the Greek throne: I have never treated it otherwise than as a joke, but to my surprise Lewis tells me the proposal was seriously made by Tricoupi.[11] one or two other Englishmen being mentioned at the same time. It is noticed also in the *Saturday Review* of this day.

21 December 1862. . . . Walpole has received from the Abp. of Canterbury the place of paid ecclesiastical commissioner: (£1,200 a year), which probably ends his political career, so far as office is concerned, for, other reasons apart, he will not sacrifice a permanent for a precarious appointment.

24 December 1862. Hatfield . . . I led the conversation, both with Lord and Lady Salisbury, to the prospects of the Conservatives for next session: and satisfied myself that Lord Salisbury is not inclined to retire, nor would willingly allow his son to be substituted for him in the new government.

1863

5 January 1863. . . . I have been deliberating whether to continue this journal or not, but on the whole decide to do so. I kept one once before, in 1855–6, but destroyed it after two years, thinking it wasted time, and served no good purpose.

11 January 1863. . . . Long conversation with Delane.[1] He talked of Turkish affairs, said the present Sultan was no better than his predecessor: he was spending the new loan lavishly on his army: the Turkish troops formerly were bad, but cost little: now, they would be no better, and would cost as much as the French: the Sultan had taken to palace-building like his brother: he was also notoriously addicted to unnatural habits and paraded his vices before the people. He, Delane, had always maintained that the attempt to keep up the Turkish empire would not do: he had supported Lord Clarendon in that view as long as Lord Aberdeen remained firm, but when his own cabinet overruled him, and decided on war, there was no more to be said: it was a subject on which Lord Palmerston would not hear reason: but events would be too strong even for Lord P.

Bulwer[2] was disgracing the country at Constantinople: living in the house of (as I understood) a Mme Aristarchi, who was in his entire confidence, and took money from everybody who had a request to make at the embassy: it was like the case of the Duke of York and Mrs Clarke: Bulwer himself was not corrupt, probably, but the Turks believed him to be so, not supposing that this sale of all favours could take place without his sanction. Bulwer ought to be recalled: Lord Cowley put in his place, Lord Granville substituted for Lord Cowley. Besides these scandals, Bulwer's pecuniary position was indecent for a minister: he was constantly pressed for payment of debts, and obliged to have recourse to strange shifts (some of these Delane enumerated).

We passed on to Indian affairs, by way of Egypt. Delane had done all in his power to promote the success of the great ship, thinking that the shortening of the Cape voyage to India wd put an end to the Egyptian question, by rendering the overland route comparatively unimportant in time of war. (It is curious that this is precisely the language which I have always held on that subject, and I think I made some allusion to it in a speech delivered on board of her when first made ready for sea.) He thought no serious danger threatened India except from the Nizam. I mentioned Nepal as likely to create disturbance if Jung Bahadur died: he seemed to dissent, urging that the Nepalese army was worthless, and that aggressive power of the govt nothing. We talked of the military executions which disgraced the English

194

victory in 1857–8: he told me he had done all in his power to keep them from the public of Europe, as being discreditable to the national character: one book, by a Mr Casper (which was quoted in the House, 1859, by Gilpin) he had persuaded the publisher to suppress. Sir J. Lawrence was mentioned: Delane now thought he would not do for Gov.-Gen. though having at first taken up his claim: thought he had a right to the peerage, would support any attempt to get it for him, with an adequate provision (I mentioned a grant of £100,000 for an estate as not unreasonable). – I answered truly, that it was an object I had never lost sight of.

He gave a long explanation of Sir Hugh Rose's[3] scrape: as might be expected, a woman is at the bottom of it: the quarrel which Rose has taken up so vindictively and foolishly is hers, not his own. He thought Rose, though quite wrong, might be allowed to remain in command another year, at the end of which period his term expires, and he can then withdraw without being disgraced. He asked whom I thought ought to succeed? I answered without hesitation, 'Mansfield.' 'So I should say,' he replied, 'but that is not the Horse Guards view. It has been offered in the event of Rose's withdrawal to Sir R. Airey and Sir W. Codrington!'[4] I expressed surprise: thence we fell to talk on the office of C.-in-C., the Duke of Cambridge's fitness, etc. Delane thought that if the Duke were to break down, which he looks upon as not improbable, that the office ought to be abolished, the Sec. of State be made acting head of the army. 'We want nothing except a general commanding the metropolitan district – give him, if you please, higher pay than the rest, but no more commanders-in-chief.'

Something was said of the party politics of the day: Delane's language was in substance as follows: a govt formed by Lord Russell cannot stand a week: there is now little real difference between party leaders: when Lord P. dies or retires, an event which cannot be far distant, something in the nature of a fusion may take place which shall include the best men of all parties. Better to wait till that time comes. I named Lord Clarendon as a possible chief: Delane shook his head, said Lord C. was much aged within the last few years, and not likely to reappear on the surface. I noticed his favour at Court, said he might be useful to manage the Queen, which was likely to be difficult. Delane thought the suspicion of court favour, backstairs influence, would do him more harm than anything else, if the public believed it. Of the Duke of Newcastle he spoke with a kind of good-humoured contempt: said he worked hard, but his mistake was doing the business that ought to be done by a clerk on £500 a year, and leaving his own undone – not giving himself leisure to exercise a general superintendence over his department.

Delane spoke in terms of high praise of the present Duke of Wellington:[5] said his ideas were always his own, original, vigorous, sometimes absurd, but suggestive: never the mere repetition of what he read in the newspapers. Thought he (the Duke) might have played a part in politics if his father had trusted him fairly: but he, the late Duke, would be satisfied with nothing less than an absolute unreasoning obedience, which in public affairs is impossible. He wanted an aide-de-camp, not a colleague.

14 January 1863. . . . Stanhope showed to R. Cecil and me an extraordinary letter from the present Duke of Wellington, written on I know not what occasion, in which he says it is well known that his father, the great Duke, was the son of a Gen. Gardner, not of Lord Mornington: that the Duke himself knew the fact, and used to speak of his reputed parent as 'Lord Wellesley's father'. I had heard the story before, but thought it too strange to be noted down as a piece of mere gossip. Lord Stanhope, however, has it under the Duke's own hand.

6 February 1863. . . . House, where nothing doing: walked back with D. who says that he is satisfied there is no such interest felt on the Ionian question as would justify the making of a motion. The truth is, no one wishes to displace Lord Palmerston, who is said to have remarked on one of the late elections, that people might talk of his losing seats, but he was all the while gaining votes. Half the country gentlemen would refuse to join in an attack upon him.

. . . In the House, Cobden came to see me, and spoke earnestly of the distress of which he takes a gloomy view. We arranged for a meeting of the Lancashire members on an early day. He did not appear to know exactly what he wanted, nor had he anything to propose: except this, that larger powers of borrowing, and for a longer term, should be given to the unions. It might come to a government grant at last, but he did not anticipate that necessity. He thought the difficulty this year would be quite as great as last, and that it could not be met, as hitherto, by subscription. (I see plainly a feeling of jealousy among Irish and English county members at the liberal scale of relief given, and at the exclusive attention which Lancashire has drawn to itself, causing distress elsewhere to remain unnoticed.)

19 February 1863. . . . Last night, at the Cosmopolitans, Thackeray[6] began to talk to me about his writings. He said the public had got tired of him: he had been twenty years before it, and now people wanted a change. I demurred: he persisted, saying that his publishers knew it well: that his last book had not paid its expenses: that the world wanted not descriptions of life and manner, but startling incidents, adventures, and so forth: that he would not write in that style: it did not suit him – but that was what hit the popular taste. Miss Evans got £7,000 for one of her novels, *Esmond*, which he thought his best, had brought him only £1,500, for a year's hard work. The publishers did not like *Esmond*: they said, 'Don't give us any more old English.' He spoke of his colleagues in literature: praised Trollope highly: could not read the sensation writers of the day, Wilkie Collins, etc.

20 February 1863. . . . Ellenborough[7] made a vigorous speech on Poland. Talking of this to my Father, I said that he was ranked by general opinion as the third best speaker in the Lords. 'He is the first in some respects,' said Lord D. 'Since Lyndhurst grew old, he has no equal for a statement, in clearness and force. It is true that he is always prepared, and cannot reply with effect.'

21 February 1863. Deaths of Lord Cottenham, Reay, and Sudeley announced. Lord Cottenham was only thirty-eight, and insane. Drink was either a cause or a symptom of his disease. He succeeded to three fortunes, one made by his grandfather, Sir W. Pepys, a master in chancery: one by his father, the Chancellor: and one by his great-uncle, Sir Lucas Pepys, in his day a fashionable physician.

Lord Reay, I imagine, left little or nothing, the vast tract of land still known as Reay's country having been sold by a former lord to the Sutherland family for £330,000.

22 February 1863. . . . The Duke of Cambridge has taken the extraordinary course of sending for Kinglake, and discussing with the latter his [the Duke's] alleged misconduct at the Alma. He admits that the charge, whatever may be its importance, is in substance true: *viz.* that at one moment in the advance he consulted Sir C. Campbell and other officers as to whether it would not be expedient to fall back: which drew from Sir Colin an indignant rebuke. It is not even imputed that his hesitation came from personal fear: and seeing that a momentary indecision in an officer who had never before seen fire, is no grave fault, society thinks the Duke had better have left the matter where it stood. But this, to a man of his excitable nervous disposition, was simply impossible. The Duke's excitement after Inkerman was so great that he had to be sent home lest he should go mad.

6 March 1863. . . . Dined with Patten, no party. He talks of the future state of parties, thinks the Carlton is ruled by a little ultra clique, which does great mischief, that Disraeli will never be accepted by the party as a leader. – Russell must follow Palmerston, but that will not last long – no one knows what is likely to come next. Spoke of my position as the most satisfactory he knew – unpledged, free to take my own line, if Ld D. should retire, looked to as a future leader, etc. I told him what is the truth that I do not think I have power of speech enough to lead either House, though I believe I could manage an office, and be useful in a cabinet. [Patten] says the reaction in favour of Conservative opinion is strongly marked in Lancashire, Bright more feared by the leading millowners than by the aristocracy – the trade unions have caused the change.

14 March 1863. . . . Disraeli has a story which comes from the King of the Belgians, that the Queen will abdicate when her son and daughter-in-law have shown themselves fit to take her place: intending to fix her residence for the rest of her life at Coburg. The person through whom this confidence comes is not very trustworthy, though well-informed, and I note it only as one of the many speculations which are afloat.

. . . At Windsor, a book is kept in which persons wishing to pay their respects write down their names: there used to be two, one for the Queen, one for the Prince: since his death the Queen has not allowed that kept for him to be discontinued, but visitors write their names in it as before – calling on a dead man. This, and other traits of a like character, are a good deal gossiped about.

24 March 1863. . . . Hartington returned for Lancashire without opposition. He made a moderate but on the whole a conservative speech. With a heavy appearance, and drawling slowness of utterance which resembles affectation, he has good sense. I do not think his abilities would have raised him to a higher position than that he might have been born in: but being born in the highest, he has enough to enable him to take his place in the world creditably.

6 May 1863. . . . Dined Grillions, the fiftieth anniversary of the club. Out of 80 members, 56 were present, my father in the chair.

7 May 1863. . . . My father put into my hands papers relating to the construction of a breakwater at Port Erin, in the Isle of Man, for which, if the Board of Trade will undertake it, the fishermen are willing to pay a tax on their boats. . . . Ld D. is much pleased at the Manxmen coming to him in their distress, notwithstanding the severance of the connection between his family and the island for upwards of a hundred years.

15 June 1863. . . . In House, a warm debate on the proposal to buy the S. Kensington exhibition buildings and land, and transfer thither all the collections of science and art. This scheme has been pressed forward by the Court with an indecent eagerness, the Queen having made no scruple of canvassing leading members personally in its favour. She is even said (but this I do not know) to have written to Delane to ask his support. To my Father and Disraeli she has expressed herself in the strongest terms, treating the question as one personal to herself. These proceedings have had their effect on official and would-be official members, of whom the great majority supported the vote. The independent feeling of the House was strongly against it. There were about 400 members present, the fullest House since the budget was opened. . . . The vote was taken before dinner: it was carried by 260 odd to 135. But this was for the purchase of the land only, the purchase of the building was postponed . . .

16 June 1863. . . . Much talk in London about the extraordinary way in which the Queen undertakes to direct the Prince and Princess of Wales in every detail of their lives. They may not dine out, except at houses named by her: nor ask anyone to dine with them, except with previous approval or unless the name of the person invited is on a list previously prepared: and the Princess, after riding once or twice in the Park, was forbidden to do so again. In addition, a daily and minute report of what passes at Marlborough House is sent to the Queen. The parties most concerned make no complaint, but others do for them, and the whole proceeding is thought ill-judged. But there is no one to say so – Leopold alone could, and his health prevents his hearing what passes, or offering advice.

2 July 1863. . . . Meeting here of about ten members of both Houses, to consider the question of American recognition. Fitzgerald[8] and Pakington were for it, all the rest thought it premature, Ld D. taking that view strongly.

. . . The vote for purchase of the Kensington buildings came on, Gladstone moving it. The House had determined from the first to throw it out, and would hardly listen to its advocate, interrupting him at every moment with laughter and derisive cheers. Disraeli supported the ministry, but did not help them. Indeed, he also failed to get a hearing. The votes were, 287 against, 121 for. I went with the majority. The feeling of members against this proposition was due to various causes. The outlay proposed would have been a waste of money – the building could never have been ornamental – but there were other feelings at work. Jealousy of Court dictation – dislike of the little agitating intriguing clique at South Kensington – jealousy also at seeing the leaders united, a combination of present and past office-holders which the House always looks upon with distrust. I do not recollect having ever witnessed in the H.C. so disorderly a scene.

3 July 1863. . . . Dined Lord Westminster's . . . Sat next Lady Waldegrave,[9] and not much attracted – she inclined to flatter, which in bad taste, as I never met her before. She talked of Harcourt, whom she evidently dislikes, though professing to take interest in his career: thinks him egotistical, conceited, unconciliatory.

9 July 1863. . . . Meeting on the American question in Ld D.'s room: ten or eleven present. All, except Fitzgerald, opposed recognition of the South: the question most discussed was, whether any offer of mediation ought to be recommended to government, or whether it would be better simply to leave the matter in their hands. The objection to the latter course is that it appears to amount to an abdication of their functions by the Opposition: and also that more than one half of the Conservatives are likely to vote with Roebuck if he divides, thus breaking up the party, and indicating an absence of united action. On the other hand, it is nearly as certain as anything can be, that mediation will do no good, that the offer will not be accepted, and may even be treated as an insult. No conclusion was come to.

16 July 1863. . . . Walking home with Patten, he talked of Roundell Palmer:[10] said he believed if he could be induced to give up his profession, then the Whigs would endeavour to make him their leader instead of Gladstone, whose dictatorial manner and want of tact give offence: Patten thought this plan likely to be carried into effect, and cited the precedents of Perceval and Ponsonby: I expressed doubts, first whether Palmer, as a friend of Gladstone, would consent to be put over his head: and next whether he would give up his profession, in which he is secure of the highest place.

28 July 1863. . . . [Among guests at Chevening were] Lord Raglan, a simple good-natured person, evidently without talent, but agreeable by an unaffected manner. Lady Raglan was less popular: she curiously resembles her brother, Lygon:[11] I have seldom seen a family likeness in ways of thinking and talking, so strong: she volunteered talking of Lord Elmley,[12] whom I scarcely know, but of whom Disraeli, Lytton, and some other good judges think highly in point of ability. She talked of him with undisguised contempt as a dreamer and visionary. There is evidently a family difference in politics: Lygon being a strong High Churchman and Tory of the bitter intolerant school – Robert Cecil's – and Elmley a moderate Conservative. The sister reflects the ideas of the former with less capacity of understanding what they mean.[13]

21 September 1863. . . . Talk with Lord Clarendon on various matters: he says the Queen is recovering fast, but greatly troubled for want of help to manage affairs: she has (in his words) 'absurdly high notions' of her prerogative, and of the amount of control which she ought to exercise over public business: wishes to be able to form a judgment independent of her ministers, but cannot do it without help: she has said as much to him in conversation. He believes she will reappear as usual in society next year.

Of the German unity movement, he thinks it will come to nothing at present, whatever it may do hereafter: the small sovereignties cannot be abolished except by force: and no one is prepared to go that length. He spoke of Prussia: was convinced the King would not give way. 'He is supported by his own family, who are more reactionary than himself: by his military staff, the only people with whom he ever converses familiarly: and by the feudal noblesse, which is poor, ignorant, proud, and follows no profession except that of arms. He is totally without ability, quite sincere, and believes himself inspired.' I asked what he meant? Lord C. continued, 'He holds the doctrine of the divine right of kings, and believes that they are guided by a direct illumination from above. He thinks this of himself, and therefore makes it a rule never to consider beforehand what he shall say on any subject.' (Here Lord C. repeated the story he had told me before as to the King's practice in that subject.) For the same reason, he is fully persuaded that it would be a crime in him to give way to the people whom he considers as democrats. God has made him a king – opposition to kings is opposition to God – for a king therefore to give way is want of faith.' He went on, 'Polignac[14] was the same. When the ordinances came out Mme —— (I lost the name) implored him to yield before an insurrection broke out. He seemed moved, said he would think of it, withdrew into his room, came out again, saying, "He had consulted the *Saint Esprit*, and was told to persevere." ' I asked what made the Prussians so slow to move? Lord C. thought the discontent among them was nearly universal, but they had not physical force on their side, the army was against them, and the officers wished for nothing better than a rising which they might repress. He could give no opinion as to how it would end.

We discussed home politics: he thought Lord Russell must be the next premier, but that he would be reluctantly followed – saw no large question likely to turn up: a dissolution would rather injure than help the party of movement. To my surprise he said that Sir R. Peel had disgusted Protestants as well as Catholics – and that ministers would not have ten Irish seats in the next parliament. He could not explain Lord P.'s partiality for Sir Robert, of whose abilities he spoke with utter contempt, as indeed do most people.

15 October 1863. . . . Lord Leitrim[15] has been removed from the Commission of the Peace in Ireland, as a punishment for a strange insult offered by him to the Lord-Lieutenant. He engaged all the rooms in the only inn of a town belonging to him, where Lord Carlisle was to have passed the night, thus compelling him to go on without stopping in the neighbourhood. He made no secret of his object in doing this, which was to gratify a personal pique for some supposed injury. Lord Leitrim is considered to be hardly responsible for his actions, and his removal cannot be regretted on public grounds: it is a question however whether an insult so petty and foolish would not have been better passed over without notice.

16 October 1863. Much talk yesterday about the late Duke of Newcastle:[16] he lived in state and show above his means, latterly becoming so much embarrassed as to be unable at times to get credit from his tradesmen for ordinary household expenses: yet while in this condition, Worksop being offered for sale, he bought it, paying (according to the Speaker) £500,000, and obtaining the money from a neighbouring banker. His chief reason was pique at not having had an offer of the property, which the Duke of Portland and some others were about to purchase between them. The result of this acquisition was to embarrass him much more, but in the end it has turned out well, the value of land having risen. He left it to his second son, who had the good sense to refuse an estate encumbered to its full value. The present Duke, on succeeding, was so poor as to say that the expense of educating his children bore hardly upon him: the Hope alliance however will end these difficulties.

Cardwell told me that the late Sir R. Peel, when attacked by Lord G. Bentinck in 1846 about his conduct to Canning, was so greatly exasperated as to propose sending a challenge to Lord G. He asked Lord Lincoln – the present Duke – to carry it, and the two men passed the whole night after that debate together, Lord Lincoln endeavouring to dissuade him. He did not succeed until next day, and even then with great difficulty. Cardwell said, the transaction appeared to him so extraordinary that he should have scruple in repeating it, if the Duke of Newcastle were not living to confirm his testimony. He had heard the story more than once from the Duke.[17]

The Speaker mentioned the extreme strictness of the rules which formerly prevailed in relation to his office. Till Speaker Abercromby's[18] time, it was forbidden to leave the Chair on any pretext, even for a minute: and on certain necessary occasions, the clerks stood up before him, extending their robes, and turning their backs, so as to shut him out from observation. It was thought that this extraordinary rigidity dated from the time of the Civil Wars, when opportunity might have been taken of the chair being vacant, to put someone else in, or otherwise infringe the rules of the House.

The Speaker related a conversation at which he was present, seven or eight years ago, between Macaulay and Lord Taunton, in which Macaulay predicted as inevitable the disruption of north and south, against the general opinion: those who were supposed to know America best arguing for its impossibility.

28 October 1863. . . . There is again an attempt being made by the old High Tories to displace Disraeli and put Gen. Peel[19] in his place. It can come to nothing, for Peel is quite unfit to lead the House, and would not, I conceive, even attempt it. Bull, Knightley, and Newdegate,[20] are mentioned as the most active in this cabal.

30 November 1863. London early: called on Sir C. Wood to discuss affairs of the sanitary commission: he began at once to tell me of the appointment of Sir J. Lawrence,[21] which, as he said, it had been necessary to decide upon in haste, as Lord Elgin's successor must go out by the mail of the 10th. Four names have been discussed: Argyll, De Grey, Lawrence, and myself: Argyll it was understood would not accept the post from family reasons: he had named me to Lord P. who had answered 'It would not be fair to ask him': the Queen had objected both to De Grey and me, on the ground that we should be wanted at home. He (Sir C.) was not wholly satisfied with the choice, but thought under the circs it was the best thing he could do. He named as objections Lawrence's objections against Queen's officers: the old quarrel on the amalgamation question, and his zeal on behalf of the missionary interest. There was also a doubt whether his health would stand. But Lawrence had done great service, he had a claim on India, and of his ability there could be no doubt. This was in substance what Sir C. Wood told me. I answered him by assuring him of my entire concurrence – I thought he could not have done better. Lawrence was then sent for, I shook hands and congratulated him, he said. 'I have something to thank you for too – I know you have always been my friend.' It was mentioned in this conversation that the Duke of Newcastle's health was such that he might probably not be alive six months hence.

1 December 1863. London: called on Disraeli: he told me of his accession of fortune, and how it came about: the amount is £40,000: the lady, a Mrs Willyams: she died aged 94: had Jewish blood in her veins: she in the first instance almost forced her acquaintance on D. who knowing nothing about her discouraged the advances she made to him.

Talk of political prospects: D. repeated what I have often heard him say before, that foreign affairs were now those on which all interest is concentrated, there are no domestic questions: Malmesbury was personally unfit for the F.O.,[22] and there was a further objection to him in his being a peer: either the premier or the foreign secretary ought to be in the Commons. This not being personal to M., might be assigned as a reason for making the change he desired. He wished me to take that post – M. to go in Cowley's place to Paris – unless this were done, he would not undertake to lead the H. of C. I did not discuss the matter, thinking it useless in our present uncertainty as to the future. He named some new men as fit for employment – Lord Devon being one.

10 December 1863. . . . Ld D. talks much of the necessity of having a cabinet ready, in case he should be called upon. He feels much difficulty in providing for young rising men, in consequence of the claims of those who have held office before. He mentioned Northcote as one who ought to have a seat in the cabinet. He was evidently aware of D.'s objection to Malmesbury, and as evidently determined not to give way to it. He spoke also of Hardwicke,[23] as necessary to him personally, as a man on whose fidelity he could rely, and who would follow him in whatever he did.[24] He wished Cairns could be Chancellor instead of Chelmsford, but did not see how it was to be managed. He said (to my surprise) that Henley expected office again, and would be discontented without it. He agreed that Walpole had behaved so ill that he deserved nothing at our hands, but would Henley accept office without him, and if not, would not those two act as a centre round which the malcontents who exist in every party would gather? He referred again to the F.O., saying, 'I suppose D. wants you to have it.' I answered, 'I thought that was his idea.' He said, 'I don't think you would like it, or that it would suit you, and the public might not be pleased to see so much power in the hands of one family.' I answered, that personally I should prefer either India or the Colonies, with the business of both of which I was more or less familiar – that I had no desire to change, but should leave the matter entirely in his hands – I would do what was thought best for the government as a whole. With this, the subject dropped. – In the above words, I expressed exactly my real feeling. But I do not expect a change of ministry for the present – and for this reason: that half the country gentlemen will not vote aganst Lord Palmerston.

11 December 1863. . . . Aspinall,[25] the recorder, . . . tells me that the Catholic families in Lancashire, such as the Gerards, De Traffords, etc., make it a rule to give their chief entertainments on Sundays, as a practical protest against the Puritan theory: I had noticed this in individual instances, but did not know it to be a custom.

18 December 1863. . . . Fleming,[26] a creature of Ld P.'s, is going about announcing that the present state of politics cannot last: that within a month from the meeting of parliament next year there must be either a dissolution or a change of ministry: I suppose this means that Ld P. feels himself to be holding office in a great measure by the support of his nominal opponents, and thinks that a new H. of C. will be wholly devoted to him.

The ultras of the Tory party lately held a conference in which they decided to choose the Duke of Marlborough[27] as their leader in the Lords – probably on account of his strong Protestant opinions – and R. Cecil in the Commons. The Duke at once declined: whether any offer was made to Cecil I do not know.

22 December 1863. . . . I have read during the last few weeks: Mommsen's history of Rome: Mackay on the Tübingen school of theology: the report and evidence of the commission on penal discipline: Renan's life of Jesus, a second time: Fezensac's memoirs: some other French biographies: part of Macculloch on taxation: the inland revenue report for last year: pamphlets, reviews, etc. My reading has not been directed to any special object.

23 December 1863. Ld D. informed me that he had been making his will, and that its chief provisions were: £30,000 for my brother, with £2,000 a year annuity for his life: £6,000 a year for my mother during life: the estate to be left in the hands of trustees – C. Stanley and E. Wilbraham – they to have no power except that of a veto on sales and on the taking of fines. The granting of leases for 999 years, without fine, to be absolutely in the hands of the tenant (i.e. myself). I told him I was entirely satisfied, which indeed I have reason to be. If the estate is to be settled at all – and such on large estates is the almost universal practice – no settlement can be made giving larger powers to the life-owner.

31 December 1863. . . . On the whole, it seems unlikely that another year can pass in such absolute repose. Personally, I have done nothing in politics, except attending to the railway business, and to committees: the few speeches that I have made in parliament have been unimportant. My health has been good: I have experienced no serious trouble or annoyance: in regard of family matters there is nothing that I could wish altered. My brother[28] is working steadily in his duty as adjutant, gaining credit for professional knowledge and willingness to work: my sister's health, which has been weak, is improving: my father, though showing some marks of age, is well, and as free from gout as can reasonably be expected. I have not gone out of my way to look for employment: but I cannot charge myself with having neglected any public duty. I have neither quarrels, nor, so far as I know, enemies: in the event of a dissolution, my return for Lynn would almost certainly be uncontested. My chief fear for the future is lest a life of such comparative indolence as I have lately had should unfit me for active occupation . . .

1864

1 January 1864. Knowsley. Attended rent day dinner, about 300 sat down.
... I received ... a curious return of the Knowsley rental ... It includes
all the estates except those in Ireland.[1] I copy it in part.

Rental for 1800	£31,881
1805	£31,984
1810	£40,271
1815	£44,566
1820	£48,614
1825	£52,494
1830	£58,331
1835	£63,094
1840	£72,616
1845	£88,638
1850	£95,199
1855	£109,121
1860	£126,196

2 January 1864. ... Made up accounts for 1863: find I have spent in all
£940 nearly: of which £200 for Lancashire distress, £127 for Lynn, £50
for charities and public objects, and £114 for books, prints, and drawings:
leaving for all other purposes £448. Total received by me since July 1851,
about £26,700, including interest on savings. Total given, up to end of last
year, for charitable or public purposes, as nearly as I can reckon, £7,900,
of which £350 in 1863. I have invested £5,600, as follows: Indian debentures
£4,000, worth £4,200 at the market rate: Natal Co. £1,000, Building Co.
£600.[2]

3 January 1864. ... My father again talked of the F.O.: said he thought it
would not suit me: he himself had been invited by the Queen[3] to hold it
along with the premiership, in 1852: the union of the two offices was in
itself impossible but apart from that reason he would have refused, and from
a motive which he thought would have influenced me. He thought we were
neither of us fond of ceremonies and forms, nor very successful, in dealing
with persons who like diplomatists are touchy in matters of form – that I
should dislike Court attendance and Court duties, of which there were many:
he further doubted how I should get on with the Queen. I repeated my
former answer – that I should greatly prefer remaining at the India Office,
the business of which I thought I understood: or going to the Colonial
Office with which also I was familiar – but that I should place myself in his

hands. I added that in any case I trusted he would not accept office again without an assured majority, and competent men to fill the places. The trials of governing with a minority and with colleagues, many of whom were incompetent, were enough: it was better not to come in a third time than to come in weak and liable to ejection at a moment's notice. In this he seemed to agree.

27 January 1864. . . . My father full of projects for his cabinet, which he expects to be required to form in the course of the present session. He appears determined on retaining Malmesbury at the F.O., with R. Cecil under him: Peel, Pakington, myself as before: Sir E. Lytton, doubtful: Carnarvon to be promoted: Lord Longford, a good working officer, the U. Sec. for War: Chelmsford to be Chancellor, but an early opportunity taken of putting Cairns in his place: Kelly Chief Baron or Chancellor for Ireland when a vacancy occurs: Northcote Board of Trade: Disraeli of course Exchequer: Henley some light office, such as Duchy of Lancaster: Walpole Home Office long enough to serve for his pension, which object it seems he puts forward openly: Hardy Pres. of Poor Law Board: Cave[4] (new) Sec. to Treasury. Some others were talked of, and to my surprise, Ld D. named Bath[5] as fit for an U. Sec.ship. Against this I protested strongly: the appointment would be a ridicule and a reproach. I do not think however that these speculations are likely to be soon put in practice. No Indian U. Sec. fixed on: it is unlikely that Baillie[6] will serve again. Hardwicke, cabinet without office.

30 January 1864. . . . Much discussion of possible future arrangements: Ld D. very anxious to make Cairns Chancellor, assigning to Chelmsford the post of President of the Council: the rest much as before: except that Carnarvon is to be Privy Seal, and manage Indian affairs in the Lords: R. Cecil U. Sec. for F.O. under Malmesbury: Fitzgerald to be advanced: Northcote Board of Trade, Henley Duchy of Lancaster: Peel, Pakington, Lytton, Disraeli, I, Walpole, Malmesbury, all to hold our old places. To my utter astonishment, he suggested Bath as an U. Sec. Against this I exclaimed, as Lord Bath is not only very unpopular in society, but ridiculous from his conceit and foolish sayings. Nothing, however, is definitively settled, nor (so far as I know) has any pledge been given except to Henley.[7] Why he should have been the exception I do not know.

1 February 1864. . . . Called on Disraeli: talk with him of the language to be held at the opening: he says, 'Criticise, but suggest nothing.' He thinks ministers are in search for a policy, that they would be ready to go into a war if encouraged by the opposition, making that their excuse with the Queen: that the event is altogether uncertain: on the whole he does not expect a change: at least not if England remained at peace: the death of Lord Palmerston would make no difference for a time: Russell and Gladstone could carry on affairs (this is what I have always thought.) He asked me what I thought was the prevalent feeling about the Danish quarrel? I said the sympathy of all whom I had met was with the Danes, but people did not feel strongly enough on the subject to wish to go to war. He concurred. He does not wish to come into office now, thinking the pear not ripe: but does not see how if called upon it would be possible to refuse. Thinks Ld D. will come into all his plans about a ministry – including the F.O. He (Dis.) has talked the thing over with Malmesbury, who, according to him, agreed that the F.O. ought to be in the Commons, and named me as his only possible substitute. We discussed various possible arrangements, as I had done with my father on Saturday.

2 February 1864. . . . I hear (indirectly, but certainly) that Lord Russell has been told of the possibility of my succeeding him,[8] on which his judgment is, 'He will make himself master of the subjects to be treated, and there will be no fault to find with his despatches: the doubt is how he will get on with the foreign ministers here.' He might have added, 'and with the Queen.' But the trial is not at hand, if indeed it ever comes off.

3 February 1864. . . . Dined Disraeli's meeting Lytton, Pakington, Walpole, Cecil, Northcote, Lovaine,[9] Burghley,[10] Palk,[11] Peel, Trollope,[12] and one or two more. Henley was not present, nor any of the lawyers. The speech was read according to custom: discussion on the war followed: a few were disposed to be warlike, Cecil and Burghley especially: but the general feeling in favour of waiting for information.

. . . Went on to the Cosmopolitans, where met Hughes, A. Russell, Higgins, Stirling, Forster, etc. Stirling talks seriously about the position of Lord Elgin's family: the widow has about £1,500 a year, the son only £900. He wants some provision made by the state, alleging Elgin's services and premature death.[13] I agree to this, and promise to promote it, if in my power.

16 February 1864. . . . Much talk with [Sir Charles] Wood: he thinks there is a marked falling off in the upper classes since 1832: young men of family no longer take the same interest in politics: there is less anxiety among great families to keep up their positions: he remembers when the Fitzwilliams thought nothing of spending £100,000 on an election . . .: now they grumble at an ordinary election subscription. It is the same with local business. The younger gentry will not serve on boards of guardians, will not attend sessions: they let the business slip out of their hands, from mere dislike of trouble. He continued long in this strain. I think he exaggerates, but there is truth in it.

A story is going about of the Prince of Wales at an officers' dinner at Windsor, having got excited in discussion about the war, and drunk confusion to the German invaders, or some such toast.

17 February 1864. . . . Dined Lord Airlie's . . . A pleasant party. Cockburn[14] very full of anecdote: told a story of his early success, the point of which was that he had received half a dozen briefs from a country attorney because the latter had been especially impressed with the respect with which so young a counsel was treated by the judge, 'taking notes of every word he said.' The judge was Lord Brougham, the case was in the Lords, and Lord Brougham had, as his manner was, made up his mind beforehand, and occupied himself while Cockburn was speaking with his private correspondence.

He talked much of Lord Westbury, and in a strain which astonished me considering that they hold high judicial office together. Said he was under the entire control of his eldest son, a worthless scamp: that the latter had been concerned in keeping a gambling house, where young men about town were plundered . . . This son exercised great influence over his father, especially in the distribution of patronage: he had lately sold the promise of a place for £1,000, which place the applicant did not obtain, and naturally applied to have his money back. Failing, he addressed himself to the Chancellor, who paid him.[15]

19 February 1864. . . . Dined Bellamy's with Disraeli and Fitzgerald. D. seems to me either growing old or in weak health: he has lost his former vivacity, and sleeps much in his seat. The party of malcontents on the Conservative side now numbers about twenty-five, and has the sympathies of many more. The leader of this section is Bentinck[16] of Norfolk. R. Cecil, though mollified by hopes of office, belongs to it: Knightley, Burghley, Newdegate, the same. Henley and Walpole, though cautious of committing themselves, encourage, as giving them importance. It might exercise some influence on affairs, were the ideas of its chiefs either entirely in accord, or practicable in themselves. But war for Denmark, language held to the U.S. which would inevitably lead to war, increased armaments, doubled income tax, and new debts, are not likely to be popular. These men are to the Conservatives what Bright is to the Liberals, only that the superiority of talent is on Bright's side.

20 February 1864. . . . Dined Speaker's: the usual party: a good deal of talk about the new malt tax agitation, which seems to be felt by most of those to whom I spoke as an embarrassment. The farmers were joining it throughout the east of England: in Hertfordshire and Suffolk it is peculiarly strong, insomuch that Lytton had lately to make a speech supporting the movement and Kelly has taken it up with the vehemence of his sanguine advocacy. The farmers do not feel what to politicians is obvious: that the abolition of the malt tax means the continuance of the income tax.

21 February 1864. . . . Cosmopolitans in evening, where met . . . a son[17] of Adams (U.S. minister) who has been serving in the American army during the last campaign. . . . He is convinced that the confederates are exhausted: says their officers as well as men are deserting (of which he gave instances): the war he considers as ended: the question now is, what terms shall be offered to the south? He thinks the general opinion is in favour of amnesty without exception, security to property, and a return to the old constitution in all matters except such as relate to slavery, which must be utterly abolished. We talked of the future of the negro race in America. I objected, that with equal rights and free intercourse there must be physical amalgamation: if this took place to a considerable extent, would not the American race be deteriorated? He admitted the risk, said it had to be incurred: after all, who were to blame? The slaveowners had themselves done more towards the mixture of the races than any other class whatever. He thought the feeling against negroes would be long in dying out, but that it was tending to diminish: a white man would now consent to sleep in the same room, and even in the same bed, with a negro: which formerly would have been out of the question.

25 February 1864. . . . Dined Stanley of Alderley's: meeting Russells, T. Taylor, Carlyle, Sir J. Acton, Argylls: pleasant party. Lord Russell had never met Carlyle before. Carlyle preached at some length after dinner, in the strain which with him is invariable. He said the Irish had never been well governed except under Cromwell: they had too much freedom to talk every man, whatever folly came into his head: what they wanted was someone to enforce silence and keep them working. They were a fine race when under control, but unfit to be their own masters. He praised the Emperor, and his way of ruling the French: said he had been in France during 1848, and felt the need of someone to put a stop to all that was going on. He talked of travel: could not see what good it did a man to make a wheel of himself: his business was to stay in the place where he had something to do – if he felt weary he ought to accept that as just a sign that there was something in him that wanted setting right – Nature made that feeling of ennui for his good, it made him think and reflect – he had no right to run away and try to shake it off by mere wandering from place to place. Railroads were a great mischief in that they encouraged people to run up and down without motive: we had far too many of them. He thought the state of the country worse and worse: nothing except talk and making of money: he almost despaired of England, unless she went through some such purification as the Americans were now undergoing. (These were not his words, but the sense of what he said at some length.) I hinted that in some matters we had improved – less meddling in foreign affairs, more care for the poor, etc. He would not have it. There was more poverty than ever, and as for war, after the Crimean folly it was impossible to say what we might not go into. He hoped that the nation was not to be judged by those who spoke for it – that there was some sense among those who kept silence – if he were to judge by speeches and newspaper writings he should think our case utterly desperate. He then turned to foreign affairs – said there was no cause in Europe worth an Englishman's troubling himself about – not even that of Italy – one might wish to see the Pope put down, as the father of all lying, but were his opponents any better?

1 March 1864. . . . There has within the last few days been posted on the walls of Buckingham Palace a handbill to the following effect: 'These extensive premises to be let or sold, the late occupant having retired from business.' The London papers suppressed it, but there is no doubt of its having been seen. – General discontent of the London tradesmen: they believe the Queen to be insane, and that she will never live in London again.

3 March 1864. . . . In House, long talk with Disraeli on malt tax, the agitation against which has spread over all the eastern counties and is growing, in his opinion, to formidable dimensions. He evidently more than half inclined to put himself at the head of it. I combat this strongly, pointing out that total repeal, which alone will satisfy the complaining parties, costs £6,000,000 yearly: that partial repeal will do nothing to remove the annoyance of excise restrictions, which is the thing most complained of: that insurance, sugar, and income tax have all of them claims to reduction at least equally strong: and that on the malt tax there is not even an entire agreement among the farmers, since those who live in counties where malt is not largely produced would prefer a reduction of income tax. D. seemed haunted by a fear that Gladstone might take up the case,[18] and draw a certain number of his followers away: we discussed this fully.

He told me of a suspicion he entertained that the Danish papers lately laid before parliament were falsified by omissions and verbal changes. This is quite possible, for the F.O. is not scrupulous in such matters, but I don't trust D.'s secret intelligence.

9 March 1864. . . . General railway bill committee, where I agreed to take the metropolitan group after Easter. It will occupy the rest of the session, and to a great extent shut me out from public debates: nothing however of consequence seems likely to be brought forward, nor do I expect a change of ministry, though Disraeli does, or professes to do so.

. . . Accident to Sir W. Jolliffe yesterday: he was shooting rabbits near a chalkpit, when a boy put his head out, at the moment of firing, received the charge, and died that night. Jolliffe is said to be much distressed.

11 March 1864. . . . News of return of the Conservative candidate, a Mr Surtees,[19] for Hertfordshire, beating H. Cowper, (Lord Cowper's brother), the late candidate for Tamworth. This contest arose out of the death of Puller, the late member: the leading gentry for the most part wished to compromise, but the farmers, carried away by the cry against malt tax, insisted on a fight and won, though Mr Surtees is neither of an old Herts family, nor very rich, nor personally distinguished. The principal importance of this choice is that it defeats Palmerston in the neighbourhood where he resides, and in the person of a member of his family. Lady Palmerston is said to make no secret of her mortification . . .

12 March 1864. Levée, to which I was obliged to go . . . though I had attended the last: it was very thinly attended. There is much discontent among tradespeople, and among that class to whom invitation to a palace ball is a mark of their social position, at the continued seclusion of the Queen. She is believed by many to be insane, or on the verge of insanity, though for this notion there is not the slightest foundation. She is on good terms with her children, except the Princess of Prussia, to whom she appears to have taken a dislike, though they are agreed on the German question: it is believed that the young lady having much of her father's cleverness was trusted by him with most of his secrets, and that this intimacy excited the morbid jealousy of the mother. She lately proposed to hand over the royal plate etc. to the Prince of Wales, which was taken as an indication that she had determined never to appear in public again: but this resolution she was persuaded to abandon. She does not like Lords Palmerston and Russell: there is no one about her qualified to advise: Grey and Phipps see more of her than anyone else, but they are mere courtiers, who try to anticipate her wishes, and dare not advise. It follows that her relations with the ministry are unsatisfactory: the more so, since she has adopted the custom of sending word beforehand that she will not allow the minister whom she receives to enter on such and such a subject, lest it should make her nervous: the forbidden topic being often precisely that on which it is most important that she should be informed. Lord Clarendon has ceased to be in her confidence: at least there is a temporary coolness, caused (according to him) by his having remonstrated too strongly against her seclusion. It seems to be thought that she is losing her popularity, and dropping out of people's recollection. Her own present idea is certainly to retain the substance of power, leaving the show of it to the Prince of Wales of whom her former jealousy is much diminished. . . . (Part of the court news above is from Lord Clarendon, part from Lord Derby, part I have picked up at various times. I have set down only what I believe to be accurate.)

Meeting at Ld D.'s including Disraeli, Lytton, Cecil, Naas, Taylor, Cairns, Peel, J. Manners, Northcote, Pakington, etc., to discuss the expediency of making a motion on the Danish question, giving notice of it before Easter. All without an exception thought it unwise: the reasons assigned being (1) that we should be abandoned by a certain number of Conservatives who do not wish to displace Lord P. – and that the ministry would thus gain the advantage of a vote of confidence. (2) That if we succeeded, the result would probably be a dissolution, which it is better to postpone as long as possible, so as to have the chance of being in power when it takes place. (3) Urged strongly by me that a motion of censure on the govt cannot be made without involving a debate, if not a decision on the question of peace or war: whence inconvenience of various kinds. If we seem to lean towards war, we go against what is undoubtedly the general feeling of the country: if, as is most likely, some of us speak for peace, some against it, we show weakness and disunion: if, what can hardly be expected, we observe on that point an entire neutrality, we fail in our duties towards the public, which expects something more from its teachers than mere recrimination and reviling of one another: and which could say with apparent truth that we had no object except to make capital for ourselves, out of a public difficulty. This latter view, I am well aware, was unintelligible to many present, especially to Disraeli: nevertheless we agreed in the result to which we came, though from various reasons.

16 March 1864. . . . Dined Sir C. Wood's . . . After dinner I got into conversation with Count Flahault,[20] who told interesting anecdotes of his service under Napoleon I. He talked of the Russian war . . . The Emperor had told him early in 1812, that the war must be an affair of two campaigns: that he would reorganise Poland in the winter, and invade Russia in 1813: had he persisted in that plan, the fate of Europe would have been different. . . . As for the Emperor himself, it is a mistake to suppose that he was difficult to approach. Anybody might say anything to him. His nephew is like him in that. 'I can give you an instance. There was a rising threatened in La Vendée and the Emperor talked to me of sending someone out to quiet the district. He proposed one of three names, Savary, Sebastiani, and someone else. I said, "Sir, don't send Savary." He asked me sharply why? I was confused, forgot myself, and answered in the first words that occurred, "Because he was the assassin of the Duc d'Enghien." When I had spoken, I felt as though I should sink into the earth. The Emperor looked me full in the face, and apart from his position and the respect due to him, his look was not one easy to meet – paused a minute, and answered, "It is a royalist district – you are right." It was fair reason for his being angry, but he showed no offence, then or later. It was impossible not to devote oneself to the Emperor. I have said to the present man, "Sir, I was the confidential servant of your uncle, and I can have no farther ambition." '

For a time in spring 1864 the Danish question receded into the background while other issues came to the fore. Stansfeld, a rising Liberal, had allowed his house to be used as a post office by Mazzinian conspirators, his defence being that he was ignorant of the contents of the letters. Guilt lay, if anywhere, with the wife, in Stanley's eyes: 'his wife is more deeply mixed up than he is aware of in the Mazzinian plots. Many stories are current concerning the lady, which I will not set down.' At the same time, Gladstone engaged in a personal quarrel with one Sheridan, the parliamentary spokesman of the insurance interest, the result being 'that Gladstone has more than ever established his character for honest imprudence', though his budget, popular with Conservatives as with opinion at large, made up for much. 'So long as Gladstone goes on taking off a penny of income tax yearly, he may do what he likes with the other half of his surplus, so far as our side of the House is concerned.'[21]

Curiously, no sooner had Stansfeld lost his job on mere suspicion of involvement with Mazzini, a blow from which his career as a younger Bright never really recovered, than Liberal England prepared to celebrate the visit of its hero, Garibaldi, whose politics were cast in much the same mould. Disraeli, always averse to enthusiasm, and mindful of the Catholic vote, stood apart, though Derby and Stanley did not.

10 April 1864. . . . D. in his most paradoxical mood, talking of Garibaldi, denying that he had ever won a battle, asserting that his Neapolitan success was due wholly to bribery, that he bought off the officers opposed to him, that his object in coming over was to collect a large fund. – Amusing at first, but his cynical affectation is apt to grow tedious. He mentioned a thing which I could hardly believe – that of the £1,200 of pension given away yearly by the Queen, and which is understood to be devoted to literature, science, art, or public services of a kind not to be recompensed by any of the departments, £500 this year is to be granted to some of the Lennox family, on the ground of their poverty: £500 more to Lady Elgin.[22] The latter is unobjectionable, but the first gift, if really contemplated, is the worst kind of job.
11 April 1864. . . . A thin House . . . Dined there, and went downstairs to smoke a cigar: in the smoking-room found Bright, declaiming, as is his custom, to a circle of friends: Ireland the subject: he said no good would be done until the estates were divided, tenant right given, the Irish church done away, the revenues partly secularised, partly divided among all sects. Nobody seems to dispute what Bright says: they all listen, which indeed is natural for he talks well, and thus he hears no opinion except his own.

The Garibaldi procession occupied over five hours in moving from the railway station to Stafford House. It was poorly got up, not much to see. There must have been 500,000 persons turned out to witness it: mostly of the poorer sort, dirty and many of them drunk . . .
16 April 1864. . . . Party at Lady Palmerston's, earlier than usual, to meet Garibaldi, who still continues the lion of London society. I saw him for the first time: he wore his uniform cloak (as I suppose it is) of coarse grey cloth, with a red shirt, or tunic, under it: a costume which he piques himself in retaining at all times. His face is manly and pleasant: his habits not equally so: he smokes in the house, spits abundantly, goes to bed when he pleases, and breakfasts before any one else is up. He has been more than once to visit Mazzini, with whom he rather desires to parade his intimacy. Our papers suppress these visits. The popular enthusiasm continues unabated. It will perplex the Continent, for there is no people in Europe among which Garibaldi's real ideas have made, or are likely to make, less way. Among the upper classes, the prevailing feeling is simple curiosity.

Lord Clarendon is gone on a mission of conciliation to the Emperor: which by his private letters appears to have been much needed.[23]

19 April 1864. . . . Great excitement produced by news of Garibaldi's sudden departure: it was planned that he should stay a month or six weeks, and visit the great towns as a means of creating agitation in favour of Italy. It was thought at first that he had been requested by ministers to withdraw, as his presence, and the reception given him, created irritation in France: this Lord P. denies: another story is, that he had come over on the invitation of Mazzini and other friends, in expectation of a general war, to arise out of the Danish affairs: but finding that nothing in that way is likely to arise, goes away disappointed: this seems probable enough. To mere flattery he is indifferent, and the pretext of health cannot be seriously put forward . . . That his visit had an object cannot be questioned: and I think it clear that in great part that object has been left uneffected. By carrying him to Stafford House, surrounding him with lords and ladies, and occupying his time with ceremonies in his honour, the Duke of Sutherland has disconcerted the projects of those, his real allies, who would have made him the hero of the trades unions. The manoeuvre has been all the more successful, because it was in some degree unconscious on the part of the performers. They thought, at the utmost, only of keeping him out of 'bad company' and not of the political risk which they have averted.[24]

22 April 1864. . . . Many enquiries of late as to Ld D.'s health: he has not suffered from gout this year, at least not to any serious extent, but his weakness and loss of appetite have alarmed Ferguson.[25] As one consequence, he has altogether shut himself up, refusing to dine out anywhere, and only on one or two occasions having friends to dine with him. This makes talk out of doors, and the belief is spread that he is not physically strong enough to hold office. What is worse, it reacts on his spirits, which, always unequal, are now more often low than otherwise. I do not think that the mischief is more than temporary but doubt Ferguson's judgment. He orders stimulants in large quantities – wine and brandy – which may be necessary but certainly do harm in the end.

23 April 1864. . . . Lord Claud Hamilton[26] full of a steam navigation company of which he is chairman – the difficulty now is to find a peer or titled person not engaged in this kind of business. Elcho[27] last week refused £1,000 a year to be chairman of the Millwall Iron Company. I have had half a dozen similar offers, which did not seem worth noting here.

5 May 1864. . . . The Queen's intrigues with the German powers openly talked of . . . The reasonable cause of complaint against our Court is, that being necessarily acquainted with the secrets of its own foreign office, it divulges those secrets in confidence to the Prussian cabinet, which is negotiating in an opposite sense. The irritation is so great that I hear it said, 'She does right not to show herself in public.' Two years and a half have sufficed to destroy the popularity which Albert took twenty years to build up.

6 May 1864.[28] ... A debate arose, though a short one, on Danish affairs: Cecil spoke vehemently, and was cheered from all sides. He did us, however, more harm than good: for he made it appear as though he wished to go to war, which is the policy which the Liberals are trying to fix upon us, calculating with reason that it will hurt us, and help them, with the constituencies. He assures me however that he does not contemplate war, thinking it too late and useless.

Disraeli and I had a long conference on the question whether any general move is to be made by the party. He wishes to avoid one if possible, thinking that a favourable division, however small the numbers, will tend to strengthen ministers: and that danger will unite them, whereas they are now much divided. Nor does he want to give them a pretext for premature dissolution. But in the event of the conference failing, he thinks (as I do) that an opposition cannot remain silent without losing reputation and seeming to abdicate its functions: and in that case it will be necessary to move a vote of censure. So far is plain sailing: but then arises the question, shall this vote be retrospective only? If it is, we shall be told that we have no policy to propose, and no advice to give. If not, what can we advise without laying ourselves open to the plausible imputation of wanting to go to war?

10 May 1864. ... Further talk with Disraeli: we agree that unless the conference breaks up unexpectedly, which is possible, there is no need of parliamentary action.

Conversation with Patten on the impossibility of carrying on the railway business on the present footing: members will not serve unless compelled: chairmen decline to attend: the House in general seems to reject this duty as dull and leading to no reward of public or parliamentary fame. Surely it is not creditable that among 650 members this should be the case.

... Disraeli has published a new edition of his almost forgotten poem, which he has dedicated to me. He sent me the volume, but I knew nothing of his intentions, and stumbled on the dedication by mere accident.

11 May 1864. ... Cosmopolitans at night, where Gladstone the general subject of conversation. It appeared to be the general conviction that he had broken with the old Whigs and placed himself at the head of the movement party. What is singular, only the night before he had held very conservative language on the principles of taxation, contending that direct taxes are vexatious, unequal, hard to raise: and that we ought in the main to adhere to our actual system, which resting on indirect taxes, undoubtedly favours property. It is felt on all hands that he is the inevitable leader: and at the same time (apart from this last move[29]) that the *hauteur* of his manners, his want of skill in dealing with men, and (what is the same thing in other words) his pedantic stiffness in adhering to his own opinions as rigidly in small matters as in great, will make him most unpopular in that capacity. He is universally respected, admired, and, except by Bright and a few of that school, disliked.

12 May 1864. . . . Dined Clarendons: a family[30] party: Lord and Lady D., F. Stanley, Talbot, and the Villiers. Lórd Clarendon very pleasant, and devoted to amusing and flattering Ld D. which he did with complete success. He abused most of his colleagues, Lords Russell and Westbury especially, and spoke of Gladstone in terms of great bitterness. He talked of the Queen, said she was quite recovered in health, and nearly so in spirits, but was afraid of being thought inconsistent if she did not persist in a show of grief. It was real enough last year, now it is only acting. Extreme dislike of England entertained by the Princess of Prussia, who has made the Queen sore on the point: the cause being the Danish sympathies of the English. Lord C. described the conference: Apponyi mild, polite, and a nullity: Bernstorff obstinate and slow – the latter as much from policy as temperament – the delays interminable, and great loss of time.

Among other things, Lord C. said of Gladstone that a physician in attendance on him had declared that he would die insane (I believe this was Ferguson.[31]) It is true that an excessive irritability has appeared in him on various occasions, and especially in the spring of 1857, when he attacked Sir G. Lewis on a financial question of no great moment, with bitterness rarely equalled in parliament.

22 May 1864. . . . Lord Russell avoided present politics, to which indeed I did not attempt to lead him, but talked freely of old histories. He said he had once possessed, but lost, a note of conversation with Napoleon at Elba,[32] about the Christmas of 1814. The ex-emperor was then enormously fat, but very restless and inquisitive, all his conversation questions. He asked especially about the state of feeling in France, and how the army was satisfied. 'I was convinced at once that he meditated a fresh attempt on the French throne: all his questions pointed that way: he had however completely decieved the commissioners residing on the island to watch him: they could talk of nothing but his content, the occupations he found for himself, and how wonderful it was that after having played such a part he could interest himself in the small affairs round him. In our conversation I said something which he seemed to take as disparaging to the profession of war: he answered sharply, "C'est un grand jeu, une belle occupation." He mentioned his apprehension of being seized by the allies contrary to treaty and sent to St Helena: I am persuaded that this fear was one of his motives for invading France. I asked Talleyrand (?) afterwards what could have led him to play so desperate a game. He answered, "Un peu d'espoir, et beaucoup de désespoir." '

Elba led to my saying, it would not have been a bad retreat to offer to the Pope, who cannot well be a subject, and yet ought not to be a sovereign, except in name. Lord R. answered that the same idea had passed through his mind, and he had desired to make the offer, but Palmerston disapproved it. Another project of the same kind which he was disposed to favour was that of cutting off a part of Rome, and leaving him sovereign within that limit with a suitable income guaranteed by the great powers. I cited the parallel cases of various deposed Indian princes. Lord R. agreed with me that the Pope would rather gain than lose in his spiritual capacity by parting with the temporal power, but said that none of his advisers thought so, nor of his opponents, which made him (Lord R.) doubt whether they were not right.

Talk, later, of Scott. When Lord R. studied at Edinburgh, party feeling ran so high that he was warned not to have anything to say to Mr Scott if he wished to be considered a good Whig. He named one of the notable men of the day as having given him this advice. Scott at that moment was peculiarly unpopular, having written a song against Fox, from whom, a few months before, he had received a political office, on the score of his literary claims. Still the advice shows what political feeling must have been in those days.

Lady Minto[33] told me that I had given great pleasure to the late Duke of Bedford,[34] when I visited Woburn in 1859, by merely taking off my hat to the bust of Fox when it was shown me. He used to mention the circumstance often. I had forgotten it – strange how intense is that sentiment, half family, half political, which binds together the leading Whigs. Lord Russell always writes at a table which has on it a small bust of Fox.

26 May 1864. . . . Long talk with Sir C. Wood . . . He disapproves Gladstone's speech[35] strongly, though agreeing that the language is so vague as to pledge him to nothing: thinks however that it indicates no settled conviction, but is only one of Gladstone's odd inexplicable freaks: would not be surprised if he were to make another speech in an opposite sense next week: believes no one in the cabinet knew that it was going to be made: the agitation cannot be revived for the present, and if tried will only damage the Liberal party. Thinks Lord P. growing weaker, and that a new administration formed by the same party cannot go on throughout a session without him: Gladstone inevitable, but most dangerous: the country wants no extremes: would be content with a Liberal–Conservative or Conservative–Liberal govt. 'Once in, if you do nothing foolish, you may stay in for years.' We talked of German politics: I found him strongly possessed with the idea that the smaller German states must some day – probably before long – disappear: but he did not believe in a single united Germany, rather in a division between Austria and Prussia, one having all the north, the other all the south, and France the Rhine.

3 June 1864. . . . Talk with Ld D. on Denmark: he very hot for war, at least so far as to wish it, but sees the difficulties: abhors the idea of declaring that you will fight only for an English interest: says it has been pain and grief to him to keep silent on the subject of the conduct of ministers: he is pressed on all sides by his friends to attack them, but hesitates, since a vote of censure at this moment would be construed as a declaration in favour of war. I agree for non-intervention, keeping clear of continental squabbles, and not undoing by a few months of fighting, all that has been done in the last ten years to make our people prosperous and contented: Ld D. a little indignant, calls this pig-philosophy and so forth, but in perfect good humour. We play chess afterwards.

Disraeli uneasy about the state of affairs, thinks the conference must break up, and that in that case it will be necessary to make some party move. He describes himself as pressed upon by the country gentlemen to attack ministers, on the ground of their doing nothing effective to assist Denmark: which means a declaration of war. To me he holds the language that he is resisting this pressure, and wants a meeting called in order to aid him in standing out against it: to my father he seems to have spoken in a different sense, and God knows if he has told either of us truth. He will however be for peace so long as the Queen is on that side, which is a considerable security. There is a struggle going on in the cabinet, Gladstone, Gibson, and most of the rest for peace, Palmerston for fighting. Lord P. wishes (I believe) to be attacked, in order that our pressure may help him to overrule his colleagues.

5 June 1864. . . . Called among others on Lady Malmesbury, who full of gossip: says it is reported in society that the Duchess of Manchester[36] is trying to attract the Prince of Wales. She has certainly thrown herself in his way on every possible opportunity.[37] Lord Bath[38] came while we were talking, but stayed only a few minutes. He quarrelled with my father for not having refused to meet Garibaldi, and more lately quarrelled with Malmesbury and Lady M. for taking the Danish against the Prussian side: having taken it into his head that the Danes are democrats.

6 June 1864. A meeting was held this morning in St James's Square of a few of the notables of the party, to consider the state of foreign affairs: I could not attend on account of the London railways, but sent a paper briefly stating my ideas. The purport of it was, that if the conference broke up, we could not avoid saying something, else we should seem to have ceased to exist as a political power: but that great caution must be used to prevent the demonstration made from appearing to be in favour of war. Ministers would undoubtedly attempt to represent us as the party of war, and such a charge, if believed, would be most damaging. It would lose us the middle class, the towns, and many supporters in all ranks. I advised that if possible no motion should be made but our policy explained by Disraeli in a manner which should make misconstruction impossible. I hear that Cecil, Whiteside, and Peel expressed themselves strongly for intervention by arms. Nothing was decided.

10 June 1864. . . . I forgot to note that after Lord Ellenborough's last speech,[39] in which he glanced at the influence exercised by the Court in favour of Germany, the Queen wrote Ld D. a violent letter complaining that he had stood by and allowed such things to be said of her. She said that she treated 'his unmanly insinuations' with 'profound contempt': she did not understand how England could so soon forget all it owed to the Prince: her style angry and undignified in the highest degree. Ld D.'s answer long, temperate, and argumentative as to the general question, of the causes of German unpopularity at this moment.

. . . There is a good saying ascribed (though obviously an invention) to the Prince of Wales. It is said that the Queen remonstrated with him about his continual smoking, on which he observed to a friend, 'that when H.M. left off her weeds he would leave off his.'

11 June 1864. . . . The Duke of Newcastle is dying at last: he has since his latest attack lost all memory of names, though not of the persons whom they represent: thus he spoke to Fortescue[40] of N. Zealand as 'that large island where we are at war with the natives' and of Gladstone as 'that very able man – my friend – who made that odd speech lately.' Such are the eccentricities of brain disease.

Adolphus Vane[41] was yesterday found dead in his bed . . . he being in confinement as insane at the time. His death is a benefit to everyone, including himself. Hereditary madness predisposed him to drink, and drinking brought out the madness. He had intervals of sanity, which made him only the more dangerous to his family. Lord Londonderry is mad: Lord Vane[42] odd, and drinks heavily: one of his children is an idiot: Ernest Vane[43] has disappeared: the last known of him is that he was supposed to be in America fighting on the confederate side: it would seem the family were doomed. They are next to the Northumberland and Beaumont families the largest proprietors in the extreme north of England: the estates, which on Lord Londonderry's death will unite in Lord Vane's hands, are supposed worth £80,000 a year.

18 June 1864. . . . Dined at home: Ld D. occupied in forming a govt, which from time to time is a favourite amusement with him, but as he alters the arrangements every time, I do not attach much importance to these projects.

23 June 1864. Breakfast at Gladstone's, meeting Sir H. Storks, Sir F. Doyle, Froude, the Bishop of Oxford, Lady A. Talbot, and others. Much talk on many things. . . . American war discussed: all blame Capt. Semmes for coming out to fight,[44] Gladstone especially, and with evident mortification at the result. Gladstone[45] spoke with astonishment of the eagerness of the 'negrophilists' as he called them, their readiness to sacrifice three white lives in order to set free one black man, even after it was shown that there was no disposition among the negroes to rise in their own defence. He could have understood the American feeling of dislike to the breaking up of the Union, but not the fanaticism of English sympathisers. I said that most of them cared little for the slaves, but a great deal for the success of the

American form of govt, naming Bright as an instance: in this G. and Mr Froude agreed. Someone said, with general assent, that this war had exhibited a quite new phase of American character – recklessness, not only of life, but of money, and a kind of volcanic force not before suspected to exist. 'Scratch an American,' added Mr Froude, 'and you find a Red Indian': a parody of Napoleon's saying respecting Russia.

Gladstone expatiated on the character of Garibaldi, saying that he was essentially a man of peace, one who believed like Cobden, in arbitration: his leading idea was that France and England by acting together should bring about a general disarmament: his own abhorrence of blood was perfectly unaffected: he had told him (Gladstone) that as a boy he hated the sight of soldiers, and could not understand how men should dress themselves up and glory in the profession of slaughtering other men. At Caprera, Garibaldi will not kill the animals he has reared, but sells them away alive, and buys food from the neighbouring country.

Among other matters, Mr G. condemned strongly the amalgamation of the war dept, saying it had greatly lessened the control of the exchequer and of parliament. The Horse Guards which used to be responsible, are now screened by the Sec. of State, while they cannot be controlled. It would have been better to have left the Ordnance Dept separate, as the Duke of Wellington framed it.

Mrs G. as usual with her, begged of all the party for a charity which she is promoting: a silly habit, which brings her into ridicule. I gave my share: some evaded her request, but that is an awkward thing to do to a lady in her own house.

28 June 1864. Meeting at this house [St James's Square] at 11, to settle the terms of a resolution condemning the diplomatic policy of ministers. I attended, partly because it was expected, partly in order to have a chance of preventing anything being inserted in the resolution that might seem to imply a wish for war.

. . . A party afterwards. Talk with M. Beust[46] on German affairs. I said, 'I understand the movement for German unity, I can conceive its being taken up warmly by the people, but I do not understand its finding support among the small states against whose independent existence the movement is obviously directed.' He laughed, and said that as for those states it was only a question of time, they might go on a little longer, or be absorbed at once, but to that it must come at last. His reply so astonished me, he representing one of these very states (though what he said is no doubt the fact) that I doubted if I had heard him rightly, and did not press the subject.

. . . Conversation with Lord Shaftesbury about labourers' houses in London. I find he accepts the conclusion to which I have long been driven, that though it is possible, and even easy, to make satisfactory provision for those whose earnings exceed 20s. a week, the large class who are unable to earn so much cannot be supplied with homes which modern refinement considers as decent, on terms which will pay to the owner. In our present state of knowledge, there is for these only the alternative of charitable assistance . . .

3 July 1864. . . . My Father has been laid up with gout, which gives no sign of getting better. He suffers much, and it is an unlucky moment. I spoke to my Mother of the possibility of inducing him to visit some German bath, but she thinks he will never consent, which I also fear. He can bear pain better than ennui: and has not crossed the Channel for forty years.

15 July 1864. . . . Walk with Patten . . . Talks of Gladstone, who he says is disgusted at being classed, as he now generally is, with the ultra-liberals: says he cannot imagine what he has said or done to earn that character, declares himself a Conservative in feeling:[47] above all is perplexed at the effect produced by his speech on reform, which he meant and believed to be moderate in tone. All this was expressed a week ago in conversation with Patten. P. is an accurate reporter, and I set down his statement within a few hours of its being made.

17 July 1864. Hatfield: the Hardwickes arrived early: he grown old and manifestly feeble: out of spirits too: which Adeane's bad health, Craven's extravagance,[48] and his own increasing infirmities amply account for.

The late debate[49] has been much written about in the newspapers, and talked of among politicians. On the whole the net results of it appear to be as follows. Ministers are stronger than they were in public estimation, since it was thought by many, and perhaps even by themselves, that they hold office on sufferance only, and could be ejected whenever Ld Derby chose to put forth his strength. I do not think this impression was at any time shared by Ld D. nor by Disraeli, who estimated their own position pretty accurately, since when the debate was in anticipation they counted on a hostile majority of from 20 to 25. But the fears of the officials exaggerated the danger: and their exultation is now proportionate. – The prospect of a dissolution is rendered more remote which is a relief to a large number of members on both sides. Something also has been lost by the ambiguous language of the motion of censure: it is argued with truth, that though an opposition is not bound to define its policy accurately, yet that they lose in moral strength by not declaring either for peace or war, for intervention or non-intervention. The truth is that on that all-important question there was no unity of purpose on either side the House. Had the matter gone further, a war-party and peace-party would have come into existence, cutting across the existing lines of demarcation: as was about to happen when the Crimean war came to an end. As a party move, the thing has failed, and as to have allowed the occasion to pass without an expression of opinion would have been simply political suicide, I do not see that we have cause to reproach ourselves. On the other hand, the peace policy, which is essentially that of the middle class, has been adopted by the House generally, and in particular by the Conservative part of it, with an apparent unanimity which was not expected, and to which I remember no parallel. This will tell on the towns, and strengthen the general feeling of content which is the support of conservative principles. There is now no quarrel between Ld D. and Manchester – meaning by Manchester not the Bright–Cobden section, but the leading merchants and manufacturers, of whom such men as Pender[50] and Fairbairn[51] are the representatives.

21 July 1864. . . . Hatfield in afternoon: met there Disraelis, Pakingtons, Carnarvon, and R. Cecil: the latter with Lady Robert were there for the first time since their marriage. It was curious to see R. in his own home looking round at the improvements, of which there are many, though none of much importance. Both he and Lady Robert were evidently nervous and ill at ease. I am glad to have contributed something, as I think I have, to this reconciliation, for the quarrel, arising merely out of temper in the first instance, was notorious in London, and did both parties harm in general estimation.

Disraeli out of spirits: says he does not now expect success for two years: which is an admission I never heard him making before.

My 38th birthday: I do not feel any older than I did at 28, and my health is better, but I am losing hair.

24 July 1864. . . . Enfield[52] tells me of a late conversation he has had with Gladstone: G. expressed himself astonished at the strength and unanimity of the parliamentary declaration in favour of peace: said it made a new era in our foreign policy: talked freely of home affairs: thought it would not do to go to a dissolution without some proof that they were really the Liberal party (his own words): the two questions on which he thought action possible were reform and the Irish church. He would not explain as to the latter – what he thought ought to be done, but talked of the establishment as a 'hideous blot' and used other strong language concerning it which I have forgotten, though Enfield quoted it at length. He declared against enquiry as unnecessary and a waste of time. This language startled Enfield, whose opinions are practically Conservative, or moderate Whig, which is nearly the same thing. I asked, 'What would the old Whig families do, if a ministry were formed, which with Gladstone at its head, should represent the ideas of Bright, Cobden, and the advanced party?' Enfield answered, 'They would withdraw their support, and form a separate party such as the Peelites constituted after 1846.' He went on to say that Gladstone had expressed to him a personal wish that the present cabinet should fall, on the ground that it had grown indolent and feeble, and wanted some years of opposition to give it new life. This may seem an odd speech from a minister but it is quite in Gladstone's line.

Lord Enfield thought Lord Carlisle could not remain long where he was, from ill health: and that the Duke of Argyll would probably succeed him at Dublin. Thought Lord Granville likely to be provided for at Paris, from which Lord Cowley is about to retire: and that in the event of anything happening to Palmerston, Lord Russell would be content to lead the Lords under Gladstone. These, he says, are the speculations current among the Whigs.

31 July 1864. . . . Talk with Walpole on a subject on which I find we think alike, the increase of centralisation in govt, and the tendency, which goes with it, to substitute paid for unpaid labour. This is popular, though it adds to expense, because it is thought, justly, to take away from the influence of leading people in their own neighbourhoods, which is naturally the desire of the radical party, but another cause contributes to the change: the general unwillingness among squires and lords to undertake any duty that gives them trouble, or requires the slightest sacrifice of time. Were I to resign the chair of the Kirkdale sessions, it would not be easy to find a substitute, and probably a stipendiary would have to be appointed: and I hear the same thing of other counties. . . . The same cause that makes the Lords adjourn at half past five, nine days out of ten, is throwing more and more of the local duty of landlords on govt officials. The end will be, people asking an awkward question 'What is the use of a class of rich men and large landowners?'

11 August 1864. . . . Talk with my father about earlier closing of session: I find he is personally well inclined to the notion of an autumn sitting, from Nov. 1 to Dec. 15, such as I proposed in *The Times* eight years ago . . . Ld D. observes with truth that railroads have introduced a bad custom of members living in the country till Easter, and coming up only when specially summoned.

Ld D. tells me of a letter which he has received from some correspondent, pointing out that of the small and partly rotten boroughs, a large majority are in the hands of Liberals. He seems much struck by the idea, and I used it to point out how little these serve any really conservative purpose. He says he has verified the statement to some extent.[53]

22 August 1864. The Lord-Lieutenancy of Ireland is going begging. It has been refused by the Duke of Devonshire, Lord Bessborough, and the cabinet generally, and is now expected to be offered to Lord Dufferin . . .

Princess Mary,[54] whose matrimonial inclinations have often amused London, is now making talk by her relations with Lord Hood, and has been sent down into Scotland to be out of the way. One of her strongest fancies was for Skelmersdale, not long before his marriage.

My father talks of his Irish administration,[55] which except the plan of national education, and the struggle with O'Connell, is but little remembered. He said the most laborious and disagreeable business he ever was engaged in was reforming the Irish civil list. Every job too gross to be sanctioned by an English parliament in the worst times was done by putting the object of it on the Irish pension list: sinecures flourished accordingly. He once passed fifteen or sixteen hours without leaving his room, having his meals brought there, engaged on a single set of papers. He found the Dublin offices corrupt, no secret could be kept: the clerks had their own friends and interests of their own to serve. He thought his chief work was the transfer of tithes from tenant to landlord, which put an end to a state of things which was in effect civil war. It had been necessary to protect the collectors of tithe by military force: and to take farm produce on the part of govt for the use of the military, when sold for non-payment of tithe, since no private purchaser would come forward. He believed that by that measure he had saved the Irish church. Next to that he reckoned the reform, although only partial, and carried out by his successors to a greater extent, of the grand jury system. The educational measure he put third. He added that no one knew what were his difficulties in dealing with O'Connell, who was not aware of the extent to which he (O'C.) was supported by a party in the cabinet.

2 September 1864. Ld D. complains of being unable to walk or shoot and has in consequence refused an invitation to Lord Chesterfield's for the middle of this month. He is occupied with Homer, otherwise the continual and absolute seclusion of his Knowsley life would be depressing. I do not think it [good] for his health, even now: and Homer is a resource which will soon fail.

3 September 1864. . . . Examined and noted a return delivered last session, showing the state of the constituencies as regards small, or rotten, boroughs. . . . Talk again with Ld D. on this subject[56] (he raising it): he seems to lay no stress on the importance of small boroughs provided that on their being disfranchised the counties receive their fair share of new members – they having less at present.

7 October 1864. . . . Reading Burton's *Dahomey*: a strange account of a strange place. He brings out one fact which is curious – viz. that the stoppage of the slave trade has led to increased massacres, as both prisoners of war and persons condemned to be sold for offences are now worthless, pecuniarily.

I hear from a private source that the Queen is bent in the event of a change of govt on making Lord Cowley foreign minister, which is probable for Ld C. paid great court to Albert, with whom he carried on a secret correspondence which the ministers were not allowed to see.

23 October 1864. Hatfield. Sir H. Bulwer[57] came from London. Much pleasant talk with him: his spirits good, though health and finances both in a bad way. (Lady Bulwer – ill-health – use of stimulants – this, it is feared, public – she at Constantinople.) He will not admit that the Turks are stationary: says we must not expect too much, must allow time, things move slowly in the East – all true, if applicable – and that a few years back their state was far worse than it is. They did not then know what they owed, or spent, or had – now there is something like a regular budget. Their debt light, trade growing – the Sultan in earnest, and doing well in the main. He has costly fancies such as building, but these are a small item in the expenses of a nation. He thinks the Turks will hold their own, as being the most warlike race, and though a minority among the whole, yet equal in strength to any of the other races separately – these hate each other quite as much as they hate the Turk.

He thinks badly of Greek prospects – I said Greece[58] wanted either a dictator or a republic, not a raw German boy sent over as a king, who was to 'reign without governing', according to the constitutional formula, which may suit England, but has never suited any other country, least of all one in so rude and primitive a state as Greece. To all this he warmly assented. He thought their tendency would be to split up into little communities, each with an interest and policy of its own – Athens and Sparta, minus the slaves and the literature.

24 October 1864. . . . My speech of last week[59] has been much criticised in the press . . . I gather that it has been a success, perhaps a considerable success. Ld D. is pleased – and the moderate Liberals, at any rate, find nothing to complain of. The more extreme partisans of both sides are disappointed at what they call its coldness of language but in this I think I have reflected pretty accurately the feeling of the educated classes – indifferent to party, not favourable to organic change, disposed towards peace, and ready to support economy and administrative improvement. Some of the Liberal papers are trying on the old device of asking 'How can you hold such opinions as you express, and yet call yourself a Conservative?' To which my answer is, or would be, were one required, that I have suggested no single measure of which even the remote and ultimate tendency can be to lessen the power of the upper classes, or increase that of the mob – which I take to be the real question at issue between the parties, so far as there is at present any.

5 December 1864. . . . Heard also of an extraordinary proposal on the part of Lord Russell to the following effect: that England and France jointly should undertake a negotiation for the purpose of inducing the Principalities to annexe themselves to Austria: who should in return cede the Venetian territory to Italy. A large sum to be paid to the government of the Principalities by way, I suppose, of indemnification for making a bad bargain: this sum to be raised by Italy, with the assistance of an Anglo-French guarantee. This scheme, or one like it, was actually laid before the cabinet, but there rejected without one voice raised in its favour except that of Palmerston.

. . . Curious story (and true) of Lord Clarendon giving the Duchess of Manchester advice not to take pains as she is doing, to attract the Prince of Wales.[60] He seems to have told her that public opinion would not endure even a suspicion of a connection of that kind, and that a large part of the unpopularity would fall on her.

1865

5 *January 1865.* . . . 'The Talbot scandal is spread far and wide . . . The woman's father, Arthur Talbot, is said to be the father of that child born two months after the marriage of the Chetwynds. The governess (Arthur Talbot's mistress) is supposed to have drugged the girl, and made the father drunk for the occasion: this was done for her own purposes to shut the girl's mouth. The question ,who was the father of that child, was all but asked one day in court . . .'

(This is extracted from a letter received by me yesterday. The girl spoken of is Arthur Talbot's daughter. Thus the case is one of incest.)[1]

21 *January 1865.* . . . Lord Granville has been in Paris proposing to the Princess Anna Murat, a relation and friend of Empress Eugénie. He was accepted, but the arrangement fell through, the lady's fortune (£80,000) not being what he expected.

22 *January 1865.* . . . Talk with F. [Stanley][2] on parliamentary preparation: advise him to train for public speaking by reading aloud, and to take lessons from Kirkel, or some other professor of elocution. He will like me have natural defects to overcome, and he cannot begin too early. . . . I urge F. not to commit himself to strong party views – which indeed he shows no desire to do . . .

23 *January 1865.* Shooting the meadows: Ld D. came out for the first time since his illness . . . I do not know what was killed, but it was a great deal. All the new planting in what was the ash plantation, and a great deal of that by the wall, is destroyed by rabbits and roe. So are most of the young trees in the pleasure ground, by hares. Ld D. encourages the white or Irish hares, which are already numerous: he will not have any of them killed. His love of shooting has grown stronger of late, especially as to the quantity of game: Ellison, the keeper in Bickerstaffe wood, has been threatened with dismissal because only 780 head were killed by five guns. Game is the almost continual subject of conversation. Disliking this state of things as a matter of taste, disapproving of it on the ground of expense, risk to watchers, encouragement of crime, and injury to farming. I yet feel the utter impossibility of interfering: (indeed to do so would be to give serious offence): while even to abstain from expressing a warm interest in the pursuit is to incur the reproach of selfish and unsocial absorption in one's own personal concerns: for Ld D. like many other men keenly interested in their pleasures, cannot understand that what he enjoys should not be equally enjoyed by those round him. The remaining alternative is to avoid Knowsley in the winter, and though staying away will undoubtedly give cause of displeasure,

I am disposed to think that it is on the whole the lesser evil. A minor, because merely personal, source of annoyance, is the ravage and destruction created among the woods, which cannot be effectually repaired during my lifetime.[3]

30 January 1865. News that Ld D. is again in the gout, and doubtful whether he shall be able to come up for the meeting of parliament.

3 February 1865. . . . Saw Disraeli: who is disinclined to make any move on the first night, thinking it useless, if, as is probable, ministers have no measures of importance to bring forward. He said there was considerable alarm as to the possibility of a quarrel with America: mercantile men were uneasy, and securities depressed, in consequence. Thought the military scheme sure to come to nothing: if indeed Gladstone were allowed to bring one forward. He knew nothing of the subjects to be discussed in the Queen's speech. There was a report of the reform question being again brought forward, but he did not believe it. If that were done, we should be in a crisis at once: otherwise it was better to let the inefficiency of the cabinet expose itself. He spoke with regret, and some annoyance, of the malt tax agitation, which he thought had been got up by Kelly mainly with a view to save his own seat: he had discouraged, and would discourage it as far as he safely could.

Dined Pakingtons, and talk on naval matters.

11 February 1865. . . . Disraeli's increasing apathy to public affairs is becoming a subject of general remark: I have myself noticed it for the last two or three years. The state of politics is sufficient to account for the change: advancing age may have also to do with it: occasional difficulty in acting with Ld D. between whom and him there is no very cordial feeling is another explanation: and possibly he is insensibly influenced by the change in his pecuniary position consequent on the old lady's legacy[4]: which makes office in that sense a matter of indifference.

12 February 1865. . . . Death of the Duke of Northumberland announced: his age was 73 . . . The Duke was as a landlord singularly liberal: he is thought to have laid out £500,000 in cottage-buildings and other like improvements. He restored Alnwick at a cost of £100,000: and leaves the property in perfect order. He was also a great builder of churches and schools. In early life he travelled far and wide: having been a sailor he retained to the last a strong liking for the naval service, and laboured zealously in 1852 for the improvement of the fleet. Unluckily Stafford's electioneering imprudences compromised him to some extent: he thought his colleagues less forward than they might have been to take up his defence (in which I think he was mistaken, for the case was an awkward one, and they could not count on a majority) and on the making up of Lord Derby's government he withdrew from practical politics. Of late he was but little seen in London . . .

14 February 1865. . . . Report about London generally believed (though not resting on any authority so far as I can learn) that Lord Palmerston will not meet his new parliament after dissolving, but retire to the House of Lords, still retaining his office. In this way he would be able to assist Gladstone while new to the leadership, and mediate in any quarrels that may arise – of which there will probably be not a few. Of Gladstone the language held on his own side the House is, 'He must lead, there is no one who can compete with him, and yet his temper and restlessness make him entirely unfit.' *The Times* is his declared enemy, his colleagues are, to put it in the mildest form, not cordial friends: with the opposition he is as decidedly unpopular as Palmerston is the reverse. His strength lies in his extraordinary gift of speech, his great general ability, and the support of the mercantile class in the manufacturing towns – not in the City, where though admired he is a good deal distrusted. To my surprise, Bright in conversation today abused him bitterly for holding out hopes to the public which he cannot realise, and for not having expressed northern sympathies in the American quarrel. But, on this last question, Bright's vehemence is hardly compatible with sanity: peace, economy, human life, free trade, personal liberty, all are as nothing compared with the one paramount idea of bringing the great popular republic out of the struggle triumphant. The language he habitually uses on this subject (I have heard it more than once) would scarcely be credible if reported. He expects a war between England and the U.S. which he says our own base and mean conduct has provoked: of the result being favourable to America he does not doubt: and he thinks it will serve us right. Not finding many to agree with him he is more than ever embittered and disgusted with life.

17 February 1865. . . . Long debate on Irish administration of justice . . . Cairns opened the case – a very delicate one to argue, without giving offence to Catholic members – with admirable tact . . . Whiteside declaimed in his accustomed style . . . Disraeli's disgust at the whole proceeding was amusing to witness: he looked at it as possibly endangering the Catholic alliance, his favourite idea since 1852, and which in point of numerical results has succeeded, though it may be a question whether the injury done by it in other ways does not countervail the gain. I think also that his habitual dislike of all independent activity among members of his party – which is quite needless since no one disputes his leadership, but also quite apparent – extends to Cairns. Whiteside he has long detested, and it must be acknowledged that Whiteside though a brilliant rhetorician, has not many other qualities of a statesman.

4 March 1865. . . . Talk, inter alia, of Gladstone, whose social unpopularity appears to be increasing. His colleagues detest him, and make little scruple in saying so – Wood and Clarendon more particularly. He is complained of as overbearing and dictatorial beyond what is permitted even to men of his eminence, while his eccentricities attract some ridicule. At a country house last Sunday (I think Lord Chesham's) he passed the evening in singing hymns with his wife, the Bishop of Oxford, who was also present, reluctantly compelled to join but revenging himself afterwards by telling the story. Between him and the Whig party there is a fundamental difference. They are sceptical, he is dogmatic and inclined to religious enthusiasm: they are oligarchic and territorial by tradition: his connections are mercantile and popular: they are bound together by close family and social ties, he is isolated, will never consent to share power, but like Peel, if he makes any friends, will choose them only among men young enough to be his pupils. Yet these differences, though fatal to friendship, may give way before the necessity of political union: at least for a time.

16 March 1865. ... There having been widely circulated a report that ministers intended supporting Dillwyn's motion on the Irish Church, I asked Sir C. [Wood] if there was any truth in it? He said, 'none', that the subject had not even been seriously discussed, so far as he knew – that for himself he thought the Irish Establishment an abomination, and believed most public men did so, but to attempt to meddle with it would be madness – that he should be sorry to answer for what Gladstone might or might not say on any question (laughing) but he was not aware of any intention to support Dillwyn even indirectly. Certainly no joint action would be taken by the cabinet.

18 March 1865. Visits ... Dined R. Cecil's at his new little house in Duchess St ... Thence Lady Palmerston's: where stayed late: Delane, as usual, conspicuous, and deeply engaged in conversation with the Premier: which is a little affectation, which both enjoy: it tells the world of their close alliance.

I insert here, having space, my note of conversation with Gladstone on the railway question (Feb. 20). He named the members of the commission as he proposed them, and seemed especially anxious that Bright should serve. He said for himself he was decidedly in favour of the plan of buying up the interest of the companies on behalf of govt and leasing them again for short terms, under stringent conditions. They had too much influence, the present companies, they were becoming a power in the state: and the waste of means by delay and diversion of traffic was intolerable. But if purchase by the State were impossible, or thought to be so, there would remain various palliative measures. The control of parliament, or of the Board of Trade, might be made far more stringent. The State could give in return:

1. Abolition of tax now levied on railways.
2. Indirect gain by abolishing other taxes on locomotion.
3. Saving of interest by taking over their debentures, the amount of which is about £100,000,000.

I asked as to this last if it were feasible, as it certainly seems to be, if the loss to the public is none, or rather if the public, by lending its credit, can make a profit, while the saving to the companies is great, how comes it that the idea has never been seriously entertained before? G.'s answer was, in substance, that there had never been convenient opportunity, time had been wanting, Sir R. Peel had hesitated, other matters had pressed, in short, it had not been thought ripe: I enquired whether the thought had ever crossed his mind of taking over the whole telegraphic system – making it a branch of the P.O.? He said yes, but he doubted the expediency: telegraphs, at least those on the present system, might be superseded and the capital invested in them be lost.

22 March 1865. . . . Lady Herbert, wife of S. Herbert, has announced her conversion to Catholicism, which has been concealed for two years, lest she should lose the care of her son, now about fifteen. Gladstone has been, as is believed, her adviser throughout. I heard as regards Gladstone the following odd story: my authority the best (I do not here set it down). This very day, at the levée, Lord Palmerston spoke anxiously to Lord Clarendon on the subject of Gladstone's religious ideas: saying that he (Lord P.) had the best reason for knowing that if G. were rejected at Oxford, and returned for a constituency like S. Lancashire, he would within six months profess himself a R. Catholic. Lord Clarendon was utterly amazed, does not recollect what answer he made, and had no opportunity of asking Lord P. for further explanation. He thinks Lord P. is misinformed, and that his idea may have arisen out of excuses made by G. for Lady Herbert, or from his language on the Colenso business, or from that held by him on the Irish church, which is to say the least ambiguous. – The last time that Lord Clarendon saw the late Lord Aberdeen, Lord A. said to him referring to Gladstone, 'You must keep that d——d fellow always in office, give him plenty to do, else he is sure to do mischief.' It is certain that of late G. has been in an excited and irritable condition, for which nothing in the state of public business appears to account: hence perhaps reports which his colleagues have exaggerated, and which have reached Lord P.

31 March 1865. . . . Lord Clarendon consults me confidentially about Ld D. whose manner on the secret committee appears to have created some talk among his brother peers. He is said to have shown great irritability, without apparent cause: as though annoyed at the whole proceeding. Other stories of the same kind reach me from other quarters. I have not myself noticed this, but explained it as probably implying the approach of a fit of gout. Other men probably suffer as much in the same way, but they keep it to themselves; with Ld D.[5] as with a boy, whatever is in his mind comes out, without reference to consequences. He appears also to have taken up warmly the case of this Edmunds – on what grounds I don't know. He is suffering from a new complaint, or rather inconvenience; violent shaking of the hand, so as to be unable to lift a cup or glass, or at times to write. Dr Ferguson says it is only a form of gout. Stimulants relieve it.

25 April 1865. . . . A cabinet met this morning, at which the budget was discussed. Whether it was finally settled, I could not gather, but the arrangements proposed were, reduction of insurance duty to 18d. instead of 3s.: reduction of income tax by twopence in the pound: both these, I believe, were agreed to: a farther discussion arose as to reduction of tea duty to one half its present amount, which involves a sacrifice of more than two millions: G. wants to do this, and in lieu of the revenue so lost to extend and increase the house tax: the plan was objected to, as complicating what was simple, and as too ambitious. I believe it was rejected, certainly it was not accepted.

This reaches me direct: I could not resist dropping a few hints to the Duke of Argyll which showed that I was cognisant of their proceedings, and enjoyed his astonished look. He may well have been astonished, for the cabinet only broke up at 4 p.m.

Lord Palmerston's illness of last week, which the newspapers have mentioned only in a casual way, was serious. Dr Drage, called in to attend him, says 'it is the beginning of the end' though it may go on for months.

Lord Russell is fixed upon as the next premier – Lord Clarendon declining to have anything to do with that place, for which he feels himself bodily and mentally unfit.

2 May 1865. . . . The budget, of which the secret has certainly been less well kept this year than usual, was confided to Delane two days before its publication, and even before the final settlement of its provisions in cabinet. Gladstone, and others of his colleagues, make no disguise of their annoyance at this unusual course, which is the act of Lord Palmerston singly.

15 May 1865. . . . Breakfast with Bishop of Oxford, and much pleasant talk . . . Some one said of Milnes – but after he had left – 'that he had done away with the two most disagreeable accompaniments of London society – introductions and invitations' – which is really a fair description of the said Milnes's frank unceremonious ways.

. . . Lord Palmerston reappeared, the first time since his illness: he was cheered of course, but would not walk up the House, coming in the back way instead, not wishing it to be seen (I suppose) how feeble his walk is.

16 May 1865. . . . Dined C. Fortescue's . . . Lady Clanricarde[6] discoursed much on the state of Ireland – very clever, with a flow of words and thought like what is related of her father. 'If Ireland had only lain on the other side of England, it would have been French long ago – and they would have been much happier as Frenchmen.' 'Ireland is overshadowed by English prosperity and greatness.' 'There is as much disaffection among us as there is in Poland.' 'In all Europe you will not find two national characters more incompatible than those of the Irish and English.' 'The chief business of the Lord-Lieutenant is to flatter the Irish people by making promises which he is not allowed to keep.' She also related an odd conversation with Gladstone – whom however she detests, so that her story must be taken with suspicion – the purport being to show that he, G., believes in phrenology. He assured her, she says, that in his own case the external shape of the head had changed with his mental progress.

18 May 1865. . . . Sir R. Peel expresses his intention of joining the Conservative party on Ld P.'s death. This purpose he does not in any way keep to himself, but rather thinks it fair to give his colleagues full notice.

4 June 1865. . . . Some political discussion with Northcote: he for giving a charter to the Catholic University, argues strongly in favour of it, cannot see any valid objection. I suggest making some attempt in the next parliament to establish a sinking fund, and reduce the debt – Northcote agrees cordially, saying it is right, whether popular or no.[7]

Van De Weyer[8] among many other things says Louis Napoleon foretold to him the approaching fall of the French monarchy, two years before it happened.

. . . Northcote talks among other things of the extreme increase of luxury among the gentry – every man now must do like the richest – no one can give a dinner without champagne, no one can live without a carriage, children must have ponies to ride, etc. . . . I think there is truth in this.

30 June 1865. . . . Strange and disagreeable stories are going about London touching the Court: founded on fact to a considerable extent, though probably not justifying the suspicion to which they lead. The Queen has taken a fancy to a certain Scotch servant, by name Brown:[9] will have no one else to wait upon her, makes him drive her out alone in a pony carriage, walk after, or rather with her, gives orders through him to the equerries, allows him access to her such as no one else has, and in various ways distinguishes him beyond what is customary or fitting in that position. There is nothing in this, most likely, except a fancy for a good-looking and intelligent dependant: but the thing has become a joke through Windsor, where H.M. is talked of as 'Mrs Brown': and if it lasts the joke will grow into a scandal. Eccentricity, solitude, and the impossibility of hearing an honest opinion are explanation sufficient. – Sir E. Landseer, to whom sundry verbal messages have been sent through this man, seems to be active in making mischief, at least he is quoted as authority for the oddest part of the story, which I do not care to set down. Lord Clarendon also gives it more publicity than is expedient.

In July 1865 Palmerston decided to dissolve, a general election was fought on no particular issue except confidence in the prime minister, and, as in 1857, Palmerston was returned with a much increased majority. At King's Lynn, Stanley had a contested election, and his non-partisan attitude proved electorally successful:

Lord Stanley (Cons.) 445   Buxton (Lib.) 401   Walpole (Cons.) 339

Seventy or eighty of Buxton's supporters voted for Stanley: without this

Liberal support his majority would not have been a very secure one.

18 July 1865. . . . [Clarendon] despondent about the state of affairs, says the inevitable political future is Russell and Gladstone, the latter will have all real power, and of him he has a deep distrust, thinks he will do anything for popularity, and ally himself with the ultras. I answered, 'Half the Whigs are really conservative, or at least moderate in opinion: if they can only agree, form a section (I do not call it a party) of their own, and control without abandoning the Liberal side of the House, they are strong enough to hold the balance.' He cordially approved, but seemed to doubt whether anything would be done, private interest and ambition being strong on the other side. Dislike and fear of Gladstone are the strongest feelings in Ld C.'s mind where politics are concerned.

19 July 1865. . . . Gladstone is at Liverpool, making effective speeches to large audiences, and canvassing along with his brother, Robertson Gladstone,[10] whose extreme violence of opinion is notorious, and will do [him] no good. Lady Brownlow, who arrived today, tells a story of Gladstone having a sister in confinement, which if true, explains some of the family eccentricities. Robertson Gladstone is on some points hardly sane: and in 1857 the minister's mind was obviously off its balance.

26 July 1865. . . . The elections are now over, the general result being that Lord Palmerston has gained about 25 seats: on a party division supposing all to vote according to their supposed sympathies he would have a majority varying from 60 to 70. But this is a fallacious test when applied to measures: among the Whigs there are at least 30, probably 40, who like Elcho, Lowe, Horsman, or Enfield, would separate from their party on any occasion where it seemed to show radical sympathies. Gladstone's speeches are watched with extreme and increasing interest: he has become the central figure in our politics, and his importance is far more likely to increase than to diminish.

27 July 1865. . . . Extract from a letter: 'The cabinet' (held yesterday) 'was a mere form: the Premier blundered over a long list of returns, nothing more nor less than what was in *The Times*: he was not "cocky". Gladstone was quiet and subdued, nobody manifested any signs of triumph: not a word of discussion about Reform: the Bright element is not thought in the ascendant in the new parliament . . .' When they parted, somebody, I fancy my informant, ventured on an expression of hope that Lord Russell would be so good as not to declare war on all the world before they met again – the joke was taken up and ended in a general volley upon the little man. Lord P. and Lord Clarendon had a private meeting this morning, and some talk about Reform: Ld P. is well satisfied with G.'s moderation in S. Lancs, and is inclined to flatter himself that Reform may remain a dead letter. Ld C. tries to undeceive him: they both admit to each other that they are sound Conservatives in heart, abhorring the notion of lowering the franchise, and determined to stand firm on the point of property as against numbers. Much inclined for a commission to enquire into the real grievances, and Reeve[11] who wished to write an article in the next *Edinburgh* on that subject has been stopped from doing so, lest there should be an appearance of dictation, if they find they are strong enough to carry it.

1 August 1865. . . . Read . . . Finlay's history of the Greek revolution[12] a strange picture of patriotism, courage, barbarism, and dishonesty. Impossible to take interest in any of their leading men . . . nor are the characteristic qualities of the people attractive, at least as described by Finlay: yet their love of country appears genuine, and their perseverance respectable. There is a curious quotation from Polybius, in which he speaks of Greek inability to keep faith in money matters, in terms which would apply to the present day.[13]

2 August 1865. . . . Ld D. tells me he has written to Disraeli, expressing in strong terms his conviction that neither of them will ever hold office again – in which opinion D. seems to agree. The question now is, whether a moderate party of Whigs and Lib. Conservatives can be formed, on the (probably) inevitable split occurring between the Whig and Radical sections. Ld Clarendon would be as fit by his social qualities as any man to bring about such a fusion: but he wants the energy, and perhaps the will, to play so leading a part.

24 August 1865. . . . I think these grounds [Knowsley] will not be exceeded for natural beauty by any in the country, notwithstanding disadvantages of soil and climate. Justice has never been done in the family to the late Lord Derby[14] whose plans were excellent, though he was too hasty in their execution, and thus left everything unfinished, besides having to alter his own work again and again. He found this place a wilderness – it had been neglected for upwards of fifty years – for his father[15] lived fashionably in London and at the Oaks during the first half of his life, and passed the second half in trying to repair, by economy, the mischief he had done to his fortune. All that we do now is to work upon, and complete his designs.

4 September 1865. Hatfield for the day: fine hot weather, pulled on the Lea, walked in Milward's park etc. Dined Carlton.

It is exactly ten years on this day since . . .[16]

I seem to myself grown younger rather than older, both in health and feeling.

5 September 1865. Left London by 2.45 train for Birmingham . . .[17] arrived about 5.30, and found Mr Boyle's house at Handsworth (Soho House, once the property of Boulton the engineer . . .) Met Lyttelton, Adderley, Dr Miller the popular preacher . . . and one or two others including the Mayor of Birmingham. Much good talk, and a thoroughly pleasant evening.

. . . The Mayor a great chemist and farmer as well as a tradesman. . . . I asked at what rate he estimated profits in Birmingham? He said 10–12% for large concerns – not more – in these the risk is less: small manufacturers from 15 to 30%, or more, but with great hazard of failure. He talked of Bright, with more dislike than approval, though himself a Liberal: said the number of his supporters among the employing class was not considerable. There is a feeling that he neglects both parliamentary attendance and local claims to a somewhat unreasonable extent: which indeed is the fact, for during weeks he never once appears in the House, nor does he show himself here, except to make a yearly political demonstration. He is considered among his constituents as a man disappointed and disgusted by failure. There is a good deal of intimidation among workmen in Birmingham: he (Mr W.) named a man employed by him as a bricklayer, who was ordered off work by the union leaders, his offence being that he got through more work in the day than trade rules allowed. This man begged to be sent to Mr W.'s farm in the country, to escape annoyance, and it was done: but the union found out his retreat, and compelled him to throw up the job he was on, under pain of expulsion. – These are the things which make employers conservative.

12 September 1865. . . . Dined with Mr Ratcliff of Edgbaston . . . He tells me the Edgbaston estate was bought by Lord Calthorpe's father or grand-father, for £23,000: it is now worth that yearly, being all built upon, and will double or treble in value.

. . . A good debate on the metric system of France. The case in its favour seems to me very strong: especially considering that we have no rival system – English weights and measures are a mere chaos – they vary in every place and every trade.

14 September 1865. . . . Gerard tells me that Lord Crawford has sold his coals near Wigan for £350,000, reserving also some annual payment in the form of a royalty. He used to work the pits on his own account.

17 September 1865. . . . Ld D. in less pain than yesterday,[18] but his attack threatens to be a long one. Frederick and I talk this over, and agree in thinking the liability to these attacks increased by ennui: he lives in almost extreme solitude, allowing no one to walk with him, receiving no guests (not one has entered the house since July except Scharf, who was there on business) and passes most of the day in his room. This is a new habit. There has been also some imprudence in diet, but not much. Ld D. thinks badly of his own health, and has often said among friends that he does not think his life worth more than three or four years' purchase. I hope and believe that expressions of this kind indicate only a passing feeling of despondency.

18 September 1865. Left Knowsley . . . To Hatfield . . . No guests. Lord Cowley has been here: he says he had from Lord Palmerston orders to tell the French govt in plain terms that the Portsmouth civilities meant nothing – that England could not and would not disarm: this message, as given, was in a style so little courteous that Lord Cowley determined if he acted upon it at all, to soften it down greatly in the delivery. He thinks that old age is telling upon Ld P. and that he is falling back on one of his old *idées fixes* – jealousy of the French. The rumours of his gout untrue: he had rashly accepted an invitation to Bristol involving a great deal of fatigue, and was persuaded almost at the last moment by his family to give up the intention.

In the *Spectator*, a clever article on my late speeches. The drift of the critic's writing is the following. 'Ld S. is not so much a liberal, or a conservative, as a neutral: disliking the power of the State, as such, seeking to limit the action of the central govt as far as possible, and inclined to hold that the importance of politics in life is overrated: agreeing in this with Mr H. Spencer.' This is just criticism, whether meant as praise or the reverse, for it expresses an idea which has been long gaining strength in my mind, that of the danger of erecting to ourselves a master called 'the State' who shall interfere in and regulate everything. Modern democracy loves such a master, and seeks to strengthen his position since he represents the universal equality of the citizen, and if you must be governed, they argue, better be governed by a minister or central authority whom you do not see than by one or many of your richer neighbours. For this reason, in France, decentralisation is entirely an upper-class movement – the workingmen think it hostile to their interest – and perhaps are right.

The *Spectator* reproaches me with not expressing an interest in the Italian or American questions – to which my answer is that it was plainly the duty of England to stand neutral in both – as is now admitted . . . Another of his comments is better – he says that I represent a reaction from Ld D.'s political peculiarities – his heat, his eagerness, his imprudence, his zeal for persons and causes, etc. This is probably true, the feeling is intelligible to me, and though unconsciously to myself, may have affected my tendencies. But I think the distaste for hot partisanship, and the wish to confine politicians within narrow limits of action, is not peculiar to myself: it seems generally diffused among educated men of middle age, and is pretty faithfully reflected in the press.

[Stanley took his holiday abroad (20 September–20 October 1865), making a walking tour of the Pyrenees in the company of Elliot,[19] a senior Colonial Office official. His diary was more concerned with fleas than with the death of Palmerston on 18 October, two days before his eighty-first birthday.]

20 October 1865. . . . Rail to London: and home at 6 p.m. exactly . . . Letters and papers all the evening: a considerable accumulation of these: no dinner, tea in my room, worked till near 12. The great bulk of my correspondence consists of requests to attend meetings, applications for money, and statements of personal grievances of the writers. It really seems as if the time and money of an M.P. were considered as public property.

22 October 1865. . . . Lady Salisbury not much better: it is a kind of nervous seizure which at first prevented, and still affects, her speech. The doctor does not think it serious. There is no suffering. The reconstruction of the ministry is proceeding without difficulty: Lord Russell its head (this had been settled in anticipation of the event): Gladstone leads H. of C. which was in any case inevitable: Lord Clarendon is offered the F.O. but hesitates till he knows more as to Lord Russell's intentions as regards reform, on which subject he (Lord C.) is very conservative. There is a general expectation that the new parliament will meet in Nov. or Dec. and that a reform bill will be brought forward.

23 October 1865. Hatfield . . . Wrote to Disraeli to propose an interview. In *Times*, a bitter attack on Lord Russell. I remember Delane telling me that he would not be able to keep the party together for a week. He is accused of acting without consultation with his colleagues as when he proposed a reform bill in 1852: of throwing them over when convenient to himself, e.g. the Duke of Newcastle in 1855 – and of living entirely in a little Whig clique, which shuts him out from the rest of the world. It is curious that for many years he has never taken in nor read *The Times*.

More court gossip, and of a disagreeable kind: the Queen's fancy for her Scotch servant, Brown, continues, and is so marked and public as to lead to general comments. It is said that the subject cannot long be kept out of the newspapers. This man is admitted to her confidence in a way that no one else is, and orders sent through him to persons of higher rank, which alone is enough to create jealousy. The Queen has repelled all friendship with subjects as beneath her dignity, and is not on good terms with any of her family, hence it is impossible that she should be warned of what is being said about her in the world.

26 October 1865. . . . Hughenden: where found D. and Mrs D. alone. He in good health and excellent spirits. It seems as if the prospect of renewed political life had excited him afresh, and that he had thrown off the lethargy which has been growing upon him for the last year or two.

27 October 1865.[20] Out nearly all day: great improvements at Hughenden: the house, which though comfortable was old and plain, is now recased, and really handsome· the garden enlarged, new paths cut through the woods, fresh plantations made, etc. – the results of the Torquay legacy. D. enjoys this place thoroughly, and is never happier than when showing it to a friend.

He asked me to be his literary executor: a trust which I accepted willingly. The mass of his own and his father's papers is considerable, as may be supposed.

Much talk on politics: of which I need set down only the general result. He is informed (which I also had heard) that at a cabinet held in August it was decided that a reform bill of some kind was necessary: but no discussion on its principles then took place. He thinks that the moderate section of the cabinet will prevail, and that a moderate, or illusory, measure will be introduced: £20 or £15 in counties, and £8 in boroughs. In that event it will be our duty to help in passing the bill (in this I cordially agreed): if on the other hand they try for a £10 and £6 franchise, a considerable secession, headed by Lowe, is inevitable: and this will probably be sufficient to defeat the measure. If the bill be moderate, the breach between Whigs and Radicals will be widened: and sooner or later considerable changes will follow. – He showed me a correspondence he had had with Ld D. in the summer, in which, pointing towards a fusion, he offered to give up the lead of the opposition, or of the House if successful. This Ld D. would have nothing to say to, and indeed I hardly think the proposal serious, for who else could lead? The object of writing, however, was to induce Ld D. to think seriously of union with the moderate Whigs. Ld D.'s reply was rather discouraging: he would lead none but a 'distinctly and avowedly conservative' government: at the same time saying that he saw no prospect of such a govt being formed. D. had on this dropped the correspondence: which indeed could at the moment lead to no practical result. He talked a good deal of Gladstone, puzzled by his persistence in High Church opinions: which he cannot think affected, for where is the motive? yet which it is hard for him to think that a man of so much talent can really hold. I named R. Palmer and my father as two other instances of orthodox opinions strongly held by minds of undoubted capacity. He did not deny the fact, but repeated his expression of perplexity.

28 October 1865. Left Hughenden early: London 11.30. – Travellers where met Ld Clarendon, and some talk on the political situation. He had seen Ld Russell yesterday, and said 'I never knew him talk so moderately or so humbly on the subject of reform before. He seemed oppressed with his responsibility, anxious to do as little as he can, and only uneasy at the idea of losing character if he does nothing.' We discussed reform: he (Ld C.) appeared to think the £6 borough franchise out of the question, and dwelt a good deal on the subject of the disfranchisement of small boroughs. I said, as I have done in public, 'I do not object to a measure of disfranchisement in itself, provided you make a fair division of the seats gained between town and country: but you must recollect that by any such attempt you increase enormously your chances of failure, since you must deal with seats held on your own side as well as on ours: and every such seat touched is a vote against you.' I urged him strongly to rely on the support of the Conservative party in the event of a moderate measure being determined upon: and expressed my belief that this support would not be limited to a bare vote in favour of the bill, but that we should discourage any attacks made on the ministry on the ground of their having broken faith with their supporters. Ld C. observed in the course of conversation 'Gladstone's temper and want of tact are what we all know: but he has looked into himself, he has been warned by a personal friend (a woman: no man could do it) and he is determined to conciliate the House if possible.'

30 October 1865. . . . Went with Lord Derby to Huyton to receive the Prince and Princess of Wales . . . The P. of Wales sat up till 3 a.m. smoking: which is said to be his usual custom: he talked a great deal, neither very sensibly nor the reverse. He is easy and pleasant in his manners: in face and figure he is growing fat, which gives an air of heaviness . . . The only thing I recollect of his talk was his expressing a wish to go to Ireland in place of the Lord Lieutenant with no political functions, but to hold a court there.

3 November 1865. . . . The royal party left this morning: Ld and Lady D. and F. Stanley are all wearied out, and I am not much better, having had on an average only from four to five hours of rest each night, with incessant occupation all day . . .

Mrs Legh of Lyme last night at the ball confided to me that her chief wish and her husband's was that he should be made a peer. The family is old, and he has a rental (she says) of £40,000 a year: but they have hardly earned a title by parliamentary importance.

I received this morning a letter from Ld Russell, asking for some conversation with me on political affairs, and fixing a day next week: private hints had previously reached me that this conversation is meant to lead to an offer of office, but as no allusion to the subject to be discussed was contained in Lord R.'s note, I could only answer it, accepting the interview.

I named the matter to Ld D. who treated it with entire indifference. On my requesting him however to explain his own view of the situation, in order that our language might be as nearly as possibly the same, he repeated with great decision that fusion or coalition was for him impossible: he must be first in his cabinet, and the cabinet must be one formed of men in whom he had entire confidence. I remarked that in the actual state of things this was equivalent to saying that he should never hold office again: which he did not seem to admit, or quite to like, and I dropped the subject. It is clear to me that he is neither prepared on the one hand to abandon his position as Conservative leader, nor on the other to make the most of it. Meanwhile he has alienated personal friends, and is less popular with the party than at any former time.

In regard to Ld Russell's offer, it is probably made only for the sake of saying that it has been made: the objections to its acceptance are overwhelming: it is seldom possible for a politician to walk singly across the floor of the House: and never so without some great change in affairs having occurred, which is not the case now: the unsettled state of the reform question would alone make a junction with the actual cabinet impossible, while it also renders their position precarious. I could not honourably abandon Disraeli without cause: nor would it be safe, considering Ld D.'s temperament, and his absolute control over estate affairs, to risk a personal rupture with him[21]: the decision therefore has not cost me a moment of hesitation or regret.

5 November 1865. . . . Much talk . . . about our late visitors: on the whole the impression is not very favourable to the Prince: he has been civil, good-humoured, and willing to please, which in his position goes a long way: but his sense is not thought much of: and people do not scruple to say that two or three years of his present course of life will do away with the little in-tellect he possesses. The Princess pleases everyone: her face is beautiful and her manners very simple and natural: it is a misfortune that she is so deaf as to be unable to follow a conversation, and often to answer at cross-purposes. They have left £50 for the servants, and something for the keepers . . .

10 November 1865. . . . Called on Ld Russell at his request, where he asked me to join his cabinet: he made the offer briefly,[22] and (I thought) as if not expecting it to be accepted. I declined, giving three reasons: one personal, that of the awkwardness of placing myself in a position of direct hostility to Ld Derby: one, the difficulty of leaving a party with which one has long acted, without special reason for such a proceeding, and especially of doing so alone: the third, the unsettled state of the reform question. Ld R. com-bated my reasons a little, but evidently felt their weight. The only remark he made which struck me was a reference to the fate of Peel and Canning, as a warning against accepting power with liberal ideas and conservative allies. He seemed to admit the difficulty of isolated action in English public life: and as his last word, intimated that a second seat in cabinet would be held open if any friend of mine were to be introduced into it, but further than this he could not go. I told him in reply I could not expect more, nor indeed so much: but hinted at the possibility of some combination of moderate men from both sides, in the event of his (Ld R.) breaking with the party of Bright and the ultras. We parted good friends: I went upstairs and sat some time with Lady Russell.

(I have heard since that Ld R. expressed himself in very gratifying terms as to this interview, saying that the result was exactly as he had foreseen, and adding remarks personally complimentary to myself.)

18 November 1865. Hatfield. The Cranbornes, who with some others have been staying here, left this morning: the quarrel between Lord Cranborne and his father is quite made up: they differ too much in character to allow of a very cordial feeling existing between them, but are on good and friendly terms. I think that after the first shock that the death of the elder brother, and [Lord Robert Cecil's] succession to his place, has been a relief to Lord Salisbury. His strongest feeling is attachment to his family as an institution – wish that its importance should continue: and of this there is now a reason-able prospect.

19 November 1865. . . . Heard (indirectly) from one of the Cowper family, an account of Ld P.'s last hours. One of his medical attendants, Dr P. Smith, is a very religious man, and insisted on his having warning of his danger: which he understood, but took little notice of, being indeed mostly in a state of lethargy. He allowed his relations to pray with him, making some signs of assent: but his last intelligible words related to Belgium, and the acknowledgment of its independence by France.

21 November 1865. . . . Talk with Lowe, who strong against Ld Russell, saying that he cannot carry a £6 borough franchise, if he tries it failure is inevitable, and at the same time both he and Gladstone are so pledged that they can scarcely avoid with honour making the attempt.

. . . Talbot and my sister[23] arrived in St James's Square . . . The Talbots describe Ld D. as in high spirits, but absolutely refusing to take either air or exercise: he will not leave the house.

22 November 1865. . . . Called on Disraeli, who just returned to town: long talk with him on affairs: but except some vague reports founded on the conversation of Whig friends, he had no new data. He showed me a letter just received from Ld D. on the subject of Irish church, which he (Ld D.) thinks is on the point of being attacked, and determines to defend to the utmost. As the question is not much discussed in the press, the only foundation for supposing an attack likely is the removal of Sir R. Peel: a step easily explicable in other ways, for the reckless rollicking fashion in which Peel disposes of affairs is as little in accordance with Irish as with English taste. In fact his appointment was a personal fancy of Palmerston's, and from the first was generally condemned. Sir R. [Peel] is in embarrassed circs, from extravagance of every kind, which makes office an object.

5 December 1865. . . . Heard of the disposition of Ld Palmerston's property. The Irish estates, which are small and encumbered, go to the Sullivan family: Broadlands to W. Cowper, who is to take the name of Temple (to which no one has a better right): whatever money there is – but it is said to be little – goes to the Ashley and Jocelyn families. Ld P. though well off was of late years always embarrassed: it is believed by his friends that the cause was, payments made in support of illegitimate children of whom he has several, and pensions to women whom he had kept long ago. – By a natural feeling, the Cowpers cannot bear to have the relationship discussed: they feel it as a discredit, the more so as the reason cannot be acknowledged.

7 December 1865. . . . Delane and Walter have disagreed as to the position which *The Times* ought to hold towards Ld Russell, and it is said D. has resigned his post as editor.

Meeting Ld Clarendon the other day, he talked with some alarm of Belgian prospects. Old King Leopold is thought dying: the Duke of Brabant is said to be more than ever in the hands of the priests: a revolution is expected: which naturally will turn to the advantage of France.

The Emperor thinks we should not fight if only Antwerp were kept out of French hands: and this might be arranged by giving it back to Holland.

8 December 1865. . . . In club, met Ld Clarendon: who talked before half a dozen people of the Albert memorial, the new hall of science to be erected in honour of the late prince, etc. The latter he thinks will cost £200,000 if built, and the subscription for it will not be one-twentieth part of that sum. He laughs at the whole thing, and only regrets the probability of its involving the Queen in trouble and pecuniary loss.

To me, he talked a good deal of the Queen: said she was 'unapproachable': if she disliked a subject, or anticipated opposition, she said: 'it made her ill to talk' or simply 'that she did not wish to have it discussed': there was no check or control upon her: no insanity, but extreme wilfulness and want of self-restraint. I asked if she had grown worse or better of late? he said there was not much change. Albert had once said to him, 'It is my business to watch that mind every hour and minute – to watch as a cat watches at a mousehole' – and he had done so, till the constant effort wore him out. He (Albert) had wished to die, and had often said so during his last illness: the Queen had repeated this to Lord Clarendon more than once, apparently unconscious of what it implied.

17 December 1865. . . . An heiress, Miss Long, . . . married Wellesley Pole, afterwards Lord Mornington: by which marriage he (W.P.) came into a property estimated at upwards of £80,000 yearly, not including ready money to the amount of £200,000: this enormous estate he completely dissipated in about ten years, neglecting and ill-using his wife, who died early. He lived to old age, supported by the Duke of Wellington: but to the last his habits of extravagance so clung to him that the money necessary for his maintenance had to be paid to a servant who took care that his wants were supplied. There seems to have been in his nature a touch of insanity: as is often seen in one member of a family where the rest are remarkable for talent. His son, the late Lord Mornington, lived mostly in Paris, an eccentric but harmless personage. He died under the age of sixty, and Ld Cowley so little expected to derive any advantage from his death that when the lawyer called upon him to announce it he did not even ask as to the contents of the will. As Ld Cowley had not of his own, official salary apart, so much as £1,500 a year, the change in his position is great.[24] He now professes himself weary of Paris, and no doubt is sincere: yet having been all his life accustomed to business, the life of a country gentleman will never suit him.

18 December 1865. London by 3 p.m. Travelled up with the Clarendons: more talk about reform: he uneasy, thinks there are signs of a storm in the distance, that if a bill were to be proposed and fail agitation would begin: that it only wants a little resistance to excite the same kind of feeling that was produced by the Duke of Wellington's memorable declaration against any reform in . . . 1830: I repeated to him what I had said to Elcho as to the composition of the new House: he evidently alarmed, fearing success much, and failure more. – No question of army or navy reductions had yet been raised in cabinet ... He showed me the despatches with which Sir H. Storks goes out, and that addressed to Gen. Eyre.

1866

1 January 1866. . . . Lord Clarendon talked freely on public matters . . . He referred again and again to the extreme difficulty of doing anything with the Queen: not obstinacy, disregard of everything except her own convenience, etc. He spoke of Gladstone as curiously altered and softened by the responsibility of power.

7 January 1866. . . . With F. [his brother] and much talk: he not pleased with the Irish estate, as too far from London, residence impossible, disturbed state of country, liability to receive no rents for a year or two in bad times: sounds me as to possibility of selling. I oppose this as it is an old family property: and say 'Do nothing in Ld D.'s lifetime, if afterwards you are of the same mind, it will be easy to arrange an exchange of the Irish lands against house-property in Liverpool or Manchester, which involves no outlay, and is a certain income'.

9 January 1866. . . . I have not set down what Lady Clarendon told me at The Grove,[1] that Ld C. had twice refused the Gov.-Generalship on family grounds: and also the offer of a marquisate with the title of Rochester.

10 January 1866. . . . W. Hornby[2] thinks well, as I do, of Ld D.'s health, which certainly improves under the singular regime which he has adopted of never leaving the house, and taking all his exercise in the form of a game of billiards after luncheon. I have seldom seen him in more equally good spirits.

13 January 1866. . . . Gregory[3] has had an offer of office, as Lowe had some weeks back: which indicates either that Ld Russell has great faith in the power of place to alter men's convictions or that the reform bill is meant to be one of a very moderate kind, for Gregory spoke against Baines's plan almost as strongly as Lowe himself.

24 January 1866. Disraeli writes from London: 'Wood remains, though he came up to town to resign. At the last moment it was discovered that [Milner] Gibson expected the office, and would resign if he did not receive it: Johnny, smarting still under the Goschen fiasco, would not face this, which would certainly have induced the immediate resignation of C. Villiers. It seems that Gibson has been for some time discontented, and declares that he is sick of the Board of Trade . . . The whole affair is utterly rotten: quite ruined: the blow will be struck from the other side. The appointment of Goschen precipitated the revolution . . . The present plan, I hear, is to meet the second reading of the Reform Bill adversely. In that case I should think it would be wise to meet it by a resolution: but at present I shall leave them to themselves. The other side will do the business . . . I suspect that Gladstone is going to terminate the Income-tax'.

25 January 1866. ... Skelmersdale[4] tells me that my old college friend Harcourt, lately made a Q.C., is earning between £10–12,000 yearly at the bar, chiefly by parliamentary practice ... Harcourt's chief defect in youth was an extremely overbearing and sarcastic manner, which got him many enemies: but this, if not wholly removed, is now kept within bounds.

26 January 1866. ... Talk between F. and Skelmersdale of a new fashion of extravagance which has sprung up among fashionable people, and does not seem likely to be put down, though it is in reality returning to an ancient and long-established abuse. At the fashionable houses it has become the custom to leave large presents to the servants not for special services rendered, but as a kind of perquisite. At Sandringham there is a regular tariff: £20 is expected from a single man, £30 from one who has a family with him: the Prince of Wales himself leaves behind about £100 at every house he visits (but this is exceptional, and in his case not amiss). The keepers at some houses expect at least £5 from each gun: and the house-servants from £5 to £10 more. The end of this system will be, to make country visiting impossible to families of moderate means, and county society still more exclusive than it is.

30 January 1866. ... Called on Disraeli: the substance of what he tells me is as follows: he believes the reform bill will be postponed till after Easter, not out of any calculation of expediency, but simply because ministers have not got one ready: he doubts whether the subject will be mentioned in the Queen's speech (but how can they help it?) He hears that Gladstone has a 'sensation measure' ready, of what kind he does not know, but believes it to relate to Ireland: whether payment of priests, or reduction of Irish church endowments, or some great project of buying up the Irish railroads. He has also got an idea that Gladstone means to sweep away the income-tax, replacing it by a tax on capital exclusively – this he seems to have picked up from one of the Rothschilds. He has been doing all in his power to hinder a revival of the malt-tax agitation, about which Kelly and some others are especially active, and which he truly says will go farther to damage the party than almost anything else can at the present time. We had also some talk of the Catholic Oaths Bill, as to which there are hopes of a compromise.

4 February 1866. ... Delane and Lord Russell seem to have quarrelled, and Lord R. gives whatever information he has to give to a new journal called the *Sunday Gazette*, which is in his interest.

... Breakfast Travellers': sat at home: wet day: Malmesbury called, and talked affairs, but told me nothing new: said a Derby and Disraeli cabinet was impossible, either we must stay in opposition, and act as a check, or form a fusion govt, if an opportunity occurred: thought Gladstone the next leader, and said my name was mentioned as his probable successor. I told him, sincerely, I neither saw nor wished that: I would serve again, if occasion arose, as Sec. of State, but did not wish for a leader's place. Called A. St.,[5] heard (through Dean Wellesley) that my name had been mentioned to the Queen in the way Malmesbury spoke of, but that she has a grudge against me on the ground that I opposed Prince Albert about the Indian army: she is right in that, and has more cause of offence than she probably knows of. Like all women, she has a kind of instinct that tells her who are the persons on whom she can exercise a personal influence: and is aware that of these I am not one. Dined A. St. meeting Disraeli and Mrs D.

9 February 1866. Here is my private intelligence as to the new reform bill. 'Above a six pound rating and nearer eight. According to returns at present received, this would add 170–180,000 to the borough franchise: and £12 or £15 for the counties. So as in all to add 200,000 to the franchise of Eng. and Wales. Returns supposed in some respects incorrect, and are to be gone over again to be verified. Not sufficient data to allow of a lodger franchise: this much regretted. Ld De Grey and Gibson wished for a distribution of seats but Ld R. holds out pertinaciously and he and G. are 'strangely moderate'. G. is supposed to prompt everything, but this is not ascertained. Bill only once discussed in cabinet. Ld R. wished for even less of a paragraph than there was in the Queen's speech. Lord ——'s expression on the question generally: 'In short a harmless measure, nothing at all, the Lord only knows what G. is about with his friends.'

11 February 1866. ... Dined A. St.: Lowe had been there, talking with violence against Ld R. as he does in all companies. His notion seems to be that he and Ld D. should both withdraw, and that a fusion should be effected with Gladstone if possible at its head. He is quite convinced of the intention and power of the H. of C. to throw out the new reform bill, whatever it may be.

19 February 1866. ... Ministers have decided to press on their reform bill, postponing their budget: the talk amongst those who best know them is that they would readily accept a defeat and drop the bill, but that Ld Russell and Gladstone object to any giving way: the others are mostly indifferent. Their language is that of men despondent as to their prospects: Gladstone, it is thought, would not unwillingly see a break-up, as Ld D. cannot form a ministry, and the reversion would almost certainly fall to him. Ld R.'s dry manners, the seclusion in which he lives, and a certain apathy, the effect of age, which is growing upon him, combine to make him very unpopular with his colleagues. He has also a knack of announcing important decisions in the newspapers without consulting them: which does not contribute to his being liked.

20 February 1866. ... *The Times* announces, as if by authority, that the reform bill will not be limited to franchise, but will include also a redistribution of seats. This resolution, if really taken, is new, as a contrary policy was very lately decided upon.

1 March 1866. . . . I dined at House with Disraeli, who assured me that Ld D. is more keen than ever for power, and prepared to make any sacrifices in order to attain it. I believe this to be true at the moment – that is, while Ld D. was excited on the subject – but not that it is true in general.

3 March 1866. . . . Some lawyer present talked of R. Palmer: said he had made during the last year £23,000, which is supposed to be more than any Att.-Gen. has made hitherto: I think it was Harcourt said this.

. . . Sefton[6] has sold to the Liverpool corporation a piece of land for a park, 400 acres or thereabouts, for £250,000: which is at the rate of £625 an acre.

15 March 1866. . . . Disraeli proposed two amendments,[7] one recognising the Act of Settlement, which ministers accepted as harmless: the other asserting the supremacy of the Queen in language, which though not offensive, nor affirming anything untrue, was obviously pointed at the Catholics and sure to be by them resisted. I had discussed this matter with him, and objected to his proposed oath, but he would listen to no argument, and I saw plainly that he felt himself pushed on by a certain section of his party. I accordingly declined to vote, though sitting through the debate. He was beaten by only 14 in a house of more than 400 members.

Talk with Lowe, and told him of the Conservative intention to oppose the second reading of the reform bill. We agreed it was best done by a resolution: this Ld D., Disraeli, and I, had all separately concurred in, and I found it his opinion also. He wished the resolution to come from his side, thinking that this would give a better excuse to wavering Liberals to come round to us: and named Grosvenor[8] as likely to move it. I told D. the conversation that had passed between us, which he agreed in, and asked me in the event of Grosvenor consenting, if I would second: which I willingly undertook. I have made no secret of my dislike to the bill, thinking that such expression of opinion might have weight with a certain number of people, as I am known not to hold extreme opinions or to be a keen partisan.

16 March 1866. . . . Attended a meeting called at Ld Salisbury's to discuss the new reform bill: Ld D. could not attend it, being in bed with gout: but Disraeli did, and delivered one of the very best speeches I ever heard him make. He went through the history of the bills of the last ten years, and asked for unanimous and uncompromising opposition to this one. There could be no doubt as to the feeling of the meeting: a feeling in which I entirely share.

. . . More of the silly gossip about the Queen and her servant Brown. She is really doing all in her power to create suspicions which I am persuaded have no foundation. Long solitary rides, in secluded parts of the park: constant attendance upon her in her room: private messages sent by him to persons of rank: avoidance of observation while he is leading her pony or driving her little carriage: everything shows that she has selected this man for a kind of friendship which is absurd and unbecoming her position. The Princesses – perhaps wisely – make a joke of the matter, and talk of him as 'Mamma's lover.' She is believed to be aware of the way she is talked about (though this cannot be certainly known) but a kind of wilfulness which is growing upon her prevents the knowledge from having any effect.

19 March 1866. . . . Ld D. though not worse is disabled with gout, unlikely to leave his bed for some time to come.

23 March 1866. . . . House, where Gladstone announced that after the second reading of his bill he would lay before the House his plan for redistribution of seats, which is a concession intended and well calculated to secure votes though logically it is indefensible. A sharp debate followed, in which the only thing noticeable was that Gladstone, for the first time since he assumed the lead, lost his temper thoroughly, and said some violent and angry things, which will be remembered against him. When angry, he becomes a radical: when not exasperated, his language is, I am told, of a conservative tendency. Thus neither party well know what to make of him. Cranborne described his speech as 'sentimental rant', rather strong language to be used to the leader of the House, but it was not an unfair description.

24 March 1866. . . . Ld D. went to Ockington for country air. He left a note offering me, in effect, the F.O. in case he should come in on the expected resignation of ministers. This did not take me by surprise, as I have long considered it certain. No answer was required. Ld D. is evidently nervous at the prospect of having to hold power under circs of peculiar difficulty.

Bright's speech is reckoned a failure: his admirers excuse it by saying that over-anxiety to avoid causes of offence prevented his giving utterance to his real opinions. This is probably true: but to many people his evident anxiety to appear moderate is more alarming than any violence.

I find the idea widely spread that Ld D. if unable to form an administration, will hand the task over to me: the Whigs generally seem to believe it. To Lowe and his friends this would be a satisfactory solution of the difficulty in which their actual position places them but the Conservatives would not, I think, accept it as satisfactory to them: and whether they did so or not I am neither physically nor mentally equal to the lead of the H. of C.

A more probable solution would be that of a coalition headed by either Ld Clarendon or the D. of Somerset: including the moderate Whigs, and a certain number of the more liberal Conservatives. It is not likely that such an administration would last long, but it might serve to bridge over an interval during which no strong govt can be formed.

30 March 1866. . . . Walk with W. Hornby and talk with him on many family affairs. He, I regret to see, thinks badly of Ld D.'s chances of life and health. Thinks him more disappointed by political failure than he will allow, and still at times eager for power. This is also Disraeli's idea, and probably true, as they see him from very different points of view.

10 April 1866. . . . Debate on Irish church . . . dull from first to last, and no division. I had prepared a speech for this occasion, but on second thoughts abstained from delivering it, for the reason that it seemed inexpedient to say at this time, with a reform discussion impending, what would probably alienate the Conservatives – and however moderately I had spoken, I think this result must have followed. The truth is, that to settle the Irish Church question satisfactorily is impossible, except by total disendowment: and the proposal of such a course is certain to set the whole north against England, while that it would conciliate the south is by no means certain. Partial disendowment is useless: the payment of priests would, it is said, be refused, though as the offer has never been seriously made, its result cannot be known with certainty.

11 April 1866. . . . Meeting at Ld Salisbury's: Ld D. spoke for above an hour, sitting, for he is not able yet to stand long. He was very well received . . . While it was going on, I received a message from Grosvenor, who came to consult me about postponing his amendment until the next stage (going into committee). He was discouraged by some secessions. I urged him most strongly not to do so, as a defeat by almost any numbers would be preferable to the abandonment of a position deliberately taken up: it wd not be understood otherwise than as a surrender. He agreed, and pledged himself not to withdraw.

23 April 1866. Breakfast and early walk with Carnarvon, who full of politics, wishes me to lead the House in the event of a new govt being formed wh I tell him is impossible: anxious about affairs, thinks England in a state of transition, dreads the growing power of the U.S. (I find this last a common feeling, and it is certainly not unreasonable): all is well while we are quiet, but in the event of a foreign war or domestic agitation what would be the resisting power of our institutions? He is not, I think, personally concerned about holding office, though liking to keep his name before the public.

28 April 1866. Cabinet held this morning, wh lasted 4 hours: in the end, after much difference of opinion ministers determined not to resign: a contrary decision was however expected, and the question 'what next?' in every one's mind. Disraeli, Ld D., and I consulted: we all agreed that if called upon he ought to make the attempt to induce the 33 seceders from the Whigs to join him: but that it was unlikely that they would consent, and if they declined the enterprise was hopeless. The numbers are Conservatives 284 (Russell Gurney was abroad, Treherne ill, last night, all the rest voted), Whig secessionists 33. These collectively do not give a majority but if they all pulled together it would be hard to defeat them. Nothing more was said upstairs: but D. came down to my room, and pressed upon me strongly the necessity of my accepting office as Premier if called upon.

Lowe would act with me, he said: he himself (D.) would serve under me: I should have the support of the whole Conservative strength, and probably that of a good many independent Whigs. He went on to discuss with me the probable arrangement of places. Our conversation lasted an hour and a half – I will not deny that with some admixture of satisfaction, it left on my mind a feeling of grave anxiety at a prospect hitherto wholly unexpected – for the thing had never occurred to me as a practical question to be decided – and it was with considerable relief that I heard at night the decision of the cabinet, which was made public as soon as arrived at.

29 April 1866. . . . [Today] Delane took occasion to tell Lady Salisbury intending it to be repeated to me, 'that a Derby-Disraeli govt would not do, that he should feel compelled to oppose it, but that the same objections would not apply to one of which Lord Stanley should be the head'. Lowe has for some time been holding the same language – I do not think the thing possible, and assuredly I do not desire it: my strength is inadequate for the post, involving as it does the lead of the H. of C. and the inevitable opposition of Gladstone and Bright, at the head of what would be either a majority, or a minority so large that the slightest defection would turn it into one.

Cosmopolitans and stayed late. The general feeling is that ministers have made a mistake in not retiring: that they would by so doing have placed us in a situation of grave embarrassment, and improved their chances of reuniting the party after a few months passed in opposition.

30 April 1866. Breakfast and early walk with Carnarvon . . . Conversation with Disraeli, Henley, Cairns, Lowe, Adderley, Mowbray, etc. on the best course to be adopted. Lowe and Disraeli are for fighting, all the rest in favour of a compromise if possible. Lowe's argument is that we can lose nothing, and may gain much, by waiting a year. D. says, 'No matter how you modify the bill, it is still theirs, and not ours, and will give them the command of the boroughs for half-a-dozen years to come'. Every one agreed that no absolute decision can be come to until this day week, when the redistribution bill is made public. I think the gen. feeling of the party is to settle the matter if possible. Obviously our policy is to avoid such a division on any important point of principle as would force govt into resignation, and if the bill is to be destroyed, to destroy it bit by bit.

1 May 1866. Called early in A. St to take leave of Lady Salisbury who leaves this evening for Homburg . . . Rumours of war grow daily more serious – Rothschild expects it (he told me so) and Apponyi told Ld D. that he did not see how it could be avoided. In Italy a war will be doubly welcome: as giving a chance of obtaining Venice, and as excusing and accounting for, national bankruptcy, which is now merely a question of time.

. . . Carnarvon tells me, among many other things, of the excessive extravagance of young men at Oxford, especially at Christ Church, which the Dean (Liddell) is much complained of for tolerating. The young Duke of

Hamilton had while an undergraduate an allowance of £5,000 a year: another kept twelve horses: in the rooms of one a single individual lost £500 at play in one night – and other instances he gave, which I have forgotten. Thus reading and a quiet life are discouraged, debts incurred, and even wealthy families crippled, while the college is discredited. We are in England too tolerant of such scandals.

6 May 1866. . . . The supposed impending war discussed by everybody: it has caused internal politics to drop into the background.

. . . Long conference with Disraeli: but we did not agree: he is eager to turn out the government, and fears nothing so much as that they may use their opportunity and drop the bill under pretext of foreign troubles or of time being wanted. I soon saw that to discuss the possibility of a compromise with him would be labour lost, and did not prolong the visit. It is after all natural and perhaps inevitable in his position he should feel as he does. To suppose that he can see Gladstone's success with pleasure would be absurd: and it is only human nature that he should look more to a personal triumph over a rival, than to the permanent effect of what he does on the party or principle which he represents.

8 May 1866. . . . Meeting of Conservative members[9] at 1, which lasted till 3.30: the result was a decision taken to oppose the second reading of the Seats Bill, Walpole, Henley, and I being the only dissentients. The precise form of procedure was not settled. Henley spoke to me strongly against this decision afterwards, and appeared inclined to separate himself from the rest. My own decision is doubtful: I dislike staying away purposely from an important division, I disapprove of parts of the bill too strongly to vote for it, and to vote against it seems to me both impolitic and imprudent. Disraeli's fixed idea is to bring his party into office, no matter for how short a term: others, like Lytton,[10] have their own purposes to serve: some, as Cranborne, abhor the idea of compromise, and enjoy a fight for its own sake: Ld D. seems undecided, but is in the main guided by Disraeli, and naturally inclines to the combative side.

. . . War has now become all but certain . . . . . . most significant of all, the Emperor of the French, in a reply to some provincial deputation, informs the world that he 'detests the treaties of 1815'. No one doubted the fact, but his taking this moment to say so shows that he approves, even if he has not secretly instigated, the quarrel now pending. It is remembered that Bismarck was at Biarritz last autumn.

9 May 1866. . . . In the afternoon I heard that the intended opposition to the second reading of Seats Bill is withdrawn: Taylor[11] on consultation with his friends found so many indisposed to join in the attack that he came to the conclusion that it would be imprudent: this he communicated to Ld D. and I suppose to Disraeli. We have therefore until after Whitsuntide to consider our cause.

10 May 1866. Breakfasted with Gladstone, meeting Mill, Froude, Bishop of Oxford, and – of all men in the world – Newman Hall, the popular preacher. Discussion between Mill and Gladstone on the question of coal exhaustion – Mill for a tax at the pit's mouth, to check waste and in particular to pay debt: G. against this (a tax of 6d per ton would give £2,000,000). Both agree that export duty impossible, though once imposed by Peel. Mill (whom I never met before) spoke little, what he said was dogmatic and sententious. He grew almost enthusiastic in praising the Americans, who seem to be to modern Liberals what the French were seventy years ago, the type and pattern of political excellence. Good talk on the whole, but rather stiff.

Railway commission: examined Chadwick, who stated and tried to defend his favourite principle that the State can and should undertake all the functions which it can possibly get into its hands. Paradoxical, but suggestive. I fear this is to some extent a growing theory – that more and more people are disposed to take the Continental view of government, the ultimate result of which is socialism.

11 May 1866. . . . Meeting at Lord Salisbury's, of conservative members of the H. of C. Speech from Ld D. on the situation of affairs, he deprecated action on the second reading of the Seats Bill, on the ground that we were not all united. Peel strong in favour of opposing at any stage. Hunt, Henley, and others for caution – I did not note on Tuesday that the meeting then held was private, only fifteen or sixteen being present: that of today was a general gathering, about two hundred attended. The feeling very cordial towards both Ld D. and Disraeli – which last year it was not always.

8 June 1866. . . . Grosvenor, who carried the failure of Hayter's motion by his speech against it, makes no secret of regretting the course he took, and accused Brand and Ld Halifax of deceiving him by unauthorised promises that the bill would not be proceeded with.

10 June 1866. . . . Cosmopolitans where much talk of the situation, foreign and internal, and especially of Gladstone, whose extraordinary state of mental excitement is the general subject of comment.[12] Some say that he has invested largely in mining speculations, and is ruined or nearly so: others that there is insanity in his family, which I believe to be true as regards one of his sisters: most people agree that if the present strain on his faculties continues, he will give way. In the midst of all this he has found time to write a paper on *Ecce Homo*, which he intended to read at some religious meeting in London, I believe in St James's parish: but some friends heard of the intention and dissuaded him.

The bill is discussed everywhere, until one becomes weary of hearing its prospects and merits argued upon: the political excitement among the upper classes is greater than it has been for the last seven or eight years: I do not believe it is shared to any considerable extent by the people.

18 June 1866. . . . House at 4.30, where debate on the substitution of rating for rental as a test of value in the franchise bill. This created unusual interest, for two reasons: (1) it was known that ministers would be strongly opposed on their own side, and thought probable that they might be beaten, (2) if the amendment were lost it became certain that the franchise bill as a whole must pass the H. of C., and in the Lords its alteration was too doubtful to be reckoned with. The actual change involved was moreover considerable, £7 of rated value being equal to £8 10s. when estimated by rental: thus the effect of the change would be materially to limit the proposed extension of the suffrage.

. . . All interest was concentrated in the division. The Cave voted almost to a man with us: of our own, only two are known to have been missing unexpectedly, though illness kept away several. Numbers, 315 to 304. The exultation of the country gentlemen is unbounded: on the ministerial side the feeling appeared to be chiefly surprise. Gladstone especially seemed, not angry, but perplexed and disconcerted. I believe he had no idea of the result, else he would not have spoken as strongly against any compromise as he did. . . . Had votes within the House been secret, the bill would at no time have had above 100 or 120 supporters. – Walk home with Disraeli, and turned in to the Carlton, where we sat a short while drinking champagne and exchanging congratulations. Home, and to bed by 3 a.m. it being already light.

19 June 1866. . . . *Times* against ministers resigning, thinks they ought to accept the amendment and go on (this is nonsense, Delane wishes the bill dropped more than anybody but wishes also to make it easy to them) . . . The Whigs, I mean the old Whig families, do not conceal their satisfaction: the want of tact, temper, and extreme haughtiness of their leader has alienated from him all that class: they feel that while he remains at the head the radical element in their party predominates.

21 June 1866. . . . In afternoon Disraeli called, sanguine of success, eager for power, and full of his projected arrangements, which he had been discussing with Ld D. They all turn on the supposition that a considerable number of the Adullamite Whigs, or followers of Lowe, will join us – which is doubtful. He insists on my going to the F.O. which I reluctantly assent to, thinking myself but little qualified for that place, but compelled to agree with D. that there is no alternative. I have however a strong impression that nothing will come of all these preparations, which perhaps made me listen to them with more appearance of approval that I should otherwise have shown. The taking of office while in a minority may be a duty and a point of honour, but I cannot think it a matter of pleasure. It is well for his own comfort that D. sees things differently. Ld D. fluctuates – at one moment desponding, at another sanguine – he is undecided and will very likely be swayed at the last moment by some accidental impulse.

The Queen refuses to leave Balmoral before next Monday, on the avowed ground that she does not choose to give up any part of her holiday. This is generally commented upon as a disregard of public duty and adds to her unpopularity. Her opinion, if she has formed one, is not known.

Met De Grey, talk with him, pleasantly and frankly, about the crisis and its causes. He blames Gladstone, but pleads, I think with justice, that the House was and is thoroughly Palmerstonian, in other words hostile to reform, and consequently that the most skilful generalship wd have failed to carry the measure through – which however is no excuse for having raised needless difficulties. The phrase 'flesh and blood' cost ten votes at least, the threat of an autumn session as many more. G. might have led the House, but he was determined to drive it: and the House is not to be driven.

23 June 1866. Conversation with Ld D. after breakfast. He tells me that the Adullamites have held a council, that the result is they decline to join him, and that consequently there is now no question of his attempting to form a govt. Their wish is for a coalition under some Whig chief of which I should be leader in H.C. (this Ld D. told me.) But as they are 40 at the utmost, the Conservatives 280, this claim does not appear altogether reasonable. Dissolution is generally talked of, and thought more probable than at first. The only alternative I hear discussed is that of a vote of confidence to be moved in the present House by some independent member.

. . . Dined Ld and Ly Cork . . . Ld Clanricarde eager to talk to me on politics, and makes no secret of agreeing in his son's views, which are hostile to any bill. Shaftesbury the same, but his complaints turned chiefly on the impossibility of dealing with the Queen: he told me of his own personal knowledge that Ld Palmerston had more than once written letters to her on important questions of public policy which he had kept about him for days, not choosing to deliver these except to the Queen herself, lest they should fall into the hands of Grey and Phipps. Thinks she has now no one to advise her, will get into trouble. Ld P. used to express alarm about her future, from the difficulty of getting her to hear any opinion, except such as she agrees in. Both these Whig peers took me aside and seemed in their several ways anxious to establish confidential communications.

24 June 1866.[13] Hatfield by early train. No guests. Out all day in fine hot weather.

25 June 1866. London: visits: letters etc. Called on Lowe, who talked with the utmost frankness, but the substance of what he said I had gathered from others. He will support a govt formed by Ld D. out of office, but fears lest if he and his friends join it they should lose their hold – such as it is – on the undecided Whigs, especially on those of the old families, who would have no one to join except Gladstone. He wants a coalition, headed by some Whig peer or by myself. – I did not argue much against these views, the question not being urgent, as it is understood that no resignation will take place at present. (This was the belief, but all wrong. June 26.)

House, where we were put off until tomorrow, as the Queen is not yet returned, and will not even on her arrival come up to town, but stays at Windsor. The delay being expected caused no disappointment.

During the last three days, the general expectation has been that a vote of confidence in the ministry would be proposed by some friend of theirs, which being carried would set them on their legs again. Crawford, the member for the City, was named as likely to discharge this duty. It now appears that they reject all such offers to extricate them from the awkwardness of their position, and the scheme is therefore dropped.

Ld D. very nervous and uncomfortable, expecting to be sent for.

26 June 1866. . . . House at 6: various reports had prevailed during the day, and no one knew exactly what to expect, when Gladstone rose, and in a speech of nearly two hours announced the resignation of the cabinet . . .

27 June 1866. Gen. Grey called on Ld D. between 10 and 11, with an invitation from the Queen to form an administration. She wishes some of the Whigs if possible included, and promises help. Her letter short and businesslike.

The Times announces formally that I am to have the F.O., approving the choice. Applications for places have already begun.

Passed a quiet day: walk for exercise: reading: letters: preparing a speech for re-election at Lynn.

Dined Grillions: party small: Gladstone one of them: he talked much and well. Cosmopolitans afterwards. Reeve very civil and friendly, offers any assistance in the way of advice or information that he can give, knowing Europe well.

Advice of the D. of Wellington to some foreign sec. (I suppose Ld Aberdeen) related by Stanhope: 'Do as much as you can of your business through your own diplomatists abroad, and as little as you can through the foreign ministers here'.

Battle in Bohemia, and victory believed to be with the Austrians, but details vague and uncertain.

A mob gathered in Trafalgar Square, on the plea of holding a reform meeting, which assembled round Gladstone's house to cheer him, then made its way down Pall Mall, and towards Elcho's house, but they were there stopped by the police. A few came to this door, but without any object, some hooting and others cheering.

28 June 1866. Meeting of 22 supporters of Ld D. I was present. All agreed that in the actual state of affairs he could not avoid trying to form a govt: that he should in the first instance endeavour to obtain Whig support: if that failed, some thought the matter ought to be reconsidered: others, that he should go on at all hazards. But about the first step there were no doubts. – It was arranged with Gladstone that the House should adjourn for a week, to give time for the new arrangements. – In the afternoon Ld D. went down to Windsor. He made an offer to Ld Clarendon to retain the F.O. – this at the Queen's request – but knowing that it could not be accepted. I have not heard of any other answers received by him.

. . . Idle day: long walk: rather anxious about the future, and uneasy, the more so as there is nothing to be done: but far less than I was when taking office in 1858.

29 June 1866. . . . I do not altogether understand what has changed Ld D.'s resolution, which a few days ago was fully taken, not to accept office unless assured of some support beyond his own party. He has, I think, been piqued by their refusal: and is also acting under the influence of Disraeli, whose invariable rule is, that to refuse office is fatal to a party.

30 June 1866 (Saturday). . . . Hatfield in afternoon . . . Spoke to Lord Salisbury about showing civility to (i.e. inviting) Delane: wh. he seemed willing to do.

It may now be taken as finally certain that the Whigs refuse to join us, and that the new ministry if formed must be composed of Conservative materials exclusively.

I hear, rather to my surprise, that Lowe who has repeatedly, and to all his friends, affirmed that he could not serve under Ld D., is now rather vexed that no formal offer has been made to him! Such are the oddities of even the cleverest politicians!

1 July 1866. Hatfield: probably the last Sunday that I shall pass in quiet and country air for some time to come: for which reason I enjoyed it all the more though not wholly free from uneasy thoughts about the future.

2 July 1866 (Monday). London early: talk with Disraeli: he wants me to take Earle[14] as my under-secretary, to which I make no objection. He sanguine and happy, Ld D. rather desponding. I in return insisted on his making no move to induce Ld Cowley to resign, which (perhaps mistakenly) I suspected was his intention.

Ld D. goes down to Windsor with the list of his cabinet – which is pretty nearly settled. . . . There has been a talk of sending J. Manners as Ld Lieut. to Ireland, with a peerage. This is objectionable in several ways, and will probably fall through.[15] . . . Chelmsford must still be Chancellor, which is a weakness,[16] but his personal popularity makes some amends. We cannot spare Cairns from the H. of C.[17]

Frederick and Constance very kindly offer to help me with diplomatic dinners by lending their house for the purpose: which puts an end to one of my difficulties, since to take and furnish a house for a few months would be absurd, and I do not suppose our tenure of office will last longer.

. . . A meeting in Trafalgar Square at night, large crowds, but the most part brought together by curiosity. They went off pretty quietly, only shouting and groaning at the Carlton.

3 July 1866. .... The Under-Secretaryship for foreign affairs has been a perplexity: indeed is so still: Stirling-Maxwell was thought of, but he has insulted the Emp. personally and won't do: Ld D. named Wharncliffe, but that is an insult to the U.S. as he ha: been the most active friend the Confederates have had in England: Cadogan is also named,[18] but (in addition to the total absence of talent) he is much connected with the Legitimists of Paris.

On the whole, the cabinet, though not brilliant, is respectable: the subordinate places are the chief difficulty.

4 July 1866. Interview with Ld Clarendon, which lasted $2\frac{1}{2}$ hours, and ranged over every subject of foreign policy. Thought we ought to have an understanding both with Russia and France about mediation, the results of the war[19] etc. The Emp. at first Prussian and Italian, but now getting much alarmed at their success, and anxious to interfere. Russia also dislikes the quarrel, and entirely Austrian. The danger of Belgian annexation continual, though not immediate. The country between Rhine and Moselle supposed what Emp. wants – Ld Cl. thinks any addition to the strength of France unpopular here, though if Prussia became a great military power that would act as a counterpoise. Drouyn de l'Huys a desperate intriguer, always prefers doing a thing by crooked ways. The Emp. reasonable except where Orleanists are concerned, when he loses all sagacity and self-control, suspects imaginary plots etc. Q. whether any designs on Luxemburg?

Danubian principalities he dwelt on at length: the substance this, they are practically becoming independent of Turkey. Turkey has claims, but if she enforces them, a war of race and religion follows, and probably Russia steps in. – Danger of Russian occupation in any case: Brunnow[20] talks of refugees, armed Poles etc. at Bucharest, danger of their exciting disturbance, and so forth, which are mere excuses.

What he said of U.S. sensible, but not new: it was impossible the Amer. govt shd not write Buncombe despatches, opinion compelled them: the best way was to negotiate privately rather than by public documents, to allow largely for their way of talking, and judge their conduct by acts rather than words. The Fenian movement, having in the States a base and great material resources, is our chief danger. If England were forced into war elsewhere, the Irish would probably rise. In the States, even their best men regarded our govt of Ireland as mere oppression. It was impossible to undeceive them. Our relations with America better than six months ago, but never cordial. He never felt sure that the Alabama claim might not crop up again. They kept it in reserve for a weapon to be used against us if necessary. – He promised to write to Ld Cowley to induce him to stay on for a short time, but he (Ld Cowley) had long contemplated resignation, having come into a good estate, and being weary with forty years of service .– In the office, no arrears. He works at night always. High praise of Hammond.

He cannot have too much work, will take all if allowed. His sole interest is the office: any chief may trust him. Murray's drafts to be looked at carefully. He (M.)[21] apt to be hard in his decisions, and offensive in style.

While we were talking came news of a complete Prussian victory in Bohemia, due, as supposed, to the breech-loading rifle they use, and which is the most destructive arm ever devised.

Dined Grillions: small party: Cosmopolitans, talk among others with Enfield, who very friendly, goes out of his way to tell me that there are 25 of the Whig party not Adullamites, who will help the new govt to settle the reform question.

6 July 1866. Friday. Went down to Windsor to be sworn in . . . Appointed a Mr Sanderson my private secretary.

It is not likely that I shall be able to continue this diary further.

My first official act was, with the consent of Ld D, to telegraph to Florence and Berlin supporting the French proposition of an armistice.

7 July 1866 (Saturday). Restless, up early, hard at work from 8.30 to near 6.30, and again two hours after dinner. Dined Travellers. Cabinet at 3, sat 1½ hour: subjects: supply of needle-guns, Fenians in Canada, a sergeant of one of the Irish regts convicted of treason, whom Sir H. Rose wants to shoot, and whose life I think we saved: foreign affairs, and winding-up of the session.

. . . Cleared the office, having neither letter unanswered nor paper unread when I left off.

Before taking office I wrote to Ld Cowley entreating him to remain at Paris – which he consents to do for the present, though making a favour of it. I have not an idea how he could be effectually replaced. Though not a man of first-rate talent, he knows the country and the people thoroughly, and can be relied on. Moreover, as the place is one not given exclusively to professional diplomatists, there will be a great scramble for it, and many attempts to get it jobbed for the interest of the party.

8 July 1866. Sunday. Hatfield for the morning, where met Lowe . . . Carnarvon was to have come, but was too busy. . . . No business, except reading up memoranda of subjects now being dealt with at F.O. Pleasant day.

9 July 1866. Busy all day from 8 a.m. At 2 the ministers came according to custom, and were received by me in state. (Levee dress). About 22 appeared successively. The audience lasted three hours. . . . La Tour d'Auvergne[22] frank and straightforward in his ways: Azeglio[23] more than half an Englishman. Altogether I like the diplomatists better than I had expected to do. Very weary at night.

. . . We learn that Prussia accepts the armistice on conditions. . . . Bulow[24] hopes in the general scramble to get back at least Schleswig in a Congress. – Musurus[25] greatly afraid that compensation to Austria will be proposed at expense of Turkey. – I reassure him on that point.

Azeglio believes the Italians would consent to leave the Pope Rome with sovereign power and dignity, provided the territory round it, now held by him, were taken away. This is exactly the compromise I have always suggested.

Italians refuse Venetia as a French gift, and want a piece of the Austrian Tyrol. The fact is, they do not like to leave off beaten, nor to owe anything to France, and they are afraid of French demands. . . . Emp. has protested that he wants no addition of territory . . . It may be so, but Savoy and Nice recur to the mind.

10 July 1866.[26] . . . There is a professorship of modern history at Oxford in the gift of Ld D. as Chancellor: vacant by the resignation of Goldwin Smith: Froude and [Thorold] Rogers are both competitors for it: and both write to me to support their claims. I named both to Ld D. giving a preference to Froude.[27]

12 July 1866. . . . Hear with regret that both Stanhope and Lady S. are deeply disappointed at not having office.[28]

13 July 1866. . . . The political situation is now as follows. The Emp. by his precipitation in answering the appeal of Austria, and promising her support, which he did in very strong terms, has compromised himself seriously. He is not willing to fight: indeed France could not arm under two months: nor has he any needle-guns, without which to go to war is, apparently, to be beaten: nor do his people desire anything so much as peace. Russia is deeply disgusted at the Prussian successes, would remonstrate and threaten to any amount, but not fight: at least I think not: certainly not alone. Armed intervention on our part would be absurd . . .

The Italians are of all the most difficult to deal with, since they want, not the results of war, but success in war itself: they want to wipe out the defeat of Custozza, and make a reputation for their army. They have in addition a dread of French demands, and an extreme jealousy of French patronage: and are not pleased at their work being done for them by their Prussian allies without their help.

The Emp. Nap. has been disappointed in all his projects. He expected a long war, which should enfeeble both the German powers: he expected the ultimate success of the Austrians, who could then give up Venice with honour, and possibly obtain a compensation in Silesia. He looked forward also to being able to interpose with authority as mediator when both the combatants had become exhausted. Instead of which his promises are useless, his threats are unnoticed. Bismarck is master of the situation: and no man is less likely to use his power with moderation. He [the Emperor] has therefore a strong personal interest in patching up a peace, however little favourable to his protégés, the Austrians: the actual state of things being as he says to Cowley, intolerable. – I intend to support his advice, after consulting the cabinet, and if Prussia and Italy be not utterly unreasonable, I do not despair of peace.

Ld Clarendon to whom I explained these views, approved them. I saw Delane, and explained to him also the state of affairs.

14 July 1866. . . . Cabinet from 3 till 5 . . . Examined today the Secret Service list, which accounts for an outlay of £14–20,000, or thereabouts yearly, the vote being £25,000. Thus there remains disposable between £10–11,000. The £14,200 is absorbed in pensions already granted, but which will diminish in course of time. Cowley receives out of it £2,000 a year in addition to his ostensible pay: Buchanan[29] £1,000, to meet increased expenses of housekeeping. I doubt whether this is a legitimate use. The grants were made by Ld Clarendon.

15 July 1866. Sunday. Hatfield for morning, where a large party: Balfours, Cadogan, Elliott, Carnarvon, etc. Lady Blanche Balfour[30] long singular in her ways: she has now gone abroad, leaving no address, and leaving her children to take care of themselves. These are brought to Hatfield accordingly.

16 July 1866. Before I left F.O. at night it was clear – not one box waiting for me, nor a letter unanswered.

17 July 1866. . . . An easy day: left off work at 5, having nothing more to do. This is not what I had expected, but the war has caused a general cessation of minor business in the various chancelleries of Europe.

Duke of Cambridge with me uneasy that nothing can be done to save Hanover, and vexed (naturally) at the fall of the small German states. He came chiefly to express his opinions, and was reasonable enough when I tried to make it clear to him that nothing could be done.

In House, debate on ballot . . . No interest in the subject.

18 July 1866. It seems that the truce reported yesterday was accepted by Prussia, but refused by the Austrians, who are bent on fighting another great battle . . .

21 July 1866. Saturday. News of five days armistice accepted by Austria. It is not known on what terms, but peace is thought likely to follow.

. . . I am forty years old this day.

The Queen sends me a letter approving the language of my despatches – which is satisfactory, as I had expected trouble in that quarter.

In cabinet, chief subjects, expenditure – Peel and Pakington both wanting more money spent,[31] Disraeli and I resisting: American federation:[32] cholera: neutrality laws, as to which I got my proposed commission sanctioned: and bills to be proceeded with or postponed.

I talked to Disraeli seriously of making the Washington mission into an embassy: which entails some extra expenditure, but would please the people of the U.S., to whom such marks of respect are by no means indifferent.

22 July 1866. Sunday. Hatfield by early train, passed day there: Eustace Cecil, Carnarvon, Shrewsbury, R. West, and others. Pleasant.

23 July 1866. . . . Mob in Hyde Park under pretence of a reform meeting: they had been warned that the park was not to be used for public meetings, whereupon they broke the rails and got in. The numbers were large. A few police were hurt, but on the whole little mischief.

. . . Spoke to Disraeli, and to H. Lennox, seriously, as to the necessity of checking Pakington's plans of expenditure, which are extravagant. He is honest and hard-working, but vain, and anxious to distinguish himself personally by another reconstruction of the navy.

24 July 1866. . . . A cabinet was called at short notice, to consider what should be done to stop rioting in Hyde Park. Under pretence of holding a reform meeting, some thousands went there yesterday evening, were refused admission, when the leaders moved away quietly, but the crowd who came with them smashed the rails, and forced their way in notwithstanding all the police could do. There was more mischief than malice in the affair, and more of mere larking than either:[33] still it had to be checked.

. . . Much doubt who is to be minister at Paris: Cowley wants to retire: Sir H. Bulwer wants the place, very clever, but disreputable, drowned in debt, and believed to be always in intrigues: Lyons, capable, but he is lately gone to Constantinople, and doing well there: a pity to move him: others in the diplomatic line I do not see. Outside it there is Malmesbury an old friend of the Emp. who however does not now like him: Stanhope, respectable but weak: Clanricarde, very clever, and his wife still more so: but his character is somewhat the worse for wear. These are all I know of.

25 July 1866. . . . Some rioting in the parks again last night, but to a less extent, and done chiefly by boys. A good deal of wanton aimless mischief, destroying trees, shrubs, etc. The effect on the respectable classes rather good than otherwise – as it shows what a mass of ruffianism we are living over: though it is fair to say that there appears to have been no malice in the proceedings, only love of destruction, noise, and fighting.

26 July 1866. Thursday. . . . Cabinet to consider what shall be done as to the riots still continuing, and especially as to the threat of holding a new monster-meeting on Monday next in Hyde Park. It was decided to refuse leave, pending trial of the legal question, and to offer those who wanted to meet the use of Primrose Hill. The letter was drafted by me, and afterwards read in the H. of C. by Walpole. In House, this offer was so far accepted by the representatives of the reformers that they undertook to discourage the holding of a meeting on Monday: which in effect settles the question. Walpole has acted sensibly enough in substance throughout this matter: but his extraordinary manner, (when he spoke of the railings being broken, and a few police hurt, he was on the point of bursting into tears) creates an impression of weakness. It is a mixture of pathos and solemnity quite uncalled for, and almost ludicrous.

Arranged with the Queen for sending first message through the Atlantic cable – a message of friendship to the U.S.

27 July 1866. . . . Cabinet about the expected riot on Monday next: we sat for a long while, and but little was settled: indeed it is greatly doubted whether any meeting will take place.

28 July 1866. Saturday. . . . Cabinet, wh. lasted two hours, Sir R. Mayne called in, he told us his whole effective force of police was 6,200 or 6,300, allowing for sick and absent on leave.

. . . Adams[34] hints at revival of the San Juan question, which was thought to be settled years ago.

Musurus reads me a long despatch on the question of the Principalities: I compliment his govt (justly) on the good sense and moderation they have shown.

29 July 1866. Sunday. Up early, and to The Grove . . . Much talk with Lord Clarendon about foreign affairs, I find his views and mine agree in most respects. Consulted him about Paris, which is just now my chief difficulty: we could think of no one outside the service: he thought on the whole it would be best to bring Ld Lyons from Constantinople, and replace him there as best we could.

30 July 1866. . . . La Tour called to talk about a Congress: as to which the state of things is as follows: Russia wants it, in order to act as a check on Prussia, and if possible save a few of the small German princes: Austria has nothing to lose by it, and may have something to gain: France does not like to oppose: though not really willing that it should be held, inasmuch as it will be a Congress where Bismarck, not Bonaparte, will hold the first place: Italy has no strong motive either way. England is simply a spectator of events. Prussia has a very strong interest that it should not take place, having the game in her hands as matters stand, and wanting nothing except to be left alone. I could not give him a definitive reply as to what our course would be, but said that it was useless to go into Congress without knowing what the basis of negotiations was to be, whether the various Powers were or were not likely to agree, and whether all wd consent to accept the award of the Congress whatever it might be – because unless that were the understanding it became simply ridiculous to enter on conferences that could lead to no practical issue. – The last condition I named, feeling sure that Prussia would not consent to it, and so that by her response, not ours, the proposal wd fall through.

31 July 1866. Saw Bernstorff[35] early, and talk of Congress: I gave him a strong hint what I expected his answer to be, and got from him, what I wanted, a strong expression of opinion that Prussia would not allow her rights acquired by conquest over North Germany to be submitted to European arbitration. Armed with this, I gave La Tour and Brunnow a conditional consent on the part of England: feeling sure that the conditions were such as could not be agreed to . . .

1 August 1866. Telegram from Bismarck, through Bloomfield, refusing a Congress at present: which as I conceive settles the affair.

... Dined at Lord Mayor's. Ld D., Disraeli, Chelmsford, Peel, and Pakington made speeches. Nothing very significant was said.

The F.O. business is curiously unequal in amount: today I have not had five hours work, while on some former days I have had eleven or even twelve hours. The staff is excellent, no arrears are allowed, everything is answered within 24, or at most 48 hours.

4 August 1866. ... Cabinet in afternoon, settling the Queen's speech: Greenwich dinner: about 40 sat down: pleasant.

... All is going wrong again between the Porte and Principalities; when we thought the dispute on the way to be arranged, it has broken out afresh, the Rumanians apparently desiring complete independence.

5 August 1866. Sunday. Unwell with sickness in the night ... Hatfield in afternoon. Met there Cranbornes, Northcote, Lytton, Beauchamp, and L. West. Pleasant.

6 August 1866. ... Received a deputation of Venezuelan bondholders: T. Baring at their head: a rascally case, but nothing except coercion can be of use: wishing to know their views, I asked them severally what they wanted me to do: no two of the party agreed.

Brunnow called, with a propn. which Russia has also made to the French govt, and on which Baron Baude[36] came a little before to speak to me. It was, in substance, that the three neutral powers should sign a declaration – in what precise form is not stated – reserving our right of taking part in the European arrangements, as having been signatories of the treaties of 1815. The object of this move is clearly a protest against Prussian aggrandisement: it is substituted for the first proposal of a Congress, which has fallen through. I promised an answer in a day or two.

Lavradio[37] came to speak about modifying the Eng. duty on wine. The Portuguese object to the alcoholic test, naturally, as being unfavourable to the strong wines which they chiefly produce. I undertook to speak to Disraeli. He wants a commercial treaty, but I threw cold water on that.

7 August 1866. ... Baron Baude came, but I could give him no answer, not having been able to see either Ld D. or Disraeli. In the afternoon I saw them, and obtained their concurrence in my proposed draft.

... Late in the day we were startled by a telegram from Paris, announcing that the Emp. has demanded from Prussia the frontiers of 1814, and something more: no details are sent: it remains in doubt whether this is an understanding or a menace: more probably the latter.

8 August 1866. ... Wrote to Ld D. on subject of the Paris embassy, which will soon be vacant: Ld Kimberley and Ld Lyons were the two I named in preference as fit. They are both Whigs, but we really have no one on our side who is at once competent for the place and desirous of filling of it.

Wrote to Northcote to urge him to set on foot a movement for repeal or relaxation of foreign navigation laws.

. . . At night, more details on the French demand.

9 August 1866. Apponyi called. I gave him an answer to his question of yesterday: in the negative: but as some consolation, gave him the news of Napoleon's demand on Prussia: which he had not heard. The Hanse Towns Min. had heard it, and came to tell me the story. It is also confirmed from Berlin.

If refused, this demand means war. The Emp. cannot advance such a claim and draw back from it, without a loss of credit compared to wh. his former failures will be as nothing. But will it be refused? Some think that Prussia, confident in her army, proud of her successes, and knowing that France is not armed, will receive the claim as a challenge, in the hope that jealousy of France will stimulate national feeling, and unite not the north only, but all Germany under one head. In that event the numbers would be nearly equal: forty millions on each side. But if the object on the part of France was to put forward this claim, it is hard to understand why the Emp. has postponed it until, by allowing Austria to be destroyed, he deprived himself of a powerful ally. The most probable explanation is, that he did not intend to take this course a fortnight ago, but has been driven into it by alarm at the extreme discontent which he sees growing round him, and which he knows to be felt by all parties in France. If he gets what he asks for, well: if not, war is a less risk than humiliation. Possibly also he counts on Russian assistance, for Russia is, if anything, more jealous than France of German power. In any case, it is a new and serious complication.

As yet, I have but few details. The Queen is excited and alarmed, cannot endure the idea of Germany, her country (for she feels it as such) being threatened. She has written to Ld D. and a cabinet will be held tomorrow – though for what purpose is not easy to say.

The idea, which naturally suggests itself, of a previous understanding with Bismarck, is negatived by many circs: the Emp. would not in that case have gone out of his way to show sympathy with Austria, which we know he did in a very marked manner. To suppose that these expressions of sympathy were only used to conceal his actual purpose, is to impute to Nap. a foolish, because useless and unmeaning, act of treachery. I believe in his vacillation rather than in deep designs long matured and concealed.

10 August 1866. Talk about Paris with Disraeli yesterday: his ideas as to appointments singular: he named Lichfield, Horsman,[38] and two or three more men unknown in diplomacy, then suggested Stanhope: at last we talked of Malmesbury. Nothing settled.

. . . Cabinet held, it was agreed among other things to instruct Cowley to ascertain the Emp.'s views about the Belgian territory, and in case of its being threatened to protest strongly. This I did by telegraph. Van De Weyer called to address a similar protest to me. He told me however privately that he had a telegram from the King, saying he had had an assurance from the French minister at Brussels that no Belgian soil would be claimed. While cabinet was still sitting, came a telegram from Loftus to effect that Bismarck refuses all cession of territory to France, saying the military strength of Germany is not increased, and he sees no claim to compensation.

Delane called to pick up news. I told him in substance what I knew, and he, to my surprise, seemed very confident as to peace being maintained: he thought Nap. would submit to the refusal, and deny having ever made the request. He confirmed my belief that the Prussian army, especially the officers, look down on the French, and say, it is as easy to march into Paris as into Vienna.

Talk to Baron Baude at the club: it is not the least odd part of these transactions, that he found great fault with, and criticised in a decidedly hostile tone, the policy of his own government, whether to draw me out I don't know.

11 August 1866. Long and curious letter from Cowley, which makes it plain that Napoleon is ill, nervous, disappointed, and in a state of mind and body which makes it equally likely that he may take some sudden and violent resolution, or that he may tamely submit to a refusal. There is no reckoning on the firmness or patience of an invalid. The original French claim appears to have extended to the whole Bavarian Palatinate, with Luxemburg: but it is thought possible that the claims may dwindle to a demand for one or two frontier fortresses, and that Bismarck, after all his blustering, may give way. He has never expressed any particular scruple about the alienation of German territory: the King has, and is much more likely to be obstinate.

The French govt is buying up breechloaders in all directions, and making large purchases of horses in this country.

12 August 1866. Sunday. Hatfield: air and exercise nearly all day: no party . . .

13 August 1866. . . . Ly S. thinks Ld Clarendon would accept Paris: being in financial troubles (as is common with him) and also miserable at having nothing to do: I say that after his refusal of office, and the reasons given, I will make no offer: but if overtures are made by any third party I shall not be sorry. His acceptance would undoubtedly be a relief to me, and an assistance to the govt: while his personal claims are so generally recognised that there could be but little jealousy on our side.

14 August 1866. Osborne by 11.30 train from Waterloo . . . The Queen . . . in good spirits about Germany: she expressed a hope that Hanover might be saved by the abdication of the King, 'who, I must say, though he is my cousin, is a very foolish man'.

. . . Dined Travellers: met Baron Baude, who full of talk: he again told me that the conduct of his govt was to him inconceivable: he did not see how if Germany were to be united against the wish of France, and Rome seized by the Italians, which would exasperate the whole clerical party, the dynasty could stand.

15 August 1866. . . . Rather perplexed about case of Venezuela bondholders who, it is evident, are being deliberately defrauded by that country. Remonstances are useless, and force is not to be applied except in the last resort.

16 August 1866. . . . Saw Sir J. Hudson today, for the first time, he came as the bearer of a message from Ricasoli, to the effect that the Ital. govt is quite sincere in desiring the friendship of Austria, now that the old cause of quarrel is removed. Ricasoli says, Italy is weary of French patronage and protection, and sees no way to escape from that except by close alliance with her former opponent. He talked much on Italian affairs. Custozza was altogether the doing of the King, who was seized with a fancy for fighting, and would not listen to his generals, all of whom opposed him, but all gave way. The blame was thrown on La Marmora, who accepts it rather than let the truth be known – Persani not a coward, as the Italian papers are now saying, but quite unfit for his place: a favourite of the King's, who likes him for his loose easy life, resembling his own. The King debauched, but likely to end as a bigot (I had heard this before).

17 August 1866. . . . Cowley writes that the Emperor's weak and nervous state makes him 'an object of pity': that it is questioned whether his illness has not affected his mind: that Drouyn says his giving way now (of this we had notice, I think, yesterday) is the first step to his downfall: that the army is greatly discontented, etc. However, all present prospect of a war is over, which is what concerns us most.

Hatfield in afternoon: no party.

18 August 1866. London by early train: F.O. till 4, but not much business. Hatfield again at night.

. . . Now that the quarrel is over, there seems to be in the mind of people here an uneasy feeling that what has happened to Austria may happen to England: that we are like the Austrians, slow and unready, apt to fail in in our first attempts, and only to put forth our strength when excited by the struggle – as was the case fifty years ago, and partly in the Crimea: that the modern tendency to make war short, sudden, and decisive tells against us: that the division of Europe into three or four great military empires still farther reduces our relative strength (Austria, Prussia, and France can each put into the field 600,000 men with little effort) and that in the event of any two great powers combining against us, even our naval superiority would become doubtful. The difficulty of recruiting even in time of peace is great: and greater as the cost of labour increases, which it seems to be doing every year.

19 August 1866. Sunday. Hatfield: no party: in the air all day.

. . . Loftus[39] thinks this peace is only a truce: that next year France will on some plea renew her demands, and press them . . . Buchanan has got a story that Napoleon wrote or sent to the Czar, asking him whether he would join in the repression of Prussian aggrandisement: which the Czar declined to do.

20 August 1866. London by early train: Hatfield again in evening.

Strange stories going about (but how far exaggerated, no man can say) of Gladstone and his oddities: how he is in the habit of going to shops and ordering large purchases – especially of china, which is/a thing he has a fancy for – which Mrs G quietly countermands afterwards, and he takes no notice, but forgets the whole transaction. If true – but such tales are apt to gather enormously in transmission – there is in this a germ of insanity. I well remember Dr Ferguson[40] predicting that G. would die mad: and Ld Clarendon repeating the prophecy with approval.

21 August 1866. . . . Ld and Ly D. came to town from Roehampton. Dined with them. Both well and in good spirits.

22 August 1866. F.O. all day. . . . Danish Min. came to see me about getting back from Prussia a part of Schleswig.

Rumour of secret treaty between Russia and Prussia, by which the latter undertakes to support Russia in her next attack on Turkey. But it rests on no authority.

Great excitement in Greece about Cretan affairs: Greek govt has applied to France for rifled guns and powder, though at peace with all the world, and all but insolvent. This is to help the insurgents, and revive the 'Eastern question'.[41] King moderate and sensible, supposed not to have known of this proceeding. The Cretans are apparently in revolt, but in what numbers, and with what chances of success, no one knows.

23 August 1866. Ld and Ly D. left for Knowsley.

Not a single diplomatist came to see me.

24 August 1866. Business light, chiefly occupied with Guatemala affairs. Hatfield in afternoon . . .

25 August 1866. Business light; nothing of importance. Hatfield in evening.

26 August 1866. Sunday. Hatfield. No guests.

27 August 1866. London early: Carnarvon came in some alarm about the rumoured new invasion of Canada by Fenians. Hatfield again in evening . . .

28 August 1866. . . . Office all day, except a meeting of such members of the cabinet as were in town to consider Monck's demand for troops. It was agreed to send two regiments.[42] This may in the end be needless, but we could not take on ourselves the responsibilities of a refusal, the demand being urgent, the message having come by telegraph, and we being therefore necessarily little informed as to the state of the case. Monck is evidently seriously alarmed and it is said he has up to this time shown great calmness and nerve in moments of supposed danger.

Greek govt sends us, through Erskine,[43] a note asking interference on behalf of the Cretan insurgents, of whose grievances we know little, but only the fact that they have taken up arms against Turkey. This is not done in any serious expectation that the demand will be acceded to, but as a bid for popularity in Greece, where the 'great idea' – that of annexing European

Turkey – is universally popular. The King is perhaps the only man who thinks his subjects would do better to attend to their own affairs, which are in the utmost disorder: and he is young, a foreigner, sick of his post, and as yet possesses little influence. If the Greeks really want Turkey, which they do, they should begin by making their govt such as might contrast favourably with the Turkish rule. Instead of that, it is, if possible, worse.

Dined Carlton.

29 August 1866. Knowsley with Ld D. who in good health and spirits . . . A messenger followed me by the afternoon train, bringing five or six large boxes.

On the way, Ld D. showed me the weekly revenue returns, which are sent to him: they are accurately made up, and give at a glance the power of comparing the present year with the last. All seems flourishing, notwithstanding the late panic: a proof that though it has seriously affected the fortunes of many rich men, it has not touched the labouring class.

30 August 1866. . . . Fresh telegrams from Monck decided us to increase the amount of reinforcements to be sent to Canada. They will now include some cavalry and artillery. I do not know whether this is wise, with our imperfect knowledge: but it is a choice of difficulties.

31 August 1866. . . . I propose to return to London on Monday [3 September], where my life will for the next five months be unvaried and monotonous. I doubt therefore whether I shall not discontinue this journal, the more so as I have but little leisure to keep it, and as most of the political events that occur are necessarily noted by me, for reference, in a different form, or discussed in letters of which copy is kept.

It is exactly five years and eight months . . . since I began to keep these daily notes . . .

1 November 1866. I begin this diary again, after an interval of two months, during which my life has passed in the interesting, but monotonous routine of office. I have not been in all more than five days absent from my post (Sundays not counted): and have established a system of hours earlier than used to prevail at the F.O. My practice is to be there, in general, at 11: having taken my exercise for the day, and answered my private letters at home. The labour is at this time of year less than it was described to me: six hours are ample to do all that the S. of State ought himself to do. There is a certain waste of time caused by the curiously unbusinesslike habits of diplomatists, who on principle never go straight to the point, but think it necessary to talk about indifferent things in the first instance, and only after some minutes come to their subject. Some of them, moreover, call without any definite reason for doing so, but merely to find out what is passing, and get materials for a despatch. On the other hand, they are all, without exception, courteous and pleasant-mannered. Brunnow is growing old and very long-winded: seldom goes away under an hour: Bernstorff is brief and decisive, more like an Englishman than most: Apponyi certainly not able, but agreeable, and thoroughly to be trusted: a gentleman in every sense, scarcely a statesman. Azeglio I like well enough, but seldom see. La Tour d'Auvergne, the Frenchman, is much respected, and I think well deserves it: he has for the last six weeks been away, and is replaced by Baron Baude, a great ultramontane in his ideas, and curiously unguarded in language. In fact he talks as if he were an English politician in opposition. Adams has never but once visited the office: he means to be friendly, but it is easy to see that the sympathy shown in England for the confederate cause has left on his mind a deep feeling of resentment, which if in power, he will probably make considerable sacrifices to gratify.

In our own diplomatic body I have made no changes of importance . . . I have made no speech in public, except a short one at Liverpool on the occasion of a dinner being given to the layers of the Atlantic cable. Northcote was in the chair.

The chief questions under discussion at the F.O. have been (1) the rescue of the Abyssinian prisoners, (2) the American war-claims lately revived, (3) the case of *Tornado*, a ship seized by the Spaniards on suspicion of being intended for a Chilian privateer, (4) Brazilian demands arising out of slave trade captures, (5) Cretan affairs, (6) the question of the Principalities (now at last settled), (7) the question of extradition generally, which has been complicated by some blundering of the Canadian authorities in the case of a man named Lamirande,[44] (8) the appointment of a commission, as promised to parlt, to revise the neutrality laws. – I know of nothing else material.

The most important event affecting the govt in the last two months is the retirement of Cairns,[45] who accepts the post of Lord Justice of appeal . . . His reason for withdrawing from political life is the weakness of his health, and the immense labour, which an Att.-Gen. has to undergo. He made it a condition of accepting office that he should be allowed so to retire if the occasion presented itself: we have therefore nothing to complain of though the loss to us in debate is serious.

. . . Bright has begun, and is still continuing, a tour of agitation in the north: his speeches have been repetitions of what he had frequently said before, eloquent, violent; they have frightened employers (who are rapidly becoming conservative) and excited some, but not a great degree of, political feeling among the masses. Except Forster, who pointedly differed from him on various matters, no person of any importance has joined Bright. Many say that he is doing his cause more harm than good.

. . . In foreign countries, much more has occurred than here: I take them one by one.

France. The success of Prussia, the demand for territorial compensation made and refused, the Emperor's acquiescence in that refusal, the failure of the Mexican project, and the approaching evacuation of Rome, have combined to create an uneasy feeling which is said to be increasing rather than subsiding. The army is to be reorganised and to be supplied with the needle-gun, to do which a large loan will be necessary: and the Emp. is anxious also to borrow in order to execute public works on a greater scale than before: which seems to be his favourite remedy when things are going badly. War is not precisely desired, but there is a fear that the Prussian govt may presume on its victories, and take liberties . . . Still I do not think that there is danger to the dynasty: What is to succeed it? The republic finished in June '48, and has shown no sign of life since: the Bourbons, both branches alike, are forgotten: and there is no general strong or popular enough to attempt an usurpation on his own account. Besides, the peasantry are all Bonapartist. The danger will be when the Emp. dies, for the Empress and Prince Napoleon can never agree – one being a fanatic for the Pope, the other not less fanatical in an opposite sense. . . . The Emp. has been very ill, but is fast mending.

The new min. of foreign affairs, Moustier,[46] professes warm sympathy with England, and desire to act in concert with us, especially on eastern affairs. Time will show whether he is sincere. Hitherto there is no reason to doubt it. His appt. was unpopular, but he seems a man of talent and energy. *Spain.* We hear but little from Crampton who is an invalid, shuts himself up, and writes only on necessary business. (It would be as well that he should retire.) But from newspapers, and private reports, I gather that the state of Spain is as bad as it can well be. The govt of Narvaez is a mere reign of terror: hundreds of persons have been deported untried, hundreds more are in prison: all education is being placed under the priests: local freedom diminished or destroyed: the press silenced and foreign journals for the most part excluded. In any other country such proceedings would create a revolution, especially where the court is anything but respectable in its moral relations and where a personal feeling of loyalty can hardly exist. But in Spain, with the priests and the army one may do a good deal.

Italy. The discontent caused by Custozza and Lissa is fast subsiding: and people begin to feel, and appreciate, the substantial gains of the war. Reductions are talked of but I cannot learn that in that way much has yet been done. The taxation is still enormous, conscription is felt as a grievance, and the priests and monks, the greater part of whose property has been confiscated, are naturally dissatisfied. This dissatisfaction has shown itself in Sicily by an open revolt, the insurgents holding Palermo for some days, and fighting hard before they retreated. Ricasoli very foolishly made light of the affair, treating it as a mere riot, which it was not, but an outbreak directed against the govt, by reactionaries and republicans acting in union. What they wanted, probably, they themselves could not tell. Italy is now fairly launched, and its future depends on itself. Newspapers swarm: there is great political activity: and the spirit of partisanship appears very strong. Ricasoli and La Marmora are both more or less discredited: but opinion does not seem to point to anyone as their natural successor. Cialdini has influence, but is described as violent and incapable from want of temper, of acting with anyone. I should imagine that for the Italians the chief danger was a certain restlessness that will lead them to displace successive administrations without cause, and a love of intrigue among their politicians. Their pressing difficulty is finance: reduction or bankruptcy is the sole alternative. They are talking of a new foreign loan.

Turkey. Principalities question, I believe, settled at last. The war in Crete goes on, with little result up to this time. There are in the island 40,000 Turks and Egyptians, and the suppression of the revolt is apparently a mere question of time. Assistance of every kind is sent from Greece, with the connivance, at least, of the government.

Greece. Brigandage undiminished, finances hopeless, anarchy everywhere: great excitement on the subject of the war, stimulated by the politicians who use the national feeling as a means of displacing one another. The King has hitherto behaved well,[47] but is wavering, in fear of losing his crown if he does not chime in with the popular wish. He is encouraged by Russia, and I suspect by his relative, the P. of Wales.

Russia. Brunnow talks much with me on the Cretan question, but has of late let it rest, since Moustier expressed himself so decidedly on the Turkish side as to show him that the attempt to revive philhellenism was hopeless, at least so far as France was concerned. I have given him no encouragement, and for the moment he seems to be content to let matters take their course.

The P. of W. goes to attend the marriage of the Czarevitch, much to the annoyance of the Queen, whose consent has been reluctantly extorted. She is jealous of him, and cannot bear his being treated as a political personage. Ld D. and I tried to get her to give the garter to the Czar (he had a fancy to have it) but to that she positively objects.

Austria. Since the conclusion of peace no event of importance has occurred there, but the state of the country seems unsatisfactory, the army has lost its prestige, the govt is unpopular, the various provinces ask for sep. and practically indep. assemblies or parliaments, wh. if refused, offence is given, and if granted, the unity of the empire is endangered. There is no statesman in whom the public has confidence. The finances are embarrassed, and on the whole it will be long before the empire recovers. Baron Beust has been named as a possible minister, but though able, he has signally mismanaged the affairs of his own country, and is detested in Germany.

Prussia. Bismarck is ill, and absent from Berlin: no one knows his plans, nor can take his place. It is questioned how far he is now master: some say the king, intoxicated with success (for he is a weak obstinate man) has taken the direction of affairs into his own hands and does not like the idea that

Europe ascribes what has been done to his minister rather than to himself. This is so natural that I incline to believe it true. The tendency of the excluded southern states, Bavaria, Baden, Württemberg, is to unite as closely as they can with Prussia, abandoning the Austrians, whom they see to be either too feeble to defend them, or too much separated from Germany to care for their interests.

United States. Alabama claims revived by Seward, but in a temperate and friendly manner. They are said to be little thought of, the people being absorbed in their internal difficulties. The elections have gone against the President . . . I do not think it will come to actual fighting, but the peace of the country is far from being restored.

. . . At home, financial affairs continue prosperous, the revenue returns show increasing trade and consumption, all is quiet.

First cabinet held today: reform the subject: three alternatives: do nothing: bring in a bill: set on foot an enquiry preparatory to a bill. All agreed that the first course was impossible: opinions varied between the two last: nothing was settled, but the idea of an enquiry seemed to please the majority. I took little part, thinking and saying that the chances of the ministry were about equally bad in any case. We should not be allowed to carry a bill, and the enquiry, if attempted, will most likely be treated as a mere excuse for evading the difficulty.

It was settled to appoint two additional judges (much wanted in the northern towns), to proceed with an index of the statutes, and to appoint a commission to enquire into the best method of making a digest of case-law.

The offer of Victoria to man and keep up an ironclad, if we will give the colony one, was discussed, but no conclusion come to.

I had (Oct. 29) a visit from P. Napoleon, usually called Plon-plon. I had never seen him before. He exactly resembles the portraits of Napoleon I: the same broad squat figure, short legs, deep chest, no neck: head growing out of the shoulders, face round and fat: every feature as in the later likenesses of the Emperor, only less idealised. He talked in an animated eager way, asking many questions not uncivilly, but abruptly, and expressing his own views with a degree of frankness which in his position seemed even extreme. He praised the Italians warmly, said they were made for parliamentary government, from their aversion for extremes: 'not like us, who if the legislative and executive differ, are ready to fight it out in the street'. The king he said was an 'honnête homme', popular, because the people knew they could trust him: Garibaldi 'une bête': the labouring classes in Italy indifferent to politics, it would be long before they asked for a share of power. All had been done by the middle class. He contrasted the north and the south, speaking with great contempt of the people of Naples and Sicily. He passed on to the Pope, whose influence in France he assured me we all exaggerated. 'I have often told my cousin, give us free discussion for three months on the temporal power, then take a vote upon it, and see if one in ten of the French people will support it. The priests are organised. Where there is organisation you can always create a factitious public opinion'.

... Of the late German war he spoke with eager interest: asked what England thought of a united Germany? I said, if he put himself in our place, he could answer the question himself: what harm would a united Germany do us? He said in France too it was regarded as a question which the Germans must settle for themselves. I asked how it would be if the south, Bavaria etc., and the Austrian provinces were disposed to join Prussia? He thought France would take it very ill. She must in that case look for compensation. 'Where', I asked, 'on the Rhine?' 'No', he said, 'what should we do with a second Venetia'. If they wished to join us, well, but they do not, they are Germans, they would be a weakness to us, not a source of strength. As to a military frontier, that is an exploded idea. He asked if England cared for any part of Belgium except Antwerp? I said yes, I would not answer for peace if any part of Belgium were touched. He: 'Of course nothing could be done without the consent of the Belgian people themselves. Conquest against their will would be an absurdity. For the rest, we are talking of the future, not of the present. The King of the Belgians is a *brave garçon*, I know him well, he will be popular. He took up the subject again. '*Les Belges étouffent*: they have not a market for their produce, nor room for their people'. He went on in this strain some time. I said it seemed to be a bad time for small states: at which he laughed again in his peculiar way.

He mentioned the French peasantry, said the strength of the country lay in them. I observed that their only political idea seemed to be the Emperor. 'And low taxes', he added.

2 November 1866. News last night of a battle in Crete, defeat of insurgents complete, loss heavy. This probably ends the war, and prevents the revival of the eastern question.

News of the appt of Beust in Mensdorff's place as Austrian prime minister. This is the Emp.'s personal choice, and is thought the greatest mistake he has yet made. . . . It is taken as a mark of hostility to Prussia: and it threatens the peace of Europe, Beust being notorious for restless ambition. On the other hand, he has undeniable talent, which is more than can be said for Austrians generally. Hatfield in aftn . . .

4 November 1866. Sunday. Hatfield. No guests. Saw Drage[48] for a local inconvenience which he does not give me much hope of being able to get rid of at once.

6 November 1866. . . . Cabinet in aftn: Hatfield again at night. Cattle plague discussed, and some relaxations adopted in the existing restrictions, after much discussion.

7 November 1866. . . . Cabinet, poor law chiefly discussed: Hardy clear and sensible, as I thought, in his proposals.

Dined at home, with a party: Carnarvon, J. Manners, Northcote, Sir A. and Ly Paget, and Malmesbury. Very busy in office, and perpetually disturbed. I do not think my health will long be equal to – not the labour for that is not excessive – but the worry and irritation of being perpetually interrupted by people who come about the merest trifles, and cannot be got to say in a few words what they have to say. The effect of these interruptions is to take away my chance of getting any exercise, for unless I read what has to be read early in the day, I have no chance of getting through it.

Reports are everywhere put about of our having had before us, and declined to entertain, the proposal of a reform bill: which is wholly untrue.

8 November 1866. Cabinet in aftn. Reform discussed, and some minor matters. The idea seemed to be, to proceed in the reform question, by way of resolution, and some resolutions were drawn and discussed: but they were very vague: I took little part in the discussion, not thinking it of much use, when the whole posture of affairs may change within the next three months. Nor do I see how without Cairns,[49] we have strength to get through the session.

9 November 1866. Dinner at Guildhall ... Admirable speech from Ld D., conciliatory towards America, and comprising nothing ...

10 November 1866. Hatfield in aftn: no party ... Long letter from Ld D. chiefly on American affairs. Tone as to Alabama claims, very moderate and conciliatory. The change in opinion on this question is remarkable. Scarcely any one would have listened to a proposal to settle it by arbitration last year: now those in favour of that course are a vast majority. The internal differences of the U.S. are far from being settled, but on that very account there is a growing apprehension that the President, or his opponents, may force on a foreign quarrel to distract attention, and reconcile factions at home. And the marvellous recovery of their finances has proved a degree of power in that country which exceeds even the expectations of those who knew it best.

13 November 1866. Busy day: at work from 9 a.m. to past 7 p.m. without interruption. Wrote a mem. on Sarawak. Consulted D. on Alabama case: he favourable to arbitration.

... Naas not altogether easy about state of Ireland. Great excitement likely to be produced at news of Stephens[50] having left America, which he is about to do, if it is not done. Troops in Ireland 19,500. Arranged (cabinet) to send a few small ships of war, gun-boats, and one frigate, to watch the coast.

Much discussion (D. of Buckingham the originator) on sending part of the Museum collections to a separate museum to be opened in East London. This agreed to, though on a smaller scale than proposed.

14 November 1866. ... Archbishop Manning came, with a request that care should be taken in case of need to protect British subjects at Rome. He talked freely of Italy: said the Italian movement and the Fenian had one origin – the idea of nationality, and implied that England had herself to thank for the troubles in Ireland. I had not seen him before – a striking intellectual face, pale and lean, very thoughtful, but yet not that of a man troubled with anxieties, the expression very peaceable.

Cabinet: I brought forward Lamirande[51] case, at Ld D.'s request: Walpole proposed various bills, for extension of Factory Act, for private executions, mitigation of punishment of death, etc. Question of making two additional Bishops also discussed, one to be at St Albans, the other in Cornwall.

A curious fact was mentioned by Naas: a bill for the better suppression of lotteries being projected, he urged as an objection that in Ireland most of the money wanted for R.C. purposes was raised in this way, no one daring, or choosing, to put the law in force.

15 November 1866. . . . Cabinet: where Northcote brought forward a variety of propositions, useful, but not very interesting, nor well understood by most.

. . . Disraeli supports principle of arbitration as to Alabama claims.

16 November 1866. . . . Cabinet in aftn, when a variety of matters discussed. Queen sends rather a peppery message complaining that she does not know what is being done in cabinet – to which the answer is that there is very little to be known.

. . . La Tour called, discussed Crete and the Hispano-Chilian war: we agreed entirely as to both.

17 November 1866. . . . Letters from Athens interesting. The state of Greece worse and worse, expected that the govt will break up, and uncertain whether any other can be formed. The King disheartened, talks of coming to ask advice of England, France, and Russia: and of proposing to the people a suspension of the constitution, the decision to be by universal suffrage, but if it goes against him he will abdicate. He is honest, but weak: his position difficult enough to try a stronger and older man. – Lyons thinks now the Cretan war is over, there will be a little breathing-time for Turkey. Servia is the only difficulty that remains of a diplomatic kind: as to finance, there is nothing pleasant to look forward to . . .

Interesting inf. from N. York as to movements of Stpehens. He is certainly coming over to Ireland next month, and if one report be correct, thinks he has 20,000 men available in Dublin: means to seize the Castle, cut the telegraph wires, call on the people to rise, and expects that if he can excite even the semblance of a civil war, the Irish will be recognised by Congress as belligerents, and the sea will be covered with American privateers. His Fenian association is said to be modelled on the revolutionary societies of France and Italy: he boasts that the arrests made in Ireland have had no effect in breaking it up. He has large stores of arms concealed in Ireland, and more being provided in America.

A good many articles in the papers on Alabama affair: all favourable to arbitration in some shape: I have not seen one of an opp. tendency. This is a singular change from last year, and shows how much we go by success.

20 November 1866. . . . Hammond tells me that Ld Clarendon used to encourage people to come to him, with or without business, and pass the whole day in talking to them: so that at 7 p.m. he has often said he had not had time to look at a paper. The consequence was, he had to sit up most of the night: to my mind a most uncomfortable way of doing one's work.

Ld D. has offered to call up Ld Percy[52] to the H. of Lds – which the latter refuses, in a sulky and rather offensive reply. His cause of quarrel is, not having had the offer of a place. A small appointment wd have been refused: for a great one he is unfit.

Sent Alabama draft to be printed for the cabinet – and very glad to have so far done with it.

. . . Cabinet: Naas' land bill discussed, though very inadequately. Also the proposed demonstration on reform to be held in London.

21 November 1866. . . . Cabinet: reform again talked about, I can hardly say discussed.

25 November 1866. Sunday. Hatfield. Messenger came down with American mail. The news they contain relates exclusively to the Fenians. They are just now in bad odour with the U.S. having voted as a body in favour of the Democratic party, which is beaten, and thereby forfeited all claim to the support of the majority. . . . According to the report of a spy set upon him, he (Stephens) boasts that he has united the Orange and Ribbon parties, they will now act together in the same lodges: he has gained many of the police, and some regts of the regular army. He is continually receiving messengers, and seems on the point of departure.

. . . Seward – whose real ideas it is hard to get at, from his excessive loquacity, frequent inconsistency, and habit of saying things he does not mean by way of sounding those he talks with – professes to desire only that the Fenian and Alabama matters should both be open questions, on which corresp. may continue – in other words, on which he may write vapouring despatches whenever it suits his purpose. This, if he means it, is so far satisfactory that it implies a wish that everything may go on peaceably.

26 November 1866. . . . Cabinet at 2.30. State of Ireland discussed: in expectation of a visit from Stephens, three more regts are ordered over: marines placed under orders: small ships detached to watch the coasts: and Ld Strathnairn,[53] who was in London, is requested to go back to his post without delay. Reform meeting of a week hence talked of: we all agreed to offer Primrose Hill, which will probably be accepted. The originators of this meeting are the Trades Unions, between whom and the Beales party, as rivals in the same business, a good deal of jealousy exists.

Alabama draft discussed, and agreed to, with the single modification that instead of suggesting the points on which we offer arbitration, I now leave it to Seward to make the proposition, confining myself to a general offer to arbitrate if we can come to terms. This is perhaps more prudent, and will make no difference. It seemed the general wish, and I agreed to it without difficulty. The draft in general much approved. The only opponent of all concession was Cranborne, who spoke with force and some bitterness, quoting speeches made by Ld D. when it was thought the Confederates were winning, and arguing that to alter our tone now would be dishonourable. He had written to me a frank and friendly letter, regretting that he must oppose. *27 November 1866.* . . . Peter Coningham, chief clerk of the F.O., died yesterday. He had been in the office since 1812. Though rough and un-polished, he was much liked . . . Hammond came into my room to tell me, and could not speak for crying.

29 November 1866. Cabinet in aftn, where we finally settled Alabama draft: and discussed Fenian affairs. Stephens has left N. York and is supposed to be on his way here. The feeling among the lower classes in Ireland is that of excited expectation: among the richer there is alarm, but less, I think, than at this time last year. Ld Strathnairn is gone over, and three more regts have been sent, making exclusive of police 22,500 men. Men of war and gunboats are watching all the ports.[54] It is certain that the present state of tension cannot last, and that either an outbreak must take place, or the whole Fenian organisation collapse.

I have today abolished two useless places in the slave trade dept, inducing the holders to retire on pensions . . .

3 December 1866. . . . F.O. at 10, and passed the day there, not expecting to be able to get out in consequence of the crowd, this being the day fixed for a great meeting of the trades unions. The crowd was however much less than anyone thought it would be, the day being wet above and muddy under foot. . . . Dined at home: much pleasure expressed that the threatened disturbance had gone off. The trades unions talked of bringing 200,000 to walk the streets: the actual number was less than 25,000: there was no excitement or enthusiasm, indeed the day was bad enough to kill it had the people been predisposed that way, which they were not.

. . . Cretan war broken out anew, chiefly by the assistance of Greek refugees, who run the blockade, and whom the Turks cannot stop. It may last some time yet.

Greece going from bad to worse: no police, disturbances every day, and the Ionians are crying out against their new govt rather more loudly than they used to do against ours.

4 December 1866. . . . Dined at home. Reform talked of: Ld D. leans to the idea of household suffrage, with plurality of votes: but a commission to be appointed in the first instance, to ascertain what the effect would be.

... Talk, among other things, of the establishment of a uniform telegraphic system throughout the U.K. – to be in connection with the G.P.O. under govt, and a single rate charged for all distances as in the case of letters – either 6d. or 1s., as experience might show to be best. Ld D. seems not indisposed to something of the kind.

5 December 1866. ... The Russians have reduced their Black Sea Fleet to such an extent as scarcely to be able to carry on the ordinary police duty. In fact they have disarmed in that quarter. The discharged sailors and officers are naturally indignant, and hold violent language about the extravagance of the Court, which compels a sacrifice of honour, and so forth. But it is a good sign for the future. Russia is borrowing £6,000,000 in this country, which according to what we hear, will for the most part be absorbed in payment of sums already expended.

6 December 1866. ... My father and mother left for Knowsley.

... Insurrection reported in the Harran,[55] beyond Damascus, which is the first result of the increased taxation imposed on Syria. It will be put down, but adds one more to the many signs which announce 'the beginning of the end'.[56]

8 December 1866. Windsor ... for an audience ... This visit wasted nearly all my available time: luckily there is but little to do.

9 December 1866. Hatfield. Party ... American mails sent down after me ... [Bruce] evidently thinks Seward failing, mentions his vague and rambling way of talking, and does not believe that he has in his mind any definite plan for the settlement of the war claims. But, whatever his mental or bodily weakness, the American minister is fully determined not to be driven out of office if he can help it, and if he thinks a quarrel, or even a war, useful to his personal interest, no scruple of conscience is likely to restrain him.

10 December 1866. ... Musurus came, with a story, which I had heard from other quarters also, of the Greek govt sending a frigate to protect the landing of the Greek volunteers in Crete. This if true, is war. I telegraphed a message to Athens, warning the King that if he forced on a war with the Porte, he must be responsible for the consequences. There is a growing feeling that the eastern question is coming on in earnest: Moustier expresses alarm, and says that Aali Pacha himself is despondent, that the Cretan war is not over: that the Turks ought to give up Belgrade, but that probably they will not: Loftus writes from Berlin somewhat in the same sense: at Petersburg it is thought that the end is approaching. The Russians, I believe, do not wish it to come yet: they are not ready: but they would desire to shake the Turkish power as much as possible, so that it may offer no resistance when seriously attacked.

11 December 1866. London early: Ld De Saumarez called, to ask that his son shd be appointed to the diplomatic service: I gave no positive answer, but am inclined to do it.[57]

... Consul Longworth from Belgrade, who is the most determined partisan of Turkey I have yet met with. He says that Servia is now a hostile province, that the Servian army, or militia, is estimated at 100,000 men if all are called out who are fit to serve: that the Servians only want Belgrade as a step to farther operations: that it is not so much a question of nationalities as of the old jealousy between Turk and Christian: they mean to have a war, and he (Mr L.) thinks it would be the best thing that could happen, as they would be put down, and Turkey relieved from one of its dangers. He says the Christians throughout the Ottoman empire are looking forward to a rising: they are set on by the Greeks chiefly, and led to believe that they will have the support of all Europe in the struggle against their masters. He will not allow that Belgrade has ceased (as is commonly believed) to be an important military post: he thinks it forms the first line of defence of the empire, the Balkans being the second, and that if really pressed, Turkey would show a power of resistance which would surprise us all. (This I think quite possible.)

12 December 1866. ... Disraeli sent to see me, and said he had received from one of the Rothschild family alarming news as to the state of France. It was thought that people were getting tired of the empire ...

13 December 1866. ... My chief employment was reading a very long mem. which professes to contain the secret history of the Fenian conspiracy: the writer speaks of the organisation as numbering in 1865 about 50,000 persons in the U.K. (those in America not counted) with from 6–8,000 stand of arms. Stephens used to represent them as three times that number: he, Stephens, much looked up to, but unpopular with the other leading Fenians on account of his refusing to trust them at all, or tell them anything, but keeping the whole direction in his own hands: obstinate in working out his plans his own way, and imprudent from relying on his own in- genuity to get him out of trouble: clever in managing men, but quite ignorant of military affairs. I believe the writer to be one 'General' Miller, from whom we receive a good deal of secret intelligence. – The latest Fenian reports point to the employment by them of Greek fire, or other such material, for the purpose of distracting attention by a multitude of incendiary fires. They seem last year to have examined the forts and magazines about Dublin, and prepared ladders etc. for an attack upon them. Miller speaks of two M.P.'s as intending to join the conspiracy, and only prevented by accident: but I suspect that, if not lying, he must have been deceived in this. He notices particularly the absence of educated or upper class men among the Fenians.

15 December 1866. ... Odo Russell writes that 'Gladstone[58] is evidently disappointed and distressed at the incapacity of the priests, the mismanage- ment of the Roman church, and the hopelessness of their case'. Neither he nor the other English politicians there are mixing themselves up in local politics.

16 December 1866. Hatfield. Long walk. E. Cecils there, and young Balfour.
17 December 1866. . . . In Crete, the insurgents are submitting, but it is
thought at Athens that they do so only for the moment, and that when a
chance appears, they will break out again. Blockade-running continues,
volunteers are poured in, and the Greek government cannot check it. The
Greek ministry has little chance of standing, but it is questioned whether
any other can be formed. The strain on Turkey is becoming serious, and
excitement increases in the other Christian provinces. All seems to make
it probable that the eastern question will come on in good earnest before long.

Greek affairs do not improve: we have today two fresh cases of outrages
on British subjects, unpunished through the prejudice of native witnesses,
and most likely the connivance of the authorities. But this last fact, though it
would justify remonstrance if capable of proof is never easy to prove: and
in truth the Greek government is wholly incapable of enforcing order and
executing justice, were it ever so well disposed.

. . . Bismarck has taken the line of refusing to see foreign ministers . . . I
believe however that it is more a matter of health, and that the great minister
is not unlikely to break down in the midst of all his success.

. . . Dined at home, Ld D. having come up . . .

. . . Musurus came, with his invariable complaint against the Greeks, in
which he is doubtless right, but what he expects to gain by saying the same
thing to me three times a week I don't know.
18 December 1866. . . . *The Times* for the first time has an article in favour of
the Cretan insurgents, advising Turkey to give up the island. This shows a
change in public feeling here: but the Turks cannot do it, without encouraging insurrection in all their other provinces.
19 December 1866. . . . Fenian reports state that Miller, the author of the
paper referred to above (Dec. 13) has quarrelled with Stephens and writes
against him in the press under his own name. He accuses S. of dishonesty,
and in return is accused of being a spy. The charge is certainly true, and
probably the others also.
23 December 1866. Highclere: met Lowes, Elliot (of the C.O.), Auberon
Herbert, Mr Kent, Sir S. and Lady Barker . . . A. Herbert is cultivated, a
gentleman, but wild and flighty as it seemed to me, sometimes saying
things which were rather clever, at others talking downright nonsense. He
has an evident wish to enter public life, but will do nothing in it. – I liked
him nevertheless.

Mr Kent the factotum of the household: something of a toady, wanting in
tact and taste, on the whole rather in the way: yet a man of some talent and
knowledge.

. . . Elliot is always good company. Lowe the same, though a little repressed by the presence of Mrs L. who has certainly grown noisy and vulgar,
she was always that way inclined, and it has grown upon her.

... Talk with C. about Canadian confederation, African settlements, colonial guarantees, and a variety of minor matters.

24 December 1866. Left Highclere early ... F.O. at 2 ... an easy day.

25 December 1866. London all morning. Hatfield in afternoon ...

... Gladstone had been ill at Rome.

26 December 1866. I took a holiday, not leaving Hatfield ... Lord Lyons writes, 'Too true that a storm is brewing in the east. Russia is playing her old game, encouraging disturbance everywhere, and claiming to be the special protector of the Christians. This is new within the last few months. Much depends on whether Greece can be kept quiet. If there is a general rising in the spring, it will lead to a desperate struggle, in which Turkey may be destroyed but at the cost of massacres in all directions. As to Belgrade, it is a danger either way. A levée en masse to defend it would shake the empire. The Sultan and govt are too unpopular with the Mussulman popn to run risks. We ought not to advise the Turks to hold out. Aali does not talk at present of yielding. Possible that he would be glad to have some pressure put upon him by the Powers as an excuse.'

27 December 1866. ... Average business at F.O. ... More papers from Greece, unsatisfactory, inasmuch as they point to the imminence of a war against Turkey, and unluckily our minister, Erskine, allows his philhellene sympathies to be much too manifest, thereby stirring up unfounded hopes among the Greek population. The King declines to open parliament in person, fearing to increase the agitation that prevails. He is helpless by his position, feeble in character, and reasonably anxious not to endanger his throne, such as it is, by going against the national will: but he will do no more mischief than he can help.

28 December 1866. Friday. Hatfield all day ... Ten boxes were sent down after me, occupying a good part of the day.

... From Paris, reports of a Russian project for putting Crete on the footing of Servia under a Christian prince. Moustier thinks the matter growing serious and that something must be done (he does not say what) to satisfy the Christian population. We shall no doubt hear more of this.

29 December 1866. ... Adderley wants me to attend a political dinner in Birmingham, and make a speech on reform: which I refused to do, thinking it needless, dangerous, and hardly compatible with my position.

... Ld J. Hay sent a letter from the Candian relief committee, asking help for the ejected villagers and families of those who have been killed in the [Cretan] war. This is a ticklish matter to deal with, as the object of the askers is to make it appear that we are supporting the insurgents if we comply, and to raise a cry of inhumanity against us if we refuse.

Hatfield again in evening.

31 December 1866. ... Buchanan writes [that] ... articles in *The Times*, and the conduct of Erskine at Athens, have led the Russians to believe that

England is favourable to the Cretan cause: which encourages Russia to talk more confidently of the necessity of something being done . . .

Disraeli has got hold of a wonderful story to the effect that it is decided at the Tuileries that Napoleon shall take Belgium, allowing Prussia to annex southern Germany as an equivalent. I have written this to Fane that he may find out what he can, but I have told him at the same time I do not believe a word of it.

. . . My room was never empty during the aftn. I do not find that habit reconciles me to these continual interruptions, which make all business requiring close attention impossible except in the early morning.

So ends a year which to me at least has been singularly full of events and interests: and which will long be memorable in Europe for the vast changes which it has seen.

1867

1 January 1867. Up early, at work by 8.30, cleared off all letters and papers: made up accounts for 1866. They show a total outlay of £1,028 nearly: arranged as follows. Lynn, £135: charities and public uses, £145, of which £100 is for the Hatfield library: loan to Hannay, £100: books, £105 nearly: prints and drawings, £45: clothes and washing £95: travelling and food, £175 nearly: Smith's wages, £50, the rest miscell.

... Revenue returns very satisafactory ... the natural growth of the revenue may be taken at 1½ to 2 millions yearly. Nothing except a war can check our prosperity.

... *Times* presses us to bring in a reform bill.

4 January 1867. . . . Telegram from Bruce to effect that Stephens is in Ireland, supposed at Lismore, disguised, and passing as a Frenchman.

5 January 1867. . . . Informed that Elcho, Anson, and others, wish to make terms with government in case of an election: they to support us if we bring forward no reform bill, we to leave their seats undisturbed. They begin to want employment, but do not choose to say so. Lowe's language is: 'Don't set yourself absolutely against reform, but ask for delay' : Ld Clarendon and C. Villiers both talk of the advantages of postponing the question, but they are not to be trusted: they always grumble and give way to their friends.

6 January 1867. Sunday. Hatfield: wet day: read, wrote etc. No messenger.

7 January 1867. . . . Despatches and letters from Washington but nothing yet about Alabama ... Bruce is active in buying up Fenian conspirators, who seem one more ready than the other to give the information required.

Called on Disraeli: discussed with him Portuguese treaty and wine-duties, as to which he is willing, and even eager, to make all the necessary sacrifices of revenue. It is estimated that to do away with the alcoholic test altogether, and reduce the duty in all cases to 1s., would involve a sacrifice of £725,000 for the first year: which, though heavy, would be rapidly made good by increased consumption. We have not yet heard from Paget what the Portuguese will be ready to concede. We talked over the budget: D. opposes increased armaments, but thinks that some increase of expenditure will be necessary, as recruits cannot be got without additional inducements. This is what Peel contends for, and it is no doubt true. D. seemed well inclined to adopt a suggestion I threw out, as to reducing insurance-duty from 1s. 6d. to 1s. per £100 insured. It is a safe proceeding, desired by the mercantile classes, and not likely to give offence in any quarter.

He then went at great length into the question of reform, as to which he has a plan ready, which does not appear to me very likely to succeed, but I have nothing to put in its place, and therefore abstained from taking useless objections.

8 January 1867. . . . Roebuck called, and asked me to send him specially to negotiate a commercial treaty with Austria. To this I could say nothing, but promised to speak to Disraeli. He also pressed very strongly the necessity of bringing in a reform bill.

. . . Delane came: talk of affairs in general: congratulates me on the absence of foreign troubles: very strong on the necessity of a reform bill. He is thoroughly friendly, in appearance, and I do believe in fact.

9 January 1867. Ld D. arrived last night in town. Dined with him. He well and in good spirits: but I think not sanguine as to ministerial prospects.

. . . Dined at home. Much discussion of eastern affairs.

10 January 1867. . . . The Irish government, having borrowed one of our cyphers for correspondence with Canada (I suppose) has contrived to lose it – probably stolen by a Fenian. We shall have to send a messenger to Washington with a new one.

Fairbairn called to talk over Sarawak. I could give him little hope of its being taken over by the State, though admitting that I should not be sorry to see that done. Sir J. Brooke recovering in part, but not likely ever to be able to return there.

. . . Easy day at office: cabinet 3 to 5, where reform discussed, and the decision taken to proceed by resolution, affirming certain general principles, and naming a commission of enquiry. I did not raise any objection, because though doubting whether this way of proceeding will answer, I can suggest nothing better. – I raised the question of Crete, but did not ask for an answer upon it, thinking the matter serious, and a little delay not likely to do any harm. – Peel brought forward his plan for an army of reserve, which I did not well understand, but we are to have it in the shape of a mem.

11 January 1867. . . . Saw Fairbairn and Abel Smith again about Sarawak. They talk of the Rajah intending, if refused here, to sell his interest to France, Prussia, or Belgium. I am sceptical as to his finding purchasers. I suggested transfer to a company in this country, which individually I should be willing to support.

13 January 1867. Hatfield: no guests: a messenger came down. Mail in from America . . . Bruce does not believe that the President has any foreign policy.

15 January 1867. . . . Brunnow called, and sat an hour (he seldom takes less) speaking out his mind about the Turks more plainly than he has ever done before. He however adheres to the declaration that Russia will not interfere in the event of a general rising in Turkey, provided other governments abstain also. I believe this to be a sincere statement, for Russian finance is very bad, and the greater part of the six millions lately borrowed has gone to pay interest upon former debts. They could hardly put an army in the field, or support it when there.

Cabinet: Peel's plan of army reserve discussed, and passed with some modification. No other business of importance. Disraeli warns me that a gigantic project of expenditure is about to be brought forward by Pakington: this I encourage him to resist to the utmost, which indeed he is well disposed to do.

Ld Russell has got hold of a strange story that the Americans have designs on Malta: a notion which he has picked up in France, and is said to be intending to make public here. He is also going to write a pamphlet on the Alabama question. (This he did wholly or in part, but was induced to suppress it: as to Malta, I suspect some mistake or confusion. The U.S. did and do want Samana[1] in the W. Indies, and there was talk of their buying a naval station in the Mediterranean – May 67.)

17 January 1867. News early this morning that F. has a son:[2] the best thing that could happen to the family. – I got, last night, Ld D.'s approval of the draft on Cretan affairs, but it cannot go till next week.

Early to the office, but found little to do. By constant attendance I have so kept down arrears, that there is now often no work on hand, especially in the morning. I intend to give up for the present almost entirely the habit of dining out, which leads to late hours, so as to reserve all my strength for office and parliamentary work.

. . . Ld D. talks to me of Pakington's projects of expenditure on the navy, which he seemed inclined to allow, if not to approve: I warned him of the opposition they will meet both in cabinet and if carried in the House . . .

18 January 1867. . . . Chief Baron Kelly[3] writes to me as to the best means of meeting certain calumnies with which he has been attacked, and which may be reproduced in parliament. They belong to a transaction which took place thirty-two years ago!

Reading, at intervals of leisure, Finlay's Greek war of independence: which I had read before,[4] but it is now specially interesting as bearing on Cretan affairs. It does not raise one's opinion of the Greek character.

21 January 1867. . . . Nothing important from Russia: except that Brunnow appears to be on system misinterpreting the language I hold to him, whether to please his government, or from simple carelessness,[5] is not clear.

22 January 1867. . . . Cabinet, where question of expenditure discussed: Peel and Pakington had between them proposed an addition to the estimates to the amount of four millions, which wd have involved raising the income-tax to sixpence: this was rejected, and a general conclusion come to, not to ask for any increase of taxation: the estimates to be cut down as best may be, by the chiefs of the departments concerned. All passed in good humour, though Peel fought hard for certain expenses, which he declared to be inevitable. We sat rather over two hours. Cranborne, from whom I had expected opposition, agreed with D. and myself in supporting economy.

23 January 1867. . . . American mails in . . . Bruce says the feeling as to war-claims is more conciliatory, and the time favourable for a settlement.

Cabinet on the Irish education question. The Catholic bishops are doing all they can to destroy the national system, and the question is whether in consideration of their undoubted power of making mischief, any concession shall be made to their demands? In the end we evaded the difficulty by agreeing upon an enquiry. There was scarcely any difference of opinion.

Telegram from Lyons says that the Sultan is likely, if not certain, to give way on the question of Belgrade:[6] which, if true, is a sign of more wisdom than Turks usually get credit for. They will by this concession disappoint Russia (which only advised the giving up of Belgrade in the confident belief that the advice would not be taken), reserve their strength for troubles nearer home, and possibly avert a civil war.

24 January 1867. Successive articles in *The Times* press for a settlement of reform. *The Times* has hitherto been friendly, but has taken its line on this question. I find a general expectation among members of the cabinet that we shall be defeated upon our resolutions: and indeed I think it likely: but the aversion to Gladstone among the old Whigs is as strong as ever. H. Cowper is purposely staying away: Sir G. Grey, it is thought, will do the same. One rumour describes G. as having come back in an extremely Conservative frame of mind. He was lately entertained at a dinner at Florence, Poerio one of the party, where he made a speech in Italian, and where Poerio expressed his gratitude for past services in a manner which made all the party shed tears – G. included. A queer scene for an English statesman to figure in.

. . . Lord Clarendon called, talked much of France, Italy, etc., but told me little that was not in despatches received. . . . He thinks the *ouvriers* are just what they were in 1848, and would begin barricade-making again if they got a chance.

25 January 1867. Ld D. slightly troubled with gout . . . New York reports Fenians breaking up, all accusing one another, calling Stephens a coward, etc.

. . . Moustier, in conversation with Fane, seems to have turned round completely on the eastern question,[7] saying that nothing can now be done with Crete except to let it be annexed to Greece, and that Thessaly must probably be separated also from Turkey. This change – which is fundamental, for M. was if anything rather too strong on the Turkish side till now – is supposed to be the doing of the Emperor personally, for to him M. is subservient to the extent of sacrificing his own opinions if he has any. But we know nothing beyond the fact that he holds this language, the reason is a mystery.

26 January 1867. Ld D.'s gout better, not much amiss now.

27 January 1867. Much talk is being caused in society by the ways of the young Duke of Edinburgh – Prince Alfred. His intrigue with Ly C. Grosvenor is so openly talked of, that the lady has not much character left: he drinks hard, leads a somewhat disreputable life, and has developed that curious tendency of lying – generally without motive, but from mere incapacity to tell truth – which belonged to the older generation of the royal family.

29 January 1867. . . . Cabinet to consider the Queen's speech: which we settled without substantial disagreement, though after much verbal criticism.

30 January 1867. . . . Talk with Egerton about the substitution in this office of printing for the continual copying-work which goes on, and by which time and labour are wasted to a great extent. Hammond opposes this, as he does all innovations.

31 January 1867. . . . Very little business: cabinet in afternoon, where discussed N. American confederation scheme, and a plan of Corry's for improving the revised code, about which I have doubts, but it is a small matter.

2 February 1867. H. Lennox called: another trouble with Pakington about his estimates, which are, as he frames them, £700,000 above those of last year, and the cabinet has insisted on their reduction by £450,000. He declines to reduce them, and talks of resigning.

3 February 1867. . . . I thought it right to let Van De Weyer know what I had heard, though not attaching much importance to it, about the employment of French agents in Belgium, charged to ascertain and report upon the state of feeling as regards annexation. He told me that system had gone on for forty years, it was nothing new, he had got possession of some of these reports, and they were as satisfactory to his govt as they must have been the reverse to those for whom they were drawn up. No wish for a change of govt existed anywhere in Belgium, though in Luxemburg there was a French party.

4 February 1867. . . . Dined Disraeli's, the usual official party. Speech read, and seemed to be approved by those who had not heard it before.

5 February 1867. . . . Meeting of parliament . . . Nothing passed to make it clear whether reform would be dealt with by a bill or by means of resolutions and – which seemed to be singular – no explanation was asked.

. . . Telegram from Brest announces the supposed landing of Stephens, the late Fenian chief. Two months ago this news would have been important

6 February 1867. . . . Long and important cabinet on the reform question. It was virtually decided to drop the idea of asking for delay, to go on as proposed by way of resolutions, but to make these resolutions preliminary to a bill. What the bill shall be is still unsettled. I have no great idea that the attempt can succeed, but it is in any case well to make it.

Discussion before the cabinet with officers of customs and excise, Disraeli and Northcote sitting with me, as to the possible danger to revenue if duties on wine were further reduced.

Dined Grillions: large party, and pleasant.

Gladstone's speech of last night is generally and justly praised for its moderation and dignity: Lord Russell, on the other hand, is as universally condemned for the bitter and purely personal tone of what he said. The Whigs only want an excuse to set him aside, and put Lord Granville in his place.

9 February 1867. . . . The intention of proceeding by way of resolution has become public, at least so far that every one believes that method will be adopted, though it has not been stated on authority.

. . . Report of Stephens having landed at Brest is confirmed. Two detectives are gone to watch him.

. . . Cabinet on reform resolutions, and a few other matters.

10 February 1867. . . . Bruce has had a satisfactory conversation with Seward, pointing to the settlement of the Alabama claim. If I accomplish this, my tenure of office, however short, will not have been useless.

11 February 1867. The Times announces that the mode of dealing with the reform question will be by resolutions – which though not openly stated, has for the last 24 hours been regarded almost as a certainty.

Reform demonstrations in the morning: which in point of numbers was a failure: the whole procession, or rather series of processions, not much exceeding 20,000. The day was fine, notice had been given for weeks in advance, and four or five times the number was expected. Everybody appeared in good humour, no excitement, and few if any accidents.

House at 4.30. Disraeli spoke for $2\frac{1}{4}$ hours in proposing his resolutions: listened to with attention and interest throughout. I did not think the speech one of his best: it was unequal, heavy in parts, and did not seem to bear as closely as one might wish on the point to be proved – viz. the necessity of proceeding otherwise than by a bill. There were however striking passages here and there. Gladstone's reply was equivocal: he evidently meant to leave it open to himself either to oppose or support, as on consideration he might think best: he was short, not (for him) effective, and seemed to speak rather because he must than because he had anything to say. The House did not seem to have made up its mind, but I am disposed to think Opposition will show fight. Their decision will turn on the votes of 'the Cave': which is itself supposed to be divided. If they agree, they can turn us out: but they are at present very far from being agreed. We must fight sooner or later, and I don't see that we can fight under circumstances more favourable.

At night, an alarm of Fenians having seized Chester: which though exaggerated, was founded on something that has really happened – what, is not clear. As many of the cabinet as could come together met at the H.O. at

10 p.m. It was there agreed to hold in readiness 500 of the Guards, and send them down if necessary.

13 February 1867. Sir P. Braila, the new Greek minister, called for the first time: he seems both intelligent and respectable, which indeed was his character when employed in the Ionian islands. He laid great stress on the recent improvement in the condition of Greece, alleging that the Greeks had not had fair play, that Otho had done all in his power to impede the working of the constitution, he had made corruption the rule, the new King was young, etc. He defended the increase of the army as a necessity: and hinted at wishing to come to some settlement with the foreign creditors. He thought the existing constitution too democratic: the King was placed face to face with a single chamber, elected by suffrage on the widest basis, with no intervening body to act as a mediator. But he added that under the present ministry there was a perfectly good understanding between the executive and the legislative. We talked of the taxes, and he admitted that of one-tenth on the produce of land to be vexatious and objectionable: but saw no present prospect of getting it reformed.

. . . Dined Grillions: pleasant.

Saw Disraeli, who sanguine as to result of the debate of the 25th: perhaps he is right, but I cannot find that anyone else is so. Heard of a meeting of ex-ministers yesterday, at which Ld Russell urged immediate action to turn out the govt. Gladstone preferred delay, but would not object to an amendment implying a vote of censure if on the 25th Ministers refused to state in detail what they meant to do. Nothing was finally decided. I wrote this to D.

His speech on Monday is generally thought a failure, being tedious, ambiguous, and not much to the purpose. It is however only fair to bear in mind that extreme caution was necessary in his position, and that on the other hand a speech of half an hour or so would have disappointed expectation.

16 February 1867. French despatches . . . Fane thinks there is some sort of understanding between France and Russia on the eastern question, but that they have not exactly come to terms.

. . . Cabinet at 1 p.m. on the reform question: Disraeli brought forward his plan of plural voting, including a savings bank franchise, an educational franchise, and one founded on direct taxation, so that, these being added to the existing franchise, the same individual might have four votes. This project Northcote, Pakington, and I opposed as certain not to be accepted by the House: and contended that if plural voting were to be accepted in principle at all, the number of votes given to the person should in no case exceed two. Peel objected to every plan by which the suffrage should be lowered, whatever the checks or counterpoises devised might be. (I have forgotten to note above that with this cumulative vote, D. proposed a reduction of the borough franchise to £5 rating.) No argument had any effect on the General, who expressed his intention to resign rather than concur in the scheme proposed. We separated at 3. Cranborne approved, but thought the House would not agree: which is also my judgment. Several gave no opinion.

Dined with the Speaker: party at Ly Derby's.

Ld Bloomfield in conversation told me that Barrington will come by his father's death into an income of something like £12,000 a year.

18 February 1867 (Monday). . . . In House, a variety of subjects: Gladstone promised support on the reform question, urging procedure by a bill instead of resolutions, and at any rate that ministers should state their plans in detail.

19 February 1867. . . . Cabinet on reform: Gen. Peel withdrew his objections, and the plan of Saturday was provisionally adopted, with the limitation of votes to two. This change in the General is the work of H.M. who interests herself warmly in the success of the measure, on the ground, which she acknowledges, that a change of government gives her trouble and annoyance: a convenient doctrine for all ministers of whatever party. I do not, for my own part, believe that the principle of double voting will be accepted by the House, but it is worth a trial. Failing to carry that we can always fall back on a more restricted franchise. That proposed in the first instance will be houschold suffrage, with rating: the difference between this and a £5 rating qualification being insignificant.

21 February 1867. . . . Walk with Carnarvon . . . talk on state of affairs: he says he knows the Whigs are thoroughly frightened, disposed to be moderate, and that Gladstone is especially anxious to take some opportunity of showing that he and Bright are not acting together. C. thinks like me that the scheme of plural voting, being new to the public, will not pass.

23 February 1867 (Saturday). . . . Cabinet: reform considered: plan for redistributing 30 seats, and effects of the new franchise proposed discussed: these I had gone over with Disraeli before. Cranborne made objections, but all the rest assented without difficulty: and indeed as to the seats, if we are to do anything we cannot well do less.

25 February 1867 (Monday). . . . At breakfast this morning Ld D. informed me, in some agitation, of the intended secession of Lds Cranborne and Carnarvon, in consequence of some new light being thrown on the results of the reform scheme as projected, by their examination of the statistics. Disraeli came at once, and we discussed the whole matter. At 12.30 a cabinet was called, and after much debate agreed to drop the plan of plural voting, and fall back on the simpler substitute of £6 rating, with some fancy franchises added. We had no option between this and breaking up the cabinet, for Gen. Peel would have joined the dissentients, having been with difficulty reconciled before. I think we have had an escape, for the double vote could not have been carried, and household suffrage, however guarded, would have alarmed many. Naas agrees with me: the rest, for the most part, regret the withdrawal of the larger scheme.

Cranborne's threat of secession was in itself legitimate, since every member of a govt has a right to withdraw from what he cannot sanction: but some feeling has been excited in the minds of his colleagues by the extreme suddenness of the act, which left no time for deliberation, and was in fact a surprise, since he had agreed on Saturday to what he refused to agree to on Monday morning. Fortunately nothing unpleasant was said, but the feeling of confidence will not be revived for a long while: the more so as Lord C. admitted that he had been discussing the government measure with various people outside – which accounts for its general purport being known.

. . . House for the statement of reform scheme. Disraeli spoke about an hour: well, concisely, and clearly: a great contrast to his performance of a fortnight ago. He explained the intended bill in detail: it was received by the House without much interest or surprise: being indeed pretty generally anticipated. Lowe, Bright, and Gladstone all spoke against the plan of proceeding by resolution: and had the best of the argument, as they well might, for in fact the resolutions have served their purpose, and may be dropped. Decency required, however, that this intention should not be announced without farther consideration and I take for granted that it will be so on Thursday, or perhaps tomorrow. Lowe threw out some hints pointing to a reconciliation with the Whig party.

Ld D. had a meeting of the party in the morning, which was well attended and unanimous: I could not be there.

26 February 1867. . . . A cabinet was held, wh. I could not attend, but I wrote to Disraeli urging the immediate withdrawal of the resolutions, with a view to anticipate any motion that might be made on the subject. This I found afterwards had been done, and I suppose everyone was agreed: there was in fact no alternative.

I took down to Windsor for audiences the Greek minister, the Haytian (a black man) and Scarlett: the Queen said little to any of them, but to me she expressed strong indignation at the conduct of Cranborne and Carnarvon.

The Liberal party held a meeting, attended by Bright and nearly all the sections of which it is composed. They agreed to support the bill, with the intention of extending it: of course calculating on our non-acceptance of the alterations which they will endeavour to introduce.

27 February 1867 (Wednesday). . . . Court at 3, where stood by the Queen while she received the diplomatists. – On the way, Ld D. hinted that the decision of Monday morning might yet be reconsidered, even at the expense of compelling the resignations then proposed. That would not in itself be an obstacle, but to alter a plan once made public, on a fundamental point, is not easy. Barrington and others tell me that the general feeling in the Carlton is one of regret that the larger plan at first contemplated has been abandoned.[8]

... Heard a bad account of Lord Clarendon's health. He has a disease which is usually fatal in the end, though it may be alleviated and kept in check for a time. His family are kept in ignorance because of its gravity.

28 February 1867. ... Serious talk with Disraeli about the state of the reform question: the matter to be decided being, can we get back to the plan originally proposed, which is evidently the safer, as well as the more popular of the two? The £6 rating would be well enough if it could be adhered to, but the House will certainly change it to £5, and this Conservatives cannot accept with honour, while to dissolve on so small a difference is not expedient: and if we resign, the bill will be equally carried. On the other hand, the secession of three members of the cabinet is a serious matter: and there is an appearance of vacillation in making a second change of plan within a few days.

2 March 1867 (Saturday). ... Musurus called to leave papers with me: the Porte refuses to listen to any proposal to cede Candia, and in a spirited reply, likens its own proceedings there to those of Russia, in Poland, except that more humanity has been shown by the Turkish forces. This I believe is true. Brunnow came a little later, with another set of papers: he professes great alarm, lest Turkey should attack Greece, which he knows as well as I do is not on the cards, but the pretence of fear is put forward as an excuse for traditional menaces.

Cabinet at 3 p.m. sat over two hours, and agreed to revert to our original plan – duality of voting, with household suffrage – the alternative adopted on Monday having clearly failed to please either party. Cranborne announced his intention of resigning, and Peel and Carnarvon, with evident reluctance, followed his example. Much argument was used to retain them, but it was clear from the first that they had made up their minds. All passed in good temper. It remains to be seen how the places will be filled up.

3 March 1867. ... Heard through H. Russell,[9] that of the 290 men who attended the meeting at Gladstone's, some 35 or 40 have communicated to him their determination not to support any move which in the present aspect of affairs, he may make with a view of turning out the government. They say they remember the policy of 1859, and what it led to. The distrust of G. is still strong among the Whigs; they dislike his religious notions, his impulsiveness, his vehemence and the absence in him of the habits and feelings of what is called a man of the world. They accuse him – whether truly or not I don't know – of liking to be surrounded, almost exclusively by young people, who look up to him, and receive what he says as an oracle. He certainly has few personal friends among his colleagues.

4 March 1867. ... Disraeli in a very short speech announced the resignation of the three ministers: and announced that he should bring in his bill on that day fortnight. . . . Gladstone took the occasion to make a speech, not exactly violent in tone, but marked by a good deal of his customary vehemence of delivery – which until now he has not shown during this session – and showing as it were an undercurrent of bitterness. He was cheered, as last year, rather warmly from below the gangway, not at all from the benches behind him.

5 March 1867. . . . The state of the reform question, and of the ministry is now more critical than it has been at any former time. There is not, so far as I can judge, much excitement or violence of feeling among the people, but a great deal of interest, and on the part of the educated classes, some not inconsiderable apprehension of possible results. The radical newspapers are of course screaming their loudest. *The Times* disapproved the resolutions (very naturally) and condemned the bill brought forward a week ago: but is anxious for a bill of some sort to pass, and not averse to its being done by the present govt, if that be possible. The party is much divided, but not disinclined to action. My idea is that after two failures we ought to stake everything on this last trick and refuse to accept modifications of the plan, except on points of detail. At the same time we are bound in consistency not to go so far as to effect a real transfer of power to the working class: which would be equally opposed to our interests and ideas. And we must give no plausible colour to the charge (sure to be brought against us) of being ready to support in office what we opposed before. If these conditions are complied with it is not likely that our bill can pass: but we shall have done our duty, and cleared ourselves of further responsibility.

After writing the above, I went down to the House, where explanations were offered by Disraeli, Cranborne, and Peel . . . I said a few words in refutation of the idea now widely spread abroad, that we are about to bring in a radical bill, and declared that we would stand or fall by our measure. This I said purposely to pledge the cabinet. I also wanted to protest against the idea that we were outbidding the Whigs in a race for popularity. I was very well received, especially by the Conservatives. Dined H.C., went home late, saw Ld D. and told him that in my judgment the fate of the ministry was settled, and all that remained was to wind up the concern as creditably as we could.

6 March 1867. . . . News that the Fenians are again busy in Ireland, and giving trouble. Cabinet at 5 p.m. but we heard little beyond what was known in the morning – that a number of outbreaks had been planned to take place at the same moment, but that they failed in every case from want both of skill and courage on the part of the insurgents. We send over a few marines, but no additional troops.

7 March 1867 (Thursday). . . . Long and earnest talk with Disraeli, Hardy, and Walpole (but all separately) on the proposed bill. D. feels assured that he cannot carry the double vote (in which I agree) and is anxious to throw it overboard altogether. But in that case we fall back on household suffrage pure and simple, with a rating check, which it may be difficult to maintain. *9 March 1867*. . . . Cabinet: reform: Disraeli anxious to get rid of the double vote plan, and fall back on a rated household suffrage pure and simple. All opposed this, though Ld D. wavered a good deal.

10 March 1867 (Sunday). Cold wet day: mostly at home: talk with Ld D. whom I find bent on remaining in power at whatever cost, and ready to make the largest concessions with that object. I regret this tendency, and went so far as I could in pointing out the interpretation which would be put upon it: what I said was received without offence, but as far as I could see, without making the slightest impression. Ld D. is however so easily unsettled in ideas, however obstinately he may defend them at the moment, that his present mood may be only temporary.

11 March 1867. . . . Short talk with Disraeli, who talks of probable, though not certain failure in the House, and consequent dissolution, but he does not wish it to be at once, thinking that to gain time may be an advantage. Dined Arlington St where much friendly talk with Lord Salisbury as to the situation. He thinks (I am afraid) that Disraeli has done himself great injury with the country by his management of the reform business.

12 March 1867. . . . Cabinet on reform bill, long, but all agreed: many details gone into.

13 March 1867. . . . There is an idea generally spread abroad that Luxemburg has been sold or ceded to France: one report says, sold for £12,000,000. If Holland has made any such bargains, the cause of her fear[10] of Prussia, otherwise inexplicable, is clear enough. But the thing is not certain.

14 March 1867. Cabinet: finished details of reform bill, which it is clear to me will not pass, but I am nearly alone in that opinion, and indeed there is no reason why I should obtrude it, having nothing better to propose.

Disturbances expected in London and Liverpool: at the latter place the Fenians are supposed to intend to burn the docks and shipping, and precautions are being taken accordingly. We are in addition threatened with a railway strike, which if it takes effect, will be a serious obstacle to the movement of troops. Reports from Ireland satisfactory.

. . . Bernstorff called, in some anxiety about the Luxemburg story, which, he says, if true is very serious, and may lead to war. The Belgian secretary came on the same business: I could only tell both that I had heard the report, but could not vouch for its accuracy.

House, where a wrangle before H. Lennox[11] was allowed to move the navy estimates. At last he did it and very well: complimented on all sides. . . . Short talk with Disraeli, who evidently despondent, though he does not admit it in so many words.

16 March 1867. . . . Bernstorff called to read me a dispatch to the effect that Baden and Bavaria have both joined Prussia in defensive alliance, with mutual guarantee of territory. . . . It is the fear of a French war that has thus united Germany. I congratulated B. warmly on this result: I knew it however before. Nothing is yet known about Luxemburg. The French papers contradict the report of the sale or cession, but they did the same in the case of Nice and Savoy.

18 March 1867. . . . In House, Disraeli brought on the reform bill: speaking well, as far as I can judge from the report but, as I was told, in the manner of a man dispirited and not expecting success. Gladstone even more confident in his manner than his words. A miscellaneous debate followed, generally unfavourable to the bill, though there were exceptions. The principle of a double vote is evidently condemned, as for my part I never doubted that it would be. Disraeli was singularly happy in his reply, which was short, animated, and to the point. But on the whole, the appearance of things is not satisfactory: and the question will now be, whether to go on with the bill, throwing overboard the double vote, but adhering to the principle of personal rating. It is possible however that a defeat on the second reading may save us from the necessity of deciding.

20 March 1867. . . . Cabinet on various matters: it was agreed to make no changes or concessions on the second reading of the reform bill, but to reserve to ourselves the right of consenting to such or not when it goes into committee if it does so.

21 March 1867. . . . Ward writes from the Hague that he has ascertained that the story of negotiations going on between France and Holland for the sale or cession of Luxemburg is true, though nothing appears yet to be settled. The information was very cleverly obtained by young Thurlow, brother of Lord T.

. . . Meeting at Gladstone's, at which it was agreed not to divide against the second reading, but to move amendments on the Speaker leaving the chair. As these will be in a liberal or rather radical sense, we must oppose them, and the question will be brought to an issue in a most satisfactory way. Gladstone and Bright were both for immediate war, but were over-ruled by the general feeling of their party.

22 March 1867. . . . Cowley entirely believes in the Luxemburg negotiations.

23 March 1867. . . . Cabinet, which lasted three hours: reform the chief subject.

24 March 1867. . . . Dined at home. Fears of the D. of Buckingham resigning, but he wrote to Ld D. to say that though reluctantly, he had made up his mind to accept the bill and go on. Hardy, who had been in doubt, had at the cabinet expressed the same opinion.

I heard today from a private source that Moustier has told Metternich that the Emp. had advanced so far in the Luxemburg business that he could not now draw back.

25 March 1867. House . . . debate on second reading of reform bill: Gladstone opened it in a speech of two hours, wholly taken up with questions of detail, moderate in its general tone, except that once being interrupted, he flew into a passion, but that was only for a minute. . . . The debate was at no time very animated, it being known that a division would not follow.

26 March 1867. . . . Bernstorff came to talk over the Luxemburg negotiation, which is now no secret. I advised his govt, if the thing were persisted in, not to make it a cause of quarrel: remembering their own large acquisitions of territory, and the advantage of conciliating France.

House . . . Disraeli closed the debate in one of his very best speeches, admirable in point of temper, tact, humour, and even argument: though this last is not generally his forte. His strongest point was showing that some of the provisions which Gladstone had most vehemently denounced, were taken from bills to which G. himself had been a party – especially that of 1854. D. before delivering this speech was in a state of nervousness and depression almost painful to witness, and quite enough to cure anyone of the ambition to be an orator.

I had to answer a question on the Portuguese treaty – or rather on the failure of the negotiations intended to lead to one.

The second reading passed, and the debate on going into committee is postponed till the 8th [April].

27 March 1867. . . . Ld Howard[12] writes that the King of Holland is loaded with debt, wants money, cannot get it, and that this is his chief reason for wishing to part with Luxemburg.

(A few hours later, I received from Brussels an intercepted telegram[13] from the Dutch min. at Paris to the government of Dutch Luxemburg, saying that for reasons of policy and strategy the Emp. reclaims the occupation of the fort and country of Luxemburg, the official demand will be made shortly.)

Disraeli's speech of last night has made a complete change in the position of the reform question and the ministry: it is certainly one of his best. Gladstone is more excited than ever, and will oppose wherever opposition is possible, but his own party is too much divided to give him effective support: at least such are the reports we receive.

28 March 1867. . . . Talk with D. about his budget. He proposes to pay off debt, and abolish the minor taxes on locomotion: which seems a safe and sensible project. He will have a surplus of about $1\frac{1}{4}$ million.

Naas showed me a curious paper, being the information of the prisoner Massey, an Irish American, captured at Limerick junction, from which it appears that the Fenians have some (though not much) communication with the revolutionary societies of Europe: two French or Belgian officers being, or having lately been, in Ireland to help them.[14] Mazzini was sounded by some of the conspirators as to his readiness to assist, but gave the prudent answer 'that he did not believe the Irish were republicans'. This man Massey's story appears to be true: he has disclosed, apparently, all that he knows, and excuses his doing so by saying that he has himself been betrayed, having been led to join the conspiracy by statements as to the strength of the Fenian leaders, in men, money, and military preparations, which proved on enquiry to be utterly unfounded.

29 March 1867. Despatches from all parts of the world. *Vienna* . . . Austria, as regards the eastern question, will support France as to Crete, but will not encourage any attempt to add Thessaly or Epirus to Greece. Beust expresses himself quite indifferent as to what happens about Luxemburg. *Bucharest*: Servians still arming, and speeding agitation wherever they have a chance: but they had only just received the news of Belgrade being given up, which will probably keep things quiet for a while. It is believed that Russia encourages them to hope for the acquisition of all Bosnia. *Paris*. Long letter from Cowley on Luxemburg: giving whole state of the affair. Holland agrees if Prussia can be brought to consent. Moustier declares that Bismarck is cognisant of the intention, will not object, but wishes the thing to be done without his being consulted. Meanwhile the K. of Prussia answers that he must have time to consider it. (Bismarck's consent is wholly inconsistent with his language to Bernstorff, but truth-telling is not his strong point.)

30 March 1867. . . . Cabinet: settled the budget, which deals chiefly with a modification of Gladstone's scheme for the payment of debt: the available surplus is in round numbers £1,250,000. We read and passed a draft despatch of mine, calling on the Spanish govt to make reparation in the case of a vessel called the *Victoria*, seized illegally more than a year ago, and in regard to which they have hitherto disregarded all appeals for justice.

31 March 1867 (*Sunday*). Bernstorff called early, to let me know what he had heard about Luxemburg: and read me a telegram which in substance declared that Prussia would not consent to the sale. (But whether this is sincere, or only part of a comedy intended to be played off to delude Europe, who knows? If serious, it means war.)

1 April 1867. . . . Erskine writes that a rising in Thessaly and Epirus is expected on a great scale: and to take place shortly.

2 April 1867. . . . Bernstorff called, on the subject of Luxemburg: I declined to give a positive answer, but let him see very plainly that I did not mean to interfere. La Tour came, talked on the same subject, and said that in his judgment it was now too late for France to draw back. He thought that Prussia would give way, but against that probability must be set the evident strong feeling aroused in Germany. Bismarck has probably encouraged the idea, and now finds that his countrymen will not allow him to keep the bargain he has made.

. . . Received with Disraeli a deputation of the reform league. Beales, their chairman, made a long pompous speech with very little in it: I thought him a charlatan: two of the other notabilities, a Mr Cremer and one Odgers, spoke fairly well, though rather vague about the use of 'H's': the only one of the party who seemed to have any real oratorical power was one Mantle, whose style was a tolerably good imitation of that of Bright. They had not much to say, except that they were in favour of manhood suffrage, and objected to all class distinctions – one speaker ingeniously arguing, that if there were to be any preference in the matter of voting, the poor should have the advantage of it, inasmuch as it was more creditable to a man to bring up a family respectably on a small income than a large one. I saw among the deputation very few faces expressive of fanaticism: they were an ordinary gathering of artisans. Being over 300 in number, and crowded together, the room was intolerable before the meeting ended. – I attended at Ld D.'s request, in his place. – Home early, troubled with a bad cold.

3 April 1867. Mr Everwyn, representing Baron Bentinck, called, and after him Bernstorff, both on the Luxemburg question: I made into despatches what they said: but it came in substance to this – France is willing to buy, Holland to sell (on certain conditions) but not unless the consent of Prussia can be obtained. This consent according to Bernstorff, the state of German feeling will not allow to be be given: and as Napoleon has gone too far to draw back, the consequences may be serious. Bernstorff went so far as to ask for English assistance in case of a war – which of course I declined in the plainest terms. He tried to put it on the contingent danger to Belgium, which I told him was an entirely separate question. We might be pledged to defend Belgium if attacked, but not to run into war for the sake of averting from her the risk of future attack.

A telegram from Paris (3 p.m.) says 'Prussian minister saw Emperor yesterday: found H.M. calm, but very determined. He said the possession of Luxemburg involved the question of his own existence'.[15]

4 April 1867. Lay late in bed to get rid of cold: Bernstorff called, with news from Bismarck that the intended cession of Luxemburg by Holland had been abandoned: which if true puts an end to present danger of war, but makes the Emp.'s position worse than before, since he will have eaten more dirt.

. . . Disraeli brought in his budget, in a speech of little more than an hour, simple, clear, and generally satisfactory: for Gladstone's budget orations of three hours, though excellent of their kind, have begun to be thought wearisome by frequent repetition. A short confused discussion followed, but on the whole D.'s plan was approved by the House.

6 April 1867. . . . Cabinet, we agreed with Corry that two ships should be sent from Malta to Gibraltar, in case of trouble with Spain, which seems likely to arise. Long discussion on the impending reform debate, but it did not seem to me that much was settled.

. . . Cowley writes that Moustier is much pleased with the language I have held to La Tour on the Luxemburg question. (It was to the effect that if the matter could be peaceably arranged, the British govt would see with pleasure a concession made to French interests and wishes which might allay the prevailing irritation and secure, without injury to anyone, the peace of Europe.) The irritation against Prussia is still increasing, and aggravated by the belief (probably well-founded) that Bismarck has played a double game, encouraging the Emperor to look forward to a compliance with his wishes, which expectation he has been compelled at the last moment to disappoint. Great efforts are making to arm the fleet with new guns of the best construction. At Paris all the talk is of war. France, it is thought, can spare from home service 320,000 men: Germany can bring into the field about 450,000. France however will have no allies in this quarrel: Russia is too busy in the east and does not wish for disturbance on her Polish frontier: Austria is held back by her state of internal disorder, and by the sympathy of her German provinces with Prussia.

It is thought by Cowley not impossible that the Emp. may himself have suggested to the K. of Holland the breaking off of negotiations, as the least unpleasant way of getting out of the difficulty. If this be true, the arrangement has been kept secret from Moustier and his colleagues. On the whole it seems most likely that the inevitable quarrel will be for the present delayed. *7 April 1867.* . . . Coleridge's amendment on the reform bill, to be discussed tomorrow, is the universal subject of conversation. The Whigs say they shall win by 40: but they are not united, and among the Liberal party generally there is a split. Our secessionists are reckoned variously – from 30 to 50: I have no means of testing these numbers, and take them as given. The object, though not stated in the resolution itself, is avowed: the movers want to substitute a £5 rating for the rating and residential franchise which we propose: in this they will be joined by all who want no bill to pass – but not, I believe, by Elcho, Grosvenor, and that party.

8 April 1867. . . . Cowley writes that the French ministers are inclined to peace, they say if there is a war Russia will make her own game in the east, Italy will seize upon Rome, there will be a general disturbance. The Emp. complains that he has been mystified by Bismarck. He says he will take no immediate step. He dislikes the idea of a conference, which has been suggested to him. He wants Prussia to give up her right of garrison to the K. of Holland: which would leave the latter free to do as he thought best: he will not consent to the fortress being razed. He wishes us to propose some compromise of the kind. Cowley suggests sounding to ascertain the state of opinion of Berlin: and thinks the most feasible solutions would be either to have the fort razed, or to hand it over to the K. of Holland on the condition that he shall not part with it.

. . . Bernstorff came to urge again the plea that if we refused to help Prussia in the matter of Luxemburg, it was probable that Bismarck would make his terms with the Emperor by consenting to the annexation of Belgium. I gave him no hope that we should interfere, saying that I did not believe the Emp. wd attack Belgium while the people were united in favour of their nationality and knowing that we were pledged to its defence. He desired that this should be considered as conversation only, saying (which was probably not true) that he had no instructions to say what he did.

House: where an unexpected scene. It appears that the divisions in the Liberal party have at least come to a head: and 50 M.P.'s of that party met together to consider what they should do as to Coleridge's (which is in fact Gladstone's) amendment. They decided not to support it: and sent him word accordingly. He thereupon decided to withdraw: saving appearances by retaining the first line of the proposed instruction, which is quite harmless – indeed, we should probably have moved it ourselves. As this *dénouement* was unforeseen, the surprise on one side, exultation on the other, and per-plexity of those who had prepared to take part in a great fight, were ludi-crous to see. The causes of this unhoped-for success have been – dislike of Gladstone among his supporters – wish to get the question settled anyhow – and above all, fear of a dissolution.

9 April 1867. . . . Much talk over the events of last night, and as is natural, great exultation on the ministerial side.

. . . The conservative secessionists, of whom the most active is Sandford, lately known as Peacock[16] (he changed his name) are now styled 'the Peacock's tail'. It is not a long tail.

10 April 1867. Letters and dispatches from Paris: full details of the Em-peror's convn with Cowley. The Emp. repeats that Bismarck in the first instance received favourably his proposals in the Luxemburg matter, and even suggested the precise form in which compensation should be given to the K. of Holland. He, Bismarck, even offered to help the transaction by putting a pressure upon Holland on the subject of Limburg. The Emp. now hopes the Powers will suggest some arrangement which he can honour-ably accept. He would be satisfied if the fortress were given back to the K. of Holland, the Prussian garrison being withdrawn. But he objects strongly to its being destroyed – which looks as if some ulterior design were in his mind. (According to one statement, it is impossible to raze the fortress, as its strength consists mainly in the natural defences created by the character of the ground.)

According to Goltz, Bismarck admits that he gave some encouragement but says it did not amount to a pledge, and that he always warned the Emp. of the possibility of German feeling making the cession impracticable. The statements on the two sides are quite contradictory as to details. Cowley goes on to say that the declaration just published in Paris is pacific in tone, but inaccurate – or something worse – as to facts. The feeling of irritation in France is intense, and war would be acceptable. The minister of war, how-ever, has warned the Emp. that he cannot be ready in less than eight months

– that is not till next spring: an important matter, as it gives nearly a year for the chance of peace being preserved.

La Tour called, and read me some papers on this subject. They were not very material, but I made them into a despatch. He volunteered to say that France must insist on the Prussian garrison being withdrawn: I asked why, as it had been there for thirty years and more? He said the circs were altered, that formerly the German confederation was divided, now it was united: formerly its action had been slow, and machinery complicated, now it was a power formidable for offence as well as defence. He seemed anxious, and owned he could not see how either side was to give way.

11 April 1867. Cabinet called to consider a proposal from a large number of the independent Liberals, Hibbert being their spokesman: what they ask is that the person who claims a vote on personal payment of rates shall be liable to pay the reduced rate only, as though he were a compounder. If this were conceded, they would support the principle of personal rating and the limitations as to residence. Pakington and Malmesbury were for yielding, all the rest – and I among the strongest – for refusing all farther concession. So it was settled.

13 April 1867. . . . The division last night was 310 against 289: of Liberals, 45 voted with us, 18 being Adullamites, and 27 supporters of the late govt: 27 stayed away: of Conservatives, there voted against us only 6: how many stayed away is not clear, but I am told about 14 or 15. It is wonderful how the party has held together under all its difficulties: and the steadiness with which we have been supported by our friends should make us the more careful not to yield any point, without absolute necessity, to our and their opponents.

15 April 1867. Van De Weyer came: anxious to obtain Luxemburg for Belgium. Bernstorff came, and read me a despatch in which Bismarck states that Germany cannot afford to give up Luxemburg on any conditions whatever. This if true would almost of necessity lead to war: but who can tell whether Bismarck means what he says?

16 April 1867. Telegram from Vienna. Beust has proposed to Prussia that Luxemburg should be ceded to Belgium, Belgium giving up to France an equivalent amount of territory. This proposition is said (I suppose by Beust) to have been well received at Berlin. But it is in direct contradiction to the despatch read me by Bernstorff yesterday!

Bernstorff called, knowing nothing, as I expected, of this telegram.

. . . Easy day on the whole. The eastern question is at an end for the moment: Omar Pasha is sent to Crete to put an end to the insurrection (he ought to have been there six months ago): Moustier finds he has gone too far, has other work on hand for the moment: and is not disposed to stir.

. . . Later in the day, I hear that the K. of the Belgians absolutely refuses to listen to any proposal for an exchange of territory: which puts an end to that scheme.

The French are growing anxious that England should interfere . . .
18 April 1867. . . . Gen. Grey called at 11, with an urgent message from the
Queen, saying that Belgium is in danger, and the Emperor must be told
that we will not allow it to be touched!

La Tour called, repeating only what he had said before: that France
would accept any settlement of the Lux. difficulty that secured the French
frontier: i.e. that was accompanied by the departure of the Prussian garrison.
He told me that in his own mind he leaned to the plan proposed by Beust
(*v.* 13 April): but he was not instructed to say anything on the subject.

Van De Weyer came later, bringing from his govt a positive refusal to
consent to any exchange of territory whatever. He denounces the whole
scheme as a trap, intended to throw on Belgium the responsibility of causing
a rupture. He was eager, almost vehement, to induce me to make a public
declaration that if Belgium were touched we would make it a *casus belli*.
This I declined doing, as no one had threatened war, and the interest felt
by the British govt in Belgium had been recently and repeatedly expressed.
Van De Weyer however appeared to think that the decisive moment had
come, and that the invasion of his country might be any day expected. It is
he who has been stirring up the Queen.

Bernstorff called later, and read a despatch in which Bismarck says that
he never consented to the Austrian proposal except so far as public opinion
would sanction his doing so, and that he now does not think it will! consequently for the present he must maintain the *status quo*. This looks more
like war than anything we have had yet.

Left the office about 5, having finished all there was to do, and by road to
the villa Lord D. has taken at Roehampton, where I never was till now: it is
down Putney Lane, a pleasant old-fashioned house, with large grounds well
shaded with trees, and a good large garden: just such a place as a man might
occupy who had business in London, yet not so much as to require him to be
there very early or very late. . . . There met F. and C.[17] who did not know
of my coming, nor I of theirs: and so passed an evening in great comfort
and pleasure, all the more because the news from Spain makes it appear
that there is no danger of a quarrel[18] in that quarter: so there was no
anxiety to spoil our enjoyment.
19 April 1867 (*Good Friday*). . . . Despatches . . . Beust's language is that
England and Austria are in the same position, both desire peace, both will
remain neutral, at any rate for the present, and he is anxious for a confidential
understanding between the two govts, and a renewal, if possible, of the old
alliance. Bloomfield appears to have answered him cautiously, which I am glad
of, for he is a meddling restless man, not to be trusted, though very clever.[19]

Cowley writes that the Emp. says he has abandoned all idea of getting
Lux. for France: but that his honour requires that the Prussians evacuate
the fortress. If that is not done, war is inevitable. He is very eager that we

should mediate, advise Prussia to give way, etc. Cowley says he is as reasonable as possible, and that the thing is at least worth trying. He has been very friendly with the King of the Belgians, but suggested to him a customs-union with France, which the King would not listen to. The reserve, 40,000 strong, is being called out for exercise: under ordinary circs it would not be called out till the winter. Orders are also being sent to England for as many breechloaders as possible.

Lyons writes that the Porte is standing at bay, will yield nothing as to Crete, is confident of the success of Omar Pasha, who is confident himself also, and will make one last effort with all its power. Meanwhile discontent grows among the Moslem popn, taxes being high, salaries not paid, the administration generally disorganised. The Turks will pay their debts honestly as long as they can, but it is likely they will soon be unable. – The number of insurgents in Crete is stated to be from 3 to 4,000 only (this on good authority) but formidable by their organisation, their power of escaping when beaten, and the sympathy of the people. Their game is to harass the troops by little skirmishes and local disturbances, without making serious resistance or exposing themselves to much loss.

The Greek govt is trying hard to raise a loan of £1,000,000 at the rate of 10%, for warlike purposes exclusively. They have failed both at London and Paris.

Telegraphed to Berlin, to ask if Bismarck really means to make a war for so small a matter? implying that in my opn he had better give way. I told La Tour (who called, but brought nothing new) what I had done, but guarded myself against the idea that a formal mediation was intended.

. . . Bernstorff called, and I spoke to him strongly (though with the reservation that I spoke unofficially) in favour of concession. He seemed to think it possible that Bismarck might have given personal pledges of which the King and govt knew nothing.

Back to Roehampton on foot . . .

20 April 1867. . . . Moustier is still hopeful of Bismarck giving way, urges strongly that we should interfere, thinks the maintenance of peace may depend upon it. Russia refuses to offer any advice: at Brussels, Rogier, as Van De Weyer had done here, expresses strong desire that the fortress should be made over to Belgium, while objecting to give anything in exchange. The fact is, in the scramble they hope to get it for nothing.

21 April 1867. . . . The reports of his [Gladstone's] financial difficulties are again current, as they were last year: but possibly quite unfounded. It seems to be thought that he has cast in his lot with the extreme party, and is little concerned at the prospect of a rupture with the old Whig families.

24 April 1867. Into London by rail from Barnes station, it raining: having started a little after 8, I was at F.O. by 9.30 a.m., an hour at which probably no Sec. of State was ever seen there before!

... Tel. from Petersburg that Gortschakoff thinks peace may be preserved by the neutralisation of Luxemburg, and with that view will propose a conference to be held there. I shall decline this, unless France and Prussia agree to abide by the decision of such conference, of which there is not much probability.

... Howard de Walden says that Rogier is in great anxiety, declaring that the safety of Belgium depends solely on England: he thinks that Prussia will not respect Belgian neutrality, and then France must enter the country in self-defence.

... Easy day at office. Left at 4 p.m. and walked back: trying a new road, I lost my way, and wandered some miles round, but well repaid by the views, and a pleasant walk. Not even London itself gives a stranger such an idea of English wealth as the multitude of villas round Wimbledon, Putney, Richmond, etc., all requiring their owners to be possessed of considerable means.

25 April 1867. ... Greek and Turkish despatches arrived late. Not much in them. The Cretan insurrection is not prospering. The insurgents will not face Turkish troops in the plain. Omar Pasha has orders to put down the rising at any cost: after which the Porte will grant liberal institutions etc. The Greeks are also greatly disappointed at not having succeeded in stirring up disturbances in Thessaly on a large scale: and some of those who have crossed the frontier are burning the villages of the Christian population, in order to punish their apathy and induce them to rise.

The Russian govt, after showing itself very hostile to that of the Principalities, has suddenly changed its policy, and is showing every possible civility. The belief entertained is that there is an understanding to allow Russian troops to pass through, in the event of war with Turkey.

27 April 1867 (Saturday). ... The telegram of last night is to the following effect: Bismarck expresses wish for peace, and disposition to accept any honourable terms of arrangement. He thinks the proper course would be for Holland to apply to the Powers, who should at her invitation propose a conference. Prussia will accept a conference: she can then make concessions to Europe which she could not make to France: but on that account she can accept no preconcerted basis.

Loftus thinks that they will accept evacuation, and a European guarantee.

... Cabinet at 3 p.m. to consider what shall be done if the reform league persist in holding their meeting in Hyde park, contrary to law. We agreed to issue a proclamation declaring any such meeting illegal, but farther steps were left for consideration.

Late in the evening I received from Bernstorff a communication to the effect that Prussia was willing to submit the question of an evacuation of Luxemburg to the decision of a conference: a declaration which if sincere, and if he adheres to it, puts an end to the risk of war.

To Roehampton, late, and very weary, but yet contented with the prospect of peace: although this conference brings abundance of diplomatic trouble with it, and will lead to many discussions in the House.

28 April 1867 (Sunday). . . . Signed a despatch agreeing to the conference, and assenting to its being held in London, if that should be desired. I suggest that it should be called by the K. of Holland. Roehampton again . . . much talk with Ld D. who well pleased with the prospect of peace, in good spirits, and fast mending in health: which I hope may long continue.

. . . American mails in: they contain no news, but Bruce again writes in terms of anger and apprehension about Seward: says his chief wish is to humiliate England, that he is probably trying to obtain British Columbia as a set-off to the Alabama claims, that he has been endeavouring to separate us from the French in China, etc. Bruce is thoroughly uneasy and alarmed. I cannot but think he exaggerates the danger, yet it is not wholly imaginary.

29 April 1867. . . . [The papers] think it doubtful whether Bismarck is sincere in his declarations. I believe he is, and for this reason, that Prussia has nothing to gain by putting off war, if she means to fight: being armed herself, and France but partially so, delay is to her a disadvantage.

. . . Azeglio came to find out if Italy would be admitted to the conference. I answered him favourably so far as my personal opinion was concerned, but could not pledge the other Powers.

. . . I saw with pleasure, but yet with some anxiety, that peace is considered as secure, and that it is here regarded as mainly the work of England. The French government is very grateful for what we have done, and I cannot detect any sign of annoyance in that of Prussia, though the effect of our interference has been rather favourable to France than the reverse. But neither party, I believe, wants a war, and they are glad on both sides to have a decent excuse for remaining at peace. Yet if, after all, a rupture should come, the disappointment felt will be proportionate to the pleasure now expressed, and we shall then be unduly blamed, as we are now undeservedly praised.

30 April 1867. Telegram from Paris that France and Prussia have agreed to suspend their armaments in view of a conference. Cowley writes that the Emp. shows not the slightest desire for war, though he says that in opposing the prevalent feeling he is staking his popularity, and that the hatred of Prussia is on the increase. *Delay will be dangerous* – I think he is right there.

It is believed that the Emp. has been negotiating with Italy on the basis of an Italian contingent of 70,000 men to be supplied in return for a subsidy of £20,000,000 (500 million francs.) I shall enquire about this.

Last night, Irish land bills in House: I heard little of the debate, but yet enough to make it plain that the House wants no such bill to pass, and that the whole thing is – except in the minds of some very few persons – an imposture. Two divisions were taken on amendments, after which we adjourned, it being evident that the majority on both sides wished the question dropped: and for this year it probably will be.

. . . An especially friendly letter from Ld Clarendon, enclosing one from Reeve, who is at Paris. Reeve says there is a strong feeling there of gratitude to England for having helped the Emperor out of his troubles.

1 May 1867. . . . Busy about conference affairs: long cabinet on the threatened Hyde Park demonstration of Monday next. Decided to issue a notice declaring it illegal, but not to resist its taking place, as in the actual state of the law the offence committed is merely a trespass: but to bring in a bill limiting more strictly the use to which the parks may be put, and imposing a penalty for violation of the restrictions.

Gave a dinner in Downing St, chiefly to diplomatists, 28 sat down. Afterwards a party, to which over 1,000 invitations were sent out. I suppose about half the number came. C. acted as lady of the house, and Sanderson made himself generally useful as aide-de-camp.

2 May 1867. . . . Van De Weyer [called] . . . wishing to find out what chance there is of Belgium getting the G. Duchy for herself: but he is too cautious to move officially in the matter. . . . The young King of Greece arrived[20] a little before 4. He sat with me half an hour, talking unaffectedly, but in a rambling confused way, repeating the same thing again and again: his manners good, but I did not carry away a high opinion of his capacity. He expressed great anxiety for the annexation of Crete: saying that if Omar Pasha succeeded in crushing the insurrection there, it would break out throughout the other European provinces of Turkey, and a general war and massacre would follow. He said this several times, as though repeating a lesson he had learnt.

. . . In House, division on the two years residence required as a qualification for the new voters. We were beaten by 80, many of our own people staying away. This result was expected, but we thought ourselves bound by pledges to take the sense of the committee.

3 May 1867 (Friday). . . . Prepared with Hammond a draft of proposals for the conference . . . cabinet at 1: sat 1½ hour, on reform and the threatened Hyde Park riot: agreed to have a meeting of the party on Monday, the situation being critical.

Bentinck came, who held, as Bernstorff had done before, very decided language as to the necessity of placing the neutrality of Luxemburg, like that of Belgium, under a European guarantee. I did not conceal from him the difficulty I felt on this point: and he thought it might be the cause of the conference being broken off. Our proposals are sent out by telegram to all the capitals.

Two means of evading the guarantee difficulty are practicable: one, to recognise simply as existing and in force, that of 1839, to which England is a party: the other, to limit the engagement entered into, to a simple undertaking on the part of all the Powers to respect the neutrality recognised in the treaty. This is a moral guarantee, while it does not pledge us to fight.

House: where debate on Hyde Park meeting: feeling divided, but not much excitement.

4 May 1867. Incessant diplomatic visits all day, on Luxemburg question. Cabinet on Hyde park, decided not to stop the meetings if peaceable, but to try the legal right by bringing actions of trespass against the leaders.

5 May 1867. . . . Answer from Berlin that they insist on neutralisation of the Duchy, and collective guarantee.

Much indignation (I am told) at the Carlton at the idea that the meeting in Hyde Park is not to be opposed.

6 May 1867 (*Monday*). . . . Fine hot day, almost like July. The guarantee question is that on which all now turns, and it is doubtful whether Prussia will give way. I have prepared a draft of convention which will be circulated next morning.

House, where reform bill in committee, all going smoothly: no division. No questions.

Meeting in Hyde Park went off quietly, without excitement, the numbers at no time great: the speeches, I am told, not much listened to: but Walpole's conduct in first announcing that the meeting was forbidden, and then allowing it, is generally blamed. We are all equally responsible, but he is the minister in whose department the matter lay, and from his somewhat weak and vacillating character there is a tendency to assume that it was his personal doing.

7 May 1867. Lay awake great part of the night, from the heat, which is extreme: but not unwell. Up at 5, worked an hour on papers, then to bed again: walk before breakfast. Somewhat troubled in mind about the conference, or rather about the guarantee which Prussia requires, and which I fear will not be well thought of here.

Conference at 3, in the large room, Downing Street: we met at a round table, Apponyi voted me into the chair, and we went to work on a draft the greater part of which had been prepared by Brunnow. We sat two hours, Fane acting as protocolist: all passed easily, except that the Luxemburg envoys had not received their instructions. Delane called late, I talked the thing over with him, and was satisfied with the favourable view he took of the proposed arrangement, as he is a good judge of opinion. I had, for form's sake, reserved my consent till the next meeting, but made it be understood that I would give way, only wishing to place on record that I did so in deference to the unanimous decision of the government. I saw also the representative of the *Telegraph*, and secured him.

Dined Travellers: House, debate on Irish church, Gladstone strong against it, but would not vote, saying the time was not opportune. The division was close, but the motion lost.

8 May 1867. . . . Great heat, such as has not been known in May for 25 years, so they say . . .

Vistahermosa came to ask for admission for Spain to the conference. I told him it was half over, and he came too late, which indeed he could not deny. It seems his govt is jealous at the inclusion of Italy.

. . . Second diplomatic dinner in Downing Street: 29 sat down: party afterwards, about 1,100 cards sent out.

9 May 1867. . . . Heat continues . . . Deputation from Luxemburg came, complaining of prospective injury to the town from withdrawal of garrison, and destruction of the fortifications: I heard their story, sympathised, but could not help them. Conference at 1 p.m. sat about two hours, and finished nearly all our business. Office, and H.C. at 4.30, where questioned about the negotiations, and nervous in answering, but it was very well received. For years no subject has caused me so much uneasiness as this, but it seems well over at last. Debate on reform bill renewed, Hibbert's amendment, which was supported by the whole strength of the Opposition, defeated by 66: a decisive majority, which makes the bill safe. Gladstone spoke with great bitterness, and (oddly enough) early in the evening, about dinner-time: as if he had meant to show that he did not claim the right of a leader, to close the debate on his side. We expected to win by 30 or 35, but were taken by surprise at the numbers.

10 May 1867 (Friday). Office early, conference at 1, sat till 2.30, occupied with very small points of detail: wasting time. Bernstorff and La Tour had not precise instructions as to the date of evacuation, and that article was deferred.

Press unanimous in congratulation at the prospect of peace being achieved. I begin to feel a little uneasiness at this new difficulty being started, but probably it is only that the govts did not expect the conference to end so soon, and thus deferred sending final orders to their representatives.

11 May 1867. Up early, walk round Hyde Park: office 11.30. Van De Weyer called, with a fresh alarm about Belgium, which appears to be the normal state of his government: La Tour came, and relieved my mind by saying that all was settled with Bernstorff, and he was authorised to sign . . .

Cabinet at 3, where Scotch reform bill the chief subject: we also decided not to send an expedition to Abyssinia. Conference at 5, where, to my great joy, we signed the treaty. I believe this to be the shortest conference on record, and it has not been the least successful. But if it fails to preserve peace, as is possible, the responsibility for a new guarantee will be heavy: and this reflection spoils any pleasure I might otherwise feel.

14 May 1867. . . . Stanhope has refused the Duchy, in a not over-civil note, indicating annoyance at having been passed over in July.[21] There remains therefore a vacancy to fill up. Grosvenor had previously declined, as we knew that he would.

15 May 1867. . . . Howard de Walden writes that the Belgians in general are well pleased with the result of the conference. A few would have liked to have Luxemburg annexed to Belgium, but the majority have sense to see that it would be a dangerous and unprofitable acquisition.

17 May 1867. . . . Fighting in Crete: as usual, both sides claim a victory . . . There is renewed diplomatic agitation at Constantinople, but Fuad Pasha declines to enter into any negotiations with the insurgents. I foresee more trouble with this eastern question.

. . . Musurus [called] . . . with his customary stock of official fictions. Then Van De Weyer, with a long story about the Belgian guarantees of 1831 and 1839, the practical object of which I could not make out, unless it was to get some confirmation of them, which is quite needless, as they are already as stringent as words can make them.

House: where reform bill again considered, and Disraeli rather imprudently pledged himself to accept an amendment, which goes to abolish the practice of compounding for rates altogether: this was not considered in cabinet and may give trouble hereafter.

18 May 1867. . . . Despatches from Paris: Moustier anxious to detach Luxemburg from the Zollverein, and wishes it united for financial purposes with Belgium.

. . . Long cabinet, chiefly on reform: but all agreed, which I did not expect. Some objections were made by me, but not pressed.

19 May 1867. . . . News that the Sultan is coming over to England – the first time since Turkey existed. What we are to do with him I have not an idea.

20 May 1867. . . . Reform debate, a powerful speech from Lowe, in his old style . . . Lowe's speech was perfect of its kind: but from over-statement of his case nearly ineffective: in fact most of it might have been described as an argument against constitutional government: and by attacking all parties as equally guilty, he in fact excused all. Nevertheless, there was truth and force in his warnings, though exaggerated: and I at least am not free from anxiety as to the future. Our justification for doing what we are doing lies in the state of feeling on both sides – on the certainty of being thrown over by our own friends if we held out (in fact they are for the most part pressing us on) and in the danger of revolutionary agitation if nothing were done.

21 May 1867. . . . Queen writes, hoping that I will prevent the Sultan's visit. How is that possible?

22 May 1867. . . . Cabinet, attended by Lord Abercorn, to decide whether capital punishment should be inflicted on any of the Fenian prisoners. Naas, Walpole, Marlborough, and I were against: all the rest in favour. So it was determined to take the worst case, and make one example. The argument for, was 'It will be thought you are afraid of the American government, and dare not punish: loyal people will be discouraged: the peasantry fear executions, and think little of sentences of penal servitude: the prisoners themselves will expect pardon in a year or two, and make light of any sentence that can be reversed.' Against, it was urged 'You are making martyrs, giving a new impulse to the cause, enabling the Fenian leaders to renew their funds, now nearly exhausted: and if a debate arises in parliament, things will be said which will act as a fresh stimulus to sedition. Besides, opinion in England is against hanging for political causes, whatever it may be in Ireland.' All agreed that as a question of justice, there could be no doubt of our right to enforce the law: it was a question of policy only.

Snow, rain, and hail, spoiling the Derby as a popular holiday. Easy day at the office. Dined Grillions: small party: pleasant. Thence Cosmopolitans with Kimberley and T. Baring.

24 May 1867. . . . The chief Rabbi of the Jews [called], with a telegram announcing persecution in Jassy,[22] massacres in the streets etc. Baron Rothschild spoke to me of this last night. I promised to do what I could, and telegraphed accordingly.

25 May 1867. . . . Cabinet, where after much discussion it was decided in deference to the generally expressed feeling, to commute the sentence of Burke, the Fenian left for execution. I am glad of this, as it was my opinion throughout: yet sorry that it was not done on Wednesday so that the appearance of indecision might have been avoided.

28 May 1867. . . . Ld D. tells me of Court troubles: the D. of Edinburgh having got leave to lay out £3,000 of public money in presents for his visit to the Australian colonies, has spent £6,000 and more, and gone off leaving the bill unpaid: which is not very unlike a fraud. The sum can however be deducted from his allowance. We believe too that the P. of W. is going to have his debts paid. They are stated at £50,000. I doubt whether the House would consent, and if it did, the debate would not be an agreeable one for the family.

29 May 1867. . . . Dined at home: played chess with Ld D. in evening, which I think we have not done for a year past. He in good spirits, though not yet looking fully recovered.

30 May 1867. . . . Cabinet at 1, chiefly on Reform bill, all pretty well agreed, and not much trouble: sat till 3 . . . House again at 9: came just in time for division on Laing's amendment, which takes away from all boroughs under 10,000 their second member: it was carried by a vast majority, many of the conservatives voting for it: I think the House was quite right in this decision, we knew how it would go, but wished that the initiative should not be with us, lest we should alienate friends whose patience has already been tried a good deal. Among the minority was Brand, the Whig whip, but whose own borough is threatened.

31 May 1867. . . . Sharp debate on Irish Universities, in which Lowe attacked Gladstone on the score of having broken faith with parliament:

Gladstone in reply almost unable to speak when he first rose, from passion: the House amused rather than interested.

1 June 1867. . . . Cowley has had a long talk with Moustier on the east: M.'s language is, that France has long tried the plan of opposing Russia, finds it does not answer, and now wishes by a semblance of cooperation to keep her in check. . . . D'Azeglio called, and Musurus, both on eastern affairs. The Italian govt anxious to interfere, wishing to act with us – chiefly as a proof of independence of France – but not knowing nor greatly caring, what advice it gives, so long as it gives some. . . . Article in *Times* on Luxemburg ratifications very complimentary to the government.

Cabinet 3.30: question: redistribution of seats: I urge disfranchisement of up to 5,000 popn, which will give 9 seats, besides the 45 second members taken from all under 10,000: this well received, but nothing settled.

(In the end it was decided to oppose the amendment, as likely to be unpopular in the House, and to create opposition to the farther progress of the bill: I opposed this decision, but the House has since taken the same view. June 5.)

6 June 1867. . . . Turkish govt telegraphs that it is willing to make large reforms in Crete, provided that the Powers will declare that they will give no countenance to efforts against its authority. This is an adroit move, as Russia will not find it easy to give the assurance required.

. . . House again, and sat till 2 a.m., when home very weary. These late sittings quite exhaust me, and I hardly know how I shall go on with them.

7 June 1867. . . . Cabinet: redistribution of seats: settled our plan, but whether the House will accept it, who knows?

11 June 1867. Called on D. at his request: Rothschild having given him some vague, but alarming intelligence[23] of intrigues now going on at Paris: I could not make much of what he said, but promised to watch and make all necessary enquiries.

14 June 1867. . . . Talk with Naas about Fenians: he evidently alarmed at the general sympathy shown for them among a comparatively respectable class of the south Irish population. Provisions and little luxuries are being constantly supplied to the prisoners by tradesmen and persons in that rank of life. It is believed another attempt will be made.

18 June 1867. . . . Debate on London and Durham universities, to which the cabinet (very foolishly, as I think) decided to give a member jointly: the two places having nothing whatever to do with one another: naturally the House objected, and several divisions were taken: in the last of which we were beaten, as we deserved to be: and so the matter will drop.

The Times writes up cumulative voting in a succession of articles, and complains grievously of its not being adopted: the secret being that Walter[24] has been the Liberal candidate for Berkshire, and would come in under the cumulative system, being supported by a large minority.

Much talk in society about the P. of Wales, and his disreputable ways of going on. He is seen at the theatres paying attention to the lowest class of women, visits them at their houses, etc. The public though inclined to be tolerant – and the more so in his case as it is well known that his mother will not let him interfere in business of any sort through jealousy – dislikes the scandal and publicity of these proceedings: while people in the higher class are annoyed by his preference for low company, and want of dignity generally.
24 June 1867. . . . Bismarck has come back from Paris satisfied that unless the French are wilfully deceiving him, there is no present danger of war. He, and the Prussians generally, are rather sore at Lord Derby's description of the value of a collective guarantee: which, to say truth, was more accurate than diplomatic. He represented it as nearly worthless, which it is, but a little ambiguity at this moment would have been more prudent.

. . . Musurus calls, with information, partly out of date, and partly contradicted by that which Ld Lyons has sent. He (M.) does not know what his own government is doing.
28 June 1867. . . . Trouble in Bulgaria, stirred up by the Russians, whose agents openly attend the meetings of the disaffected.

No sensible progress making by the Turks in Crete: even where Omar Pasha's army makes way, and the insurrection is put down, it beings again as soon as the troops are gone. Great distress and famine over the greater part of the island.

House: reform again: long and sharp debate on a clause, not itself especially important, but as to which the cabinet appears to have considered itself pledged. We voted, but left our friends free to do as they pleased: (indeed they would not have followed us) and they threw it out. Gladstone lost his temper as usual . . .
29 June 1867. Ld D. again attacked with gout and rheumatism: the latter a new complaint for him.

. . . Trouble at Court: it appears that there is a plan formed to hoot John Brown at the approaching review, if he appears with the Queen: and the thing has been considered serious enough to justify a warning being given on the subject to H.M. How she will take it no one knows.

. . . La Tour called, to read consular despatches from Crete: it is clear he considers the game up, and the cession of the island to Greece inevitable. Cowley's despatches, received this morning, indicate also that such is the opinion of the French govt.
30 June 1867. . . . Windsor with my mother in evening . . . The Queen in the best of humours, very large, ruddy, and fat (the tendency increases rapidly) but complaining of her health, saying the work she has to do is too much for her, that she is almost knocked up – and so forth.

. . . Heard from Paget that John Brown is not to appear at the review, where he would certainly have been hooted. The Queen unluckily parades this man about London behind her carriage, in his Highland dress, so that every street boy knows him. Paget . . . grieved at the stories in circulation: feels sure (like most reasonable people) that there is no real foundation for them – or in plain words that J.B. is not a favoured lover – but says plainly that he has great influence, that she consults him about everything, has him in her room at all hours etc. He argues truly, that if anything were amiss there would not be all this publicity. Talks of the P. of W., thinks he has got into a thoroughly bad set, that they treat him without respect, that he will see no one else – hopes the Princess may bring him round. Parallel of George IV suggested, not by me.

5 July 1867. . . . The Queen consents to stay at Windsor to receive the Sultan which is right: but she writes to Ld D. complaining of her health[25] and has sent Dr Jenner to him to confirm her words. From Dr Jenner's report it seems that there is really so much weakness of nerves, and liability to excitement, that any great departure from her usual way of life, or more than ordinary agitation, might produce insanity. He declares he is willing if called upon to make a report to this effect to the cabinet: but to what purpose, since by the nature of the case it cannot be made public? Meanwhile, her growing unpopularity has thoroughly alarmed Grey, and those about the Court who take a personal interest in her.

. . . Good debate on cumulative vote . . . I have always thought the plan of cumulative voting sound and just in principle, if applied in a country where electoral divisions were equal, in such manner that every constituency should have three members. But this cannot be the case with us: and in England the diversities actually existing in representation supply, though in a rougher and less perfect manner, the securities desired for the minority.

6 July 1867. . . . It is exactly twelve months since the present government accepted office. The time has passed slowly, as is always the case when there is much to do and to think of: there has been anxiety, at times irritation, at others exhaustion and overwork: on the other hand is to be set the absence of *ennui*, constant, and in general not disagreeable employment, and whatever pleasure arises (I do not rate it highly) from the possession of power. On the whole, I do not actually dislike official life, and am willing that it should continue for the present: but I do not know that as master of Knowsley I should be of the same opinion: and in any case I should be sorry to look forward to a long term of what – however honourable – is really slavery. I have passed only two weekdays out of London since Oct. last.

. . . Cabinet: where the Queen's state very seriously discussed: it was decided not to press her about the review, which is to be postponed altogether. It seems that Dr Jenner says any strong excitement (and very little excites her) produces violent fits of bilious sickness, and if Nature did not provide this relief the effect on her mind might be dangerous.

17 July 1867. . . . Last joke about H.M. 'Why is the Queen penny wise and pound foolish?' 'Because she looks after the browns and lets the sovereigns take care of themselves.'

19 July 1867. Early, after breakfast, La Tour called: in some agitation of mind: saying that the Turkish government has declined the proposed enquiry into Cretan affairs. He appeared to think that this refusal could not be accepted by France, and that she must thenceforth concert her measures with Russia in order to compel a change of policy.

. . . Much talk about a coalition between the Whig opposition in the Lords, and the malcontent Conservatives, to support some amendment to the reform bill, which, as they calculate, will compel the ministry either to resign or withdraw the bill. Grey, Carnarvon, Cranborne, Lowe, are actively engaged in this project, and they appear to have secured the support of the *Times*. We shall see the result.

21 July 1867. . . . Buckingham palace at 2, having been appointed to meet the Sultan at a private audience: this lasted about three-quarters of an hour . . .

Most of the Sultan's conversation consisted – as at a formal interview was inevitable – of compliment and commonplace: yet what he said about Crete showed that he understood the situation. He spoke of his wish to improve the position of the Christian races and the administration generally: of the necessity of time: of the reforms that had already been made: of the dishonest conduct of the Russians, who excited discontent wherever they could, and then pointed to it as an evidence of misgovernment: (his expression was 'they light the match themselves, and then cry "fire" '): of the impossibility of his ceding Crete, or taking steps which would necessarily lead to its cession. Some other things he said, which I do not now recall. I assured him in strong but general terms of our determination to respect the independence of his government: but urged that if possible he should avoid a direct rupture with France and Russia. We conversed through Fuad Pasha as interpreter. I don't know whether he translated faithfully. Fuad told me, more emphatically than the Sultan had done, that they could not give up the island: they might yield it to force, if the Great Powers chose to use force for in that case they would not be responsible to their own people: but cede it voluntarily they could not. I said nothing, but could not help thinking they were right.

29 July 1867. . . . Disraeli tells me that the Rothschilds are confident of peace, and consider the Danish question as being virtually settled.

1 August 1867. . . . A short discussion on Irish railroads: Gladstone strongly in favour of their purchase: we postpone action, and demand farther inquiry, which indeed is necessary, as many details are wanting.

3 August 1867. . . . Feeling singularly well and in spirits, which one would not expect after the life of the last six months.

8 August 1867. . . . Much talk with Greek minister about present state of affairs. He seems fair, candid, and intelligent: the latter a common quality among his countrymen, the former quite the reverse.

10 August 1867. . . . Cabinet 3.30, much talk, and little done. It is a common complaint among us now that we can arrange no business when together: for want, I think, of some one to keep order, which Ld D. does not do, and no one else can. However, there was today but little to be discussed.

12 August 1867. . . . Arranged to make Sanderson a personal allowance of £100 a year (out of my own pocket) in addition to his salary, which I think not adequate to the work he does.

13 August 1867. . . . The Belgian chargé [called], introducing M. Rogier, over in England for a few days: M. Rogier talked with me for some time: a large stout man, with a big voice, reminding me of Lord Ellenborough. Very eager to get Luxemburg, and also to have the support of the British government in the Scheldt dispute. I do not give much hope on either point.

House at 2, answered questions: . . . sitting again at 9, stayed till past 1. Utterly sick and weary of this life, which involves continual waste of time, which can be very ill spared. My papers, no doubt, follow me to the House: and some business can be done there: but a great deal cannot: and arrears grow upon me, while the physical exhaustion produced by heat and late hours is very trying.

15 August 1867. . . . Lord Cowley in conversation told me that the Mexican idea had been in the Emperor's mind ever since 1854: that it was originated by the Empress, and pressed on by her: and that when the news of Maximilian's execution arrived, the Emperor burst into tears, had a 'scene' with the Empress, and was so ill as to be unable to go to some ceremony which he was to have attended the day after.

18 August 1867. Hatfield: fine day: out of doors from breakfast to dinner. Morier came in afternoon.

19 August 1867. London by 8.55 train . . . went to call on the young King of Greece at Marlborough House: he civil but weak: confirming my impression from a first interview.[26] He talked in a very odd way, asking me among other things whether I considered Turkey as a Christian Power? I really did not know what he meant, and said so, and he did not explain: but I suppose he intended to hint that the rules of European diplomacy ought not to apply to a non-Christian state. He kept repeating the same thing again and again. The only subject on which he talked was Crete. I was with him half an hour. – House at 3.30 for the last time . . . Hatfield by 5.5 train: walk in the park.

20 August 1867. London by 10 . . . Council at Windsor . . . Walk from Paddington to King's Cross, where caught the train to Hatfield. Morier, Elliot (of the C.O.), Lady Brownlow, the guests.

21 August 1867. . . . Cabinet, where little settled. I pressed on my colleagues the reorganisation of the education dept, for which my plan is to detach it from the Privy Council, create a separate minister of education (who might also have charge of the museums, picture galleries, and the like), and in order to avoid increasing the number of paid offices, connect the Duchy of Lancaster with the Presidency of the Council, so that the former shall in effect be merged in the latter. This scheme I explained, and it was well received. Back to Hatfield by 6 p.m. train . . . Found Odo Russell, and the Clevelands, besides the party of yesterday.

Settled with Morier the Austrian negotiation. He is very clever, very hard-working: something of a dreamer, full of German ideas.

22 August 1867. London by 8.55 train . . . Brunnow very friendly, and moderate in his language about Crete. I forgot to note that the K. of Greece on Monday reverted two or three times to the proposal that the Sultan should cede Crete for a sum of money down: I answered, that in principle I saw no objection, since the inhabitants themselves no doubt desired the transfer: but that there were two objections: one that the Sultan would not choose to sell: the other that Greece had not the means of buying.

23 August 1867. . . . Euston at 10, Huyton at 3 . . . all I saw in good order and great beauty. No guests or family, only Ld and Ly D.

24 August 1867. Boxes by post . . . France and Russia continue to press for the Cretan enquiry: the Porte gives the same answer as before: consent if it be limited to questions of administrative reform: otherwise refusal. – The Greek govt is arming, and trying to buy ironclads . . . They have nothing to lose: the state of the country being hopeless as it is.

25 August 1867 (Sunday). Boxes by post . . . Church: luncheon with Hale: talk with him on local matters . . . Tired and not very well, I do not know why.

26 August 1867. . . . Walk 11 to 3. Returned home, and almost perplexed what to do with my time. I have been so long busy every day and all day, Sundays excepted, that I scarcely know how to use leisure when it comes.

28 August 1867. With Hale early, to look at an estate now offered for sale . . . I had no hesitation in advising Ld D. against the purchase . . .

30 August 1867. Took leave . . . Noted the great beauty of country when near Lancaster, and thence most of the way to Carlisle: which revived in my mind an idea I have long entertained of buying land in this district when available, to be ultimately a refuge for the family when smoke and building shall have made Knowsley uninhabitable: a result which seems to be nearer than I used to think it . . . Aberdeen about 4 a.m.

31 August 1867. . . . Arrived Balmoral . . . Soon after I had arrived, the mail came in . . . It would seem that Napoleon is satisfied of the impossibility of finding in Austria an ally against Prussia: and the chances of war are so far diminished. He has also been strongly pressed to take a position in eastern affairs more friendly to Turkey:[27] with what result we do not yet know.

2 September 1867. . . . Dined with the Queen: H.M. in good spirits, talking more freely, and with more enjoyment, than ever I heard her. At night, smoked with P. Christian: an honest quiet gentleman, who will not set the Thames on fire.

3 September 1867. . . . The Greek government, bankrupt as it is, is getting built for itself some four or five small ships of war: Tricoupi saying openly that they shall be at war with Turkey before next summer.[28]

. . . The Queen today breakfasted and wrote her letters in the open air, in the garden, the day, though fine, being as cold as an ordinary English October. She drives out late in the afternoon in an open carriage, and does not return till 8 p.m. when all is quite dark. Her love of exposure to the weather, and her dislike of heat and close rooms, are almost morbid.

4 September 1867. . . . Dined with the Queen . . . H.M. in good, even high spirits, laughing and talking without restraint.

7 September 1867 (Saturday). Left Balmoral about 8 . . . to Euston by 4.40 on Sunday morning. Thence home . . . being just 21 hours from door to door.

9 September 1867. . . . Heard that Ld D. is again attacked by gout, and rather sharply: the result, I fear, of his inevitable attendance in the H. of Lords, when not half recovered from a former illness.

10 September 1867. . . . Apponyi confirmed what I had heard as to the peaceable nature of the Salzburg conference: and also as to the influence which his government had exercised over that of France on eastern affairs: the fruits of which are beginning to be apparent.

Adams brings me Seward's answer on Alabama claims, which though somewhat vague and obscure, is on the whole satisfactory, inasmuch as it accepts the conditions of arbitration proposed by us.

11 September 1867. . . . Fresh confirmation, from various quarters, of the change of policy of the French government in the east.

. . . Pakington [called], with a story of the French govt having sent him their new Chassepot rifle, under condition of secrecy as to the trial of it, whereupon the War Dept allows the result of these trials to get into the newspapers. I told him to say nothing about it: they don't read our papers much, and very likely may never see the report. . . . Hatfield by 6 p.m. train.

12 September 1867. Hatfield all day . . .

13 September 1867. Office by 11.30: busy till 4, when left again for Hatfield.

14 September 1867. Hatfield: long drive in the direction of Hoddesden, where the woods are extensive and the country very beautiful. No guests.

15 September 1867. Hatfield. Out nearly all day.

16 September 1867. . . . Russian despatches: the idea of Cretan annexation appears to be at last dropped by Gortschakoff: a great and unexpected change, due partly to the Emperor's interview with Fuad, partly to the military success of Omar Pasha and the exhaustion of the insurgents:

partly perhaps also to the corresponding change which French policy appears to be undergoing. The Czar himself is no doubt more moderate than his advisers.

17 September 1867. . . . Long talk with Northcote on Abyssinia, we agreed on nearly all points: I embodied our joint views in a despatch.

. . . Dined Carlton: long talk with Hunt, whom met there, about Abyssinian expenses: he thinks they have not as yet reached a million, including all that is ordered.

19 September 1867. . . . Hatfield by 5 p.m. train.

20 September 1867. . . . Finished all work by 2 p.m. and back to Hatfield . . .

21 September 1867. . . . Hatfield by 6 p.m. . . . Large party to meet the Queen of Holland.

22 September 1867. Hatfield: large party . . . The Queen [of Holland] very talkative, very clever, very odd: easily excited: seems devoted to Lord Clarendon in particular: not the least formal, not causing stiffness, as royal people almost always do.

I shook hands with Carnarvon on meeting, but declined all private conversation with him: and indeed he did not seek it.

23 September 1867. . . . I heard this morning of the Q. of H. a story too strange and extraordinary to set down here, unless in cypher. It will not be forgotten, but I note the hearing of it that the time and place may be preserved.

25 September 1867. . . . Stagnation of business complete: there has been nothing like it since I came into this office.

26 September 1867. Letter from Disraeli; wishing to have a session specially for Abyssinia, confined to that subject, without a Queen's Speech. I doubt if such an arrangement is possible.

Letter from Ld D. dwelling on the necessity of the minister at Washington being a man of rank: which I do not believe important.

Wrote . . . to the Queen a long letter on replacing Lowther [at Berlin] . . . she wants Morier there, or rather the Crown Princess does, in order that he may help her in intriguing against Bismarck: which is just why I will not send him. . . . Then to Euston . . . Arrived Knowsley about 11.30. Family party.

27 September 1867. . . . Northcote called, on his way to Balmoral. He discussed with Ld D. and me the question of a November session, and also the wording of a despatch containing instructions for Sir R. Napier, about which we have had some correspondence.

28 September 1867. . . . With F. at 3 to Huyton to receive the Queen of Holland: five carriages brought her and her suite.

29 September 1867. . . . Some talk with the Queen, who says the Salzburg visit was an idea of the French Empress, who blames herself, justly, for the Mexican catastrophe, and wanted to make what amends she could to the

Austrian court. There was no other motive. She says peace is certain for 1868, but for 1869 she will not answer.

1 October 1867. Up early, to Huyton with F. at 9: to see the Queen off: she leaves Southampton for Cherbourg tonight. . . . Many boxes: the arrangement as to the K. of Hanover's fortune is at last made, and the treaty signed: a good end of a matter which though not important has been troublesome.

2 October 1867. . . . All I have heard in Lancashire confirms the impression that there is as yet no sign of reviving trade. Things are as bad as they have ever been in the towns. Even building land is in no demand.

3 October 1867. . . . The Queen writes to Ld D. again pressing Morier for Berlin, which is manifestly an intrigue against Bismarck, conducted by the Crown Princess. Ld D. to whom I explain the circumstances supports me steadily.

14 October 1867. . . . Disraeli writes, from Rothschild's information, that the Emp. is no longer master of the position, that there is a secret treaty between Italy and Prussia, and that the Prussians are about to spend a million and a half on ironclads, to be built in America, as they would be stopped in the event of war if built here.

. . . Talk with [Gathorne] Hardy: he expects another Fenian outbreak of some sort, and various incendiary attempts: says the country is in a state of panic: and complains of the want of skilled detectives. Ours have no practice in dealing with any except the criminal classes.

15 October 1867. . . . Disraeli came to discuss various matters. He sketched out to me the outline of his intended speech at Edinburgh.

16 October 1867. . . . Disraeli came at my request to discuss the Roman trouble, he agreed with me in thinking that interference would be at any rate premature.

17 October 1867. Left London by 10 a.m. train for Manchester, where a dinner given in the Free Trade Hall to Ld D. and the ministry. About 800 sat down, and 1,200 more looked on. The Premier's reception was enthusiastic: he spoke about an hour, his voice feeble, but in other respects the speech effective.

18 October 1867. . . . Elliot has seen Moustier on his way to Constantinople. Moustier avowed to him with perfect frankness that the secret of the anti-Turkish policy lately pursued by France, was that a war in Germany was expected, and the support of Russia desired! This at least is plain speaking.

19 October 1867. . . . The order for French troops to leave for Rome has not yet been given: and the Emperor apparently does not wish to give it, if he can obtain his object without the use of force. He has told the Italian govt that if an Italian army crosses the papal frontier, it will be a *casus belli*: and that French troops will very shortly be at Turin. If, on the other hand, they can put down the Garibaldian movement and undertake to respect the papal territory, France will take no step. The question of the Pope's future position in Italy they are willing to reserve for future discussion.

Nothing is known, at least nothing is avowed, as to any secret under-standing between Prussia and Italy.

Erskine writes from Athens that the Greek govt, seeing that they will not have the support of the Great Powers, have deferred their scheme of going to war with Turkey. The emigration from Crete goes on as before.

21 October 1867. . . . D'Azeglio called while I was out, saw Sanderson, and expressed himself as hopeful that no expedition would take place. I went to talk over the whole matter with Disraeli: whose views concurred with mine in every respect. . . . Dined Travellers: met Azeglio, and much talk with him.

22 October 1867. Slept ill: a little out of sorts . . . Azeglio called: long convn with him, on which I founded a draft. He is quite satisfied with what we have done.

It seems that the French expedition to Rome is, if not abandoned, at least suspended . . . that the Garibaldian volunteers have been defeated: that the King has, in substance, complied with the demands of France . . . The danger now is that the party of action, beaten and angry, may turn against the monarchy, which has failed to help them in their need.

28 October 1867. . . . Buchanan writes that the Russian F.O. has changed its tone, talks of non-intervention in Crete, abuses the Greeks for having thought that they could compel Russia to act, as Cavour forced the Emperor's hand: in short, they are backing out of a false position: and they say the illusions still entertained at Athens will soon be at an end.

. . . Hatfield by 5.25 train.

29 October 1867. . . . Letter from D. of Buckingham, to the effect that H.M. is not in very good humour at my having taken the part of the Italians in this dispute.

30 October 1867. . . . Telegram from the Queen, who afraid (very unnecessarily) that we shall get mixed up in this Italian complication. I send an answer that ought to satisfy her. She has never been in good humour since the failure of her attempt to get Morier placed at Berlin.

1 November 1867. . . . Erskine writes from Athens that brigandage has begun again, and that the Greeks are getting tired of having to feed the Cretan refugees, of whom there must be between 30 and 40,000 in Greece. They cost £20,000 a month, or one-fourth of the whole revenue of Greece. It does not, however, appear that the Cretans have any idea of giving up the struggle. On the contrary, they are confident they can hold out through the winter.

Elliott writes that Fuad will give the Cretans all they want, short of autonomy. He thinks that if they had the choosing of a Prince, they might begin with one of their own people, but the next step would be to elect the King of Greece in that capacity: from which to complete annexation the distance is not great.

2 November 1867. . . . Disraeli looked in, just returned from his Scotch demonstration. I went to the Austrian embassy, and had an interview of an hour with Beust. Dined there . . .

3 November 1867. . . . Beust called upon me at 3 p.m. and sat an hour. He afterwards called on Lord D. He is an eternal talker, very clever, very restless, cannot leave things alone, inclines always to the sanguine view of things, his activity immense, but I do not think he adheres steadily to any plan. Vanity and the desire of playing a great part are very obvious in his conversation.[29]

4 November 1867. To Windsor for a Council, the business purely formal . . . Drafted two despatches on the Roman question. I do not absolutely decline the conference proposed by France, but suggest various difficulties in the way of accepting the invitation, not conceding my opinion that they are practically insuperable.

I hear from Berlin that Bismarck holds similar language, adding that if we decline, he shall do the same. He does not see, he says, why he should be called upon to repair the mistakes committed by other people. He thinks the Pope ought to be a sovereign, and so personally independent, but that it does not matter whether his territory is large or small, and for what he loses in that respect a money compensation may be given. This is exactly the view I have always taken.

. . . At night, despatches from Constantinople. There is now no doubt of the rejection by the insurgents of Aali's proposals: and that nothing except the concession of complete autonomy will give a chance of saving the island. Fuad is supposed to think, that if it comes to cession, there will be less loss of dignity in yielding to an intervention of all the Great Powers, than in offering fresh terms to the insurgents and thereby acknowledging that they are masters of the situation.

Note. The Queen this morning remarkably civil about Germany etc., seems to have recovered from her ill-humour, which a week or ten days ago was very marked.

5 November 1867. Telegram this morning announcing the defeat of Garibaldi, and consequent evacuation of papal territory by insurgents.

. . . The Greek minister [called], who seems convinced that Crete will be at last annexed to Greece: in which I suspect he is right . . .

Cabinet at 3: much talk, and little settled: but we arranged that the question of the Fenians tried at Manchester should be brought before us on Thursday.

6 November 1867. . . . Ld D. (who came up on Saturday last) again seized with gout.

7 November 1867. . . . Saw Baude, and advised withdrawal of French troops, if not from Italy altogether, at least from Rome to Civita Vecchia. My reasons for this advice are stated in a draft addressed to Ld Lyons.

. . . Cabinet at 3, Ld D. absent from govt. Sentences of Manchester Fenians discussed, but no final decision. Question raised of prosecuting the *Irishman* newspaper, and certainly the articles produced were treasonable enough: but Naas, Hardy, Disraeli, and I all objected, thinking the risk of failure great, and the advantage small: and it was determined to do nothing at present. The most vehement for prosecuting were Chelmsford and J. Manners. One of the articles under consideration was a violent attack on Judge Keogh: and it appeared that he himself had deprecated any notice being taken of it, on the rather singular ground that in that case he should be marked out for assassination. It seems there is really in Dublin an assassination committee: supposed to number about 25 members, of whom 7 are now in custody. There have been sent to penal servitude, in all, between 35 and 40 Fenians. It is thought that the publicity given to the Sheffield outrages has done mischief, putting murder into people's heads: especially as Broadhead and Co. got off without punishment. Incidentally it was mentioned that one of the articles complained of was from the pen of Isaac Butt: once a Conservative M.P., now a pauper, and with a ruined character.

9 November 1867. . . . Lord Lyons writes that Beust is much disappointed at not having succeeded in inducing me to join with him in his proposal of a joint manifesto on the Cretan question.

10 November 1867. . . . Bread-riots at Barnstaple, Exeter, and other places. Troops sent to Oxford to stop rioting there. Distress getting severe at the east of London. Revenue returns showing a falling off. Altogether, a gloomy prospect for the winter.

12 November 1867. . . . Cabinet at 4. Queen's Speech read and partly considered: also the Manchester Fenians: but our chief business was the renewing of the contracts of P. and O. company, which we agreed to, at £400,000 a year for twelve years, and a guarantee of 6%: high terms, I thought, but nobody would compete with them, and they are masters of the market.

13 November 1867. . . . Delane [called], who to my satisfaction says that though the Abyssinian expedition is an unsatisfactory affair (in which I quite agree) there is no help for it, and that it will not be seriously attacked in parliament. Talk with him as to the conference:[30] his view of it is much the same as mine, indeed all the world here seems of one mind on the subject.

14 November 1867. . . . Cabinet at 4 p.m., sat two hours, considering the speech.

17 November 1867 (Sunday). . . . In afternoon, walk with Northcote: called to enquire at Grosvenor Gate, Mrs Disraeli being very ill. Hatfield by 6 p.m. train.

18 November 1867. . . . Working up Abyssinian papers. Dinner at the Clarendon, given by Disraeli, but owing to his wife's serious illness he was not able to attend. I took the chair. Speech read etc. as usual. Fenian deputation at the Home Office: who being refused an audience, became noisy, abused Hardy, almost in his hearing, and refused to go till the police were sent for.

19 November 1867. At home all morning, preparing for the debate of the afternoon, and made more anxious by the doubt which exists whether I may not have to take the lead, in Disraeli's absence, should Mrs D. die which is thought possible. It is a position for which I am utterly unfit: yet who else can hold it?

... House at 4.30 ... Gladstone followed, temperate and courteous, and expressing in well-chosen words his sympathy with Disraeli's personal troubles. D. answered, and for the first time since I have known him was unable to speak audibly when he first rose, from emotion.

20 November 1867. ... Cabinet at 3: Irish University education discussed: and some Abyssinian matters: and the question of the condemned Fenians at Manchester. We ended by being all of one mind, to commute the sentence of Shaw, who was not proved to have used any deadly weapon: and to leave the other three for execution.

21 November 1867. ... Paid Noel £100, in aid of workingmen's associations: a quasi-compulsory subscription, as all the cabinet give.

22 November 1867. ... From Athens I hear that brigandage, so far from being repressed, and as was thought, extinct, is more rife than ever, and that the Greek govt has sent off a good many of the banditti whom it could induce to surrender, to Crete, where as the minister observes, there is nothing to rob, and they can do no harm. This proceeding, however, they appear to have discovered.

23 November 1867. ... Cabinet at 3, discussed postal contracts at length, London cattle-market, and prospects of Fenian disturbance in London.

27 November 1867. ... Cabinet at 4: Disraeli absent. Principal question discussed, the absence of charities and government buildings from rating. On the whole, the feeling was against all such exemptions, but we settled nothing.

30 November 1867. ... Cabinet at 3, where much discussion on the Fenian business. Hardy says that arms are being bought in large quantities, a thing which there is no legal power to stop. The disaffected in every town, so provided, will be more than a match for the police. Arms are sometime seized, but there is no legal right to do this, and the owners would have a legal remedy. The arms are mostly revolvers, and made in Belgium. He thinks some legislative remedy ought to be provided, such as requiring all guns to be registered, or the like. We were all, however, of opinion that the case was not strong enough to justify us bringing in a bill. It could not be carried, nor could we state our reasons fully. He evidently expects an outbreak. Some discussion afterwards on education, but vague and without result. Disraeli was not there.

. . . Read some numbers of the *Glasgow Free Press* and the *Dublin Weekly News* – violently treasonable . . . The feeling among the Irish peasantry seems to be growing worse and worse: the language now openly held is, that neither the church nor the land grievances are what they complain of, they want independence, and nothing else.

1 December 1867. . . . Despatches: Lyons writes . . . that it would be worth while for the Porte to make almost any sacrifice in the Cretan business that would serve to bring back France to her former eastern policy.

Elliot says there are reports of changes, but the Sultan professes entire confidence in Aali and Fuad, only he says there is more work than they alone can do. He is not well pleased with Omar Pasha, who he thinks deceived him by too sanguine reports and promises of immediate success. He will offer almost any terms to the Cretans, but is determined to resist all proposals for cession of territory. There are general predictions of a rising in the spring. Ignatieff again holds violent language, saying that Crete must be annexed to Greece, nothing else will now settle the question. I begin to think he is right.

4 December 1867. . . . I heard at Windsor that the Queen refusing to allow an equerry to be in attendance when she is driven about by John Brown, and the possibility of a Fenian attack upon her being thought to make precautions desirable, she is followed in these drives by two of the suite, who keep at a distance, and are armed with revolvers.

7 December 1867. . . . Home by 5 p.m. well pleased that the session, short as it was, is over, for parliamentary attendance interferes very inconveniently with office work. Ours is a strange system: a minister during half the year, passes about 40 hours weekly in the House: he has to prepare for debates: and all his administrative duty must be done in the mere leavings and fragments of his time.

9 December 1867. . . . Cabinet at 12, sat nearly four hours, wasting time, as I thought, for after all but little was settled. We talked of education, and the idea was much discussed of, as it were, turning the flank of the religious difficulty by paying only for results, leaving the school to be set on foot and managed as the parties establishing it may think best. This seemed to be approved by several present. Then arose a discussion on Vancouver's island and British Columbia, and it appeared clear that neither one nor the other could be held against the U.S. in the event of a war, without a totally disproportionate expenditure of force. Then Ireland: question of prosecuting the *Irishman* for an article manifestly seditious, but as usual, no decision come to.

10 December 1867. Lord and Lady Derby left for Knowsley.

15 December 1867. Hatfield. Walk morning and afternoon. Young Balfour[31] arrived, a fine handsome lad, and clever.

17 December 1867. . . . At 1 p.m. met Disraeli, Hardy, the Chancellor, Pakington, Corry[32] and D. of Buckingham: called together by Hardy, who has received a multitude of Fenian communications. One informant speaks of 155 Fenian and republican clubs in London alone, all unknown to the police. Several announce projects for blowing up the Houses of Parlt, and assassinating the Queen. Another reported plan is to seize the P. of W. on his way to or from Sandringham. From Philadelphia comes a story of an association whose object is to hire houses in various parts of London, fill them with combustibles, and set them on fire at the same time. A Fenian has been heard to threaten the burning of the theatres when full, and the destruction of public buildings. The police report on Fenian evidence, that three men are told off to assassinate Ld D., Hardy, and me. Monck telegraphs (and this is the most serious, as being in some degree authenticated) that a ship is to sail for Dieppe ostensibly, really for the Bristol channel, from New York, with a party on board whose object is to murder the Queen etc.

I cannot say that I attach much importance to any of these stories, but no doubt they justify some precautions. Hardy says that we have no detectives, and that a new force will require to be organised, independent of Sir R. Mayne. We agreed to hold a cabinet on Thursday. – I cannot but think that most of this evidence is mere gossip, and that we are acting with more haste and fuss than is necessary: but no doubt excess of caution is a fault on the right side . . .

18 December 1867. . . . Meeting of cabinet ministers in town again today: agreed to detain the suspected Fenian privateer: many arrangements of detail were talked of, and some were made.

19 December 1867. . . . Breakfast with Ld D. who inclines to agree with me as to the non-necessity for strong measures: I believe that Disraeli is recommending them from an idea that by exciting a panic he will make the work of government in the approaching session easier, and divert attention from party-fights. But it is a doubtful and dangerous policy.

. . . Cabinet at 3, which lasted three hours: not much settled, except that we will not ask parliament to meet earlier than usual, that we will strengthen the metropolitan police, increase number of detectives, and take other precautionary measures that may be necessary. The Queen, it appears, is alarmed and angry: she wants Habeas Corpus suspended, militia embodied, in short preparation made to meet an armed insurrection: notwithstanding which, she resists obstinately all suggestions that she should allow herself to be attended when driving about, especially after dark.

20 December 1867. Breakfast early with Ld D. and saw him off to Knowsley . . . Went over to speak to Disraeli about some rather hasty orders given by Corry as to the seizure of the supposed Fenian privateer. I fear in his Irish zeal he has gone beyond what international law will justify. I said so to the cabinet, but with everybody talking at once, and the prevailing anxiety to do something that should look energetic, I could hardly get a hearing. D.

(whom I found closeted with Mayo) agreed, and I sent over to the Admiralty to suggest some farther discussion. Corry afterwards came to the F.O. and was very reasonable. He agreed to modify the instructions given . . .

29 December 1867. Hatfield: walk in morning: boxes by post and messenger . . . The Cretan trouble goes on as before: the Greek govt give encouragement, and, as is said, promises of support, in public debate of the Assembly, but the speeches are revised for publication, and the strongest passages omitted. So writes Erskine.

31 December 1867. Hatfield all day. . . . Ld and Ly Cairns arrived: much talk with him. He thinks the prospects of the Irish church gloomy, but that its disendowment if effected, would also involve that of the English establishment, while it would alienate the Protestants, and do nothing to conciliate the Fenian sympathisers.

. . . Fenian panic somewhat lessened: though the successful robbery of arms at Cork, and attack on a martello tower at or near Queenstown, show that there are plenty of desperate adventurers ready to risk their lives for a chance of making mischief.

In foreign affairs, nothing gives me real uneasiness except the negotiations with America: it is impossible to say what may happen in that country, where the Irish vote is powerful, and parties are utterly reckless of consequences, if they can secure a momentary advantage. A war between France and Germany, though disagreeable, would not for us be dangerous: and I think the English people would have sense enough not again to engage in a Crimean quarrel.

1868

11 January 1868. . . . To Disraeli to discuss education: he is willing to create a minister of education and a minister of health, two plans which I have often pressed upon him: but does not see his way to a measure till the meeting of the new parliament. I tell him that to do nothing this year will disappoint expectation: unless the time be completely filled up with other business. He says nothing is settled, we may consider it again. Hatfield by 5.25 train.

18 January 1868. . . . Disraeli writes on the education question: it seems that he and Ld D. do not entirely agree as to whether a bill shall be brought in or not: the practical difficulty is to do anything while R. Montagu[1] is the nominally responsible minister: though industrious and quick, his total want of tact makes it impossible that he should be entrusted with the conduct of an important measure.

. . . Elliot writes that the proceedings of the Russians in Crete have caused great irritation. They have been taking off refugees without even the form of asking leave from the Turkish authorities, and are alleged to have supplied provisions and stores to the insurgents still in arms.

19 January 1868. . . . Called on Disraeli to discuss an education scheme. We are to consider it in cabinet on Tuesday. D. was better pleased with it than I am: but I want further details.

21 January 1868. . . . Cabinet at 3: D. of Marlborough brought forward his scheme for education: good, I thought, in the main, but I doubt whether as a whole it will be sanctioned by his colleagues.

24 January 1868. . . . Delane called: he anticipates an outbreak in Ireland next spring: wants a new Devon commission to enquire into land-tenures, arguing that the landlords' side of the case has never been fairly stated, and that in this way, many prevalent fallacies will be exposed: thinks an education bill ought to supplement, not to supersede, local rating: which is our view also: and supports me entirely on the Alabama claims.

28 January 1868. . . . Sir M. Montefiore[2] [called] to thank about Servian Jews, and ask for protection to be continued.

Cabinet at 3 on education question: all orderly, contrary to our usual custom, and a good discussion. Opinion was strong in favour of an educational census, and of the creation of a minister of education as a separate department: on other points we were divided.

. . . Unsatisfactory accounts of Ld D. He makes slow progress, has no appetite, and is extremely weak. But the doctors think he goes on well.

30 January 1868. . . . Talk with Goschen about many things: he alarmed at the spread of pauperism, or rather at the growth of a new feeling about paupers. What is claimed for them is not merely support, so that they shall not starve, but comfort while so maintained: and he argues that no one will provide for his own future, if the unpopularity and disgrace attaching to the workhouse are done away. There is truth in this. He thinks political economy is in danger, it has never been popular in any country: and is disbelieved in by Americans, Australians, etc.

31 January 1868. ... Cabinet at 4, where discussed amendments on the India bill of 1858, and the elections bill about to be brought in, whereby the trial of election petitions is transferred from parliament to the judges. We were pretty well agreed on all points.

... Ld Cairns very despondent in his views as to church matters: says if the Irish church goes, which he sees to be probable, the English will follow within twenty years.

1 February 1868. ... Cabinet on education: nearly all agreed that the education dept ought to be reconstructed: the D. of Marlborough however held out, and threatened resignation. We separated without any agreement being come to. All however passed in perfectly good humour.

Heard of Lord Exeter being obliged to shut up Burleigh for a long while to come,[3] as also to sell some estates, in consequence of the unsuccessful speculations and extravagances of his father.

4 February 1868. ... Talk yesterday with Disraeli about the education difficulty: he has various plans for meeting it: and among other things, expects to get back Gen. Peel into the cabinet, which I told him I considered as hopeless.[4]

... Cabinet at 3. Education discussed, no settlement arrived at, but the general tone friendly. A committee of cabinet appointed to discuss the question.

5 February 1868. ... O. Russell says Mazzini is in London, and is believed to be in communication with the Fenians.[5]

8 February 1868. ... Spoke to Mayo last night about the appointment of a new Devon commission to enquire into the Irish land system, which I agree with Delane would be useful as tending to dispel a multitude of existing delusions. Mayo is well inclined, but thinks the selection of men to serve upon it will not be easy.

Fergusson,[6] one of Lord Bute's trustees, tells me of him: how he has been on the verge of turning papist, and may still: how his income (or rather, I suppose, rental) is £130,000 a year, and increasing: his tastes studious, and turn of mind theological etc.

12 February 1868. ... Travellers, where talked over with Barrington[7] Ld D.'s illness. He expects that Ld D. will shortly wish to retire, that Disraeli will take up the reins, but will not be able to manage the concern: after that, all is uncertainty.

I had in the evening a singular message from Disraeli through Taylor asking me to put my name on the committee of one of the candidates for

Cambridge, Mr Cleasby:[8] his rival is B. Hope,[9] against whom D. entertains a personal dislike since his speeches of last year. I said I would consider the matter, meaning this as a refusal, since I see no reason for meddling in a business which does not affect the interests of the government. It seems that J. Manners has, not very wisely, given his name as a supporter of Hope.

15 February 1868. . . . By 11.45 was at office: where found nothing, and for some time sat idle. Since 1866, there has been no such diplomatic calm as at this moment. For how long?

. . . Cabinet at 3.30: discussed the expediency of arresting Train, who is giving treasonable lectures at Cork and thereabouts. Agreed to stop his lectures, but not arrest him, as that is the thing he most wishes.

Question of a new Devon commission discussed, but no result was come to.

Corry talks of new iron-clads, but will reduce the African squadron. Talk of various motions coming on, of the Irish reform bill, etc. Broke up at 5.30.

In the early hours of 17 February Stanley found a telegram summoning him at once to Knowsley, where his father lay ill, and asking him to bring a second doctor with him. When they arrived, his father's condition, though still precarious, was past the crisis, which had been exaggerated by the local doctor, who had burst into tears during the night from strain. Nevertheless, this short but violent illness marked the end of Derby's career.

18 February 1868. . . . Ld D. this morning announced to me his intention to retire from official life, saying that it was irrevocably fixed, that it was for him a matter of life or death, the doctors had said he must have months of complete repose before he could recover, and this while he had his present position was impossible. He would write to Disraeli shortly, but wished me to prepare him for the communication. I did not attempt to dissuade my father from his purpose, believing him to be right, and that a longer continuance in office would probably kill him. I wrote to D. accordingly. My mother has told me that for the last few weeks Ld D. has constantly been oppressed with the sense of business left undone, and of responsibility for measures in advising which he could have no share.

20 February 1868. Called on Disraeli at his request to discuss the situation. We talked for an hour. I promised him cordial co-operation and support. We tried to arrange the necessary changes.

22 February 1868. . . . Musurus about Greece: he says the Greek govt has sold the gun-boats[10] it lately purchased in England, to the Cretan committee, and that they are being used as blockade-runners. As this proceeding, if it has really taken place, would be equivalent to a fraud practised on England (since the Cretan committee could not have been allowed to build ships here on their own account) I have promised to enquire into it.

Cabinet at 3.30: sat two hours: nothing known or guessed of Ld D.'s resignation having been sent in. Church-rates: Irish land: ecclesiastical titles bill etc. discussed. We agreed to a new Devon commission, and a limited land-bill.

In the early spring the eastern question showed signs of life, only to disappear from view again almost at once. France sought, without success, to act with Britain to re-assert the Crimean system: but since Russia, perhaps looking to the benefits of a coming Franco-Prussian war, chose to do nothing, nothing needed to be done. France expressed some contrition for her pro-Russian part in the Cretan imbroglio in 1867, and sought to press Britain into activity against 'refugees'; and, disturbed by lost influence at Bucharest and by a general belief that Rumania would declare its complete independence, France tried to persuade Stanley not to take Rumania too lightly. The Turks opportunely produced an intercepted Russian despatch warning the Rumanians against premature action, while British despatches from Russia argued that there was now every desire to prevent the eastern Christians from starting a war. Since supposed Russian designs did nothing worse than cause a fall on the Bourse, Stanley was able to have no policy worth speaking of during 1868 so far as the eastern question or Crete was concerned. Russian pressure ceased at almost the same time as Stanley had first shown himself willing to consider the cession of Crete to Greece as practicable.

24 February 1868. . . . Disraeli sent for me, in some agitation, to talk over the state of affairs: he had scruples about kissing hands etc. till he had heard again from Lord Derby, lest it should be thought he was acting with indelicate haste. We agreed to telegraph to Knowsley, and apply for sanction, so that no feeling of that kind should be possible. I did so, and wrote to Ld D. later to explain.

26 February 1868. . . . I went at 2 to call on Disraeli, and found his arrangements prospering. . . . Cairns has accepted: Chelmsford expresses annoyance openly, but will soon recover his temper: Walpole wishes to retire, saying that his position in the cabinet without office, is anomalous, which is true, but the reason is, that he is influenced by his wife, who hates D. I see no reason why he should be pressed to remain, but the Queen wishes it. Northcote and Hunt[11] are the two talked of for the exchequer, but the inconvenience of moving N. at this moment is obvious, and Hunt, though not in the first rank, is sensible and laborious. He would in fact be subordinate to Disraeli: and at the present time it is not likely that any important financial changes will take place.

27 February 1868. F. came to breakfast: he reports no marked improvement in the last three days. It seems the Queen has given him [Lord Derby] much annoyance, in his weak state, by her way of writing, which was curt and totally without expressions of sympathy or regret. Knowing her disposition, I am not surprised, but he has always entertained some illusions about her. She seems to have told him he had better resign at once, in order to save her trouble.

29 February 1868. . . . [Musurus] is evidently looking to be governor of Crete: indeed he said so in so many words, alleging that since his wife's death he could not bear to live in London.

1 March 1868. [At Knowsley] . . . Found Ld D. wonderfully recovered, his spirits excellent, voice clear and strong, but he is still very weak in the limbs. He talked to me of the Queen's way of writing to him, about which he was at first very sore: but I think he now understands her nature. She is civil to persons in power under her, whose good will contributes to her comfort (and not always to them): but sees no reason for wasting civility on those who can no longer be of use to her.

2 March 1868. Left Knowsley by 8.15, Euston 2.30, and arrived just in time for a cabinet on Irish affairs. We discussed education, land, church: the latter subject slightly, the two first fully. It was impossible for anything to be more orderly and well managed than the proceedings: which was not formerly the case. I kept a note of what passed, but the substance was, that we agreed without dissentients to Mayo's plan for a Catholic college, to have a charter: and also to his bringing in a bill including the greater part of what was in that of last year, and at the same time proposing the appointment of a new Devon commission. The church question was approached with great caution, Cairns being known to have strong opinions upon it. The general wish seemed to be, to commit ourselves as little as possible, and endeavour to tide over the present session, leaving church matters to be dealt with by the new parliament.

3 March 1868. . . . Cabinet at 3.30: the business almost exclusively Irish: Catholic University: land question: church: etc. The most important decision come to was to support, at least not to oppose, the repeal of the eccles. titles act. (I have kept a note of the proceedings.)

15 March 1868. . . . The effect of the debate on Ireland, so far as it has gone, is to bring out in a marked way the tendencies of the House. The Irish church has been left almost undefended, no one not an Irishman had a good word to say for it: on this subject the change of feeling is marked: it seemed as if the Fenian trouble had turned a languid sentiment of disapproval into an active determination to get rid of the thing altogether. On the land the state of opinion is wholly different: there is willingness to give a measure of tenant-right, without any strong conviction that it will be of much use, but a steady determination to resist all such projects of confiscation as those of Bright and Mill: perhaps I should say of Mill only, for Bright has greatly softened down his scheme, and now confines it to a plan of voluntary purchase. *30 March 1868.* [In the debate on the Irish Church] ... The case which I had to argue was one of extreme delicacy, for it is impossible not to see that even on our own side, the feeling is all but universal that some great change must take place in the status of the Irish Church: the only line to take was, therefore, to decline to pledge ourselves until the new parliament. On the whole, I felt and feel satisfied,[12] having said nothing that can compromise either myself or the ministry.

13 April 1868. Late last night the news reached me of Ld Salisbury's sudden illness: and this morning that of his death. I had seen him on Saturday well and cheerful. ... He was within a few days of ending his seventy-seventh year. Ly S.[13] had been warned just in time to arrive from Knole (where she had gone for a visit) while he was still living. – Though the sudden death of an old man is not an event to be wondered at, or for himself to be regretted, it raises feelings in the mind of those who have long known him familiarly, of a very painful kind. For twelve years Hatfield has been to me like a home,[14] and the sudden breaking of a tie of such old standing affects me more than I am willing here to set down. A happy family circle broken up – the widow – the children – the uncertain future. I will make no farther note on this subject.

19 April 1868. ... Some talk at the clubs yesterday in consequence of a seditious placard having been posted up in Pall Mall (and I suppose elsewhere) calling on the Queen to abdicate in favour of the P. of W. as she will not perform her social duties. It does not appear to have been widely circulated.

22 April 1868. .... Cabinet at 4 p.m. Discussion as to our course, but we were all agreed in substance, (1) not to resign, (2) not to dissolve on the old constituencies, (3) not to press on any measures except such as are absolutely necessary, e.g. the Scotch and Irish bills, and those reduced to franchise bills only. I made a full note of the discussion.

23 April 1868. .... Disraeli much excited by intelligence, which he has from the Rothschilds, that Prussia contemplates disarmament. I did not understand why he felt so strongly on the matter, but discovered at last that he thought, by taking advantage of early information, that we might represent this to the French, as our doing, and possibly induce them to give some promise of disarmament in their turn: when the result being made public, England in general would reap much credit, and the ministry in particular be strengthened. I doubt the feasibility of this combination, ingenious as it is.

Budget in House: Hunt did his work well and clearly: the plan adopted seemed to meet with general acceptance, though Gladstone made strong declarations in favour of reduction of expenditure generally.

26 April 1868. News came of the storming of Magdala, and death of Theodore, with slight loss on our side. Thus ends, more fortunately than could have been expected, a war on which we embarked with extreme reluctance, and only from a sense of the impossibility of doing otherwise. It has cost £5,000,000,[15] or nearly so, but the money has been well spent, for it has proved not only that an English army could fight, which was not doubted, but that it can march and shift for itself in an extremely difficult country, which was not thought to be our strong point.

4 May 1868. . . . Cabinet at 11, when the question of resignation or dissolution seriously discussed: we all agreed to go on for the moment, but in the event of the opposition making our places untenable to consider anew whether to resign or dissolve on the old constituencies. To the latter alternative I entertain a very strong objection, and believe that others do the same. It would be probably useless, and certainly vexatious.

. . . I regard the crisis as postponed only, not averted. If the opposition have a majority, not on Irish Church only, but on all questions, they may make it impossible to carry on business: but whether they have or not remains to be seen: they certainly had not last year.

9 May 1868. . . . Cabinet at 2, where settled the answer to the address on Irish resolutions, with little difference of opinion except as to words: then took Scotch reform bill which Disraeli wished to deal with by adopting one of the amendments moved from the opposite side: this was disliked, and in the end he agreed to postpone it, and take the Boundaries bill first: which gives us the advantage of having a fight in a case in which we are clearly right, and where all our friends will stand by us. If we win, our situation is satisfactory, and we can afford to make concessions on other matters with a good grace: if we lose, the alternative of resignation or immediate dissolution is placed before us at once. Either way the present suspense is terminated: which is an advantage.

14 May 1868. . . . House, where Boundaries bill discussed, in a very conciliatory spirit on the part of the opposition. It was evident that they had found their party unwilling to agree on an attack, and they confined themselves to the fair and reasonable proposition of referring certain disputed cases to a committee. This we agreed to, but a good deal of difficulty and confusion arose as to the precise scope and functions of the committee. The debate, however, was perfectly good-humoured.

19 May 1868. . . . At 2 a cabinet, which sat for an hour and a half. All except myself were in favour of dissolution, if the House did not agree to rescind its vote of last night on the rating question. I agreed to try whether the rescinding might not be accomplished, but reserved my opinion as to the advantage of a dissolution, which I cannot believe in as likely to be of any use: and it is not justifiable if undertaken without a reasonable prospect of success.

4 June 1868. . . . Cabinet at 1, where we settled to bring in a bill which should if possible shorten the interval before the general election takes place: sat till 3 . . .

5 June 1868. . . . Death of Lord Shrewsbury[16] announced at the age of 64. He had so managed his affairs, that though with the title he came into at least £40,000 a year, all on which he could lay his hands was gone, and it was only by the assistance of his friends that he was able to live in England. How he brought about this result no one knows, for he lived poorly, but he had a passion for speculations of all kinds, and was the dupe of every projector who came to him with a plausible story. Personally he was disliked, his manners being rough and even repulsive. I believe that the bulk of his property was so settled that he could not greatly injure it.

Robertson Gladstone, brother to the ex-minister, has been making a speech at Liverpool in which he declares that the persecutions undergone, and still to be undergone, by his brother have no parallel since those to which the founder of Christianity was exposed! This was a little too strong for his audience, especially as he did not say what the persecutions in question were. He took the opportunity of contradicting the prevailing report of G. being ruined.

(I have since heard that Mr R. G. has been for some time past in a state of mental excitement, and more or less under medical care.)[17]

10 June 1868. . . . Cabinet at 5: Hunt much annoyed at the count-out of last night, which he alleges was purposely arranged by Taylor:[18] on whose dismissal he was inclined to insist, making his own resignation the alternative: we managed at last to quiet him, and the matter dropped.

. . . Tankerville[19] talks of the ways of the young men now entering the world: the prevalence of a low style of life: drinking in the morning is common: gambling and betting almost universal: they get these habits at the public schools, where absolutely nothing else appears to be learnt. He says he was warned against Eton, as the worst of all, for his own son, but finds Harrow not much better.

18 June 1868. . . . Called . . . to sign a paper relating to some part of Ld Salisbury's will. At his door met the present Ly S.[20] who very friendly, rather to an embarrassing extent, considering my relations with her husband, which she professed to ignore. But better so than a quarrel.

28 June 1868. Hatfield by early train: passed the last day that I shall ever pass there, chiefly in the woods and gardens. Since the spring and summer of 1855,[21] that house has been constantly open to me, I have lived in it as my own home, and it was with reluctance that I went through the pain of this leave-taking. No other place can ever have connected with it the same associations: no years of my future life can be like those that have elapsed since I came to know it well. I returned by the evening train to London in a mood which was not cheerful, and tried, but with little success, to drive out depressing thoughts by attending to such business as I found awaiting me.

5 July 1868. . . . Either the continued heat and drought, or constant residence in London, has affected my health, so that I fall asleep in the day, and feel incapable of much exertion: which is with me a new thing.

7 July 1868. . . . Another wrangle in the Lords: there have been three or four lately: Carnarvon, the most bitter and vehement, though not very effective against ministers: it is said his wife pushes him on, being ambitious both of political and fashionable distinction: Salisbury on the other hand is more quiet and conciliatory, and seems to feel himself at home in the Lords, which he never did altogether in the Commons.

8 July 1868. . . . Invitation from Carnarvon to Highclere, which looks as if he had not given up the idea of our acting together, notwithstanding his present vehemence: I declined it, civilly, but rather coldly.

13 July 1868. Navy estimates got through . . . H. Corry very ill: H. Lennox did the work, and did it well.[22]

21 July 1868. . . . Not well, partly from bilious derangement, partly exhaustion from bad air and late hours . . . My forty-second birthday: I hope the next will not be passed in the F.O. of which after two years I begin to have had quite enough.

26 July 1868. [In private conversation] . . . I said that the priests did not care that Ireland should be prosperous in the English sense of the word – better farmed, better housed, the people better clothed. These things were to them, if not indifferent, at least of very minor importance: what they want is that Ireland should be Celtic, Catholic, full of national feeling and religious zeal, and densely peopled. Of the danger and misery of over-population they never think.

28 July 1868. . . . Cabinet 2.30: chief business the settling of Queen's speech, which was read: it is short, and harmless: the only sentence which raised discussion was the last, relating to the Irish church. In the draft, Disraeli had framed it as a strong manifesto on the Protestant side: I took the lead in opposing this, and others (Duke of Marlborough for one) joined, not objecting to the substance of what was to be said, but thinking the Queen ought not to be made to say it. In the end we agreed to substitute other words drafted by Cairns, which if somewhat unmeaning are at least free from objection.

1 August 1868. . . . F. has had the offer of Du Cane's[23] place (civil lord of the admiralty) vacant by Du Cane's going to Tasmania. He is obliged, but hesitates, as he thinks attendance in London may interfere with his canvass. I say on the whole he had better accept. He is, I think, a little nettled at the place having been asked for him by Ld D. as in fact it was, without his knowledge or consent . . .

On 6 August Stanley left London for the continent, to be in attendance on the Queen at her villa near Lucerne. He returned on 6 September. Neither his diary nor the Queen's published letters say anything of interest about his visit.

26 August 1868. . . . Sir H. Bulwer[24] has come forward as a Liberal candidate and makes no secret of his expectation that he shall succeed me in the F.O. He offered his services to Disraeli a year ago: I doubt his being accepted by either party: unless he were to make his terms with Gladstone, and obtain what he lately wanted, a special mission to Washington.

5 September 1868. . . . H. Lennox wants to be made Irish secretary in Mayo's place, and writes to me to help him. He is fit for it in some respects,[25] but I doubt his temper, which dealings with Irish members would be likely to try rather severely.

14 September 1868. . . . D. says the elections are extremely difficult to speculate upon, the results will be unexpected in many places: he thinks the Conservatives ought to gain in England, and probably to hold their own in Ireland, but Scotland is their weak point. He did not think the violent party would be strong in the new parliament, their way of writing and talking seemed as if they anticipated disappointment. He said the Queen was more than friendly: expressing herself anxious that even if out of office we should be strong. He had *carte blanche* for the new bishop . . .

I mentioned in conversation the late French loan to D., and the extraordinary extent to which it had been taken up by the people. D. said it confirmed him in the opinion he had long held, that France was a richer country than England: partly in consequence of the more saving habits of the people, partly because so large a part of their wealth came directly from the soil, which yielded more than ours, and an income so obtained was less liable to fluctuation than one which came from manufactures or commerce . . .

9 October 1868. . . . Disraeli at 3, to talk over the situation generally: he is sanguine as usual, talks of 300 seats as secure,[26] and allowing the same number to the other side, reckons on one half or more of the odd 58. I receive his statements with caution, but on the whole it does seem likely that the new voters will be more favourable than we could have ventured to expect, and that we shall at least be a strong opposition.

25 October 1868. . . . R. Johnson[27] talked a good deal of the negro question. He thought it would settle itself, though not in the way desired by philanthropists: that the African race, uncared for, and unfit to take care of itself, would die out. It was known, he said, that of the four millions of negroes one million had disappeared already: and he had no reason to suppose that the state of things which led to this result had changed. The principal loss was caused by the neglect of children, whom their parents would allow to die, rather than take any trouble about them when ill.

26 November 1868. . . . Disraeli tells me that the Queen has declared to him that she would sooner abdicate than consent to the disestablishment of the Irish church.

27 November 1868. . . . Left F.O. about 5.30: home: tired, and slept before dinner, which I hardly ever do. The sedentary life I am compelled to lead does me no good, in point of health, and I shall not regret a change.

28 November 1868. . . . Cabinet,[28] where all agreed, without one dissentient voice, in the policy of immediate resignation.

7 December 1868. . . . La Tour called, uneasy, and reasonably so, at the expected rupture between Greece and Turkey: the Porte having announced that unless the laws of neutrality are better observed in future, and certain definite concessions made, they will break off diplomatic relations, close the ports against Greek ships, and give subjects of Greece notice to quit Turkey. This ultimatum however is not to be sent until Saturday, and it is hoped that meanwhile Greece will give way. In the actual situation of the government, it is difficult to see what can be done: but after consultation with Hammond, considering the urgency of the case, I framed a telegram of warning and advice to the Greek government, which pledges the F.O. to nothing, and may possibly be of some use. It is however on the cards that objection may be taken to my having said anything, when de facto I have ceased to be a minister.

. . . My work at F.O. is nearly over, and not to my regret: much of it was interesting, but the constant interruption and disturbance from visitors, the tendency of diplomatists to waste time in unnecessary talk, the impossibility, at this time of year, of getting air and exercise without neglecting official duty, and the difficulty of escaping, even for a few hours, from telegrams and despatches, make the post trying to health and temper. I want rest, and feel that I want it.

. . . Dined Travellers, where much talk with Lord Clarendon on F.O. matters.

9 December 1868. . . . Windsor by special train . . . Council held, after which we severally gave up our seals. The Queen very civil to me, said 'she was sorry to take them back, they had never been in better hands.'

11 December 1868. Busy on letters and papers till 11, when to Lord Clarendon to talk over with him the state of matters in F.O. It seemed to me that our views were generally in accordance. He looked ill and worn, and dwelt much on his own reluctance to take office again, which I should have believed, but for knowing the efforts which his family and friends have made to put him there, and it is hardly to be supposed that they would have done this without his consent. He told me that Bright had consented to join with extreme reluctance, and had only given way after a two hours discussion with Gladstone: in which the latter urged him to the utmost. . . . Bright feels that he has lost independence and power, and subsided into a Whig official: he knows too that most of his colleagues regard him as a prisoner in their camp rather than as an ally. It is strange that he did not ask for two seats in cabinet besides his own: he might have had them if he had stood out for terms.

. . . Note of some points touched on between Ld Clarendon and me:

The Queen: indifferent to business, except where pressed on by relations: jealous lest anything should be kept back from her, but interferes little, and only where Germany is concerned, or Belgium. Tendency of Belgians to claim a kind of exclusive British protection, which is not our interest to give. Unluckily H.M. encourages this disposition.

The Office: . . . Hammond - indefatigable, but will do all himself - result, when he is ill or away nothing goes on. He will not train the men under him as he ought. Sanderson the best of the juniors . . .

Diplomatists: get rid of Crampton[29] and Bloomfield[30] - both worn out - the rest fairly good. O. Russell, West,[31] Lumley,[32] Morier, Lytton,[33] all fit for high places . . .

Foreigners: caution against Brunnow's reports, which are never reliable, and less so since with old age, the habit of incessant talking has grown upon him.

R. Johnson: friendly, but very loose in his way of doing business.

La Tour: friendly, communicative, generally accurate in his reports: no fault to find. Bernstorff concise, business-like, not disagreeable to deal with, but very touchy - this is the character of his government and the more noticeable, as Prussians certainly are not given to respect the feelings of other people, being curiously harsh and rough in their dealings. Apponyi quite accurate, very pleasant to do business with, a little inclined to be slow and long-winded, but that is his only failing.

We discussed Seward's extraordinary vacillations: I saw Ld C. was like myself, half inclined to think he wants money: unless he is negotiating with Grant for a seat in the new cabinet, which would explain his conduct. Ld C. regards him as representing the very worst type of American politician: and I agree.

27 December 1868. . . . Lowe says of Bright, when asked how they got on together, 'I am paid £5,000 a year to love him, and I intend to love him dearly.'

29 December 1868. . . . Saw W. H[ornby] and understand from him that the S. Lancs. election will cost our side, in all, about £8,500: I do not know how much of this Ld D. contributes. He and F. both agree that the cost of the N. Lancs. contest will be exactly double, £17,000: of which £10,000 is Ld D.'s share. . . . Gladstone, W. says, did not expect defeat till late on the day of polling: both then and at the nomination his temper was painfully exhibited: he said something insulting to the High Sheriff on the hustings, and was obliged next day to send a written apology.

1869

13 January 1869. . . . Letter from D. (who supposes me at Knowsley) saying that he is living alone, sees no one, but is occupied and content.

. . . . Called on Disraeli, whom I found well, and in good spirits: we discussed the situation, but agreed that the less done at present the better. I found D. agreed with me, that one of the chief difficulties of the cabinet would be the Irish land question: Irish officials are pledging themselves to fixity of tenure, or something very like it, and that it does not seem likely that an English parliament, composed as at present, will grant. The 'national' party in Ireland argue ingeniously that it is desirable the Imperial legislature should have the settling of the church question, which if left to Irish hands would create dissension between Catholic and Protestant: that the land must then be given to the tenant, on a fixed perpetual payment: that the effect of these two measures will be to destroy the interest which is now felt by the English clergy and the landowners, in the maintenance of the Irish connection: and to do away with causes of dispute between Catholic and Protestant: they will then both only remember that they are Irish, and unite in demanding separation, which England will not greatly care to refuse. I note this reasoning, absurd as it appears on this side the Channel, because I believe it really to embody the views of the bulk of the Irish people, or at least of that large minority whom they allow to represent them.

27 January 1869. . . . In papers, death of Ernest Jones[1] announced, aged 50. He had just been chosen by ballot as Liberal candidate for Manchester in the event of Birley's seat being vacated. He used to appear at the Kirkdale sessions, but had little practice: his extreme vehemence being against him as an advocate. He did not appear to me to possess much intellectual capacity: but being honest, and thoroughly in earnest, might have given trouble in parliament. He is reported, and I believe truly, to have refused the succession to an estate of £2,000 a year, offered by a relative on condition of his giving up politics. His principal object was the redivision of land among the people, so that fewer might live in towns, and more on their own produce. – He once, a good many years ago, borrowed a small sum of me, who did not know him, being as he said in urgent want:[2] but he asked for it like a gentleman. He was then by way of having given up politics.

7 February 1869. . . . Called on Disraeli, who talked little politics, and evidently thinks there is nothing to be done for the present. He gave an amusing description of having been taken out hunting in Yorkshire, by no means to his own satisfaction, but he appears to have acquitted himself better than could be expected from a man who never rides. Talked of Houghton, 'another Boswell, but without a Johnson': of Burghley under the new regime, etc.

16 February 1869. . . . Dined Travellers: met there Carnarvon, and some friendly talk with him, the first since the schism of 1867. But we both kept clear of politics.

17 February 1869. . . . Wilson Patten came . . . he talks of the state of things in Dublin, says the corruption he found exceeded all that he had expected, or could have believed, though prepared for a good deal: no person was ever recommended to him on the ground of merit, everything was and is treated as a matter of bargain and jobbing. Altogether he seems to have been thoroughly disgusted with his post, as from the first he expected to be.

27 February 1869. . . . Invited to dine with Lord and Lady Salisbury. I declined, as being engaged, and should probably have declined in any case: but the invitation looks as if he wished to ignore past differences.

3 March 1869. Meeting of late cabinet at Grosv. Gate to discuss Irish bill: it was agreed without a dissentient voice that a division must be taken on the second reading, by way of protest, though with no hope of success, or even of making a good division: that it would be better taken on a direct negative than on any amendment, however ingeniously framed: but that considering the immense inducements held out both to the landed interest and to the poorer occupiers, in the way of money to go directly into their own pockets, there was not much prospect of being able to modify the scheme in any material point. What could or should be attempted in the Lords might remain for consideration at a later stage. D. acknowledged to me that he did not at all see his way. He thought that after this success the violent party would give Gladstone a good deal of trouble: e.g. by raising the land question, 'that of the Church in England, etc.'

15 March 1869. . . . Dinner there with Disraeli, and much talk: he out of spirits, says he thinks the monarchy in danger, which he never did before: not from immediate causes, nor from any feeling against it of a strongly hostile character, but from gradual loss of prestige: the Queen has thrown away her chances, people find out that they can do as well without a court, etc. Nothing as to party prospects, which are obviously hopeless.

8 April 1869. Meeting of late cabinet at Grosv. Gate to discuss amendments in the Irish bill: but nothing very definite was settled, except that we would endeavour to save some of the endowments. Cairns told us that the Lords would not throw out the bill on the second reading, though they might amend it in detail. This is right and wise. The Irish Protestants give no help: they only call names and talk violently, to little purpose.

15 June 1869. . . . Looked in at the Lords. . . . Lytton had meant to speak, but took fright and ran away, as he did ten years ago in our House . . . (Note. This was the reform debate of 1859. He was to have opened it one night on behalf of ministers, when nervousness prevailed, and he disappeared from the House: by good luck he was found and brought back just in time, and his speech was greatly admired, as it deserved to be.)

20 June 1869. . . . Much talk with Disraeli: he says that the amendments to be moved will be moved by Lds Salisbury or Grey: Cairns declines to take any part, I suppose as thinking that they will come more properly from some peer who has voted for the second reading. But they will take counsel together. The problem to be solved is, what is the utmost that can fairly be secured for the Protestants without endangering the bill on his return to the Commons. If it can be passed I believe very few on our side will desire to prolong the controversy.

D. was more animated – I might almost say, more violent – in speaking of the life peerage bill – than I have heard him on any subject. It is a favourite aversion of his. He declares if it comes down to our House he will personally do all he can to throw it out.

4 July 1869. . . . Saw Constance who tells me a strange story of how Ld Clarendon is likely to offer the Madrid vacancy to Lord Howden,[3] an old man, long retired from diplomacy, and who lives no very reputable life in France. He (Ld C.) dislikes the idea, sees all the objections that will be made, but is under some mysterious engagement[4] to Ld H. the nature of which his family don't understand. . . . The family dislike the whole business extremely, and Ld C. himself is, they think, both anxious and annoyed on the subject. – I know from other sources that Ld H. has been boasting that he has the appointment in his pocket if he pleases to go. – Another story: Odo Russell[5] was offered Washington early in the spring, *vice* Thornton, whom Ld C. would have moved to Madrid: Russell however saw the outcry which so rapid an advance would cause, and had the good sense to refuse. The appointment would have been cried out against everywhere as a job. Ly C. is the chief mover here: she is ambitious for her children, and not scrupulous. Ld C. probably has not much more scruple, but is a better judge of opinion, and sensitive to abuse.

16 July 1869. . . . The House is evidently weary of the Irish question: and not in an angry mood, though unwilling to give way on any really important point. Gladstone's own temper is visible and audible whenever he rises to speak: but he has so far restrained the expression of it as to have said nothing particularly offensive, though the mixture of anger and contempt in his voice is almost painful to witness. With all his splendid talent, and his great position, few men suffer more from the constitutional infirmity of an irritable nature: and this is a disease which hard mental work, anxiety, and the exercise of power, all tend to exacerbate. Disraeli is quite aware of the advantage which he possesses in his natural calmness: and takes every opportunity to make the contrast noticeable.

25 July 1869. . . . Heard . . . an exact version of what passed previous to the negotiation between Granville and Cairns. It seems that at the cabinet held on Wednesday [21 July], Gladstone and Argyll were strongly in favour of dropping the bill, and beginning an agitation: Bright did not side with them, thinking the result would probably be the overthrow of the H. of Lds, and though not himself objecting to this solution of the difficulty, he thought it premature, and likely to create social disturbance. He was therefore inclined to be moderate. His opinion impressed the others, who all agreed, and in the end Gladstone gave way. Fresh trouble arose when Granville communicated the terms of Cairns' arrangement: Gladstone refusing at first to have anything to say to them, fearing that he should be accused of sacrificing principle to office, and so forth: Ld G. had to hint at resignation before obtaining his colleague's consent, which was rather extorted than given: D. of Argyll is said to be even now much annoyed, foreseeing radical defections.

29 July 1869. . . . I heard today another version of the manner in which the Irish compromise was carried through the cabinet. It came, indirectly, from Lowe, and did not much differ from that which I had had before, except in the one respect that Lowe represented himself as warmly in favour of the arrangement, whereas according to Lord Clarendon he had treated it with a certain contempt. Anyone acquainted with Lowe's manner and way of talking will see that these stories are easily reconcilable.

30 July 1869. . . . Committee, where discussed report . . . I left the House at 6, glad to think I shall not see it again this year. It has given me little pleasure, and I cannot claim to have achieved any success there. But with the settlement of the Irish church question a new scene in politics opens: and I am henceforth more free to act independently of party than was ever possible while Lord Derby remained a political leader. The chief difficulty which I feel, and long have felt, in deciding questions of policy, is that on many of them my reason tells me that the party of innovation must succeed, and that resistance is foolish: while at the same time I have not the slightest sympathy with the movement or its authors. E.g. the ballot which in some shape I regard as inevitable, and may perhaps acquiesce in rather than oppose it, but which is avowedly pushed forward with the view of lessening the power of the upper and middle over the lower classes. To questions of land, and the distribution of property, the same argument applies still more forcibly. It is hard to choose between what you feel to be distasteful, and what you know to be impracticable: and for a moderate man, of aristocratic sympathies, and detesting political enthusiasts, this is often the only alternative.

23 August 1869. . . . Thinking seriously of writing a pamphlet on the Irish land question: I have time, and the requisite knowledge, and a strong opinion as to what ought and ought not to be done. But if this is attempted, the present and next month is the most suitable opportunity.

24 August 1869. Holwood:[7] where found Lady Bulwer and the A. Russells staying, and Lord and Lady Russell come for a visit. Ld R. appeared infirm, and walked with some difficulty, but talked cheerfully and with a certain animation. He began by saying he had a great deal to say to me, and then explained his views as to Irish land, which are sound and moderate enough: not averse to a moderate bill of compensation for improvements but wholly opposed to the idea of the modern radical party – fixity of tenure and the like. He sat under the old oak which is said to be that where Pitt and Wilberforce discussed together the abolition of the slave-trade. . . . I looked at the old man with interest: he has played a great part, and represents a bygone generation. His love of political business is unabated, though bodily weakness forbids his ever taking an active part again.

8 September 1869. . . . Finding Ld D. dwelling much on the idea of selling his Irish estates, I suggested to him the expediency, if he did so, of re-investing the amount in land to be purchased in North Lancashire, for my brother: by which means the influence of the family will be increased: and I know from F. himself that it is what he wishes.

28 September 1869. . . . Ld D. talks much of selling his Irish estate, being disgusted at the turn which affairs have taken, and at the ill-feeling which exists among the tenantry, though full half the rental of the estate has for many years been spent in improving it. As he asked my opinion, I urged him not to act in haste, as it is hardly possible that the feeling of distrust in the security of Irish property can increase: and a forced sale at the present time would be to sacrifice the property. He acquiesces so far as to consent to fix a reserve price . . . this, in my belief, is equivalent to deferring the whole transaction. . . . The acreage is 6,887 acres: the rental £7,681: there are also 233 acres of bog and plantation, and receipts other than rents amounting to £289, chiefly arising from rents reserved in perpetuity, on estates with which no other connection is retained . . . There are in lease 3,071 acres, held by 21 tenants. The tenants without leases are 127. The largest farm contains about 360 acres: there are eight others above 100 acres. The average sum remitted to England for the last few years has been about £5,000. There has been in the last thirty years an increase of rent to the extent of about 25%.

Lord Derby's death was neither a sudden blow nor a painful struggle: he gradually grew weaker, while his family gathered round at Knowsley, with little doubt in their minds as to the outcome. His deathbed,[8] like his funeral on 29 October, concerned only his immediate family. Only his last phrases of note are worth mention. To little Eddy Stanley, who said he was very sorry for Grandpa, he replied 'Grandpa is very sorry for himself': and again when asked his state, he answered 'Bored to utter extinction.'

29 October 1869. . . . After luncheon the will was read. Its main provisions were known to me already, but I was relieved to find that there were not many legacies, as the existing burdens are almost more than I know how to clear off.

Roughly put, the state of things is as follows. All the land, and the London house, are mine for life, under trustees, whose powers of inter-ference however are extremely limited. F. declining the Irish estates, these also come to me on the same conditions. The gross receipts from all are, in round numbers, a little under £170,000 yearly. My mother has £6,000 a year for her life, with an immediate legacy of £3,000: F. has £125,000, besides £80,000 settled on him before, or in all £205,000: and I reckon minor legacies with probate and succession duty, as probably making up from £50–60,000 more. This added to the old debt, of £420,000, makes a permanent charge on the estate which will not fall short of £680,000 or four years gross rental.

Walk with Hale[9] when the business was ended: renewed discussion with him as to the means of clearing off this load of debt,[10] which I shall never be quite happy till I have done, or at least put in the way of doing. In talking with him I reckoned the time to be allowed for that purpose as 14 years, at the rate, in round numbers, of £50,000 a year: of which £30,000 to be from savings, and the remaining £20,000 from sale of detached lots, chief rents, etc.
30 October 1869. My mother, F. and C. left together for London. My mother has told C. that she does not intend ever to return. This decision does not surprise me, and I think it will be adhered to. She has never much liked the place, prefers London, and the associations of Knowsley can now only be painful.
14 November 1869. . . . Strange stories of H. Russell,[11] the D. of Bedford's heir, who at present manages the estate for him. He was always singular in his character, soured and disgusted with the world, without apparent reason, and inclined to avarice: but of late his love of money has become nothing less than a form of insanity. He has told his two brothers, not in jest, or as an excuse, but quite seriously, that when he becomes D. of Bed-ford he will not be able to afford to continue the allowance of £1,000 a year now made to each of them, having a family of his own to provide for. (The income of the dukedom exceeds £300,000 a year, and is quite free from debt.) He complained of his wife opening a bottle of soda water the whole of which was not drunk, saying it cost sixpence. He has quarrelled with the Duke's agent for spending too much money, though the property was always administered with rigid economy. It appears as though his head was turned by the vastness of the fortune which will be, and already is practically his. A warning, and perhaps one needed by all who come into a similar position.
15 November 1869. . . . Saw Malmesbury . . . he tells me that Cairns has resigned the lead of the opposition, which I did not know, but am not

surprised to hear, as he took it reluctantly. His alleged reason is that he wishes to attend to the appeals, which as an ex-chancellor, he conceives to be his special duty: and that he cannot do that and act as leader both. Malmesbury says it is now a question between Salisbury and myself. Salisbury's energy and talent are admired, but he is thought rash, and not entirely trusted: and there is also the drawback that he cannot, or rather will not, act with Disraeli. I asked why M. could not himself return at least for a time to his old post? He said he could not do it while D. was leader, and told me a story of what he considered an uncandid treatment of him when my father resigned: which resolved itself into this, that D. had spoken slightingly to him of the claims of the D. of Marlborough and to the Duke in nearly the same terms of him (M.). I am afraid there is strong intrinsic probability that this story is true, but it is a small matter and the real fact is that ever since 1852 the two men have disliked one another. He (Malmesbury) and Salisbury both wish Hardy to be Conservative leader in the Commons: he has eloquence and a certain energy, but no great mental range. He would please the church party, but on the whole he is scarcely strong enough for the place.

I said little, and indeed M. did not in any way invite me to an expression of opinion: but from the little I did say, I allowed it to be inferred that my wish was at present to remain as far as possible uncommitted.

26 November 1869. . . . O'Donovan Rossa,[12] a prisoner sentenced for a long term for having taken part in the Fenian outbreak of 1867, is returned member for Tipperary . . . it will open the eyes of people here to the real wishes of the middle and lower class in Ireland. I am convinced that in the southern counties at least nine out of every ten men, if fairly appealed to, would be in favour of separation from England: and the tenth man would not be very heartily against it.

11 December 1869. Cairns . . . told me that on consideration he had decided to return for the opening, thinking it more decorous not to throw up his leadership in haste, nor to seem to desert his friends. He said the wish that I should succeed was almost universal. That Salisbury declares nothing shall induce him to be leader, and this without reference to his quarrel with Disraeli: he does not wish, he says, ever to be in a position that will compel him to take office again. Cairns thinks this language is sincerely held, though it does not follow that S. may not change his mind. That the divergence of my views from those commonly held by Conservatives on such questions as that of the University tests is perfectly understood and allowed for, and that the party are willing to accept me with these drawbacks. That there is no need of an immediate decision: it may be well to take some months, even after the session has begun, to consider the matter. I gave no opinion, and he asked for none.

He predicts a mild land bill, and the acceptance of denominational education by the cabinet: in which case the Liberal party will infallibly be split in two. He says that the failure of Gladstone's health is generally expected among his supporters: and they are prepared to put forward Granville as Premier, Cardwell as leader of H.C. The latter a weak appointment, but inevitable if Lowe and Bright mutually decline to act under each other.

Strange story of Gladstone frequenting the company of a Mrs Thistlethwaite, a kept woman in her youth, who induced a foolish person with a large fortune to marry her. She has since her marriage taken to religion, and preaches or lectures. This, with her beauty, is the attraction to G. and it is characteristic of him to be indifferent to scandal. But I can scarcely believe the report that he is going to pass a week with her and her husband at their country house – she not being visited, or received in society.

14 December 1869. . . . Malmesbury called . . . and confirmed the story of Gladstone's going to visit the Thistlethwaites! A strange world! He also says that the Liberal party expect him (G.) either to die or break down, and have arranged that Cardwell shall lead the Commons. (It is worth notice that most of those with whom I have had occasion to talk during the last few months look forward with no apparent regret to some such change – they admire G. but distrust him.)

Malmesbury agrees with me that the ballot in some form is inevitable, and that the H. of Lds will have great difficulty in resisting a measure which essentially concerns the other House.

19 December 1869. Called on Motley[13] . . . I asked his opinion as to the future of the negro race in the States: would they amalgamate with the whites, die out, or hold their own as a separate race? He said he disbelieved altogether in amalgamation: nature was against it: those who talked most about it would dislike the idea of intermarriage with negroes as much as their neighbours. All that law could do had been done for the negro: he had civil and political equality: legislation could not turn him white, nor make him the equal, intellectually, of the white man. He (Motley) believed in the inferiority of the race, though some of his enthusiastic friends in New England would not agree with him. He did not say they would die out, but he thought they would dwindle, and be pushed aside by the white immigrants . . .

The year closed with a short visit to Hughenden, which Derby had rarely visited during the period of his semi-residence at Hatfield.

23 December 1869. Walk to a village called Downley, where saw the process of chairmaking . . . The common towards Bradenham in great beauty. Juniper grows luxuriantly. Cottages much improved: D. is doing them up one by one, and spends, he tells me, all the rental of the estate upon it.

Noticed in the woods a fine beech-tree girdled round and killed, evidently by design: D. says that when any labourer thinks himself aggrieved, or has a quarrel with his employers generally, his revenge is apt to take the form of some act of mischief of this kind.

Very little passed between D. and myself as to present politics. We both rather avoided the subject. He admitted to me that though still willing to exert himself for the benefit of the party if necessary, his interest in it was diminished, he had obtained his object, and if he never held office again, he should not feel that his life had been a failure. He had often doubted whether he should go on with the leadership in the Commons: the fatigue was considerable: but he saw no one in whose hands he could leave it, and that circumstance had decided him.

24 December 1869. London again by early train . . . Nothing passed between D. and myself as to current events: our talk was almost entirely of the past and future, of literature, philosophy, history – everything rather than politics. I can see that he wishes me to be Conservative leader in the H. of Lds, but recognises the impossibility of my assuming that post at once, even if on other grounds I desired it.

. . . Hughenden has been increased by several purchases within the last few years, and is now a compact estate of 1,200 acres, a large part of which is covered with beechwood.

NOTES TO THE TEXT

Introduction

1 See William Matthews, *British Diaries 1442–1942* (1950) and John Stuart Batts, *British Manuscript Diaries of the Nineteenth Century: An Annotated Listing.*

2 We also need diaries to understand what went on in parliamentary debate. Hansard's apparent comprehensiveness makes one liable to forget how much it omits even of what took place in the chamber. Such questions as how empty the House was, who was drunk, and whether a speaker met an icy or a warm reception, are not in Hansard. Stanley faithfully records each time Gladstone lost his temper, a central political fact about Gladstone, but invisible in Hansard. Given the absence of sophisticated journalism, only the diary of an intelligent parliamentarian can make sense of the debates of this period.

3 Miss M. Pearlstine of the University of Cambridge is engaged on a biography of the diarist. Accordingly, no account of Stanley's life is given here. In any case, the diaries are important not for what they tell us of their author, but for what they reveal of other people.

4 But see Sir Edward Russell, *That Reminds Me* – (1899), 278–91, for a genial sketch of the diarist in later life. Russell was editor of the *Liverpool Daily Post.*

1849

1 Edward Stanley, fourteenth Earl of Derby (1800–69), premier 1852, 1858–9, 1866–8; cr. peer, as Lord Stanley, 1844; succ. father as Lord Derby, 1851.

2 Benjamin Disraeli (1804–81), premier 1868, 1874–80.

3 J. C. Herries (1778–1855); served under successive administrations, 1823–30; secretary at war 1834–5; president, board of control, 1852: financial expert.

4 Charles Cecil John Manners, sixth Duke of Rutland (1815–88); M.P. (Cons.) Stamford 1837–52, Leics. N. 1852–7; as Lord Granby, led Protectionist party in the Commons for a month, 1848, resigning from incapacity; succ. father 1857; d. unm. and was succ. by his brother, Lord John Manners of 'Young England'. Took no part in successive Cons. ministries, but included in draft cabinets of 1849, 1850, 1851 (see below, 23 Mar. 1849, 25 June 1850, 27 Feb. 1851). Described as 'pseudo-Russian' in Crimean War (Malmesbury to Stanley, 21 Oct. 1855). Like Disraeli, he nourished a hopeless passion for Lady Forester (Disraeli's Lady Bradford), whom his father forbade him to marry (Lady Cardigan, *My Recollections*, 154).

5 Lord George Bentinck (1802–48), protectionist leader in the Commons, 1846–7: the diarist's predecessor as M.P. for King's Lynn.

6 Sir R. Peel (1788–July 1850), premier 1834–5, 1841–6.

7 Robert, Viscount Jocelyn (1816–54), eldest son of the third Earl of Roden, a prominent Irish Protestant leader and landowner; m. 1841, Lady Frances Elizabeth Cowper, y. d. of fifth Earl Cowper, and step-daughter of Palmerston; M.P. (Lib.–Cons.) King's Lynn 1842–54; followed Peel in 1846; a significant channel of communication between Palmerston and the Derbyites in the early 1850's.

8 Augustus Stafford O'Brien-Stafford (1811–57); known as Stafford O'Brien until 1847: M.P. (Cons.) Northants. N. 1841–57; secretary to admiralty, 1852.

9 Feargus O'Connor (1794–1855); M.P. (Chartist) Nottingham 1847–52; pronounced insane June 1852.

10 Sir J. Graham (1792–1861), first lord of admiralty 1830–4, 1852–5; home secretary 1841–6.

11 Charles Gordon-Lennox, fifth Duke of Richmond (1791–1860); succ. father 1819; postmaster-general 1830–4; president, Royal Agricultural Society, 1845–60.

12 George, fourth Earl of Aberdeen (1784–1860), foreign sec. 1828–30, 1841–6, premier 1852–5.

13 Anthony Ashley Cooper, seventh Earl of Shaftesbury, philanthropist (1801–85; styled Lord Ashley 1811–51, succ. 1851; M.P. 1826–51; never held cabinet office.)

14 J. W. Henley (1793–1884), M.P. (Cons.) Oxfordshire 1841–78; president, board of trade, 1852 and 1858–9; resigned over reform, 1859: declined home office, 1866.

15 John Stuart (1793–1876), M.P. (Cons.) Newark 1846–52, Bury St. Edmunds, 1852: held legal office, 1852–71: kt., 1853.

16 Spencer Walpole (1806–98): M.P. (Cons.) Midhurst 1847–56, Camb. Univ. 1856–82; home secretary 1852, 1858–9, 1866–7.

17 James Parke, first Lord Wensleydale (1782–1858); judge 1828–55; cr. life, then hereditary peer, 1856; generally Liberal.

18 Thomas Pemberton (1793–1867): cr. Baron Kingsdown, 1858; member of Judicial Committee of Privy Council from 1844: took surname of Leigh, 1843.

19 Charles Henry Lord March, later sixth Duke of Richmond (1818–1903); succ. 1860; president, poor law board, 1859; president, board of trade, 1867–8; lord president 1874–80; first secretary for Scotland, 1885–6; M.P. (Cons.) Sussex W. 1841–60.

20 W. E. Gladstone (1809–98), four times premier.

21 Henry Labouchere, first Baron Taunton (1798–1869); president, board of trade 1847–52, colonial sec. 1855–8; cr. peer 1859.

22 John Wilson-Patten, first Baron Winmarleigh (1802–92); cr. peer, 1874; chief sec. for Ireland, 1868; a Lancs. M.P. 1830–74 and a family friend; of liberal inclinations, the diarist calling him 'a sensible, moderate politician, unbiased either by passion or by ambition' (Stanley diary, 4 June 1857).

23 In the diaries D. always denotes Disraeli, Lord or Ld D. (from 1851) the diarist's father.

24 Richard Bagge (b. 1810), younger twin of (Sir) William Bagge, Bt., of Stradsett Hall, Norfolk (1810–80), M.P. (Protectionist) Norfolk 1837–57, 1865–80.

25 For the Bentinck family interest at Lynn, created by Lord William Bentinck about 1820 because the seat was 'secure and cheap . . . and it would give me pleasure to transmit it as my legacy to the family', see John Rosselli, *Lord William Bentinck: The Making of a Liberal Imperialist, 1774–1839* (1974), 74–7, 90–6. Lord George Bentinck succeeded to the seat when his uncle went to India in 1828, and held it until his death in 1848 vacated it, without a contest, for Stanley, who was on tour in America at the time. His father settled the matter for him by receiving a deputation from Lynn 'who promised the individual support of the two sections, and guaranteed not only your return, but almost answered for their being no contest' (Lord Stanley to his son, 31 Oct. 1848). The Radical leader in Lynn put his name to the requisition to young Stanley. The whole negotiation took place, appropriately, at Newmarket, with neither the candidate nor most electors knowing what was afoot.

26 Probably Sir Thomas Bateson, Bt. first Baron Deramore (1819–85), M.P. (Cons.) Londonderry 1844–57, Devizes 1864–85; a Lord of the Treasury under Derby, 1852.

27 See M. Brock, *The Great Reform Act* (1973), 300, for the meeting of 13 May 1832.

28 John Charles, third Earl Spencer (1782–1845); as Lord Althorp, chancellor of the exchequer 1830–4; succ. 1834.

29 R. L. Sheil (1794–1851), 'Irish orator and Whig placeman' (see below, 5 July 1850, 2 June 1851).

30 Hugh, Lord Ebrington, second Earl Fortescue (1783–1861), Whig M.P. for Devonshire in 1830–32; succ. father, 1841.

31 Lord John Russell, first Earl Russell (1792–1878), cr. peer 1861; premier 1846–52, 1865–6.

32 Richard Cobden (1804–65).

33 Henry, first Lord Brougham and Vaux (1778–1868), lord chancellor 1830–4; strongly reactionary in later life.

34 Thomas Baring (1799–1873), second son of Sir Thomas Baring, second baronet; educ. Winchester; head of Baring Bros. and Co. 1828–71, chairman of Lloyds 1830–68, director of the Bank of England 1848–67. Baring was offered the Exchequer should occasion arise (see below, 16 Feb. 1851). Stanley, in his post-mortem speech on the 1851 crisis, alluded to him when he referred to the colleague whose private affairs prevented him from serving (Greville, ed. Fulford, vi 276). He allegedly declined Derby's offer of the Exchequer in 1852 and 1858 (D.N.B., *Modern English Biography*). Though Greville thought him 'the most sensible and respected of the Derbyites' (Greville, vi 404), he had an unacknowledged family, brought up to expect no more than a competence, though he was worth one or two millions (Stanley diary, 4 June 1865). The diarist noted (4 Apr. 1851) that 'though the House contains no higher authority on mercantile topics, few members sit oftener silent'.

35 Dr William Whewell (1794–1866), Master of Trinity Nov. 1841–66; never a bishop.

36 Henry, third Marquess of Lansdowne (1780–1863), Whig minister 1806–58.

37 Charles, second Baron Colchester (1798–1867); paymaster-general 1852, postmaster-general 1858–9.

38 Edward, second Baron Ellenborough (1790–1871); succ. to barony, 1818; served in Conservative ministries, 1828–30, 1834–5, Sept.–Oct. 1841, Jan.–July 1846, Mar.–June 1858; gov.-gen. of India, 1841–4; cr. earl, 1844.

39 Henry, third Earl Grey (1802–94), son of Lord Grey of the Reform Bill; succ. 1845; styled Viscount Howick 1807–45; M.P. (Lib.) various seats 1826–45; junior office 1830–4, secretary at war 1835–9, secretary of state for war and colonies 1846–52.

40 George Villiers, fifth Earl of Jersey (1773–1859); held household office in Conservative administrations, 1830, 1834–5, 1841–6, 1852; succ. 1805.

41 Cornwallis, third Viscount Hawarden (1780–1856); succ. 1807; lord-in-waiting 1841–6, Feb.–Dec. 1852; rep. peer of Ireland 1836–56; voted for repeal, 1846.

42 Thomas, second Earl of Wilton (1799–1882); held household office, 1835; succ. his maternal grandfather, 1814; one of three brothers holding distinct peerages (Westminster, Wilton, Ebury).

43 But cf. below, 5 July 1850, 13–14 Feb. 1851.

44 James, eighth Earl of Elgin (1811–63), governor-general of Canada 1846–54, postmaster-general 1859–62, viceroy of India 1862–3; succ. as earl 1841 and cr. baron (U.K.) 1849.

45 Lord John Manners, later seventh Duke of Rutland (1818–1906); M.P. (Cons.) Newark 1841–7, Colchester 1850–7, Leics. N. 1857–85, Melton 1885–8; succ. brother, 1888; in all Conservative cabinets 1852–92.

46 Edward, third Earl of Powis (1818–91); succ. 1848; voted with ministers on Don Pacifico (diary, 17 June 1851).

47 (Sir) Charles Adderley, first Baron Norton (1814–1905), M.P. (Cons.) Staffs. N. 1841–78; president, board of trade, 1874–8; cr. peer, 1878.

48 Probably Henry James Baillie (1804–85), M.P. (Cons.) Inverness-shire 1840–68: held minor office, 1852.

49 Henry Ker Seymer (1807–64), M.P. (Cons.) Dorset Feb. 1846–64; Fellow of All Souls 1831–5.

50 George Bancroft (1800–91), U.S. historian.
51 Thomas Spring Rice, first Baron Monteagle (1790–1866), Whig minister; chancellor of the exchequer, 1835–9; cr. peer, 1839.
52 George Tierney (1761–1830), Whig leader.
53 Joseph Hume (1777–1855), radical.
54 John Bright (1811–88), radical.
55 Cf. below, 10 May 1850, 20 July 1850, 20 Feb. 1851.
56 Sir Allan Napier MacNab, Bt. (1798–1862), commander of loyalist volunteers in 1837–8 rebellion; premier of Canada 1854–6; contested Brighton as a Conservative, 1859.
57 John Singleton Copley, first Baron Lyndhurst (1772–1863); lord chancellor Apr. 1827–Nov. 1830, 1834–5, 1841–6; b. in Boston of U.S. loyalist family; Disraeli's mentor.
58 Sir Francis Head (1793–1875), lieut.-governor of Canada 1835–8; Sir George Arthur (1784–1854), lieut-.governor of Upper Canada 1848–41.
59 For Ellice's contrary version, see below, 25 Aug. 1861; for the most recent opinion on this well-known claim by Brougham, see M. Brock, *op. cit.*, 383, n. 116.
60 Sir Charles Wood, first Viscount Halifax (1800–85), chancellor of. the exchequer 1846–52, president of the board of control 1852–5, first lord of the admiralty 1855–8, secretary for India 1859–66, lord privy seal 1870–4; cr. peer, 1866.
61 James Howard Harris, third Earl of Malmesbury (1807–89); M.P. (Cons.) Wilton June–Sept. 1841; foreign secretary 1852, 1858–9, lord privy seal 1866–8, 1874–Aug. 1876; in the confidence of Derby and Palmerston; a friend of Louis Napleoon from the 1830's; wore rouge. In 1856 the diarist described his character thus: 'Known to me intimately, as I served under him in the F.O. Rather reactionary in opinion, but not beyond the limits of common sense: his judgment on indifferent matters sound: goes at once to the point, has no illusions, no favourite theories: a good judge of character, agreeable in conversation, fond of anecdote, a little inclined to exaggeration in story telling, but this of a harmless kind: no malice, good temper, considerable patience: in six months of official life, with many annoyances, I never saw him irritated: very industrious, gave up his whole time to labour while in power, now fond of politics, though he never took to them till the Protectionist schism: better versed in diplomacy than in home affairs: knows nothing of the theory or science of politics, but his good sense stands him in its stead: does not speak on subjects which he has not studied: does not do himself justice: his style both as a writer and speaker is uncouth: the ideas clever, but expression defective. A man of the world and of society: unpopular with the puritans in consequence of alleged irregularities in private life: and with the newspapers, on account of Tory opinions bluntly expressed. His real claims are very far above his reputation: he might have played a considerable part if earlier put in training for office. A personal friend of the French Emperor: contributed to bring about the Anglo-French alliance'. Malmesbury was also notable for contributing 'really clever' squibs on himself and the Derby ministry, anonymously, to *Punch* (Stanley's notes, 8 Jan. 1853).
62 Gladstone moved an address on this subject, 5 July 1849.
63 George Smythe, seventh Viscount Strangford (1818–57); M.P. (Cons.) Canterbury 1841–52, when defeated; in 'Young England' movement 1842–4; under-secretary for foreign affairs, Jan.–July 1846 (see below, 17 Aug. 1852) and a free trader; fought the last duel on English soil, 1852; succ. his father, 1855; married a fortnight before his death.

1850

1 George Frederick Young, protectionist militant (1791–1870); shipowner and shipbuilder, and chairman of the General Shipowners' Society; M.P. (Lib.) Tynemouth 1831–8, (Cons.) Scarborough 1851–2.

2 (Sir) William Hutt (1803–82), M.P. (Lib.) Hull 1832–41, Gateshead 1841–74; vice-president of the board of trade and paymaster-general, 1860–5.

3 William Beresford (1797–1883), protectionist whip 1846–52, M.P. (Cons.) Harwich 1841–7, Essex N. 1847–65; secretary at war March–Dec. 1852.

4 Edward Cardwell (1813–86); sometime Fellow of Balliol and barrister; junior office Feb. 1845–July 1846, minister 1852–5, 1859–66, 1868–74; cr. viscount, 1874.

5 Philip Henry, fifth Earl Stanhope (1805–75), only son of the fourth earl, whom he succ. 1855; previously styled Lord Mahon; junior minister 1834–5, July 1845–July 1846; a free trade conservative; M.P. (Cons.) 1830–2), 1835–52; an historian of some note. His house at Chevening was, with Hatfield, the only country house where the diarist really felt at home.

6 Richard Grosvenor, second Marquess of Westminster (1795–1869), Lord Steward of the Household 1850–2; succ. father, 1845; K.G. 1857.

7 Cf. below, 9 and 24 Feb. 1851.

8 W. J. Fox (1786–1864), radical and dissenter; M.P. Oldham 1847–52, Dec. 1852–7, Oct. 1857–62.

9 Henry, Earl of Arundel and Surrey, later fourteenth Duke of Norfolk (1815–60); M.P. (Lib.) Arundel 1837–Aug. 1851, Limerick city 1851–2; succ. father 1856.

10 John Arthur Roebuck (1801–79), M.P. (Lib.) Bath 1832–7, 1841–7, Sheffield 1849–68, 1874–9; chairman, Administrative Reform Association.

11 John Macgregor (1797–1857), M.P. (Lib.) Glasgow 1847–57; joint secretary to the board of trade 1839–47; writer on tariffs and trade.

12 Sir Edward Buxton, Bt. (1812–58), M.P. (Lib.) Essex S. 1847–52, Norfolk E. 1857–8; an Anglican.

13 George, eighth (Scotland) and first (U.K.) Duke of Argyll (1832–1900), at this time a Peelite; lord privy scal 1852–5, followed by office in Liberal governments.

14 Archibald William (Montgomerie), thirteenth Earl of Eglintoun (1812–61); succ. 1819; lord-lieut. of Ireland 1852, 1858–9.

15 *Claims and Resources of the West Indian Colonies. A letter to ... W. E. Gladstone.* (London, 1850). The diarist subsequently wrote *Farther Facts connected with the West Indies. A second letter to ... W. E. Gladstone.* (London, 1851).

16 Rev. Hugh McNeile (1795–1879), leader of popular protestantism in Liverpool; cr. Dean of Ripon, Sept. 1868.

17 Isaac Butt (1813–79), professor of political economy, Trinity College, Dublin, 1836, and a Protestant; first entered parliament in May 1852 as a Derbyite; leader of Irish home rule party 1870–9; regarded by the diarist from about 1870 as ruined in personal character by his liaisons and debts (see also below, 7 Nov. 1867).

18 Edward, thirteenth Earl of Derby (1775–June 1851), the diarist's grandfather, was a steady if quiet Whig who had first entered the Lords in 1832 as a baron created by Grey.

19 Over the Don Pacifico case.

20 Robert (Jocelyn), third Earl of Roden (1788–1870); succ. 1820; connected, through his son Lord Jocelyn (see above, 23 Mar. 1849), with Palmerston; a grand master of the Orange Society, he was dismissed from the Irish magistracy following an affray in July 1849.

21 John Thomas (Freeman-Mitford), second Baron Redesdale (1805–86); cr. Earl of Redesdale, 1877: a noted Chairman of Committees and Deputy Speaker of the House of Lords, 1851–86. Disraeli in 1880 called him 'narrow, prejudiced, and utterly unconscious of what is going on in the country'.

22 George (Eden), second Baron Auckland (1784–1 Jan. 1849), gov.-gen. of India 1835–41, first lord of the admiralty 1846–9.

23 Henry Hardinge, first Viscount Hardinge of Lahore and King's Newton (1785–1856), governor-general of India 1844–8; succ. Wellington as C.-in-C., 1852–5; cr. peer 1846. Though twice a senior minister under Peel, he joined Derby in 1852 (Mar.–Sept.) as Master-General of the Ordnance.

24 Dr George Tomlinson (d. 1863), an old friend; Bishop of Gibraltar 1842–63.

25 Lord Henry Gordon-Lennox (1821–86), third son of fifth Duke of Richmond; M.P. (Cons.) Chichester Feb. 1846–1885; minor office 1852, 1858–9, sec. to admiralty 1866–8, chief commissioner of works 1874–6 (resigned, to relief of cabinet, in wake of financial scandal). Married 1883. See Blake, 325–7.

26 Arthur, second Duke of Wellington (1807–84), M.P. (Cons.) Aldeburgh 1829–32, Norwich 1837–52; styled Lord Douro 1812–14, Marquess of Douro 1814–52; succ. father 1852.

27 (Sir) Fitzroy Kelly (1796–1866), solicitor-general July 1845–June 1846, July–Dec. 1852, attorney-general 1858–9; judge July 1866.

28 Princess Mary (1776–1857), fourth d. of George III, m. 1816 her cousin William Frederick, second Duke of Gloucester (1776–1834), known as Silly Billy.

29 Edward S. Cayley (1802–62), M.P. N. Riding 1832–62.

30 Cf. above, 7 May 1849, and below, 13–14 Feb. 1851.

31 H. R. H. Adolphus Frederick (1774–1850) seventh and youngest surviving son of George III; cr. Duke, 1801; viceroy of Hanover 1816–37.

32 Sir Samuel Morton Peto, Bt., contractor (1809–89), M.P. (Lib.) Norwich 1847–54, Finsbury 1859–65, Bristol 1865–8; his firm failed, 1868.

33 Samuel Jones Loyd, Baron Overstone (1796–1883), banker; cr. peer 1850.

34 (Sir) Thomas Wilde, Baron Truro (1782–1855), attorney-gen. 1841, 1846, lord chief justice 1846–50, lord chancellor 1850–2. He m. secondly, 1845, Augusta Emma D'Este, d. of H.R.H. Augustus Frederick, Duke of Sussex, son of George III.

35 Sir John Campbell, first Baron Campbell of St Andrews (1779–1861); law officer in 1830s; cr. peer, 1841; chancellor of duchy, 1846–50; chief justice, Queen's Bench, 1850; lord chancellor 1859–61.

36 Sir Robert Rolfe, Baron Cranworth (1790–1868), lord chancellor 1852–8, 1865–6; cr. peer 1850.

37 Cf. above, 5 June 1849, and below, 20 Feb. 1851.

38 H.R.H. George, second Duke of Cambridge (1819–1904), only son of Adolphus Frederick, first Duke, the seventh and youngest surviving son of George III; C.-in-C. 1856–95.

39 Baron Christian Bunsen (d. 1860), German ambassador to England 1841–54.

40 Lionel Nathan de Rothschild, Baron of the Austrian Empire (1808–79), senior partner of Rothschild and Sons; M.P. (Lib.) City of London 1847–68, 1869–74, but unable to sit until 1858.

41 Constantine Henry (Phipps), first Marquess of Normanby (1797–1863); cr. marquess 1838; senior minister, 1834–41; ambassador to Paris, 1846–52; minister to Florence 1854–8.

1851

1 Stanley probably left Knowsley for Hughenden on 13 Jan. 1851 (Stanley to Disraeli, 8 Jan. 1851, Hughenden MSS. B/XX/5/54). His date of departure from Hughenden is not clear, but Disraeli was back in London on the evening of 20 Jan. (M. and B., iii 274).

2 Cf. Disraeli to his sister, 22 Jan. 1851, in R. Disraeli, *Lord Beaconsfield's Letters 1830 to 1852* (London 1887), 237: 'Young Stanley's visit to Hughenden, though hurried, was very agreeable. He seemed charmed with the hill country, after Lancashire, and with everything else. Having no horses, we took long walks together – one day to

Hampden, which pleased him much, another to the Abbey, no one there, so we rambled all over the park; the view of Hughenden from the heights is quite marvellous. I had never seen it before ... We walked to Denner Hill and its sylvan neighbourhood and on Sunday, after church, we walked on the hills in view of Dashwood's Park till we got to West Wycombe Church'.

3 Cf. the account of Disraeli's rural pleasures in Blake, *op. cit*,, 409–10.

4 The comment on Byron comes from his father's preface to the fourth edition of *The Literary Character* (1828). His views on Gibbon and Voltaire were also inherited: cf. James Ogden, *Isaac D'Israeli* (Oxford 1969), 81, 120.

5 An opinion repeated later in Disraeli's *General Preface to His Novels* (1870) in even stronger form.

6 Disraeli's claims were in each case groundless. But cf. Disraeli to Mrs Brydges Willyams, 20 Apr. 1862, Brydges Willyams MSS., after hearing Meyerbeer, 'this great genius'; 'He, like most celebrated composers, and even singers and musicians, is a child of the great House of Israel'.

7 Cf. below, 5 May 1853.

8 Probably Lord Henry Lennox.

9 Samuel Phillips (1814–54), a Tory journalist of Jewish origins, who had vilified Disraeli in 1847–8 and aided him in 1848–9, had then lost contact with Disraeli except for some friendly approaches in 1852. His censures in 1854 have no obvious explanation. *The Times*, 17 Jan. 1854, contained a long unsigned review, alternatively adulatory and contemptuous, of *The Rt. Hon. Benjamin Disraeli, M.P. A Literary and Political Biography* (London 1854). Stanley called Phillips's review 'the bitterest and most masterly of all his writings' (diary, 21 Mar. 1851). Phillips compared Disraeli's influence over Stanley, with Hogarth in mind, to that of a 'questionable beldame' over a girl freshly arrived from the country. Cf. below, 21 Mar. 1851.

10 After the 1852 election Stanley pressed Disraeli to win over Palmerston (Stanley to Disraeli, 19 July 1852, Hughenden MSS., B/XX/5/554).

11 The first number of the *Press*, the outcome of discussion going back at least as far as May 1849, in which the younger Stanley was a central figure, was published on 7 May 1853. On 8 Jan. 1851, Stanley had written enthusiastically to Disraeli: '... for my own part, I am willing to give all the time and trouble that can be spared from the House' (M. and B., iii 490–1).

12 In Dec. 1850 Disraeli had asked to consult Lord Stanley about 'a great financial scheme which he is concocting with Herries' (Lord Stanley to Malmesbury, 2 Dec. 1850, Malmesbury, i 267). Derby's opinion was in favour of fighting for 'relaxation of the monetary laws and an amendment of the poor law', i.e. broadly items 1 and 3 of Disraeli's plan. Disraeli twice divided the House with motions on agricultural distress, on 13 Feb. and 11 Apr. 1851, reducing the Government majority to 14 and 13 respectively.

13 Cf. below, 1 Feb. 1851.

14 Disraeli's *Lord George Bentinck: a Political Biography*, although not published till Dec. 1851, had been begun in autumn 1850. On 10 Sept. 1850 Disraeli had written to his sister that, faced with 'two immense chests of George Bentinck's papers from the Duke of Portland – materials for a memoir, long contemplated', he would 'be glad to get to Hughenden tomorrow, having before me enormous labour, which nothing but solitude, study, and abstinence can beat down, if indeed they can . . .' (R. Disraeli, *op. cit.*, 233).

15 This passage first appeared as 'Disraeli in 1851: "Young Stanley" as Boswell', ed. L. Colley and J. Vincent, in *Historical Studies* (Melbourne), vol. 15 no. 69, Oct. 1972. It is reprinted here, with minor changes, by kind permission of the editor.

16 Charles William, third Marquess of Londonderry (1778–1854); succ. his half-brother 1822; ambassador to Vienna 1814–23; see also below, June 1852, for his 'betrayal' on formation of 1852 ministry.

17 Gilbert, second Earl of Minto (1782–1859), succ. 1814; minister to Berlin 1832–4, first lord of the admiralty 1835–41, lord privy seal 1846–52; envoy to Italian states, 1847–8.

18 Sir Robert Harry Inglis, Bt. (1786–1855), M.P. (Tory) Dundalk 1824–6, Ripon 1828–9, Oxford University 1829–54; s. of an East India Co. director: educ. Winchester and Christ Church; priv. sec. to Lord Sidmouth; succ. father 1820; in Feb. 1829 defeated Peel in Oxford Univ. by-election; denounced Wellington's attempt to form a govt in May 1832; opposed Maynooth grant and repeal to corn laws; supported Ashley on factory reform. He declined Stanley's offer of cabinet membership in the 1851 crisis (see below, 27 Feb. 1851). There is no memoir.

19 George, tenth Earl of Winchilsea (1791–1858); succ. 1826; extreme protectionist and protestant; fought duel with Wellington 1829.

20 Cf. above, 26 Mar. 1850, and below, 24 Feb. 1851.

21 William Nicholas Keogh (1817–78), M.P. Athlone 1847–56; sol.-gen. (I.) 1852–Mar. 1855, att.-gen. (I.) 1855–6; judge 1856–78.

22 George William Frederick (Villiers), fourth Earl of Clarendon (1800–70); diplomatic career 1820–39, including envoy to Madrid 1833–9; succ. uncle 1838; lord privy seal and chancellor of duchy 1864–5, foreign secretary 1865–6, 1868–70. Refused Palmerston's offer of choice of posts other than F.O., 1859; refused F.O. from Derby 1866.

23 Cf. above, 7 May 1849, 5 July 1850.

24 (Sir) Joseph Napier, first bt. (1804–82), att.-gen. (I.) 1852, lord chancellor of Ireland 1858–9, vice-chancellor of Dublin University 1867–82. Cr. bt. 1867.

25 Charles, third Earl Fitzwilliam (1786–1857), Whig M.P. 1806–33; succ. 1833.

26 Sir John Cam Hobhouse, first Baron Broughton (1786–1869), president of the b. of c. 1835–41, 1846–52; cr. peer 1851.

27 Cf above, 26 Mar. 1850, 9 Feb. 1851.

28 Charles John (Canning), second Viscount and first Earl Canning (1812–62), third, youngest, and only surviving son of George Canning; succ. his mother as viscount, 1837; M.P. (Cons.) Warwick 1836–7; under-secretary for foreign affairs 1841–6, commissioner of woods and forests Mar.–July 1846; postmaster-gen. 1852–5, gov.-gen., then viceroy 1855–62; cr. earl 1859.

29 Cf. below, 26 Feb. 1851.

30 Cf. below, 1 Mar. 1851, and 3 Jan. 1864, where the date given (1852) may be a mistake for 1851.

31 Sir Stratford Canning, first Viscount Stratford de Redcliffe (1786–1880); cousin of Canning: diplomatic career 1807–33: M.P. (Tory) 1828–30, 1831–2, 1835–42; ambassador to Constantinople 1841–58; cr. viscount Apr. 1852.

32 Gladstone reached London at half past ten, having no idea that he would be summoned on his arrival. Newcastle at once tried to dissuade him from joining Lord Stanley, partly on the grounds 'that if we held off now the crisis must end shortly in placing the *summa rerum* in our hands'. A note from Lord Stanley had been awaiting Gladstone for some days, but Beresford then arrived with fresh and urgent requests that he should see Stanley: Gladstone went, was offered a wide choice of offices, and told, what he had not expected, that Lord Stanley proposed a five or six shilling duty on corn. Gladstone felt 'an intense relief at the very first moment when he spoke of a duty on corn and so put me out of the question'. Gladstone then went to consult Canning, who shared his views, and returned to give Lord Stanley his refusal 'at which he did not show the least surprise'. For these details, see *The Gladstone Diaries*, 26 Feb. 1851.

33 Algernon (Percy), fourth Duke of Northumberland (1792–1865), first lord of the admiralty under Derby in 1852.

34 Henry Thomas Lowry-Corry (1803–73), M.P. (Cons.) Tyrone 1826–73; second son of the second Earl of Belmore, and bro. of third Earl; married Shaftesbury's sister; comptroller of the household 1834–5, a lord of the admiralty 1841–5, sec. to admiralty 1845–6, 1858–9, vice-president of council 1866–7, first lord of the admiralty 1867–8. Not employed in Derby's 1852 government.

35 In Dec. 1851 Ashley lamented his loss of connection with the protectionists in a manner suggesting that he never knew of the above intention (Hodder, *Shaftesbury*, under 25 Dec. 1851).

36 Sir E. Sugden, Lord St Leonards (1781–1875), solicitor-general 1829–30, lord chancellor of Ireland 1834–5, 1841–6, lord chancellor 1852; cr. peer 1852.

37 Charles, fourth Earl of Hardwicke (1799–1873); lord-in-waiting 1841–6 (resigned over repeal), postmaster-gen. 1852, lord privy seal 1858–9.

38 Brownlow (Cecil), third Marquess of Exeter (1795–1867); succ. 1804; court office 1841–6, 1852, 1858–9.

39 James, second Marquess of Salisbury (1791–1868); succ. 1823; lord privy seal 1852, lord president 1858–9. His second wife Mary (1824–1900) married the diarist in 1870.

40 Henry Pelham (Pelham-Clinton), fifth Duke of Newcastle (1811–64); lord of the treasury 1834–5, woods and forests 1841–6, chief sec. for Ireland 1846, col. sec. 1852–4, sec. for war 1854–5, col. sec. 1859–64; succ. father 1851.

41 Ernst Philipp Ivanovitch, Count de Brunnow (1797–1875), Russian minister in London 1840–54, 1861–74; cr. Count 1871.

42 H.R.H. George, second Duke of Cambridge (1819–1904); succ. father 1850; commander-in-chief 1852–95.

43 Premier 1801–4 and Pitt's successor.

44 George Henry Moore (1811–70), Mayo squireen, leading figure among the independent Irish, and father of the author; M.P. Mayo 1847–57, 1868–70. The diarist knew Moore in Ireland in 1844–6: 'a clever, gay, good-humoured, and remarkably impudent Irishman, with the capacity to become a considerable person, but devoid of perseverance, and supposed to be compromised by transactions on the Turf. He assumed the post of leader of the priest-party, but has since been forced to give way to the greater earnestness and genuine fanaticism of Lucas. At this time he made some noise, and was thought likely to do more than he has since in fact effected' (diary, 18 Mar. 1851).

45 Sir George Grey, second baronet (1799–1882), Whig M.P. 1832–74; junior office 1834–41, chancellor of duchy 1841, home sec. 1846–52, 1855–8, 1861–6; colonial sec. 1854–5, chancellor of duchy 1859–61.

46 Adam (Duncan-Haldane), second Earl of Camperdown (1812–67); succ. father 1859; a lord of the treasury 1855–8; as Lord Duncan, M.P. (Lib.) 1837–52, 1854–9.

47 William Williams, merchant and radical reformer (1789–1865), M.P. (Lib.) Coventry 1835–47, Lambeth 1850–65.

48 Hugh, third Earl Fortescue (1818–1905), M.P. (Lib.) Plymouth 1841–52, Marylebone 1854–9; lord of treasury 1846–7, sec. to poor law board 1847–51; called to Lords 1859 and succ. 1861. His wife had refused an offer of marriage from Louis Napoleon.

49 John S. Russell, first Baron Hampton (1799–1880); educ. Eton and Oxford, but did not graduate; changed name to Pakington 1831, inheriting his aunt's estates 1846; deeply rooted in Worcs., where he was chairman of quarter sessions 1834–58, but also owned Little Milford colliery, Pembrokeshire, and in 1847 discovered iron ore on his Welsh property; M.P. (Cons.) Droitwich 1837–74; cr. bt. by Peel, July 1846, and peer

by Disraeli on losing seat, 1874. For his early standing, see R. Disraeli ed., *Lord Beaconsfield's Correspondence with his Sister 1832–1852*, p. 90; for his suggested leadership of a Conservative reunion in Nov. 1848 (because 'all his liaisons are with Peel's party, whilst all his votes have been with us') see R. Stewart, *The Politics of Protection*, p. 138. His papers show no contact with Lord Stanley, Bentinck, or Disraeli in 1846–51. He was colonial sec. 1852 (carrying N.Z. constitution), first lord of the admiralty 1858–9 (announced decision to build first ironclads), 1866–Mar. 1867, war office 1867–8, first civil service commissioner Nov. 1875–80; offered home office by Derby, Feb. 1859. An experienced legislator who had carried 'improving' bills in 1840, 1844, 1847, 1850, Pakington was a success in 1852 (below, June 1852) though hostile to Disraeli, wishing Palmerston to lead (below, Nov. 1852). Disraeli returned his contempt in 1853, when Pakington was talked of as leader with 'ultra' support (Greville, ed. Fulford, vi 404–5; below, 17 Mar. 1853). In policy Pakington consistently sought 'moderate reform, and progressive improvement' (election address, *The Times*, 9 Apr. 1859), e.g. promoting education bills in 1855 and 1857, supporting the Jew Bill in 1857, urging a uniform £8 ratal franchise in 1859, seeking a church rates compromise in the late 1850's, promoting the movement for boys' reformatories in concert with Lord Stanley and probably Northcote; romantically moved by the New Social Movement of 1870, his unsound views caused Derby anxiety; president of Social Science conference 1871; president of N.U.C.C.A. 1874. With Stanley as a fellow-spirit, Northcote and Adderley as associates, he was in advance of his party on social issues in the mid-1850's, his education bills being attacked as 'the secular system in disguise' by R. Cecil, and by Disraeli on party grounds; in 1857 Pakington had to be dissuaded from leaving the front bench on this issue. His main achievement was to obtain a R.C. on popular education, 1858. Though a regular attender at Disraeli's Saturday shadow cabinets of Mar.–July 1855, he had no private contact with him, and his papers contain no comment on Disraeli; there are however signs in 1855–9 of his developing a relationship with Derby. Interests: archery, skating, family life.

Throughout the ministerial crisis of 1851 Pakington was on a tour abroad, returning to London only on 4 Mar. 1851 (i.e. after Lord Stanley's appeal in the Lords on 28 Feb. for new blood). On 11 Mar. he 'wrote to Lord Stanley to tell him that I should join his party', receiving 'a long and interesting answer' next day (Pakington's diaries, Worcs. C.R.O. 705/349/2). On 11 April Pakington became engaged to his third wife, and he took little part in politics during the rest of 1851.

See Hampton MSS., Worcs. C.R.O.: *D.N.B.*; H. and R. Pakington, *The Pakingtons of Westwood* (1975); and an unpublished paper by Mrs B. Montagu.

50 He was the only Conservative to vote for Gladstone's Home Rule Bill in June 1886.
51 William Forbes Mackenzie (1807–62), junior whip Apr. 1845–Feb. 1846 (resigned), joint sec. to treasury Feb.–Dec. 1852, becoming chief whip briefly following Beresford's downfall; M.P. Peebles 1837–52, Liverpool July 1852, but unseated on petition June 1853, and not again returned. Established closing of Scottish pubs at 10 p.m. and on Sundays.
52 George, third Baron Forester (1807–86), M.P. (Cons.) Wenlock, 1830–74; succ. brother, 1874; household office 1852, 1858–9.
53 Possibly Douglas Brown (1820–92), barrister (1847) and recorder of King's Lynn 6 Jan. 1869–1885.
54 J. W. Croker (1780–1857), Tory man of letters, portrayed as Rigby in Coningsby.
55 Charles Newdegate (1816–87), M.P. N. Warwickshire 1843–85.
56 Henry Drummond, F.R.S. (1786–1860), M.P. (Cons.) W. Surrey 1847–60. In the parliament of 1847–52 there were two Henry Drummonds on the Conservative side.

57 Henry Grattan (1789–1859), second son of the the orator, and M.P. Dublin City 1826–30, Meath 1831–52; see below, 16 May 1851. A protestant Repealer and member of the Reform Club.

58 Thomas Wakley (1790–1862), editor of the *Lancet*; M.P. (Lib.) Finsbury 1835–52.

59 Between 14–30 Nov. 1850 no less than 78 works on papal aggression were published (Hodder, *Shaftesbury*, ii 335).

60 Sir Henry Winston Barron Bt. (1795–1872), M.P. Waterford City 1832–47, 1848–52, 1865–8.

61 William Henry Magan (1820–61), M.P. (Lib.) Westmeath 1847–59; retired army officer.

62 John O'Connell (1810–58), third son of Daniel O'Connell; M.P. 1832–Aug. 1851, 1853–7; clerk of the hanaper in Ireland, 1856.

63 A free trade Liberal won Boston in 1849 by 422 to 321. On his death, a Protectionist was elected by 368 to 251 (22 Apr. 1851).

64 (Sir) Edward Bulwer-Lytton, Bt., previously Lytton Bulwer, first Baron Lytton (1803–73), M.P. (Lib.) St Ives 1831–2, Lincoln 1832–41 (Cons.) Herts. 1852–66; colonial sec. 1858–9; cr. bt. 1838, peer July 1866.

65 *Letters to John Bull, Esq. on affairs connected with his landed property, and the persons who live thereon*. Pp. 104. Chapman and Hall: London 1851.

66 Richard More O'Ferrall (1797–1880); M.P. (Lib.) Kildare 1830–47, Longford Apr. 1851–July 1852, Kildare 1859; junior office 1835–41, P.C. 1847, gov. of Malta 1847–51.

67 James Whiteside (1806–76), M.P. (Cons.) Enniskillen Apr. 1851–Feb. 1859, Dublin University 1859–66; solicitor-gen. (I.) 1852, attorney-gen. (I.) 1858–9; like Cairns and Fitzroy Kelly, saw better prospects in judicial than in ministerial office in July 1866, becoming Lord Chief Justice (Ireland).

68 Richard Southwell (Bourke), sixth Earl of Mayo (1822–72), chief sec. for Ireland 1852, 1858–9, 1866–8, viceroy of India 1868–72 (assassinated); succ. 1867; M.P. (Cons.) Kildare 1847–52, Coleraine 1852–7, Cockermouth 1857–67.

69 John Gibson Lockhart (1794–1854), editor of *Quarterly Review* 1825–53; son-in-law and biographer of Sir W. Scott; auditor of duchy of Lancaster 1843 to death.

70 Robert Knox (d. 1859), editor of *Morning Herald* 1846–58; colonial official 1858–9.

71 Louis Adolphe Thiers (1797–1877), historian, and a leading politician under Louis Philippe; premier 1870–3.

72 Sidney Herbert, first Baron Herbert of Lea (1810–61); held office 1834–5, 1841–6, 1859–60; cr. peer 1860.

73 François Guizot (1787–1874), premier of France 1840–8.

74 John Philpot Curran (1750–1817), Irish orator.

75 Hon. G. C. G. F. Berkeley (1800–81), M.P. W. Gloucs. (Lib.) 1832–47, (Protectionist) 1847–52.

76 The thirteenth Earl, the diarist's grandfather, d. 30 June 1851.

1852

1 *Diaries and Correspondence of James Harris, first Earl of Malmesbury* . . . Edited by his grandson, the third Earl of Malmesbury. Bentley, 1845.

2 (Sir) Frederick Thesiger, first Baron Chelmsford (1794–1878), Cons. M.P. 1840–58; sol.-gen. and kt. 1844; att.-gen. 1845–6, 1852, lord chancellor 1858–9, 1866–Feb. 1868, being made to give way to Cairns 'without the month's notice that would have been given to a cook' as he said.

3 Viscount Jocelyn (Peelite) 637; Lord Stanley (Cons.) 550; Robert Pashley (Lib.) 385.

4 Robert Adam Christopher-Nisbet-Hamilton (1804–77), M.P. (Cons.) Edinburgh 1831–2, Lincs. N. 1837–57, chancellor of duchy (outside cabinet) 1852. His surname was Dundas to 1836, then Christopher to 1854, then as above.

5 William (Lowther), second Earl of Lonsdale (1787–1872), M.P. (Cons.) 1808–41; succ. father 1844; vice-president of board of trade 1834–5, postmaster-gen. 1841–5; lord president 1852.

6 George, sixth Earl Cowper (1806–56), Lady Palmerston's eldest child by her first marriage; a Whig junior minister in 1834. Beresford was secretary at war and Christopher had the duchy.

7 Georgiana Charlotte Mary (Wellesley) (1817–78), dau. of Henry, first Baron Cowley by a sister of the Lord Salisbury who served under Derby in 1852 and 1858–9. She m. Bulwer Dec. 1848.

8 Sir J. Brooke, rajah of Sarawak (1803–68); rajah from 1841. Brooke's operations against piracy were called in question by Hume and Cobden, and Aberdeen granted a commission of enquiry, but the charges of inhumanity were not upheld.

9 Richard, second Duke of Buckingham and Chandos (1797–1861); succ. 1839; lord privy seal 1841–2, resigning over corn laws; by 1848 ruined by folly and had to sell Stowe.

10 Alexander Cochrane-Wishart-Baillie, first Baron Lamington (1816–90), M.P. (Cons.) 1841–6, 1847–52, 1857, 1859–68, 1870–80. An original member of 'Young England'; cr. peer 1880.

11 George, third Baron Harris (1810–72), gov. of Trinidad 1846–54, gov. of Madras 1854–9, lord-in-waiting 1860–3; supporter of Palmerston.

12 James, tenth Earl and first Marquess of Dalhousie (1812–60), succ. 1838; Peelite minister 1843–6, gov.-gen. of India 1848–56.

13 (Sir) James Emerson Tennent, Bt. (1804–69), M.P. (Cons.) Belfast 1832–41, 1842–5, Lisburn 1852; sec. to the India Board 1841–5, civil sec. to Ceylon govt. 1845–50; perm. sec. to poor law board, Mar.–Sept. 1852, sec. to board of trade 1852–67, cr. Bt. 1867; advised protectionists on Ceylon controversy and on handling of the press; seen by diarist as able and slippery.

14 William Frederick Augustus Delane (1793–1857); barrister, manager of *Morning Chronicle* to 1847, treasurer of county courts in Kent and Surrey, Mar. 1847 to his death; financial manager of *The Times*.

15 William Henry Lytton Earle Bulwer, first Baron Dalling (1801–72), second of three sons of Gen. Bulwer, and elder bro. of first Baron Lytton, novelist and Cons. minister; M.P. (Lib.) 1830–7, 1868–71 (but see below, 26 Aug. 1868); minister at Madrid 1843–8, Washington 1849–52, Florence 1852–4, and Constantinople 1858–65; cr. peer 1871; one of Lady Salisbury's circle in the 1860's.

16 (Adm.) Sir George Francis Seymour (1787–1870), c.-in-c. on the N. American and W. Indian station Jan. 1851–Nov. 1853.

17 (Sir) John Crampton, second bt. (1805–86), career diplomatist; chargé d'affaires in U.S. 1847–9, 1850–2, minister to U.S. 1852–7; envoy to Spain 1860–9; succ. as bt. 1858.

18 Abbott Lawrence (1792–1855), U.S. minister in London (resigned 1852).

19 Henry Unwin Addington (1790–1870), envoy to Madrid 1829–33; perm. under-sec. at F.O. 1842–54.

20 (Sir) Edward John (Stanley), second Baron Stanley of Alderley (1802–69), Whig M.P. 1831–41, 1847–8; cr. peer 1848, succ. father 1850; paymaster-gen. 1841, under-sec. for foreign affairs 1846–52, paymaster-gen. Feb. 1852, Dec. 1852–5, vice-president of board of trade 1855–8; postmaster-gen. (in cabinet) 1860–6.

21 Stanley's notes relating to 3 Sept.–19 Nov. 1852 were lost when he came to write the present document in 1855.

22 Charles Pelham Villiers (1802–98), anti-corn law leader; M.P. (Lib.) Wolverhampton 1835–85, Wolverhampton S. 1885–98; president of poor law board 1859–66.

23 (Sir) William Shee (1804–68), M.P. co. Kilkenny 1852–7; cr. first R.C. judge since 1688, in 1863, and kt., 1864.
24 Derbyite Whip.
25 The Duke of Wellington's funeral.
26 Ralph Bernal Osborne (1808–82), M.P. (Lib.) 1841–65, 1866–74; sec. of Admiralty Dec. 1852–Feb. 1858; a 'favourite of the House' on account of supposed wit.
27 Fitzroy James Henry (Somerset), first Baron Raglan (1788–1855), military sec. to Wellington 1827–52; c.-in-c. in Crimea, 1854; eighth s. of fifth Duke of Beaufort.
28 Sir John Buller Yarde-Buller, Bt., first Baron Churston (1799–1871), M.P. (Cons.) Devon S. 1835–58; cr. peer 1858.
29 Daughter of Queen Victoria's half-sister, Princess Feodora of Leiningen, by Prince Ernest of Hohenlohe-Langenburg. She was 17 when Napoleon, then 45, courted her.
30 Probably William Barnard (Petre), twelfth Baron Petre (1817–84); a Liberal; held Grand Cross of the Order of Pius IX.
31 Nicholas Wiseman (1802–65), archbishop of Westminster and cardinal 1850–65.
32 An English professional beauty; created Comtesse de Beauregard. Cf. André Maurois, *Miss Howard and the Emperor* (1957), p. 63.

1853

1 This was in fact based on Lord Ossulston's account of the situation in Huntingdon-shire. 'In that country no farmer dares place his ricks together, lest they should be burnt all at once: but scatters them about singly here and there. No assistance can be got in case of accidental conflagration. There seems to be among the labourers of the midland counties a general hatred of both farmers and landlords' (Stanley's notes on Malmesbury, Liverpool Record Office).
2 Christian Friedrich, Baron von Stockmar (1787–1863), political factotum of the Coburgs, and private adviser to Victoria and Albert.
3 George, seventh Earl of Carlisle (1802–64), Whig M.P. (as Lord Morpeth) 1826–48; chief sec. for Ireland 1835–41, with cabinet seat from 1839; chief comm. of woods and forests 1846–50, chancellor of duchy 1850–2; lord-lieutenant of Ireland 1855–8, 1859–64. See below, 18 Apr. 1861.
4 (Sir) William George Hylton (Jolliffe), first Baron Hylton (1800–76) cr. Bt. 1821; M.P. (Cons.) Petersfield 1830–2, 1837–8, 1841–66; under-sec. at home office Mar.–Dec. 1852; chief whip 1853–9; P.C. 1859, cr. peer 1866. See *A Politician in the Fifties: A Selection from the Correspondence of the Right Honourable Sir William Jolliffe, Bart., M.P. (Lord Hylton)*. London: John Murray, 1905, and the important collection of Jolliffe's political papers in the Somerset County Record Office.
5 Samuel Lucas (1818–68), editor of *The Press*, 1853, *Once a Week* (1859–65). *The Shilling Magazine* (1865).
6 But cf. below, 20 June 1869. The topic which inspired Disraeli in 1851 was the Jewish settlement of Palestine.
7 Cf. below, 21 Dec. 1862.
8 Ulick John de Burgh, fourteenth Earl and first Marquess (I.) of Clanricarde (1802–74); succ. as earl, 1808; m. Canning's daughter 1825; cr. marquess 1825; foreign under-sec. 1826–7; minor office 1830–4; ambassador to Russia 1838–41; P.M.G. 1846–52; refused Granville's offer of Paris embassy in Jan. 1852; mortified at omission from Aberdeen ministry; his appointment as lord privy seal, Feb. 1858, precipitated Palmerston's downfall.
9 John (Ponsonby), first Viscount Ponsonby (*c.* 1770–1855), diplomatist; ambassador to Constantinople 1832–41, to Vienna 1846–50; cr. viscount 1839: uncle of third Earl Grey.

10 On 5 Apr. 1853 Ponsonby wrote to Grey describing a visit from Lord Henry Lennox 'on Saturday last'. Lennox produced credentials from Disraeli dated Friday afternoon. Lennox, after discussion with Ponsonby, then produced a memorandum on the present state of parties, which Ponsonby enclosed to Grey. The memorandum was really a very ordinary proposal for Grey to join Derby. Lennox gave assurances that, in the event of Derby retiring, Grey would become leader, and that Stanley warmly concurred in the intrigue. Grey replied to Ponsonby, 6 Apr. 1853, with a firm rejection, saying '. . . I consider this Administration as upon the whole the best that can be hoped for at present, and I am therefore anxious for its continuance'. Lennox replied, 8 Apr., trying to renew his overtures. (Grey declined office from Derby in 1858). I am obliged to Mr Robinson for the above information from the Earl Grey papers, 3rd Earl, 1st Viscount Ponsonby file (University of Durham, Department of Palaeography and Diplomatic).

11 Cf. above, Jan. 1851.

12 Sir William Goodenough Hayter, first Bt. (1792–1878), M.P. (Lib.) Wells 1837–65; Lib. chief whip 1850–9.

13 Lord Alexander Lennox (1825–92), M.P. (Cons.) Shoreham 1849–59, who had in Jan. 1853 expressed himself 'intensely disgusted at his brother Henry's *engouement* for Disraeli' (Liverpool Record Office, notes on Malesbury).

14 Cf. below, 5 July 1861, 3 Nov. 1865.

15 Thomas Challis (1794–1874), hide and skin salesman, lord mayor of London 1852–3; M.P. (Lib.) Finsbury 1852–7.

16 Henry (Somerset), seventh Duke of Beaufort (1792–1853); A.D.C. to Wellington 1812–14.

17 Rev Edward James Geoffrey Hornby, Rector of Bury (b. 1816), son of Rev Geoffrey Hornby (1780–1850), also Rector of Bury. The latter was nephew of the twelfth Earl of Derby, and brother-in-law of the thirteenth.

18 Thomas Wrigley (1808–80), partner with his father in papermaking concern; chairman of Bury Banking Co.; sheriff of Lancs. 1872.

1854

1 Camille Hyacinthe Odillon Barrot (1791–1873), a leading French politician of the Orleanist period.

2 Lord Robert Arthur Talbot (Gascoyne-Cecil), third Marquess of Salisbury (1830–1903), M.P. (Cons.) Stamford Aug. 1853–68; sec. for India 1866–Mar. 1867 (resigned), 1874–8, foreign sec. 1878–80, premier 1885–6, 1886–92, 1895–1902.

3 William Drogo (Montagu), seventh Duke of Manchester (1823–90), styled Viscount Mandeville 1843–55; M.P. (Cons.) Bewdley 1847–52, Hunts. 1852–5: held court office Mar.–Dec. 1852.

4 Richard (Butler), second Earl (I.) of Glengall (1794–1858); succ. 1819; repr. peer (I.) 1829–58.

5 Miles Thomas (Stapleton), eighth Baron Beaumont (1805–54); succ. father 1839.

6 Sir Edward Cholmeley Dering, eighth bt. (1807–96), M.P. (Lib.) E. Kent 1852–7, 1863–8.

7 See above, page 159.

8 Edward ('Bear') Ellice sen. (1781–1863), M.P. (Lib.) Coventry 1818–26, 1830–63; joint sec. to treasury 1830–2, sec. at war 1833–4. Founding chairman of Reform Club, and brother-in-law of Grey of the Reform Bill.

9 George Hamilton Seymour (1797–1880), priv. sec. to Castlereagh 1822; followed diplomatic career; minister at St Petersburg 1851–Feb. 1854.

10 In July 1854 Stanley wrote, and sent, a weird anonymous letter to Newcastle, urging him to give up the War Office. 'The Govt of India either has been, or within few

days will be, offered you. Accept it. By so doing you will save your character, retrieve your finances, and stand well for the Premiership: a high post, but one which with the support of Albert and the *Times*, you may both get and hold. . . . Not the talents. of Wellington can save one holding your place . . . You will be reviled, perhaps ruined, unjustly. . . . You will come back, rich and renowned, to find Mr Gladstone leading the Commons'. (Derby MSS., miscellaneous, Liverpool Record Office).

1855

1 Just before the ministerial crisis the diarist was more concerned with social reform than politics. On 11–15 Jan. 1855 he had paid his first visit to Pakington at Westwood, to discuss the projected Education Bill in which his host was wholly absorbed. This visit led to a new political friendship which influenced Stanley much in 1855–7.

2 Cf.Phillimore to Gladstone, 31 Jan. 1855, Add. MSS. 44277 f.2: 'Did I tell you that a few weeks ago Ld Stanley told me that if Palmerston were Premier he (Ld S.) would not oppose his Government'.

3 Col. Thomas Edward Taylor (1811–83), M.P. (Cons.) co. Dublin 1841–death, chief whip *c*. 1860–8; chancellor of duchy, Nov.–Dec. 1868, 1874–80.

4 Stanley's companion of his Welsh tour was Lord Robert Cecil, the future premier (and eventual supplanter of the diarist in Conservative politics.) It is characteristic of Stanley's diary that we only know this personal detail from other sources.

5 Sir William Molesworth, eighth Bt. (1810–22 Oct. 1855), M.P. (Lib.) Leeds 1837–41, Southwark 1845–55; first commissioner of the board of works Jan. 1853–July 1855; colonial sec. July 1855–death.

6 This was the famous occasion on which Lord Derby *may* have said: 'What the devil brings you here, Edward? Are you going to be married or has Disraeli cut his throat?' (Henry Greville's *Diary*, ii 263). Stanley's apology for missing the Norfolk meeting for a reason he could not reveal, found its way into the *Times* (cf. Greville, ed. Fulford, vi 168, for Disraeli's tart comment on Stanley's idea of secrecy). Malmesbury's printed diaries do not discuss the episode.

1856–57

1 In August 1855 Stanley went on a tour of Wales with Lord R. Cecil, later premier. In September he came to know Lady Salisbury much better; from the spring and summer of 1855 he regarded Hatfield as a second home (cf. below, 4 Sept. 1865, 13 Apr. 1868, 28 June 1868).

2 'Notes taken during the year 1857', Liverpool Record Office 920 DER 46/1.

3 *Loc. cit.*, 26 Mar. 1857.

4 See below, 31 Aug. 1866, for proof that the later series of diaries began 1 Jan. 1861.

5 As early as Feb. 1856, Stanley wrote a long letter to his father announcing his intention of giving up Conservative politics and devoting his time instead to 'good works' of a public nature. (There was never any question of his opposing his father publicly in politics, however much he disagreed with average Conservative opinion.) Characteristically, he never sent the letter.

6 For criminals, however, he advocated remission for good conduct, gradual transition to freedom at the end of the sentence, and the provision of employment on public works for ex-convicts. 'Criminals are driven back into crime by the impossibility of finding work . . .' he wrote. As a leading Lancashire magistrate, he observed that 'drunkenness is, in one way or other, the immediate cause of nine-tenths of the crime'.

7 Malmesbury to Stanley, 10 Sept. 1856, Liverpool Record Office.

8 Pakington to Stanley, 30 Oct. 1857, *loc. cit.*
9 Same to same, 7 Sept. 1856, *loc. cit.*
10 Stanley to Pakington, 16 Jan. 1855, *loc. cit.*
11 *Ibid.*
12 *Ibid.*
13 Pakington to Stanley, 19 Jan. 1855, Liverpool Record Office.
14 Stanley to Pakington, 18 Jan. 1855, *loc. cit.*
15 Pakington to Stanley, 7 Sept. 1856, *loc. cit.*
16 Disraeli wrote to Pakington, 5 Jan. 1855, Hampton MSS., Worcs. C.R.O., sharply and rudely rebuking him for improperly introducing the question 'on his own responsibility alone'. Pakington replied (7 Jan., *loc. cit.*) claiming the right to legislate 'as an independent M.P. not as the organ of a party'. In Jan. 1857 Disraeli again wrote deprecating Pakington's action in raising the subject of education (Disraeli to Pakington, 27 Jan. 1857).
17 Pakington to Stanley, 18 Jan. 1855, Liverpool Record Office.
18 Pakington to Stanley, 18 and 29 June 1855, *loc. cit.*
19 Cf. Pakington to Stanley, 30 Oct. 1857, *loc. cit.*, saying that the Mutiny had driven education and everything else out of his head, and that what he really wanted to see in the 1858 session was the replacement of parliamentary reform by Indian reform, carried through by Palmerston with support from a Derbyite opposition.
20 Pakington to Stanley, 5 Nov. 1857, *loc. cit.* Pakington's doctrine of the need for combination, which in 1856–7 temporarily ran parallel with Derby's doctrine of the need for absorption, had its practical side. In January 1857 he entertained Cobden and Gladstone successively at Westwood, with foreign affairs the uppermost topic (Pakington to Stanley, 12 Jan. *loc. cit.*) Pakington, like Stanley, thought the bombardment of Canton more inexcusable than Sinope (*ibid.*)
21 Disraeli told Greville of Stanley's 'exceedingly curious' opinions; George Smythe informed him that Stanley was 'a real and sincere democrat' (Greville, ed. Fulford, vi 166.)
22 Pakington to Stanley, 6 Feb. 1855, *loc. cit.*, replying to Stanley's suggestion, 5 Feb., that Derbyites should support Russell against Palmerston. Pakington wrote 'Attack upon Pam certainly – I quite concur in that – but why support Lord John?'
23 Pakington to Stanley, 24 Sept. 1856, *loc. cit.* In using education as their *cheval de bataille*, Pakington and Stanley were well aware that they were stealing Russell's brightest clothes. In 1855 Pakington acted in haste without consulting colleagues 'because I know accidentally and by chance that Lord J. R. is preparing a Bill . . .' (Pakington to Disraeli, 7 Jan. 1855, Worcs. C.R.O.)
24 Stanley presided at the first conference on Reformatories, 20 Aug. 1856, and was active in supporting the related project of Industrial Schools for street arabs in 1857. A particular political merit of these schemes was that radical millionaires like Hadfield denounced them noisily, thus showing the Tories as the people's (and the children's) friend.
25 For an allusion to coquetting between Gladstone and Disraeli, see *Leaves from the Diary of Henry Greville*, Edited by the Countess of Strafford, Third Series (London 1904), p. 11, for entry of 5 Feb. 1857.
26 For the situation in late 1856 and in the two 1857 sessions, see George Saintsbury, *The Earl of Derby* (1892), 99–105; (Sir Hylton George Hylton Jolliffe, third Baron Hylton), *A Politician in the Fifties: A Selection from the Correspondence of the Right Honourable Sir William Jolliffe, Bart., M.P. [Lord Hylton]*, (priv. pr. London, John Murray, 1905), 39–47; Wilbur Devereux Jones, *Lord Derby and Victorian Conservatism* (1956), 213–19; M. and B. iv 58–82.

27 Walpole, Pakington, and Lytton met at Knowsley with Lord Derby to settle the course to be taken in parliament, 'but nothing was settled'. Cf. Derby to Jolliffe, 11 Jan. 1857, Somerset Record Office DD/HY box 18: '. . . I am afraid it will be v. difficult to keep the party together and still more so to satisfy them – but I will do my best. 'Walpole and Pakington will meet here on Mon.; and so, thanks to your suggestion will Lytton, who is evidently much pleased at being asked. He can however only stay one night: but even that may do good. Let me know if you hear anything of Diz. I will write to him as soon as I hear he is in England'.

28 What Stanley feared was that if income tax were lost, then placing the whole burden of taxes on trade would not be acceptable for long, and the final result would be taxation of property. 'Progressive' support for income tax thus had a reactionary *arrière-pensée*.

29 For the letters, see M. and B., iv 60–3. During 1856, Stanley wrote, he had come to 'the conclusion that a seat on the front Opposition bench was inconsistent with the political position into which I had gradually and half-unconsciously passed . . .' This did not mean decisive separation, for the events of 1855 had shown the Derbyites could only hold power in a coalition 'all moderate politicians might join . . .'

30 For Pakington's threatened secession, see M. and B., iv 63–4.

31 Gladstone was seen as unusually close to rejoining the Derbyites at this time. Derby wrote to Jolliffe (11 Jan. 1857, *loc. cit.*) 'Gladstone however is, I know, expecting to hear from me and v. hungry though v. cautious. I will write to him shortly, but only to express my readiness to talk with him confidentially on the state of public affairs. I am sure it is good policy not to seem too eager to effect an understanding . . .'

32 From the second report on competitive examinations for entry to the Civil Service.

33 In a normal year (1853), 227 local and personal Acts were passed. The highest figure since 1800 for public Acts passed was 196 in 1814–15.

34 From information taken from the Administrative Reform Association.

35 George Duncan (1791–1878); retired Dundee merchant; M.P. (Lib.) 1841–57 (re-tired).

36 Liberal chief whip.

37 Fitzroy Kelly's plan gave a vote to anyone with an income of £100 p.a. from any source: also to members of any profession (army, navy, law, medicine, church).

38 Disraeli argued (20 May) that, in the case of England, 144 county members represented 9–10 m. pop., but 319 borough members only 7 m. pop.

39 Stanley noted numbers of petitions received by the Commons as an index of apathy. The yearly average was 176 (1785); 205 (1800–05); 899 (1810–15); 10,218 (1852–6); 13,867 (1856 alone); 1459 (1857 sess. I), 4847 (1857 sess. II).

40 On 30 Jan. 1857 Stanley had read Sir A. H. Elton's pamphlet *The Ballot a Conservative Measure*. Elton's views (sufficiently indicated by the title) were 'in substance mine: I believe it to be also Disraeli's, who is a good judge in such questions. But years must pass before this view becomes acceptable to the agricultural party'.

41 Sir G. C. Lewis was Palmerston's chancellor of the exchequer 1855–8.

42 Robert Vernon Smith, first Baron Lyveden, president of the board of control 1855–8.

43 On the occasion of a visit to Manchester to address the Cotton Supply Association.

44 James Platt (1823–57), M.P. (Lib.) Oldham Apr.–Aug. 1857.

45 Home secretary 1855–8.

46 Liverpool Record Office 920 DER 46/2.

1858

1 See above, 4 Apr. 1853.

2 Herman Merivale (1806–74), perm. under-sec. for colonies 1848–60, for India 1860–74.

3 Sir Thomas Frederick Elliot (1808–80), assistant under-sec. for colonies 1847–68 (retired on pension). Went on walking tour of Pyrenees with the diarist in 1865.

1859

1 Capt William Hay (1794–1855), ensign 1810, capt in dragoons 1824–9, inspecting superintendent of Metropolitan Police 1839–50, second commissioner 1850–5.

1860

1 Notes of a visit to Paris, made in spring 1860 with Wilson Patten, and copied into diary for 15 Jan. 1863: original not traced.
2 This entry comes from a section entitled *Extracts from a notebook of 1860* which was copied into the flyleaves of the 1863 diary. The original has not been traced.
3 Ernest Charles Jones, chartist (1819–69): a barrister who often practised before Lord Stanley at the Kirkdale sessions. For Stanley's view of Jones, see below, 27 Jan. 1869. Jones first approached Stanley, without previous acquaintance, in a letter of 27 June 1860 from a Kensington address. He enclosed 'a copy of one of my recent volumes of poems', and a laudatory article on himself from the *Saturday Review*. Jones reviewed his sufferings, including the death of his wife 'after an agony of three years with cancer' which had left him with four children, two of them very young. He mentioned that his wife was a daughter of Mr Edward Stanley of Ponsonby, late M.P. for Cumberland. Jones stated 'I have abandoned political life in *disgust*' and sought a living at the bar. 'My return to the bar is, practically, the same as a beginning.' He therefore sought £15 to £20 to fend off the pressure of tradesmen's debts, which 'would place me in safety, and give me breathing time to advance in my profession.' Stanley endorsed the letter 'Ansd., sending £20. I do not want it repaid to me, but when he can spare it he may hand on the amount to any deserving person in difficulty, laying same injunction on him.' Jones replied, again from Kensington, with thanks, 30 June 1860. Jones wrote again to Stanley, 12, 16, and 18 May 1862, from 55 Cross St, Manchester, seeking the requisite testimonial from Stanley as chairman of quarter sessions in order to apply for legal posts in Wigan and Salford. Stanley sent a testimonial, but noted 'Can't interfere further.' The above letters are in Liverpool Record Office, 920 DER miscellaneous.
4 G. W. M. Reynolds, journalist and chartist (1814–79): founded *Reynold's Weekly Newspaper*, 1850.

1861

1 I.e. since his father inherited the estates. For further accounts, see below, 2 Jan. 1864.
2 The total invested in securities at the end of 1861 was £4,500.
3 Victoria, daughter of Lord John Russell by his first wife, married H. M. Villiers, 16 Apr. 1861.
4 John Wilson-Patten, first Baron Winmarleigh (1802–92): cr. peer, 1874: chief secretary for Ireland, 1868: a Lancashire M.P. since 1830 and a family friend.
5 George Melly (1830–94), M.P. (Lib.) Stoke 1868–74: stood as Liberal at Preston, 1862, and Stoke, 1866.
6 Charles John, first Viscount Colville of Culross (1818–1903), nephew of ninth Lord Colville in the Scottish peerage: held posts at court, 1852–8: master of buckhounds, 1866–8: lord chamberlain to Princess Alexandra, 1873–1903: representative Scottish peer, 1852–85: cr. U.K. baron, 1885, and viscount, 1902.
7 Charles Richard, sixth Earl De La Warr (1815–73): brother of Lady Salisbury (who was later the diarist's wife); committed suicide at the Bull Hotel, Cambridge.
8 Cf. Disraeli to Derby, 28 Jan. 1861, printed M. and B., iv 295.

9 Lord Lincoln, later the sixth Duke of Newcastle, married Henrietta Adela, daughter of Henry Thomas Hope of Deepdene. Surrey, 11 Feb. 1861. Hope died on 4 Dec. 1862, leaving £300,000 in money to his widow, as well as the life interest in 'his vast landed estate', after which they were to pass to his daughter (diary, 21 Feb. 1863).

10 Georgiana Susan, who married Sir Charles Du Cane, K.C.M.G. of Braxted Park, Essex, 25 June 1863.

11 Lord Adolphus Frederick Charles William Vane-Tempest (1825–64), third son of Charles, third Marquess of Londonderry, and Frances, the great lady who was Disraeli's friend. He married Susan, only daughter of the fifth Duke of Newcastle (Gladstone's Peelite colleague of the 1840's and 1850's), thus adding to the latter's notorious ill fortune in domestic as well as political matters. He was uncle to Lord Randolph Churchill, whose mother was a Vane: see also 7 July 1862, 11 June 1864, below.

12 Richard Spooner (1783–1864), fifth son of Isaac Spooner of Elmdon Hall, Warwickshire: partner in his father's bank at Birmingham: M.P. (Cons.) N. Warwickshire 1849–64: leader of anti-Maynooth party.

13 Francis, seventh Duke of Bedford (1788–1861). See below, 14 May, 5 June 1861, 22 May 1864.

14 William, eighth Duke (1809–72), only son of the above: died unmarried, and was succeeded by his cousin.

15 Francis Charles Hastings Russell, ninth Duke (1819–91), who married Elizabeth Sackville-West, sister of Lady Salisbury the diarist's future wife. The later diaries are well-informed on the Russell family in all its branches. Hastings Russell was father of the tenth and eleventh Dukes. Before succeeding to the title, he sat for Bedfordshire 1847–72.

16 Abraham Hayward (1801–84), Whig man of letters.

17 The most popular Conservative daily paper.

18 Edwin James (1812–82); M.P. (Lib.) Marylebone 1859–61; an unsuccessful actor, then barrister (1836) and Q.C. (1850–62, when name removed); recorder of Brighton, 1855–61; visited Garibaldi and present at skirmish before Capua, 1860; disbarred 1861, with debts of £100,000, and went to New York, where he appeared as lawyer and actor. Returning to London in 1872, he was articled to a solicitor in 1873: wrote and lectured on U.S. subjects. According to Sir B. Brett, James had the unique distinction of betraying a client for cash. In return for £1,000, he induced his client to give up certain victory for a compromise (diary, 17 Aug. 1871). See also 18 Apr. 1861.

19 Stanley strongly approved of Wood's tenure of the India Office, and appears to have been consulted on most, perhaps on all, major developments in Indian affairs, including the choice of viceroy. The diaries include frequent accounts of their deliberations, which rarely involved any disagreement: another aspect of the party truce of 1859–65, in fact.

20 John Harvey Lewis (1812–88), M.P. (Lib.) Marylebone 1861–74: supporter of ballot and Irish disestablishment: contested Bodmin, 1857, and Hull in 1859 (twice), apparently as a Liberal.

21 Probably, from the context, Henry Arthur Herbert of Muckross, co. Kerry, (1815–66), M.P. (Lib.) Kerry 1847–66; Chief Secretary for Ireland, 1857–8.

22 Liberal whip.

23 For a further referencees to Disraeli's wish to remove Malmesbury, and Derby's determination to retain him, see below, 1 Dec. 1863, 4 Jan., 30 Jan., and 1 Feb. 1864.

24 Cf. Malmesbury, *Memoirs*, ii 243–4, for the renewal in December 1861–January 1862 of a compact similar to that entered into in respect of the session of 1860: see also M. and B., iv 293–4 for Palmerston's statement of the terms of the compact. Stanley appears to be alone in referring to church rates as part of the arrangement.

25 The diarist omits to mention Derby's stipulation 'that in the general support we are prepared to tender you he does not include that of a Reform Bill' (Malmesbury to Palmerston, 29 Jan. 1861, Broadlands MSS.)

26 Andrew Steuart, M.P. (Cons.) Cambridge borough 1857–63 (took C.H.).

27 Dr Forbes Benignus Winslow (1810–74); opened private asylum at Hammersmith 1847.

28 See above, 23 March 1861, and below, 5 June 1861.

29 Gladstone had announced the Postmaster-General's cancellation of the contract for the carriage of mail from Galway to America, thus demolishing dreams of a second Liverpool in the west of Ireland (*Parl. Deb.*, 3, vol. 162, col. 2094, 16 May 1861).

30 Sir James Weir Hogg, Bt. (1790–1876), Indian magnate, and chairman of East India Co., 1852–3: member of Council of India, 1858–72.

31 In the main division on Gladstone's proposed repeal of the paper duties, ministers won by 296 to 281, majority 15; on Horsfall's motion for reducing duties on tea instead of on paper, ministers won by 18.

32 Sir Fitzroy Kelly (1796–1880), Conservative politician and lawyer: solicitor-general under Peel 1845–6, under Derby 1852, attorney-general 1858–9: lord chief baron 1866–75: kt. 1845: M.P. (Cons.) Ipswich 1835, Cambridge 1843–7, E. Suffolk 1852–66.

33 Col Taylor (1811–83), M.P. (Cons.) co. Dublin 1841–83, Conservative whip; Chancellor of Duchy of Lancaster Oct.–Dec. 1868, 1874–80.

34 Edmund Hammond, first Baron Hammond (1802–74): foreign office official 1824–73, becoming permanent under-secretary, 1854.

35 William Page Wood, first Lord Hatherley (1801–81), second son of a London hop merchant, Lord Chancellor 1868–72.

36 Sir F. Thesiger, first Lord Chelmsford (1794–1878), Lord Chancellor 1858–9, 1866–8.

37 Sir Edward Sugden, first Lord St Leonards (1781–1875), Lord Chancellor of Ireland 1835, 1841–July 1846 ,serving under Peel; cr. peer and Lord Chancellor, 1852; declined Derby's offer of the same post, 1858.

38 Perhaps William Entwistle (1808–65), M.P. (Cons.) S. Lancs. 1844–7; banker and chairman of Leeds and Manchester Railway.

39 Sir Robert Gerard, first Baron Gerard of Bryn (1808–67): A.D.C. to the Queen, March 1867: cr. peer, 1876. Gerard never stood for parliament, but was at this time considering contesting the newly created extra seat for S. Lancashire, on specifically R.C. lines.

40 For the diarist's fear of his father, see also below, 3 Nov. 1865.

41 David, thirteenth Earl of Buchan (1815–98); succ. 1857, his brother having previously died; became R.C.; bankrupted for trifling sum (1894).

42 See below, 14 Oct. 1861.

43 Richard, second Duke of Buckingham (1797–1861); succ. 1839; by buying estates with borrowed money and other extravagances, he became ruined within eight years of succeeding. The contents of his mansion at Stowe were sold in a forty days sale. He 'had the talent of inspiring ruffians with enthusiasm, of charming creditors, and of taking swindlers in' (Disraeli to M. Corry, 11 Sept. 1866.)

44 Fortescue was offered the post by Newcastle on behalf of Palmerston (11 July). Fortescue objected to moving from his under-secretaryship at the Colonial Office. Newcastle said he must accept, unless his seat was in danger, but added that the proposed reshuffle 'would weaken the Govt – couldn't last beyond March'. Lady Waldegrave advised him to accept (17 July). Armed with local warnings of a severe contest in Louth, he went to see Sir G. Grey and Brand (18 July). Brand said he had been chosen 'as most likely to conciliate our Irish friends or quondam friends' but 'of course any risk of defeat would never do'. (It later emerged that Carlisle, the

lord-lieutenant, had strongly supported Fortescue). After 'painful suspense', Fortescue was told that Palmerston had dropped the idea. There was no direct refusal, and no interview with Palmerston. On 22 July Russell asked Fortescue's opinion of Sir R. Peel jnr. for the post, 'which *he* was in favour of . . . I said it would be a bold experiment, but I saw a good deal in its favour'. Fortescue was glad that the offer fell through, partly because it would have meant separation from Lady Waldegrave. See Carlingford's diary (transcript), Somerset County Record Office. I am grateful to Dr T. Dunne of Mary Immaculate College, Limerick, for clarifying this point.

45 Edward ('Bear') Ellice, the elder (1781–1863), whip in Lord Grey's ministry 1830–2.

46 Cf. above, 7 June 1849.

47 For William IV's peculiar habits of exaggeration before he came to the throne, see The Countess of Strafford ed., *Leaves From The Diary of Henry Greville*, *Third Series* (London 1904), p. 13.

48 See above, 1 Aug. 1861.

49 Presumably Lady Salisbury.

50 Sir William Jolliffe, first Lord Hylton (1800–76), M.P. (Cons.) 1830–2, 1837–8, 1841–66; under-secretary, home office, 1852; chief whip 1853–9; cr. peer, 1866.

51 Derby had turned ill with a decided attack of gout, combined with a bilious affection, about 14 September, and his recovery was slow, though by the 26th he was well enough to sit with the family in the evening.

52 Sir Robert Peel (1822–95), son of the premier, and Chief Secretary for Ireland 1861–5: thereafter became a Conservative by degrees, but in 1886 was the only member of his party to vote for Home Rule, and thereafter stood as a Gladstonian Home Ruler.

53 *The Times*, 23 Nov. 1861, p. 7. Stanley had promised in 1854 to give the electors of Lynn an annual survey of public affairs and of his part in them. This he fulfilled, except in 1860 (and later in 1862 and 1863, when there was nothing to discuss.) As far as 1860 was concerned, Stanley had liked neither the reform bill of that year, nor the manner in which it was opposed.

Surveying European developments, Stanley stressed in each case that Britain was not and should not become directly involved. In America, where he expected the North to win and then find its problems had only begun, he equally deprecated intervention and urged strict neutrality, though by no means supporting the Union cause on its merits.

At home Stanley looked forward to certain progress, especially in finance, where the only problem lay in which taxes to reduce first. The 'Conservative' reaction of the sixties he saw as a myth: progress might be slow but was inevitable. He declined to support abortive private bills for electoral reform, but named some grave administrative reforms as ripe for attention: patents, land transfer, Admiralty reform, purchase of commissions, education, church rates, consolidation of statute law. On church rates he undertook to continue to vote against the rate, but did not think a settlement likely, some people relishing the controversy as an advertisement.

54 Robert Grosvenor, first Baron Ebury (1801–93), third son of first Marquess of Westminster; Whig M.P. 1826–57, cr. peer 1857.

55 Probably Thomas Edward Wilbraham (1820–84) of Delamere, Cheshire, country gentleman, and trustee of the Stanley estates under the will of the fourteenth Earl (see below, 23 Dec. 1863).

1862

1 The cotton famine caused by the American civil war.

2 Frederick William Robert, fourth Lord Londonderry (1805–72): fourth Marquess, succeeding his father in 1854: died 'after long seclusion in consequence of mental

disease' (*The Times*, 27 Nov. 1872): his wife became R.C. in 1855: like his half-brother Adolphus, already insane (see above, 6 Mar. 1861), he was uncle to Lord Randolph Churchill on his mother's side. For general comments on the family, see below, 11 June 1864.

3 Similar views were expressed by Cobden to Bright, 7 Aug. 1862, B.M. Add. MSS. 43652 f. 37–9, and by Cobden to Paulton, 13 Aug. 1862, B.M. Add. MSS. 43662 f. 240–5. (In Jan. 1861 Cobden had proposed Swiss mediation.) After autumn 1862 Cobden dropped thoughts of intervention and came to the view that the North must be allowed to win. I am grateful for help on this point to Dr K. Fielden, Cobden's biographer.

4 George (Egerton), second Earl of Ellesmere (1823–62); succ. 1857; a Conservative supporter of Palmerston.

5 The future fifth Earl of Hardwicke (1836–97) married Lady Sophia Wellesley, younger daughter of the first Earl Cowley, 16 Feb. 1863.

6 Lord Granville, in search of a second wife, had made three unsuccessful proposals to the beauty who became Lady Otho Fitzgerald.

7 Charles John (Manners-Sutton), second Viscount Canterbury (1812–69); a Conservative; d. unmarried; son of the famous Speaker of 1817–34.

8 Sir Henry Drummond Wolff (1830–1908), politician, diplomatist, and member of the Fourth Party; secretary to the high commissioner for the Ionian Islands, 1859–64, taking part in arranging their transfer to Greece; received a pension from the Greek government on relinquishing office; deeply distrusted by the diarist especially in the 1870's.

9 Cf. below, 23 June 1864.

10 See below, 19 Dec. 1862. For Disraeli's comments, 9 Dec. 1862, see Blake, 419.

11 G. Tricoupi(s), Greek diplomatist and statesman (1832–96); three times premier.

1863

1 J. T. Delane (1817–79), editor of *The Times* 1841–77.

2 (Sir) William Henry Lytton Earle Bulwer, first Baron Dalling and Bulwer of Dalling (1801–72); the second of three brothers, the youngest of whom was Lord Lytton the novelist; ambassador to Turkey, 1858–65; cr. peer, 1871.

3 Sir Hugh Rose, first Baron Strathnairn (1801–85), C.-in-C. India 1860–5.

4 Sir R. Airey, first Baron Airey (1803–81), Q.M.G. in Crimea; Q.M.G. of the forces, 1855–65; Gov. of Gibraltar 1865–70; and Sir W. J. Codrington (1804–84), C.-in-C. in Crimea from Nov. 1855; Gov. of Gibraltar 1859–65; twice refused the rank of Field-Marshal.

5 Arthur Richard (Wellesley), second Duke of Wellington (1807–84); succ. his father, 1852: M.P. (Cons.) Aldeburgh 1829–32, Norwich 1837–52; gave general support to Palmerston's two administrations; never held office, but his wife held court appointments 1843–58, 1861–68, 1874–80.

6 W. M. Thackeray (1811–Dec. 1863); 'his last book' was probably a reference to *The Adventures of Philip* . . . (1862).

7 Edward, first Earl of Ellenborough (1790–1871): succ. as second baron, 1818, and made earl, 1844; gov.-gen. of India 1841–6; president of board of control 1828–30, 1834–5, 1841, and Mar.–June 1858; first lord of the admiralty under Peel, 1846.

8 Sir W. R. S. Vesey-Fitzgerald (1818–85), M.P. Horsham 1852–65, 1874–5; under-secretary for foreign affairs 1858–9: Governor of Bombay 1866–72.

9 Frances, Lady Waldegrave (1821–79), four times married, lastly (Jan. 1863) to Chichester Fortesque, first Lord Carlingford. Sir W. V. Harcourt, the Liberal politician here referred to, was her nephew, and in the 1850's she had not only made him her protégé

but played him off against Fortescue, who disliked him. Her liking for Harcourt in fact continued after her marriage, as her husband acknowledged after her death.

10 Roundell Palmer, first Earl Selborne (1812–95), Lord Chancellor 1872–4, 1880–5.

11 Frederick Lygon, sixth Earl Beauchamp (1830–91); President of Oxford Union and Fellow of All Souls: M.P. (Cons.) Tewkesbury 1857–63, W. Worcs. 1863–66; junior office, 1859; Lord Steward, 1874–80: Paymaster-General, 1885–6, 1886–7; member of council, Keble College.

12 Cf. diary, 4 June 1864: 'Lord Beauchamp, who succeeded to the title only a few months ago, is dying. F. Lygon succeeds: Pakington says the estates are £40,000 a year rental, and probably clear, for the late Lord B. loved money, and saved a good deal. . . . The family are consumptive.'

13 Henry Lygon, fourth Earl Beauchamp (1784–Sept. 1863) had held the title since 1853. His son, the fifth Earl, the Lord Elmley of the above passage, died of consumption aged 37 in Mar. 1866, unmarried. Lord Elmley was M.P. (Cons.) W. Worcs. 1853–63: his father had held the seat 1832–53. Despite scattered evidence of the fifth earl's friendship with Disraeli, the present Lord Beauchamp has no surviving Disraeli correspondence.

14 Prince Jules de Polignac (1780–1847), president of council of ministers under Charles X, 1829–30.

15 William, third Earl of Leitrim (1806–78); murdered, with his clerk and coachman, in co. Donegal; his funeral disturbed by a mob which tried to drag the coffin from the hearse: active in relief during the famine.

16 Henry Pelham, fourth Duke of Newcastle (1785–1851), Gladstone's patron. The purchase of the Worksop estate in 1838 cost £370,000, but other land bought on borrowed money in Notts. brought the total in two years to £450,000; see John Martineau, *The Life of Henry Pelham, Fifth Duke of Newcastle, 1811–64* (1908), 68–70.

17 For slightly differing versions of the story, see Martineau, *op. cit.*, 80; and Arnold Haultain ed., *Reminiscences by Goldwin Smith, D.C.L.* (New York, 1911), 175–7.

18 James Abercromby, first Baron Dunfermline (1776–1858), Speaker 1835–9.

19 Gen Jonathan Peel (1799–1879), brother of the premier; a great patron of the turf; war minister 1858–9, 1866–8; M.P. 1826–30, 1831–68; expected to return to cabinet in 1868 (see below, 4 Feb. 1868). The diarist speaks of the diplomatist Sir Robert Morier as Gen Peel's son.

20 Charles Newdigate Newdegate (1816–87), M.P. (Cons.) N. Warwickshire 1843–85; Sir R. Knightley, first Lord Knightley (1819–95), M.P. (Cons.) S. Northants. 1852–92; Bull, (or Ball?) I cannot identify with any member of this date.

21 (Sir) John Laird Mair Lawrence, first Lord Lawrence (1811–79), viceroy of India 1863–8: cr. baronet, 1858, and baron, 1869.

22 Cf. above, 19 Apr. 1861, and below, 4 and 30 Jan., 1 Feb. 1864.

23 Charles Philip, fourth Earl of Hardwicke (1799–1873); followed naval career; M.P. 1831–4; succ. 1834; Lord-in-Waiting 1841–6; Postmaster-General, 1852; Lord Privy Seal, 1858–9.

24 Hardwicke had, however, been refractory in 1852: see above, June 1852. For his failing health, see below, 17 July 1864.

25 J. B. Aspinall (1818–86), Recorder of Liverpool 1862–86.

26 Henry Fleming (d. 1876), assistant secretary to the poor law board 1848–59, and its permanent secretary 1859–71.

27 John Winston, seventh Duke of Marlborough (1822–83): succ. 1857: M.P. Woodstock 1840–5, 1847–57: Lord Steward of the Household 1866–7, Lord President of the Council 1867–8: Lord-Lieutenant of Ireland, 1876–80.

28 Frederick Stanley, sixteenth Earl of Derby (1841–1908), the diarist's brother, entered the army as a lieutenant in the Grenadier Guards in 1858, becoming a captain in 1862. He retired from the army in 1865, becoming M.P. (Cons.) Preston 1865–8, Lancs. N. 1868–85, and Blackpool 1885–6.

1864

1 The rental, including the Irish estates, was in 1863 about £144,000, all figures being of course gross.

2 Lord Stanley's income would thus appear to have been about £2,000 p.a., of which he spent half on himself, and gave away or invested the rest. His aim was to donate for public purposes 'one third of my total receipts: which is the proportion I fixed twelve years ago' (diary, 4 May 1864). The citizens of Lynn, a borough in rapid decline, found great difficulty in maintaining the benefactions they had received from Stanley – baths, a library, and an Athenaeum (diary, 4 Mar. 1864).

3 The Queen's object was presumably to exclude Palmerston. As Palmerston refused office, and Derby probably did not want Palmerston anyway, but had two adequate names available, Malmesbury and Stratford Canning, the problem was unreal. Evidence on the point is lacking. But cf. above, 25 Feb., 1 Mar. 1851, for a similar proposal in that year of which this may be a misdated recollection.

4 Sir Stephen Cave (1820–80), M.P. (Cons.) Shoreham 1859–80; paymaster-general 1866–8, 1874–80; barrister of Inner Temple, 1846.

5 John Alexander (Thynne), fourth Marquess of Bath (1831–96); succ. 1837; see also below, 5 June 1864.

6 Probably Henry James Baillie, P.C. (1804–85), M.P. (Cons.) Inverness-shire 1840–68; joint secretary to board of control, 1852.

7 Henley received no post under Derby in 1866.

8 At the Foreign Office.

9 Algernon George (Percy), sixth Duke of Northumberland (1810–99); styled Lord Lovaine 1830–65, Earl Percy 1865–7; succ. his father, Aug. 1867; vice-president, Board of Trade, Mar.–June 1859; Lord Privy Seal 1878–80; freemason and scientist.

10 William, third Marquess of Exeter (1825–95); succ. Jan. 1867; M.P. 1847–67; held minor posts, 1866–8, 1874–5.

11 Sir Lawrence Palk, first Lord Haldon (1818–83); M.P. (Cons.) Devon S. 1854–68, Devon E. 1868–80; succ. father as fourth baronet, 1860; cr. peer, 1880.

12 Sir J. Trollope, first Lord Kesteven (1800–74); M.P. (Cons.) S. Lincs. 1841–68; succ. father as seventh baronet, 1820; pres. of the poor law board, 1852; cr. peer, 1868.

13 James, eighth Earl of Elgin (1811–64), viceroy of India 1862–4; see also below, 10 Apr. 1864.

14 Sir Alexander Cockburn (1802–80), lord chief justice since 1859.

15 The son disappeared to the continent with all the money he could raise, leaving heavy gambling and other debts behind him (diary, 14 June 1864).

16 George W. P. A. Bentinck (1803–86), M.P. (Cons.) Norfolk W. 1852–65, 1871–84.

17 Charles Francis Adams jnr (1835–1915).

18 Gladstone abolished the malt tax in his budget of June 1880.

19 H. E. Surtees (1819–95), M.P. (Cons.) Herts. 1864–8.

20 Comte de Flahault (1785–1870), Bonapartist officer, politician, and society figure; recognised to be Talleyrand's son; A.D.C. to Murat and to Napoleon; m. the Baroness Nairne and Keith; his eldest daughter m. (1843) Henry, fourth Marquess of Lansdowne (1815–66), the Adullamite leader; the Lord Lansdowne of the Entente Cordiale was therefore Talleyrand's great-grandson.

21 17, 18 March 1864: 8 April 1864.

22 Cf. above, 3 Feb. 1864.

23 Clarendon was commissioned to try and arrive at an understanding with the Emperor about the approaching conference on the Danish question, and to smooth over misunderstandings arising from Garibaldi's visit (see Sir H. Maxwell, *The Life and Letters of the fourth Earl of Clarendon*, ii 291.)

24 Stanley had said to Bright, 'I wonder if it ever occurs to the Duke [of Sutherland] that if Garibaldi had his way, there would be no Dukes of Sutherland' (R. A. J. Walling ed., *The Diaries of John Bright*, 1930, pp. 275–6.)

25 Probably Dr Robert Ferguson (1799–1865), physician extraordinary to the Queen from 1857. See above, 12 May 1864, 20 Aug. 1866.

26 Lord Claud Hamilton (1843–1925), second son of the first Duke of Abercorn.

27 Sir Francis Wemyss-Charteris-Douglas, tenth Earl of Wemyss (1818–1914); succ. 1883, prior to which he was known as Lord Elcho; a leading Adullamite.

28 The diarist spoke freely to Bright in the smoking room on 6 May, saying Derby was unwilling to come in without prospect of a majority, and that Palmerston would not go to war for Denmark. 'Emperor not disposed for war, and rather favoured Denmark united with Sweden and Norway. Spoke of Ireland, on which Lord Stanley made use of phrase, "that infernal Irish Church", but did not see how it could be dealt with, and thought no change short of extinction would be of any use. America: I condemned the tone of Lord Derby in speaking of the seizure of the 'rams' at Birkenhead, in which Lord Stanley did not differ with me.' (Walling, *op. cit.*, 277–8.)

29 See below, 26 May and 15 July 1864. Speaking for the government on Baines's motion to lower the borough franchise, Gladstone enunciated the principle that substantial numbers of artisans were morally entitled to vote (*Parl. Deb.*, 3, vol. clxxv, col. 324, 11 May 1864.)

30 Frederick Stanley, the diarist's brother, married Lady Constance Villiers, eldest daughter of Lord Clarendon, on 31 May 1864.

31 See above, 22 Apr. 1864, and below, 20 Aug. 1866.

32 Cf. Spencer Walpole, *The Life of Lord John Russell* (1891), 79–80; John Prest, *Lord John Russell* (1972), 15.

33 Emma, Lady Minto (d. 1882); m. William, third Earl of Minto, 1844.

34 See above, 23 Mar. 1861.

35 See above, 11 May 1864, and below, 15 July 1864.

36 Countess Louise d'Alten (1864–1911), Duchess of Manchester (1852–90), Duchess of Devonshire (from 1892).

37 Cf. below, 5 Dec. 1864.

38 See above, 27 and 30 Jan. 1864.

39 *Parl. Deb.*, 3, vol. clxxv, cols 606–10 (26 May 1864), implying that the Queen was a 'difficulty of the greatest magnitude' where Germany was concerned, in preventing ministers 'carrying out a purely English policy.'

40 Chichester Fortescue, first Lord Carlingford (1823–98); cr. peer, 1874; M.P. (Lib.) co. Louth 1847–74; at this time Newcastle's under-secretary at the Colonial Office, 1859–65.

41 For Adolphus Vane, see above, 6 March 1861; and for Lord Londonderry, see above, 7 July 1862.

42 George, Earl Vane, fifth Marquess of Londonderry (1821–84); succ. his father as Earl Vane in 1854, and his half-brother as Marquess in 1872; died of apoplexy. Two of his daughters died in childhood.

43 Lord Ernest McDonnell Vane-Tempest (1836–85), the youngest brother of the fifth Marquess. He married into the Durham gentry in 1869 and had a son in 1871.

44 On 19 June 1864 Capt Raphael Semmes (1809–77) of the Confederate commerce raider *Alabama* had engaged U.S.S. *Kearsarge* outside Cherbourg, and his ship was sunk. The *Alabama* had previously captured 82 U.S. merchantmen.

45 For Gladstone on the U.S., see also above, 21 Nov. 1862.

46 Friedrich Ferdinand Graf von Beust (1809–86), Saxon and Austrian statesman; minister-president of Saxony (1858), chancellor of Austria (1866); subsequently Austrian ambassador in London (until 1878) and in Paris (1878–82). A Protestant.

47 But see below, 24 July 1864.

48 Adeane (d. 1870) and Craven were his sons-in-law.

49 On the Danish question. Ministers won by 313 to 295, a majority of 18 (9 July). Stanley spoke, denying that Disraeli's motion hinted at war, and identifying himself strongly with a policy of non-intervention.

50 Sir John Pender (1816–96), textile merchant and telegraph magnate; probably the diarist's closest friend in the business community.

51 (Sir) William Fairbairn, first Baronet (1789–1874); cr. Bt, 1869; manufacturing engineer at Manchester and shipbuilder at Millwall; built nearly 100 bridges. The diarist held shares in his firm.

52 George (Byng), third Earl of Strafford (1830–98); succ. father 1886; Lib. M.P., as Lord Enfield, 1852–74; cr. baron, 1874; held junior office 1865–6, 1871–4, 1880–3.

53 Cf. below, 3 Sept. 1864.

54 H.R.H. Princess Mary (1833–97), younger daughter of Adolphus Frederick, first Duke of Cambridge, son of George III. She married Francis, Duke of Teck (1837–1900) in 1866: the future Queen Mary was born in 1867.

55 As Chief Secretary for Ireland, 1830–33.

56 Cf. above, 11 Aug. 1864.

57 Cf. above, 11 Jan. 1863.

58 For the diarist's views on Greece, see also below, 1 Aug. 1865.

59 See *The Times*, 20 Oct. 1864, p. 8 for Stanley's review of public affairs in the Town Hall at Lynn. Stanley saw the constitution as working well, nearly all grievances having been removed, but he did not expect the absolute calm of the last few years to continue, although the turbulence of the 1830's and 1840's was unlikely to return. He stressed the duty of both parties to keep the state within narrow bounds. Turning to the past year, he saw 1864 as the beginning of a new era in British diplomacy, based on non-intervention. He applied this principle to the questions of the unification of Germany and Italy, to the white colonies, which he wished left to their own devices, and to Africa, where existing commitments should be jealously scrutinised. The white colonies must eventually become independent; the others should if anything be seen as a source of weakness.

On the Eastern Question, Stanley was curiously specific. The break-up of the Turkish empire was only a matter of time and it was not our interest to antagonise the emerging races by prolonging it. He admitted the English interest in the neutrality of Egypt and the independence of Constantinople, but otherwise saw no cause for anxiety if Turkey lost imperial power, and he predicted that this would soon be a practical question. 'The Turks have played their part in history; they have had their day and that day is over; and I confess I do not understand . . . the determination of our older statesmen to stand by the Turkish rule whether right or wrong. I think we are making for ourselves enemies of races which will very soon become in Eastern countries dominant races, and I think we are keeping back countries by whose improvement we, as the great traders of the world, shall be the great gainers . . .'

60 Cf. above, 5 June 1864.

1865

1 Mrs Blanche Chetwynd, eldest daughter of the Hon and Rev Arthur Talbot, successfully sued her husband, William Henry Chetwynd, for divorce on grounds of adultery with cruelty; he brought counter-charges, claiming that her first child referred to above was not his, and that his wife smoked a pipe. They had married in 1854 when she was 18 and he 42 (see *The Times*, 17 Dec. 1864–22 Jan. 1865). Rumour added that, Mrs Chetwynd having become a Catholic, it was the priests who had promoted the divorce, she having some fortune of her own to which they sought access (diary, 21 Jan. 1865). For Stanley's connection with the Talbots, see below, 21 Nov. 1865.

2 His brother, who was shortly to be returned for Preston; see above, 31 Jan. 1863.

3 The trees were a particular point of friction, since the diarist had made them his special concern since about 1860.

4 Cf. above, 1 Dec. 1863.

5 Derby had good news shortly afterwards when his first grandson, the future seventeenth Earl, was born to Frederick and Constance Stanley (Apr. 1865). Until then there was a distinct risk that the estate would eventually pass to distant relatives who were unworthy or worse.

6 Harriet, Lady Clanricarde was the only daughter of Canning the statesman. She married in 1825 and died in 1876. Her son, Lord Dunkellin (1827–67) moved the amendment which brought down Russell's government in 1866. The family had quarrelled with ministers over the Galway mail contract in 1861 (see above, 23 May 1861).

7 Northcote instituted a sinking fund in his budget of 1875.

8 Sylvain Van De Weyer (1802–74), Belgian minister in London 1831–67.

9 John Brown (1826–83), the Queen's personal attendant.

10 Robertson Gladstone (1805–75), Liverpool merchant and politician, and elder brother of the premier; never recovered from his wife's death in 1865, neglecting his affairs and sitting 'silent and unkempt in his empty house'; became a Unitarian; for another comment on his lack of balance, see below, 5 June 1868.

11 Henry Reeve (1813–95), Whig publicist and editor of Greville's journal; ed. *Edinburgh Review*, 1855–95.

12 George Finlay, *History of the Greek Revolution* (2 vols, 1861). For the diarist's previous views on Greece, see above, 23 Oct. 1864. For further adverse comment provoked by reading Finlay, see below, 18 Jan. 1867.

13 For the diarist's views on Greece, see also above, 23 Oct. 1864.

14 Edward, thirteenth Earl of Derby (1775–1851); zoologist and patron of Lear; father of the premier.

15 Edward, twelfth Earl of Derby (1752–1834); founded Derby and Oaks; great patron of cock-fighting.

16 Cf. below, 13 Apr., 28 June 1868.

17 To attend the meeting of the British Association.

18 Derby had been in bed with gout (diary, 13 Sept. 1865).

19 Sir Thomas Frederick Elliot (1808–80), assistant under-secretary for colonies, 1847–68.

20 The day of Palmerston's burial.

21 Cf. above, 5 July 1861.

22 Cf. John Prest, *Lord John Russell* (1972), 404, where the Duchy of Lancaster is named as the post under discussion.

23 Emma Charlotte Stanley (d. 1928) m. Oct. 1860 Col. the Hon. Sir W. P. M. Chetwynd Talbot (d. 1898), brother of the eighteenth Earl of Shrewsbury.

24 The extravagant fourth Lord Mornington, Wellington's brother, died in 1857 and was succeeded by his son (by Miss Long, the heiress of Draycott, Wilts.), the fifth Lord Mornington, who died unmarried in 1863, when his titles went to his cousin, the second Duke of Wellington, but the Wiltshire estate went to his other paternal cousin, the first Earl Cowley (1804–84), son of the first Baron Cowley (1773–1853), Wellington's youngest brother.

1866

1 Clarendon's house.
2 Sir William Wyndham Hornby (1812–99), K.C.B., J.P., D.L. (Middx. and Lancs.), Admiral (retired 1864), Commissioner of Prisons 1877; his father was the brother of the wife of the thirteenth Lord Derby. Hornby looked after Knowsley, as well as being a companion to the premier, and was confirmed in his post as comptroller by the diarist when he succeeded in 1869.
3 Sir W. H. Gregory (1817–92), M.P. (Lib.–Cons.) Dublin 1842–7, co. Galway 1857–72; gov. of Ceylon 1872–6; supported Derby's reform bill, 1859, and opposed Russell's, 1866; refused junior Admiralty post from both Russell and Derby, Jan. and June 1866 (Cowling, 107) though Smith puts his refusal of Russell in autumn 1865 (F. B. Smith, 56).
4 Edward Bootle-Wilbraham, second Baron Skelmersdale (1837–98); succ. grandfather 1853; held household office in Cons. ministries, 1866–98: cr. Earl of Latham, 1880; married Clarendon's second daughter, 1860; a Freemason. The diarist's mother was Skelmersdale's aunt.
5 Arlington St, home of Lord Salisbury.
6 Fourth earl of Sefton (1835–97): succ. father, 1855; left over £273,000; lord-lieut., Lancs.
7 To an oaths bill.
8 Hugh Lupus Grosvenor, first Duke of Westminster (1825–99), second son of the second Marquess of Westminster; M.P. (Lib.) Chester 1847–69; cr. Duke, 1874: Master of the Horse, 1880–5.
9 For attendance, see below, 11 May 1866.
10 Lytton sought a peerage, which he gained when his party took office.
11 Conservative chief whip.
12 Cf. below, 20 Aug. 1866.
13 Sunday.
14 Ralph Anstruther Earle, Disraeli's private secretary, was appointed, to his apparent satisfaction at the time, to be Secretary to the Poor Law Commissioners; cf. M. and B. iv 446. Edward Christopher Egerton, an unobtrusive figure, was eventually appointed Stanley's under-secretary; Sir R. Knightley took pride in having refused Derby's offer of this post at some point in July 1866 'because he would not serve under Disraeli' (Julia Cartwright ed., *The Journals of Lady Knightley of Fawsley 1856–1884*, London 1915, p. 174.)
15 On Saturday 30 June Derby offered Manners a choice between his old office (Works) and that of Chief Secretary for Ireland, *vice* Naas. On Monday morning Manners and Naas arranged between themselves to retain their former posts. On Monday evening Derby returned from Windsor with permission to offer Manners the Lord-Lieutenancy, with a peerage, saying 'It will be salvation if you consent'. Manners, who had not been consulted, reluctantly accepted, but when the *Times* denounced the appointment the following morning he persuaded Derby to release him. The Duke of Abercorn was appointed. See C. Whibley, *Lord John Manners and his Friends* (1925), ii 136–40 Manners refused the Chief Secretaryship again in July 1868; in Apr. 1868 he refused the Governor-Generalship of Canada (Whibley, ii 144).

16 Chelmsford was warned by Derby that his appointment could only be temporary (M. and B. iv 443; Whibley, *Lord John Manners and his Friends*, ii 143–4). Disraeli wrote of him to M. Corry, 'I believe he knows that I recommended Lord Derby not to reappoint him . . .'

17 Cairns took the attorney-generalship on condition that he could give it up for judicial office, which he did on 29 Oct. 1866; see below, 1 and 8 Nov. 1866.

18 Edward, first Earl of Wharncliffe (1827–99); succ. father as second baron, 1855; acrostics editor of *The Owl*, 1864; railway chairman; cr. earl 1876. Henry, fourth Earl Cadogan (1812–73); succ. 1864; captain of the yeomen of the guard 1866–8.

19 The Austro-Prussian war. Prussia defeated Austria at Sadowa on 3 July. An armistice was signed on 22 July, followed by the Peace of Prague on 23 August.

20 Russian ambassador.

21 James Murray, assistant under-secretary.

22 French ambassador.

23 Italian ambassador.

24 Danish ambassador; see below, 22 Aug. 1867.

25 Turkish ambassador.

26 On 10 and 11 July Stanley was absent from London most of both days attending to his uncontested re-election for Lynn, where he made a speech of an hour (at 11 a.m. on 11 July) in the town hall (see *The Times*, 12 July 1866, p. 5). Stanley tried to give a historical analysis of the failure of the 1866 reform bill, blaming not so much the Palmerstonian character of parliament, as the action of the Whig cabinet in ruling out compromise. The majority of Conservatives, Stanley said, would have settled for £8 rental in towns and £20 rental in counties. He blamed Gladstone for bringing popular pressure to bear on the House; this was a mistake, for if a minister showed distrust of the House, it would reciprocate. Stanley said as little as possible about future prospects for reform, but admitted that the question must be settled by compromise if possible. He stressed that his colleagues had not wished to form a government on narrow party lines, and that many Whigs had stood aside only on grounds of scruple about changing sides for apparent presonal gain. He predicted unexciting debates in 1867, with the incoming cabinet mainly winding up routine business.

On foreign policy, he denied that a Conservative ministry meant war, and preached a policy of non-intervention as a vital concern of the landed interest and 'of our own poorer classes at home, of whom we are trustees'; praised Napoleon III, and made clear the importance he attached to friendly relations with the U.S.

27 Derby appointed Stubbs.

28 For repercussions, see below, 14 May 1867.

29 U.K. ambassador to Russia.

30 Mother of the premier; widowed 1856, died 1872.

31 On behalf of the War Office and Admiralty respectively.

32 i.e. Canadian federation.

33 Cf. Monty Corry (who was looking after Mrs Disraeli) to Disraeli, 24 July 1866: 'The people in general seem to be thoroughly enjoying themselves, and I believe she sympathises with them.'

34 U.S. minister in London. For rarity of his visits, see below, 1 Nov. 1866.

35 Prussian minister.

36 French diplomatist.

37 Portuguese minister.

38 Both were leading Adullamites (Whig rebels).

39 Lord Augustus Loftus, U.K. ambassador to Prussia.

40 See above, 22 Apr., 12 May 1864, 10 June 1866.

41 See also above, 11 Jan. 1863 (Delane on Turkey); 23 Oct. 1864 (Stanley on Greek defects); 24 Oct. 1864 n. 1 (Stanley on Turkish disintegration); and 1 Aug. 1865 (on Greeks as depicted by Finlay.)

42 Cf. below, 29 Nov. 1866, for the despatch of regiments to Ireland; in both cases hardly the action of a cabinet expecting serious unrest in England. Lord Monck (1819–94) was governor of Canada 1861–8.

43 Edward Morris Erskine (1817–83), fourth son of second Baron Erskine; attaché at Munich 1835; minister at Athens 1864–72, at Stockholm 1872–81.

44 Cf. below, 14 Nov. 1866.

45 Cairns, disappointed of the Woolsack, was Lord Justice of Appeal 29 Oct. 1866–Feb. 1868; cr. Baron Cairns of Garmoyle, 26 Feb. 1867. Cf. above, 2 July 1866, and below, 8 Nov. 1866.

46 Appointed 1 Sept. 1866, *vice* Drouyn de l'Huys, following the failure of French policy in the August crisis (see M. R. D. Foot, 'Great Britain and Luxemburg 1867', *English Historical Review*, July 1952, p. 356).

47 Cf. above, 28 Aug. 1866.

48 His doctor.

49 Cf. above, 2 July, 1 Nov. 1866. Disraeli wrote to Corry 'Only think of Cairns asking for the Lord Justiceship! It is a great blow for the party and mainly for myself. For he was my right hand in debate and with him I was not afraid to encounter Gladstone and Roundell Palmer. Now I have got them both without the slightest assistance.'

50 The leader of the Fenian movement.

51 'A French refugee who having robbed a bank and escaped to Canada, was there delivered up, by some sharp practice on the part of the French agents of police, and considerable neglect on our side' (diary, 1 Dec. 1866). See *The Times*, 9 Nov. 1866, p. 8.

52 Algernon George (Percy), eighth Duke of Northumberland (1810–99), styled Lord Lovaine 1830–65, Earl Percy 1865–7; Freemason, antiquary, scientist, Irvingite (married d. of Henry Drummond); junior office 1858–9; succ. father Aug. 1867; lord privy seal 1878–80.

53 First Baron Strathnairn (1801–85), C.-in-C. Ireland 1865–70.

54 Cf. above, 13 Nov. 1866.

55 Word and place uncertain.

56 Cf. Stanley's speech at Lynn, 19 Oct. 1864: 'I believe the breaking up of the Turkish Empire to be only a question of time, and probably not a very long time' (*The Times*, 20 Oct. 1864, p. 8).

57 The son was appointed attaché. The father, the third Baron, was an obscure Conservative backbencher.

58 Gladstone was passing the winter in Rome.

1867

1 In the Dominican Republic.

2 Victor Albert Stanley, the second of the diarist's eight nephews by his brother Frederick, sixteenth Earl of Derby. Until the nephews came along, there had been anxiety that the estates and title might one day pass to ne'er-do-well relatives who were not gentlemen.

3 Formerly Sir Fitzroy Kelly.

4 For previous comment on Finlay, see above, 1 Aug. 1865.

5 Brunnow was past his prime, having entered the diplomatic service a little before the Congress of 1818 (diary, 7 Apr. 1867.)

6 On 21 Feb. 1867 a telegram confirmed that all Servian demands in connection with this fortress, would be met by Turkey.

7　France was seeking the support of Russia in order to set the scene for the Luxemburg question. For Moustier's avowal of this, see below, 18 Oct. 1867. For previous Anglo-French harmony, see above, 1 and 16 Nov. 1866; for premonitions of the new Franco-Russian alignment, see above, 28 Dec. 1866, 15 Jan. 1867.

8　For the background to the Carlton revolt in favour of household suffrage see Sir Edward Russell, *That Reminds Me* – (1899), pp. 248–52.

9　Hastings Russell, Lady Salisbury's brother-in-law.

10　The Dutch minister had recently given Stanley a long story about the danger of a Prussian attack on Holland, based on slender evidence of Prussian military espionage (diary, 25 Feb. 1867). Bismarck had hinted to an English diplomatist that he attached more importance to Holland than to the Rhine frontier; this Stanley noted as 'a straw in the wind' (diary, 6 Mar. 1867.) For Clarendon's mention of Luxemburg, see above, 4 July 1866. Cowley wrote to Stanley on 12 March that he was 'almost sure there was something in the wind' about Luxemburg; the French had started their bid for cession by Holland on 28 February (M. R. D. Foot, 'Great Britain and Luxemburg', *English Historical Review*, July 1952, p. 358).

11　Lord Henry Lennox was Secretary of the Admiralty. Stanley several times remarked on his parliamentary skill.

12　The sixth Baron Howard of Walden (1799–1868), minister at Brussels from 1846 to his death.

13　Cf. Foot, *op. cit.*, p. 363, n. 1.

14　Cf. *Lothair* (Oxford Novels edition, ed. V. Bogdanor), ch. 27, p. 91, where the professional revolutionary, Captain Bruges, just returned from Ireland, comments on the Fenians 'No real business in them. Their treason is a fairy tale, and their sedition a child talking in its sleep'. Stanley, and presumably other senior ministers, received much elaborate information, not included here, about European secret societies, passed on through official channels from would-be informers. It was the imagination of these informers rather than of Disraeli that provided much of the revolutionary background to *Lothair* (1870). For Mazzini and the Fenians, see also below, 5 Feb. 1868.

15　This was at once sent to Disraeli with the message, 'Dear D. The enclosed has just come in. I don't see how war can now be avoided. Yrs. S.' (Foot, *loc. cit.*).

16　G. M. W. Sandford (d. 1879), M.P. (Cons.) Harwich 1852–3, Maldon 1854–7, 1859–68, 1874–78; changed name from Peacocke, 1866.

17　His brother and sister-in-law.

18　The *Victoria*, a U.K. vessel, had been outrageously treated by the Spanish, who had acted as if they thought Britain incapable of retaliation. Stanley had taken a strong line and had been prepared to enforce it by reprisals, presumably on Palmerstonian lines (diary, 7 Apr. 1867). See also above, 6 Apr. 1867.

19　For Stanley's distrust of Beust, see also below, 3 Nov. 1867.

20　For Stanley's second interview with the King, see below, 19 Aug. 1867.

21　See above, 12 July 1866.

22　In Rumania.

23　See below, 29 July and 14 October 1867, and above, 24 May 1867, for other evidence of Rothschild's role.

24　John Walter (1818–94), proprietor of *The Times*, and grandson of its founder; M.P. (Cons. or Lib.–Cons.) Nottingham 1847–59, (Lib.) Berks. 1859–85.

25　For the Queen's attacks of nervous vomiting, see Whibley, *op. cit.*, ii 121, citing Manners' journal of 6 July 1867.

26　See above, 2 May 1867.

27　See below, 10, 11, and 16 Sept. 1867.

28 See below, 19 and 28 Oct. 1867.
29 Cf. above, 19 Apr. 1867.
30 The conference proposed by France on the Roman question.
31 Arthur Balfour, later premier.
32 Henry Thomas Lowry Corry, first lord of the admiralty Mar. 1867–Dec. 1868.

1868

1 Lord Robert Montagu (1825–1902), second son of the sixth Duke of Manchester; M.P. (Cons.) Hunts. 1859–74, Cons./H.R. Westmeath 1874–80 (retired); vice-president of the council, with responsibility for education Mar. 1867–Dec. 1868; an R.C. 1870–82; an energetic and unpredictable controversialist. The 1868 education bill was introduced in the Lords, where it did not get beyond a second reading.
2 Sir Moses Haim Montefiore (1784–1855), leading opponent of anti-semitism; connected by marriage with the Rothschilds.
3 This was short-lived; for Exeter's hospitality at Burleigh to gatherings of Conservative leaders in Jan. 1871 and Jan. 1872, see *inter alia* Julia Cartwright ed., *The Journals of Lady Knightley of Fawsley 1856–1884* (1915), 212–14, 226–7.
4 Gen. Peel never returned to office. At the end of February Cranborne was also sounded, but refused peremptorily (M. and B. vi 596; Lady G. Cecil, *Salisbury* i 291). On 13 February, a day before Disraeli received Derby's decision to retire, Disraeli had in effect offered Derby's job to Granville (Fitzmaurice, *Granville* i 519–20).
5 Cf. above, 28 Mar. 1867.
6 Sir James Fergusson, Bt., under-secretary at the Home Office; the original of Lord Culloden in *Lothair*?
7 George William (Barrington), seventh Viscount Barrington (1824–98), M.P. (Cons.) Eye 1866–80; held household office 1874–80, 1885–6, Aug.–Nov. 1886; sometime priv. sec. to Derby, when premier; cr. Baron Shute of Beckett (U.K.) 1880, but known by his Irish title; an intimate of Disraeli in his last years, though described as 'stupid and uninteresting' (Disraeli to Lady Bradford, 16 Nov. 1879).
8 (Sir) Anthony Cleasby (1804–79), barrister 1831, Q.C. 1861; serjeant at law Aug. 1868, baron of Court of Exchequer Aug. 1868–79; kt. Dec. 1868; Icelandic scholar; contested Surrey 1859, and the Cambridge University byelection (result, A. J. Beresford Hope, Cons., 1,931, Cleasby, Cons., 1,400).
9 Alexander James Beresford-Hope (1820–87), M.P. (Cons.) Maidstone 1841–52, 1857, Stoke 1865–Feb. 1868, retiring to represent Cambridge University Feb. 1868–death; High Church owner of *The Saturday Review*; attacked Disraeli as 'the Asian mystery', 1867.
10 See above, 24 Aug., 3 Sept. 1867.
11 George Ward Hunt (1825–77), M.P. (Cons.) Northants. N. 1857–77; fin. sec. to treasury 1866–8, chanc. of exchequer Feb.–Dec. 1868, first lord of admiralty 1874–7.
12 But cf. Bright's *Diaries*, 30 Mar. 1868: '. . . Speech altogether weak, and badly spoken, or rather *read* for he speaks from a written speech.'
13 Lady Salisbury lost her first husband in April 1868, her father and her younger sister in February 1869, her mother in January 1870, and her eldest brother (by suicide) in April 1873, thereafter becoming prone to attacks of depression which in turn affected her second husband's attitude to his work. (She married the diarist 5 July 1870.)
14 Cf. below, 4 Sept. 1865, and below, 28 June 1868.
15 The final cost of the Abyssinian war was £9,000,000 (M. and B. v. 45).
16 Henry John (Chetwynd-Talbot), twenty-first Earl of Shrewsbury (1803–68); succ. as Earl Talbot of Hensol 1849, and as Earl of Shrewsbury 1856; household office 1852, 1858–9; left under £50,000.

17 See above, 19 July 1865. Cf. Stanley diary, 5 July 1868: 'Robertson Gladstone's extraordinary speech of the other day explained: he has since shown signs of mental disturbance, and is under medical care.'
18 Conservative whip.
19 Charles (Bennet), seventh Earl of Tankerville (1810–99), M.P. (Cons.) N. Northumberland 1832–59; succ. father 1859; household office 1866–8; became R.C. 1879.
20 Georgina (*née* Alderson), Countess of Salisbury (1827–99), wife of the premier.
21 Cf. above, 4 Sept. 1865, 13 Apr. 1868.
22 Cf. above, 14 Mar. 1867, and below, 5 Sept. 1868.
23 Sir Charles Du Cane (1825–89), M.P. (Cons.) Essex N. 1857–68; civil lord of admiralty 1866–Aug. 1868, gov. of Tasmania 1869–74, chairman of board of customs 1878–death; translated *Odyssey*.
24 Sir H. Bulwer, first Baron Dalling and Bulwer (1801–72); ambassador at Constantinople 1858–65, M.P. (Lib.) Tamworth 1868–71; cr. peer 1871.
25 Cf. above, 13 July 1868. Lennox was thought of again for this post in 1874, but rejected by Disraeli because of his involvement in dubious companies.
26 Disraeli told the Queen on 27 September that the party committee on elections predicted 330 seats for the Conservatives (*Q.V.L. 1862–78*, i 538).
27 Reverdy Johnson (1796–1876), U.S. minister to London 1868–9; generally sympathetic to the South and uneasy about Emancipation.
28 Dated 27 Nov. 1868 in *Queen Victoria's Letters 1862–78*, i 558.
29 Sir John Crampton (1805–86), career diplomatist; minister to Madrid 1860–July 1869 (retired on pension).
30 John Arthur Douglas (Bloomfield), second Baron Bloomfield (1802–79), career diplomatist 1818–71; ambassador to Austria 1860–71.
31 Lionel Sackville-West, second Baron Sackville (1827–1908), career diplomatist 1847–88, including Washington 1881–8; succ. brother 1888. The diarist's wife was West's sister.
32 John Savile-Lumley, later Savile, first Baron Savile of Rufford (1818–96), career diplomatist 1841–88; minister at Brussels 1868–83.
33 Edward Robert (Bulwer), second Baron, and first Earl of Lytton (1831–91); career diplomatist, then viceroy of India 1876–80; succ. father 1873.

1869

1 See above, 29 July 1860.
2 Jones also received help from the Royal Literary Fund (diary, 28 Apr. 1869), of which Stanley was sometime chairman. In the 1880's the diarist set up one of Ernest Jones's sons as a commercial traveller, apparently out of regard for his father.
3 John Hobart Caradoc, second and last Lord Howden (1799–1873), ambassador at Madrid 1850–8; held no subsequent office, despite what is said above.
4 Clarendon's younger children were reported as having been provided for by Howden, 'which is singular, as there is no connection between the families' (diary, 17 Jan. 1869). Howden, an R.C. convert, left them £10,000, although no relation (R. E. Chester Waters, . . . *The Chesters of Chicheley* . . ., London 1878, ii 688).
5 Odo Russell, first Lord Ampthill (1829–84), brother of ninth Duke of Bedford; m. 1868 Lady Emily Theresa Villiers, Clarendon's third daughter; sole representative of H.M.G. at Rome, 1858–70; assistant under-secretary at the F.O., 1870–1.
7 An estate taken by the dowager Lady Salisbury after her husband's death; later bought by Derby.
8 Derby received the same medical attention as the cottagers on his estate. Dr Gorst of Knowsley, Derby's local doctor, was paid £300 a year to attend the poor gratis.

Derby had moreover instituted a social security scheme in the 1850's, for the cottagers on his estate, with contributions from employee and employer, designed to ensure no one went to the workhouse or had to ask for charity.

9 The Knowsley agent.

10 A first step was taken the following day, when Derby arranged to reduce his household expenses (house, stables, gardens, park, and game) at Knowsley to a firm £20,000 a year. Previously they had probably been about £30,000 a year.

11 Lady Salisbury's brother-in-law: see above, 23 Mar. 1861.

12 J. O'Donovan Rossa (1831–1915), elected Nov. 1869 but as a convicted felon declared ineligible to take his seat.

13 John Lothrop Motley, historian and diplomatist (1814–77), author of *The Rise of the Dutch Republic* (1856), U.S. minister to Vienna 1861-7 and to London Mar. 1869–Nov. 1870.

INDEX

Except in the cases of Lords Aberdeen, Derby (the 14th Earl), Malmesbury, Palmerston, Sir John Pakington, and 'Wales, Prince of', where the form of name is that given here, the form adopted for the names of noblemen is that followed in the *Dictionary of National Biography*, with cross references from the names not used.